THE POWER OF PRINT IN MODERN CHINA

Studies of the Weatherhead East Asian Institute, Columbia University

STUDIES OF THE WEATHERHEAD EAST ASIAN INSTITUTE, COLUMBIA UNIVERSITY

The Studies of the Weatherhead East Asian Institute of Columbia University were inaugurated in 1962 to bring to a wider public the results of significant new research on modern and contemporary East Asia.

For a complete list of books in the series, see page 373

The Power of Print in Modern China

INTELLECTUALS AND INDUSTRIAL PUBLISHING FROM THE END OF EMPIRE TO MAOIST STATE SOCIALISM

Robert Culp

Columbia University Press
New York

Columbia University Press
Publishers Since 1893
New York   Chichester, West Sussex
cup.columbia.edu
Copyright © 2019 Columbia University Press
All rights reserved

Library of Congress Cataloging-in-Publication Data

Names: Culp, Robert Joseph, 1966- author.
Title: The power of print in modern China : intellectuals and industrial
publishing from the end of empire to Maoist state socialism / Robert Culp.
Description: New York : Columbia University Press, [2019] | Includes
bibliographical references and index.
Identifiers: LCCN 2018046101 (print) | LCCN 2018057965 (ebook) | ISBN 9780231545358
(electronic) | ISBN 9780231184168 (cloth : alk. paper)
Subjects: LCSH: Publishers and publishing—China—History—20th century. |
Shang wu yin shu guan—History—20th century. | Zhonghua shu ju—History—
20th century. | Shi jie shu ju (Shanghai, China)—History—20th century. |
China—Intellectual life—20th century.
Classification: LCC Z462.3 (ebook) | LCC Z462.3 .C85 2019 (print) |
DDC 070.50951/0904—dc23
LC record available at https://lccn.loc.gov/2018046101

Columbia University Press books are printed on permanent
and durable acid-free paper.
Printed in the United States of America

Cover design: Milenda Nan Ok Lee

Cover photo: photograph by Francis E. Stafford, Hoover Institution Archives,
© Stanford University.

Contents

List of Figures vii

Acknowledgments ix

List of Abbreviations xiii

Introduction 1

PART I Recruiting Talent, Mobilizing Labor

I Becoming Editors: Late Qing Literati's Scholarly Lives
and Cultural Production 27

II Universities or Factories? Academics, Petty Intellectuals,
and the Industrialization of Mental Labor 53

Part I Epilogue: War, Revolution, Hiatus 87

PART II Creating Culture

III Transforming Word and Concept Through Textbooks and
Dictionaries 95

IV   Repackaging the Past: Reproducing Classics
Through Industrial Publishing   126

V   Introducing New Worlds of Knowledge: Series Publications
and the Transformation of China's Knowledge Culture   155

PART III   Legacies of Industrialized Cultural Production

VI   Print Industrialism and State Socialism:
Public-Private Joint Management and Divisions of
Labor in the Early PRC Publishing Industry   185

VII   Negotiated Cultural Production in the
Pedagogical State   214

Conclusion   248

Notes   263
Bibliography   323
Index   353

Figures

Figure 1.1   Zhonghua Book Company Editing Department circa 1916   41

Figure 2.1   Zhonghua Book Company Editing Department circa 1924   56

Figure 2.2   Eastern Library, Commercial Press, 1930   80

Figure 2.3   Eastern Library and the Commercial Press Editing Department after the Japanese attack of January 1932   80

Figure 3.1   Celebrating establishing the constitution   99

Figure 3.2   A dialogic context for presenting information about geography   110

Figure 3.3   Inscriptions for *Cihai* from Cai Yuanpei, Wu Jingheng, and Chen Lifu   119

Figure 4.1   Sun Yuxiu and Shen Yanbing circa 1920   134

Figure 4.2   Sample page from *Sibu congkan*: a Song edition of *The Book of Changes (Zhou yi)*   135

Figure 4.3   Example of Zhonghua's imitation-Song font from the sample book of *Sibu beiyao*   145

Figure 4.4   Example of the string-bound edition of *Sibu beiyao*   146

Figure 4.5   Sample book for *Gujin tushu jicheng*   149

Figure 5.1   Titles from the Complete Library showing their call numbers   165

Acknowledgments

This project analyzes changing patterns of collective cultural production in twentieth-century China. Various forms of collaboration, in turn, have made this book possible. Over the past decade, I have had the good fortune to cooperate with Wen-hsin Yeh and Eddy U on four conferences and an edited volume. Our shared exploration of intellectuals and knowledge production in twentieth-century China shaped my approach and interpretations at every stage of this project. I thank them both for their challenging questions, perceptive suggestions, and generous support.

In Shanghai I have enjoyed long-term friendships with scholars in the History Department at Fudan University and the History Institute at the Shanghai Academy of Social Sciences. Questions, comments, and research guidance during visits, lectures, and conference presentations at both institutions greatly enriched this book, for which I am grateful. My special thanks go to Zhang Zhongmin and Zhou Wu for sharing their insights on cultural production and book history in modern China.

I presented a preliminary exploration of this topic and two finished chapters from the book at Columbia University's Modern China Seminar. Each time, thoughtful discussion impacted my understanding of the chapters at hand and the project as a whole. For the past fifteen years I have benefited from the collegiality of the seminar's participants and its organizers—Eugenia Lean, Robbie Barnett, and Chuck Wooldridge. Given those long-standing connections with Columbia, I am thrilled that this book is being published as one of the Studies of the Weatherhead East Asian Institute. I am also grateful to the Warner Fund of the Columbia University Seminars Series for providing extra support for publication of this book.

The history of cultural production and history of the book in China have flourished in East Asia, Europe, and North America over the past two decades. It has been energizing to work on this project as this field has grown. The debt I owe to the many brilliant scholars now publishing in this area will be apparent from the notes in the following chapters. As often happens, new sources have helped fuel the growth of that scholarship. My work was greatly enriched by the publication of diaries from some key figures in China's publishing industry, such as Zhang Yuanji, Shu Xincheng, Jiang Weiqiao, and Wang Boxiang, and library access to diaries by Bao Tianxiao and Sun Yuxiu. I thank Sun Huei-min and Wang Youpeng for helping me work with some of that material. Online collections of books and periodicals have made it possible to survey series publications and track books' dissemination in new ways. Archival resources are revealing more and more of the internal workings of organizations like the publishers discussed here. I am grateful to the Shanghai Municipal Library, Shanghai Municipal Archive, Zhonghua Book Company, and the Lexicographical Publishing House Library for sharing their rich collections of late Qing, Republican, and early PRC materials. A brief stint as a consulting editor gave me some unexpected firsthand insights into the work life of a staff editor.

This book's arguments and interpretations have been shaped at every turn by the comments and suggestions of many generous readers and listeners. I thank Tom Mullaney and the anonymous reader from Columbia University Press for their smart questions and productive advice on the complete manuscript. Many colleagues have read or heard portions of this book, as conference papers, lectures, or finished chapters, and provided invaluable guidance. They include Cynthia Brokaw, Shana Brown, Janet Chen, Sherman Cochran, Nara Dillon, Michael Hill, Tze-ki Hon, Joan Judge, Rebecca Karl, Paize Keulemans, Eugenia Lean, Li Renyuan, Barbara Mittler, Rebecca Nedostup, Elizabeth Perry, Christopher Reed, Arey Ling Shiao, Eddy U, Nicolai Volland, Fei-hsien Wang, Timothy Weston, Wen-hsin Yeh, Peter Zarrow, and Zhang Qing. Chapters or sections of this project were presented in talks at Brown University, Harvard University, Princeton University, the University of Alabama, Beijing Normal

University, the Shanghai Academy of Social Sciences, and Sun Yat-sen University. I am grateful to the audiences at each of these institutions for their very helpful feedback.

At Bard two faculty seminars generated valuable guidance for framing this topic for readers outside the China studies field. My special thanks go to Tabetha Ewing for our discussions of book history, to Omar Cheta for his guidance on business history questions, and to Li-hua Ying for all her support and timely advice on difficult translations. The interlibrary loan staff at Bard College's Stevenson Library have tirelessly tracked down every obscure Chinese volume I have requested over many years. Thanks, too, to two generations of students in my seminar the Power of Print, whose perceptive questions and creative interpretations helped me to approach my own work in new ways.

Finally, I thank the Weatherhead East Asian Institute's Ross Yelsey for all his support going into the publication process. And I am grateful to Cae-lyn Cobb, Miriam Grossman, Monique Briones, Leslie Kriesel, Mike Ashby, and Anne Routon at Columbia University Press for their expert guidance through the review and editorial process.

Funding for the research and writing of this book was provided by grants from the Bard Faculty Research Fund (2007–2008, 2009–2010, and 2014–2015), the National Endowment for the Humanities Summer Stipend Program (FT-56939-09), the Visiting Scholars Program of the International Center for the Study of Chinese Civilization at Fudan University, and a Scholar Grant (GS021-A-13) from the Chiang Ching-kuo Foundation for International Scholarly Exchange. Without this generous support, this project would not have been possible.

Portions of chapter 1 were previously published in "New Literati and the Reproduction of Antiquity: Contextualizing Luo Zhenyu and Wang Guowei," in *Lost Generation: Luo Zhenyu, Qing Loyalists and the Formation of Modern Chinese Culture*, ed. Chia-ling Yang and Roderick Whitfield (Saffron, 2013). Parts of chapter 2 were included in "Mass Production of Knowledge and the Industrialization of Mental Labor: The Rise of the Petty Intellectual," in *Knowledge Acts in Modern China: Ideas, Institutions, and Identities*, ed. Robert Culp, Eddy U, and Wen-hsin Yeh (Institute of East Asian Studies, University of California, Berkeley, 2016). Sections of chapter 3 first appeared in "Teaching *baihua*: Textbook Publishing and the Production of Vernacular Language and a New Literary Canon in Early Twentieth-Century China," *Twentieth-Century China* 34, no. 1

(November 2008): 4–41 (copyright © 2008 Twentieth Century China Journal, Inc.). I am grateful for permission to republish that material here. Additional portions of chapter 3 were drawn from "Chuangzhi *Cihai*: Zhonghua shuju yu Zhongguo xiandai yuyan yu sichao de chansheng" 创制《辞海》：中华书局与中国现代语言与思潮的产生 (Making *Cihai*: Zhonghua Book Company and the production of modern Chinese language and thought), in *Zhonghua shuju yu Zhongguo jin xiandai wenhua* 中华书局与中国近现代文化, ed. Fudan daxue lishixi et al. (Shanghai: Shanghai renmin chubanshe, 2013), and "Dingyi xiandaixing: *Ciyuan* yu xiandai Zhongguo yuhui de chuangzhi" 定義現代性:《辭源》與現代中國語彙的創制 (Defining modernity: *Ciyuan* and the creation of the modern Chinese lexicon), in *Jindai Zhongguo zhishi de jiangou* 近代中國知識的建構, ed. Peter Zarrow and Zhang Zhejia (Taipei: Zhongyang yanjiu yuan, 2013). Some material from chapter 5 was included in "Wei putong duzhe qunti chuangzao 'zhishi shijie': Shangwu yinshuguan yu Zhongguo xueshu jingying de hezuo" 为普通读者群体创造'知识世界'——商务印书馆与中国学术精英的合作 (A world of knowledge for the Circle of Common Readers: Commercial Press's partnership with China's academic elite), *Shilin* 史林, no. 3 (2014): 92–108.

In all my work I depend on the love, support, and good humor of my family. I dedicate this book to Katie, Autumn, and Lizzie, who have lived with these editors for a long time. It's time we move on to a new cast of characters.

Abbreviations

GPA   General Publishing Administration (Chuban zongshu 出版總署).

HZS   Zhonghua shuju bianjibu 中华书局编辑部, comp., *Huiyi Zhonghua shuju* 回忆中华书局 (Remembering Zhonghua Book Company), 2 books in 1 vol. (Beijing: Zhonghua shuju, 2001 [1987]).

PRCCS1949   Zhongguo chuban kexue yanjiusuo 中国出版科学研究所 and Zhongyang dang'anguan 中央档案馆, comps., *Zhonghua renmin gongheguo chuban shiliao (yijiusijiu nian)* 中华人民共和国出版史料 (一九四九年) (Historical materials for publishing in the People's Republic of China [1949]) (Beijing: Zhongguo shuji chubanshe, 1995).

PRCCS1950   Zhongguo chuban kexue yanjiusuo 中国出版科学研究所 and Zhongyang dang'anguan 中央档案馆, comps., *Zhonghua renmin gongheguo chuban shiliao (yijiuwuling nian)* 中华人民共和国出版史料 第二卷 (一九五零 年) (Historical materials for publishing in the People's Republic of China [1950]) (Beijing: Zhongguo shuji chubanshe, 1996).

PRCCS1953   Zhongguo chuban kexue yanjiusuo 中国出版科学研究所 and Zhongyang dang'anguan 中央档案馆, comps., *Zhonghua renmin gongheguo chuban shiliao (yijiuwusan nian)* 中华人民共和国出版史料 (一九五三年) (Historical materials for publishing in the People's Republic of China [1953]) (Beijing: Zhongguo shuji chubanshe, 1999).

PRCCS1954   Zhongguo chuban kexue yanjiusuo 中国出版科学研究所 and Zhongyang dang'anguan 中央档案馆, comps., *Zhonghua renmin gongheguo chuban shiliao (yijiuwusi nian)* 中华人民共和国出版史料 (一九五四年) (Historical materials for publishing in the People's Republic of China [1954]) (Beijing: Zhongguo shuji chubanshe, 1999).

PRCCS1956   Zhongguo chuban kexue yanjiusuo 中国出版科学研究所 and Zhongyang dang'anguan 中央档案馆, comps., *Zhonghua renmin gongheguo chuban shiliao (yijiuwuliu nian)* 中华人民共和国出版史料 (一九五六年) (Historical materials for publishing in the People's Republic of China [1956]) (Beijing: Zhongguo shuji chubanshe, 2001).

PRCCS1957–   Zhongguo chuban kexue yanjiusuo 中国出版科学研究所 and
1958   Zhongyang dang'anguan 中央档案馆, comps., *Zhonghua renmin gongheguo chuban shiliao (yijiuwuqi, yijiuwuba nian)* 中华人民共和国出版史料 (一九五七，一九五八年) (Historical materials for publishing in the People's Republic of China [1957–1958]) (Beijing: Zhongguo shuji chubanshe, 2004).

PRCCS1959–   Zhongguo chuban kexue yanjiusuo 中国出版科学研究所 and
1960   Zhongyang dang'anguan 中央档案馆, comps., *Zhonghua renmin gongheguo chuban shiliao (yijiuwujiu, yijiuliuling nian)* 中华人民共和国出版史料 (一九五九，一九六零年) (Historical materials for publishing in the People's Republic of China [1959–1960]) (Beijing: Zhongguo shuji chubanshe, 2005).

PRCCS1961   Zhongguo chuban kexue yanjiusuo 中国出版科学研究所 and Zhongyang dang'anguan 中央档案馆, comps., *Zhonghua renmin gongheguo chuban shiliao (yijiuliuyi nian)* 中华人民共和国出版史料 (一九六一年) (Historical materials for publishing in the People's Republic of China [1961]) (Beijing: Zhongguo shuji chubanshe, 2007).

PRCCS1962–   Zhongguo chuban kexue yanjiusuo 中国出版科学研究所 and
1963   Zhongyang dang'anguan 中央档案馆, comps., *Zhonghua renmin gongheguo chuban shiliao (yijiuliuer, yijiuliusan nian)* 中华人民共和国出版史料 (一九六二，一九六三年) (Historical materials for publishing in the People's Republic of China [1962–1963]) (Beijing: Zhongguo shuji chubanshe, 2009).

PRCCS1964–   Zhongguo chuban kexue yanjiusuo 中国出版科学研究所 and
1966   Zhongyang dang'anguan 中央档案馆, comps., *Zhonghua renmin gongheguo chuban shiliao (yijiuliusi nian zhi yijiuliuliu nian)* 中华人民共

和国出版史料 (一九六四年至一九六六年) (Historical materials for publishing in the People's Republic of China [1964–1966]) (Beijing: Zhongguo shuji chubanshe, 2009).

SMA   Shanghai Municipal Archive

SYJ   Shangwu yinshuguan 商务印书馆, comp., *Shangwu yinshuguan jiushinian, 1897–1987—Wo he Shangwu yinshuguan* 商务印书馆九十年 1897–1987—我和商务印书馆 (Ninety years of Commercial Press, 1897–1987: Me and Commercial Press) (Beijing: Shangwu yinshuguan, 1987).

SYJ2   Shangwu yinshuguan 商务印书馆, comp., *Shangwu yinshuguan jiushiwu nian, 1897–1992—Wo he Shangwu yinshuguan* 商务印书馆九十五年 1897–1992—我和商务印书馆 (Ninety-five years of Commercial Press, 1897–1992: Me and Commercial Press) (Beijing: Shangwu yinshuguan, 1992).

ZSA   Zhonghua Shuju Archive

THE POWER OF PRINT IN MODERN CHINA

Introduction

I n the sixty years after the abrogation of China's civil service examinations in 1905, publishing became a career outlet and a context of cultural activity for a wide spectrum of educated people. Late Qing literati like Sun Yuxiu 孫毓修 (Xingru 星如), who had failed the provincial examinations multiple times, made careers in the publishing industry, as Sun did when he joined the Commercial Press Editing Department in 1907. A generation later, foreign-educated academics, like Harvard-trained meteorologist Zhu Kezhen 竺可楨, had stints working in publishing, while others, such as New York University PhD sociologist Sun Benwen 孫本文, wrote extensively for publishers' lists. Beginning in the 1910s, waves of Chinese-educated young people, such as Jin Zhaozi 金兆梓, who graduated from Hangzhou Prefectural High School and later dropped out of Beiyang University, made lives for themselves as compilers and editors, as Jin did when he worked at Zhonghua Book Company starting in the 1920s. For men like Jin, who was working in Zhonghua's Shanghai Editing Department and contributing to the revision of its signature dictionary *Cihai* in the early 1960s, careers in publishing begun during China's Republican period (1912–1949) extended well into the first two decades of the People's Republic of China (PRC) (1949–present).[1]

The intersection of these different kinds of literate people in the Editing Departments of China's three largest publishers—Commercial Press (Shangwu yinshuguan, founded 1897), Zhonghua Book Company

(Zhonghua shuju, founded 1912), and World Book Company (Shijie shuju, founded 1921)—made them lively sites of cultural production. At the height of their capacity during the late 1920s and early 1930s, each publisher concentrated from several dozen to several hundred intellectuals in their editing department. At any given point from the late Qing through the start of the Sino-Japanese War (1937–1945), the combination of these publishers accounted for the vast majority of textbooks approved by the government and sold to students.[2] But they also produced series publications whose titles numbered in the hundreds or even thousands, standard reference books of nearly every kind, multiple nationally circulating journals, and massive collections of republished classical texts. Their offices, in short, were major centers of intellectual life in modern China, and their publications were key features in the Chinese cultural landscape.[3]

The publishers' emergence as intellectual centers was facilitated by the epochal shift in Chinese cultural politics that started at the turn of the twentieth century. The end of the civil service examinations (1905), establishment of a modern school system that introduced foreign learning (1902), and the fall of the last imperial state (1911) pried apart the mutually constitutive relationship between Confucian learning, government service, and the literate elite that had characterized Chinese life since the fourteenth century, if not earlier.[4] What now constituted legitimate knowledge was open to question, and the monopoly of Confucian learning failed to guarantee elite status as it once had.[5] Just as importantly, government office was no longer the ultimate prize of the educational process. Those without advanced classical education could now find their way into government service. By the same token, an elite education might not necessarily lead to political office. Moreover, political office itself increasingly failed to provide an honorable career path, as militarists controlled governments and elected officials proved to be both corrupt and ineffective. With the end of the imperial order, the route for educated people to attain meaningful careers with social status and cultural authority was no longer clear.

This book analyzes why commercial publishing emerged in this dynamic context as a key institution for literate elite cultural activity, and it explores how cultural production from the leading publishers developed and shaped Chinese thought and culture in the twentieth century. Certainly, publishing was not the only career option for the educated elite. Careers in education, especially higher education, attracted many.[6] So, too, did new professional fields like law, medicine, engineering, and journalism.[7] As political turmoil continued throughout the first half of the twentieth century, revolutionary activism itself became a career path for talented educated people.[8] But publishing was an attractive career choice, for it provided the educated elite with a way to play a prominent role in public life and to use the novel power of industrial capitalism to transform Chinese culture. Moreover, even when literate elites pursued careers in other professions, academic fields, or even revolutionary activism, they still depended on the publishing industry to disseminate their ideas and make their reputations. In short, publishing provided a vital medium for China's literate elite to forge new roles and identities for themselves in the modern world.

Over the course of the twentieth century many aspects of Chinese culture and intellectual life were transformed. Classical language was replaced by a written vernacular with a dramatically new lexicon and distinct conventions of writing. New systems of ideas were introduced from abroad and indigenized by being synthesized in distinctive ways and related to China's most pressing social, economic, and political problems. China's long legacy of classical learning changed from being viewed as the universe of all legitimate knowledge to being considered China's distinctive national heritage. Book publishing played a vital role in realizing each of these cultural changes and others. Publication served to extend new cultural forms and ideas to the growing Chinese reading public. But just as importantly, the publishing process itself fundamentally shaped how those systems of ideas and cultural practices took material form and found expression in public life. So, this book demonstrates how the cultural activities and work practices of literate elites in China's largest publishing companies proved vital to two of the most important long-term changes in twentieth-century China: the making of the modern intellectual and the creation of modern Chinese culture and thought.

Twentieth-century China was an age of revolution, so we have understandably focused on key moments of intellectual and political upheaval—the Hundred Days Reform, the Qing New Policies, 1911, May Fourth, the vernacular language movement, the National Revolution, and the Chinese Communist Revolution—to explain many aspects of social and cultural change. But the material form that new culture and systems of ideas assumed resulted from concrete techniques of book production that developed gradually and organically in publishers' editing departments through the daily activities of executives and staff editors. Moreover, intellectuals' embodiment of new social roles was the product of gradual shifts in literate elites' daily work lives, modes of cultural activity, and patterns of sociability. By shifting focus to editors' daily practices in the editing departments of China's largest publishers, we can capture glacial movements that are more difficult to discern than the eruptions of major political and cultural events but in the long run were, I contend, just as fundamental to shaping the landscape of Chinese modernity.[9] The ways literate elites worked to make books affected who they were and how ideas and cultural forms found expression.

Print Capitalism, Print Industrialism, and Intellectual Labor

By the early twentieth century, China's educated elites had already been engaging in publishing activity for several centuries. China's woodblock (xylographic) publishing industry flourished throughout the Ming (1368–1644) and Qing (1644–1911) dynasties.[10] With multiple regional publishing centers, late imperial publishers furnished examination candidates with classical texts and commentaries as well as many kinds of examination aids. They also published a wide range of literature, how-to books, almanacs, and practical guides for medicine and other fields that reached readers throughout the empire. Kai-wing Chow has demonstrated that beginning in the late Ming, publishing became a prime area of literati activity.[11] Many scholars wrote to publish, especially those who were unsuccessful in the civil service examinations. Chow establishes that writing examination aids, compiling new collections of classics, penning prefaces for others' writings, and publishing literary works allowed literati of all stations to earn income and build their reputations while exercising cultural influence, even to the extent of shaping the interpretations that found favor in the examination system.

Chow and other scholars of late imperial Chinese publishing also portray a system that was highly commercialized. In fact, the extent of commercialization during the late Ming and high Qing periods compares favorably to the conditions in early modern Europe that Benedict Anderson has identified as "print capitalism" and which he sees underpinning the rise of nationalism in Europe and the Americas.[12] Certainly, publishers like Mao Jin, the seventeenth-century Changshu scholar-merchant who cashed out his land and pawnshops because of poor returns to establish a publishing concern that Kai-wing Chow estimates at its height employed forty to fifty block carvers and more than one hundred employees overall seems as capitalist as his early modern contemporaries in Europe and North America.[13] If print capitalism is associated primarily with profit-driven textual production for a broad market of readers, it was part of the Chinese cultural and economic landscape from at least the sixteenth century.

But Christopher Reed argues persuasively that a key transition in the publishing field occurred with the introduction of mechanized print technology, marking a new stage of development in Chinese publishing beginning in the late nineteenth century.[14] Given the importance of this industrial shift, I characterize this later period with the term "print industrialism," since so many aspects of what Anderson associates with "print capitalism" were features of Chinese publishing throughout the late imperial period (1368–1911). In China, the mechanization of print industrialism allowed the centralized mass production of books on a far greater scale than was possible with woodblock publishing. Industrial mass production provided the means to generate a greater diversity of texts in greater number. Both the variety and mass scale of mechanized production were essential elements of the cultural and social power of industrial publishing in the twentieth century that China's educated elites sought to harness.

China's leading publishers used printing technology developed abroad, as well as the corporate form of the joint-stock company governed by a board of directors.[15] However, industrial book production in twentieth-century China also evolved in distinctive ways that were inflected by cultural precedents and the dynamic social, economic, and political contexts of the early twentieth century. One typical approach in China that was uncommon elsewhere was to combine the functions of publishing, printing, and distribution in one company. Another central feature of the Chinese publishing process, as it developed first at Commercial Press in the first decade of the twentieth century and then at Zhonghua Book Company in the 1910s and World Book Company in the 1920s, was in-house production of many manuscripts in large editing departments. Chinese publishers initially developed this system and maintained it to meet the needs of textbook production (chapter 1), which was their most lucrative product. Rapid shifts in curriculum standards meant that publishers frequently had to produce new series of textbooks every few years, for which having a large stable of experienced authors on hand was a practical solution. Japan's Golden Harbor Press (Kinkōdō), which collaborated with Commercial Press during the late Qing, had developed a similar system of in-house compilation of textbooks by the company's own editorial staff in the 1880s to respond to the early Meiji (1868–1911) system that allowed publishers to produce their own textbooks subject to government approval. But this strategy for textbook production was undermined by greater Japanese government control of textbook publishing starting in 1903 and never became a generalized model for book production in Japan as it did in China.[16]

In the early twentieth-century United States, where the size and extent of the textbook market compared to China, the main textbook publishers contracted independently with groups of educational reformers, teachers, and, later, leading experts in schools of education to write textbook manuscripts.[17] During the same period, American publishers of cheap genre fiction created "fiction factories" of pseudonymous writers to reproduce mysteries, romances, or Westerns according to an editor's formula. But these techniques were not used at the leading general trade publishers that occupied similar market positions to Commercial Press and its competitors.[18] Instead, most leading American publishers solicited manuscripts from authors working independently, with editors in a small office collaborating with the authors on revision or altering manuscripts themselves to meet market expectations.[19]

Once established for textbook publishing, China's commercial publishers' globally distinctive large editing departments were then used to produce a wide range of publications, including reference books, book series, classical reprints, and journals through coordinated collective production. Full-time staff editors (*bianyi, bianji*) working for the companies compiled (*bian*) from existing materials and translated (*yi*) from foreign languages many texts, as Meng Yue has clearly shown.[20] Yet they also authored a great many texts (especially textbooks and series titles) and much material (for reference books and journals). Publishers' patterns of large-scale mobilization of educated people for collective textual production resembled in some ways the major compilation projects of the Qing period, such as the *Veritable Records* of the Qianlong reign, which occupied nine hundred scholars, or Ruan Yuan's compilation of the *Collected Glosses on the Classics* (*Jingji zuangu*), which employed forty scholars.[21] These precedents of large-scale collective compilation projects most likely naturalized the development of large editing departments in the context of Chinese industrial publishing.

But the goal of Republican-period commercial publishers, first and foremost, was to make a profit, while late imperial officials focused exclusively on mobilizing scholars to pursue a major cultural enterprise. And it will become clear that the recruitment and organizational dynamics in Republican editing departments assumed unprecedented new forms. After 1949, Commercial Press and Zhonghua Book Company continued using the editing departments and compilation strategies developed in the first half of the twentieth century because they advanced the PRC state's pedagogical goals.

Although the basic structure of large editing departments continued from the late Qing through the early PRC periods, dynamics of intellectual labor in these companies changed significantly over time. Industrial production of books involves two different kinds of intellectual labor. What I call managerial labor connotes conceptualization of the product and the planning and organization of its production and marketing.[22] But for cultural commodities like books, the manipulation, generation, and organization of symbols, images, and text are equally fundamental to creating the product.[23] This second form of intellectual labor involves making the content and form of the book.

Over the course of the first two-thirds of the twentieth century, the relationship between these two dimensions of intellectual labor and how they were each configured changed significantly in China's leading publishers. During the late Qing and early Republic, literati with similar intellectual backgrounds and overlapping social connections working in editing departments generated a collaborative approach to book production, following dynamics characteristic of literati study societies (chapter 1). There was little structural differentiation between managerial labor and content formulation. Executive editors and staff editors cooperatively conceptualized and executed publishing projects. As economic competition intensified and editing departments grew, managerial labor was increasingly concentrated in the hands of just a few people, usually executive editors (*zhubian*), the editing department director (*bianyisuo suozhang, bianjibu buzhang*), or general manager (*zongjingli*) (such as Wang Yunwu, Lufei Kui, Shu Xincheng, Xu Weinan, or Shen Zhifang) (chapter 2). In terms of the translation, compilation, writing, and editing of books, industrialized production led to commodification of knowledge and routinization of mental labor in assembly lines of text production that paralleled developments elsewhere.[24]

Systematic recruitment and training, coordinated group production, assignment of discrete tasks, and orientation of individual work to the collective goals of the corporation were all common features of publishing work at Commercial Press, Zhonghua Book Company, and World Book Company starting in the 1920s and 1930s. During this process, there were instances where publishing executives borrowed explicitly from foreign models, most notably Wang Yunwu's embrace of Taylorism and "scientific management" in 1930 (chapter 2). More commonly, however, Chinese publishers developed their own organizational strategies organically in response to intensifying competition and demand throughout the first half of the twentieth century. Many of their management approaches leveraged distinctive features of China's cultural and social milieu to meet corporate goals of productive efficiency.

After 1949 agents of the PRC state increasingly controlled managerial labor at Commercial Press and Zhonghua Book Company (chapter 6). Initially, from 1949 through 1953, both publishers continued to operate as private companies, and the state intervened in management primarily through working with the companies to demarcate areas of publishing specialization. After 1954 government-appointed cadres served directly as company director (*shezhang*) and editor in chief (*zong bianji*). They played key roles in determining companies' publishing plans and organizing the production process. But because the prior organization and personnel in both publishers' Editing Departments persisted into the 1960s, many experienced editorial staff continued to have a hand in management at several levels, even as production processes continued to follow pre-1949 models.

Dimensions of Cultural Production

Different generations and kinds of Chinese intellectuals in the twentieth century engaged in industrial publishing because of its tremendous productive power. Since books are at once commodities and media for transmitting ideas and circulating symbols, making books generates complex chains of social effects. Manufacturing books, in other words, is productive in several different ways that I track through the chapters that follow. At its most basic level, book manufacturing is economic production of a consumer commodity, for the book is a material object with a market value that is circulated, sold, and bought. But by giving material form to systems of ideas and cultural expression, books also produce knowledge in society and have impact on the cultural field. Further, by circulating as signs under the name of their authors, editors, or compilers, books also produce their producers in complex ways.[25] As they reach consumers, books additionally define communities of readers. By exploring each of these aspects of publishing, this book illuminates distinctive features of material economic production, knowledge and cultural production, and social production in modern China.

Economic Production

In their seminal work on the history of publishing, *The Coming of the Book*, Febvre and Martin emphasize that from the start the printed book in Europe was a commodity governed by concerns about capital investment and markets, like any other good.[26] Commercial concerns drove book production in China as well. Industrialization of book production allowed Chinese publishers to expand and diversify greatly the kinds of books and titles they published to appeal to different kinds of readers. To supply plural markets, publishers needed to mobilize the intellectual labor that could generate diverse genres of text with highly varied content. Coordinating the investment in talent (*rencai*) to be able to produce particular kinds of texts for specific markets was a central calculus for publishers in organizing their editing departments, and it is primarily this kind of capital investment that I focus on in the following chapters, although investments in machinery, paper, and retail outlets were also vital.

Before 1949 publishers sought to manage investment in talent by recruiting editorial staff in competitive labor markets to maximize the reading communities they could reach with products to increase profits. During the early PRC, cost-effective allocation of personnel (*fenpei*) to meet the demand from various segments of the reading public continued to be a concern as publishers sought to realize the aims of socialist construction while maximizing efficiency in a context with severe resource constraints. So, even though corporate profit ceased to be a driving motive during the Maoist period, before and after 1949 publishers thought in terms of adjusting numbers and kinds of editing personnel to be able to satisfy demand from variegated reading communities.

This book's focused consideration of the recruitment, training, and management of staff for technical work to produce cultural commodities contributes to a nascent scholarship on recruitment, training, and management of technical staff in modern Chinese enterprises.[27] By assessing how different groups of intellectuals were recruited into publishing companies at different historical moments, it illuminates the operations of labor markets and work dynamics for China's literate elite. In particular, it portrays how publishers competed with employers in the educational sector, government, and a host of emerging professional fields to secure necessary staff. Editors' mastery of techniques for writing and compiling particular categories of texts, as well as their understanding of the publishing process itself, fostered some degree of specialization over time. This limited specialization was captured in the term "publishing circles" (*chubanjie*), which came to be commonly used during the Republican period. But publishing work, like education, was always relatively accessible to a wide range of literate people. It was bounded by a fairly low threshold of technical skill or knowledge, and it was never governed by an association or licensing exam that would allow it to constitute itself as an exclusive profession on a Western model.[28] So publishing work never became professionalized to the same degree that law and medicine, for example, did during the Republican period;[29] rather, it remained open to a broad cross section of intellectuals, who used it for a range of objectives.

This book also provides a social ethnography of the work lives of editorial staff in three of China's leading capitalist enterprises, contributing to an emergent social history of professional and clerical labor in industrial corporations in the Western-language literature on China.[30] It opens a window onto how work to produce cultural commodities for a mass market shaped the daily lives of China's educated elite, from the period of competitive capitalism through the early years of state socialism. New forms of systematic training and standardized procedure configured intellectuals' work lives in unprecedented ways, but elements of literati leisure culture continued to characterize social life in the field of publishing, right into the 1960s. Editing departments also served as key sites for intellectual exchange and a whole host of cultural activities throughout this period. Their integration of practical efficiency and various forms of elite cultural practice characterized the distinctive form of Chinese cultural production that emerged in postimperial China.

Knowledge Production

As text commodities circulate to readers, they also serve to produce knowledge and culture. The proliferation of books certainly made knowledge, new and old, accessible to diverse communities of readers over the course of the twentieth century, as demonstrated most clearly perhaps with the textbook.[31] But the knowledge effects generated by increased book production were not limited to the transmission or circulation of established forms of knowledge.[32] Rather, the formulation and organization of ideas in texts also serves to configure and create systems of knowledge. For instance, Latour analyzes a process that he calls amplification, through which various mediations extend the findings of empirical scientific and social scientific research into different modes of public representation.[33] Likewise Foucault in *Archaeology of Knowledge* emphasizes how systems of knowledge are constituted by discursive fields, which are "made up of the totality of all effective statements (whether spoken or written), in their dispersion as events and in the occurrence that is proper to them."[34] Discursive fields, for Foucault, extend across the borders of specific texts and contexts of articulation. But insofar as he sees the enunciation of statements as a key step in the creation of systems of knowledge, the material production of texts is vital, for it allows those statements to have a social presence.

As China's major commercial publishers produced series, reference books, textbooks, and collections of classical texts, they generated the discursive fields through which new systems of thought were configured.[35] Publishing undoubtedly has played this vital role in many other contexts throughout the world, but the specific cultural and historical dynamics in twentieth-century China conditioned that process in several key ways. For one, the instability of institutions of higher learning in the early Republic, and after 1927 a Nationalist government that sought to shape higher education for its own ends, meant that the publishing sector was a privileged site for defining academic disciplines and formulating foundational knowledge in Chinese. Publishers' economic autonomy provided intellectuals with an outlet to configure disciplines and courses of study on their own terms (chapter 5). In addition, production of Chinese-language monographs and textbooks, through creatively synthesizing foreign scholarship, was vital to indigenizing new forms of Euro-American thought for Chinese scholarly and educational circles, challenging the hegemony of foreign-language textbooks and monographs.[36] Further, publishers' pursuit of mass markets, in concert with Confucian and nationalist ideas about the need to cultivate the citizenry, meant modern Chinese scholarship found a general reading market at a time when academic and popular or middlebrow readers' markets elsewhere were increasingly bifurcated.[37]

Distinctive features of classical scholarship as it developed in China's late imperial period also shaped the significance of the large-scale republication of classical texts that Shanghai's publishers undertook during the Republican and PRC periods (chapter 4). As in early modern Europe, print reproduction of classics democratized access to ancient texts.[38] But the virtual monopolization of rare editions during the Ming and Qing by private collectors primarily in the lower Yangzi region meant that the twentieth century's reprint series exploded class- and region-based barriers that had constituted intellectual hierarchies for centuries, giving such republication a special salience in twentieth-century China.[39] In addition, selection of editions and publishing formats configured the very archive for the twentieth-century project of "reorganizing the national heritage" (zhengli guogu).[40] In sum, publishing constituted the fundamental first step in the twentieth century's academic revolution, not its by-product or culmination.

Moreover, the publishing process itself could substantively change how knowledge and culture were packaged and presented. Developments elsewhere compel us to be attentive to this possibility. For instance, in his classic study of the publication of quarto and octavo editions of the Encyclopédie in eighteenth-century France, Robert Darnton demonstrates how the text was by turns condensed and expanded to meet the needs of various publications by provincial editors, who unceremoniously altered the text of elite scholars like Diderot and Rousseau.[41] "Publishers," he tells us, "in general had a cavalier attitude toward the written word in the eighteenth century. Books that now look like classics were thrown together casually and reshaped from edition to edition or even in the course of one printing."[42] Similarly, in twentieth-century China, staff editors were responsible for reframing and rewriting academic knowledge for textbooks, reference books, classical reprints, and series publications to make it accessible to broad markets of readers. New concepts central to modern academic knowledge consequently reached most readers in forms packaged by low-ranking staff members working in leading publishing companies rather than directly from the pens of leading intellectuals. Staff editors even played a key role in shaping the form through which ideas were expressed by writing the language textbooks that modeled the written vernacular (*baihua*) for students (chapter 3).

Social Production

Beyond producing profitable commodities, systems of knowledge, and forms of culture, publishing was also socially productive in a number of different ways. By "socially productive" I primarily mean how the publication of text enabled authors, editors, and publishers to define themselves socially in various ways, claiming different forms of status and recognition. I draw here from the work of Pierre Bourdieu. In his theorization of the "field of cultural production," for example, he analyzes the production of literary texts and artistic works by authors and artists as strategic moves to establish their reputations in relation to others.[43] Bourdieu explains that cultural works, apart from their economic value, also allow for the accumulation of symbolic capital, which "consists in making a name for oneself, a known, recognized name."[44] Authors and artists are characterized, or can claim particular positions in this field, by the kind and degree of critical recognition they receive and the relative market for their work. Recognition by other artists or writers, celebration by the dominant social and political elite, or acceptance by a mass market all establish authors' reputations in different ways and configure hierarchical rankings among them. Likewise, in *Homo Academicus*, Bourdieu describes research, publication, and public presentation (in the form of journalism, symposia, lectures, etc.), in contrast to institutional positions and control of examinations, as strategies for claiming prestige and influence in the academic field.[45] He argues that by adopting different research methods, as well as by presenting research in different genres and venues, scholars can strive to position their disciplines and themselves in competitive hierarchies of authority and prestige.

As authors and editors wrote for commercial publishers in twentieth-century China, they also established themselves socially in relation to dominant or emergent hierarchies of social and cultural value. New generations of scholars returned from study abroad, for example, wrote monographs representing their areas of specialized research for the series publications of the major publishers (chapter 5). These publications, as much as prestigious positions in elite universities, served to define them as leading scholars in their disciplines. At the same time, their writings' ability to find a market of general readers established the relevance of their discipline and their work for China's nation-building project. But the social production involved in publishing was not limited to elite scholars and prestigious authors. Staff editors could claim different kinds of social recognition based on their roles in the process of cultural production. Literati compilers of reprinted classical texts established themselves as classical scholars, experts in bibliography, through their work on major collections. Even staff editors writing boilerplate prose for textbooks and reference books could aspire to status as intellectuals because of their association with major cultural projects and their work with their brushes or pens rather than their hands.

In addition, from the late Qing through the early 1960s, publishers' editing departments served as contexts for various forms of cultural practice that marked the editors and scholars working there as intellectuals (chapters 1, 2, and 7). They served as forums for various kinds of intellectual exchange akin to study societies and literary associations. They were educational contexts where young scholars could use publishers' library resources for self-cultivation or apprentice with experienced publishing hands or established scholars. In addition, elite patterns of commensality, social drinking, and connoisseurship associated with the production and consumption of books characterized daily life at these companies through the early PRC period. All these practices contributed to forms of distinction that defined the Chinese intellectual.[46]

Specific features of China's cultural and academic fields and historical development created a calculus for social production different from the mechanisms Bourdieu describes for nineteenth- and early twentieth-century France. For one, the limited formalization of the academic domain in late Qing and Republican China meant that institutional academic resources were neither as stable nor as powerful as they were in the context Bourdieu describes in *Homo Academicus*. Moreover, because of the long history of convergence between scholarly and literary achievement, the academic field and field of cultural production in the early twentieth century were not highly differentiated and autonomous from each other. The fluid movement of literate people between academic institutions and publishing houses is one indication of this lack of relative differentiation. Both factors enhanced the impact of cultural production in the publishing field on academic and scholarly hierarchies. Further, the foreign academic disciplines introduced to China in the early twentieth century coexisted with classical Chinese scholarship to offer competing standards for academic and cultural evaluation. While the former claimed increasing prestige and power over the course of the twentieth century, the latter was never completely eliminated or marginalized, even in the early PRC.

In addition, Chinese political and cultural elites' preoccupation with mobilizing the citizenry for national salvation and, after 1949, socialist construction meant that the marketability of publications was a powerful basis of legitimation. A mass readership did not just connote profitability or indicate a lack of academic seriousness and rigor. Rather, it also represented the work's and the author's contribution to the project of nation building through educating and cultivating the nation's citizens. This symbolic value associated with mass-market accessibility complicates the opposition between autonomy and heteronomy that Bourdieu sees to be fundamental to the modern French cultural field. In twentieth-century China, art or scholarship "for its own sake" always ran the danger of seeming to be problematically disengaged from the central preoccupation of national survival.

This book is primarily a study of book production rather than consumption. But in line with Chinese publishers' concern with accessing important markets of readers, at key moments I consider how their choices about what kinds of texts to publish, and how to publish and market them, also helped to shape communities of readers. My approach here is informed by book-history scholars like Roger Chartier and Anindita Ghosh, who have demonstrated that we cannot assume a ready correspondence between sociological categories and communities of readers.[47] Rather, they suggest that textual packaging, genre, voice, style, content, and language can all play a part in shaping the formation of reading communities by influencing how accessible and appealing particular kinds of texts have been for different kinds of readers. Marketing and distribution also function to configure reading communities.

In Republican China, publishers strove to organize textbooks, series publications, reference books, and even some classical reprints to make them accessible to an imagined "general reading public" (*yiban dushu jie* or *duzhe qunzhong*). Insofar as theorists and political leaders envisioned modern citizens to be grounded in Western learning and global civilization, the "reading public" correlated to the emergent ideal of the national citizenry. A rough measure of the dimensions of the reading public they imagined can be generated by adding together the fully classically literate readers inherited from the late Qing, who had been capable of competing in the imperial examinations and would have continued to be active readers during the Republican period, with the numbers of students in the modern primary and secondary schools established after 1902. David Johnson estimates the former to have numbered roughly 5 million during the Qing period.[48] As of the early 1920s, there were roughly 6.8 million primary and secondary students nationwide.[49] By the late 1930s, there were approximately 18.4 million primary students (1936) and 522,625 secondary students (1935).[50] Taken together, these figures suggest a general reading public during the 1920s and 1930s in the range of 12 to 24 million. Given an overall population of roughly 400 million during this period, the major publishers' formulation of the general reading public defined the national community in a rather circumscribed way, excluding a much larger number of people who had more marginal forms of literacy.[51] But as a group of potential customers, the general reading public was significant in absolute terms. Reaching the "general reader" promised publishers both a substantial market and the greatest impact for their publications. Textbooks and reference books offered the best chance to capture the broadest cross section of individual customers (chapter 3). Institutional customers, like libraries, schools, or government offices, provided access points for most readers to more expensive large-scale series and reprint publications (chapters 4 and 5). At the same time, publishers continued to produce publications like photolithographed reprints of rare classical texts or synthetic monographs of cutting-edge academic scholarship that they pitched to elite reading communities. In this register, publications became vehicles for social distinction.

Bourdieu generally describes the field of cultural production with the metaphor of a competitive marketplace for economic, symbolic, and cultural capital. The economic side of this calculus was greatly dampened with the establishment of state socialism in China during the 1950s, as open labor markets were replaced with the centralized system of personnel allocation and profit ceased to be a central imperative for publishing companies.[52] Yet the competitive field of cultural and symbolic status continued to be operative, and Chinese authors and editors still sought recognition through their cultural work.[53] With the transformation of the political field, however, the system of values informing judgments about different cultural and academic works shifted in at least two important ways. For one, an emphasis on economic development—or socialist construction (*shehui zhuyi jianshe*)—enhanced the privileged status of technical and scientific work to an even greater extent than it had during the Republican period. In addition, cultural and academic work was increasingly evaluated according to the extent that it advanced socialist political agendas, or its "redness."[54]

The accumulation of symbolic capital through cultural production and cultural practice in the publishing field allowed everyone working in and for the publishers' editing departments to establish themselves as intellectuals (*zhishifenzi, zhishijieji*) in some sense.[55] They ranged from the leading academics and literary figures that contributed manuscripts to the staff editors working on group projects that I call petty intellectuals (*xiao zhishifenzi*), who had basic modern educations but lacked the cultural recognition, authority, mobility, and economic independence of leading scholars (chapter 2). Modern Chinese intellectuals, in other words, were defined in part by the production of published writing for a consuming public.[56] By focusing on how intellectuals built their reputations through participation in industrial capitalism and the cultural marketplace, I bring a new perspective to research on the intellectual in modern China, for much of the existing literature emphasizes the formative power of social movements and political parties in creating the modern intellectual.[57] In emphasizing dynamics of the cultural marketplace, my approach dovetails with recent work spearheaded by Nicolai Volland and Christopher Rea and others on the "cultural entrepreneur."[58] But where they focus primarily on the cultural innovations and initiatives of exceptional literary and business figures, this book demonstrates how a large cast of characters used their cultural production work to claim recognition as modern intellectuals. In fact, the relatively unknown "petty intellectuals," who did practical work on publishers' most lucrative products, such as textbooks, reference books, and classical republication projects, emerge in this book as unsung heroes of twentieth-century publishing. Without them, China's cultural transformation in the twentieth century might never have happened as it did.

By tracking these distinct dynamics of production, I capture the economic, intellectual, and social dimensions of industrial publishing and demonstrate their close interrelation. The material form of the book commodity, and its ability to generate profits for the first half of the twentieth century, made it a medium for constructing and disseminating new systems of ideas. Widespread circulation of textbooks, reference books, classical reprints, and series publications legitimized those ideas, contributed to reorganizing the national heritage, and generally helped transform the cultural field, while also constituting distinct communities of readers. At the same time, intellectuals benefited materially from their work as authors, compilers, and editors, and they benefited socially as the circulation of their works made their reputations. In China's modern publishing companies, material, cultural, and social processes of change were intertwined and mutually constitutive.

Power in Production

Industrial book production provided a vehicle for Chinese intellectuals to produce new forms of culture and new roles for themselves. But publishing houses were also cultural arenas and social contexts marked by shifting tensions among various forms of social, cultural, economic, and political power. We see those power relations playing out along several different vectors. The diverse kinds of intellectuals that publishers hired possessed varying forms of academic, social, and cultural capital, which differentially affected their positions in labor markets and in the companies. Changes in the organization of book production itself conditioned intellectuals' work in distinct ways. Moreover, the PRC state's interventions in the publishing industry during the transition to socialism in the 1950s made political power a fundamental force in book production in unprecedented ways. Intellectuals in the publishing industry operated among these cross-cutting "force relations."[59]

For the first half of the twentieth century, publishing companies recruited editors in open labor markets. During the late Qing and early Republic, with the end of the examination system and fall of the imperial state, the large numbers of Confucian-trained literati now had limited career options. Their cultural capital could easily be converted to win them positions in just a few fields, such as journalism and education, without investing in study overseas or in specialized training for new fields. Different combinations of exposure to foreign learning, examination success, distinction in classical scholarship, and access to social networks served to make them attractive recruits for publishing companies.

A decade later, students returning from overseas study with foreign degrees had high levels of academic capital in Republican China.[60] But in the late 1910s and early 1920s, academic and professional positions that corresponded to the specialized fields of their training were not necessarily available. Even when returned scholars could secure academic appointments, a crisis in higher education funding in the 1920s undermined the attractiveness of those positions.[61] Consequently, for the first half of the 1920s, returned scholars were drawn to work in publishing, but their specialized degrees made them relatively expensive and mobile, able to move into professional fields (e.g., law, medicine, engineering), government office, or academic institutions once they stabilized beginning in the late 1920s.[62] High school and college graduates had moderately high levels of academic capital for the time but even fewer career outlets, giving them limited leverage in the Republican labor markets.[63] Teaching, clerical work in business or banking, and journalism provided possible career alternatives.[64] Compared with these options publishing seemed attractive both for its pay and for allowing young graduates to live in the cultural center of Shanghai, find outlets for their intellectual interests, and participate in the cultural communities that editing departments became.

Changing relations of power characterized publishing companies' work dynamics as well. As increased competition made productive efficiency a central imperative of all the publishers in the 1920s and 1930s, managerial labor became monopolized by a relatively small group of general managers and executive editors who supervised staffs increasingly composed of petty intellectuals. Consequently, managers and executive editors dominated the process of defining product lines and organizing the labor systems, which conditioned the work of authors and editors in various ways. For instance, publishers imposed strict word limits and stylistic templates on series publications to which even elite scholars writing for the publishers had to adhere. Moreover, as managers organized production processes for textbooks and reference books according to industrial divisions of labor on the model of the factory assembly line to maximize efficiency, staff editors came to perform discrete tasks of textual production for publications planned and coordinated by others.

Despite these growing structural constraints, academics and staff editors also operated as a modern Chinese version of a "creative class" "whose economic function [was] to create new ideas, new technology and/or new content."[65] Publishers depended on their editors and authors to develop innovative content for new products, whether advanced academic monographs or serviceable textbooks for the school system. To achieve that goal, publishers gave even petty intellectual staff editors opportunities to take initiative to write books and articles. They also fostered a vibrant cultural and academic environment to encourage the germination of ideas. Consequently, a fundamental tension at the core of industrial capitalism between creative innovation and systematization for productive efficiency found full expression in Republican-period Chinese publishing companies.[66] But the forms that tension assumed and how it resolved at different historical moments were shaped by the postimperial Chinese context marked by ongoing legacies of late imperial culture, mass production of cultural commodities to promote mobilization for national salvation, and a literate elite seeking to reconstitute itself in the modern world.

After the founding of the PRC in 1949, the Chinese Communist government intervened in publishing in unprecedented ways. This book's exploration of state involvement provides the first detailed study in English of the dynamics of book publishing in the Mao era, and it illustrates how that system developed, in part, through adaptation and reorganization of pre-1949 publishing companies like Commercial Press and Zhonghua Book Company. Examination in chapter 6 of the publishers' corporate restructuring reveals that the process of reorganization and state intervention was ad hoc, uneven, and often improvised, not fully planned, systematic, nor strictly organized on a Soviet model. Thus, the experience of the leading publishing companies reinforces recent work on the early PRC that views Mao-era state-building and development projects as more serendipitous, adaptive, and opportunistic than programmatic and teleological.[67] In addition, these major capitalist companies, rather than avoiding state involvement, petitioned for public-private joint management in 1953, giving us a basis to revisit vital business-history questions about how enterprise reform transpired during the early PRC period.[68] Publishers' and editors' hopes for maintaining enterprise integrity and continuing to contribute to cultural development, as well as seizing opportunities to secure access to key segments of the book market, mitigated concerns about changing the ownership regime.

Once the transition to socialism occurred in 1954, Commercial Press and Zhonghua Book Company had state and party representatives on their boards and in their management. In addition, publishing plans and products were both subject to review and vetting by the Ministry of Culture and Central Propaganda Department. Yet the PRC state was not only a "propaganda state" bent on using media to transmit political messages to mobilize its people for political action.[69] It was also a pedagogical state that sought to instill knowledge in its citizens for socialist construction.[70] The knowledge that the state sought to produce, through the activities of intellectuals, and relate to its citizens, through both media and education, differed from propaganda in several ways. It had to be empirically validated, have practical efficacy for socialist construction (i.e., "seeking truth from facts"), and be able to pass tests of legitimacy with technical specialists operating both inside and outside the Chinese cultural context (i.e., having "universality").[71] Because of the state's pedagogical agenda, during the first seventeen years of the Maoist period, Chinese publishers like Commercial Press and Zhonghua Book Company still depended on the knowledge and skills of the "creative class" of experienced staff editors and specialized intellectuals to produce particular kinds of books to disseminate knowledge and transform Chinese culture. As a result, intellectuals and publishing hands working with or at these companies had some leverage to negotiate with state and party cultural administrators over the aims and operations of industrial publishing. Thus, early PRC publishing was characterized by what I term a negotiated form of cultural production whose dynamics continued to be shaped by the personnel and precedents of the Chinese publishing industry during the era of competitive capitalism. This picture of negotiated cultural production contrasts markedly with an image of the media under state socialism as being fully dominated from the center by the party and state as in the propaganda state model. Well into the 1960s Chinese intellectuals continued to be able to use publishing as a platform to influence culture and society while also pursuing their own personal and intellectual agendas, as they had since the final years of the Qing empire.

Structure of the Book

This book is organized both chronologically and thematically to capture historical developments and to highlight specific forms of book production and their social and cultural impact. Part 1 provides a chronological account of the formation and development of the leading publishers' editing departments during the late Qing and Republican periods. Chapter 1 analyzes Zhang Yuanji's formation of the Commercial Press Editing Department by recruiting late Qing literati primarily from the lower Yangzi (jiangnan) region, a strategy Zhonghua Book Company came to emulate in the 1910s. The literati editors' mastery of the Confucian classics combined with some modern learning allowed Commercial Press and Zhonghua to draw on one pool of editors to produce a wide range of modern and classical books. These editors, in turn, shaped the work culture at the publishers by introducing both literati leisure culture and collaborative approaches to book production modeled on literati study societies.

Chapter 2 follows the development of the major publishers' large editing departments from the 1920s through the 1940s. The cultural-reform movements and academic developments of the late 1910s and early 1920s motivated Commercial Press and Zhonghua to seek new talent for their Editing Departments in order to keep up with reader demand for new content that literati editors could not provide given their limited foreign learning. During the early 1920s, Commercial Press hired scholars who had studied overseas, and Zhonghua recruited leading cultural reformers to inject new life into their Editing Departments. These scholars pioneered monographic book production that diversified the publishers' lists, but they were far too expensive and mobile to retain as a permanent staff. So starting in the 1920s the two leading publishers and the newly formed World Book Company turned to recruiting recent graduates of the Chinese school system as staff editors. In the face of intensifying competition and demand, the companies developed an industrial model of book production in their editing departments, with staff editors working according to refined divisions of labor under executive editors to produce textbooks, reference books, and series for a mass market. But literati, academics, and staff editors together created vibrant intellectual environments in editing departments, where they pursued their own projects and enjoyed forms of leisure and culture that marked them as scholarly elites.

Part 2 explores how the publishers' production of different genres of text shaped the development of twentieth-century Chinese culture while also contributing to the social production of several types of modern intellectual. In chapter 3 I describe the production of language textbooks and the encyclopedic dictionaries *Ciyuan* (1915) and *Cihai* (1936). Together language textbooks and *Ciyuan* introduced and helped standardize the modern Chinese lexicon and consolidate the conceptual changes introduced through the late Qing reforms. *Cihai* defined the terms and concepts that modern academic disciplines, social movements, and political parties introduced during the 1920s. Language textbooks written by staff editors during the 1920s and 1930s also provided models for vernacular writing that shaped student prose from this generation onward. As a result, literati and petty intellectual staff editors played significant roles in some of the twentieth century's most lasting linguistic and conceptual changes.

Even as companies were publishing modern textbooks and dictionaries, they also reprinted classical texts, which is the focus of chapter 4. From the 1910s through the 1930s, Commercial Press and Zhonghua Book Company mobilized economic and human capital to publish the *Collection of Chinese Classical, Historical, Philosophical, and Literary Works* (*Sibu congkan* 四部叢刊), *Essential Writings from the Four Categories of Learning* (*Sibu beiyao* 四部備要), and the *Complete Collection of Past and Present Books and Illustrations* (*Gujin tushu jicheng* 古今圖書集成). They drew on the expertise and rare-book collections of literati editors and their colleagues to compile these major collections that served to democratize classical learning for late Qing literati and a new generation of students moved by calls to "organize the national heritage" (*zhengli guogu*). Through their compilation work, literati editors like Sun Yuxiu and Zhang Yuanji established themselves as scholars of editions and classical bibliography. By contrast, efforts to reprint in its entirety the *Complete Book of Four Treasuries* (*Siku quanshu* 四庫全書) by collaborating with Republican states proved much less successful.

Chapter 5 focuses on publishers' series publications, which presented Chinese readers with literature from throughout the world and synthetic monographs covering the fields of modern science, social science, and humanities. Some leading series, like Commercial Press's Complete Library (Wanyou wenkou 萬有文庫) and World Book Company's ABC Series (ABC congshu ABC 叢書), aimed at the general reading public. But others, such as Commercial Press's University Series (Daxue congshu 大學叢書) sought to reach academic and professional readers with specialized studies presenting cutting-edge research. Writing studies for these different kinds of series enabled authors, whether outside academics or staff editors, to represent fields of knowledge within China and to present themselves as experts in particular areas of study. At the same time, they mapped out the disciplines and scholarly approaches in a global system of knowledge and they adapted those approaches to China's educational and cultural needs through a form of writing I characterize as synthetic construction.

China's leading publishing companies were some of Republican China's foremost capitalist enterprises, yet Commercial Press and Zhonghua Book Company managed to thrive during the early period of Chinese state socialism. Their transformation and publishing activities are the focus of part 3. In chapter 6 I discuss both publishers' reorganization as public-private joint-venture enterprises (*gong si heying qiye*). Over time they each took on distinct areas of specialization within the framework of state planning, with Commercial Press focusing on translating Western humanities, social science, and science scholarship and Zhonghua Book Company reprinting classical texts and producing reference books. Managers in the two companies, and party and state cultural administrators, saw benefits from working with each other, which provided for a cooperative relationship that left intact many of the institutions and personnel that the commercial publishers had developed during the Republican period.

For the PRC state, publishing served a fundamental role disseminating knowledge for the purpose of socialist construction, generating the distinctive form of negotiated cultural production that is the focus of chapter 7. Party and state cultural administrators depended on the content knowledge and publishing experience of academic experts and staff editors to produce the books necessary for their cultural projects. To realize those projects, the two sides negotiated over the architecture of publishing plans and the framing and content of particular series and books. Concern for efficiently meeting demand for publications for specific segments of society provided a basis for publishers to continue to use personnel and production methods developed under competitive capitalism for book manufacturing under state socialism, even as more "socialist" modes of collective production were tried and abandoned. These common dynamics of book production enabled academics and staff editors to find avenues to pursue their own agendas and contribute to cultural exchange through publishing work in ways similar to those of the first half of the twentieth century.

The extreme politicization of culture during the 1960s, which culminated in the Cultural Revolution, destroyed the system of negotiated cultural production developed during the 1950s and interrupted intellectuals' activities in the publishing field. As the concluding chapter demonstrates, the cultural politics of production came to trump productive efficiency for socialist pedagogy during the Cultural Revolution decade (1966–1976). Certain vestiges of negotiated cultural production and pre-1949 publishing dynamics, however, might still be animating the Chinese publishing industry today.

PART ONE

Recruiting Talent, Mobilizing Labor

CHAPTER I

Becoming Editors

Late Qing Literati's Scholarly Lives and Cultural Production

4. Store up talent.

—ZHANG YUANJI'S NOTES FROM A LUNCH MEETING ON GOALS FOR
COMMERCIAL PRESS, MARCH 27, 1916

In 1907 Sun Yuxiu was at loose ends.[1] Son of a family of rural intellectuals from just west of Wuxi, Sun showed early academic promise. He won the *xiucai* degree in 1895, tested into Jiangyin's new-style Nanjing Academy (Nanjing shuyuan 南菁書院) the same year, and gained higher stipend status in the 1896 examinations. But thereafter his progress stalled. He failed three successive provincial examinations at Suzhou and turned to traditional havens of unsuccessful literati—teaching and serving as a private secretary—but neither offered stable, long-term employment. Sensing the shift of intellectual climate, Sun studied English with a Protestant missionary and pursued whatever modern education he could. With the abrogation of the civil service examinations in 1905, Sun's struggles deepened as he bounced from one uncertain short-term engagement to another, without even the hope of possible future examination success to motivate him.

As he floundered, Sun tried his hand at translating *Carpenter's Geographical Reader*. In the course of shopping the manuscript to various publishers in the spring of 1907, Sun approached Commercial Press through an intermediary, who used the preface of the translation as an introductory text. Sun's timing, for once, was fortuitous. Head of the Commercial Press Editing Department, Zhang Yuanji 張元濟, was recruiting scholars who could compile textbooks and reference books for the rapidly growing publisher, which was in the process of publishing textbooks for the newly launched modern Chinese school system. After a short meeting with Zhang, Sun

[27]

was hired to a joint appointment in the Editing Department's English Division and the Chinese Division for a monthly salary of one hundred yuan. The publisher also purchased one portion of the manuscript of his translation for two hundred yuan. Soon thereafter, Sun bought some Commercial Press stock, which vested him in the company. For the next sixteen years, until his death in 1923, Sun translated foreign texts, compiled children's literature, evaluated classical editions for the library, and helped Zhang Yuanji prepare the classical reprint series *Sibu congkan*. In short, he found both a job and a career at Commercial Press.

He was not alone. For the generation of scholars left stranded by the end of the civil service examinations, the introduction of foreign learning, and ultimately the end of the imperial order, commercial publishing companies like Commercial Press and Zhonghua Book Company provided a vital career outlet from the first years of the twentieth century into the early 1920s. As each publisher built up an editing department to produce textbooks, reference books, and journals, it sought to recruit talented men with multiple skill sets, as the epigraph from Zhang Yuanji relates. Over years, if not decades, working for a publisher provided scholars like Sun with a steady income, an outlet for their scholarly activities, and a ready-made community of like-minded colleagues. In turn, this generation of classically trained scholars with reformist proclivities and some exposure to modern Western learning shaped the work culture of each publisher in decisive ways. This chapter explores the symbiotic relationship between China's emergent commercial publishers and the last generation of late Qing literati during the first two decades of the twentieth century.

The Search for Talent

Xia Ruifeng 夏瑞芳 partnered with Bao Xian'en 鮑咸恩, Bao Xianchang 鮑咸昌, and Gao Fengchi 高鳳池 in 1897 to found Commercial Press primarily as a printing company.[2] Opportunities for textbook publishing after the turn of the twentieth century compelled Xia to reach out to reformist literati based in Shanghai, first Cai Yuanpei 蔡元培 and then Zhang Yuanji, to head an Editing Department (*bianyisuo*) that could compile textbooks for the emergent school system initiated by the Qing New Policies in 1902 and 1904. Expansion of schools and growth of the textbook market compelled the publisher to hire new editors to compile textbooks.[3] Commercial

Press benefited in multiple ways from its location in Shanghai. The foreign concessions afforded some measure of protection against Chinese political authorities. As a gateway for the import of foreign technology, Shanghai allowed them ready access to advanced printing machinery. It also allowed them to acquire capital for expansion, as they did through a partnership with the Japanese textbook publisher Kinkōdō starting in 1903.[4] Moreover, Shanghai was a key node in an expanding network of urban transportation centers that allowed Commercial Press to grow a nationwide system of branch stores and affiliated retailers to expand its market.[5]

Perhaps most important, though, was Shanghai's location at the heart of the lower Yangzi region, which gave Commercial Press access to the extensive human capital constituted by the scholarly elite concentrated in Jiangsu and Zhejiang.[6] Beginning in 1903, when Zhang became editorial director, through 1921, Zhang and Gao Mengdan, who succeeded him, actively recruited scholars, many of them from the Jiangnan region, to work in or for the Editing Department. Zhonghua Book Company, whose leaders worked first for Commercial Press, replicated many of the same patterns of scholarly recruitment after its formation in 1912. The result was that into the 1920s both companies depended primarily on late Qing literati to write, compile, translate, and edit their publications.

Surveying Zhang Yuanji's detailed diary reveals a process of constant recruitment of compilers and editors that allowed Commercial Press to produce varied publications. Zhang's entries during the 1910s show him managing on nearly a daily basis recommendations for prospective authors and editors from colleagues inside the publisher and his large network of acquaintances outside it. Zhang, Gao Mengdan 高夢旦, and other leading figures in the Editing Department, such as Jiang Weiqiao 蔣維喬, Zhuang Yu 莊俞, Du Yaquan 杜亞泉, and Sun Yuxiu, evaluated candidates' capabilities in relation to the publisher's ongoing publication agendas. Hiring involved complex determinations regarding whether to bring a scholar into the Editing Department full-time, keep them on retainer as a consultant or regular contributor, or pay them manuscript fees or royalties for particular projects. Zhang and his colleagues also considered salaries for particular individuals in light of the pay scales of editors and compilers doing similar kinds and quality of work in an effort to systematize compensation during the course of these decades.

Editorial staff came to Commercial Press mostly through recommendations. This approach privileged personal relational networks in a pattern inherited from the late imperial period, when personal secretaries and other professional staff were often chosen by recommendation and personal introduction.[7] Once a scholar was introduced, Zhang and his colleagues considered the person's background and experience, related them to various publication projects, and evaluated whether to hire them, in what capacity, and according to what pay scale.[8] In each instance, Zhang considered the prospective candidate in light of his educational background and work experience to gauge his potential value to the company. But he also considered how much salary the candidate would command given his previous work record. Tan Lianxun 譚廉遜, with high school teaching experience and a recommendation from leading editor Jiang Weiqiao, could be hired with a salary of around forty yuan per month and was an easy choice.[9] Dong Maotang 董懋堂 could demand a somewhat higher salary because of previous positions and required more careful consideration.[10] At the same time, Zhang sought to relate candidates' skills to particular projects or needs at the publisher. For instance, Zhou Jimei 周寄梅 had exceptional English skills for the time because of study at the University of Wisconsin, which made him an attractive hire.[11]

Hiring a scholar to work as a compiler or editor for the Editing Department staff constituted a long-term commitment and carried the expectation that the staff member would contribute to a range of projects. Zhang also contracted with scholars outside the company to do specific writing, compiling, translating, and reviewing tasks. Most commonly, the publisher bought finished manuscripts from scholars for fixed prices, which allowed it to secure copyright.[12] Manuscript prices, depending on the length and complexity of the books in question, ranged from roughly one hundred yuan to several hundred yuan per volume. A consistent feature of Jiang Weiqiao's work at Commercial Press during the first two decades of the twentieth century was to review manuscripts offered to the company for sale, revealing a constant flow of material into the publisher from outside authors.[13] For shorter pieces, especially fiction and translation, Commercial Press paid authors or translators by set rates per thousand characters, which ranged from two to four yuan.[14] Manuscripts were not always purchased with cash, however. Occasionally, authors were compensated, in whole or in part, in the form of a certain number of free books.[15] Some authors also arranged to be paid in royalties.[16] Once they had acquired a manuscript by purchase or royalties, companies could protect their right to be the sole publisher of a book by registering it with the Shanghai

Booksellers' Guild and the Shanghai Booksellers' Trade Association, which Fei-hsien Wang argues played the key role of policing the book market during the Republican period.[17]

Beyond authors who either became permanent staff members or sold manuscripts from outside the publisher, Commercial Press also maintained a range of long-term consulting or contract relationships with many scholars, who were paid by salary or on a piecework basis for consistent part-time work. For instance, in 1912 for compiling dictionaries on a part-time basis, the company considered paying two scholars each salaries of one hundred and two hundred yuan per month.[18] In another example, beginning in 1913, after several false starts with other prospective editors, Zhang hired Yu Shaohua 郁少華 to revise Commercial Press's *English-Chinese New Dictionary* (*Ying Hua xin zidian*). Yu worked outside Commercial Press but was offered graduated payments of one hundred fifty yuan per period in which he would complete separate sections of the dictionary (up to *G*, up to *N*, up to *S*, and through the end).[19] Whether paid piece rate or salary, in each of these instances scholars not formally on staff maintained a long-term relationship with Commercial Press.

All the hiring practices discussed here depended on interpersonal networks among literati.[20] Leaders at Commercial Press, staff working in the Editing Department, or their friends and professional acquaintances outside the publisher recommended people for new staff positions or to contribute to specific projects. Those recommended could be friends, relatives, classmates, or residents of a common native place. Colleagues also recommended or recruited scholars known by reputation or by previous publications, whether they had been written for Commercial Press or other publishers. In all cases, however, personal or intellectual relationships, which formed the strands of the literati social network, provided the basis for hiring or engagement. In this way literati culture facilitated industrial book production.

Throughout this period, Zhang Yuanji and the other leading editors at Commercial Press sought to systematize rates of pay across these different kinds of work. In terms of staff within the Editing Department, requests for salary increases were evaluated in relation to other employees doing similar work, with a goal of some degree of parity across the staff. For instance, in June 1912 Zhang set the starting salaries at the same level of sixty yuan per month for two incoming staff editors who were introduced separately.[21] In May that year Du Yaquan asked for monthly salaries of three employees to be raised by ten yuan each because of increased responsibilities or effective work.[22] But in August Zhang hesitated to give pay raises to two of the editors in an effort to maintain some parity among staff.[23] In October 1912, Du Yaquan reported that a valued editor was in danger of being poached by a school offering a higher salary, and he convinced Zhang and Gao Mengdan to raise the editor's salary the following year.[24] In these various examples taken from one year, we see Zhang Yuanji, Gao Mengdan, and other leading figures in the Editing Department seeking to establish parity in pay for similar grades of staff while also responding to labor markets for teaching, government service, and other kinds of writing that provided literati with other work opportunities. Efforts to standardize pay also extended to writing purchased by contract. For instance, when Wang Zhonggu 汪仲谷 introduced Lu Qiuxin 陸秋心 to compile and translate fiction, Zhang Yuanji quoted him seemingly fixed rates of pay: "Told him that the highest level was three yuan per thousand characters, next two and a half yuan, and then two yuan, with short stories being the most useful."[25] Bao Tianxiao likewise cites standard rates for manuscript fees ranging from two to three yuan per thousand characters.[26]

By the time Hu Shi 胡適 visited Commercial Press in the summer of 1921, when he was recruited to become the new head of the Editing Department and consulted for suggestions about how to reorganize it, pay for the editorial staff was stratified, ranging from less than thirty yuan per month at the entry level to more than three hundred yuan a month for a select few.

MONTHLY SALARIES FOR THE COMMERCIAL PRESS
EDITING DEPARTMENT (1921)[27]

300+ yuan: 2 people
250–300 yuan: 1
200–250 yuan: 4
150–200 yuan: 8
120–150 yuan: 17
100–120 yuan: 5
70–100 yuan: 14
50–70 yuan: 17
30–50 yuan: 46
0–30 yuan: 62

These hierarchical pay rates reflected the differences in background, experience, and mobility mentioned in the discussion of editorial staff recruitment. At the same time, these tiered rates of pay also reflected the efforts by Zhang and Gao Mengdan to establish rough wage parity for each stratum of editorial staff. Most generally, Zhang Yuanji and his colleagues succeeded in their main objective: pooling a large group of talented men for wages that were standardized at a relatively low rate. By 1921 Commercial Press's editorial staff was impressively large, with 176 members. Of that total number, 139 (79 percent) earned less than one hundred yuan per month, and 108 (61 percent) earned less than fifty yuan per month.

In 1912, Commercial Press employee Lufei Kui 陸費逵 secretly teamed up with several colleagues to establish Zhonghua Book Company, which became Commercial Press's leading competitor. In its basic organization, Zhonghua followed the Commercial Press model, recruiting a large Editing Department with a permanent staff. Other former Commercial Press Editing Department colleagues, like Dai Kedun 戴克敦 and Shen Zhifang 沈知方 (芝芳), formed the core personnel of the new company. This pattern of experienced editors joining a new publishing company at its founding, as would subsequently happen with World Book Company and Kaiming Bookstore, constituted one of the main patterns of horizontal mobility among companies for editorial staff during the Republican period.[28] In 1913, a year after its founding, Zhonghua Book Company's Editing Department had a staff of seventy to eighty compilers and editors; by 1916 the number had grown to more than a hundred.[29] These large editing departments with permanent staffs that wrote, compiled, and revised texts represented a distinctively Chinese approach to publishing that persisted, with some alterations, through the Republican period and into the 1960s. This model contrasted starkly with that of contemporaneous Western publishers, which operated with just a handful of acquisition and copy editors.[30]

Such large stables of talented men were affordable at this time because late Qing literati were seeking new sources of income and outlets for their abilities after the end of the civil service examination and the Qing empire. As the accounts drawn from Zhang Yuanji's and Jiang Weiqiao's diaries suggest, large numbers of literate men persistently sought work in the publishing industry during the first two decades of the twentieth century. Permanent large editing departments were also economically rational for the publishers because of the dynamics of the Chinese book market at this time. Through the early 1920s, textbooks constituted a major proportion of each company's business. For instance, in the early 1920s Commercial Press estimated that it had sold upward of fifty million volumes (*ce*) of just its *Republican Chinese Language Textbook* (*Gonghe guowen jiaokeshu*), which had been developed after the 1911 Revolution.[31] During Zhonghua's first few years, when textbooks were its main product, by 1916 the company grew to do more than one million yuan of business annually, earning more than two hundred thousand yuan in profits and building up two million yuan in base capital.[32]

Yet frequent changes in textbook standards meant that publishers needed to be prepared, every few years, to produce whole sets of textbooks in the course of a few months.[33] In the words of longtime Commercial Press textbook compiler Zhuang Yu, "Each time the educational system was modified, textbooks immediately changed. Often before a book would be fully issued, we would have to quickly compile the second book [on the same subject]."[34] Having a bull pen of well-educated men and capable writers made such rapid production of large numbers of diverse textbooks possible. At the same time, other kinds of publications and services that had large market demand, such as journals and correspondence schools, also required constant production of text.[35] For other kinds of lucrative large-scale publications, especially reference books, simultaneous mobilization of large numbers of compilers was also quite effective. Commercial Press and Zhonghua Book Company developed and sustained their large editing departments because they allowed the publishers to rapidly generate large amounts of text for the genres of product most important for their business. Once they had assembled these large groups of editors, they could also encourage them to write, translate, or compile specific additional projects that had market potential, such as fiction, monographs, or republished classical texts. Still, the possibility of soliciting manuscripts on specific subjects by purchase, word count, or royalty provided an alternative model of mobilizing talent that complemented the publishers' main approach of keeping a large Editing Department with a permanent staff. These arrangements by independent contract also continued to be used by commercial publishers through the late Qing and early Republican periods.

Hybrid Learning as a Cultural Resource

The late Qing literati who made up the large permanent staffs at the Commercial Press and Zhonghua Book Company Editing Departments during the first two decades of the twentieth century had classical educations, and many of them had competed, with varying degrees of success, in the civil service examinations. Yet many were also attracted to new forms of Western and Japanese learning, which they acquired through formal or informal channels. As a result they had hybrid intellectual backgrounds on which they could draw for their compiling and editing work. In addition, many of them sympathized with and at times participated quite actively in movements for constitutional reform, social change, and political revolution that marked the late Qing and early Republic. Their plural backgrounds and social experiences inevitably shaped the dynamics of their work at the modern publishers.

Mao Dun's 茅盾 (originally Shen Yanbing 沈雁冰) memoir provides a vivid snapshot of the personnel in the Commercial Press Editing Department when he joined it in 1916. He quickly discovered that it was populated primarily by former officials, degree holders, and personal secretaries, men well trained in the classical tradition who sometimes also had some degree of Western learning and were also often committed to late Qing and early Republic agendas of reform and revolution. For instance, Chen Chengze 陳承澤, Xu Ke 徐珂 (style name Zhongke 仲可), and Wu Zengqi 吳曾祺 (Yiting 翊庭) were all provincial degree holders (*juren* 舉人) with different mixes of classical and modern educational backgrounds.[36] As with Sun Yuxiu, other editors Mao Dun encountered had not achieved political positions or great success on the examinations but still had invested intense effort in classical learning, even while acquiring some modern education. In fact, most of the leading figures in the Commercial Press Editing Department from its earliest years, such as Zhang Yuanji, Gao Mengdan, and Zhuang Yu, were classically trained scholars who also had some Western learning and were committed to projects of social and political reform.[37]

The leading figures in Zhonghua Book Company's Editing Department during the 1910s paralleled the late Qing literati group at Commercial Press in their academic backgrounds and reform predilections.[38] For instance, Fan Yuanlian 範源廉, who directed the Editing Department from 1912 to 1916, was a native of Xiangyin, Hunan, and in 1898 studied under Liang Qichao at the Shiwu School, imbibing the combination of classical scholarship and modern learning that characterized Kang Youwei and Liang's reform movement during this period.[39] After the failure of the Hundred Days Reform in Emperor Guangxu's court in 1898, Fan studied in Japan, where he established accelerated courses in politics and law and in teacher training. He also subsequently served as an adviser to the late Qing Ministry of Education. Zhang Xiang 張相, Zhonghua's leading textbook compiler and assistant director of the Editing Department, was a child prodigy and a *xiucai* degree holder.[40] But before entering publishing he spent most of his career teaching at modern schools in his hometown of Hangzhou. Dai Kedun's 戴克敦 career trajectory was quite similar. Also a *xiucai* from Hangzhou, Dai taught at Hangzhou's Qiushi Academy before joining Commercial Press as an editor.[41] One of the creators of Zhonghua Book Company with Lufei Kui, Dai replaced Fan as the director of the Editing Department in 1916 and held the position until his death in 1925. Coming out of the same milieu of classical education and social reform as the leading intellectual figures at Commercial Press, Fan, Zhang, and Dai set the tone for the Zhonghua Editing Department during the 1910s and early 1920s. Other key figures in the Zhonghua Book Company Editing Department, such as Xie Meng 謝蒙and Xu Yuangao 徐元誥, shared elements of these men's background in classical learning, study in modern schools, and reform or revolutionary commitments.[42] As with Commercial Press, then, Zhonghua Book Company's Editing Department included its share of classically trained scholars who had acquired some degree of modern learning, at times through overseas study, and reformist or revolutionary inclinations.

Commercial Press editor Jiang Weiqiao's detailed diary affords some insight into this group's intellectual influences as well as how their social, cultural, and political experiences informed their activities in the two publishers' Editing Departments. Jiang initially had a classical education and prepared for the civil service examinations in his youth.[43] But exposure to publications from the Jiangnan Arsenal on Western technology caused him to shift his focus to modern learning and educational reform beginning in 1895. When he started working for Commercial Press in 1903, he was already teaching at the Patriotic Girls' School of the Patriotic Education Society (Aiguo xueshe) and translating and writing for the radical newspaper *Subao*. At the same time, Jiang was studying English and other subjects while also participating actively in educational-reform activities. For instance, in 1905 he taught chemistry in the China Education Association's mobile lecture course (*tongxuesuo*) while studying physics and biology; in later years he also studied botany, for which he collected samples.[44] Though based in Shanghai, he remained active in social-reform efforts in his hometown of Changzhou, such as the Changzhou Library (Changzhou tushuguan), Anti-Foot-Binding Association, and a primary school.[45] In Shanghai he was an active member of the Jiangsu Provincial Education Association.[46] In December 1910 he participated in the Tianshi Hygiene Association's (Weishenghui) queue-cutting party at Zhang Garden and cut off his own queue, much to his own relief and his wife's chagrin.[47] Further, in the aftermath of the 1911 Revolution, he cooperated with Jiang Kanghu in forming the Chinese Socialist Party, for which Jiang Weiqiao was elected the first vice-chairman.[48] All these activities mark him as an active member of the reformist camp.

Beyond his social-reform efforts and political involvement, however, Jiang celebrated living in Shanghai as an opportunity to learn and grow intellectually. At the end of 1903, for instance, he gushed, "This year living in Shanghai, the knowledge gained from my experiences and what I learned from education was ten or one hundred times that of other years."[49] In fact, Jiang's meticulous annual review of his reading materials also shows him to have been steeped in the reformist intellectual currents of the late Qing. In 1903 he read volumes 24 to 32 of the *New People's Journal* (*Xinminbao*) and volumes three to five of *New Fiction* (*Xin xiaoshuo*). In 1904 he read, in part, more of the *New People's Journal*, volume 21 of *Free Marriage* (*Ziyou jiehun*), and one volume of *Travels in the New World* (*Xindalu youji*), along with much of the *Hanfeizi* and *Huainanzi*.[50] In 1905 Jiang's readings concentrated on education, psychology, and philosophy.[51] In 1906, besides a series of books on natural science, Jiang focused more systematically on timely themes of political reform, reading a *Preliminary Discussion of Constitutional Government* (*Xianzheng peilun*), one volume of lectures on government, law, and finance from Waseda University, and the first volume of *Constitutional Government Magazine* (*Xianzheng zazhi*), as well as translations of Darwin's *Origin of Species*.[52] In 1907 and 1908 he continued reading about law, politics, and society, along with Yan Fu's translation of a book on logic.[53] In 1909 he wrote a critical review of Yan Fu's translation, faulting him for choosing overly obscure classical terms to translate basic concepts.[54] At the same time, as the momentum for constitutional reform and local self-government grew, Jiang read practical guides to political organization and civic action, such as *Essential Knowledge About Elections* (*Xuanju xuzhi*), *Key Points of City, Town, and Township Self-Government* (*Cheng zhen xiang difang zizhi yaoyi*), and *Essential Knowledge for Assemblymen* (*Yiyuan xuzhi*).[55] Even as he read widely in newly introduced currents of Western thought, Jiang also consistently read Mahayana Buddhist sutras and commentaries along with books about Buddhism, which was the focus of his religious and ethical life.[56] In combining readings on statecraft and practical concerns with classical literature on ethics and self-cultivation, Jiang continued a major pattern of literati intellectual life.

Jiang's broad readings in politics, law, ethics, education, psychology, and science exposed him to many of the most powerful new intellectual currents of the late Qing. His reading syllabus shows him to have kept up with current events and debates, even as he continued to read classical literature. This hybrid world of intellectual influences was characteristic of many late Qing literati in Jiangnan. These intellectual currents, and the reformist or revolutionary sympathies of this generation of compilers and editors, shaped the contours of the textbooks, reference books, and journals that they wrote during the late Qing and early Republic. At the same time, their background in classical scholarship could also provide a resource on which to draw for new publications. Generally speaking, work at a publisher could provide an outlet for various intellectual commitments.

Reproduction of Literati Culture in a Modern Industrial Workplace

The presence of classically trained scholars in the editing departments of the major publishers shaped the work culture of those companies, even as it allowed for the production of a diverse range of print commodities for the market. From the late Qing into the 1920s, Chinese literati reproduced the habitus of elite scholarly culture at the center of the commercial publishers, which were quickly becoming leading institutions of China's emergent industrial capitalism.[57] That habitus was marked, in part, by the predominance of personal and ascriptive networks in recruitment and organization, a generalist work style, and practices associated with a literati lifestyle, such as social commensality, drinking parties, book-buying excursions, and a shared masculine living space. Several of these historically rooted aspects of the late Qing literati's reconstituted elite scholarly practice might at first glance seem to run counter to the emergent industrialization of mental labor in the publishing sector, a process that would take structural reforms and two generational shifts to complete (as chapter 2 demonstrates).

Yet in large part the literati habitus in fact proved to be economically beneficial, for those practices enabled late Qing literati and the publishers to adapt flexibly to the variegated and changing market conditions of the first two decades of the twentieth century. We have already seen evidence of the economic efficacy of some practices characteristic of late imperial literati culture in the previous discussion of staff recruitment. Hiring of editorial staff occurred primarily through personal introductions and recommendations.[58] Similarly, manuscripts were most often introduced or solicited through personal contacts. In both these ways, literati relational networks helped to fuel the growth of China's modern industrial publishing. Literati leisure culture, in the form of banquets, drinking parties, and poetry gatherings, further sustained the networks that facilitated staff recruitment and manuscript solicitation. This leisure culture also helped to euphemize the demands for profit and efficiency associated with the publishers as modern capitalist enterprises. New modes of group association modeled on the study society, a central organizational form for late Qing and early Republican social and political reformers, supported compilation of textbooks and reference books. Moreover, a generalist work style enabled publishers to tap one pool of talent to produce a wide range of publications. Literati cultural practices, in short, helped to underpin the development of industrialized cultural production during the first two decades of the twentieth century.

Workplace Organization

Literati working in the commercial publishing companies adopted late imperial patterns of scholarly practice that shaped the internal organization and work culture at the major publishers. For one, the early editing departments were organized according to broad and vague categories of learning. At the time when Mao Dun joined the Commercial Press Editing Department in 1916, for instance, it was separated into divisions for English, Chinese (*guowen* 國文), science (*lihua* 理化), and dictionaries (*cidian* 辭典), with small groups focused on working on each of the magazines the company published.[59] During the same period, Zhonghua Book Company's Editing Department was similarly divided along general lines and by genre more than subject area. Its key divisions were for textbooks, "ordinary books" (*putong tushu* 普同圖書), English publications, dictionaries, magazines, and illustrations.[60]

In practice, the boundaries between these divisions were very fluid, and the work culture of these editing departments reflected literati culture and an eclectic, generalist approach to scholarship and writing. Mao Dun, in his memoir, brilliantly captured the atmosphere of Commercial Press's Editing Department office:

> The Editing Department was on the second floor of a large three-story, rectangular Western-style building. On three sides were windows, and in the front at the entrance were three reception rooms separated by partial wooden partitions, with doors and windows for each. Another wooden partition separated these meeting rooms from the large hall of the Editing Department [*bianjibu dating* 編輯部大廳]. Within this large hall was the English Division, Chinese Division, Science Division, and each periodical's editorial group, but because the number of people in each division differed and the large hall had only this area, it was not possible to divide it into small rooms with a regular shape, and we could only work all mixed together in an interconnected space. When one saw it for the first time, with large and small tables lying this way and that, packed closely together, with the loud sound of voices, it in fact seemed like a teahouse.[61]

The absence of spatial separation between departments reveals the relative lack of functional differentiation within Commercial Press's Editing Department, and Mao Dun's comparison to the teahouse captures its affinities with one cultural preserve of late imperial literati.[62] Zhonghua's Editing Department was organized in much the same way (figure 1.1).

Rather than subject matter, discipline, or academic background providing the organizational logic for functional subdivisions within editing departments, memoirs and diaries describing Commercial Press suggest that familiar patterns of native place and kinship relations, along with factional affiliations, were decisive. In the Commercial Press Editing Department, the Chinese Division, directed by Wujin 武進 native Zhuang Yu, was the preserve of the Changzhou faction; the Science Division, under Du Yaquan, was dominated by people from Shaoxing 紹興; and Huzhou 湖州 (Zhejiang) natives, Mao Dun included, made up a plurality of the staff in the English Division.[63] Jiang Weiqiao introduced several fellow Changzhou natives into Commercial Press, recommended their manuscripts, and maintained close contact with them in the Editing Department, especially Zhuang Yu.[64] An extensive network of Fujianese scholars, including Gao Mengdan, Zheng Zhenwen, Chen Chengze, Wu Zengqi, and Jiang Boxun

Figure 1.1 Zhonghua Book Company Editing Department circa 1916. The top photo is of the General Editing Division, the Dictionary Division, the English Division, Magazine Division, and the Illustration Division. The lower photo is of the Textbook Division and the Ordinary Book Division. All the divisions are in one large hall separated by double rows of bookshelves, similar to the organization at Commercial Press described by Shen Yanbing. *Zhonghua shuju wunian gaikuang* 中華書局五年概況 (The general situation at Zhonghua Book Company in 1916) ([Shanghai]: Zhonghua shuju, 1916)

江伯訓, also populated Commercial Press, exerting great influence in the company.[65]

Family ties provided other kinds of informal organizational networks in publishing companies. During the 1910s and 1920s Zhonghua Book Company was interlaced with close family connections. Zhonghua cofounder Dai Kedun 戴克敦 was joined in the company by family members Dai Kegong 戴克恭 and Dai Keshao 戴克紹. Staff member Jin Zhaoyan 金兆梒 was followed by his brother Jin Zhaozi 金兆梓, who joined the company in 1922. And, in 1916, Zhonghua's Editing Department included brothers Ouyang Pucun 歐陽溥存 and Ouyang Hancun 歐陽瀚存.[66] Family ties were similarly influential even in the much larger Editing Department at Commercial Press. Mao Dun found that the core members of the English Division he joined in 1916 were the brothers Zhou Youqin 周由廑 and Zhou Yueran 周越然, who had established a secure position for himself and his brother by having invented the very successful English correspondence course.[67]

From the first decade of the twentieth century into the 1920s, then, the editing departments of the major publishers were organized by patterns of ascriptive affiliation in relation to specific sectors of the labor market that had characterized elite social and intellectual life throughout the late imperial period. These patterns seem to have been intensifying amid the increasingly competitive demographic and market conditions that developed beginning in the late eighteenth century.[68] Kinship, native place, and other personal ties created strong networks, which structured factions that competed for resources and influence and that conditioned each individual's career opportunities.

Dynamics of Intellectual Labor

The low degree of functional differentiation in the organization of editing departments, ascriptive networks that extended across formal institutional boundaries, and the large numbers of literati with classical training and limited modern learning combined during the first two decades of the twentieth century to create an environment where editors worked more like Confucian generalists than specialists in an academic discipline or a technical field. This lack of specialization is readily apparent when we track the activities of particular individuals. Mao Dun, within his first several years in the Editing Department, corrected exercises for a correspondence school in the English Division; translated English books on Western material culture with Sun Yuxiu in the Chinese Division; collaborated with Sun on a compilation of Chinese fables (*yuyan* 寓言) drawn from classical sources; translated children's literature; reviewed, wrote, and translated pieces for *Student Magazine* (*Xuesheng zazhi* 學生雜誌); and helped Sun select and proofread rare editions of classical texts to be reprinted in the *Collection of Chinese Classical, Historical, Philosophical, and Literary Works* (*Sibu congkan* 四部叢刊).[69] Mao Dun was, in short, anything but a specialist. In fact, he characterized his work at the publisher as that of a "handyman" (*daza* 打雜).[70]

His experience was not unique at the time. Many of his colleagues also wore several hats. Sun Yuxiu was an erudite scholar of editions of rare books, an English translator, and compiler of children's fables.[71] Du Yaquan was director of the Science Division, which might have required the most specialized knowledge of any division at Commercial Press at the time, but also edited *Eastern Miscellany* (*Dongfang zazhi* 東方雜誌), which was extremely eclectic in its content.[72] Chen Chengze was recruited to Commercial Press to manage compilation of books on law and economics, but he also wrote extensively on philology and was part of the Chinese Division when Mao Dun met him in 1916.[73] Between 1903 and 1912, Jiang Weiqiao compiled language, history, and moral-cultivation textbooks, drafted entries for the comprehensive dictionary *Ciyuan*, wrote specialized articles and editorials for *Education Monthly* (*Jiaoyu zazhi* 教育雜誌), reviewed an astounding range of manuscripts, wrote reports on the Nanjing Enterprise Promotion Exhibition in 1910, and drafted revolutionary chronicles as the 1911 Revolution occurred.[74]

The late Qing literati's generalist work style, which fit with late imperial patterns, ran counter to systematic disciplinary organization of commercial publishers' editing departments and the specialization of staff members who could harness discrete professional training to produce specialized publications. During these early years, such lack of disciplinary focus might in fact have been a virtue, for exposure to specialized modes of foreign knowledge was limited among the reading public. Demand was greatest for broad introductory texts, and a range of literati could be mobilized, as needed, to translate and compile such works. Little specialized knowledge was needed, for example, with Sun Yuxiu's and Mao Dun's translations of English texts on Western food, clothing, and shelter.[75] At the same time, the publishers' investment in rare-book republication projects (discussed in chapter 4) suggests that public interest in a wide variety of classical scholarship remained lively throughout the early twentieth century, so that literati editors' classical learning continued to be relevant. Market conditions, in short, allowed late Qing literati to continue working as generalists even as they incorporated various kinds of Western learning into their scholarly repertoires.

Changing patterns of literati academic exchange also shaped the dynamics of cultural production in the commercial publishing companies. Specifically, the study society (*xuehui* 學會) and various other forms of voluntary association (*shetuan* 社團), such as education associations, self-government organizations, and social-reform groups like anti-foot-binding societies, became a central part of elite public culture during the last decade of the Qing and the first decade of the Republic.[76] As noted, Jiang Weiqiao, Zhang Yuanji, Lufei Kui, Du Yaquan, and other leading figures in the Commercial Press and later Zhonghua Book Company Editing Departments played active roles in many of those organizations.[77] Consequently, the patterns of collective inquiry, horizontal exchange, and cooperative cultural work that characterized those societies found expression in the work dynamics of the major publishers.

How new forms of horizontal association shaped work practices at Commercial Press can be seen most clearly from Jiang Weiqiao's descriptions of textbook compiling during the late Qing. In his diary, Jiang describes collaborative processes of planning, compiling, and editing that drove textbook production, which was the core of the company's business at this time. For instance, on December 2, 1903, as Commercial Press prepared to compile its first comprehensive lower-primary language textbook, Jiang met with Zhang Yuanji, Gao Mengdan, and two Japanese advisers from Golden Harbor Press to discuss the textbook's basic organization in great detail, down to the number of new characters to be introduced in each chapter and their complexity.[78] Jiang compiled eight chapters overnight, and they provided the basis for a second discussion by the same group the following day. That day Jiang compiled five more chapters, working collaboratively with Zhang Yuanji. The following day he continued to compile collaboratively with Yang Chiyu in the morning, and he met with the Japanese consultants again in the afternoon.[79] This process of periodic meetings and collaborative compilation continued throughout December and into 1904 as they produced this textbook that would serve as a template for other Commercial Press textbook publications.[80]

In his memoir, Jiang described in some detail the dynamics of the round-table discussion meetings during the compilation and revision process of the Newest Textbook series.

> With the roundtable meetings at that time, discussions were most detailed when we were just starting the *Newest Lower-Primary Chinese* [textbook]. With the first two volumes, with nearly every lesson we wrote we discussed until there were no objections before finalizing the manuscript. After the third and fourth volumes, each person individually wrote a draft according to the principles [we had determined] and, after the draft was completed, handed it over for discussion. There were also those where one or two people discussed it beforehand. At that time there was no lack of interesting material. For instance, when I had compiled a particular lesson, I used the character "cauldron" [*fu* 釜], and Gao Mengdan wanted to change it to "three-legged cauldron" [*ding* 鼎]. I said, "Three-legged cauldron is too archaic and uncommon; we can't use it." Gao said, "Three-legged cauldron is really an everyday word. How can you say it is not common?" I said, "How is it that three-legged cauldron is used every day?" And Gao said, "How is it that three-legged cauldron is not a word used every day?" So the two of us argued until we were really going at each other. Later we made detailed distinctions and only then understood that in Fujianese [*Minyu* 閩語] they call "cauldron" [*fu*] "three-legged cauldron" [*ding*] and do not call it "cauldron" [*fu*]. We both clapped our hands and had a good laugh.[81]

We see here a work process that resembles the collaborative learning and debate of the study society in almost every way. The goal was group consensus on every aspect of the project, as they seem to have achieved with the first two volumes of the textbook. Compilers sketched out initial drafts that were then offered for group review and commentary. When there were differences of opinion, competing views were discussed in great detail. As Jiang relates it, even individual characters could be the focus of heated debate.[82]

The study-society dynamic was not limited to textbook drafting and editing. Dictionary compilation seems to have followed similar patterns.

With China's first major encyclopedic dictionary, *Ciyuan*, for example, the initial group of compilers was composed of just five or six people, but the project grew in scale over time, and ultimately fifty people were listed as compilers for the project.[83] Responsibility for researching and drafting entries for particular terms was shared out to individual compilers. Then compilers would review one another's work and meet to work out problems with particular definitions or etymologies.[84] In this process of shared work, group problem-solving, and collective review, we see similar dynamics to those of the textbook-compilation process described by Jiang.

The importance of this collaborative model of book production is reflected as well in the story of Zhonghua Book Company's founding. Anticipating the imminent fall of the Qing empire in the fall of 1911, Lufei Kui, who at that time was editor of Commercial Press's *Education Monthly*, spearheaded compilation of primary and secondary textbooks suitable for the forthcoming Republican polity. To accomplish this, Lufei secretly gathered at his house a group that included other Commercial Press staff members Dai Kedun, Shen Zhifang, Chen Yin 陳寅, and Shen Yi 沈頤 to collectively compile a complete new set of Republican textbooks.[85] Even when defying Commercial Press to start their own company, Lufei Kui and his colleagues used its style of collaborative compilation to create its signature product.

Day-to-day accounts of corporate management in the late Qing and early Republican Commercial Press also suggest that a culture of active consultation extended from the earliest years of the century into the 1910s. Jiang Weiqiao's and Zhang Yuanji's diaries repeatedly refer to discussions within the staff, especially regarding long-term planning and questions related to the development of individual projects.[86] For example, in the immediate aftermath of the Wuchang Uprising, Commercial Press held an editorial meeting (*bianyihui*) to strategize about pacing the completion, typesetting, and publication of particular projects, delaying a number of publications pending the outcome of the revolution. Four days later Gao Mengdan and Zhang Yuanji talked with Jiang Weiqiao about compiling a revolutionary chronicle of the contemporaneous events.[87] Similarly, in 1916 when Commercial Press was approached by an American about compiling, publishing, and distributing Chinese materials for a business-correspondence school that was already running successfully in the United States, Zhang immediately consulted with a group of colleagues that included Gao Mengdan, Gao Fengchi, and Bao Xiancheng.[88] In these and many other cases, then, we see the dynamics of elite literati study societies at play. Both long-term editorial planning and daily practices of compilation and editing were characterized by horizontal exchange of ideas, collective problem-solving, and energetic debate.[89] These practices reflected the dynamics of elite voluntary association and republican politics that characterized the late Qing and early Republic in which leading figures in Commercial Press and later Zhonghua Book Company took an active part. Through these collaborative processes, editors and compilers at the publisher engaged not only in the mental labor of producing content for publications but also in the organizational and managerial work of planning, designing, and coordinating projects.

Habits of Daily Life and Leisure

Beyond shaping the recruitment process and organizational structures of publishers' editing departments according to past practice, late Qing literati also fashioned work lives that continued many familiar patterns of elite daily life.[90] Mention has been made of Mao Dun's characterization of the large hall of the Commercial Press Editing Department as being like a teahouse, one of the signature sites of local elite activity. A number of editors at Commercial Press during the 1910s and early 1920s also lived in an all-male dormitory run as a joint partnership by stewards in the Editing Department.[91] This living space accorded with the living arrangements of elite male sojourners when studying in academies, sitting for the examinations, or, often, working in government offices.[92]

At the same time, though, Editing Department work at Commercial Press was increasingly governed by the clock, apropos the industrialization of Chinese publishing, with the expectation that compilers and editors would keep regular hours at the office each day. We see this clearly with Jiang Weiqiao. In the fall of 1913, for instance, when he returned to work at Commercial Press after a stint working in the provisional Ministry of Education at Cai Yuanpei's invitation, Jiang's diary shows him going to the office at nine every morning except Sunday without fail.[93] Regular attendance at the office was expected. The company also sought to rationalize work schedules and maximize the time of its salaried staff in other ways. For example, starting at the beginning of the lunar new year in 1907, Commercial Press introduced a schedule of rotating night work in the Editing Department by which each compiler would work three hours (6:00–9:00 p.m.) one night per week. Significantly, all Editing Department staff participated, even Gao Mengdan and Zhang Yuanji, for whom Jiang Weiqiao substituted several times.[94] From Jiang's account of his daily work routine, the schedule of Editing Department work seems to have been rather systematized.

Yet Commercial Press also incorporated significant flexibility into the system. For one, during the hottest days after the so-called Slight Heat (*xiaoshu*) of July 7–21, the Editing Department shifted for a month to a half-day schedule, which started at 8:00 in the morning instead of 9:00.[95] Moreover, Mao Dun explains how an annual bonus-pay system granted editorial staff significant scheduling flexibility over the course of any given year. Each editor was guaranteed a bonus month of pay that they could collect in total at the end of the year if they worked every day; alternatively, they could use those days as collateral for taking leave from the office. Further days could be taken off if one did not mind deductions in pay.[96] Such a schedule allowed literati editors to choose how they would arrange their time in relation to various writing and editing projects, whether for the publisher or not, creating open, flexible schedules conducive to scholarship and writing.

Editorial staff took advantage of this flexibility to pursue their own projects, in conjunction with their work at the publisher. Between 1905 and 1907, Jiang Weiqiao, for example, teamed up with colleague Xi Boshou 奚伯綬 in their spare time to translate a *Higher Level Botany Textbook* (*Gaodeng zhiwuxue jiaokeshu* 高等植物學教科書).[97] Lufei Kui, perhaps foreshadowing his eventual secret founding of Zhonghua Book Company in 1912, was discovered at the beginning of 1910 to be independently compiling textbooks for sale, separate from his duties at Commercial Press.[98] Likewise, Mao Dun recounted how he read books on classical textual criticism and other material from the Hanfenlou Library during downtime working in the Editing Department.[99] Sun Yuxiu was able to continue his life passion of the study of editions, even as he translated Western books and wrote children's literature for the company.[100] Despite the company's effort to rationally structure the editors' work time, there were still opportunities for them to pursue their own intellectual interests and do their own work on company time. The ability of scholars to continue their own intellectual projects provided an important intangible benefit of working at the publisher.

Further, in spite of the ways that work at Commercial Press's and Zhonghua Book Company's Editing Departments came increasingly to run by the clock and to be oriented toward the demands of industrial production, editors consistently re-created some of the central dynamics of literati leisure culture. As Jiang Weiqiao expressed in his diary, when he joined Commercial Press, "in the Editing Department Yang Chiyu [楊赤玉], Zhuang Boyu [莊伯俞], and Xu Furu [徐福如] are fellow [Changzhou] natives and comrades. After work we talk together and gain some of the joys of friendship."[101] Dinner parties, poetry circles, farewell banquets, book-buying excursions, and courtesy visits punctuated editors' lives during the late Qing and early Republic, much as it had the lives of elite literati during previous centuries.[102] These forms of literati leisure culture were woven into the daily routines and work lives of editors and compilers in the industrial publishers.

Jiang Weiqiao recorded in his diary numerous dinner parties, drinking excursions, and poetry parties with friends and colleagues. For example, when periodic Commercial Press colleague and fellow Changzhou native Yang Chiyu passed through Shanghai in the fall of 1907, Jiang invited him out to dinner with Editing Department colleagues Yan Lianru, Gao Mengdan, and Shen Duoshan to the Jiuhualou.[103] Gentleman's drinking parties were just as common. For instance, on April 18 the following year, "At seven in the evening, Zhang Juweng [Yuanji] invited people for a drink. Together with Zhuang [Yu], Shen [Yi], and Dai [Kedun] went to his house. Mr. Sun Xingru [Yuxiu] was there first, and [Gao] Mengdan and [Lu] Weishi came in succession. We drank to our heart's content and talked with animation until ten and then dispersed."[104] This group included many of the late Qing literati who were mainstays of the Editing Department, taking the lead on many of the textbooks, reference books, journals, and classics published or republished during the late Qing.[105]

In getting together to eat and drink outside of work, they created close bonds and warm feelings, fostering an atmosphere of leisure in conjunction with the intellectual engagement and economic profitability that were the company's explicit goals. As during the late imperial period, the exchange and sharing of poetry also provided a means to build personal and intellectual bonds, with Jiang and his friends meeting at other times to "give a banquet to recite [poetry] together."[106] Though working for one of China's most modern industrial enterprises, the late Qing literati in the Commercial Press Editing Department continued many of the leisure practices that characterized elite scholarly culture throughout the late imperial period. These practices sustained the intellectual networks that, as noted, were the main conduits by which the publishers recruited staff and solicited manuscripts through recommendations. Moreover, the informal sociability cultivated by means of shared eating, drinking, and the exchange of poetry likely underpinned the study society practices that served as one important way of organizing cultural production in the late Qing and early Republican publishers.

When we look further, social commensality seems to have been integral to the operation of the company at all levels, providing a cultural foundation for business activity. Zhang Yuanji regularly held a banquet at the beginning of the year for integral members of the Editing Department, renewing the relations of patronage and comradeship that underpinned that group.[107] A welcome-home banquet for Zhang Yuanji and Gao Mengdan, who had been traveling in Japan toward the end of 1910, provided a forum for Zhang to present an account of their travels to colleagues.[108] In fact, Zhang Yuanji's diary reveals that some of the most sensitive business of the company was conducted over meals.[109] For example, the question of who would replace Gao Fengchi as Commercial Press general manager was discussed by a small group of company leaders over dinner at Zhang Yuanji's house on April 15, 1916.[110] The Shanghai restaurant Yipinxiang seems to have been the default venue for shareholders' meetings during the late Qing.[111] If there was any tension between the commercial motives of the modern industrial publishing company and many late Qing literati's emphasis on cultural and intellectual values, the common ritual of social commensality might have helped to mute that tension by integrating both in a common field of elite cultural practices. Hard-nosed business concerns were assimilated into a familiar repertoire of literati culture.

Overall, commercial publishers' editing departments became places where literati could enjoy themselves in familiar ways by living and writing, eating and drinking together. The familiar environment of scholarship they re-created for themselves allowed them to pursue their personal intellectual agendas even as they produced for the capitalist market. In these ways, work at the publisher became not just a way of making a living, although it always most certainly was that. It also provided means for personal enjoyment and intellectual fulfillment. These factors, as much as a reliable salary, drew late Qing literati to the commercial publishers, as they would continue to draw subsequent generations of Chinese intellectuals.

China's first commercial publishing companies were some of the most technologically advanced and commercially aggressive institutions of China's emergent industrial capitalism.[112] But to operate during the failing days of the last Confucian empire and its aftermath, these publishers depended on the last generation of the scholarly elite from the late imperial period. Some of those scholars, especially in the lower Yangzi region, mastered not only classical literary culture; they also gained rapid exposure to foreign languages and modern learning. This hybrid intellectual background allowed them to compile, organize, and edit the wide range of texts required by Commercial Press and Zhonghua Book Company during the first two decades of the twentieth century. Both publishers developed large, standing editing departments that produced primarily internally the publications—textbooks, journals, and reference books—that were most vital to their economic success and cultural influence. Permanent staffs of talented scholars with diverse intellectual backgrounds facilitated constant production of text to meet changing market demand. This approach to textual production became a distinctive feature of modern Chinese publishing, differentiating it from publishers in other parts of the world in the age of print industrialism.

The late Qing literati who crafted the diverse print commodities offered by these publishers constructed a work culture shaped by the habitus of late imperial literati culture and the political reform milieu of the late Qing and early Republic. At one level, their work culture can be seen to be at odds with key aspects of industrial modernity. Recruitment through relational networks can appear to undermine open, competitive, and meritocratic forms of systematic hiring. A generalist work culture might limit specialization and functional differentiation. Moreover, fluid and open-ended organization of the workplace and work time seem diametrically opposed to the compartmentalization of time and space that has accompanied industrialization in the Euro-American world and various colonial contexts.[113]

Yet from another perspective, we can see how late Qing literati's deployment of an elite late imperial work style paid dividends for the publishers. Recruitment through personal networks, a generalist work style, amorphous lines of organization, and even fluid arrangement of work time and space enabled publishers to tap with the utmost flexibility a single pool of scholars who had both classical training and some exposure to modern Western learning. That flexibility allowed for production of print commodities that served the highly differentiated print markets of the early decades of the century, which required, for instance, both modern textbooks and reprints of ancient classics, studies of philology and inscriptions as well as surveys of Western law and science. Leisure practices like drinking parties, banquets, poetry readings, and book-buying excursions sustained the literati networks that allowed Commercial Press and Zhonghua Book Company to recruit new talent, solicit new manuscripts, and gain access to rare books for republication projects. Some of the seemingly least "rationalistic" practices of literati culture contributed materially to the development of industrial publishing. Moreover, they helped to consolidate the commitment of late Qing literati to the modern industrial publishing enterprise by providing an outlet for personal enjoyment and intellectual fulfillment over and above a living wage.

The new forms of horizontal voluntary association and collective intellectual inquiry developed by China's intellectuals in the late Qing and early Republic also shaped the development of modern publishing. The study society provided a model for a form of cultural production that Commercial Press's leading editors, all social and political reformers active in late Qing organizations, readily adapted for compiling textbooks and reference books. Inviting dialogue, debate, and collective effort, it was a republican mode of production for an era of constitutional reform and Republican politics. These collaborative dynamics allowed literati staff editors like Jiang Weiqiao, Sun Yuxiu, and Zhuang Yu at Commercial Press to participate in the managerial dimension of mental labor at the publisher as well as in the intellectual labor of content production. But by the late 1910s and early 1920s, introduction of foreign intellectual currents, shifting market demand, and new educational patterns generated modes of recruiting and organizing labor in the publishing companies that threatened the positions of the late Qing literati along with their ways of producing books.

CHAPTER II

Universities or Factories?

Academics, Petty Intellectuals,
and the Industrialization of Mental Labor

D uring his break from Beijing University in the summer of 1921, China's leading young scholar, Hu Shi, served as a consultant for Commercial Press. While meeting with Gao Mengdan and a group of younger editors, Hu painted an inspiring picture of the capitalist publishing company as a protoacademic organization.[1] He proposed that each year the company could send one or two young scholar-editors abroad to study. Heavy investment in its library would allow it to serve as a research resource for the Editing Department and the public at large. Commercial Press could set up laboratories so its editors could pursue all kinds of scientific research. Restructuring editors' work time would allow more flexibility for their cultivation. And groups of editors could work in segregated rooms according to division, akin to academic departments, instead of being mixed together in one large office space. All told, the reforms Hu proposed envisioned reorganizing Commercial Press to operate like a university or a research institute, with specialized scholars pursuing independent research with institutional support.

But in the fall of 1921, as Hu Shi's nominee to direct the Commercial Press Editing Department, Wang Yunwu, prepared to assume that post, he mapped out a very different model of book production. Wang conceptualized a process of manufacturing text that could be broken down in component units, which in turn could be saved and combined in different configurations for different products.[2] He viewed most textbooks, reference books, and encyclopedias as genres for which compilers in the press could be mobilized to write text, using different strategies of dividing labor.

> Now each person has strengths and weaknesses. Not only do they differ by academic discipline, but even in one discipline there are those who are good at the big picture and those who are good at the details; there are those who are good at choosing materials and those who are good at composing the manuscript. So we should regard the whole staff in the department as an organism, as with the hands and the feet, the ears and the eyes, each fulfilling their strengths and supplementing for their weaknesses; only this will do.[3]

Although he used an organic metaphor, the process Wang described mirrored a division of labor akin to the assembly line, as became clear in his accompanying description of textbook production. As Wang foresaw it, an editor with rich knowledge and expertise would outline the textbook.[4] A second familiar with the content and pedagogy would select and compile the material. A capable writer, in turn, would integrate the material and write it up. A fourth, most likely the initial outliner, would review the final product. What Wang proposed here was a collective production process with a manager who conceptualized the project and compilers and writers who generated and worked with textual raw material. The goal was organizing the authors, compilers, translators, and editors of a wide range of texts to create a product coordinated and packaged by executive editors.

These divergent visions of how editors should work grew out of publishing companies' efforts to recruit new personnel and reorganize their editing departments to meet the growing demand for cutting-edge scholarship after the New Culture Movement and the development of modern Western academic fields in China. They also sought to produce standard products like textbooks and reference books more efficiently. By the end of the 1910s publishing leaders recognized that the late Qing literati who had predominated in Commercial Press's and Zhonghua's Editing Departments for the previous two decades could not produce the more specialized and in-depth books necessary to meet this new demand. But who would replace them? And how could publishing companies best organize and mobilize their staffs to meet this new market demand in a cost-effective way? Should China's major publishing companies be more like universities and research institutes or more like factories? Should editors and compilers function like a scholarly elite or industrial workers? And who would decide?

Recruiting and Reorganizing

Both Zhonghua Book Company and Commercial Press moved to recruit new kinds of editors and to reorganize their Editing Departments in 1920 and 1921, soon after the May Fourth Movement in 1919. Zhonghua acted first, with General Manager Lufei Kui taking the lead after the company weathered a financial crisis in 1916 and 1917. In January 1920 he requested permission from the board of directors to add staff to the Editing Department based on the general improvement of the press's economic situation.[5] He subsequently hired Zuo Shunsheng 左舜聖 to join and then lead a New Books Division (Xinshubu) within the Editing Department.[6] Zuo was a leading member of the Young China Association (Shaonian Zhongguo xuehui), a group of young, reform-minded intellectuals, and he actively recruited colleagues from the association to populate the New Books Division.[7] They included Zhang Wentian 張聞天, Chen Qitian 陳啓天, Yu Jiaju 余家菊, Cao Chu 曹芻, Jin Haiguan 金海觀, Li Da 李達, and Tian Han 田漢, who all spent varying lengths of time in the Zhonghua Book Company Editing Department during the early to mid-1920s.[8] While some of these young intellectuals had studied abroad by the time they joined Zhonghua's Editing Department, they were not widely recognized at the time as leading academics in their own right.[9]

The introduction of the New Books Division was part of an overall reorganization of the Zhonghua Editing Department. As noted in chapter 1, it had originally been organized by genre more than category of knowledge, with divisions for textbooks, ordinary books (*putong tushu* 普同圖書), English publications, dictionaries, magazines, and illustrations.[10] After the reorganization, besides the New Books Division there were divisions for Chinese literature, history, and geography, national language (*guoyu*), mathematics and science, national heritage (*guogu*), Western literature, and fine arts.[11] Out of these new organizational units and their staff came new publications like the New Culture Series, the Young China Association Series, and the Little Friend Library (Xiao pengyou wenku).[12] By drawing on the network of colleagues and associates in the Young China Association

（一）所 輯 編

（二）所 輯 編

Figure 2.1 Zhonghua Book Company Editing Department circa 1924. *Zhonghua shuju shisan nian gaikuang* 中華書局十三年概況 (The general situation at Zhonghua Book Company in 1924) ([Shanghai]: Zhonghua shuju, 1924)

and affiliated groups of intellectuals, Zuo Shunsheng fostered a dynamic of collaborative book production similar to that of the study-society model developed at Commercial Press and Zhonghua during the first two decades of the twentieth century. Lists and journals were filled by coordinating among the interests, initiatives, and expertise of a group of like-minded peers in a common organization contributing to a range of publications.[13]

In the spring of 1921 Commercial Press also began to reorganize its Editing Department. Gao Mengdan first sought to convince Beijing University professor Hu Shi to succeed Gao as Editing Department director, which would have reprised the process in the late Qing when Zhang Yuanji had been hired to build up the Editing Department and launched new publishing initiatives. But Hu was hesitant to leave Beida, and Gao could convince him only to visit Commercial Press as a consultant from July 17 to September 7, during summer vacation.[14]

During that time Hu Shi went to the Editing Department nearly every day, participating in meetings, interviewing staff, and joining in the literati leisure culture discussed in chapter 1, replete with dinner parties and book-buying excursions. These discussions and meetings generated stimulating ideas for transformation of the Editing Department. A frequent refrain in those discussions was how to attract and retain talented editorial staff.[15] Just as importantly, some staff members, like Zheng Zhenwen 鄭貞文, who had been educated in Japan, called for reorganization of the main editorial units according to the categories of learning in the secondary-school curriculum.[16] Others suggested arranging separate rooms for different groups of editors, giving staff full summer vacations, and providing funds for overseas study.[17] As revealed in the chapter's opening passage, Hu Shi also suggested expanding the Hanfenlou Library to make it more a research library and establishing laboratories to allow scientific research.[18] In combination, these suggestions created an image of the publishing company that was more like a university or research institute that would be organized according to categories of academic knowledge and would facilitate staff in developing expertise through research and overseas study.

Still uncertain, though, was who would replace Gao Mengdan as Editing Department director, since Hu Shi remained hesitant.[19] Fortuitously, over the summer in Shanghai Hu Shi renewed his friendship with Wang Yunwu, his former English teacher, whom Hu subsequently nominated for this position.[20] Once Hu Shi recommended Wang, he went through a long vetting process with the publisher's leadership, "the mother-in-law looking over the son-in-law," as Hu put it in his diary. The process culminated with Wang's being hired on a trial basis starting in the fall of 1921 as assistant director of the Editing Department, with Gao Mengdan temporarily continuing to serve as director.[21] After Wang submitted suggestions for reforming the Editing Department at the end of the year, the General Affairs Office appointed him director to replace Gao in January 1922.[22]

Although Wang Yunwu was not a leading scholar like Hu Shi, he was probably a better choice for what Commercial Press sought to accomplish. Wang was largely an autodidact who had never trained seriously for the imperial examinations and had only limited formal schooling, but he had read extensively in English to familiarize himself with the world of thought beyond China's borders.[23] Wang also came from a family of small businessmen, had been apprenticed to a hardware store in his youth, and had worked in the early Republican government as a secretary and minor official. This combination of broad learning and street smarts would allow him to view texts and ideas instrumentally and to commercialize academic culture.[24] Ultimately, Wang Yunwu went on to become one of China's leading cultural entrepreneurs.[25]

Wang began his tenure as director of the Editing Department with ambitious plans for reform, drafted in November 1921, which informed many of his initiatives at the publisher during the 1920s and 1930s. In terms of optimizing existing personnel and supplementing them with new talent, he asserted that among the resources the company needed most were "those who have specialized learning in one field"; "those who deeply understand educational principles or are rich in experience with secondary and primary school textbooks, and who are able to know the requirements of students and the actual situation of textbooks"; and "those skilled in foreign writing and able to write works or translate."[26] To address the first and third of these needs, Wang actively recruited scholars who had recently returned from study overseas.[27] They included Zhu Jingnong 朱經農, who had studied education in the United States; Tang Cheng 唐鉞, who had a doctorate in psychology from the United States; Zhu Kezhen 竺可楨, who had studied meteorology at Harvard; and Duan Fuqun 段撫群, who had studied mathematics in the United States. Later in the 1920s, Wang further recruited other leading, foreign-educated intellectuals to be editors. For instance, China's best-known interpreter of modern science, American-trained chemist Ren Hongjun 任鴻雋, came to direct the Physics and Chemistry Division. Legal scholar Zhou Gengsheng 周鯁生, who had studied at Waseda University in the late Qing and received advanced degrees at the University of Edinburgh and the University of Paris, became head of the Law and Economics Division.[28] Tao Menghe 陶孟和, who had studied sociology at the London School of Economics and became one of the leading figures in the discipline during the 1920s and 1930s, worked in the General Editing Division (Zongbianji bu) and as a compiler for the encyclopedia project before becoming director of the Law and Economics Division.[29] Other scholars Wang hired who had studied abroad or were respected young scholars from Chinese universities included He Bingsong 何炳松, Gu Jiegang 顧頡剛, and Zhang Qiyun 張其昀. In sum, a number of leading figures in Chinese academic circles worked for periods of varying length at Commercial Press during the 1920s.

As he hired this group of young scholars, Wang also reorganized Commercial Press's Editing Department to be much more specialized and functionally differentiated. His basic goal was "to consider adjusting the original divisions of the Editing Department so that they accord more closely with the characteristics of academic courses of study [*xueshu fenke*]."[30] After reorganization, the Editing Department had nine major divisions that corresponded to the categories of modern academic learning: Chinese (*guowen* 國文), English (*yingwen* 英文), Philosophy and Education (*zhexue jiaoyu* 哲學教育), History and Geography (*shidi* 史地), Law and Economics (*fazheng jingji* 法治經濟), Mathematics (*shuxue* 數學), Natural Science and Physiology (*bowu shengli* 博物生理), Physics and Chemistry (*wuli huaxue* 物理化學), and the Miscellaneous Works Division (*zazuan bu* 雜纂部).[31] Within Commercial Press's new organizational system, Wang also established more specialized groupings for compiling and editing magazines, reference books, and encyclopedias.[32] Special committees were formed for three different dictionary projects and for the massive encyclopedia project, which had six subordinate departments. In addition, agencies were established for eleven different magazines. Within this new organizational framework, the scholars Wang hired oversaw compilation of reference books and portions of the encyclopedia, directed production of textbooks, and produced titles for the many different series he initiated.

As foreign-trained scholars gathered at Commercial Press during the mid-1920s, it became an academic center that competed with China's emergent university system, providing intellectuals with an alternative platform for scholarly production. While working at the publishers, foreign-trained scholars also shaped the dynamics of production during the 1920s and 1930s by writing relatively specialized works that expressed their understanding of a particular academic field (explored through analysis of series publications in chapter 5). Editors with specialized advanced training wrote books that surveyed particular fields, explored specialized topics, or introduced new methodologies in a monographic style of book production. Euro-American norms of academic writing were introduced into Chinese publishing circles through the presence of this new generation of scholars in the Commercial Press Editing Department. This monographic approach to book production even influenced textbook production. Secondary textbooks penned by young academics working as editors like Tao Menghe and Zhang Qiyun during the mid-1920s synthesized methods drawn from Western scholarship on topics such as social issues and geographical systems.[33]

Even as they reorganized their Editing Departments, Commercial Press and Zhonghua Book Company also continued to acquire book manuscripts from writers and scholars working outside the publisher, either buying them outright or offering authors royalties.[34] Journalist and fiction author Bao Tianxiao, for instance, maintained close relationships with both Zhonghua and Commercial Press, where he had worked for a time during the 1910s. In his diary entries of the 1920s, he notes committing several manuscripts to the two companies, sometimes accepting manuscript fees and other times taking payments in royalties.[35] Bao generally received royalties of 10 percent or manuscript payments of three yuan per thousand words. World Book Company similarly arranged for authors and scholars outside the company to contribute manuscripts to projects like its ABC Series.[36] In these cases and others, publishers used manuscript fees and royalties to get access to monographs and literary texts beyond those produced by their own staff.[37]

Petty Intellectuals as Staff Editors

One constraint on hiring foreign-trained academics as staff editors was that they were relatively expensive. Wages for well-educated scholars had to be competitive with salaries in universities during the 1920s and 1930s, which ranged from a low of one hundred twenty yuan per month for an instructor to as high as five hundred yuan per month for a full professor.[38] During the early 1920s, Commercial Press and other Shanghai-based publishers had an economic advantage, since Beijing's universities had trouble meeting pay schedules because militarist administrations diverted educational funds elsewhere.[39] But over the long term, foreign-trained academics' expertise generated multiple work opportunities, which allowed them to demand a high wage and to move fluidly into government and academic positions. For instance, Zhu Kezhen, who began work at Commercial Press in 1925, was invited to teach at Tianjin's Nankai University in 1926 and engaged by Cai Yuanpei in 1927 to direct the Meteorology Institute at Academia Sinica.[40] Tang Cheng was hired away by Qinghua University in the summer of 1926.[41] Tao Menghe established the Social Survey Department in Beijing in 1926.[42] And in 1924 Ren Hongjun left Commercial Press to serve as vice president of National Southeastern University in Nanjing.[43] Thus, while it was beneficial to hire some specialized academics, they were too expensive and mobile a group to be the main editorial staff for a commercial publisher. As Zhonghua's Editing Department director in the 1930s Shu Xincheng put it, "If we want to fulfill some undertakings in terms of education and culture, naturally we need specialized knowledge, but because of economic constraints, we cannot support [yanghuo] specialized scholars [zhuanmen de xuezhe]."[44]

Instead, during the 1920s and 1930s, the three main publishers recruited heavily in the growing pool of recent high school and college graduates to engage staff editors.[45] These groups, in Wang Yunwu's parlance, "have common knowledge and are able to gather materials and compile them" and "are strong in classical Chinese and modern Chinese and are able in a short time to complete lively manuscripts."[46] Possessing basic common knowledge and mastering functional prose writing would allow them to generate the text used in reference books and textbooks, which were key products at these publishers.

These recruitment patterns are immediately apparent from World Book Company's staff expansion in the early 1920s. Shen Zhifang, who previously had worked at both Commercial Press and Zhonghua, founded World in 1921.[47] Initially, the publisher focused on publishing fiction, which required limited in-house editorial staff. Starting in 1924, however, World Book Company dove headfirst into the lucrative textbook market, in a bid to compete with the two leading companies.[48] This commitment led, in turn, to a drive to recruit staff members from the ranks of high school and college graduates to engage in the necessary compiling work. As a news item in a company journal revealed in 1924, "This company's Editing Department Primary School Division, because it is hurrying to compile textbooks and teaching methods, recently additionally recruited five editorial staff, all of whom are normal school or high school [*zhongxue*] graduates and have taught for many years. They will either translate or write, mostly to provide teaching materials."[49] Later the same year, World further hired St. John's College teacher Jin Yuxiu 金聿修 and Wusong Fishery School teacher Lu Yunbiao 呂雲彪 to serve as editors in the Primary School Division.[50]

World's recruitment strategy directly paralleled that of Commercial Press and Zhonghua Book Company, which also drew on the corps of recent modern school graduates with teaching, editing, or administrative experience for their staff editors throughout the 1920s and 1930s.[51] Zhonghua's compilers and proofreaders for the encyclopedic dictionary *Cihai*, for example, were recent students or graduates of universities or normal schools, and many assisting staff members were higher-primary or lower-middle-school graduates.[52] For basic editorial work, large publishers like Zhonghua could draw on a large group of high-school- and college-educated literate men with basic academic and writing skills who would work relatively cheaply.

More systematic data on the education and work backgrounds of staff editors can be drawn from material on Commercial Press's trainees and newly hired compilers during the 1930s. Tables 2.1 and 2.2 list the trainees recruited by Commercial Press in 1934 and the incoming compilers and translators recruited in 1936. Recruits for both kinds of entry-level positions had fairly high levels of education for China as of the 1930s. This was especially true of the trainees, who were expected to bring new talent into the company from some of China's best universities. The prospective compilers and translators recruited by Commercial Press in 1936 generally had less-elevated academic backgrounds. Besides Cai Qimin, Guan Huaicong, and Zeng Xinshan, most of the nascent compilers had only secondary educations. However, almost all of them had previous teaching, editorial, or proofreading experience, suggesting that these technical skills were more important to the publisher than a specialized academic background. In fact, these recruits could be shifted easily among a wide range of writing and editing tasks at the company. The selectivity of the examinations that generated both the trainees (ten out of twenty-eight who sat for the exam)[53] and the translators and compilers (seven out of forty)[54] indicates the demand for positions in the publisher and the relatively large pool of educated people from which the company had to choose. This surplus of educated people resulted from increased secondary and higher education during the Republican period with limited work opportunities.[55] It allowed Commercial Press, Zhonghua Book Company, and World Book Company to limit labor costs for staff editors while mobilizing significant numbers of school graduates with modern education to contribute to large compiling and editing projects.

TABLE 2.1. COMMERCIAL PRESS TRAINEES (1934)[56]

Tan Jun, 譚俊, 22, native of Wujin, Jiangsu. Graduate of the History Department of National Central University's Liberal Arts College.

Wang Qixi 王啟熙, 25, native of Minhou, Fujian. Graduate of Mechanical Engineering at National Communications University. Previously served as an editor at *Children's New Life Weekly*.

Zhang Yuli 張毓黎, 24, native of Minhou, Fujian. Graduate of the Economics Department at Guanghua University's Business School. Previously served as a clerk at the Directorate of Posts and for a foreign business firm.

Wu Shengzu 吳繩祖, 24, native of Zhongshan, Guangdong. Graduate of the History Department at Jinling University's Liberal Arts College.

Wu Zeyan 吳澤炎, 21, native of Changshu, Jiangsu. Graduate of the Sociology and History Department at Daxia University's Liberal Arts College. Previously served as an editor at the *Huanian Weekly* agency and an assistant researcher at the Zhongshan Cultural Education Center (Zhongshan wenhua jiaoyuguan).

Wu Pengfei 吳鵬飛, 24, native of Yuyao, Zhejiang. Graduate of the Liberal Arts College at Fudan University. Previously taught high school.

Song Jiaxiu 宋家修, 25, native of Liling, Hunan. Graduate of the Economics Department at National Shanghai Business Academy. Previously served as a teacher at a vocational school.

Dai Daxi 戴搭熙, 24, native of Ningxiang, Hunan. Graduate of the Law Department at National Wuhan University. Previously served as a high school teacher.

Wang Yanfan 王衍蕃, 24, native of Minhou, Fujian. Graduate of the Accounting Department at Daxia University's Business School. Previously served as a staff member of Shanghai's Kailang Brothers' Company.

TABLE 2.2. COMMERCIAL PRESS NEW COMPILATION AND TRANSLATION STUDENTS (1936)[57]

Zhao Jing 趙靜, 29. Graduate of Zhejiang Provincial First Middle School. Attended Tongwen Academy. Previously served as a high school teacher.

Cai Qimin 蔡棄民, 28. Graduate of Daxia University. Previously served as a high school teacher.

Mu Jixiang 沐箕香, 26. Attended Zhejiang's Chunhui Middle School. Previously served as a compiler (*bianyiyuan*) at a publishing company (*shuju*).

Cao Chensi 曹沉思, 22. Attended Yokohama's Zhonghua Public School (*gongli xuexiao*). Graduated from Shanghai's Guanghua University Affiliated Middle School and attended the university. Previously served as a proofreader at a publishing company.

Zeng Xinshan 曾新山, 25. Graduate of the Law School of Japan's Tokyo Imperial University.

Guan Huaicong 管懷琮, 29. Graduate of the Economics Department of National Labor University. Previously served as a high school teacher.

Li Kenong 李克農, 19. Attended Zhejiang's Haining Middle School. Previously served as a proofreader at a publishing company.

As the foregoing example from Commercial Press suggests, the leading publishers increasingly used the more objective method of competitive examination to recruit editorial staff rather than more particularistic approaches like recommendation, ensuring new recruits would have a common base of background and skills.[58] At times the publishers used extreme methods to ensure that the examinations would be blind, such as not even revealing the name of the company doing the recruiting, suggesting a heightened concern for objective judgment.[59] The recruitment examinations themselves tested applicants' writing ability in Chinese, Japanese translation (Commercial Press only), basic mathematical skills, the ability to translate from Chinese to English and vice versa, and common knowledge in a range of subjects, including government, law, history, geography, natural science, and current events.[60] This wide range of topics indicates the publishers sought recruits with broad basic backgrounds. Increasingly systematized recruitment, based on objective measures of talent and education, promised a relatively uniform staff that could be moved easily among production tasks.

Systematic training followed objective forms of recruitment. The development of routinized training was clearest at Commercial Press. After they entered the publisher, trainees cycled through each of its departments, receiving education and hands-on training in each.[61] The trainees recruited in 1934 rotated among the following departments on a regular schedule: Secretarial Office (Mishuchu 秘書處), Distribution Department (Faxing-suo 發行所), Compilation and Review Committee (Bianshenhui 編審會), printing factories (*yinshuachang* 印刷廠), and the Printing Plate Factory (Zhibanchang 製版廠).[62] Trainees had to learn the rules of various sections and offices, and managers and section heads lectured them about aspects of publishing on a rotating schedule. Each trainee was to keep notes regarding what they learned at each stage of the training, which were reviewed by company managers. Trainees were graded on their performance in the various sections and departments.[63] The rigorous and comprehensive nature of the training provided each trainee with knowledge and skills for each of the major departments in the company, allowing them to adapt easily to jobs at various places in the production process. But even when such systematic approaches were not used, staff often progressed through a staged process of training, from basic proofreading, research, translation, and writing work to more complex, independent writing projects.[64]

Publisher recruitment of recent high school and college graduates as staff editors meant that the Chinese publishing pattern of large editing departments continued through the 1920s and 1930s. At the same time, the leading publishers flourished. After Wang Yunwu's reorganization efforts in 1922, the Commercial Press Editing Department grew to between two hundred and two hundred forty editors (not including administrative staff and proofreaders).[65] Since the vast majority of these had been recently hired, the 1920s marked a period of transition from an Editing Department dominated by literati to one dominated by new school graduates, with a small number of more elite academics added in.[66] At Zhonghua, from 1930 to 1937, the Editing Department staff ranged from a low of one hundred to a high of one hundred sixty-seven.[67] Maintaining these large staffs demanded significant investment from the publishers. Based on the table of wages for the Editing Department Hu Shi compiled in 1921, a highly conservative estimate for the monthly salaries for Commercial Press editorial staff that year would be approximately 10,000 yuan per month, which would work out to 120,000 yuan per year, or 130,000 yuan with the bonus month factored in.[68] By 1930 Wang Yunwu estimated that Commercial Press's editorial staff salaries amounted to 200,000 yuan annually.[69] Over the decade of the 1920s, Commercial Press's profits frequently hovered in the neighborhood of 1 million yuan annually.[70] From 1930 to 1937, annual wages for Zhonghua Book Company's somewhat smaller Editing Department ranged from a low of 74,692 yuan in 1932 to a high of 139,299 yuan in 1936.[71] But during the same period the company consistently earned annual profits ranging between 176,000 yuan and 247,000 yuan.[72]

Wang Yunwu's trip to Japan, the United States, and Europe in 1930 drove home the realization that by comparison globally, the editing departments of China's leading publishers were extremely large.[73] This realization seems to have planted a seed to reform the editing department by reducing its size and more rationally dividing tasks between something resembling acquisition editor and copy editor functions. Japan's attack on the Commercial Press factory and office complex on Baoshan Road during the Battle of Shanghai in January 1932 gave Wang an unexpected opportunity for that reorganization. As part of Japan's invasion of Shanghai that started on January 28, Japanese forces bombed the company, reducing to ruins and ash its main office, main printing factory, warehouses, schools, Editing Department, and library.[74] In response, the company immediately suspended operations and laid off all its workers.[75] When the company resumed operations in August, it did so with a skeletal staff. The General Management Office, which now incorporated the editorial staff, had a total staff of 140 people, compared with a previous staff of 380 in the management office and 200 plus in the Editing Department.[76]

After reorganization of the company that fall, the Editing Department was replaced by a Production Department (Shengchanbu 生產部), which had a Compilation and Review Committee (Bianshen weiyuanhui 編審委員會) within it that initially had only seventeen staff members divided into six reviewing editors (*bianshenyuan*) and eleven compilers (*bianyiyuan*).[77] Wang sought to shift Commercial Press's approach to publishing more specialized books whose manuscripts would be acquired through contract with intellectuals and writers working outside the press.[78] Still, committee rules also made provisions for hiring assistant compilers (*zhuli bianyiyuan*), who were not listed in the committee's staff, and magazine agencies also had dedicated editorial staffs.[79] In addition, Commercial Press continued to have compilers, editors, and proofreaders working on special dictionary and reprint projects as well as in other areas of the company, such as the Proofreading Department.[80] Overall, while the numbers of staff performing compiling and editing functions was smaller than before, Commercial Press still maintained comparatively large groups of editors at the company for in-house production of textbooks, periodicals, and reference books.

As high school or college graduates with wages ranging from twenty to one hundred yuan per month, staff editors were situated squarely in the group that Wen-hsin Yeh has labeled petty urbanites.[81] This pay range, for instance, corresponded to that for most reporters, proofreaders, and staff editors working in Shanghai's newspapers during the 1920s and 1930s.[82] It ran somewhat lower than national-bank and foreign-enterprise employees, corresponded fairly closely to municipal-government employees, and on average exceeded the wages of retail staff and most teachers.[83] Occupying this middle status, staff editors felt acutely the concomitant economic and social pressures of their unstable position in urban society. These economic pressures were exacerbated by rising costs of living, which one author estimates increased by 40 percent between 1925 and 1930, with particularly sharp increases in food and housing.[84]

An article on "The Livelihood of Shanghai's Middle-Class Society" in the *Advancing Virtue Quarterly* (*Jinde jikan* 進德季刊), journal of the Colleagues' Association to Advance Virtue (Jindehui 進德會), a social organization at Zhonghua Book Company dominated by the editorial staff, clearly signaled the class and status-group sentiments of the publisher's editors.[85] After detailing a modest family budget of roughly fifty yuan per month, the author mapped out the economic challenges his peer group faced when trying to live within it. "Even if those in Shanghai's middle-class society [*zhongdeng shehui*] serve in each organization or business, their monthly income at the most is 70 or 80 yuan and at the least is 40 or 50 yuan, or 20 or 30 yuan. Now when the cost of living rises daily and everything becomes more expensive, the various expenditures [*yongxiang*] will all increase."[86] Though they earned more than industrial workers, those in midlevel society, the author argued, were ultimately worse off. They depended completely on their employers for their salaries, without the ability to strike for higher wages like workers.

Moreover, unlike workers, who had no pretense and could live with utter frugality, those in middle-class society needed to maintain a certain lifestyle worthy of their status as literate, educated people.

Although they do not have the capability to support their own living situation, they also must consider their dignity [*timian*]. If they go out to meet a guest, they must always wear a long gown. . . . At home they also cannot do things with manual labor [*laoli*], like cooking, washing clothes, making tea, or buying vegetables. For all these things they must rely on other people and cannot do it themselves. They cannot have a plentiful income, but they also cannot live like a person in the lower level of society.[87]

The concerns in this article were echoed by another colleague, Jiang Bozhen 蔣伯震, who also lamented that middle-class professionals had limited incomes but status expectations associated with being a literate elite that required certain kinds of clothing, food, housing, and social interactions.[88] Jiang further emphasized that "the real suffering of the middle class is that their spiritual desires cannot be satisfied. Because the middle class are mostly people who have received a middle school education or higher, they have their own ideas, have aspirations, and their appetite for knowledge is strong, so they often wish to study profound learning. Further, because of the position they occupy and the work they do, they especially must study at all times to make use of it."[89] Together, these articles suggest staff editors felt the pinch of limited incomes in Shanghai, where the cost of living was increasing quickly, while at the same time aspiring to a standard of living and quality of life comparable to the urban professional class. Because they faced the economic pressures associated with the petty urbanite status group more generally yet also engaged in literate work and were recognizable as intellectuals, as Jiang Bozhen indicates in his article, we can characterize them as "petty intellectuals" (*xiao zhishifenzi*). As such, they at once shared experiences with but were distinct from both industrial print workers and the elite academics who held elevated positions in the Commercial Press Editing Department or submitted manuscripts from outside the publishers.

Even as publishers recruited most editorial staff from the ranks of recent high school and college graduates, they also installed Editing Department directors who were leading intellectuals with impressive reputations to oversee that work. Illustrated in the preceding is one approach to this with Wang Yunwu's reorganization of the Commercial Press Editing Department. There, leading scholars like Tang Cheng, Tao Menghe, Ren Hongjun, and Zhou Gengsheng directed specialized divisions within the Editing Department. Later, when Wang served as general manager, American-educated historian and educator He Bingsong was chosen to direct the Editing Department. Zhonghua and World similarly brought in leading scholars to head particular projects or the whole Editing

Department. Shen Zhifang at World Book Company, for instance, courted Xu Weinan 徐慰南, who taught at Fudan's Experimental High School (Shiyan zhongxue), with a salary of five hundred yuan and a car service to bring him to work.[90] Xu was able to use his connections with scholars, artists, and writers to arrange manuscripts for the ABC Series and other publications. Zhonghua Book Company at the same time recruited Shu Xincheng first to write a textbook, then to oversee its signature dictionary project, *Cihai*, and finally to run the Editing Department altogether in 1930.[91] Subsequently, his contract was renewed repeatedly, and he served as Editing Department director until his retirement in 1953, effectively shifting the focus of his promotion of education from his own writing to carrying out what he called administration of writing (*zhuzuo xingzheng*).[92] At all these publishers, intellectuals hired as directors became administrators of others' writing, disaggregating cultural production into writing and its management.

Mental Labor and Flow Production

The organization of editing departments composed of large numbers of staff editors with basic modern learning and writing competence coincided with development of a form of textual production based on an industrial model akin to a factory assembly line. As noted at the start of the chapter, Wang Yunwu described just such a production process when he was preparing to take over the Commercial Press Editing Department. Wang in fact started to implement something similar to this production model with his initiative to produce a Chinese encyclopedia, with executive editors overseeing staff editors executing discrete research and writing tasks.[93] With the reorganization of the Editing Department, by 1924 Wang had created an encyclopedia committee, which he headed, that had six departments with an overall staff of thirty-one. Each department was directed by one of the leading young scholars he had recruited—namely, Tao Menghe, Tang Cheng, Cheng Yingzhang 程瀛章, Bing Zhi 秉志, and He Bingsong, with one directed by the experienced older editor Fu Weiping 傅緯平.[94] Besides organizing staff editors to translate foreign encyclopedia entries, Wang also hired university students on summer vacation to do translating work.[95] Wang further experimented with an incentive system that projected each staff member's monthly productivity translating or writing text at a rate of two to three yuan per thousand characters and rewarded them for surpassing those targets.[96] All in all the departments of the encyclopedia project worked like assembly lines for textual production, with staff editors translating and writing under the coordination of foreign-trained academics. This industrial workshop model was replicated for other large-scale Commercial Press projects like Zhang Yuanji's *Rare Editions of the Twenty-Four Dynastic Histories* (*Bainaben ershisi shi*) and Wang Yunwu's *Zhongshan Dictionary*.[97] As I have demonstrated elsewhere, Zhonghua's flagship dictionary, *Cihai*, was produced using similar dynamics.[98] Overall, by the 1930s Zhonghua was keeping careful track of the production of each of its staff editors on a daily, weekly, and monthly basis.[99]

Besides large-scale publications like encyclopedias, dictionaries, and reprint projects, publishers produced textbooks and other publications for a popular audience in similar ways. Yang Yinshen's 楊蔭深 early career at Commercial Press, where he was initially hired as a proofreader, reveals how a range of texts were produced by staff editors writing fungible content that was solicited, configured, and reviewed by executive or senior editors.[100] First Yang was drafted to write synopses of books collected in the Complete Library (Wanyou wenku 萬有文庫) for Commercial Press's advertising circular, *Publishing Weekly* (*Chuban zhoukan* 出版週刊). Later, he wrote a wider variety of book introductions for the circular and took a hand in its editing when it was short-staffed. Then, starting in 1936 reviewing editor (*bianshen*) Huang Shaoxu 黃紹緒 directed Yang to revise Sun Lianggong's 孫俍工 *High School National Language Textbook* to fit the new curriculum standards issued that year by the Ministry of Education. In 1937 Huang further assigned Yang to compile language textbooks for vocational schools. With both textbooks, the overall organization of the readers was reviewed and vetted by senior editors like Huang and Fu Weiping. In these and other revision projects to which Yang was assigned during the mid-1930s, senior editorial directors set the publishing agenda, defined the nature of the project, and set the parameters for Yang's compilation or editorial work. Yang, as an entry-level staff editor, carried out the proofreading, writing, and annotation work he was assigned, producing content to help keep the flow of Commercial Press's publications moving. But Yang also experienced a consistent expansion of his work responsibilities as he successfully completed his assigned tasks, reflecting a meritocratic environment that allowed editors to rise in stature and do more interesting and challenging work over the course of their careers at a given publisher.[101]

So, during the 1920s and 1930s, groups of editors translated, compiled, and wrote textbooks, journals, and a range of reference books seemingly just as they had during the preceding two decades. But the common feature of coordinated group work masked substantial differences in power relations and work dynamics. In the earlier period, directors and staff editors were peers working in collaborative relationships characterized by horizontal communication, where together they planned publications, decided on their methods, and reviewed the content that they themselves produced. By contrast, during the 1920s and 1930s, executive editors like Wang Yunwu and his academics, Shu Xincheng and Shen Duoshan, Shen Zhifang and Xu Weinan, set publishing agendas and organized coordinated systems for generating, integrating, and reviewing text. Staff editors, who had lower levels of education and academic status, produced fungible text for coordination by executive editors or revised and repurposed it under executive editors' direction. Consequently, during this later period two distinct forms of mental labor—the planning and management of the productive process and the production of textual content—were decoupled. This distinction between planning and coordination, on the one hand, and textual production, on the other, was formalized at Commercial Press after the establishment of the Compilation and Review Committee (later again a department [bu]) in the fall of 1932 after the January 28 Incident.[102] General Manager Wang Yunwu served simultaneously as the committee's director. He and a small group of reviewing editors (bianshenyuan) were responsible for drafting publishing plans, selecting manuscripts solicited from outside, and directing the writing, translating, and revising work of the committee/department's compilers. Compilers (bianyiyuan), for their part, were to "compile and edit [bianji] each kind of textbook, reference book, and periodical" under direction from the director and reviewers. Likewise, at Zhonghua Editing Department director Shu Xincheng assigned manuscript reviewers, made final decisions on acceptance, and supervised each stage of the editing, typesetting, and proofreading processes.[103] Editing Department leaders fully controlled the planning and management aspects of textual production, while staff editors generated content, like workers on a textual assembly line.[104] This process allowed the major publishers to optimize the output of their large editing departments while minimizing expense by depending primarily on recent graduates of the modern Chinese school system, who had basic modern learning and functional writing skills.

As noted, these patterns of large-scale mobilization of educated people for collective literary production resembled in some ways the major compilation projects of the Qing period, which also depended on the labor of large groups of underemployed scholars and had high degrees of division of labor.[105] However, they differed from the dynamics in Shanghai's leading publishers in that the Qing-era projects were orchestrated by the state or leading scholar-officials whose goals were academic or cultural political. At Commercial Press, Zhonghua, and World, the aims were primarily commercial. That is not to say that the publishers never considered the cultural, social, or political value of their publications. Part 2 illustrates the many ways agendas for cultural reform, national construction, and educational development motivated their initiatives. But as Shu Xincheng noted at the time, "Because it must plan for the company's survival, [the publisher] has to be attentive to business. . . . If something is closely related to education or culture but the company would experience a relatively great loss, we also have to abandon it."[106] Efficiency and marketability conditioned publishing managers' choices about all aspects of the production process. Further, Qing-era scholarly projects operated on a patronage model, whereas intellectual labor in the commercial publishers became primarily a wage-labor relationship. The result was a process of cultural production that was increasingly market driven, impersonal, and instrumentalized for mass production.

As staff editors were integrated into collective labor processes that mirrored flow production, with discrete productive tasks that could be timed and coordinated according to the principles of Taylorism, or scientific management (*kexue guanli*), the organizational structure limited their independence and control over the purpose and process of intellectual labor. Instead, project editors or editing department directors increasingly dominated the managerial dimension of compiling and editing work, setting publishing agendas and subdividing work to create efficient divisions of labor. These directors consequently controlled production of content through the dynamics of the labor market and wage-labor relations, and staff editors became increasingly subject to mechanistic labor processes.[107] Staff editors, however, had some opportunities to transition from content production to managerial positions through successful compilation work. Zhonghua's Jin Zhaozi offers one clear example of such mobility. Jin was first hired to compile textbooks during the early 1920s but rejoined the Editing Department as director of the vital textbook division after a short stint in government during the late 1920s.[108] Cases like Jin's suggest that while the differences in work roles between content producer and production manager were significant, effective editors could cross from one to the other, creating an incentive of upward mobility.[109]

Staff editors could also follow their own intellectual agendas by writing books and articles outside their regular work routines and selling them to the press for manuscript fees. Wang Boxiang 王伯祥 (1890–1975) offers a prime example. He graduated from Suzhou's First High School (Diyi zhongxue) and taught in several schools before working in Commercial Press's Editing Department for a decade between 1921 and 1932.[110] Despite his limited academic background, Wang wrote a series of monographs for the publisher, following the pattern of academic writing that foreign-trained academics introduced to the press during that decade.[111] His detailed diary reveals how in 1927 he took advantage of half-day afternoons during Commercial Press's summer vacation period and evenings and weekends during the rest of the year to write the *History of the Taiping Heavenly Kingdom Revolution* (*Taiping tianguo geming shi*), drafting at home roughly a thousand characters or a chapter at each sitting. His work on that historical monograph coincided with his work compiling a high-school-level Chinese history textbook for the publisher, which he wrote each morning at the office.[112] While juggling the two projects and negotiating various social obligations, Wang finally submitted the fifty-thousand-character manuscript at the end of November, expecting a manuscript fee of one hundred fifty yuan (at a standard rate of three yuan per thousand characters).[113]

Such a project allowed Wang to engage in scholarly work while supplementing his income, evading to some degree the more mechanized kinds of textual production under an executive editor typical of textbook and reference-book production. But Wang could not fully escape either the structural expectations of the publisher or the economic constraints of his petty intellectual status. When he turned in the manuscript he expressed aspirations for a more thorough scholarly inquiry into the Taiping movement that was not formulaic (*bagu*) and constrained by "limits of time and style." "Later," he said, "I should concentrate my effort on this and finish a perfect 'Specialized History of the Taiping.'"[114] The next day, however, because of economic considerations he confronted the sober reality of having to turn his attention immediately to monographs on the Sino-Japanese War and the Three Kingdoms that Commercial Press expected from him for series publications.

I plan to first do "Annotation of the Three Kingdoms" and can hand over the manuscript within the year, then at the New Year I will not experience straitened circumstances, otherwise the New Year will be very difficult. My family's expenses in recent years have increased by the day. Fortunately, I can depend on writing manuscripts for a little money to make it up, but my body is frail and I cannot endure sitting with perseverance, so I am fearful about writing manuscripts. What can I do?![115]

Moonlighting writing manuscripts for the company allowed a petty intellectual like Wang to pursue some of his scholarly interests and write something other than the boilerplate prose of textbooks and reference books. But financial considerations were primary, and his writing had to fit the agendas of the publisher, as defined by its managing editors. They favored short monographs covering topic areas in their series publications rather than the more in-depth study Wang really wished to write.[116] Economic considerations, for both the company managers and Wang, conditioned how he wrote and the form it took.

Labor Activism and the Cultural Politics of Intellectual Labor

As the writings by Jiang Bozhen and others in the Zhonghua staff journal *Advancing Virtue Quarterly* suggest, staff editors occupied a "middle" position, suspended between industrial workers and the urban professional elite. On the one hand, they faced serious economic constraints and the increasing routinization and mechanization of mental labor, experiences similar to those of the working class. On the other hand, they had relatively high levels of education for the time and worked with their pens and brushes in ways similar to more high-profile groups of intellectuals. Assessing the action staff editors took in the labor protests that erupted periodically at Commercial Press and Zhonghua Book Company from the mid-1920s through the early 1930s reveals the ways in which they might have self-identified and affiliated in relation to industrial workers and academics or the urban professional elite.

Both publishers experienced significant labor unrest in the wake of the May 30 protests, and in each case Editing Department staff expressed solidarity with their company's industrial workers. Strikes at the end of August 1925 brought together workers across each company's departments. At Commercial Press, on August 22 staff in the Distribution Department (Faxingsuo) struck over wages, work time, and treatment.[117] They were soon joined by the print workers' union and by staff in the General Affairs Office and Editing Department, which organized a "colleagues' association" (*tongrenhui*). Each group chose representatives, who formed a Strike Central Executive Committee that presented the conditions raised by the different groups of staff and negotiated with management. The representatives from the Editing Department were Chinese Communist Party (CCP) member Shen Yanbing (Mao Dun), Ding Xiaoxian 丁曉先, and Zheng Zhenduo 鄭振鐸.

The groups' solidarity might have been built in part on the collective action taken in support of industrial workers striking during the high tide of the May Thirtieth Movement in June of that year. During those protests, workers and staff had agreed to donate to the fund to relieve striking workers between 5 percent and 50 percent of their pay, depending on their monthly wage. Moreover, the Editing Department independently donated 10 percent of its special savings account, which amounted to 3,568.82 yuan.[118] Members of the Editing Department, such as Ye Shengtao, Zheng Zhenduo, and Wang Boxiang, played key roles in this process of mobilization, and published the journal *Justice Daily* (*Gongli ribao*).[119] The common expression of nationalist sentiments underpinned the connection among these groups of workers who had distinct backgrounds and roles within the company.

In August, strike demands included calls for increased wages, reduced work time, regular holidays, the distribution of bonuses, and provisions for relief and severance pay for fired or laid-off workers.[120] But there were also distinctive demands related to each department. For instance, members of the Editing Department called for the company to send colleagues with five years of service or more to "study overseas or to do academic investigation [*xueshu shang zhi kaocha*]" with pay, suggesting they were more interested with generating opportunities for academic enrichment and higher education than in more immediate livelihood concerns. After several rounds of negotiation, the company accepted some of the demands but not others and agreed to raise wages progressively for groups making fifty yuan per month or less, starting at 10 percent and increasing by 5 percent or 10 percent increments for each cohort in a ten-yuan range.[121] Significantly, these increases affected staff editors on the lower end of the Editing Department pay scale but not those with greater seniority or status. As for paid sabbaticals, the company offered to consider them on a case-by-case basis according to the company's needs and opportunities.

Zhonghua Book Company also experienced labor unrest involving all its divisions in August and early September 1925.[122] But a more sustained and contentious confrontation occurred in 1927 after the Northern Expedition.[123] Initially, in early April 1927 the Printers' General Labor Union (Yinshua zong gonghui) had mediated an agreement between management and each of Zhonghua's departments for better pay and working conditions. Later that year, however, the company pushed back against that agreement by suspending operations on July 3, 1927, claiming economic hardship because of the wage increases imposed during the spring. A standoff between management and the combined representatives of the staff association extended throughout July. Finally, on July 26 with strong public support from editorial staffs at Commercial Press and World Book Company, the Shanghai Municipal Government's Bureau of Agriculture, Industry, and Business led by Pan Gongzhan 潘公展 stepped forward to mediate, with support from other organs of the Nationalist government. After the government threatened to confiscate a share of Zhonghua's property in order to compensate the locked-out workers, the company agreed to resume operation on August 1. Subsequently, on August 18 the company's management signed an agreement with representatives of each sector of the company's workers and staff that locked in more modest wage increases and established procedures for the company to lay off workers by providing them with two months of severance pay. Later that fall, Zhonghua took advantage of this second agreement to fire some three hundred workers and undermine the CCP organization at the company.

In these protests of the 1920s, the context of anti-imperialist struggle and mobilization for national unification seems to have fostered a sense of solidarity between editorial staff, industrial workers, and office and retail staff. CCP organizational ties that encompassed both industrial workers' unions and intellectuals, like Shen Yanbing, undoubtedly reinforced those connections.[124] But the collapse of the United Front and suppression of CCP activities in both labor unions and among intellectuals altered the environment in which staff editors acted politically, leading them to self-identify and voice their interests in different ways. This shift comes through clearly in the response of the Commercial Press editorial staff to

Wang Yunwu's effort to institute aspects of Taylorism into the operations of the Editing Department in 1931.

As I have recounted in detail elsewhere, Wang Yunwu returned from a study tour to Japan, Europe, and the United States in 1930 enthused about Taylorism and eager to apply it to all aspects of company management.[125] For the Editing Department, in January 1931 he proposed a system of quantifying production for proofreading, translation, composition, review, and compilation, offering editorial staff bonuses if their rate and quantity of work surpassed the established standards. Wang's proposal triggered a storm of protest in the Editing Department mostly because editors felt that the mental labor and cultural production they engaged in could not be quantified according to a piecework system in the same way manual factory labor could. In general, the editors seemed most concerned with the status implications of being associated with mechanized, manual labor versus creative intellectual work in a society that historically had distinguished social status precisely in this way.[126]

The following year, in the fall of 1932, Mao Dun, who had worked at Commercial Press for more than a decade during the 1910s and 1920s, wrote a short story that reinforces this interpretation of the status identification of staff editors as of the early 1930s. The story, "Wartime" (You di er zhang), focuses on the January 28 Incident, whose action included the destructive Japanese bombing attack on Commercial Press. Mao Dun's story traces the diverging fates of the company's editor, Mr. Li, and his neighbor, the print worker Xiang.[127] Mao Dun's central theme is to recognize and celebrate the working class's nationalist resistance, but for our purposes the story is significant for the way it describes a significant gulf in social and cultural status between the editor and the print worker. In Mao Dun's words, "Although Hsiang [Xiang] was a neighbor and they both worked for the same firm, since one was a 'gentleman' in the editorial department and the other only a worker in the printing press, the two seldom met."[128] With his intimate knowledge of the publishing world, Mao Dun recognized that even petty intellectuals working as staff editors in the publishers claimed distinction from the working class because of their literate work. That distinction was highlighted by Mr. Li's ability to relocate his family to the relative safety of the International Concession and depend on a modest cushion of a hundred yuan from the company's pension advance even as Xiang left his wife destitute when he joined a work gang supporting soldiers at the front.

Despite the increasing routinization of textual production and the limited wages the leading publishers offered staff editors, Mao Dun's story, Jiang Bozhen's essay, and the editors' reaction to Wang Yunwu's scientific management proposal all suggest that they fundamentally identified themselves as scholars more than as industrial workers. Cultivation of an academic environment in publishers' editing departments and fluid interactions between different tiers of intellectuals fostered this kind of self-identification. The ability to live a scholarly lifestyle and consider oneself an intellectual allowed staff editors to make a significant status claim in Republican society, offering some compensation in symbolic capital for their limited wages and work autonomy.

With reorganization of editing departments in the early 1920s, editorial staff had argued for improvements to company facilities that would foster a more scholarly atmosphere and allow for staff members' intellectual development. As noted, Hu Shi's visit sparked calls by editors for Commercial Press to improve library facilities, provide more sustained summer vacations, set up laboratories for scientific research, and support paid sabbaticals, a proposal echoed during the company's strike in the summer of 1925. Similar appeals were made at Zhonghua Book Company, as captured in an article by Zuo Shunsheng in 1922 in the *Advancing Virtue Quarterly*.[129] Zuo started by celebrating the "craze" (*re*) for language study at the publisher, where classes in English, Japanese, Esperanto, and Chinese had enthusiastic volunteer student bodies ranging from ten to thirty or forty. Building on this enthusiasm, Zuo expressed hope that courses in French, Russian, and German could be offered in the future.

Viewing these educational opportunities as beneficial for both the company and its staff members, Zuo further advocated for two more improvements. First, he called for expansion and reorganization of the library. Second, he suggested that the company keep samples of the scientific instruments it manufactured to "form a small 'laboratory' to make it easier to provide proof when compiling science books and so colleagues enthusiastic about science can also use it for experiments."[130] In the offering of supplemental courses, a research library, and lab facilities, Zuo saw the potential for Zhonghua to become an academic institution as much as a commercial one, in keeping with the vision developed contemporaneously by Hu Shi and the young editors he talked with at Commercial Press. As Zuo put it, "In this way Zhonghua Book Company after five years will not only be a commercial institution that exclusively manages the book trade but at the same time an organization for academic research, and it will certainly be able to make even greater contributions to the Chinese cultural undertaking."[131] Young intellectual editors were attracted by the prospect of a workplace that opened avenues for research and learning, approximating the atmosphere of a university or research institute.

Commercial Press and Zhonghua did, in fact, invest in fostering an academic environment in their companies during the 1920s and 1930s. For one, they organized and maintained substantial libraries, which became prominent features of both companies. Beginning in 1907 Commercial Press invested in the Hanfenlou Library, which during the late Qing was managed by Wu Zengqi. Wu was a Qing-era provincial degree holder who was an expert in ancient literature, so he assiduously collected rare books (*shanbenshu*), with help from Zhang Yuanji and Sun Yuxiu.[132] Despite the Hanfenlou's impressive collection of rare books, by the time of Hu Shi's visit, he and younger staff in the Editing Department complained about the need for more modern, Western books and called for expanded library facilities, for which there was broad support in the company.[133] By 1925 Commercial Press had established the expanded Eastern Library (Dongfang tushuguan), a five-story complex with one hundred seventy thousand Chinese-language volumes along with fifty thousand volumes of books and periodicals in Western and Japanese languages (figure 2.2).[134] The library soon became one of Shanghai's cultural landmarks but was tragically destroyed in the Japanese bombing of Commercial Press's Baoshan Road complex in January 1932 (figure 2.3).

Zhonghua Book Company followed suit and developed its own library collection to support its Editing Department. Started in 1916 as the Zhonghua Book Company Book Depository (*cangshulou*), by 1920 the collection had accumulated about ten thousand volumes.[135] As of 1925 the collection had grown to sixty thousand volumes, became organized by subject category, and was renamed the Zhonghua Book Company Library. When Shu Xincheng was hired to direct the Editing Department in 1930, he assumed simultaneous direction of the library and expanded its collection to include Chinese and foreign reference books, the textbooks of all China's major publishers, and a variety of rare books. In 1935 this expanded

Figure 2.2 Eastern Library, Commercial Press, 1930. Virtual Shanghai, http://www
.virtualshanghai.net/Asset/Preview/dbImage_ID-1989_No-1.jpeg, accessed August 27,
2018; originally from Institut d'Asie Orientale

Figure 2.3 Eastern Library and the Commercial Press Editing Department after the
Japanese attack of January 1932. Shangwu yinshuguan 商務印書館, comp., *Shangwu
yinshuguan fuye hou gaikuang* 商務印書館復業後概況 (Commercial Press's general situation after its revival of operations) ([Shanghai]: [Shangwu yinshuguan], [1934]).

library moved with the Editing Department to the company's new factory complex on Macao Road.

For editors at the publishers, these libraries became resources for intellectual development. In his memoir describing his work at Commercial Press, Mao Dun remarked several times about taking time for personal reading, at times drawing material from the Hanfenlou Library.[136] He expressed the value he attached to his independent reading in response to Sun Yuxiu's concerns about his poor starting salary by saying, "I am not here for profit or fame. I just seek the richness of the Hanfenlou's book collection, with its complete Chinese and foreign books, ancient and modern, so that I can read a little."[137] Regardless of whether these were Mao Dun's exact words, they suggest that self-study and a bookish lifestyle were primary motivations for some young people working at the publisher. Similarly, Commercial Press Editing Department staffer Lu Tianbai 盧天白 later waxed rhapsodic about having time to read quietly in the Eastern Library in the year before it was destroyed in the January 28 Incident.[138]

The publishers also facilitated editors' supplemental study in various ways. As previously mentioned, after the strikes in 1925 Commercial Press was at least willing to consider supporting editors going abroad for further academic study. We see similar dynamics at Zhonghua Book Company, where editors like Ma Runqing 馬潤卿, Zuo Shunsheng, and Zhang Wentian took leaves of absence to engage in further study abroad. In regard to Ma Runqing, the announcement of his study plans in *Advancing Virtue Quarterly* stated, "After work [while working in the English Division of the Editing Department] he has still studied literature and law, working diligently without fatigue. Moreover, because learning has no limits, he has resolved to go to America and enter university to further work at literature and law, hoping to reach the summit of achievement."[139] Also, as noted, Zhonghua supported further study at home by offering supplemental courses at the company itself. At times it also subsidized staff members' study elsewhere. For instance, Lu Jialiang 陸嘉亮 recalled positively the way Zhonghua Book Company had supported Editing Department staff, as well as workers in other departments, in pursuing supplemental study for self-improvement during the 1930s, going so far as to reimburse school tuition for staff members with passing grades.[140]

While library resources and supplemental courses certainly gave editors opportunities for personal development through study and research, perhaps the most powerful way that a scholarly atmosphere was created and sustained at the publishers was through the kinds of formal and informal association that developed among editors at each company. At Zhonghua editor Li Jinhui 黎錦暉 sought to formalize a scholarly community in 1923 through institutionalization of a Spare-Time Compilation and Translation Society (Gongyu bianyishe). He began his appeal to colleagues by offering a criticism of the monotony that characterized their routine editorial work on a mass-production model: "During the day we are restricted by regulated and mechanical work, and the aim of work is mostly for our physical needs."[141] In contrast, this organization was meant to create a context for mutual learning and self-initiated projects of reading, writing, and translation that would be "a good dose for sweeping away depression and cultivating our bodies and minds."[142] Meeting weekly for mutual support, they would discuss independent writing and compilation projects, which would inspire new avenues of learning.

It is not clear whether Li's proposed society was ever institutionalized, but even when scholarly collaboration was not formalized in an organization, editors interacted around shared intellectual interests and research or writing projects of various kinds. Gao Juefu's 高覺敷 memoir offers a vivid example. Gao entered Commercial Press's Editing Department in 1926 after getting a degree in Hong Kong. He worked in the Philosophy and Education Division under Tang Cheng and likened it to having tested into a graduate school, with Tang serving as his adviser.[143] Reading in the foreign journals that Tang ordered as reference materials for the division facilitated Gao's intellectual development. Further, as his intellectual interests migrated toward developmental psychology, Gao successfully petitioned to use Commercial Press's Shanggong Primary School as a lab to study linguistic and cognitive development. As school principal, he invited visiting scholars to lecture on educational psychology, exposing the teachers to that field.[144] For Gao, then, work at Commercial Press was like being at a university, affording him opportunities for intellectual development and independent research.

Gao further describes the sense of intellectual community that was fostered by the presence of a large group of leading academics and young scholars in the Editing Department.

The academic atmosphere of the Editing Department was pronounced, and after the May Fourth Movement it was even more vigorous and completely renewed. At that time the experts in each discipline included Zhu Kezhen, Zhu Jingnong, He Bingsong, Tang Cheng, Zheng Zhenwen, Zhou Changshou, Li Shicen, Ye Shengtao, Shen Yanbing, Zheng Zhenduo, Hu Yuzhi, Yang Xianjiang, and Zhou Yutong, so that it truly could be said that the talent was plentiful and the achievements were countless. In this kind of academic environment, one was influenced imperceptibly by what one saw and heard and unconsciously transformed, so that it spontaneously gave rise to my feelings of worship of them and consequently encouraged my interest in scientific research.[145]

Fluid interaction between elite scholars and staff editors allowed the latter to feel like members of an intellectual community, encouraging them to pursue independent research and participate in collaborative projects.

Wang Boxiang's writings also reveal these dynamics.[146] At Commercial Press, Wang worked mostly as a compiler of history and geography textbooks, with nearly every diary entry during the 1920s starting with a report on which textbook he had worked on that day. So he had more than his share of the monotonous, mechanical textual production described by Li Jinhui. But he also shared in a wide range of scholarly and cultural activities that were generated by the lively group gathered at the press during the 1920s and early 1930s. For instance, when Wang's friends Zheng Zhenduo and Ye Shengtao started distributing *Literature Weekly* (*Wenxue zhoubao*) out of Zheng's house, Wang Boxiang got involved doing a great deal of the legwork, such as gathering subscriptions and addressing envelopes.[147] His involvement stemmed from participation in the Literary Research Association (Wenxue yanjiuhui), which incorporated other colleagues from Commercial Press.[148] Significantly, in order to help his friends with the journal, Wang found himself siphoning time away from his own writing and from Japanese classes that he was taking at Commercial Press, which were taught by his Editing Department colleague Xie Liuyi.

From this evidence, Wang's life at Commercial Press was replete with intellectual and cultural activities that strayed far from his primary compiling and editing work, which could be routine and mechanistic. At the same time, Wang shared with his colleagues a lively intellectual leisure culture. Wang's diary is full of references to visits with his closest friends, which included Ye Shengtao, Zheng Zhenduo, and Zhou Yutong 周予同. This expandable group frequently went on outings around Shanghai, met to eat and drink, surveyed the bookstores, and went to watch opera or films.[149] These activities were in many ways continuous with the forms of literati leisure that Commercial Press and Zhonghua editors had participated in during the late Qing and early Republic. Besides providing a counterbalance to the routines of mechanical text production, they also allowed men like Wang to continue to live the lifestyle and embody the leisure culture of the Chinese scholarly elite. That leisure culture and a range of literary and scholarly pursuits marked staff editors as intellectuals and cultured people, even as they faced limited incomes and operated in increasingly mechanized work environments. Those activities further enabled staff editors to maintain strong social networks that included a wide range of scholars, providing them with a powerful form of social capital.

Mental Labor in the Age of Mechanical Reproduction

During the 1920s and 1930s China's publishing circles faced increased market demand for more diverse products, which fostered a drive for production captured most concisely in Wang Yunwu's slogan for Commercial Press to publish "one new title per day" (*ri chu xinshu yizhong*). Growing numbers of modern school students and graduates, younger and Western educated, with an interest in global trends of thought and culture, fueled this demand. Industrial print technology made it possible for the publishers to supply books to this growing market, but they needed to generate fresh content for each title. Zhonghua Book Company and Commercial Press responded in part by hiring foreign-trained academics and cultural trend makers who cultivated a monographic style of book production in publishers' editing departments during the 1920s. But publishers also turned to cheaper recent graduates of domestic colleges and high schools for staff editors. They populated large editing departments that continued to make China's publishing sector globally distinctive. Further, publishers developed systems of book production using division of labor and flow production, especially for the textbooks and large-scale reference books that were the companies' economic mainstays. The speed and scale of industrial book manufacturing shaped how books were written, compiled, reviewed, and revised.

As factory-style book production developed under imperatives for increasing volume and efficiency, staff editors, like industrial workers elsewhere, lost control over the dynamics of their labor, which was increasingly shaped by requirements of the production system itself. Within this overall trend of alienation of control of cultural production, a small group of managers and designers organized and managed the system of production to which authors, compilers, and editors were subject.[151] In Republican China's domain of cultural production, during the 1920s and 1930s intellectual labor bifurcated. On the one hand there developed a level of planning, oversight, and review controlled by executive editors like Wang Yunwu, He Bingsong, Lufei Kui, Shu Xincheng, Shen Zhifang, and Xu Weinan. On the other hand, petty intellectual staff editors proliferated, filling discrete positions in divisions of labor generating fungible text—textual assembly lines—that could be flexibly integrated into textbooks, reference books, and journals, depending on market demand and company initiatives. These dynamics differed markedly from those of the two preceding decades, when editing department directors and staff were part of a common intellectual stratum as literati and shared in processes of planning and production according to the study-society model (discussed in chapter 1).

Despite increasingly routinized work and wages suppressed by continuous oversupply of literate people, staff editors during the 1920s and 1930s found some fulfillment in publishers' editing departments. They created opportunities for upward mobility through effective work. They carved out time for their own writing and editing projects. They pursued self-cultivation using company resources like libraries and supplemental education, which publishers provided primarily to enhance their cultural production. And they built relationships with colleagues and leading academics at the publishers that allowed them to view themselves as members of a community of scholars, not as industrial workers. Several of these practices resemble the phenomenon of *la perruque*, or "making do," as theorized by Michel de Certeau. As with "making do," staff editors' activities gave them some satisfaction but did not fundamentally alter the emergent power structures inscribed in the system of production. In fact, those activities may even have enabled those systems by making work at the publishers more sustainable for staff editors over the long term. Many staff editors, including the group featured in this chapter like Yang Yinshen, Jin Zhaozi, and Wang Boxiang, worked in publishing companies for many years, if not decades.

Yet we can also go beyond Certeau by acknowledging that participation in the cultural life at the publishers paid staff editors real dividends in social capital, through association with leading scholars, and cultural capital, by providing them with a basis to claim status as a scholar or intellectual. In the Chinese cultural context, relationships with mobile and publicly recognized intellectual figures were valuable resources for staff editors. Moreover, working with the brush or pen still marked an important status distinction between "gentlemen" and workers in postimperial society. Thus, Chinese cultural preferences for literary work as a marker of cultural distinction and as a basis for elite association helped underpin development of an industrial mode of cultural production by ensuring the dedicated commitment of the compilers and editors who produced content for the publishers. Petty intellectuals, like these staff editors, with basic modern educations and writing skills, in practice constituted the vast majority of the intellectual stratum in modern China. Along with primary- and secondary-school teachers, newspaper reporters and editors, and many different kinds of clerical staff and government functionaries, they were largely anonymous and invisible, yet their activities contributed materially to China's cultural production and the transformations of the first half of the twentieth century, whose dynamics I explore in part 2.

Part I Epilogue

War, Revolution, Hiatus

For China's Shanghai-based commercial publishers, the start of the Sino-Japanese War in 1937 triggered an extended crisis that lasted through the founding of the People's Republic of China in 1949. Companies adjusted to changing wartime conditions in two phases. Between Japanese occupation of the lower Yangzi region in the fall of 1937 and the start of the Pacific War in December 1941, the publishers moved as much of their Shanghai facilities as possible into the relative safety of the International Concession. Still, the losses were great. World Book Company had its main factory complex in Hongkou occupied almost immediately by Japanese forces.[1] Commercial Press and Zhonghua Book Company also lost facilities in Shanghai and Beijing and faced growing restrictions in Shanghai. But they also took advantage of their diversified production centers in Hong Kong to set up alternative managerial offices.[2] Both publishers further sought to ensure access to markets in China's interior, with Commercial Press moving initially to build a factory in Changsha, while exploring other possible sites in Guilin, Kunming, and Ganxian, and with Zhonghua developing a subsidiary main office in Kunming.[3] In the second phase, after Pearl Harbor and the concomitant Japanese occupation of Hong Kong and the foreign concessions in Shanghai, the Nationalist Party's wartime capital of Chongqing became the main center of publishing activities from 1942 until the end of the war.[4]

Wartime disruption led to dramatic reductions in all these companies' editorial staffs. With the onset of the war, for instance, at the end of 1937, Zhonghua pared down its editorial staff in Shanghai to 25 people, since it had limited access to inland markets. Laid-off editors received six months of severance pay at 60 percent of their salaries.[5] As operations revived in Hong Kong, Zhonghua's editorial staff there rebounded to 42 to 46 members between 1938 and 1940, but this was still far short of the prewar high of 167.[6] After Zhonghua's General Management Office (Zong guanli chu) was established in Chongqing in 1942, it contained a Compilation and Review Department (Bianshenbu), with a skeleton staff of 25, directed by longtime staff editor Jin Zhaozi, which included old colleagues from Shanghai such as Ge Suicheng 葛綏成 and Yao Shaohua 姚紹華.[7] Commercial Press similarly developed a number of compilation and review (*bianshen*) offices. Besides a remnant group in Shanghai, compilation and review offices or departments initially were set up in Changsha, Hong Kong, and Chongqing, with the last becoming the main center for editorial functions after 1941.[8] But as with Zhonghua Book Company, these were skeletal staffs compared with the prewar period. In Chongqing Commercial Press operated with between 5 and 10 editors working primarily under the leadership of veteran Su Jiqing 蘇繼廎 to maintain flagship journals like *Eastern Miscellany*, reprint reference books and titles from the University Series, and solicit new manuscripts.[9] Soon after the war's start, then, the large, coordinated editing departments at the major publishers ceased to exist and function as they had during the previous four decades.

Their reduction corresponded to the relative decline of the book market during the war. Early in the war Commercial Press's leaders predicted limited purchasing power would lead to a drop in regular book sales, so after having worked to diversify its publications during the 1930s, by 1939 they came to focus again on publishing textbooks as their economic mainstay. According to a report in the board of directors' meeting that year, "After August 13 [1937], because we foresaw a weakening in the purchasing power of ordinary books for general use, and this company's financial strength was not as great as before, we again changed our policy and still use most of our strength to print and sell textbooks."[10] However, by 1942 in Chongqing, Nationalist Party policies for national standard textbooks threatened to undermine the major publishers' competitive advantage in even this fundamental market.

In 1938 the Ministry of Education formed a committee for compiling national standard textbooks for the primary level, whose manuscripts were completed in 1942, after several changes in curriculum standards. With a mandate from Chiang Kai-shek, the ministry began publication of these textbooks in 1942, using Zhengzhong Book Company (Zhengzhong shuju 正中書局) as the main printer and distributor.[11] Zhengzhong had been set up with major backing from the Nationalist Party during the late 1920s.[12] Zhengzhong's capacity for printing and distribution was limited, however, and it could not keep up with demand for textbooks.[13] Consequently, the government encouraged formation of a consortium for textbook printing and distribution composed of China's seven largest publishing companies: Commercial Press, Zhonghua Book Company, Zhengzhong Book Company, World Book Company, Great East Book Company (Dadong shuju 大東書局), Kaiming Bookstore (Kaiming shudian 開明書店), and Wentong Book Company (Wentong shuju 文通書局).[14]

After extended negotiations, these companies formed the Seven-Company Associated Supply Office (Qijia lianhe gongying chu 七家聯合供應處) on April 19, 1943. The companies divided up the rights to a certain percentage of textbook production and distribution, based roughly on a calculation of each press's production capacity and historical share of the textbook market. However, Zhengzhong Book Company gained a disproportionate share because of its close ties to the Nationalist government.[15] Companies were in turn responsible for contributing a corresponding percentage of the fifty million yuan that would provide the start-up capital for the joint distribution company. The proportions of capital and market share were distributed as follows: Commercial Press, Zhonghua Book Company, and Zhengzhong Book Company 23 percent each; World 12 percent; Dadong 8 percent; Kaiming 7 percent; and Wentong 4 percent.[16] Although established to address wartime exigencies, the system of unified compilation and coordinated distribution on a share basis by the major publishing companies continued into the postwar period. The system was expanded in April 1946 to eleven companies overall. At this time the proportional stakes of Zhonghua Book Company and Commercial Press each declined by 2.5 to 3 percent to about 20 percent each, while World's share was reduced by 2 percent.[17] This consortium system granted each publisher a certain level of production for and sales in the captive market for textbooks. But because the textbooks were centrally compiled by the National Office of Compilation and Translation, one of the main ratio-nales for commercial publishers to maintain large editorial departments was gone.

With shares of the textbook trade effectively frozen during the years of the Pacific War and postwar periods, publishers sought to diversify their other publications. As Zhonghua general manager Li Shuming explained to the board of directors in 1943, "Now, because of the constraints of the current situation, we must change our policy and emphasize publishing ordinary books. Besides first reviving *New Zhonghua* magazine, addition-ally we will print more books of benefit to resistance and construction, and science and literary books. We expect in the future to be able to put out more than ten titles a month."[18] In practice, Zhonghua did publish sev-eral periodicals, high school textbooks, and an impressive range of series publications, but most of these book manuscripts were solicited from out-side the publisher.[19] Similarly, Commercial Press reprinted reference books, continued publication of the University Series, as well as publishing the High School Series (Zhongxue congshu) and a selected collection of texts from the Complete Library (Wanyou wenku).[20] In each of these cases, however, Commercial Press, too, was primarily reprinting published material in new formats or, as with the University Series, drawing in man-uscripts from outside the company, further obviating the need for large groups of compilers and editors.[21]

After the end of the Pacific War, in a context of civil war and economic crisis, the book market continued to be depressed, and production chal-lenges continued for all the major publishers, as Zhou Wu and Nicolai Vol-land have established.[22] Hyperinflation undermined the public's purchasing power. Access to newsprint was strictly controlled and its cost exorbitant, constraining efforts at large-scale publishing. Government con-trols tightly limited the scope of potential content. Endemic conflict because of the Civil War limited access to internal markets. These condi-tions (as I explore in chapter 6) provided the impetus and backdrop for the restructuring of the major Shanghai publishers as public-private joint-management (*gong si heying*) ventures during the early 1950s. For our pur-poses here, the more immediate impact of these challenges was to preclude the reconstruction of large mass-production–oriented editing departments in the immediate postwar context. As of 1950, Zhonghua Book Compa-ny's Editing Department had a staff of sixty-two compared with a prewar level of one hundred seventy.[23] After Commercial Press's Compilation and Review Department moved from Shanghai to Beijing, in the spring of 1951 it had a staff of just eighteen.[24] Both publishers would spend much of the next decade rebuilding their productive capacity.

PART TWO

Creating Culture

CHAPTER III

Transforming Word and Concept Through Textbooks and Dictionaries

I n 1934, more than a decade after the Ministry of Education mandated the use of vernacular language in primary- and secondary-school language courses, the National Language Unification Preparatory Committee (Guoyu tongyi choubeihui 國語統一籌備會) was complaining about textbooks. The committee of linguists, cultural reformers, and educators assembled by the Ministry of Education had a primary mandate to supervise the unification of spoken-language pronunciation, but committee members were also concerned about the quality of the written vernacular students were learning. The committee voiced its alarm: "In primary schools, since promulgation of the 'national language' course, besides selecting and using ready-made vernacular works, textbooks compiled and circulated by publishing companies are also numerous. The written style used in them is often nondescript [*bulun bulei*], with the syntax and parts of speech randomly designated by the author or compiler; some [words] fundamentally do not fit the parts of speech while others are incorrect, dialect expressions. If they are not inspected, the influence will be boundless."[1] As a result, the committee proposed that it have access to language textbooks during the review process so it could assess the language, even as the Ministry of Education evaluated books' content and pedagogical qualities.

The committee's concern with publishing circles' linguistic influence was reasonable. Since the first decade of the twentieth century, textbooks and dictionaries had played a key role in shaping the modern Chinese lexicon and writing style. Late Qing and early Republican language text-books and dictionaries, especially Commercial Press's *Ciyuan*, standard-ized and defined the neologisms that provided the terms and concepts for modern Chinese thought and culture.[2] Beginning in the 1920s language textbooks served as models for the written vernacular language (*baihua* 白話). And Zhonghua Book Company's encyclopedic dictionary *Cihai* introduced the language of new academic disciplines and political parties. By the mid-1930s the transition from a world of classical prose embedded in a Confucian intellectual tradition to one of the written vernacular translating modern, Western concepts was well under way. Textbooks and dictionaries played key roles in forming the new linguistic and conceptual universe.[3]

Dictionaries and textbooks were by no means the only texts introducing new styles, terms, and concepts, but they served a vital function because of their didactic and authoritative qualities. Scholars of dictionaries in the Euro-American world have observed how even dictionaries that explicitly aimed to offer a description of contemporary language use have come to be viewed as being normative and paradigmatic, setting standards for proper usage.[4] Similarly, textbooks, as pedagogic resources, have an authoritative quality that legitimizes their content. In the words of Michael Apple and Linda Christian-Smith, textbooks "participate in cre-ating what a society has recognized as legitimate and truthful."[5] In a con-text where language is in flux and a subject of instruction, textbooks' formal elements are also normative in important ways. That is, they offer students standard forms of modern prose writing to emulate, as well as models of distinctive modern genres of text, such as diaries, meeting minutes, sur-vey reports, letters, accounts, and many others. In this way, dictionaries and textbooks from Commercial Press, Zhonghua Book Company, and World Book Company provided China's educated young people with for-mal models and a stable lexicon for modern writing, giving practical sub-stance to *baihua*.

Significantly, the authors of these texts usually were not leading intel-lectuals and language reformers. Rather, they were in most cases the staff editors in the editing departments at the leading publishing companies. In a setting in which the lexicon was in rapid flux and scholars were just for-mulating standard grammars, a staff editor's choice of terms, framing of definitions, and formulation of textbook content provided students with their first, authoritative models of language use. This process explains the concern of the scholars and officials in the National Language Unification Preparatory Committee. More than a decade too late, they had realized that a motley crew of petty intellectuals operating with minimal government oversight was playing a key role in the transformation of the written Chinese language, one of the most fundamental and lasting of cultural changes in twentieth-century China.

Introducing New Terms and Concepts

Under Zhang Yuanji's leadership, Commercial Press effectively created the modern Chinese textbook as a genre, in step with the Qing government's introduction of educational reforms in 1902 and 1904.[6] The Newest Textbook series (Zuixin jiaokeshu), first published between 1904 and 1908, was the first complete set of primary and secondary textbooks produced in China, providing prototypes for many other textbooks of the late Qing and early Republican periods.[7] The series also grabbed a considerable proportion of the market share during the last decade of the Qing, going through multiple printings before 1911, and so can be viewed as the most representative example of late Qing textbooks.[8] Commercial Press's business grew roughly sixfold from 1903 to 1912, based largely on its textbook sales.[9] Consequently, its Chinese language (*guowen*) textbooks provide us with a valuable resource for interpreting how new terms and concepts reached students in China's first modern schools.

The central figures in Commercial Press's Editing Department took the lead in compiling the primary and upper primary language textbooks in the Newest Textbook series. Using the consultative compilation strategy described in chapter 1, Zhang Yuanji, Gao Mengdan, Jiang Weiqiao, Zhuang Yu, and Yang Yutong combined forces to craft these textbooks. Reflecting both their classical educations and reformist impulses, they wrote the textbooks in an accessible *wenyan* style while at the same time seeding them densely with a modern lexicon that related to students' new ideas about politics, culture, society, and history.[10] These terms had been percolating in translated texts and dictionaries since the middle of the nineteenth century, but they were given new fixity and authority through their inclusion in the leading language textbooks of the era.[11] By focusing on terms that illustrated new social and political dynamics, we can see how the reformist literati editors shaped the definitions of terms and concepts to fit with their own political, social, and cultural agendas.

The textbooks' project of introducing students to the language of modernity was signaled in part by their organization.[12] Chapter titles and themes were often single terms that the lesson then defined and explained, almost in the format of a glossary. The textbooks included lessons on abstract new terms such as "constitutional monarchy" (*junzhu lixian* 君主立憲), "patriotism" (*aiguo* 愛國), "citizenship" (*guomin* 國民), and "occupations" (*zhiye* 職業) but also chapters on the material culture of modernity, including "railroads" (*tielu* 鐵路), "telephones" (*dianhua* 電話), "companies" (*gongsi* 公司), "museums" (*bowuyuan* 博物院), and "parks" (*gongyuan* 公園). Explaining these modern terms, in turn, often entailed using many other loan words and return graphic loans that were transforming the modern Chinese lexicon.[13]

For example, after an opening chapter that presented the Qing government's edict declaring the trajectory and timeline of constitutional preparation, the next several chapters in Commercial Press's higher primary school language textbook offered a discussion of the idea of constitutional monarchy that incorporated a wide range of new terms, or terms whose meanings were changing dramatically in the first decade of the twentieth century[14] (figure 3.1). The chapter contrasted "constitutional monarchy" (*junzhu lixian* 君主立憲) with both "autocracy" (*zhuanzhi* 專制) and "democracy" (*minzhu* 民主). It explained that in a constitutional monarchy the government's policies were shaped in part by "public opinion" (*yulun* 輿論). Such opinion was expressed openly in a "parliament" (*yiyuan* 議院) or a "local assembly" (*yihui* 議會). Here the people were described as the main constituency of the "state" (*guojia* 國家) and were seen to have certain rights, such as the right to free "speech" (*yanlun* 言論) and to security of their "property" (*caichan* 財產). The textbooks introduced terminology that helped make comprehensible the political changes under debate during the late Qing, debates in which the literati editors at Commercial Press played an active role.

The meanings of the new terms in these textbooks reflected broader discussions of social, cultural, and political change occurring across many different media during the late Qing and early Republic. Commercial Press's lower-primary reader, for example, focused its last lesson on a comparative discussion of Chinese and European "civilization" (*wenming* 文明), introducing students to the powerful Japanese loanword that ranked nations

Figure 3.1 Celebrating establishing the constitution (*qingzhu lixian*). Gao Fengqian 高鳳謙, Zhang Yuanji 張元濟, and Jiang Weiqiao 蔣維喬, [*Zuixin*] *gaodeng xiaoxue guowen jiaokeshu* 最新高等小學國文教科書 (Newest higher-primary Chinese textbook), 8 vols. (Shanghai: Shangwu yinshuguan, 1907).

on a linear scale of progress.[15] Significantly, the primary content of *wenming* in this lesson was technological. Europe's academic learning, trade, and military power were portrayed as more advanced than China's because of Europeans' successful use of printing, the compass, and gunpowder, all of which were seen to have originated in China. In other lessons, "civilization" was associated with current Western values of care for public spaces like parks, attentiveness to the division and organization of time, and civil treatment of strangers.[16] Association of "civilization" with trade and military capacity, on the one hand, and new modes of public culture, on the other, resonated with the dominant social Darwinist discourse circulating in China during the early twentieth century.[17] In these passages, the textbooks channeled dominant European and Japanese conceptions of civilization and civility that differed greatly from ideas of ritual propriety (*li* 禮) and elite cultural literacy (*wen* 文) that had been most powerful in China during the late imperial period.[18]

After the 1911 Revolution, Commercial Press domination in the text-book market was momentarily challenged by the rise of Zhonghua Book Company.[19] But despite the rise of a strong competitor and establishment of a new political regime, Republican language textbooks introduced new terms that were loanwords or return loanwords with new meanings even as their style continued to follow the patterns of late imperial *wenyan*.[20] In fact, early Republican textbooks were often written in a somewhat less-accessible style that was further removed from everyday language. Some educators noted at the time a movement away from new-style prose and spoke of it as a reversal of a progressive trend in the language of educa-tion.[21] Still, lexical change continued apace, exposing students to a new vocabulary that gave them tools to discuss modern society, culture, poli-tics, and technology.

Defining the Terms of Modernity

Contemporaneous to its textbook publishing, Commercial Press compiled dictionaries aimed to capture the modern lexicon. Company leaders Zhang Yuanji and Gao Mengdan both supported dictionary compiling, which they viewed as a vital part of modern cultural life that demonstrated a nation's cultural level.[22] They first published the *New Character Dictionary* (*Xin zidian* 新字典), initiated in 1906 and issued in 1912, which innovated through its presentation of explanations, organization, as well as its use of illustrations, indexes, and appendixes.[23] However, they also sought to pro-duce a dictionary of terms and phrases that would help readers negotiate the increasingly Westernized language of China's coastal cities. *Ciyuan*'s lead editor, Lu Erkui, identified 1903 and 1904 as the moment when the proliferation of translated books in Shanghai introduced new terms that became widespread but difficult for many people to understand.[24] *Ciyuan* promised to serve as a compass to guide readers through the emergent Westernized lexicon.

For dictionary compilation, just as with textbooks, Commercial Press depended on its editorial staff of late Qing literati, with their diverse intellectual backgrounds. The dictionary's compilers eventually reached fifty people and included company stalwarts like Jiang Weiqiao, Du Yaquan, Zhuang Yu, and Sun Yuxiu, who were also serial textbook compilers and contributors to other projects.[25] They worked in the collective, collaborative fashion that characterized the Commercial Press Editing Department during this period. The result was a rigorous process of compilation that entailed various kinds of collective research.[26] Reports of this strenuous research process, publication of laudatory reviews of the dictionaries by foreigners in Commercial Press's own journal *Education Monthly* (*Jiaoyu zazhi*), as well as inclusion of leading young scholars like Guo Bingwen 郭秉文 and Meng Sen 孟森 among the project's compilers all served to reinforce the intrinsic power of *Ciyuan* as an authoritative text.[27]

Ciyuan's content, in turn, reflected the social and political reform currents of the late Qing and early Republic in which many of the dictionary's compilers took an active role. The inclusion of new terms, which encompassed neologisms, redefined character combinations, and transliterations, recognized them as acceptable elements of the modern Chinese vocabulary. Further, by settling on specific definitions of new terms, *Ciyuan* contributed to fixing the meanings of newly introduced, and sometimes hotly contested, concepts that had social, cultural, or political relevance during this period. The dictionary also helped circulate Western knowledge in China through encyclopedic entries on the people, places, and things associated with world history and global modernity. In transmitting these global currents of thought to the Chinese reading public, *Ciyuan* sometimes also naturalized terms and concepts that later became central to the New Culture Movement (1915–1925) during the late 1910s and early 1920s. With sales of several hundred thousand sets in its first decade or so, the dictionary had substantial social impact.[28]

Ciyuan incorporated the fluid, shifting rhetoric of society and politics that gained power and salience through the political movements and intellectual debates of the 1890s and following decade. For instance, the dictionary grounded the language of sovereignty and rights that had been tentatively introduced as contested terms during the late Qing. It defined "sovereignty" (*zhuquan* 主權) as "the state's authority [*guojia zhi quanli* 國家之權力]."[29] Yet the dictionary also introduced the language of citizenship, defining the "citizen" (*gongmin* 公民) as "designating local people who have civic rights [*gongquan* 公權] and can elect assemblymen."[30] Turning, then, to *gongquan*, we see a broad definition of civil rights, which incorporated not only the power to petition the government but also "rights to participate in state institutions," associated directly with suffrage, and "civil liberties" (*ziyouquan* 自由權), such as "the freedoms of assembly, association, publication, and speech, as well as freedom of religion."[31] Similarly, the dictionary equated *renquan* 人權 with the English term "personal right" and defined it in terms both broad and narrow: "The broad meaning refers to all the rights that humankind can advocate. The narrow meaning just refers to the right to human dignity [*rengequan*] within human rights."[32] In light of the contested nature of ideas of rights in late Qing discourse, *Ciyuan* gave these terms a distinctly liberal cast, with an emphasis on civic participation and personal freedoms. Less visible here is the stress on collective security and welfare that Stephen Angle suggests was central to discussions of *quanli* during the late Qing,[33] a fact that likely reflects the constitutionalist and revolutionary proclivities of many of Commercial Press's editorial staff. As noted with the review of Jiang Weiqiao's diary in chapter 1, Commercial Press editors involved in compiling *Ciyuan* were steeped in the late Qing liberal intellectual currents of constitutional reform, which invariably shaped their translations of terms like "sovereignty" and "civic rights." Further, given Jiang's review of Yan Fu's translations, we see them reflecting critically and self-consciously on the best terms to relate new, foreign concepts. Literati editors fixed standard definitions of terms that resonated with their cultural and political proclivities.

Ciyuan also related distinctly new conceptions of humanity that were rooted in the Darwinist worldview and the globally comparative framework of race, both of which found expression in the entries for specific terms listed under the character *ren* 人. The entry for "race" (*renzhong* 人種), for instance, defined it as "the types of people in the world. Because of differences in skin color, skeleton, language, and so forth, they are divided into five kinds."[34] A table specified this division into skin-color-based groupings of yellow, white, black, brown, and red, thereby fixing those stock distinctions that had circulated broadly in late Qing and early Republican social discourse.[35] Further on, *Ciyuan* included the term for the modern European academic field of ethnology (*renzhongxue* 人種學)—"A field of learning that researches the systems and characteristics of human races and investigates their mutual relations"—which suggested that the fivefold racial typology presented in the entry on race was grounded in modern, Western science.[36] Here the literati editors gave the language of race and a new conception of human categorization through phenotypic characteristics specific content in terms of global racial distinctions whose authority was underpinned by association with an emergent Western science, as well as by their very inclusion in the authoritative dictionary.

Not all the new language collected in *Ciyuan* related to high-flown concepts and abstract terms like "sovereignty," "rights," and "race." Like contemporaneous textbooks, the dictionary also contained many new terms that named objects, institutions, and practices that were central to the material culture and daily experience of modern urban life. For instance, *Ciyuan* collected terms describing material features of daily life, such as the Japanese-derived "rickshaw" (*renliche* 人力車), "concrete" (*renzaoshi* 人造石), "parks" (*gongyuan* 公園), and metric units of measurement (e.g., *gongjin* 公斤, *gongchi* 公尺, *gongli* 公里), providing handy reference for modern readers.[37] It offered extensive definitions for certain modern institutions, such as companies/corporations (*gongsi* 公司) or insurance (*baoxian* 保險), that explained their dynamics and functions, at times formulating what were essentially brief explanatory primers.[38] In this modality, the dictionary took on a pedagogical function, documenting, for example, not only the forms that corporations in China did take but also the forms they might take, based on foreign models. In general, *Ciyuan*'s collection of new terms associated with the objects and institutions of modern life contributed to determining the modern vernacular lexicon. At the same time, as an encyclopedic dictionary, *Ciyuan* shared in Commercial Press's larger pedagogic project of exposing Chinese readers to a new world of people, places, and things. To do so, it incorporated extensive lists of transliterated terms that were a feature of the entries for certain characters (such as *yi* 伊) deemed most useful for their sound values rather than their intrinsic meaning.[39] The global reach of the terms signals the cosmopolitanism into which *Ciyuan* invited its readers. It served at once as a reference book, in case its readers encountered transliterated names like Aeschylus (Yishiqi 伊士奇) or Ibrahim Pasha (Yibulaxin 伊布拉欣) as they read, and as a prototextbook that Chinese readers could delve into to explore the world.

In opening up to a world of ideas in this way, *Ciyuan* also introduced terms and concepts that had, perhaps, limited circulation and salience during the late Qing and early Republic but would become fundamental to the cultural politics of the New Culture Movement. For instance, a new language of self, subjectivity, and personhood that entered China during the first two decades of the twentieth century was collected and codified in *Ciyuan*, providing a powerful vocabulary for the challenges to Confucian forms of relational ethics and the claims of self-definition that were central to the New Culture project. For example, *Ciyuan* incorporated new loanwords for "subject" (*zhuti* 主體) and "subjective" (*zhuguan* 主觀),[40] and it defined them in terms that would support claims of individual dignity, consciousness, and self-expression that became more prominent during the late 1910s and early 1920s. Here "subject" was defined in contrast to objects and was associated with bearing rights and duties: "For instance, we say people are the subjects of rights and duties."[41] Similarly, the concept of "subjectivity" was linked to both consciousness and agency: "If I use my consciousness to study something and know it, it is called subjective"; "If I act toward external things, then the subjective belongs to myself and the objective belongs to the things outside the self."[42] Together these terms expressed a vision of the subject as a rights-bearing person with consciousness and agency, a formulation of the person that would become vital to New Culture efforts at social and cultural reform.

This view of the subject echoed in the dictionary's definition of "personhood/human dignity" (*renge* 人格), which it said "connotes in law having the qualifications of autonomy and independence. Such as, slaves and prisoners have no personhood/human dignity."[43] The associations of autonomy and independence, contrasted pointedly with the condition of servitude and imprisonment, gained authority through the connection with legal discourse even as the term became available for other social uses. Those associations made "independent personhood" (*duli renge*), according to Wang Zheng, a fundamental term of New Culture discourse, serving, for instance, as a powerful basis for women's claims of equality and independence.[44] It would be simplistic to suggest that in *Ciyuan* we already see a fully developed articulation of the forms of personhood, self, and subjectivity that emerged in New Culture discourse. However, the dictionary introduced those terms as legitimate elements of the modern Chinese lexicon, and it embedded in those terms concepts that associated fully realized personhood with autonomy, agency, and consciousness that would underpin the arguments of the next generation of reformers.[45]

Thus, as the first comprehensive dictionary of terms and phrases published after the end of the imperial state, *Ciyuan* provided a powerful medium for the generation of literati reformers with mixed intellectual backgrounds at Commercial Press to shape the Chinese lexicon and conceptual field during the early Republic. As a cultural text *Ciyuan* operated on several levels at once. In conjunction with the textbook series published at the same time, it collected the new terms associated with modern life and institutions, marking them as legitimate elements of the Chinese vocabulary.

Further, it codified the concepts and fixed the definitions of terms associated with the political, social, cultural, and economic changes initiated and encouraged by reformist literati of the late Qing and early Republic. Literati reformers lent these terms and concepts authority by their very inclusion in the dictionary but also by rooting them in new fields of science and law and by associating them with the modern West. *Ciyuan* also operated as an encyclopedia in miniature, offering readers a ready primer and reference for a world of history, geography, science, and culture outside China. In defining terms integral to new philosophies and sciences drawn from a wider world, *Ciyuan* further introduced concepts that could later be mobilized for social criticism in the context of the New Culture Movement.

Modeling Vernacular Writing

Although early Republican textbooks continued to relate new terms and concepts to students, many educators and intellectuals were still critical of the lack of change in pedagogy in primary and secondary schools after the 1911 Revolution.[46] Concomitant criticism of language instruction led to a growing chorus for change in the language of China's textbooks.[47] As literary scholar Zheng Guomin notes, many educational reformers during the 1910s believed teaching students language closer to contemporary spoken language would allow for more rapid spread of education by building on the language students already knew and used, would enable them to be more active and independent learners in keeping with modern educational models, and would teach them a practical language used in contemporary life rather than that of antiquity.[48]

At the same time, participants in the self-proclaimed literary revolution and language-reform movement viewed promotion of vernacular writing as the key to both modernizing Chinese culture and creating a unified mass citizenry.[49] In April 1919, leading figures in this movement, most notably Zhou Zuoren 周作人, Hu Shi, and Qian Xuantong 錢玄同, participated in the Ministry of Education's National Language Unification Preparatory Committee, in which they called for revising primary-school textbooks using vernacular national language.[50] In their proposal, they argued that "one should regard each kind of textbook used in primary schools as the headquarters [*dabenying* 大本營] for spreading national language," revealing what they saw to be the strategic centrality of textbooks to their movement.[51]

To these reformist intellectuals, disseminating their version of modern language through schools was a key move in marking its official status and spreading its influence in the linguistic and cultural marketplace.[52] This proposal was the culmination of several years of effort by educational organizations and language reformers to begin to change the basic written language of education, in the face of various forms of institutional and cultural resistance, so that it would conform more closely to language that students encountered every day.[53]

Taking measure of the growing trend, Commercial Press in October 1919 began the process of converting its primary-level Chinese readers into the vernacular language.[54] This early commitment to vernacular textbooks allowed Commercial Press to issue the *baihua* New Form (Xinti 新體) textbooks simultaneous with the Ministry of Education's January 1920 announcement that all primary textbooks should be written in the vernacular starting in the fall of that year.[55] Language reformers' ideological projects here merged with the commercial aims of publishers to generate quickly a new generation of vernacular textbooks. Commercial Press and Zhonghua Book Company both issued full sets of vernacular readers starting in the fall of 1920. In 1921 Zhonghua established a National Language Division, directed by Li Jinhui, within its Editing Department.[56] The leading companies also published new sets of vernacular-language readers after new primary and secondary curricula were drafted by the National Federation of Education Associations (Quanguo jiaoyuhui lianhehui 全國教育會聯合會) in 1922 and 1923. The new curricula were drafted in conjunction with promulgation of the American-style New School System (Xin xuezhi 新學制).[57]

World Book Company, which previously had not directly competed with Commercial Press and Zhonghua Book Company in the textbook market, viewed the curriculum reforms of the early 1920s as an opportunity to break into that lucrative market. The publisher explained its motivation to publish textbooks in terms of rapidly changing pedagogical methods, which required corresponding new teaching materials; the need for publication of more textbooks to satisfy demand from growing numbers of schools and students; and, following a social Darwinist logic, the need for competition among publishers to generate progress in teaching materials.[58]

With a place as big as China, just having the several sets of textbooks that have already been published, truly one cannot speak of any competition. If one really wants competition, one certainly must put out several times more the current number [of textbooks] to enable educational circles to collectively experiment and compare, and only then can there be hope of progress.

Based on the foregoing reasons, this company has the motivation to compile textbooks.[59]

To gear up for increased textbook production World Book Company added editorial staff to the Primary School Division of its Editing Department, selecting people with at least high-school or normal-school educational backgrounds and some teaching experience. It also solicited teaching materials and suggestions about approaches to compiling textbooks from educational circles, with several thousand people responding to the latter inquiry.[60] Curricular reform, of which language change was a part, created an opportunity for World Book Company to compete with Commercial Press and Zhonghua.

The revised curricula of the early 1920s offered a dramatically new vision for how, and what, language was to be taught in primary and secondary schools. The Ministry of Education's directives of 1920 called for all lower-primary language instruction (in so-called citizens' schools, *guomin xuexiao*) to change to the vernacular. In the draft curricula issued in 1923, vernacular language was to provide the main content for reading and writing instruction at the primary level. Moreover, the 1923 curriculum also called for roughly half the readings overall at the lower-middle-school level to be in the vernacular. They were to be organized on a sliding scale, starting with a high of 75 percent vernacular in the first year, 50 percent vernacular in the second, and 25 percent vernacular in the third year.[61]

But as noted cultural reformer Hu Shi argued in an article in 1920, there were as yet no government-established standards for vernacular writing.[62] Language reformers and linguists started to write grammatical guides in the early 1920s, several of which were published by Zhonghua Book Company, but they were not accessible models from which students could learn directly.[63] Advocates of language reform, like Hu and his colleagues, instead expected that models of vernacular writing would arise organically from the writing in a range of media, like textbooks and newspapers. In practice, though, most major Chinese newspapers continued to use classical language for roughly two-thirds of their content well into the 1930s because its concision allowed more space for profit-making advertisements.[64] Moreover, newspapers lacked the textual authority of state-approved textbooks. Language reformers' emphasis on textual publication to generate language models granted textbook compilers great leeway in, and great responsibility for, crafting new forms of vernacular writing. In this section I draw examples from three prominent primary-level language textbooks, one published by each of the main commercial publishers during the key period of language reform: a Zhonghua text from the initial period of promotion of vernacular language in the primary schools (1920–1921); Commercial Press's immensely successful New School System primary language textbook by Zhuang Shi 莊適[65], Wu Yanyin 吳研因[66], and Shen Qi 沈圻 of 1923;[67] and World Book Company's lower primary reader by Editing Department director Wei Bingxin 魏冰心 from the early 1930s.[68] I also make occasional references to Ye Shengtao's Kaiming Bookstore textbook of 1932 to illustrate how the approach of the three major publishers compared with other contemporary textbook writing.[69] All these textbooks presented students with models of writing that approximated spoken language by creating contexts for lessons that emphasized oral exchange and exposition.

Textbooks frequently set up contexts of dialogue between characters to provide a framework for presenting an oral form of written language. An example from Wu Yanyin and Zhuang Shi's New School System textbook, recounting a story about Benjamin Franklin, was characteristic:

"Mother, I bought a pipe!" His mother said, "How much did you buy it for?" He said, "I gave him all the pence you gave me." His brother looked over the pipe and said, *"Ayou!* You've been cheated [*shangdangle*]! This pipe is worth just one pence! How could you have given him all your pence?" Franklin heard this, threw down the pipe, and cried, sobbing. His mother comforted him saying, "When buying something, you cannot pay too high a price. This is a very good lesson! In the future pay attention to this."[70]

This typical dialogue is highly colloquial, including slang terms like *shangdangle* 上當了, exclamations like *ayou* 啊喲, and exhortative sentence-final expressions like *ba* 罷 and *ya* 呀. Primary-level national-language textbooks were filled with narrative accounts that included large amounts of dialogue, whether between human characters or animal protagonists in vignettes drawn from or approximated fables and fairy tales.[71] These strategies of dialogue naturalized the use of spoken-language vocabulary and phrasing.

Textbooks also created contexts for orally based writings in other ways. For instance, they often created scenarios that set up a spoken presentation of material that otherwise could be presented in an expository manner. Hu Shunhua and his colleagues at Zhonghua used this strategy repeatedly in their 1920 textbook. In presenting material on national geography, for example, they used the device of having an older brother present a description of the tour he had taken around China to his younger brother.[72] The resulting monologue created a context for information about geography, culture, and social activities to be presented in a colloquial style. Another way to do this was through personification, where objects literally spoke for themselves. For example, in Wei Bingxin's World textbook, basic facts about electricity were presented through a personified monologue: "I am called electricity and I live in the sky. Originally I was quite carefree. Many years ago I was led down from the sky by a youth named Franklin, then people and I came to know one another."[73] By letting objects speak, textbooks could relate a whole array of ordinary knowledge in a more oral language than the easy classical style that had predominated in late Qing and early Republican textbooks.[74] Though used mainly at the primary level, dialogue and personification were also sometimes used in secondary-level textbooks, when authors sought to create a framework for spoken-language presentation of content.[75] In general, the creation of scenarios focused around oral presentation and exchange allowed the publishers to craft a version of the written language that tacked closely to speech patterns.

Textbooks also presented students with new models of vernacular writing in genres like letters, diaries, notes, reports, lectures, and various kinds of journalistic genres. The forms for letters were especially vital because of the importance of this genre of writing for literate people and the complex prescriptions for address, signature, and presentation in the classical language during the late imperial period. An example from Wei Bingxin's textbook of letters between friends is telling. They addressed each other in familiar terms as "my brother" (*wuxiong*) and signed off in highly colloquial form expressing very modern sentiments: "I wish you progress!" (*zhu ni jinbu*), and "I wish you happiness!" (*zhu ni kuaile*).[76] Hu Shunhua's textbook, by contrast, offered a model of a letter between business associates. Some features were somewhat more formal: the correspondents addressed one another as "mister" (*xiansheng*), the first letter used a conventional expression of thanks, and they used the banker's form of writing numbers. But the basic style was still fairly colloquial, if clipped and precise: "Please buy on

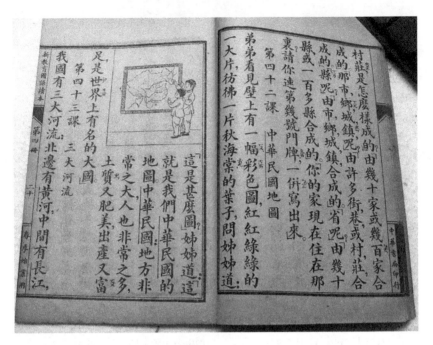

Figure 3.2 A dialogic context for presenting information about geography. Hu Shunhua 胡舜華 et al., [*Xin jiaoyu jiaokeshu*] *guoyu duben* 新教育教科書國語讀本 ([New education textbook] national-language reader), 8 vols. (Shanghai: Zhonghua shuju, 1920–1921), 4:20.

my behalf one bolt [of silk fabric] of the natural color. Now I am remitting fifteen yuan of silver currency. Once it is purchased, please give it to the post office to mail. Thank you very much for taking all this trouble [*fei nide shen, ganxie de hen*]."[77] In general, these textbooks provided multiple examples of how to write letters in an accessible, vernacular style, escaping the complex formal requirements of classical letter styles.[78]

Similarly, with other genres the textbooks offered students alternative vernacular models to genres of long standing in the classical written tradition. For instance, in World Book Company's primary national-language reader, we get a model diary entry from a student who presents a vernacular account of an outing with a classmate that included snatches of dialogue between them.[79] Likewise, in the Zhonghua Book Company New Education series national-language textbook, Hu Shunhua and his colleagues used the device of presenting a school newspaper to introduce students to models of different genres of vernacular writing, specifically news reports, commentary (*pinglun*), and short fiction.[80] A brief example from the commentary genre suggests how the textbooks presented writing formulas that reflected the vernacular writing of the day and provided ready models for students to emulate: "Truly dependable learning is not completely what is taught by the teacher. Mostly it is derived from self-study [*zixiu*]. If one cannot study by oneself, one certainly cannot seek learning, so we should emphasize self-study."[81] In these cases, and with other genres ranging from lectures to reports and notes, the textbooks offered models for vernacular writing that students could follow.[82]

As most of this section has emphasized, primary-level language textbooks, by incorporating contexts that favored spoken language, presented students with a version of vernacular writing grounded primarily in oral-language conventions. At higher grade levels, textbooks introduced students to what I call a professionalized vernacular, whose conventions depended heavily on patterns of writing in European languages. We see this stylistic variation most clearly with social scientists working in the publishers who wrote secondary-level textbooks. For instance, Tao Menghe 陶孟和, a leading sociologist who was in the group of foreign-trained scholars Wang Yunwu hired during the mid-1920s, wrote a *Social Issues* (*Shehui wenti* 社會問題) textbook for the high school equivalent of civics class under the New School System curriculum. Tao, trained in Great Britain in sociology, wrote in a social science style that differed greatly from late Qing *wenyan* styles but also diverged from patterns of everyday speech. Instead, his writing was characterized by repetition and enumeration, as well as long, dense, complex sentences that used extensive modification, qualification, and embedding. Further, he employed a highly abstract vocabulary of borrowed terms that were often not explained or illustrated. Note the following passage, which relates some of those prose characteristics even in translation:

Anything that is a social activity [*huodong* 活動] of course influences society. Within society, change in each thing, such as changes in organization [*zuzhi* 組織] and relations [*guanxi* 關係], changes in custom [*fengsu* 風俗] or habit [*xiguan* 習慣], or changes in feeling [*ganqing* 感情] and thought [*sixiang* 思想], are nothing more than one kind or many kinds of development [*fazhan* 發展] and transformation [*bianhua* 變化] in social activity. These kinds of development and transformation are known as society's process [*chengxu* 程序]. War and revolution [*geming* 革命] certainly are large-scale social processes, and as for other transformations, anything sufficient to influence all of society or a part of it are social processes. Social life is formed [*goucheng* 構成] by social activity and social processes.[83]

In contrast to late Qing and early Republican textbooks, which, as discussed, explicitly introduced, illustrated, and defined a modern lexicon, Tao's writing here is saturated by a new, abstract language of organizations, relations, transformations, and processes, none of which are defined or explained. Further, many of the foreign stylistic patterns that literature scholar Edward Gunn argues shaped post-1918 Chinese vernacular writing are features of Tao Menghe's writing in this textbook.[84] Tao includes sentences that are long and complex, incorporating various kinds of modification and embedding. Word order in many places followed conventions of European languages, and imported patterns of figurative constructions, verb-phrase constructions, and liberal use of *yu* 於, meaning "to," "toward," or "for," were quite common.[85]

Vernacular prose in these textbooks took the form of Western-influenced social science writing, with extended causal chains, frequent qualification and exemplification, and an abstract vocabulary of borrowed social science terminology. As such, it was open to the criticism of leftist writers like Qu Qiubai 瞿秋白 and Mao Dun that May Fourth intellectuals were developing a new arcane language based on Westernized syntax, style, and vocabulary that was just as distant from spoken vernacular as *wenyan* had been.[86] Works such as Tao's, however much they were intended to simply relate new ideas with transparent, vernacular prose, in fact presented students with an alternative model of vernacular writing that built less on colloquial spoken language than on new modes of academic and professional discourse that were significantly influenced by European and Japanese vocabulary and stylistic conventions. That language paralleled the dominant discourse in the scholarly monographs in the publishers' series publications that I explore in chapter 5.

Reading the Readers

The vernacular-language textbooks received mixed reviews. Some were positive, lauding the textbooks for rich content and exposing students to new forms of language. A review of Commercial Press's New School System reader in the professional journal *Primary Education* (*Chudeng jiaoyu*), for instance, asserted that "the material with literary quality has also increased, and they greatly emphasize repetition of new characters, words, and phrases."[87] Similarly, Ministry of Education reviewers lauded World Book Company's first national-language textbook for its rhymes, which made it accessible to students: "Inside it is mostly rhymed language, which is convenient for children in their early years of studying."[88]

But the textbooks also faced criticism from conservatives as well as progressive reformers. Conservatives dismissed the new readers as "dog-and-cat education," mocking the focus on fables and stories about animals meant to make the books more accessible.[89] More telling, though, might have been criticism from other reformers, who debated whether the textbooks were fulfilling the goals of the language-reform movement. Some questioned whether the restrictions on numbers of characters used and requirements for repetition made the textbooks wooden and uninspiring: "Under these heavy restrictions, can creative textbooks be compiled? No wonder that even though [the publishers] add the signboard 'new' to the names of the textbooks, the content in fact is insufferably hackneyed!"[90] More fundamental criticism had to do with the nature of the language in the textbooks and whether the publishers should be making fundamental decisions about the proper form of the Chinese language. For instance, Shen Shoumei's review of World Book Company's primary-school national-language textbooks from the 1920s raised fundamental questions about whether the writing in the textbooks was really a written form of the spoken language or whether the authors still depended on classical writing for substantial amounts of the content.[91] Similarly, as mentioned at the start of this chapter, the National Language Unification Preparatory Committee questioned whether the textbooks were actually written in a recognizable vernacular.[92]

Despite these criticisms, evidence suggests that national-language textbooks quickly gained wide currency in primary education during the 1920s and 1930s. During the 1920s, local governments directed local schools to start teaching national language using the new textbooks, and publishers correspondingly reached out to local governments to promote their products.[93] Further, multiple examples from local primary schools in the lower Yangzi region suggest that many schools switched decisively to teaching vernacular language using textbooks by the major publishers during the early and mid-1920s. Teachers' reports in 1924 and 1925 on Chinese-class teaching practices in private, public (*gongli* 公立), township (*xiang* 鄉), and county schools in rural Jiading 嘉定, Qingpu 青浦, Jurong 句容, and Chongming 崇明 counties all reveal teachers using the vernacular national-language readers of the leading publishing companies.[94] Even in instances where teachers seem to have been using their own teaching materials, as in the case of Qingpu County Second Primary School (Qingpu xianli di'er xiaoxuexiao 青浦縣立第二小學校), their lessons followed the organization and dialogic style of the mainstream readers.[95] Such evidence suggests vernacular national-language textbooks were reaching students in local schools. In this way, staff editors at commercial publishing companies like Zhuang Shi and Wu Yanyin, Hu Shunhua, and Wei Bingxin provided the primary models of vernacular writing for several generations of Chinese students during the 1920s and 1930s.

National Standardization in Wartime

As noted earlier, the Sino-Japanese War decisively shifted the nature of textbook publishing in China. The fight for national survival, resource constraints, and limited and variable markets allowed the Nationalist government for the first time to assert centralized control over textbook compilation. After 1942 the National Office of Compilation and Translation compiled most primary and secondary textbooks. The major publishers, including Commercial Press, Zhonghua Book Company, and World Book Company, took responsibility only for printing and distributing the national standard textbooks.

Despite the centralization of textbook compilation, the commercial publishers' approaches to national-language textbook compilation continued to shape how the written vernacular was presented to students through the 1940s. An immediate postwar example of a standard national-language and common-knowledge textbook compiled by the National Office of Compilation and Translation reveals textual strategies that parallel closely the national-language textbooks of the 1920s and 1930s.[96] In particular, the textbook used large amounts of poetry and song, along with narrative with extensive dialogue, thereby presenting students with a written form of spoken language. For example, to relate a lesson about water hygiene, the textbook had a story about a child who got an upset stomach from drinking cold water, prompting his mother to chide, "You cannot drink water that has not been boiled."[97]

Similarly, a lesson discussing the elements most essential for life (air, water, rice, wheat, meat) was set up as a discussion between a teacher and his students, with each student presenting an argument.[98] For sections that could have been written in expository prose, they also used personification and self-narration, as in an account by a personified form of coal that explained how it had developed over millions of years from organic matter.[99] Also common were narrativized "lectures" or "stories" that allowed spoken-language presentation of the common-knowledge material, such as a tale about Sima Guang as a child that was common to many textbooks but was here presented by a student speaker.[100] In general, the textbook's emphasis on narrative and spoken language, whether in the form of song, dialogue, or monologue, normalized for students vernacular language that was a written version of the spoken form, as had been common during the 1920s and 1930s.

The National Office of Compilation and Translation textbook also followed earlier national-language textbooks by the major publishers in presenting students with models of vernacular versions of common genres of writing, such as diaries, letters, and reports. Note the following letter, which also related common knowledge about fruits and plants.[101]

Paternal Aunt [*gumu* 姑母]:

Mother told us that tomatoes have lots of nutrients. In the garden we grew many plants, and now the tomatoes are already ripe. We often heard Mother say that Paternal Aunt loves to eat tomatoes. Today some people are going into the city, so we are taking advantage of the occasion [for them] to carry a basket. Paternal Aunt, I am guessing you will love to eat even more the tomatoes that we grew. Respectfully wishing you

Peace and health! [*jingzhu ankang* 敬祝安康]

Respectfully yours [*jingshang* 敬上], your niece Xiaoming

SEPTEMBER 18

Significantly, while the main text of the letter is written in an orally based vernacular, the salutation reincorporates coded language of respect that reflects something of the formality of earlier approaches to letter writing. That formality suggests a gradual softening of the boundary between vernacular and classical written language that promoters of the vernacular-language movement, and commentators on textbooks, had promoted in earlier periods.

The textbook also provided models of vernacular writing in various other genres of text, as had textbooks of the 1920s and 1930s. For example, one lesson replicated a diary entry by a student character who was a representative to the school's student self-government organization. The entry used a written form of the spoken language to recount the activities and decisions of the self-government organization, modeling both the content and form of diary entries.[102] In turn, the narrative describes the student self-government organization drafting a "Hygiene Joint Pledge" (Wei-sheng gongyue), which was then reproduced in the text, offering a model for the kinds of lists of injunctions and guidelines that became ubiquitous in China beginning in this period.[103] In general, the National Office of Compilation and Translation followed closely the models of language textbooks produced during the 1920s and 1930s by presenting a version of written vernacular that was rooted in the dynamics of the spoken language while also providing models of vernacular writing for letters, diaries, and other genres of text. Its language textbooks were barely distinguishable from those published earlier by Commercial Press, Zhonghua Book Company, and World Book Company. In this way, the approaches taken by editorial staff in the major commercial publishing houses continued to shape how the vernacular language was taught even after the state took control of textbook compilation.

The *Sea of Words* and the Proliferation of Technical and Political Language

During the decades when vernacular-language advocates promoted changes in writing styles that were codified in textbooks, the Chinese lexicon continued to change rapidly. These changes created an opportunity for Zhonghua Book Company to produce a comprehensive dictionary that could challenge, and in some ways surpass, Commercial Press's *Ciyuan*. A 1937 advice-column response to a reader about whether to purchase *Ciyuan* or Zhonghua's recently published *Cihai* reveals key differences between them. "It has already been many years since Commercial Press's original and supplement sections of *Ciyuan* have been published. Because of society's evolution

[and] changes in the political situation, new terms for science and to describe and name things mostly are not incorporated. . . . Zhonghua's *Cihai* has been published most recently . . . , and the content and the kinds of terms collected naturally are relatively richer."[104]

As the columnist suggests, *Cihai* specially captured several new kinds of vocabulary, including scientific and academic terminology, as well as language associated with the social and political movements growing out of the May Fourth period. It also offered more extensive and nuanced explanations of academic and political terms, providing a more sophisticated perspective on foreign concepts and systems of knowledge.

Cihai's distinctiveness resulted from the astute leadership of Shu Xincheng and Shen Duoshan 沈朵山 (Yi 頤). Initially, Zhonghua had launched the *Cihai* project in 1915 right after publication of *Zhonghua's Great Dictionary* (*Zhonghua da zidian*) and Commercial Press's *Ciyuan*.[105] However, under dictionary compiler Xu Yuangao 徐元誥 and Editing Department head Fan Yuanlian's 范源廉 leadership, the word and phrase dictionary, meant to supplement Zhonghua's earlier character dictionary, made little progress. The manuscript compiled by the mid-1920s, in fact, differed little from the earlier *Ciyuan*.[106] When Lufei Kui sought to give the project new life by hiring educational reformer Shu Xincheng in 1928,[107] Shu's assessment was that "in the original manuscript there were too many old terms that were already dead and too few new terms that were popularly used."[108]

In response, Shu and Shen Duoshan, who succeeded Shu as *Cihai*'s primary editor when Shu became director of Zhonghua's Editing Department in 1930, took an alternative approach. Shu first had editorial staff read widely in contemporary books and journals to capture common new terms and had them translate material from Western reference books to buttress *Cihai*'s encyclopedic entries.[109] Shen Duoshan continued this practice, having his staff read widely in fiction and opera from the late imperial period and designating Liu Fanyou 劉範猷 to read important recent newspapers, journals, and books to identify new terms.[110] To carry out this wide-ranging survey of modern and late imperial writings and compile thousands of new entries, Shu and Shen organized a group of twenty to thirty staff editors with high-school and college educations.[111] As I have described elsewhere, the *Cihai* Editing Division operated through discrete divisions of labor, where petty intellectual compilers had responsibility for specific categories of common terms and encyclopedic entries in one or more specific subjects.[112] When more specialized knowledge was necessary, the editors turned to experts inside or outside the company to help draft and review the entries, supporting the claim in the "Editor's Outline" that "anything in this book related to specialized science was written by experts, and the selection of entries was systematic."[113] For instance, the publisher appealed to linguist Li Jinxi for help to review several dozen linguistic terms, tapping into his expertise.[114]

The result of the wide-ranging surveys of contemporary writings commissioned by Shu and Shen was that *Cihai* in fact captured important additions to the Chinese lexicon. One significant addition was terminology associated with the new academic disciplines and professions that took root in China during the 1920s and 1930s. As the executive editors articulated it in their opening statement, they identified "important terminology for the professions of agriculture, industry, and commerce in society" as well as "frequently seen and used technical language [*shuyu*] from science and literature and the arts."[115] In addition, *Cihai* also incorporated the vocabulary of the social and political movements that had emerged in China in the decades since *Ciyuan*'s publication, thereby consolidating and normalizing a language of social radicalism, political mass activism, and party politics.

Cihai identified, defined, and thereby helped legitimize the new vocabularies associated with social mobilization, cultural reform, and mass activism that emerged from the milieu of the New Culture and May Fourth Movements during the late 1910s and 1920s. For instance, *Cihai* newly incorporated the vocabulary of class, with entries defining the proletariat (*wuchan jieji* 無產階級) and bourgeoisie (*youchan jieji* 有產階級, *zichan jieji* 資產階級), who were defined in Marxist terms according to whether a person owned property or worked for their livelihood.[116] Further, the dictionary had extensive entries on terms like "the final stage of capitalism" (*ziben zhuyi zuihou jieduan* 資本主義最後階段) and "class struggle" (*jieji douzheng* 階級鬥爭).[117] Following Lenin, it associated the former with the growth of monopolies and imperialism. The entry for "class struggle" offered a classical Marxian analysis of class struggle as the motor of history, with emphasis on the crisis of capitalism that would lead to the end of capitalist society. Other words associated with social-reform projects that *Cihai* introduced had prescriptive as well as descriptive dimensions to them, such as "mutual aid" (*huzhu* 互助).[118] Phrases like "mutual aid" were not just new terms but new concepts in Koselleck's sense. In this case, *Cihai*'s definition contrasted mutual aid with social Darwinist ideas of competition, which

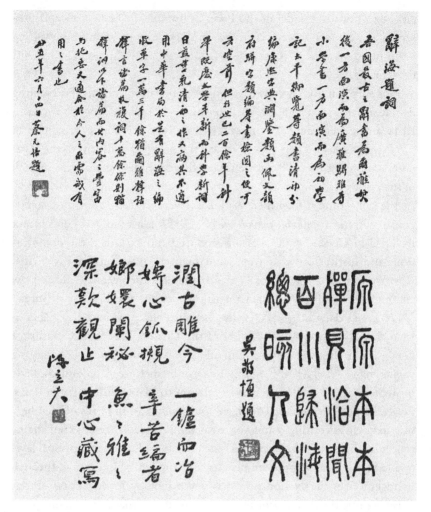

Figure 3.3 Inscriptions for *Cihai* from Cai Yuanpei, Wu Jingheng (Zhihui), and Chen Lifu. Inscriptions by cultural and political figures like these helped to legitimize *Cihai* as an authoritative text. Shu Xincheng 舒新城 et al., eds., *Cihai* 辭海 (Shanghai: Zhonghua shuju, 1936).

became widespread starting in the late Qing, and associated it instead with Kropotkin's anarchism, preserving the idea of an alternative pole of cooperative self-organization that became influential during the late 1910s and early 1920s. This anarchist perspective was reinforced by inclusion of the Chinese term for "communalism" (*gongshe zhuyi* 公社主義), which the dictionary defined as a political system based on a federation of self-governing city-states, on the model of the Paris Commune.[119] These concepts preserved an approach to social activism in stark contrast with the prevailing Leninist ideologies of both the Nationalist and Chinese Communist movements.

Not surprisingly, however, given its publication during the Nanjing decade, *Cihai* also included the new terminology of the Chinese Nationalist Party and government. For instance, it defined the Three Principles of the People (*sanmin zhuyi* 三民主義) as "the political platform of the Chinese Nationalist Party."[120] It then offered independent definitions of each of the principles, emphasizing the goal of freedom and equality for each.[121] At the same time it identified Nationalist Party rule as a form of democratic centralism (*minzhu jiquan zhi* 民主集權制), a term and concept not included in *Ciyuan*.[122] *Cihai* also introduced and explained the organizations and institutions that were fundamental to Nationalist Party rule. *Cihai*'s entry for *zhong* 中, or "central/middle," for instance, glossed the central party and government institutions of the Central Party Bureau (Zhongyang dangbu 中央黨部), the Central Political Committee (Zhongyang zhengzhi huiyi 中央政治會議) of the Central Executive Committee (Zhongyang zhixing weiyuanhui), and the Academia Sinica (Zhongyang yanjiu yuan 中央研究院).[123] In other cases, the dictionary redefined previously introduced modern terms in relation to Nationalist Party policies. For example, *Cihai* defined "citizen" (*gongmin* 公民) in terms of membership in a self-governing county or town and involvement in its civil affairs, reflecting the party's shift away from democratic politics at the national level to a focus on local self-government as construction.[124] In general, through its inclusion of the Nationalist Party's terminology for ideas and offices, *Cihai* became the first dictionary to document systematically the introduction of a Leninist party's political jargon, which marked one of the most dramatic changes in spoken and written Chinese during the twentieth century.

Along with documenting political vocabulary, *Cihai* included among its encyclopedic terms major recent political events, both Chinese and foreign, no matter how sensitive they might have been. The inclusion of these proper nouns, especially those that were more politically fraught and sensitive, was debated at the company. Shu Xincheng recounted in his diary a telling exchange between himself, *Cihai* editors Shen Duoshan and Zhang Xianzhi, and longtime Zhonghua Book Company stalwart Jin Zhaozi on just this question. They wanted to leave out sensitive recent political events to avoid trouble, but Shu argued they were responsible for incorporating recent events and for countering and correcting inaccurate or distorted foreign accounts.[125] In the end, Shu's view won out, and *Cihai* included numerous brief accounts of recent political events.[126]

Yet inclusion of recent historical events and politicized terminology exposed *Cihai*'s publishers to just the kinds of criticism that Shu Xincheng's colleagues had perhaps anticipated. A 1943 article by Zhou Shushan in the Nationalist Party–affiliated organs *Central Weekly* (*Zhongyang zhoukan*) and *Victory Magazine* (*Shengli zazhi*) illustrates the challenge faced by nonpartisan publishers in representing politicized events, institutions, and activities.[127] The article parsed in great detail six different entries, including those for Sun Yat-sen and the Chinese Nationalist Party, finding large and small "mistakes" with the narrative in each. For instance, in commenting on the passage on the Wuchang Uprising, it states, "It briefly says 'it is called this because Li Yuanhong first spearheaded the revolution at Wuchang.' . . . It must be known that Li Yuanhong not only was not the person spearheading the revolution but also was forced to serve as commander of the Hubei Army, and he also was dragged out from under his bed by party members."[128] As independent publishers operated in an increasingly partisan political environment, the content of their publications faced scrutiny by those with specific political agendas, especially in regard to encyclopedic entries on recent or current events.

A further important cultural and intellectual shift from the 1910s through the 1930s was the rapid development of Chinese academic life, which was marked by the influx and institutionalization of new academic disciplines and professions.[129] *Ciyuan* already had included much terminology from Western systems of thought and foreign academic culture, such as the names of academic fields, legal and mathematical terminology, and the vocabulary and concepts of evolution. However, as Chinese scholars returned from studying abroad and set up departments, institutes, and journals dedicated to modern academic disciplines during the 1920s and 1930s, they introduced and elaborated more extensive new lexicons of specialized terminology and proper names that represented an alien and rapidly changing landscape of knowledge in China. Moreover, Chinese intellectuals' growing understanding of the internal complexity and developmental process of foreign academic fields and theories compelled *Cihai*'s compilers to offer more comprehensive, robust, and nuanced explanations of Western systems of thought. Reference books like *Cihai* thus reinforced the transformation in China's knowledge culture that monographic series publication effected, a process I explore in depth in chapter 5.

By incorporating a new academic vocabulary, *Cihai* helped modern readers learn how to traverse the landscape of foreign learning. The dictionary is filled with numerous entries from natural sciences like botany, biology, chemistry, physics, and mathematics. They identify the Chinese versions of scientific terms and gloss them with the Latin, notational, or English equivalents that each discipline used for a global system of symbols. For instance, *Cihai*'s entry for the character *gong* 公 includes all the measures of the metric system (*gongli, gongjin, gongfen,* etc.), as well as a number of essential mathematical terms, such as "common numerator" (*gongfenzi* 公分子), "common denominator" (*gongfenmu* 公分母), and "common factor" (*gongyinshu* 公因數).[130] These entries were both more comprehensive and systematic than what *Ciyuan* had offered. At the same time, *Cihai* presented extensive explanations of the terms that made them comprehensible to common readers. For example, it provided a detailed explanation of the key biological concept "symbiosis" (*gongsheng* 共生), a term not included in *Ciyuan*, that offered concrete examples of three different dynamics of symbiosis.[131] In another instance, *Ciyuan* briefly had defined "infectious disease" (*chuanranbing* 傳染病) as "an illness where a virus can infect another person" and listed a few examples.[132] By contrast, *Cihai*'s entry "infectious disease" took most of a column, defining the phenomenon in detail and describing different kinds of transmission processes.[133] Together, these brief examples suggest how *Cihai* incorporated modern scientific terms and concepts in more comprehensive, systematic, and thorough ways than had *Ciyuan*.

Cihai also included extensive terminology from the social sciences and humanities that had the potential to cross over into more general discourse. At the most basic level, *Cihai* described a great many fields and concepts not captured in *Ciyuan*. For example, *Cihai* included an entry on "folklore" (*minsuxue* 民俗學), which had emerged as an important field among progressive intellectuals in China during the 1920s and 1930s.[134] *Cihai* also comprehensively surveyed the spectra of theories and methods associated with each modern scientific and social scientific field, where *Ciyuan*'s editors had often limited themselves to identifying disciplines themselves. For instance, under the character *zhu* 主, *Cihai* included an impressive list of philosophical and psychological theories not mentioned in *Ciyuan* that captured the diverse intellectual landscape of modern Western thought.[135]

zhuwo shuo 主我說 (egoism)

zhuzhi shuo 主知說 (intellectualism)

zhumei shuo 主美說 (aestheticism)

zhuyi shuo 主意說 (voluntarism)

zhude shuo 主德說 (moralism)

zhuguan shuo 主觀說 (subjectivism)

zhuqing zhuyi 主情主義 (sentimentalism or emotionalism)

zhuguan de xingxhi shuo 主觀的形式說 (subjective formalism)

This theoretical language provided resources for a wide range of intellectual stances. Moreover, particular entries for the terms could provide genealogies for the philosophical perspectives that were rooted in Western thought. For instance, the entry for "intellectualism" connected it back to Descartes, Spinoza, Aristotle, Plato, and others. These attributions gave this new terminology the authority of association with Western intellectual history, even while the diversity of terms revealed the contested and dynamic nature of the conceptual field they represented.

As these examples suggest, the development of academic disciplines in China led to more complex and nuanced understanding of Western scholarship and the concepts they related. This transformation comes through clearly in how *Cihai* defined the important concept of "race" (*renzhong*) in contrast to how it had been defined in *Ciyuan*. As noted, *Ciyuan* offered a brief, matter-of-fact definition of "race" and also presented an accompanying table that categorized people by skin color. *Cihai*, by contrast, identified three competing theoretical approaches to racial distinction, starting with Blumenbach's emphasis on skin color and head shape, then more recent techniques focused on cranial measurements, and finally categorization according to natural systems (*ziran xitong fenleifa* 自然系統分類法, natural classification), which tended to situate populations by place.[136] The entry revealed clearly how different forms of classification generated diverse typologies, and even how practitioners of the same system could produce somewhat different classifications. Instead of presenting a self-explanatory typology, *Cihai*'s entry gave the term for "race" a specific genealogy in European scholarship, identified competing theories, and grounded these distinctions in competing methodologies.

Taking this example as indicative, we see that in *Cihai* foreign-derived neologisms continued to be legitimized and naturalized as elements for Chinese discourse, but they were also situated with more specificity in Western intellectual traditions that revealed the concepts' methodological infrastructures and their contested histories. To return to Koselleck's distinction between term and concept, *Ciyuan* had presented "race"/*renzhong* more as a bounded, specific, and self-explanatory term, while *Cihai* presented it as a contested and changing concept. *Cihai*'s approach to presenting academic fields and theories in all their complexity, full of internal tensions and debates, corresponded to the contemporaneous trend of publishing synthetic monographs on each discipline and debate (see chapter 5). The publications of both genres marked publishing circles' contributions to the development of Chinese academic life. *Cihai*'s status as a comprehensive dictionary, a seminal reference book from one of China's largest publishers, helped to legitimize the terms and concepts it presented and the ways it defined them. It also made manifest how academic knowledge was open and debatable at a time when the Nationalist Party sought to become an absolute arbiter of scientific legitimacy and determine absolute meanings.[137]

The transformation of the Chinese lexicon and the shift from writing predominantly in the classical to the vernacular language were arguably two of the most important and lasting cultural changes of the twentieth century. Publications from the three major publishing companies played a substantial part in realizing these changes. Dictionaries and textbooks of the late Qing and early Republic introduced modern terms covering all aspects of society, culture, economics, and politics. From the 1920s through the 1940s, national-language readers and other textbooks taught students two different versions of vernacular writing, while also providing models for writing various genres of text. The 1936 dictionary *Cihai* captured the post–May Fourth politicization of language and the explosion of academic terminology and concepts during the 1920s and 1930s. As authoritative texts that presented standard versions of terms, concepts, and styles, language textbooks and dictionaries taught young people directly how to interpret a new intellectual and cultural landscape and how to write and express themselves in new ways. By fixing the definitions of key concepts like "race," "citizenship," and "rights," *Ciyuan* and *Cihai* played vital roles in producing knowledge during the Republican period.

These transformative textbooks and dictionaries were not written primarily by leading language reformers, linguists, or academics.[138] Nor were they formulated by state actors, even though at times they were sanctioned by state institutions. Rather, late Qing literati editors in the Commercial Press and Zhonghua Editing Departments created *Ciyuan* and the formative late Qing and early Republican textbooks. A later generation of petty intellectuals, serving in the Editing Departments of all three major publishers, took the lead in crafting the national-language readers, from which most students learned vernacular writing. Under Shu Xincheng and Shen Duoshan's direction, they also compiled *Cihai*, which became the most authoritative comprehensive dictionary of the twentieth century. A consideration of both sets of publications reveals how literati and petty intellectuals transformed modern Chinese culture through their intellectual labor.

At the same time, it is important to recognize how staff editors' cultural activities were framed and inspired by others. The trends of conceptual and linguistic change textbooks and dictionaries concretized, such as the vernacular-language movement, the social reforms of the May Fourth period, and development of new academic disciplines, were initiated and thematized by leading intellectual figures. Just as importantly, within the publishing companies, executive editors set the publishing agendas and organized work processes. As seen in Shu Xincheng's decision to collect new terms for *Cihai* from contemporary publications and to include entries summarizing recent historical events, staff editors usually worked within parameters defined by others. But without staff editors' labor, which fed the productive industrial capacity of the leading commercial publishers, the language-reform movement and the dissemination of new intellectual currents and concepts might have remained unrealized. Ultimately, competition to create more distinctive and successful products in the competitive market for textbooks and reference books helped drive this major cultural change.

CHAPTER IV

_____

Repackaging the Past

Reproducing Classics Through Industrial Publishing

I
n January 1919, in the waning days of the lunar year, Commercial Press editors Sun Yuxiu and Shen Yanbing took the train to Nanjing. Their aim was to review the editions of ancient books held in Jiangsu province's Jiangnan Library,[1] which contained the books from several prominent private collections. Drawing on his skills as a scholar of editions, Sun was helping Zhang Yuanji formulate the catalog and access the best rare editions for what would become the *Collection of Chinese Classical, Historical, Philosophical, and Literary Works (Sibu congkan* 四部叢刊*).*[2] Sun and Shen faced an uphill battle. Despite prior approval from the provincial government, the library administrator, Wang Zhenzhi 汪振之, only grudgingly allowed them to review titles for four days, citing the coming lunar New Year holiday. Sun and Shen seized the moment, evaluating books from as early as they could gain access to the library each day until the lamps were lit in the evening, braving the numbing damp cold of the Nanjing winter. Despite the short time frame and bureaucratic constraints, Sun Yuxiu worked at a prodigious rate, reviewing some 181 titles in the four days, returning to Shanghai on the night train on January 18.[3]

This would be the first of four trips Sun Yuxiu would make to Jiangnan Library in 1919, at the height of the New Culture Movement and precisely the moment when the May Fourth protests were about to explode. Sun invested much of his own time and energy as well as the efforts of young compilers Shen Yanbing, Sun Kanghou, and Jiang Zuoyu. Throughout the year, Sun and Shen reviewed and collated rare editions, arranged the photographing of select books, and proofed and reviewed the resulting negatives. Altogether the work on *Sibu congkan* represented a remarkable investment of human editorial resources along with financial capital to purchase and access rare books, demonstrating Commercial Press's ongoing commitment to classical republication, even as it pursued textbook and monograph projects that advanced various cultural reform agendas. Soon thereafter Zhonghua Book Company would initiate its own massive classical publishing projects, *Essential Writings from the Four Categories of Learning* (*Sibu beiyao* 四部備要) and *Complete Collection of Past and Present Books and Illustrations* (*Gujin tushu jicheng* 古今圖書集成). Publishing old books was a major priority for both companies, even though most Euro-American scholarship emphasizes their contributions to progressive cultural-reform projects.

What motivated Commercial Press and Zhonghua Book Company to take on these classical publishing projects during the high tide of cultural reform, and how did they leverage their editorial resources to realize them? When publishing leaders discussed classical publishing, they used a language of "circulation" (*liutong* 流通), "transmission" (*liuchuan* 流傳), and "preservation" (*baocun* 保存) that had both synchronic and diachronic aspects. In historical terms, preservation and transmission emphasized the continuity through time of the cultural canon, a concern that had both ancient and more recent Confucian dimensions and one many literati editors shared.[4] But following Joseph Levenson, we can also see ways in which during the first half of the twentieth century the philosophical and literary texts transmitted from the ancient past started to change their valence, from being perceived by literati primarily as living artifacts of universal civilization to records of an evolving national culture.[5] This new emphasis on the national community and its historical roots comes through clearly in the publishers' repeated use of the terms "national heritage" (*guogu* 國故), "national essence" (*guocui* 國粹), and "national learning" (*guoxue* 國學) when promoting publication of classical texts.[6] In this framework ancient books could provide a cultural basis for a historically rooted identity that underpinned national strength. As articulated in Zhonghua's promotional material for *Sibu beiyao* in the 1930s, "If this book is spread throughout the country and widely seen, national learning will prevail, the national essence will be preserved, culture will revive, and the nation will flourish again."[7] As Meng Yue has observed, this link to national welfare made the threat of losing national heritage to foreign governments or individuals particularly sensitive.[8] At the same time, late Qing literati like Sun Yuxiu had a vested interest in establishing their credentials as classical scholars while also making more widely available rare classical texts that had long been sequestered in private collections, democratizing access to knowledge.

Production strategies for classical publications depended on the kinds of social, cultural, and economic capital publishers could mobilize, which varied over time and by project.[9] By the 1910s and 1920s both Commercial Press and Zhonghua Book Company had accumulated enough financial capital to allow them to invest strategically in rare books for republication. At the same time, they each leveraged the human capital in their Editing Departments for classical republishing projects. The late Qing literati in Commercial Press's Editing Department tapped their social networks for expertise and textual access, while at the same time drawing on their classical learning to make strategic decisions about the selection of titles and editions. Zhonghua's leaders took a workshop approach to textual production, organizing large groups of low-ranking scholars with practical competence to proofread and touch up large-scale publications. The resulting publications transformed the landscape of classical scholarship during the Republican period by configuring the classical canon and at once democratizing and hierarchizing textual access.

Mobilizing Literati Networks, Converting Capital: *Sibu congkan*

Zhang Yuanji and Sun Yuxiu collaborated to produce *Sibu congkan*. Both were late Qing literati, but they had different levels of cultural achievement and recognition, which conditioned their roles in and approach to this project. As noted in chapter 1, Zhang had been awarded the *jinshi* degree (1892) and served in the Hanlin Academy, though he had also been involved in the 1898 Reform Movement, after which he was persona non grata with the Qing establishment.[10] Based on his academic achievement, he carried a high level of academic capital forward into the Republican period. Sun Yuxiu, by contrast, never achieved a degree higher than *xiucai* (1895), despite repeated efforts at the examinations, and studied a mix of foreign and Chinese learning as a young adult.[11] Yet Sun came from a family that embraced books and scholarship independent of the civil service exams. And through a combination of self-study, training at Nanjing Academy, and informal study with book collector Miao Quansun 繆荃孫, Sun had some background as a scholar of editions (*banbenxue* 版本學) and skill with the difficult parallel prose style (*piantiwen* 駢體文).[12] As mentioned, Sun compiled a diverse range of publications for Commercial Press, as did many literati editors, but he flourished during the 1910s, when he gradually came to specialize in work with classical texts: judging purchases for the Hanfenlou Library; selecting titles for republication; and conducting a range of collating, proofreading, and annotating work to facilitate those projects.[13] Zhang Yuanji's commitment to classical publishing provided an outlet for Sun Yuxiu's scholarship and compilation work.

In consultation with Miao Quansun in the spring of 1909, Zhang decided to begin publishing rare old books held in the Hanfenlou Library, relying heavily on Sun Yuxiu.[14] Through this republication work, Zhang and Sun sought to earn a profit from continued interest in classical scholarship but also to "'extend the life' of the ancients, with the emphasis on disseminating rare ancient books that were already declining each day."[15] They tested the market and experimented with tapping literati networks for books and expertise with a relatively small series of reprinted classical texts called *A Collection of Obscure Books from the Hanfenlou* (*Hanfenlou miji* 涵芬樓秘笈), which began publication in 1916 and concluded in 1921.[16]

Planning for *Sibu congkan* started in 1915 and extended to 1919. The project was announced in a statement, "Explanation of *Sibu juyao*" (四部舉要說略), which was published in March 1915 in *Shenbao* and *Fiction Monthly* (*Xiaoshuo yuebao*).[17] The publisher explained the project by decrying the loss of old books and difficulty of access to them: "Knowing what is new and reviewing the past are equally important. Since Xian[feng] [1851–1862] and Tong[zhi] [1862–1875], China has passed through many events and old books are being lost by the day. Now the difficulty seeking books and the feebleness of national learning have never been worse than at this time." In turn, Commercial Press expressed six benefits or virtues (*shan*) of the project. First, whereas previous collections had focused on obscure volumes, they would publish "books recited in every home, which like practical necessities [literally, cotton, silk, beans, and grain] are what the four classes of people cannot be without for one day." Second, they would not alter the books collected, as had been done with previous collections during the Ming and Qing, but rather would preserve the original text. Third, by using quality originals, they could avoid errors. Fourth, they would gather books in one place to save time and effort. Fifth, slight reduction of page size while using large-character formats would make the books easy to both store and use. Sixth, the volume size and paper quality would be uniform to relate a fine aesthetic sense. In sum, the articulated goals were to bring together scattered rare volumes that otherwise would be inaccessible to make them available in their original form for the everyday scholarly pursuits of a broad public. Further, they sought to price the set reasonably enough that they could circulate readily (*liutong*), for that was when books had real value.

Within this overall framework, the initial focus was on organizing the catalog that would fulfill the bibliographic vision of the project. Zhang Yuanji and Sun Yuxiu conducted a multisided discussion between each other and a whole range of colleagues and mentors to prioritize different titles and editions, making key decisions about which books should be included and which excluded. For instance, on May 19, 1915, Zhang Yuanji wrote to Fu Zengxiang 傅增湘[18] explaining the *Sibu congkan* project and asking for his feedback on an appended catalog: "If there are places we should increase it or reduce it, we also seek that you indicate it. But if there are increases, there must be corresponding reductions, because it will influence the sale price."[19] Zhang also asked Fu to evaluate whether there were high-quality original editions available for some of the texts Commercial Press did not have in the Hanfenlou and to suggest alternatives.[20] Zhang Yuanji and Sun Yuxiu were then left to sort through the commentary of multiple scholars and coordinate between themselves to decide on the final version of the catalog.[21] Zhang and Sun together tapped networks of expertise that extended far outside Commercial Press to configure a collection of distinctive scholarly value. To do so they took advantage of the social capital they had built up over their careers and recruited scholars who had no immediate economic stake in Commercial Press into a common intellectual enterprise anchored in a commitment to classical scholarship.

Once it was decided that the collection would offer photographic reprints of rare publications rather than typeset versions of more common editions, an equally pressing concern was getting access to high-quality editions to photograph and reprint.[22] Zhang and Sun had to coordinate between what the publisher had in the Hanfenlou Library or could acquire for it, on the one hand, and, on the other, what they needed to borrow from public and private collections.[23] Throughout the process of compiling *Sibu congkan*,

Zhang Yuanji and Sun Yuxiu continually sought to buy fine rare editions when they could to supplement the collection at the Hanfenlou Library.[24] During 1919 and 1920, in the midst of publishing *Sibu congkan*, Zhang and Sun's correspondence reveals persistent exchanges about whether to buy certain books and at what cost.[25] For these purchases Zhang Yuanji depended on Sun Yuxiu's expertise in the study of editions to judge the quality and value of each text. Zhang, in turn, calculated how much the company could afford to spend on particular volumes or sets of books.

At the same time Zhang and Sun both tapped networks of friends, family, and acquaintances to borrow rare editions of key volumes to photograph and republish.[26] Zhang and Sun also lent books from their own collections to the project. Sun, for instance, provided seventeen titles from his Xiaolutian collection.[27] Incorporation of his books in a major collection like *Sibu congkan* helped establish Sun's reputation as a significant collector. In general, inclusion in *Sibu congkan* seemed to hold some attraction to the scholars they approached, who offered their books generously. We see this in Ye Dehui's comment to Xia Jingguan about lending his books for republication: "The volumes I have stored at home I will not have any scruples about lending enthusiastically, and I should also do my best to introduce my friends' collections."[28] Association with a project of this scale guaranteed scholars no small degree of recognition as book collectors and masters of classical learning in an era when the official markers of distinction, once formalized in the imperial examination system, had already been dismantled. As Bourdieu argues, ownership of fine cultural objects and exhibiting the taste to appreciate them can serve as a powerful sign of cultural distinction.[29]

One particularly large private collection Sun and Zhang sought to use was Qu Liangshi's 瞿良士 Pavilion of the Iron Harp and Bronze Sword (Tieqin tongjian lou 鐵琴銅劍樓) in Changshu. As recounted in Zhang Yuanji's diary, Zhang and Sun worked to cultivate a relationship by personally visiting the Qu family home in Changshu for several days in October 1919.[30] The trip included meals together, visits with other local literati, some with their own book collections, as well as shared reading of books and appreciation of paintings and rubbings of inscriptions. Through these shared practices of connoisseurship, a form of embodied cultural capital, Zhang and Sun built powerful relational bonds with Qu Liangshi that lasted for years.[31] Their visit culminated in presentation of a list of books they sought to reprint and plans to send a crew to photograph them at the Qu family residence the following spring.[32] Ultimately, Commercial Press incorporated twenty titles from the Qu family library into *Sibu congkan*.[33]

At the same time, Zhang and Sun also sought access to a major public collection, Nanjing's Jiangnan Library (Jiangnan tushuguan), which had absorbed into its collection some valuable rare-book collections of scholarly elite families.[34] After Sun Kanghou 孫康候 (Jun 峻) made an initial survey of the library's holdings,[35] at the start of 1919 Zhang Yuanji "decided to ask [Sun] Xingru to go to the Nanjing Library to select books that can be printed for *Sibu juyao* [*Sibu congkan*]."[36] After the initial trip to Nanjing, Sun Yuxiu and Shen Yanbing returned there in mid-April and went directly to the provincial governor's office to get approval to borrow books to be reprinted in *Sibu congkan*. Despite several long waits, they never met with the provincial governor, Qi Yaolin 齊耀琳, himself, but they did eventually meet with a section head, who informed them that the governor had read the documents Commercial Press had submitted and would support the publisher's borrowing and reprinting of the library's materials.[37] Although many details about the process of photographing the materials remained to be resolved, Sun and Commercial Press had secured access to a valuable collection of books. In turn, Governor Qi Yaolin came to be listed as one of the "initiators" (*faqiren* 發起人) of *Sibu congkan*.[38] Through association with this prestigious collection, Qi presented himself as a cultural patron in a way similar to scholar-officials of the late imperial period. Commercial Press here traded cultural capital for textual access to create a more valuable and marketable product.

Sun Yuxiu's detailed record of the books he reviewed in Nanjing reveals the kinds of mental labor that went into compiling a reprint series like *Sibu congkan*. Sun's passion for his work led to long, grueling days in the library, as is captured in the following description of his first visit to Jiangnan Library with Shen Yanbing in January 1919. "Already brought up forty-two rare books [*shanbenshu*], calculated the number of pages for twenty titles. In the afternoon read until dusk, and the two courtyards had lights for the dark; hands and feet all froze. [Sun] Kanghou finally left at nightfall, but [our] two voices [Sun's and Shen Yanbing's] had still not stopped."[39] Sun Yuxiu made a careful record of each of the books he reviewed. He focused first on the rarity of the edition as well as the value of the paratext that framed and supported the text. We get some sense of these concerns from his notes on a fine Ming edition: "*Meng Haoran Collection* [*ji*], four chapters [*juan*], two volumes [*ce*]; Ming edition. Preface by Yicheng's Wang Shiyuan, and a preface by Wei Tao. Ten lines [per half page], eighteen characters [per line]. Printed beautifully."[40]

At the same time, Sun had to evaluate the quality of the printing and paper, the size of the volumes, and how they compared with editions available in the Hanfenlou or other libraries Commercial Press had access to. For instance, he made note of "*Wei's Suzhou Collection*, six volumes, Ming printed edition. Same as the one at the company [Commercial Press], but this copying and printing are relatively advanced."[41] Similarly, where editions corresponded, he considered how to supplement existing texts by collating in volumes, sections, or pages from this collection.[42] Sun carefully prioritized which books from the library Commercial Press sought to photograph to reprint and how portions of particular publications could be coordinated with others to reconstitute whole books and collections.[43] After some negotiation, it was decided to photograph the Jiangnan Library's books in Nanjing, with two photographers coming from Shanghai to do the work.[44] During a fourth visit by Sun Yuxiu to Nanjing in June 1919, work finally got under way, with Sun overseeing part of it.[45] Subsequently, Jiang Zuoyu 姜佐禹 remained in Nanjing to monitor the photography, and Shen Yanbing reviewed the photographic negatives that were sent back to Shanghai daily.[46] In the end forty-two titles from Jiangnan Library were incorporated into *Sibu congkan*.[47]

Throughout this process the labor of a number of low-ranking literati was necessary to realize publication of *Sibu congkan*. First and foremost, Sun Yuxiu drew on deep classical learning, the publication history of a remarkable range of texts, and almost photographic recall of which editions were available in which collections to strategically select particular texts for collection and republication. In turn, Sun's work was supported by capable scholars like Sun Kanghou, Shen Yanbing, and Jiang Zuoyu who also had some bibliographic expertise, could follow Sun's notations, discriminate among the texts reproduced, check photographic prints against originals, and properly collate sections of texts to make cohesive wholes. Commercial Press's active recruitment of marginalized literati made such staffing possible.

At the same time, Commercial Press's literati leadership used conventional patterns of patronage and commensality to develop functional working relations with Jiangnan Library's staff. For instance, Mao Dun describes in his memoir how Sun Yuxiu treated the library staff to meals to break

Figure 4.1 Sun Yuxiu (*left*) and Shen Yanbing (*right*) circa 1920. Liu Hecheng 柳和城, *Sun Yuxiu pingzhuan* 孙毓修评传 (A critical biography of Sun Yuxiu) (Shanghai: Shanghai renmin chubanshe, 2011).

down the barriers between them. "The Nanjing branch manager arranged in advance for us to live at the Longpanli Jiangnan Library's guest room and also sent a cook to specially manage our food, and the sumptuous courses were fine and plentiful. At each meal Sun Yuxiu invited the library head and high-level members of the staff, and in this way suddenly everyone was on friendly terms and all matters went smoothly."[48] As during the late imperial period, shared meals created interpersonal bonds that facilitated business transactions. At the same time, Commercial Press strategically distributed largesse to smooth its work. Specifically, in July 1919 Zhang Yuanji directed that sixty-five yuan be sent to Jiang Zuoyu in Nanjing to distribute among the library staff, starting with Director Wang Zhenzhi.[49]

Through coordinated access to some of the lower Yangzi region's most valuable collections of rare books, Zhang Yuanji and Sun Yuxiu engineered an impressive collection of 323 titles in twenty-one hundred volumes (*ce*) issued in six print runs starting in May 1920. Sun Yuxiu's responsibilities remained intense during the production process. Beyond collating different editions and volumes of particular texts, finding ways to supplement where there were missing pages or sections, he also provided extensive notes on the edition of each text used in the collection and oversaw the proofreading and corrections.[50] From 1919 to 1923 *Sibu congkan* was a major focus of Sun Yuxiu's work at Commercial Press. It allowed him to concentrate on the bibliographic work that was the primary interest of his scholarly life. In one of history's ironies, delayed printing of the last section of *Sibu congkan* prevented Sun Yuxiu from seeing the published text in its entirety before his death early in 1923.[51]

Yet Sun had significantly shaped the extant classical canon through his selection of particular editions for *Sibu congkan*, which became a landmark publication. Scholars with other perspectives could question the books one

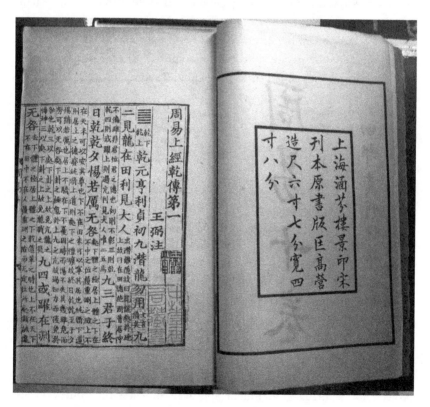

Figure 4.2 A sample page from *Sibu congkan*: a Song edition of *The Book of Changes* (*Zhou yi*)

selected for preservation, and they could also challenge choices of edition and print run.[52] A more fundamental criticism, however, revolved around the whole approach of choosing to focus on the oldest and rarest editions. As one commentator put it, "With the current *Sibu congkan*, expert collators [*jiaokanjia*] or those who love antiquity will certainly consider it important, but those with elementary learning will certainly not find it convenient."[53] Given mistaken characters, missing pages, and random marks of various kinds in the original publications, all but the most expert classicists would need to compare any given rare edition photographed and reprinted in *Sibu congkan* with an annotated one in order to follow it. They would also require some guidance in how to approach the text. The very strategy of focusing on rare editions made the collection most useful to a relatively small group of collectors and classicists with the expert knowledge to evaluate and interpret them. From this perspective, then, *Sibu congkan* can be viewed as an elitist project whose main constituency was Zhang Yuanji's and Sun Yuxiu's own literati peers. Yet for that reading community, *Sibu congkan* democratized access to rare editions that previously had been sequestered in private collections like the collection of the Qu family. By 1934 it had been printed three times, with more than five thousand sets sold in the first two print runs.[54]

The Limits of State Stewardship: Preserving *Siku quanshu*

On the heels of completing *Sibu congkan*, Commercial Press pursued an even larger republication project: reprinting the Qianlong-era *Complete Book of Four Treasuries* (*Siku quanshu*) in its entirety. The scale was several times that of *Sibu congkan*, with 3,460 books (*bu*) in 36,275 volumes (*ce*), constituting 2,290,916 pages.[55] In contrast to *Sibu congkan*'s scattered texts, the *Four Treasuries* were concentrated in the form of three extant collections, the most complete and well preserved of which was stored in the Wenyuange 文淵閣 in the Palace Museum. Another intact collection that had been stored at the Wenjinge 文津閣 at the Summer Palace in Rehe was moved to the Capital Normal Library (Jingshi tushuguan). But the seeming advantage of the books' concentration soon came to confound the project, for securing government approval to access the collection and funds to support its republication complicated multiple attempts by Commercial Press to reprint it during the 1920s.

In 1924 Commercial Press initiated its own effort to reprint the *Four Treasures*, which they connected to the company's thirtieth anniversary, after a failed government effort in 1920.[56] Given the massive size of the project, they made several adjustments in an effort to make it commercially viable.[57] For one, they planned to reduce slightly the size of the text so that multiple pages of the original would fit on one printed page, thereby limiting the expense of both printing and paper. Further, they planned to print it in four different formats to target distinct audiences and kinds of customers. With two of the sets they also planned to use imported Western paper so as not to exhaust Chinese paper stocks. By these means, Commercial Press sought to lower the capital expenses for the project, limit its time frame to five years, and reduce somewhat the purchase price, which the company projected would be three thousand yuan per set for the two collections that would be printed on Western paper.

In explaining the motivation for this project, Commercial Press emphasized most a concern for preservation of cultural resources during a time of turmoil and conflict.

When the Hong and Yang incident [Taiping Rebellion] arose, the Wenzong and Wenhui [collections in Zhenjiang and Yangzhou, respectively] were lost in succession. During the United Army's intrusion [in 1860], the Wenyuan [Pavilion, at Yuanmingyuan] was also reduced to ash. The Wenlan [Pavilion] [in Hangzhou] fortunately survived, but the remaining volumes besides those that were stolen are now less than half the number. Currently there are really just three complete ones. The Wenyuan set is in the palace. The Wensu and Wenjin sets were one after the other moved into the capital, five planets gathered in the constellation for literature [*wu xing ju kui*], which can be said to be a grand occasion. But with having the three sets gathered in one corner, having a vast, unsystematic collection is a concern. The Ming period's *Yongle Compendium* also at one time formed three sets, but by the Qianlong period, there were already omissions, though there were still more than twenty thousand *juan*. During the Boxer Uprising, some were turned into ashes and some circulated among the people, and only several dozen volumes were stored in public institutions. If we take that [the *Compendium*] as a method for this [the *Four Treasures*], is it possible not to be fearful?[58]

In this shorthand history, company leaders emphasized how domestic turmoil and foreign invasion had led to the destruction or degradation of four of seven sets of the *Four Treasuries*, leaving just three remaining. They drew a powerful analogy to the *Yongle Compendium*, which had eroded over a few centuries to just a remnant of its former glory. At the same time, they went on to point to clear foreign interest in the collection, seeing it as a monument that represented Chinese culture in world civilization. At this juncture, it seems, fear of foreign cultural appropriation was less acute as a motivator than concerns about domestic and foreign political turmoil undermining cultural heritage preservation.

The challenge for Commercial Press was getting access to the books themselves. For *Sibu congkan* Commercial Press had sent teams of photographers to Nanjing and Changshu, but with the much larger *Four Treasuries* project, the company sought to transport it to Shanghai and do the photographing and printing work at the its main office and factory complex. "In February 1924 we specially sent representatives to the capital to the Qing court's Imperial Household Department [Neiwufu] to discuss borrowing it and transporting it to Shanghai to photographically reprint. We received approval from the Imperial Household Department. But because its significance was relatively great, we needed first to consult with the cabinet [Guowuyuan]."[59] Negotiations with the cabinet and its ministries were extended and involved, entailing detailed discussion about how to physically move such a large collection from Beijing to Shanghai. Gao Mengdan and Commercial Press Beijing branch office manager Sun Zhuang appealed to the Ministry of Communication to arrange special rail cars for the transfer and to reduce costs for transporting the books in accord with the shipping rates for educational materials.[60] In the end the ministry resisted Commercial Press's proposed cost reductions but directed the regional railway administrations to arrange special shipping methods for the books, which they in turn coordinated with the publisher.[61]

From April 5 to 7, 1924, Commercial Press workers began boxing and preparing to ship the Palace Museum collection of the *Four Treasuries*. But one-third of the way into the work, on April 8 the Secretariat (Mishuting) of the president's office issued a public pronouncement suspending the planned shipment from Beijing to Shanghai.[62] The pronouncement expressed concern over the potential for loss or damage to this collection, which had immense cultural value.[63] In response, Zhang Yuanji wrote to the premier reprising the publisher's arguments about the need to conduct the work in Shanghai because of the scale of the project, which would occupy the better part of the publisher's physical plant and personnel.[64] He further emphasized that the company's newly built steel and cement library had special rooms dedicated to storing the *Four Treasuries* that would protect the collection from any damage. Premier Sun Baoqi 孫寶琦 was not swayed. In response he wrote,

> Overall, because the *Four Treasuries* has bearing on culture it should urgently be published in order to widely circulate. But there are those that advocate doing it according to the original book's style and not changing it, and there are those that advocate publishing it in Beijing. For the time being, this is difficult to resolve. We need to plan comprehensively before we can settle on a program. If you have time you can come to Beijing to discuss it together, and perhaps it will be easy to resolve.[65]

By raising questions about the basic approach to the project, Sun Baoqi effectively returned the project to the discussion and planning stage. Why the Beijing government came so far in cooperating with Commercial Press only to suspend the process at the last minute is unclear. Some at the time attributed it to the fact that Commercial Press refused to pay a significant bribe of sixty thousand yuan to one of President Cao Kun's protégés.[66]

The following year, however, the government in Beijing changed, and Duan Qirui's cabinet proved much more positive about reprinting the *Four Treasuries*. In particular, Minister of Education Zhang Shizhao 章士釗, a cultural conservative who simultaneously was reversing the ministry's previous promotion of vernacular language education, strongly supported the project. After initial discussions about reprinting select portions of the collection and having the printing carried out by the Ministry of Finance's Printing Section, Zhang Shizhao reached out to the Commercial Press leadership about printing the whole collection.[67] The contract stipulated thirty full-sized sets of archival quality to be stored in libraries in China and abroad, as well as eighty sets in reduced size that Commercial Press would sell at a market price of three thousand yuan per set. This time the Ministry of Education proposed to ship to Shanghai the Wenjin Pavilion set stored at the Capital Normal Library, over which it had direct authority.

Once again, however, China's disrupted political situation intervened to confound the project. With the entire Wenjin collection boxed and ready to transport as of October 20, the outbreak of a military conflict made it impossible to ship the books from Beijing to Shanghai. By the time peace was reestablished the following spring, Zhang Shizhao was no longer in charge at the Ministry of Education, and the political will to continue this project had dissipated.[68]

Twice within two years Commercial Press had prepared a shipment of the *Four Treasuries* to go to Shanghai for photographing and printing only to have the project cut short by political interference and disruptions. The contrast with the preparation and execution of *Sibu congkan* is stark. In that case Zhang Yuanji and Sun Yuxiu had been able to mobilize literati networks to create a valuable assemblage of rare classical works. Where political access to books was necessary, as with the Jiangnan Library collection, Zhang was able to trade cultural capital for political support. With the *Four Treasuries* project, divisions within the government and frequent changes of leadership disrupted the long-term planning necessary for a project of this size. The destabilized Republican governments of the Beiyang government period could not fulfill the role of cultural steward that Chinese states had historically played. Much more successful were commercial publishers like Commercial Press, which could mobilize social, cultural, and economic capital for large-scale cultural production. They were confounded most when they had to contend with unstable modern states that had inherited the cultural artifacts of the late imperial period.

The relative stability of the Nationalist government after 1928 provided better conditions for Commercial Press to collaborate to republish the rarest titles in the *Four Treasuries*. The removal of the Wensu Pavilion's *Four Treasuries* collection to the northeast in 1928 meant that it fell under Japanese control after the Manchurian Incident in September 1931, making some preservation of the remaining two sets of the collection an even more pressing issue.[69] In 1933 Commercial Press worked with head of the Central Library Planning Office Jiang Fucong 蔣復璁 to conclude a contract for publication of a group of rare volumes that would be decided on by an editorial board composed of fifteen experts.[70] Among leading classical scholars a fierce controversy ensued over whether the collection should be composed of volumes from the *Four Treasuries* itself or rare earlier editions of titles held in the *Four Treasuries* that were unaffected by omissions, Manchu censorship, or errors in the compilation process of the original collection.[71] By the fall of 1933 the editorial board settled on 231 titles to be reprinted; Commercial Press began the photographic work and prepared to issue advance order forms in January 1934, with full publication occurring in 1935.[72] Ultimately, cooperation between the commercial publisher, intellectuals, and officials of a stable government allowed at least some part of the *Complete Book of Four Treasuries* to be published.

Popularizing National Heritage: *Sibu beiyao*

Zhonghua Book Company's answer to *Sibu congkan* and, to some extent, the *Complete Book of Four Treasuries*, was *Sibu beiyao*. Zhonghua initiated the project in 1920, while Zhang Yuanji and Sun Yuxiu were right in the midst of preparing *Sibu congkan* for publication. Moreover, the model for *Sibu beiyao* was a Qing-era collection drawn from the *Complete Book of Four Treasuries*, the *Assembled Essentials of the Complete Book of Four Treasuries* (*Siku quanshu huiyao* 四庫全書薈要), which had selected 473 titles from the larger collection to reprint for scholars' access.[73] Indeed, Zhonghua's leaders' goal was to reprint selectively the most essential books from the four categories of knowledge for scholars to use so readers would not be overwhelmed by the number and complexity of China's printed canon and confused by the multiple editions, some quite expensive, circulating in bookstores.[74]

This connection to the *Four Treasuries* had a personal salience for Zhonghua Book Company founder and general manager Lufei Kui. His ancestor from five generations before, Lufei Chi 陸費墀 (d. 1790), had been a *jinshi* of 1767. In addition to serving in the Hanlin Academy and Grand Secretariat, Lufei Chi had worked on the *Complete Book of Four Treasuries* as chief collator and then as the official overseeing installation of several of the completed collections, altogether staying involved with the project on and off for seventeen years.[75] Given this history, which Lufei Kui recounted and referred to in his explanation of the book's origins, it seems that for him *Sibu beiyao* was, in part, an effort to reclaim and establish publicly a family heritage of classical scholarship.

For Zhonghua Book Company as a whole, the broader motivation for publishing *Sibu beiyao* was associated with ease of access to the most important classical texts. As offered in one explanation of the project, "China's books are so many, if scholars want to research Chinese learning, what books should they read? Which books are most important? People with elementary learning have a difficult time and no way to start. With finely carved books, editions mostly do not survive; the cost to buy them is great, and it is not easy to find them."[76] Rather than emphasizing rare, early editions that scholars fetishized for collection and preservation in their own right, Zhonghua emphasized "commonly circulating fine editions" (*tongxing shanben*) that were "essential" for practical scholarship.[77] If we review the selections for the classics section (*jingbu*), for instance, we see numerous editions chosen from Ruan Yuan's publication projects, some from the Xuehaitang's classical publishing ventures in the nineteenth century, and some texts self-published by Qing scholars.[78] In Lufei Kui's words, "With these books [we have] selected the essentials to collate and print and published them in succession so they can both supply the demand from society's libraries and facilitate the needs of scholars studying national learning, so perhaps it will be some small help!"[79]

In fact, an emphasis on practical use led to selection of more accessible recent publications that were often annotated by leading scholars, so that a mechanism for guiding readers was built into the work itself. Again we can see this with Zhonghua's selections for the classics (*jing*).[80] The publisher chose annotated versions of the classics from the Han and Tang, as well as the late imperial standard of Zhu Xi's annotated version of the Four Books. But further, "Classical scholarship by the Qing period had the finest commentaries, so we also compiled *Notes and Commentaries of the Thirteen Classics* of the Qing period."[81] So *Sibu beiyao* included commentaries, studies, and annotated works on specific texts by notable Qing-era Confucian scholars like Wang Yinzhi 王引之, Li Yongchun 黎永椿, Duan Yucai 段玉裁, Liu Baonan 劉寶楠, Jiao Xun 焦循, Zhong Wenzheng 鍾文烝, Chen Li 陳立, Hong Liangji 洪亮吉, Zhu Bin 朱彬, Hu Peihui 胡培翬, Sun Yirang 孫詒讓, and Sun Xingyan 孫星衍, among others.[82] At the same time, in the proofreading process they corrected mistakes that had been transmitted from woodblock edition to woodblock edition in the past. They also incorporated annotated versions of the dictionaries, character books, and interpretive guides for the classics that provided resources for the kinds of philology and textual research that had come to dominate scholarship during the Qing period. In short, the collection was designed to provide an integrated small library of texts to facilitate scholarly research. As one commentator put it, "Systematic and orderly compilation like this can simply be said to be one set [of books to show] the history of classical studies' development."[83]

Reviewing model syllabi or reading lists for classical studies during the late Qing and early Republican periods largely confirms Zhonghua's claims. Zhang Zhidong's curriculum for classics at Hubei's School for Preserving the Heritage (Cungu xuetang 存古學堂) corresponds to the general approach Zhonghua's editors took with *Sibu beiyao*. That is, it included the full range of core classical texts, commentaries from different historical periods, and many examples of recent scholarship from the Qing.[84] Similarly, Liang Qichao's "Essential Syllabus of Introductory Books for National Studies" of 1923 also included the full range of classical texts along with commentaries and scholarship of different periods, stretching into the late Qing and early Republic.[85] In response to Liang Qichao's syllabus and an even more extensive one offered by Hu Shi, Lufei Kui himself formulated a list of the most basic classical readings in each of the four categories. He emphasized focusing on a small group of fundamental reprinted original works (often the Zhonghua editions reset in imitation of the Song font) coupled with some recent critical scholarship.[86] In practice, *Sibu beiyao* integrated these approaches by focusing on reprinted classical texts coupled with a selection of critical commentaries, thereby offering, as advertised, a comprehensive resource for basic classical scholarship. By contrast, *Sibu congkan*, with its focus on early, rare volumes and its photolithographed format that took up much more space per title than the typeset *Sibu beiyao*, did not include these later commentaries.[87] As a result it omitted the critical scholarship of the Qing that was informed by several generations of evidential studies research and that evaluated the provenance and fundamental meanings of key texts within the classical tradition.

By emphasizing "commonly circulating fine editions," Zhonghua's leaders lowered expectations about finding the earliest extant and distinctive editions. This less-selective approach dramatically reduced the need for the enormous front-end investment of intellectual labor by discerning scholars of editions that Sun Yuxiu and his colleagues had engaged in during the 1910s and early 1920s when preparing *Sibu congkan*. The work of selecting titles and editions was left mostly in the hands of Ancient Books Division (Gushubu) director Gao Shixian 高時顯 (style name Yehou 野侯), with help from colleague Ding Fuzhi 丁輔之.[88] By contrast, since Zhonghua's leaders had decided to typeset and reprint the books in *Sibu beiyao*, the most intensive investment of labor was in proofreading to make sure the typeset version accurately reflected the original woodblock versions of the books. In fact, *Sibu beiyao* had a dedicated group of ten proofreaders who mutually divided the work. While this work certainly required some expertise to be able to follow difficult text and grasp obscure characters, it expressed a different order of competence in classical scholarship than that exhibited by Sun Yuxiu as he weighed the value of publications of different eras and printers.

The decision to typeset and reprint the books in *Sibu beiyao*, instead of using photographic reprinting as Commercial Press had with *Sibu congkan*, was facilitated in part by invention of a new font that aesthetically expressed a classical flavor. Zhonghua Book Company compiler Ding Fuzhi's family in Hangzhou were book collectors that had owned the Hall of Eight Thousand Chapters (Baqianjuan lou). In 1921 the Ding brothers, who "were gifted at literature, calligraphy and painting, and engraving," developed a fine imitation-Song font that allowed classical texts to be reset in a font that evoked the earliest woodblock printing of the Song period (figure 4.3).[89] Although *Sibu beiyao* was typeset and reprinted, Zhonghua also produced and sold editions in a string-bound format (figure 4.4). Together, the imitation-Song font and string binding used the physical qualities of the text as icons to demarcate classical Chinese knowledge from the new forms of foreign knowledge entering China at the time that were published in hardbound or paperback Western formats. National learning was physically distinguished from Western learning. Production of books in these formats catered to a form of nostalgia that associated reading classical texts with an overall aesthetic experience that was enhanced by certain material qualities of the text. At the same time, the Song font and string binding mitigated the contrast between the photolithographed early editions collected in *Sibu congkan* and the more common later editions collected in *Sibu beiyao*.

Regardless of the aesthetic quality of the font and the ability to present a unified text throughout, the decision to typeset and reprint *Sibu beiyao* opened Zhonghua up to criticism. Specifically, Commercial Press, which had photographically reproduced the texts in *Sibu congkan*, published an advertisement suggesting implicitly that mistakes in copying and typesetting would lead to numerous errors in the published version of *Sibu beiyao*. Commercial Press's criticism, though certainly self-interested and intended to establish the superior quality of its own publication, raised serious

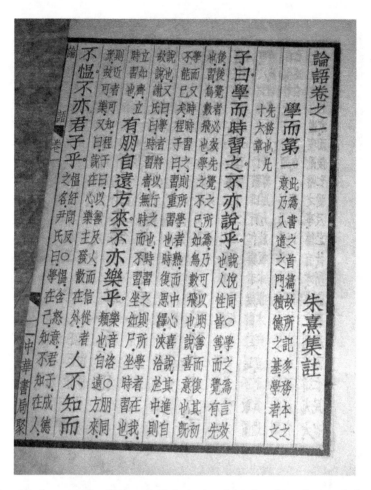

Figure 4.3 An example of Zhonghua's imitation-Song font from the sample book of *Sibu beiyao* (chapter 1 of Zhu Xi's annotated version of the *Analects*). *Sibu beiyao yangben* 四部備要樣本 (Sample book of *Sibu beiyao*) ([Shanghai]: Zhonghua shuju, n.d.)

concerns for the reading public. Lufei Kui responded in advertisements by proclaiming the rigor of his company's proofreading practices, but he also counterattacked aggressively by asserting that photographic reproduction itself could generate problems by transmitting mistakes and confusing stray marks and smudges. A mark in the wrong place, he contended, could turn "big" (*da* 大) into "dog" (*quan* 犬) or "too" (*tai* 太). To further protect Zhonghua's integrity, the company published an advertisement offering a reward

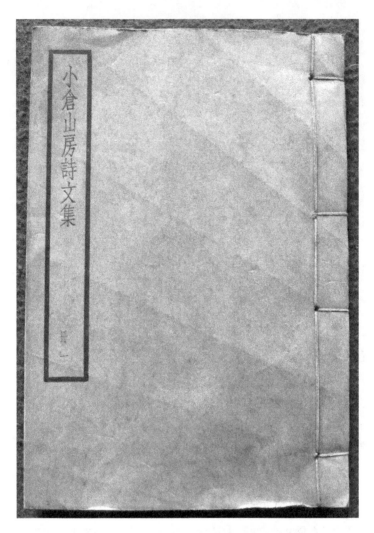

Figure 4.4 Example of the string-bound edition of *Sibu beiyao*

of one yuan for each error a reader found in the text.[90] In fact, scholars like Ye Shengtao pointed out numerous errors in *Sibu beiyao*'s proofreading, but these could be identified and improved in subsequent print runs.[91] Despite these errors and Commercial Press's critical advertising campaign, *Sibu beiyao* sold out all its initial print runs in the 1920s, prompting plans to reprint it in new formats starting in 1934, making it a truly popular collection of classical texts.[92]

Photographically Preserving Collected Classics:
Gujin tushu jicheng

Zhonghua Book Company followed the success of *Sibu beiyao* with an even more ambitious and large-scale project. The *Complete Collection of Past and Present Books and Illustrations* (*Gujin tushu jicheng*) differed from the other kinds of collected classical works discussed in this chapter. As a category book (*leishu* 類書) it drew material from a wide range of classical and contemporary texts and organized that material according to particular topics and themes.[93] Compiled initially by Chen Menglei 陳夢雷 and completed as a government project, sixty-four sets were published in brass movable type during the Yongzheng reign in ten thousand chapters (*juan*).[94] Zhonghua's director of the Ancient Books Division Gao Shixian raised the prospect of reprinting this massive collection on the heels of completing the first printing of *Sibu beiyao* in 1926, suggesting that Zhonghua by this point considered having a major classical republication project going to be a normal part of doing business. As presented in the introduction to the project, Zhonghua's leaders believed that the thematic organization of this collection offered advantages for conducting research, since it brought together large bodies of material from a range of sources on particular topics and themes.[95] As with *Sibu beiyao*, Zhonghua Book Company emphasized practical scholarship.

It also emphasized the concerns with transmission (*liuchuan*), which incorporated issues of both preservation and access. In their introduction to the project, Zhonghua's leaders recounted in some detail the limited availability of the publication.[96] Originally, only sixty-four sets had been printed during the Yongzheng reign, and the collection was not reprinted until the Guangxu reign.[97] These later reprints were either riddled with mistakes, not intact, or inaccessible. Overall, Zhonghua's leaders made the case for republication based on limited availability and circulation.

But these very factors made publication a challenge. How could Zhonghua get a clean and complete version of the collection to work from? From the outset Shu Xincheng argued for the importance of working from an intact copy of the Yongzheng-era movable brass type edition rather than from the flawed Guangxu-era reprints. Yet it was not until the mid-1930s that Zhonghua was able to acquire a copy to serve as the master manuscript for the reprint.[98] Still, the set they found included sixty-some volumes that had been hand copied to fill in missing printed volumes. In a photographic reprint, such inconsistencies in font quality and size were unacceptable, so Zhonghua hunted extensively for printed volumes to supplement. Eventually, the Zhejiang Provincial Library agreed to loan the company the necessary volumes from the Wenlan Pavilion.[99] Zhonghua here used a combination of the book market and literati networks to reconstruct the text it sought to reprint.

An equally pressing question was how Zhonghua would print and publish a collection of this scale. As Tongwen Book Company's travails during the Guangxu period showed, conventional lithographic reprinting of the full-sized text could be prohibitively expensive, and Zhonghua's leaders were mindful of not creating a book that its customers could not purchase. The solution they settled on was to use a three-*kai* format, which was about the size of half a newspaper page, thus allowing them to print the equivalent of nine pages of the original text on one printed page, which brought the final price to about eight hundred yuan (figure 4.5).[100]

As with *Sibu beiyao*, *Gujin tushu jicheng* required little intellectual labor on the front end to discriminate among extant editions and to collate compatible editions as had been true of *Sibu congkan*. Instead, the most labor-intensive parts of the process involved editing, proofreading, and touch-up work, not to mention the printing itself. As Sun Luoren 孫犖人, who was involved in the publication, recounts, the production process was organized by a refined division of labor and coordinated work patterns characteristic of industrial labor: "The work adopted the style of assembly-line production [*liushui zuoye*], on one side editing the manuscript and on another laying out the mounting [*fa biao*], on another side proofreading, and on yet another touching up, photographing, reviewing the lead sheet samples, making the plates and doing the printing, and setting the binding and layout."[101] We see here a multistep production process that coordinated mental and manual labor.

To edit, proofread, and touch up, Zhonghua assembled large teams of people with basic understandings of classical texts and calligraphy. As described by Sun Luoren, who coordinated the printing portion of the project, Zhonghua set up a temporary facility to allow proofreaders and touch-up staff to work at upright tables that could hold the large, newspaper-size printed sheets. They ended up hiring roughly twenty additional staff members so that they could maintain a continuous process of touching up proofs, with the company's own workers working at night and part-time employees for this project working during the day.

Figure 4.5 Sample book for *Gujin tushu jicheng*. Nine pages of original text were arranged in three rows of three on one page, with borders being erased to give a sense of continuous text. *Gujin tushu jicheng yangben* 古今圖書集成樣本 (Sample book for *Complete Collection of Past and Present Books and Illustrations*) ([Shanghai]: Zhonghua shuju, n.d.).

The company's colleagues introduced and recruited a group of more than twenty temporary workers who had culture and the ability to write the old Song-style characters [*lao Songti zi*] of ancient books, paying them on a piecework basis. At the same time Division Head Lufei Shuchen [陸費叔辰] appointed Comrade Chen Zhonghe [陳仲和] to serve as the manager at the temporary workshop. [They] specially worked the day shift and had the company's own touch-up staff work the night shift. Working day and night in this way, they sped up the rate of progress of the touch-up work.[102]

If we assume that the company's own workforce was roughly the same as that of the temporary workers, this project required roughly forty people to check and retouch proofs by hand. As recounted by Sun Luoren, these were scholars with basic educations in classical texts and calligraphy rather than refined experts in the study of editions like Sun Yuxiu. But as at Commercial Press, Zhonghua's publishing agendas for old books created employment opportunities for these classically trained scholars. They were just a lower tier of scholars, distinct from the credentialed elite like Zhang Yuanji who had passed the civil service examinations and classicist experts like Sun Yuxiu who were recognized masters of certain kinds of knowledge and technique. Zhonghua's strategy of mobilizing larger numbers of modestly trained scholars as editors, proofreaders, and calligraphers for this project parallels the shift in editorial workforces more generally. As discussed in part I, we see a turn from late Qing literati with extensive classical learning or the first generations of foreign-trained experts to petty intellectuals with basic educations and functional literary competence who worked in assembly-line production processes.

Democratizing Classical Learning

When Commercial Press and Zhonghua Book Company leaders discussed the motivation for publishing these collections of classical texts, they used a language of transmission (*liuchuan*), broadening circulation (*liutong*), and popularization (*puji*). They sought to give scholars access to titles and editions that were difficult to find and use. In the words of an advertisement for Commercial Press's *Siku quanshu zhenben*, the goal was "circulating a collection of obscure books for national learning."[103] To a certain extent, republication itself guaranteed wider access to these books, which had often been held in small numbers in collections usually not accessible to the public. But at the same time, the serious investments in book acquisition, expert mental labor, materials, and production that went into these series meant they also sold for amounts that limited access in a different way.

The purchase price of most of these collections of reprinted classics made them too expensive for most individual consumers. When purchased through advance order, *Sibu congkan*'s version on Lianshi paper cost 600 yuan (four payments of 150 yuan each), while the version on Maobian paper cost 480 yuan (four payments of 120 yuan each), with postage added.[104] *Sibu beiyao*'s set price for the first collection of four hundred volumes was 160 yuan; with full payment up front it dropped to 80 yuan, and four installments through advance order cost 90 yuan.[105] When extended out over the five collections that made up the full set of two thousand volumes (six *kai*), the cheapest advance order price would have been 400 yuan, with the full price possibly ranging considerably higher for other installment-payment plans.[106] The *Gujin tushu jicheng* and *Siku quanshu zhenben* were both even more expensive. The latter, published in one thousand nine hundred sixty volumes (*ce*), cost 800 yuan for the first collection.[107] As noted, Zhonghua's leaders struggled to bring the price for *Gujin tushu jicheng* below 1,000 yuan per set by eventually deciding to print nine original pages on one three-*kai* page, for a final list price of 800 yuan.[108] In general, the prices for these collections put them beyond the reach of most private customers.

But individual customers were not necessarily the main anticipated buyers for these large-scale collections. Instead, for both publishers institutional consumers building up library collections might have been the most obvious customers. In their statements explaining the motivation for producing *Sibu congkan* and *Sibu beiyao*, both companies indicated that they viewed libraries as important potential customers. As mentioned, Lufei Kui asserted that one goal of publishing *Sibu beiyao* was to "supply the demand from society's libraries."[109] Likewise, when Sun Yuxiu introduced *Sibu congkan*, he suggested that elites opening a library would be one possible use for the collection.[110] The potential of these compilations to provide base collections for libraries was echoed in cultural circles. For instance, Chen Gaoyong 陳高傭, in a commentary on the publication of *Sibu beiyao*, asserted, "Each cultural institution's establishment of libraries generally is not very complete . . . with books like *Sibu beiyao* that are both economical and perfect, no matter what, they should find a way to buy a set."[111] As centers for research and cultural dissemination, libraries, schools, research organizations, and government offices that purchased these collections could give a larger public access to them.

In practice, one important strategy the publishers used to market these collections was to directly contact government offices to encourage schools, government institutions, and libraries to purchase them, a strategy made use of also for series publications (*congshu*) (taken up in chapter 5). For instance, in 1922 Zhonghua Book Company board member Yu Fu 俞復 contacted the director of the Jiangsu Department of Education to convince him of the value of *Sibu beiyao* for the schools and libraries in his jurisdiction. "Since the sale price is cheap, buying it for use is relatively convenient. Now we have already publicized an advance-sale agreement and will issue books by period. Each school and library especially should buy it in advance to provide for scholars' examination."[112] Commercial Press also reached out to government authorities in hopes that they would encourage schools and libraries within their jurisdictions to buy *Sibu congkan*.[113]

Through the mechanism of sales to schools and libraries, Commercial Press and Zhonghua Book Company made classical texts widely accessible during the Republican period. Collections like *Sibu beiyao* included the standard scholarly editions and commentaries necessary for basic classical education and research. Insofar as these texts paralleled those of many late imperial woodblock publishers, Zhonghua Book Company can be seen as continuing a trend in popular publishing of literati resources begun in the late imperial period.[114] But Zhonghua differed from its late imperial predecessors by using modern industrial publishing technology and labor practices while selling to modern institutions like public libraries and schools. At the same time, both publishers also published the rare books and fine editions that were essential to more arcane forms of bibliographic, philological, and historical research. To the extent that many of the latter kinds of texts had been sequestered in the private libraries of the lower Yangzi region or the imperial collection itself, the companies' republication projects broke that monopoly and democratized classical learning in important ways.[115] Although these reprinted texts were not readily affordable for the average consumer, aggressive sales to schools and libraries made multiple sets of these texts widely accessible in ways they historically had not been. Even commentators critical of a collection like *Sibu congkan* could grant that the publication of such a collection made accessible books that had previously been out of most people's reach.[116] Such broadened access to the fundamental texts of a classical tradition can be seen as a prominent dynamic of mass publishing in a global comparative context.[117]

From the 1910s through the 1930s, just as these collections were being published, "reorganizing the national heritage" (*zhengli guogu* 整理國故) became a watchword among reformist intellectuals.[118] Such calls for basic education in the classics and renewed critical scholarship fostered new reading publics for classical texts, among groups like university faculty and students.[119] But it was not young, modern-educated scholars like Hu Shi, Gu Jiegang, or Fu Sinian but the older generation of late Qing literati like Zhang Yuanji, Sun Yuxiu, Lufei Kui, Gao Shixian, and Ding Fuzhi who did some of the most fundamental work of that reorganization: selecting, collecting, and republishing large collections of classical texts. As with the dictionaries and textbooks discussed in chapter 3, intellectuals working in publishing circles, outside the main institutions of higher learning, had a huge impact on the cultural trends of the modern period by producing the texts that became the basic resources for various kinds of intellectual inquiry. These late Qing scholars utilized the social and cultural capital of the late imperial period, especially the mobilization of social networks and the study of editions, to create these series. Modern, industrial cultural production here depended on forms of cultural knowledge and social practice that had long histories. But at the same time, industrialized printing infrastructure, assembly-line production, and the publishing companies' unprecedented distribution systems made possible the publication and dissemination of a large number of extensive book collections that fulfilled a deep-seated Confucian imperative to preserve the cultural tradition and nonelite Qing scholars' aspirations to democratize knowledge. Through this classical publishing, Shanghai's commercial publishing companies, more than the unsettled Republican state, served as the primary stewards of China's cultural heritage.

As a selective process, republication inevitably reconfigures and reconstitutes classical traditions, even while preserving and passing them on. Insofar as these republished texts came to constitute the most accessible source base for classical scholarship, they played a fundamental role in production of knowledge about the Chinese past. In reviewing the collections discussed here, several dynamics of reconfiguration are most obvious, although experts in classical thought and literature can undoubtedly identify subtler though no less substantial impacts resulting from compilers' selection of particular texts and editions. As noted, Commercial Press's publication of selections from the *Complete Book of the Four Treasuries* raised sensitive questions about whether to reproduce texts altered for political reasons during the Qing period or to substitute ostensibly more "authentic" earlier editions. At the same time, the exclusion of Qing-era commentaries from *Sibu congkan* resigned to silence a whole era of critical scholarship that had opened the classical tradition to unprecedented scrutiny, while *Sibu beiyao* made them readily available to Republican scholars. Further, Zhang Yuanji and Sun Yuxiu's emphasis on early, rare editions from the Song, Yuan, and Ming in constructing *Sibu congkan* perpetuated what one could call the bibliographic fetishism of the Jiangnan elite. In this way, that collection encapsulates in printed form the values of connoisseurship and refined consumption associated with that group. This elitist mentality of tasteful selectivity stood in some tension with the overall project of circulation and dissemination that inspired these projects. But it also contributed to building Zhang's and Sun's reputations as classical scholars and rare-book collectors, cementing their cultural authority in vital ways.

CHAPTER V

Introducing New Worlds of Knowledge

*Series Publications and the Transformation of
China's Knowledge Culture*

I n the fall of 1932, Commercial Press general manager Wang Yunwu
sent letters to dozens of leading scholars throughout China inviting
them to join a University Series Committee (Daxue congshu weiyuanhui).[1] He called upon the scholars to help Commercial Press formulate
a comprehensive catalog that would support the university curriculum for
all China's universities, solicit manuscripts from their colleagues and students, and review manuscripts in their fields of expertise.[2] Wang's goal for
the University Series was to provide university-level textbooks in Chinese
for each subject area and discipline in China's system of higher learning. By
the spring of 1933, Wang had consolidated an editorial committee of more
than fifty prominent scholars. As of that summer dozens of academic manuscripts were in various stages of preparation, review, and production for
Commercial Press, contributing to its postreconstruction goal of publishing "one new title each day."[3] Publication of the University Series would
continue through the rest of the Nanjing decade, the War of Resistance to
Japan, the Civil War, and into the 1950s, after the founding of the People's
Republic, well after Wang Yunwu had left Commercial Press.

The University Series exemplifies the close partnership that developed
between China's commercial publishers and its leading scholars during the
1920s and 1930s. That partnership yielded multiple large-scale series publications, including Zhonghua's New Culture Series (Xin wenhua congshu), Commercial Press's Complete Library (Wanyou wenku), and World

Book Company's ABC Series (ABC congshu), that offered readers thousands of volumes on virtually every subject of modern learning. The series benefited both the publishers and the scholars. Publishing companies were able to diversify their product lines and satisfy the growing demand for more in-depth studies of each academic discipline. For their part, scholars could publish books that helped establish their disciplines and their reputations while also earning extra income through royalties or manuscript fees. As these publication series grew in size and diversity over the decades, the landscape of Chinese intellectual life was reshaped.

A persistent tension in these series was how popular or professionalized they would be. China's publishers here confronted a global quandary. At roughly the same time in the United States, for instance, we see a divergence between "middlebrow" publications that "popularized" academic knowledge for a mass public, on the one hand, and, on the other, increasingly specialized and narrow academic publishing.[4] In Republican China this tension took shape in discussions about how much series would present "ordinary knowledge" (*changshi*) to the "general reading public" (*yiban dushujie*) and to what extent they would be specialized or professionalized (*zhuanye*). In fashioning the Complete Library during the 1920s, Wang Yunwu sought to elide this tension by offering general readers a comprehensive collection of monographs that introduced the newest academic learning in China in accessible ways. In practice, these two extremes proved difficult to balance. In the late 1920s World Book Company offered an ostensibly more popular alternative in the ABC Series, which explicitly sought to make ordinary knowledge more accessible. Soon thereafter, Wang Yunwu himself aimed to capture the more specialized academic market through publication of the University Series. Nonetheless, certain overlaps in the kinds of authors who wrote for the series and the books deployed for them meant that relatively specialized academic writing continued to reach China's general reading public through the Republican period, into the 1950s, blurring strict hierarchies among readers.

To examine the dynamics of cultural production for series publications, I make extensive use of prefaces (*xu* 序, *xuyan* 序言), introductions (*liyan* 例言), reading instructions (*fanli* 凡例), postscripts (*bawen* 跋文), reference-book lists, and other kinds of paratext. Paratext supplements the main text in ways that potentially reframe it and reveal information about its course of production.[5] In Republican China, prefaces to academic books were a hybrid cultural form. They increasingly incorporated new discursive modes influenced by Western academic norms, such as explaining the book's provenance, locating it in a discursive field, documenting the material used, mapping a research strategy, and acknowledging help from mentors and colleagues. Yet we also see continuation of some late imperial patterns, where the preface served as a forum to praise the author and work and to frame it in relation to an existing literature and intellectual genealogy in order to lend it credibility.[6]

The prefaces of series monographs illuminate the relationship between authors and the publishers as well as processes of intellectual production during this formative period for China's academic disciplines. In particular, they indicate that the dominant mode of academic production from the 1920s into the 1950s was what I call synthetic construction. That is, series authors frequently drew on a range of seminal work by foreign authors that they then synthesized to represent a particular subject or a field and connected to the Chinese context. My interpretive approach to this writing strategy is informed by the work of Lydia Liu, who has alerted us to how translation is a "translingual practice" that reconstitutes language and concepts in a new cultural and intellectual context, and Michael Hill, who asks "how a translation relates itself to local political and cultural discourses."[7] Through series monographs, we can see these Chinese academics reconfiguring fields of knowledge for China through their selection, interpretation, juxtaposition, and representation of foreign scholarly work.

New Culture and New Books

Publication of book series to introduce Western learning to China had started during the late nineteenth century. As Benjamin Elman's pathbreaking research on the history of science has shown, missionary translators and government translation bureaus produced several series of translations of seminal works and introductory textbooks focused on natural science, mathematics, and social science starting in the 1870s and continuing through the turn of the century.[8] But several changes in the decades between the late nineteenth century and the 1920s led to resurgent demand for more extensive and more specialized series publications on foreign knowledge. For one, these decades witnessed the consolidation of modern academic disciplines and their institutionalization in research universities in the United States, Europe, and Japan, generating fields of learning that were increasingly elaborated and professionalized.[9] At the same time, self-funded and government-supported overseas studies exposed increasing numbers of Chinese students to these newly institutionalized academic disciplines, whose methods they brought back with them to China.[10] In addition, New Culture calls for thoroughgoing cultural reform encouraged more exhaustive and in-depth inquiry into foreign systems of ideas, without the filter of Protestant Christianity, which had inflected the early translation projects in which missionaries were involved. These trends culminated in a new era of publishing series focused on foreign learning.

Zhonghua Book Company moved first to compile books addressing new cultural and intellectual currents in 1919 and 1920. Zhonghua established a New Books Division (Xinshubu) in its Editing Department in 1920 and recruited editorial staff from the members of the Young China Association (Shaonian Zhongguo xuehui), an active force in New Culture activities during the early 1920s.[11] Zuo Shunsheng 左舜生[12] soon assumed leadership of the New Books Division, and he immediately reached out to the network of young intellectuals who were active in the Young China Association and the New Culture Movement more broadly to secure manuscripts on new research topics. These manuscripts became the basis for the New Culture Series. "So I still sent out thirty or forty special letters seeking manuscripts, and I asked them to introduce other friends who were appropriate for carrying out this kind of work. Before about two months, I received a number of replies from inside and outside the country, and there were already more than a dozen agreed-upon manuscripts. So I made a great fanfare and in each of Shanghai's newspapers issued a so-called new book advance notice of publication!"[13]

Among the main group of authors, thirteen had studied abroad, fourteen had teaching positions in universities or higher normal schools, and four worked in the Zhonghua Editing Department at some point during the 1920s. Several in the group published multiple books in the series, topped by German-educated engineer Ma Junwu 馬君武, who published seven titles in all.[14] Ma, it seems, had been sitting on several translation manuscripts, such as Darwin's *Origin of Species* and Haeckel's *Monistic Philosophy*; Zuo's solicitation provided a convenient outlet for publication.[15]

Overall, the series was dominated by translated foreign works and overviews of particular topics that synthesized foreign scholarship. Historian Zou Zhenhuan calculates that twenty-six of forty-three titles, more than 60 percent, were translations.[16] As William Alford has shown, there were virtually no legal constraints of copyright on Chinese companies publishing translations of foreign works throughout the Republican period, creating a lucrative commercial opportunity.[17] Other books drew together material from foreign scholarship and synthesized it to provide an overview of particular subject areas or included revised lecture notes prepared for teaching college classes to survey a subject area. We see this approach with Miao Fenglin's 繆鳳林 record of Liu Boming's 劉伯明 lectures about modern Western philosophy at Southeastern Higher Normal University in Nanjing and Liu Bingli's lectures for a course on social problems at National Jinan University.[18]

Many of the topics addressed central areas of concern for intellectuals involved in the New Culture Movement. For instance, Yu Jiaju's 余家菊 translation of Rudolf Eucken's study of philosophical theories of the meaning and value of human life spoke to contemporary debates on the "philosophy of life."[19] The series also included more leftist themes as well, reflecting the trends of social thought during this phase of the New Culture Movement. For example, future Chinese Communist Party member Li Da 李達 translated a Dutch introduction to historical materialism, with the recommendation that "anyone who wants to study, criticize, or oppose socialism at the very least must read this book twice."[20] Cai Yongchang 蔡詠裳 and Dong Shaoming 懂紹明 translated a book by an American journalist on women's situation in the Soviet Union, a title that addressed social reformers' overall interest in women's issues and in social and political conditions in the USSR after the Russian Revolution.[21]

There was also a heavy concentration of social science work that aimed at analyzing the central dynamics of modern society, economics, and politics to contribute to China's overall process of development. For instance, Ma Junwu translated five titles by the Austrian political economist Eugen Philippovich on development policies of various kinds, which Ma characterized as "national livelihood policies" (guomin shengji zhengce 國民生計政策). Ma viewed these studies as providing a resource for those who would promote economic development in China, as he articulated in the preface of his study of transportation policy.[22] Later in the arc of the series, by the late 1920s and early 1930s, it also included several works summarizing Western social theories and social science methodologies.[23] These books aimed to provide tools for a Chinese readership to grasp an increasingly complex society. For example, Xu Sitong noted that the social sciences were developing quickly in response to the increasing social complexity of modernizing societies.[24] His book was intended to guide people through the variety of social theories that had been formulated in the foreign academic literature.

The New Culture Series' focus on issues of social and cultural reform, social theory, and social policy reflected its genealogy as an organic outgrowth of the New Culture Movement, as mediated by members of the Young China Society. But the list's very focus and cohesion, rare in later series, could equally be perceived as a problem as readers in the 1920s sought access to broader vistas of knowledge. We get a taste of this demand for more comprehensive publications encompassing a wider range of subjects from a review of the New Culture Series in the journal *Youth Society Semimonthly (Shaonian shehui banyuekan)*.

> The World Series and New Culture Series are already being compiled. If in speaking of the meaning of new culture it is wholly limited to philosophy, literature, and sociology, then there is nothing I can say. If we say that the meaning of the new culture encompasses something a little broader, then I feel that "A Record of Ordinary Knowledge" [Changshilu] and "Specialized Books on Higher-Level Science" [Gaodeng kexue zhuanshu] [the narrower sense of science] are not necessarily less important.[25]

The author signals here a nascent demand for more comprehensive publications covering a broader range of disciplines and subjects in modern series publications, in both more generalist and more specialized registers. It was just this broader demand that Wang Yunwu sought to address when he launched his ambitious program of series publications at Commercial Press in 1922.

Complete Libraries for the General Reading Public

When Gao Mengdan hired Wang Yunwu to direct the Editing Department at Commercial Press in 1922, Wang immediately identified that Commercial Press published "books related to the new learning" in a piecemeal way.[26] In fact, redressing this issue was part of Gao and Zhang Yuanji's motivation for hiring a new director of the Editing Department. Wang viewed the new students and graduates of the Chinese school system as a potential market for more specialized books, and he viewed the positive response to past Jiangnan Arsenal publications as one confirmation of that market.[27] In response, Wang developed a comprehensive plan for publishing multiple series of books, with a target of one hundred titles for each, that would greatly expand Commercial Press's overall list of publications.[28] When compared with Zhonghua's New Culture Series, the scale and diversity of Wang's plan was enormous. For Wang each major field of learning provided an opportunity to publish dozens of books on more specific topics. Fields and subjects, here, became placeholders for potential print commodities that Wang hoped Commercial Press could supply to a Chinese market of readers eager for exposure to modern, Western thought. Wang, the autodidact from a petty bourgeois commercial background, showed no scruples about commodifying new fields of learning.

The idea that all members of the Chinese reading public should encounter new fields of learning like forestry, scientific knowledge about cotton fibers, or the economic theories of Friedrich List marked a major transition in China's "knowledge culture."[29] By "knowledge culture" we mean the cultural practices and schemas that inform judgments about legitimate knowledge, its categorization, as well as its representation and circulation, including how open and accessible it is socially.[30] By the early 1920s, Confucian culture no longer provided the primary basis for judgments about what constituted valid knowledge, even in the hitherto privileged domains of ethics, politics, and social theory.[31] Instead, Western sciences and academic disciplines were taken as the standard, creating an imperative for the educated Chinese public to have some knowledge of those fields. This imperative was clearly reflected in the promotional material about the series Commercial Press began publishing in the 1920s. In listing the main objectives for the Complete Library, which, starting in 1929, integrated all the series published earlier in the 1920s, the introduction to the series stated that a primary goal was to "instill the learning necessary for human life in the general reading public [*yiban dushu jie*]."[32] This new knowledge culture reflected a hegemonic conception of civic republicanism and mass nationalism framed by early twentieth-century political theorists and promulgated widely over the following decades.[33] This vision posited a national public of conscious, active, modern citizens who could contribute to national development. In this political context, academic knowledge was perceived as being able to contribute to the collective project of nation formation through wide dissemination rather than marking a closed circle of individual readers as cultured and elite. The imperative to educate a modern citizenry created a rationale, and a business opportunity, for Commercial Press's large-scale publishing of each series during the 1920s. Wang Yunwu could imagine the entire "general reading public" being potential customers for books about Western academic subjects.

Publication of the series was possible only through the coordinated efforts of a large number of intellectuals, many of whom had the most current and sophisticated understanding of foreign sciences, social sciences, and humanities available in China at that time.[34] Given the great diversity of subjects and titles included in the combined series he proposed, Wang inevitably had to solicit or accept manuscripts from scholars working outside the company for many topics, often purchasing manuscripts so the company could secure the copyright.[35] Still, for the first collection of the Complete Library, which was compiled primarily before Commercial Press's reorganization of the Editing Department in 1932, scholars whom Wang had recruited to work for the publisher often contributed to the series in multiple ways, producing significant portions of it.

The example of Harvard-trained meteorologist and geographer Zhu Kezhen 竺可楨 gives some sense of how the foreign-educated intellectuals Wang recruited in the 1920s facilitated the publisher's massive publication of series during the 1920s and 1930s.[36] Wang Yunwu hired Zhu to serve as director of the History and Geography Division of the Editing Department in the mid-1920s, and he contributed to producing these series in multiple ways.[37] For the series Chinese Translations of World-Famous Works, Zhu reviewed Zhang Qiyun's translation of Bowman's *The New World*. For the National Learning Small Series he wrote a volume called *Chinese People's Cosmological View* (*Zhongguo ren zhi yuzhouguan*). For the New-Era History and Geography Series, Zhu reviewed books on the Mongolian problem, world geography, and human geography. And for the Universal Library he wrote the volumes *Meteorology* (*Qixiangxue*), *A Short History of Geology* (*Dizhixue xiaoshi*), and *Geography* (*Dilixue*). Zhu's varied activities suggest how the Editing Department staff Wang recruited produced extensive content for the series that was at the cutting edge of Chinese scholarship at that time.

By 1929 the titles in Wang's series were mounting to the level where he felt confident introducing the Complete Library,[38] which packaged all the discrete series published during the previous decade as a comprehensive product. Working from a base of roughly four hundred volumes that had been produced by 1929, Wang sought to fill in and expand these series to a complete set with one thousand titles printed in two thousand volumes.[39] The goal was to generate the whole series in five installments between 1929 and 1931. In practice, the January 28 Incident of 1932, which destroyed much of the Commercial Press complex, delayed completion of the first collection until the end of 1933.[40] When purchased by advance order, the whole series cost three hundred sixty yuan; when purchased by regular installments, the total price was four hundred twenty yuan.[41] The second collection of titles for the Complete Library, which included an expanded list on national learning (*guoxue*), significantly more Chinese translations of famous foreign works, a series on natural science, and one on modern problems or issues (*xiandai wenti*), included seven hundred titles in two thousand volumes. It was completed only in 1939, two years after the start of the Second Sino-Japanese War.[42] The achievement was, nonetheless, impressive. Within two decades Commercial Press had organized and published a comprehensive collection of Chinese and Western science, social sciences, humanities, and literature, despite the destruction of most of the company's physical plant in 1932 and the onset of a war that engulfed the publishing center of Shanghai in 1937.

In terms of content, the Complete Library offered the average reader foundational texts in all the major Western academic disciplines and literary traditions, as well as basic materials for Chinese "national learning" (*guoxue*).[43] The component series were complementary. The encyclopedic Universal Library (Baike xiao congshu), which contained the largest number of titles in the first collection, offered short monographs on many modern topics and fields of learning as well as aspects of Chinese thought, literature, and culture. Each series dedicated to an academic discipline (history and geography, natural science, pedagogy, etc.) contained more indepth studies, on the principle "each volume concentrates on discussing one issue." According to Li Jiaju's calculation, titles focused on science, technology, and medicine numbered 323, or 30.97 percent of the total, while books concerned with history, philosophy, and the social sciences (economics, politics, psychology, education, law, geography, sociology, and anthropology) numbered 405 titles, or 38.82 percent of the total.[44] Clearly, the publishing of scientific texts remained a major priority, as it had since the late Qing. The significant proportion of publications in areas like economics, education, law, and politics reflects the concern with understanding and managing society and social problems that gained momentum during the Republican period.[45] Continued publication of many works in the fields of history, geography, and philosophy indicates how late imperial scholarly patterns continued to shape book markets and publishing priorities in the twentieth century. The series Chinese Translations of World-Famous Works contained two hundred fifty translations of iconic Western scholarly works, philosophy, and literature, providing even more specific background in particular subjects and fields. The Complete Library, in sum, allowed for both breadth of coverage and progressive depth of learning on a whole range of modern subjects. At the same time, the Complete Library also included a substantial number of classical Chinese texts and scholarship in the National Learning Basic Series and the Student National Learning Series.

Wang Yunwu's consolidation of large series into the Complete Library revealed his capacity to vary packaging to create new products.[46] He increasingly viewed written text as malleable content that he could shape and reorganize into a whole range of products rather than viewing the book as a discrete object that was the inspiration and creative product of an autonomous author.[47] In Chinese Translations of World-Famous Works, for instance, the series editors bundled numerous translations by Yan Fu and Lin Shu from earlier in the twentieth century as representative examples of world-famous scholarship and literature.

Such repackaging could help to keep production costs down for large-scale publications like the individual series and the Complete Library. Still, the price of the Complete Library (three hundred sixty to four hundred twenty yuan for each collection) was clearly prohibitive for many individual readers and households during the 1920s and 1930s.[48] However, as with the reprint series of classical texts discussed in chapter 4, Wang Yunwu's marketing strategy was not aimed at individual consumers but at libraries or institutions (schools, companies, government offices) and individuals or groups intent on establishing or building a library. In explaining the inspiration for the Complete Library, Wang referenced the slow growth and development of libraries in China and his intention that this series publication could, in effect, provide a complete, instant library.[49] "My ideal thus was to help each locality, school, and organization, as well as even many families, for an extremely low price, set up libraries that were similar in shape [to Commercial Press's Eastern Library, Dongfang tushuguan] but smaller in proportion and simplify to an extreme degree these libraries' classifying, cataloging, and other management work."[50] The Complete Library's books, with their uniform covers and forms, had cataloging numbers on the side and came with catalog cards for each title that allowed customers to immediately create a card catalog and shelving system for the books (figure 5.1).

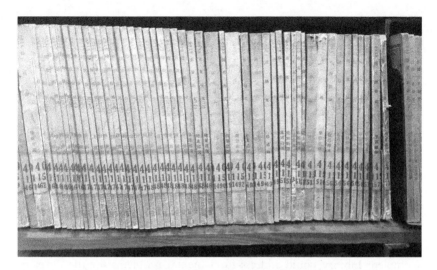

Figure 5.1 Titles from the Complete Library showing their call numbers. The call numbers in black on the bottom were provided by Commercial Press with the original publication; the numbers in red were added by the library where the books are currently held.

Wang and Commercial Press thus emphasized a marketing approach for this large-scale publication that identified institutions and institution builders as the most likely potential customers. It was a strategy that balanced the economic constraints of Republican China with the intellectual ambition to expose the whole reading public to the broadest possible cross section of modern learning. In contrast, American publishing strategies such as Book-of-the-Month Club and Pocket Books, clearly targeted individual consumers. Wang's strategy of identifying libraries and library builders as the main consumers of this massive collection of Commercial Press books was also related to his own experience as a self-taught man.[51]

In practice, Commercial Press directly targeted institutional customers with marketing appeals and emphasized the series' ability to provide a base collection for a library. As the journal *Reading Monthly* (*Dushu yuekan*) recounted,

> For the Complete Library published by Commercial Press, previously because the books were numerous and the price was too great, private individuals mostly could not afford to buy it, so the market demand was very small and the loss of money great. Later the

manager, Wang Yunwu, used lots of techniques, besides widely publishing advertisements in each large newspaper every day, also repeatedly contacting each area's library and public organizations, and now the Complete Library's market demand has increased greatly over what it was previously.[52]

As I have elaborated elsewhere, the publisher's branch managers directly contacted provincial and municipal governments throughout the country, sending promotional materials like samples, and urged them to direct their subordinate organs and educational institutions to purchase the series, which many governments accordingly did.[53] In promoting the series to regional and local government leaders, Commercial Press's branch managers emphasized the underdeveloped state of China's libraries and argued that the Complete Library could address fundamental problems for the development of libraries, such as the cost of building a collection, choosing texts to make a balanced collection, and developing a system to categorize and organize the books. To make purchase of the series more attractive, Commercial Press offered various discounts, especially when provincial governments coordinated orders with subordinate units to order several dozen sets at once. To help subordinate institutions purchase the series, provincial governments could also provide matching funds or approve creative financing arrangements to take advantage of time-sensitive advanced purchasing agreements. In the end, many local governments, schools, and social organizations ended up purchasing the Complete Library, thereby spreading knowledge from all over the world to all corners of the country. The print run of five thousand sets of the first collection of the series was sold out by the time the second collection was launched in 1934.[54] The excitement and anticipation palpable in the announcements of the sets' arrival at school libraries throughout the country suggest how the series satisfied a nascent demand for comprehensive new learning.[55] By targeting these kinds of institutions for sales, the Complete Library became most accessible to secondary students and higher, government officials, and emergent professional elites.

The Case for Ordinary Knowledge

The scale of Commercial Press's series publications put pressure on its competitors to keep up with both the size and diversity of the Complete

Library while also differentiating themselves in some way. Zhonghua Book Company, for instance, was, by the mid-1930s, offering readers more than eighty distinct libraries (*wenku*), collections (*ji*), and series (*congshu*) in ten different thematic groups, many of them targeted at young readers.[56] But many of the lists were small and relatively undeveloped, featuring just a handful of titles.[57] World Book Company's response was to launch the ABC Series, which was designed to be at once comprehensive and accessible, in ways similar to Commercial Press's Universal Library. Developed quickly in 1928 and 1929, in step with Wang Yunwu's bundling of Commercial Press's series in the Complete Library, the ABC Series constituted a sustained effort to compete with Commercial Press's extensive series publications.

World's founder, Shen Zhifang, and leading editor, Xu Weinan 徐慰南, titled their collection the ABC Series with the goal of emphasizing the basic, accessible nature of the titles in the series. As Xu put it in his introduction to the series, "In Western languages the explanation of ABC is each kind of learning's steps and outline. Each kind of learning in the West has its ABC."[58] He went on to emphasize the popular nature of the material the series would present. "Just as with the ABC books in the West, we want to take each kind of learning and popularize it and universalize it, to make everyone have an opportunity to obtain each kind of learning and make everyone able to find access to each kind of learning. We want to liberate each kind of learning from the grasp of the intellectual class and disseminate it to give to the whole populace. The ABC Series is popular university education and the fountainhead of new knowledge."[59] Echoing in Xu's statement is a powerful rhetoric of mass education, bringing knowledge to the people, and liberation of knowledge from an intellectual elite that paralleled a range of progressive educational projects during the 1920s.[60] World Book Company sought to differentiate its series as being more popular and accessible than existing series published by rival companies.

At the same time, however, World Book Company sought to compete in terms of both the comprehensiveness and quality of its publications. As with Commercial Press's series, Shen Zhifang and his colleagues organized the ABC Series according to modern academic units. They first divided the whole series into five large sections: (1) literature and arts (*wenyi*); (2) politics and economics (*zhengzhi jingji*); (3) philosophy (*zhexue*); (4) education, history, and geography (*jiaoyu shi di*); and (5) science (*kexue*).[61] Each section was then further broken down into topical categories. "For example, the Literature and Arts Section is divided into (1) National Learning group [*guoxue zu*]; (2) Literature group [*wenxue zu*]; (3) Western Literature group [*Xiyang wenxue zu*]; (4) Folklore group [*minsuxue zu*]; (5) Arts group [*yishu zu*]."[62] Shen Zhifang here followed Wang Yunwu in viewing each discipline and subfield of academic learning and culture as a category for potential commodities. This system of discipline-based organization, which corresponded to academic methods and subjects of instruction in the modern schools, differed fundamentally from late imperial techniques of organizing knowledge. During that period, four broad categories of textual genre predominated (the *sibu*, as outlined in chapter 4), along with what Elman has called the topical arrangement of compendia or encyclopedia.[63] The organization of series publications thus marked a fundamental shift in the way knowledge was ordered in China.

Despite the populist thrust of the series' promotional rhetoric, Shen Zhifang and Xu Weinan also sought to produce high-quality books that could compete with those published by Commercial Press and Zhonghua. To do so they strove to get the support of "famous scholars, specialists, and diligent students" who could write top manuscripts.[64] In writing about the series authors in their journal *World* (*Shijie*), however, the publisher distinguished between the many scholars returning from overseas who had a title but proved to be ineffective scholars and teachers and those who were in fact knowledgeable and effective.[65] Given Commercial Press's active recruitment of returned foreign scholars for its Editing Department throughout the 1920s, it is difficult not to read the magazine's vignette about a teacher with a master's degree from an American university who cannot teach effectively as a dig at just those foreign-trained scholars who were working at the publisher. Still, World Book Company, too, depended, in part, on this tier of returned scholars and leading academics to publish its ambitious series.

The mix of different kinds of authors involved in World Book Company's ABC Series both paralleled and departed from Commercial Press's approach to staffing the Complete Library in several ways.[66] As at Commercial Press, several editors from the publisher's own Editing Department—Zhu Yixin 朱翊新, Wei Bingxin 魏冰心, Lu Dongping 陸東平, and Fan Yunliu 范雲六—contributed volumes. These were confined primarily to educational topics, reflecting the focus on textbook writing of World's Editing Department. But generally speaking, from the start World Book

Company relied more heavily on contributors outside the company to serve as authors for the series. The company tapped Shanghai-area universities for potential authors: specifically, six faculty members from Fudan University and three from the University of Law and Politics, two of whom contributed more than one volume. In addition, it drew widely from faculty at other schools scattered throughout the country and officials in government office. It also solicited a number of manuscripts from the growing urban professional groups and literate elite, such as engineers, editors of other publications, and literary or arts professionals, such as writers, literary critics, or artists. All told, World Book Company depended more heavily on authors outside its own Editing Department, an approach that was more economical than building a stable of authors as Commercial Press had initially done under Wang Yunwu.

In keeping with Xu Weinan's emphasis on elementary learning in the ABC Series' announcement, the list included a number of books on practical features of modern life. For example, it incorporated books on topics such as insurance, finance, surveying, industrial and commercial management, company law, drawing, advertising, and photography. In addressing such nuts-and-bolts topics, the series drifted toward offering readers something like how-to books or the kind of household and industrial general knowledge Eugenia Lean sees Chen Diexian having promoted in his Collection of Household Knowledge (Jiating changshi huibian).[67] This approach eroded somewhat the boundary between theoretical and practical learning that had been a hallmark of the late imperial period.[68] The ABC Series also incorporated several titles on topics like social distribution and the women's movement that preserved the socially progressive impulses of the New Culture Movement and the early phase of the National Revolution that were captured in Zhonghua's New Culture Series.[69]

However, many more of the titles in the ABC Series introduced new fields of learning similar to Commercial Press's thematic series from the early and mid-1920s. Books on various kinds of literature, Chinese and Western, social science fields like sociology, anthropology, and economics, not to mention more applied fields like law, engineering, urban planning, and government administration were all included. In addition, there were many titles on various aspects of education and philosophy, but only a small number of books (ten titles as of 1929) focused on science and technology. As with Commercial Press's and Zhonghua's series, with the ABC

Series we see authors filling out a subject area that accorded with their own expertise. For example, the American-trained sociologist Sun Benwen 孫本文 wrote two monographs, one on the field of sociology and another on population theory, for the series.[70] Engineer Yang Zheming 楊哲明 wrote no fewer than five titles for the ABC Series, which together covered the fields of urban planning, administration, engineering, and roads.[71] In sum, the ABC Series paralleled those initiated by Wang Yunwu in offering introductions to a wide spectrum of Western academic and technical fields.

At both publishers, though, editors imposed constraints on length and expectations about stylistic accessibility that affected the forms books assumed in the ABC Series and the Complete Library. Authors of books for the ABC Series repeatedly cited how word limits, in the range of between thirty thousand and eighty thousand characters, conditioned their choices in terms of breadth of coverage as well as depth and complexity of examples.[72] Authors also strove to make their writing accessible and easy to understand. Similar constraints conditioned the volumes in Commercial Press's Complete Library. When initially organizing the series, Wang envisioned a target length for each title of twenty thousand to forty thousand characters.[73] In practice, the national learning series, Chinese translations of famous Western works, and the history and geography series titles ran somewhat longer, in the range of forty thousand to a hundred thousand characters. The other thematically organized series, however, including the encyclopedic Universal Library, had titles of twenty thousand to forty thousand characters.[74] As with the ABC Series, many Commercial Press authors described how spatial constraints compelled them to select the most essential elements of their field and present the information in a general way for the nonspecialist, sparing extensive detail.[75] As Shen Qianyi 沈乾一 put it in the preface to his *Chinese Medicine*, "Because of restrictions of length, in this book I had to try my best to be succinct."[76] Consequently, many volumes in both series included in their titles such phrases as "short history" (*xiaoshi* 小史), "elementary introduction" (*qianshuo* 淺說), "schematic history" (*lueshi* 略史), "general discussion" (*gailun* 概論), or "outline" (*dagang* 大綱 or *gangyao* 綱要).[77] They had, in other words, the character of an overview or survey of a field or topical area rather than that of an in-depth research monograph. The forms dictated by Wang Yunwu and Shen Zhifang, as well as the goal of comprehensive coverage of whole fields of knowledge, came to shape the organization and content of individual titles in the series.

Specialized Monographs and the Academic Book Market

As mentioned, in the fall of 1932 Wang Yunwu invited a distinguished group of scholars in a wide range of fields to join a committee to coordinate and oversee a collection of more specialized books, the University Series.[78] In reaching out to these intellectuals, Wang stressed two factors.[79] First, he argued that Chinese academic development had been constrained by a lack of Chinese-language textbooks in specialized fields. Depending on foreign-language textbooks was costly for university students and forced them to make extra efforts to read material in a foreign language. In addition, when more specialized books suitable for college-level textbooks were published, they were isolated and not coordinated in any way. In contrast, Wang offered a vision of a comprehensive and organized set of Chinese-language university textbooks for all subjects: "If the whole country's specialized scholars could work together and cooperate, drawing up an entire plan for the subjects proper for universities, and further have all the nation's specialized scholars, according to the subjects in the plan, divide responsibility for writing so there is no duplication, it is expected that through this cooperation, with the implied meaning of dividing labor, after three to five years, these kinds of university books can certainly accumulate over time and present a magnificent sight."[80]

Based on this pitch, by the spring of 1933 Wang Yunwu had recruited more than fifty members of the University Series Committee, which settled at fifty-four members.[81] Only a handful, specifically Wang himself, He Bingsong, and Fu Weiping, were active members of Commercial Press's Compilation and Review Committee, the successor of the Editing Department. The rest were primarily leading academics at universities throughout the country, many of whom had earned advanced degrees from foreign universities. Among them were many familiar leading scholars and educators, such as Hu Shi, Jiang Menglin 蔣夢麟, Fu Sinian 傅斯年, Zhang Boling 張伯苓, Luo Jialun 羅家倫, and Weng Wenhao 翁文灝. Included as well were several intellectuals in the Nationalist Party who played key roles in educational administration during the Nanjing decade, such as Wang Shijie 王世杰, Zhu Jiahua 朱家驊, and Cai Yuanpei. Still, a number of scholars active on the committee had been members of the Commercial Press Editing Department during the 1920s, including Ren Hongjun, Zhu Jingnong, Zhu Kezhen, Bing Zhi, Tao Menghe, Tang Cheng, Zheng Zhenwen, Zheng Zhenduo, and Gu Jiegang. Others, such as Ma Junwu and Guo

Renyuan, had been involved in World Book Company's ABC Series. As with the *Siku quanshu zhenben* project, the editorial committee provided Wang with a mechanism to formalize relationships with leading intellectuals without bearing the burden of paying their ever-growing salaries.

Wang planned for the committee to "(1) Draw up an overall catalog [*quanmu*] for the University Series. (2) Introduce or collect manuscripts for the University Series. (3) Review [*shencha*] book manuscripts for this series."[82] In some ways, the first of these steps was the most challenging, for it entailed drafting a comprehensive curriculum that would balance the approaches of all China's universities. Commercial Press's Compilation and Review Committee made a first pass at compiling the overall catalog for the series, then the committee sent it out for review to members of the University Series Committee.[83] After compiling the suggestions, Commercial Press published a preliminary catalog and again solicited suggestions from the committee, which it incorporated into a final version of the catalog in the summer of 1933.[84] The process culminated in an expansive catalog divided into 8 "colleges" (*xueyuan*), 33 "departments" or disciplines (*xibie*), and 737 subjects (*kemu*).[85] The colleges encompassed the humanities, science, law, education, agriculture, engineering, business, and medicine.

By reaching out to scholars throughout the country, Wang and his colleagues had formulated a comprehensive curriculum for higher education that coordinated the distinctive approaches of China's various universities, something the Nationalist Party was able to execute fully only during extraordinary wartime conditions.[86] At a time when the Ministry of Education was intervening more directly in colleges and universities nationally, Commercial Press provided a forum for Chinese intellectuals to formulate their own vision of higher education.[87] The catalog certainly reflected Nationalist Party concerns for cultivating technical education to support national construction, with 153 subjects outlined for natural science (*li*) and 196 subjects outlined for engineering (*gong*).[88] Yet it also included very robust curricula in humanities fields (136 subjects) like literature, philosophy, and history, which the party was actively trying to discourage. Commercial Press operated as a competing center for organizing academic life in modern China by providing intellectuals with a platform to express their vision of higher education. It could do so because the publisher offered a mechanism—industrial publishing—that would allow intellectuals to realize that vision in a set of specialized textbooks for each academic subject area. For the company, the University Series catalog provided a prospectus for some 737 publications across a range of disciplines, which allowed it to diversify once more its products for a new and growing audience at the highest level of the school system.

Commercial Press first tapped into its own backlist to jump-start the series. The Compilation and Review Committee selected existing titles that fit the subject categories in the University Series catalog and submitted them to the committee for review.[89] These titles included popular publications from the 1910s and 1920s, such as Hu Shi's *History of Chinese Philosophy* (*Zhongguo zhexue shi dagang*), a translation of H. G. Wells's *The Outline of History* (*Shijie shi gang*) by Liang Sicheng and others, and Lü Simian's *Vernacular Chinese History* (*Baihua benguoshi*). Selecting titles from its backlist allowed Commercial Press to repackage existing publications, leveraging fungible text to fashion new products. Although, some commentators questioned whether in some instances Commercial Press had created some subject categories in order to accommodate existing works rather than applying existing works to subjects that were viewed as desirable on first principles.[90] In practice, by 1935 the titles that were published and approved clustered in the humanities (35 of 136 subjects), education (23 of 46 subjects), and law (36 of 81 subjects).[91] In contrast, the sciences (17 of 153 subjects), engineering (10 of 196 subjects), and other technical fields had very few existing publications to draw on, creating an opportunity for intellectuals in those fields to craft books that would provide new titles for the company.

As noted, Wang and his colleagues expected the University Series Committee to solicit and recommend manuscripts. By the spring and summer of 1933, Wang was already fielding suggestions of possible publications for the series, which the committee had to coordinate with the newly formulated subject areas and existing titles.[92] Aside from the fees for reviewing manuscripts,[93] the ability to solicit and recommend manuscripts would have been an attractive motivation for participating in the committee, for it offered intellectuals an opportunity to support their patronage networks by channeling publishing opportunities toward their students and colleagues. The company offered authors a standard 15 percent royalty for each title.[94] But perhaps more importantly, it invited a scholar to write the monograph that would represent a subject in the comprehensive curriculum of the University Series catalog. With a projected word length of one hundred fifty thousand to three hundred thousand characters per title, the University Series allowed authors to explore complex academic topics in greater depth than had been true of the titles in the Complete Library or the ABC Series.[95]

In response, Commercial Press drew a steady stream of manuscripts. As of 1935 185 titles were in the process of being compiled for the University Series, with large numbers coming in the technical fields that were most underrepresented in the existing list.[96] These books contributed to a diversification of the publisher's production, such that in the five years prior to 1937, books for general use, like those in the Complete Library, and university textbooks surpassed the quantity of textbooks the company published.[97] For example, in 1935 Commercial Press published 781 titles of ordinary books compared with 103 titles of textbooks, and the business in ordinary books and magazines surpassed that of textbooks, which together garnered the company an overall profit that year of 1.04 million yuan.[98] In 1936 ordinary books constituted 41 percent of the company's business (compared with 32 percent for textbooks), and the company earned profits of 1.19 million yuan.[99]

When the Sino-Japanese War started in the summer of 1937, many manuscripts completed in the late 1930s awaited publication until later in the war or the postwar period, when Commercial Press's printing facilities were stable enough to resume publication. Authors' prefaces reveal how the vicissitudes of war affected the material production of books that committed authors continued to write regardless of wartime displacement and disturbance. For instance, Li Chaoying's 李超英 comparative study of public finance systems built on an English volume about the Chinese public finance system the author had published in 1936. The revised and expanded Chinese manuscript was completed in 1940, but the manuscript and plates of the first printing in Hong Kong in December 1941 were destroyed with the Japanese invasion and occupation. Fortunately, Li had kept a copy, which was finally published in Chongqing in 1943.[100] Reprinting existing titles for the University Series and publishing new titles, which required relatively little editorial work, became a key area of publication for Commercial Press in Chongqing during the War of Resistance.[101] A survey of extant copies of the University Series held at Shanghai Municipal Library reveals that as many as seventy-four new titles in the series were first published during the war (in Changsha or Hong Kong and then Chongqing) and in the postwar period. Even with the displacement and disruption of war, the project of filling out the library of academic publications continued, serving as an important economic resource for Commercial Press.

Producing Scholarship and Academic Reputations

Despite minor variations in the goals and composition of the series offered by the three major publishers, when surveyed from the early 1920s into the late 1940s we see certain common features of their production. Together, these aspects combined to form a distinctive dynamic of Chinese monographic book publishing in the Republican period. These series all offered Chinese intellectuals opportunities to craft books that covered a particular field or subject, at once establishing that field and their reputations in the public domain. But instead of presenting original research, authors most often synthesized the foreign literature that dominated a field or subject and sought to make it relevant to the Chinese context of nation building, self-defense, and national construction. Through this process, authors sometimes made arcane academic subjects the purview of a broad readership in a way that linked learning to the nation's welfare.

Contributors to series publications frequently cited an absence of Chinese-language works in their field as a primary motivation for wanting to write a book for the series. Authors in Commercial Press's Pedagogical Series (Shifan congshu) repeatedly emphasized the need to publish books on particular subfields of education in order to provide a basis for their development in China.[102] As series author Wu Junsheng 吳俊升 expressed, he revised his lecture notes on educational philosophy at Beida to publish as a monograph in the series in part "because in publishing circles works having to do with educational philosophy are still too few."[103] Common to these publications, and many others in the Complete Library, was the goal of publishing particular works to address needs in the education field more broadly by establishing a specific subfield, providing foundational academic resources in the Chinese language, or introducing methods essential to the development of the field.[104] Similar concerns were expressed in many of the prefaces of books in Commercial Press's University Series, which often focused on very specialized subject areas.[105] But even with the more popular ABC Series, authors often noted a dearth of books in a given subject area that their book was meant to address.[106]

By writing or translating foundational works, intellectuals contributed to developing particular fields or subfields in China while also grounding their own reputations through public discourse. By promoting a discipline, they established themselves as authorities and experts both in academic circles and in the public eye. For instance, Liu Binglin 劉秉麟 implicitly claimed broad expertise in political economy by producing synthetic overviews of Adam Smith, Friedrich List, and David Ricardo for the Universal Library series, essentially surveying the key figures in the political theory field to inform the understanding of Chinese readers.[107] Similarly, by publishing no fewer than five books for the ABC Series on various aspects of urban planning and administration, Yang Zheming introduced the discipline while also establishing himself as one of China's leading experts in it.[108] We see a similar dynamic with sociologist Sun Benwen, who published two volumes in the ABC Series (one on demography and another on sociology), edited a short series on sociology for World Book Company, and for the University Series published books on principles of sociology, social psychology, and four volumes on China's modern social problems. This prolific output over two decades helped develop the field of sociology in China while also identifying Sun Benwen as one of its leading experts.[109] In short, monographs in series served to establish disciplines, fields, and scholars.

Supporting prefaces by well-known, leading scholars could give books and their authors a powerful endorsement in a form similar to how prefaces had been used in China during the late imperial period.[110] Rhetorically, authors themselves could also use prefaces and introductions to explicitly claim expertise on a certain subject. For example, in the preface of his introduction to Malthus's *On Population*, Lin Kui 林骙 demonstrated command of the critical Western literature on Malthus and his informed opinions about the relative importance of different editions of the author's work.[111] By contrasting his nuanced views with reductionist interpretations, Lin established himself as an expert in Malthus's thought while making the case that understanding it was essential for "late developers" (*houjinzhe*) like China. Similarly, in Dong Wenqiao's 董問樵 study of national defense economics, written for the University Series and published during the war, the author claimed expertise based on a decade of study in Germany, England, and France.[112] Those claims were reinforced by references to encouragement of his research by leading defense scholars Jiang Baili and Yang Gengguang. Dong could also point to the wartime context to establish the vital nature of his work.[113] By demonstrating expertise in published specialized work that had current relevance, Chinese scholars claimed status and intellectual authority in their society in a different idiom than had Confucian scholars during the late imperial period, relating foreign scholarship to China's place in a competitive world. At the same time, by speaking as experts through a popular medium intended to expose the public to modern knowledge, Chinese scholars escaped the tension between specialized knowledge and popularization that began to confront American scholars at this time.

When we turn our focus to how these books were written, we also find many common features. Immediately striking is the large percentage of books that grew out of collections of lecture notes for classes at universities.[114] For example, Wu Shirui's 吳世瑞 preface explained in detail how he progressively built up his lecture notes over successive terms at three different schools to serve as the basis for his monograph, *Principles of Economics*.[115] Intellectuals teaching in China's new universities responded to the lack of appropriate Chinese-language textbooks by putting together compilations of lecture notes, often circulated to students in printed form, that provided the basis for monographs published by the major publishers.

To form these lectures and the monographs that grew out of them, the scholars most often engaged in a process I characterize as synthetic construction. They drew from wide collections of mostly foreign academic literature, synthesized them from their own intellectual perspective, incorporated material about China, and related the subject to the Chinese context. In exploring this process of synthetic construction, I seek to build on and extend Meng Yue's insightful characterization of late Qing and early Republican compilers at Commercial Press as taking part in what she calls transcompilation, which produced "many 'translations' that were actually paraphrases, interpretations, expansions, or contractions."[116] Reflecting on the later period of the 1920s through the 1950s, we see certain continuities in that Chinese intellectuals were actively engaging new systems of foreign thought even as they introduced them into the Chinese context. However, as described in chapter 2, many intellectuals of the 1920s and later often had extensive exposure to Western learning and disciplinary expertise from long periods of study overseas and a depth of knowledge in particular subject areas that far surpassed that of late Qing literati. Thus, the Republican-period series certainly included many translations of individual foreign works and occasional original research monographs, but they incorporated many more synthetic works. The authors of these studies shaped their subjects according to the scholar's own intellectual background, analyzed tensions and debates in the scholarly literature, and connected that scholarship to the broader sociopolitical context at the time they were writing. The resulting synthetic monographs fit perfectly the leading publishers' demand for books that could "cover" particular fields or subjects.

Examples of the synthetic construction process are evident across the different series discussed here. Sun Benwen's introductions to the field of sociology for the ABC Series and the University Series illustrate how Chinese scholars could synthesize and reformulate foreign theories in different scales of book published in distinct lists.[117] In his brief overview of the field of sociology for the ABC Series, Sun emphasized that "the arrangement of the material in this book emerges from the author's own individual judgment and is not based on the established precedent of any sociology book."[118] Sun was not, in other words, directly translating the approach of a single seminal work, and he articulated a distinctive approach that related social activity to culture (*wenhua*) and attitudes (*taidu*). Further, although he acknowledged drawing on the American sociological literature, he also viewed himself as going beyond previous scholars in focusing on the significance of social behavior, the distinguishing of social elements, the relationship between social standards and social control, and the relationship between cultural maladjustment and social problems.

In his later study *Principles of Sociology*, written for the University Series, Sun explicitly distinguished his work from earlier translations of Western works and emphasized his synthetic approach of combining different arguments and perspectives.[119] Sun continued his emphasis on culture as being fundamental to how human communities could adapt to their conditions and survive, an emphasis that he related back to two American scholars who influenced him, William Ogburn and William I. Thomas.[120] Yet he also related that concern with cultural development as a means of adaptation for survival to the specific context of postrevolutionary China.[121] Further, Sun intentionally used examples from China wherever possible to connect the subject matter to local conditions. In sum, Sun took a synthetic approach to sociology and sought to relate sociological theory to Chinese concerns and Chinese dynamics.

We see similar dynamics in Zhong Luzhai's book *Comparative Education* for the University Series.[122] As with other texts in these series, Zhong began writing up his own lecture notes because there were no appropriate textbooks for courses on this subject. Further, when friends studying in the United States encouraged him to translate a book in this subject by a professor at Columbia University, Zhong passed because he found that the book omitted what he felt were essential subjects. Instead, Zhong incorporated material from that book into his own synthetic approach. Further, throughout the book Zhong would "whenever necessary bring up issues of reform in Chinese education, because the objective of studying comparative education is researching foreign educational systems and methods to serve as lessons or points of reference to improve our country's education."[123] Like Sun, Zhong integrated and reconciled disparate material and approaches while at the same time relating the subject to the Chinese context and agendas.

But Chinese scholars often did not work alone. Beginning in the late 1920s, as Chinese academic life became more specialized and professionalized, prefaces reveal how authors depended on colleagues to review their writing and suggest additions and revisions. For instance, in the preface to his study of educational philosophy for the Pedagogical Small Series, Wu Junsheng recognized help from various mentors and colleagues: "Beijing University president Mr. Jiang Menglin previously read the original manuscript and made corrections while also bestowing a preface. The Central Political School professor Mr. Meng Xiancheng instructed the author a great deal and wrote several letters correcting this book's content. Beijing University professor Mr. Tang Yongtong also read the original manuscript and had corrections."[124] By mentioning leading scholars like Jiang Menglin and Meng Xiancheng, Wu implicitly certified the value of his work. He also indicated how his work was the product of collaboration with others. With publication in the 1930s and 1940s of the University Series, whose books were written primarily by university-based academics, mention of consultation with and review by colleagues became ubiquitous.[125] In his preface to the college-level sociology textbook discussed in the preceding, Sun Benwen thanked no fewer than sixteen colleagues at various institutions.[126] At one level Sun's thanks to colleagues replicates the familiar acknowledgments in American academic writing, which is no surprise given his long period of study in the United States. But we also see signs here, and in the prefaces of other scholars in Sun's generation, of the reconstitution of scholarly networks in modern academic institutions. As intellectuals reviewed one another's work and made suggestions, they re-created in a new institutional context the kinds of collaborative literati networks, continuous with the late imperial period, that we saw providing the basis for republication of classical texts. Academic writing at the highest level remained a collaborative process in China.

Prefaces also reveal ways that Chinese intellectuals depended on unpaid labor of various kinds to produce their writings. In an era before typewriting was common outside business and government contexts and word processing was unimaginable, various forms of textual organization (*zhengli*) and copying (*chaoxie*) were essential to producing books. With the University Series publications, we see multiple instances of teaching assistants (*zhujiao*) and wives doing this work.[127] Zhang Yinian's 章頤年 mention of both kinds of assistance in the preface to his book on mental hygiene was characteristic: "The work of organizing and copying was divided between teaching assistant Ms. Sun Wanhua in the Educational Psychology Department at Daxia University, Shanghai Municipal Central District Experimental Primary School teacher Ms. Lu Guchu, and my wife, Zhaohua."[128]

The dependence on unpaid female labor in the household or the workplace is telling. In the thousands of titles published in the series discussed in this chapter, the number of women authors can be counted on one hand, suggesting that they could rarely claim public recognition as modern intellectuals. Yet as male scholars sought to make companionate marriages with educated young women, their wives could support their intellectual enterprise through the extremely time-consuming work of manuscript organization and copying, as well as, one suspects, other forms of editorial and intellectual work that escaped comment.[129] Women striving for higher education similarly provided a pool of academic labor on which senior male faculty members, acting as mentors and patrons, could draw. While publishers rewarded the mental labor of male intellectuals with manuscript fees and royalties, the labor supplied by their wives, sisters, and female students, assistants, or colleagues was completely unpaid and virtually unrecognized. As a result, in some significant way industrial publishing of scholarly books in China was subsidized by unpaid, highly gendered forms of household and academic production.

By publishing academic books, China's commercial publishers became a leading force shaping the development of intellectual life in modern China. Commercially savvy publishers Wang Yunwu, Shen Zhifang, and, to a lesser degree, Lufei Kui saw an opportunity in the proliferation of scholarly fields and subjects entering Republican China. As they set up competing series, each subject area came to denote a potential commodity that they could produce and sell, with the support of Chinese intellectuals. For those intellectuals, collaboration with the publishers was an opportunity not just for remuneration in the form of salary, manuscript fees, or royalties. In addition, through cooperation with the publishers, intellectuals could use those companies' substantial productive resources to influence the course of Chinese academic development. By writing individual volumes or multiple titles, intellectuals shaped the development of particular fields and subjects. The thousands of translations and synthetic studies published in series from 1920 into the early 1950s served to define, in large part, what modern learning meant to a Chinese reading audience. Through participation in organizing a grand publishing project like the University Series, intellectuals also played a part in designing the structure of Chinese academic life apart from the government intervention that impinged on universities beginning in the 1930s. The economic independence of commercial publishers insulated them from government interference and provided intellectuals with a platform for scholarly expression and a mechanism to imagine a new academic landscape. Thus, publishers in China offered intellectuals a valuable institutional resource for knowledge production apart from the university.

With the resulting series publications, intellectuals and publishers sought to avoid the bifurcation of publishing markets into a popular or middlebrow market, on the one hand, and, on the other, a specialized elite market, as was happening at that very moment in the United States. For the companies, the commercial imperative of trying to maximize sales militated against resigning intellectuals' writings to a narrow market of specialists. We see this even with the more specialized titles of the University Series books, which were pitched both as textbooks for university courses and, in some cases, as reference books for a whole range of readers.[130] Most authors, too, sought a broader readership based in part on the belief that their academic field had potential to contribute to China's national development. This perspective certainly animated scholars of more applied fields like engineering and the natural sciences. But it also inspired those in the humanities and social sciences, who viewed the Chinese people's social and cultural development as a fundamental prerequisite of China's becoming truly modern.

Here the Confucian predilection that knowledge, however seemingly arcane, could be socially and politically transformative informed Chinese intellectual development.[131] Equally important was the logic of national citizenship, which posited a mass public of conscious, active, modern citizens who could dedicate themselves to national construction. In this political context, academic knowledge could contribute to the collective project of nation formation rather than marking individual readers as cultured, which was a primary dynamic in the contemporary West. Consequently, large-scale publishing of scholarly work depended on and contributed to what could be called China's civic republican knowledge culture in the twentieth century. Within that framework, knowledge had value for its potential to inform and underpin a multidimensional project of national development, which spanned economic, political, social, and cultural domains. Moreover, it was geared to a broad public of readers who, as citizens, could contribute to that developmental project. In practice, that readership—and thus the nascent citizenry constituted through print—was made up of secondary and higher-level students, urban professionals, and government workers whose institutions had the resources to buy large collections like the Complete Library.[132]

Writing books that introduced academic fields to a general audience and established their relevance to nation formation also provided authors with a powerful way to establish their reputations. This mode of self-making differed from the logic of heteronomy versus academic exclusivity—that is, writing only for other experts—that Bourdieu saw as operative in the modern French academic and cultural fields.[133] At the same time, writing academic texts for a mass market imposed certain constraints on Chinese scholars. As noted, Wang Yunwu and Shen Zhifang established standards of length and style with the goal of ensuring accessibility to a broad market of readers. Authors had to work within these parameters to have access to the public that would allow them to make their fields and their names.

PART THREE

Legacies of Industrialized Cultural Production

CHAPTER VI

Print Industrialism and State Socialism

*Public-Private Joint Management and Divisions of Labor
in the Early PRC Publishing Industry*

On the evening of January 28, 1954, representatives from Commercial Press and Zhonghua Book Company attended a banquet hosted in Beijing by leading figures in the PRC government's General Publishing Administration (Chuban zongshu; hereafter GPA).[1] The banquet concluded a series of meetings held throughout January between GPA officials and representatives of each publisher's administrative staffs and boards of directors. The discussions formulated the conditions for each of the two commercial publishers becoming public-private joint-management enterprises (*gong si heying qiye*) with new publishing mandates. That May Commercial Press would become the Higher Education Publishing Company, and Zhonghua Book Company would become the Finance and Economics Publishing Company. Both publishers would continue to maintain their original imprints, but they were taking a significant step toward state control. The new corporate structure would entail state representatives joining the boards of directors and assuming key positions on the companies' management teams.

Despite the dramatic nature of the institutional transformations involved, the interactions between the government and company representatives must have felt comfortingly familiar. Present at the banquet were Zhou Jianren and Ye Shengtao, both of whom had worked for Commercial Press during the 1920s and early 1930s. The director of the GPA during the negotiations was Hu Yuzhi, who had also worked at Commercial Press during the same period. Representing the companies in these meetings were figures like Chen Shutong, Shi Jiuyun 史久芸, and Dai Xiaohou 戴孝侯 for Commercial Press and Shu Xincheng and Lu Wendi 盧文迪 for Zhonghua Book Company, all of whom had been involved in publishing for many years, witnessing the dramatic changes of the war and postwar periods, even as their companies remained intact. Meeting with the GPA concurrently, representatives of the two old competitors were fully aware that the other company was going through the same process of corporate restructuring. Moreover, their discussions involved a range of familiar practical issues, encompassing each company's assets and liabilities, their long-term publishing strategies, and staffing for new publishing goals. Concluding the meetings with a banquet accorded with practices of literati commensality that reached back to the end of the Qing empire.

As this brief account suggests, Commercial Press and Zhonghua Book Company both experienced significant changes in their institutional structures during the 1950s. Each publisher became a public-private joint-management company with significant state involvement, and state agencies determined their publishing areas as part of a nationwide division of labor for cultural production. Yet key members of the former publishers' boards of directors, management personnel, and editorial staffs remained involved in both companies well into the early Mao period. Moreover, institutional practices and publishing goals that had been generated by the commercial publishing dynamics of the Republican period shaped both companies until the eve of the Cultural Revolution. By 1958 Zhonghua Book Company was independently reconstituted as the government's dedicated publisher of classical texts and reference books, with a staff that included many old publishing hands from the Republican period. A reestablished Commercial Press became responsible for Chinese translations of foreign scholarship, much as it had been during the 1920s and 1930s. But neither company had followed a straight path to state management mapped out in advance by the CCP's cultural cadres according to a pre-established model.

Managing the Transition

The disastrous condition of Shanghai's publishing industry in 1949 is difficult to exaggerate. In his detailed study of Shanghai publishers during the late 1940s, Zhou Wu quotes extensively reports from a forum on the publishing industry convened by the newspaper *Dagongbao* (*L'Impartial*) in April 1948 that documents a range of challenges. In the forum, *National Literature Monthly* (*Guowen yuekan*) editor Zhou Yutong 周予同 noted that publishers' activities were undermined by the difficulty of getting access to paper and the uncertainty of the Nationalist Party's censorship regime. The Writer's Study's (Zuojia shuwu) Yao Pengzi 姚蓬子 also observed that the contraction of the postal system during the Civil War functionally limited metropolitan publishers' business networks. Kaiming Bookstore's Xu Diaofu 徐調孚 illustrated that the capital costs for producing books outpaced the prices of the books themselves. Moreover, Great China Book Company's (Da Zhongguo tushuju) Ding Juntao 丁君陶 asserted that inflation increased the cost of most people's basic needs so greatly that they had no disposable income for books.[2] Kaiming Bookstore's 1950 petition for public-private joint management echoed these complaints.[3] Apart from damaging material losses from the War of Resistance, during and after the war Kaiming faced significant Nationalist Party censorship. Further, during the Civil War period, runaway inflation sparked significant increases in Kaiming's operating expenses. World Book Company seems to have been in even worse condition, with high levels of debt and wages in serious arrears. By the fall of 1949 the company's managers were planning to sell off equipment and materials and to rent out the company's retail storefront on Fuzhou Road in order to remain in business.[4]

Commercial Press and Zhonghua Book Company shared these woes. For instance, Zhou Wu cites letters from board member Zhang Yuanji that show him trying to sell Commercial Press's rare books and paper matrices to keep the company afloat, as well as appealing for help to former Commercial Press colleagues who were now in the CCP.[5] As Zhonghua Book Company's leaders recounted in a report in 1950, "From victory [in the War of Resistance] to the liberation of Shanghai, that short period, what we mainly relied on for maintenance was printing currency and distributing paper, and although we made every effort to carry out our fundamental business of the publishing enterprise, there was not much achievement."[6] Despite the difficult economic circumstances, Zhonghua published several series to provide resources for school libraries, revived magazines like *Zhonghua Education Circles*, and produced audiovisual materials for education. The company also published the progressive journal *New China Semimonthly* (*Xin Zhonghua banyuekan*).

As the tide of the Civil War turned after 1947, leaders at both publishers shifted their focus from corporate survival under Nationalist rule to positioning themselves to operate under Communist rule. For instance, Dai Xiaohou, who worked on Commercial Press's management team from the late 1940s through the mid-1950s, recounts how directors Zhang Yuanji and Chen Shutong brought Xie Renbing 謝仁冰, a founder of the Committee to Promote Chinese Democracy who had CCP connections, to the company as assistant manager and director of the Editing Department in 1947. They also hired underground party member Zheng Taipu 鄭太樸 to serve as a compiler for the publisher in 1949, although he passed away while traveling to Shanghai.[7] At Zhonghua, "in the name of employing staff with natural science and engineering and foreign language [expertise], we hired several Russian-language compilation and review staff. Further in response to an invitation from Mr. Shen Yanbing [Mao Dun], who was going to the Soviet Union, we relied on him to buy a large number of Soviet books and periodicals. At the same time the printing factory used the pretext of additionally buying materials to buy Russian-language copper matrices [tongmou]."[8] These maneuvers positioned Zhonghua to be able to meet new demand for Soviet publications after the Civil War.

As the CCP founded the new state, it put in place a much more centralized system of media control than the Nationalist Party had attempted to implement. Volland explains how both late imperial Chinese models of didactic cultural leadership and Soviet models of propaganda control encouraged this approach, even though the operation of Sanlian Bookstore under indirect CCP guidance during the 1930s and 1940s offered an alternative model.[9] In a series of directives during the fall of 1950, the new PRC government reorganized much of the publishing industry under the direct control of the GPA. The activities of the state-run New China Bookstore (Xinhua shudian) expanded to monopolize most distribution of books and magazines. The GPA also assumed direct control over major portions of the printing industry. At the same time, under the umbrella of the New China Bookstore, state-owned People's Publishing Houses (Renmin chubanshe) were established nationally and regionally to publish political books, and the Education Press (Jiaoyu chubanshe) was set up with support from the Ministry of Education to publish textbooks.[10] State management of much printing and distribution infrastructure, along with monopolization of the key publishing sectors of political books and textbooks, quickly gave the PRC state control over certain segments of the publishing industry and increased leverage over private publishers.

Within this new system of state control, some private companies were targeted for elimination, restructuring, or absorption by the government. One such publisher was World Book Company, which had large stakes held by Nationalist government officials that exposed the company to rapid government takeover. Nationalist Party leaders like Li Shizeng 李石曾 had held more than half the company's capital, which the PRC government took over, giving it a controlling share in the company. It planned to use this controlling share to decommission the publishing and distribution arms of the company while transforming the printing arm into a joint public-private enterprise that preserved the rights of those who held commercial shares.[11] In practice, it was difficult to distinguish World Book Company's assets and shares from those of the umbrella investment company, the World Agency (Shijie she), organized by Nationalist Party figures Li Shiceng, Wu Zhihui 吳稚暉, and Zhang Jingjiang 張靜江.[12] But by February 1950 the GPA had established a process for taking military control of World Book Company and its many branches.[13]

Nevertheless, many private publishing companies continued to operate, including Commercial Press and Zhonghua Book Company. The new publishing policies, which were mapped out in the first national publishing conference in October 1950, affected them in two major ways. First, the conference determined that "publishing institutions should gradually dispense with distribution and printing work, entrusting distribution and printing duties to monopoly public and private distribution and printing institutions."[14] To this end the GPA encouraged the leading publishing companies—Commercial Press, Zhonghua Book Company, Sanlian Bookstore, Kaiming Bookstore, and Lianying Bookstore—to integrate their distribution networks of branch stores into a unified distribution company that would be separately managed.[15] Xie Renbing spelled out the calculus for Commercial Press. "Is this beneficial to Commercial Press? Of course it is beneficial. It is quite apparent that if we do not participate, the other four companies can still establish a unified distribution organization; in terms of the government, it already has a state-managed bookstore and it has no need to carry loads for Commercial Press. But if we turn around and think about ourselves, if we do not participate, naturally we will be isolated."[16] The danger of marginalization and having only limited distribution outlets compelled these large private publishers to participate.

In the fall of 1950, the GPA coordinated negotiations among the five publishers that ironed out procedures for combining the distribution outlets of each company under a unified management structure.[17] On January 1, 1951, the five companies formed the China Book Distribution Company (Zhongguo tushu faxing gongsi), with each company transferring over its branch offices and many of its distribution staff, as well as contributing to the overall capitalization of the new, combined company.[18] Formation of the China Book Distribution Company had complex implications. From the government's perspective, it could take advantage of the distribution infrastructure China's leading publishers had developed over half a century while prying bookstores away from private corporate owners' proprietary control. Private distribution networks became cooperative and, with state involvement, increasingly "public." That network also dramatically supplemented the nascent state-run distribution system represented by the New China Bookstore. For the publishers, book distribution now had just two outlets—the New China Bookstore system and the China Book Distribution Company system—which represented a significant loss of commercial autonomy. But the private companies were also freed from the considerable expense and difficulty of running their own nationwide distribution systems, especially in the challenging market conditions of the late 1940s and early 1950s.

The second major outgrowth of the early PRC publishing policies was a push toward coordinated division of labor among China's public and private publishers, with each company developing a specialized focus in its publications.[19] As Xie Renbing colorfully expressed it, "In the conference people pointed out that we published a *Ciyuan* while their company [Zhonghua] published a *Cihai*; their company published a *Tushu jicheng*, and ours published a *Congshu jicheng*. This naturally dissipates strength, and work is duplicated and wasted. Now the government, in order to correct past mistakes, is leading each company in specializing and dividing labor."[20] Within this overall mandate, each publisher's leaders sought to carve out an area of specialization that balanced state imperatives for certain kinds of publications with the company's existing editorial resources.

In 1950 Zhonghua Book Company's Editing Department had a staff of sixty-two divided into sections (*ke*) for politics, economics, philosophy, education, Russian language, literature, fine arts, children's literature, history, geography, mathematics, physics, and chemistry (*shu li hua*), industry and agriculture, biology, medicine (*yiyao*), and hygiene.[21] Initially, it outlined a publishing trajectory focused on agriculture, education, medicine, and Russian-language materials.[22] In the National Publishing Conference, the GPA mandated that Zhonghua emphasize agriculture, medicine, and hygiene, but leaders in the Zhonghua Editing Department in fact felt ill-equipped to focus intensively on the latter two categories. Instead, they advocated for shifting the focus to change its direction of specialization to foreign language, introducing the Soviet Union, and agriculture, taking advantage of the Russian-language editorial staff they had assembled in the previous few years.[23] Throughout 1951 the Editing Department reached out to various other academic, governmental, and media units to arrange sources of manuscripts that corresponded to its areas of specialization, and it expanded the editorial staff to seventy-three.[24] At the beginning of 1952, the main office of the Editing Department moved to Beijing, with a work group continuing to operate in Shanghai. In Beijing the Editing Department built connections to ministries and academic units focused on agriculture and the Soviet Union.[25] It also came under increasing state oversight as its publishing plans were submitted to the GPA for regular approval.[26]

After the National Publishing Conference in September 1950, Commercial Press had a mandate to focus on science and technology books, as well as children's books and reference books.[27] With this decision made about the company's publishing orientation, GPA director Hu Yuzhi pegged Yuan Hanqing 袁翰青, former head of the Bureau to Popularize Science (Kexue puji ju) in the Ministry of Culture, to be Commercial Press's new editor in chief.[28] Besides preparing to relocate Commercial Press's Editing Department to Beijing, Yuan also sought to reorganize it to align more closely to its new publishing mandate of scientific and technical books. In part, he recruited staff from his former unit in the Ministry of Culture. At the same time, he arranged for Commercial Press to absorb the private People's Base Publishing Company (Minben chubanshe) run by Wang Tianyi 王天一, which before and after the war had published three separate journals to popularize science, medicine, and agriculture.[29] The resulting Editing Department combined members of the original Commercial Press staff, members of Wang Tianyi's company, and some of Yuan's former colleagues in the Ministry of Culture. By 1952 Commercial Press's publishing plans had accordingly come to focus primarily on science, technology, and medicine, with some attention to reprinting classical books.[30]

Within the framework set up at the first national publishing conference, private publishing companies continued to produce fairly large proportions of available books well into the early 1950s. Zhou Wu, for instance, cites a report by Hu Yuzhi to the Culture and Education Committee, noting that in 1951 private publishers produced roughly half of all titles published nationally, dominating all sectors outside political publications, the social sciences, and textbooks.[31] A 1954 report from the GPA's CCP leading group to the Central Propaganda Department indicates that private companies still played a significant role in PRC book publishing even two years later.[32] As of the end of 1953, there were two hundred ninety private publishers nationwide (more than two hundred fifty of which were in Shanghai). Together they produced 53 percent of the titles published that year, 25 percent of the volumes for all books besides textbooks, and 54 percent of all illustrated books.

The Five Antis Campaign of 1952 further extended state and party control over private businesses like Commercial Press and Zhonghua Book Company. Aimed explicitly at various forms of business malpractice and tax evasion, the Five Antis Campaign functioned through a combination of confessions by company managers and criticisms from employees operating through party-run labor unions, all overseen by the CCP.[33] At Zhonghua the campaign started on February 1, 1952, with discussions between labor and management that led to the company's union organizing an Inspection Committee for Increasing Production and Practicing Economy (Zengchan jieyue jiancha weiyuanhui), to which the Business Management Committee sent Pan Daren 潘達人 and Zhong Jizhou 鐘吉宇 to act as representatives.[34] Management also formed a small working group to study relevant documents, and a period of investigation and discussion extended from March 3 to April 10. Starting on March 30 Zhonghua participated in district-level study and confession meetings for the campaign under Shanghai's Putuo District Committee to Increase Production and Practice Economy and transmitted a confession to authorities on April 3. But throughout April and May the company-level committees continued to collect documents and confessional materials, leading to a more extensive report compiled between May 22 and 24.[35]

The process culminated in a meeting called by the union's Five Antis Committee on May 25. In the meeting worker and staff representatives concluded that management's representatives had been thorough in their self-criticism, and measures like "shipping back overseas machinery, materials, and paper, as well as remitting overseas funds" fostered confidence about production.[36] Later that summer the Shanghai Municipal Committee to Increase Production and Practice Economy judged Zhonghua to be a "law-abiding company" (*shoufahu*), assessing an overall levy of 18,392,998 yuan on illegal income.[37]

The Five Antis Campaign seems to have been more extended and complicated for Commercial Press. Already in 1951 members of the GPA's party group suspected the presence of hidden assets, continued involvement in the company by Wang Yunwu, who had fled to Taiwan with the Nationalists, and a lack of openness on the part of Commercial Press's leadership.[38] As at Zhonghua, Commercial Press formed a Committee to Increase Production and Practice Economy in January 1952, with substantial union, CCP, and Youth League participation.[39] Confessions by managers and inspections by workers and staff generated a letter of confession that was sent to the Shanghai Book Trade Association on February 6. The letter of self-criticism identified six improper business practices between 1949 and 1951. These included selling off newsprint purchased in the United States, which was considered a form of "currency arbitrage" (*taohui*); shipping books from Hong Kong in teak boxes to import teak wood (used in the printing process) without paying the proper import duty on it; providing a food and carfare subsidy for inspectors from the East China Postal Supply Office; allowing Education Bureau representatives from Wuhu to take some gifts gratis; avoiding a printing tax; and switching from imported to domestic paper for textbooks without adjusting the price accordingly.[40] In reality, all these were minor offenses, many of which probably reflected common business practices during the late Republican period.

Further investigation in February and March, however, turned up nine more problems, which the company duly reported.[41] On April 4 company representatives participated in the Huangpu District International Trade Industry's Self-Assessment Public Criticism Small Group (Zibao gongping xiaozu), which judged the company to be half law-abiding and half law-breaking. They further participated in the Huangpu District News, Publishing, and Printing Industry Mutual-Aid Mutual-Criticism Small Group, which continued into May, but the group could not immediately resolve the Commercial Press case because of its complexity. Later, on May 22 Commercial Press received a preliminary verdict of half law-abiding and half lawbreaking.[42] In the end, however, the Shanghai Municipal Committee to Increase Production and Practice Economy imposed a verdict of "basically law-abiding" on Commercial Press and levied relatively modest exactions.[43] This generally positive final verdict undoubtedly removed a dark cloud from over the publisher.

However, the half-year process of self-assessment and public meetings, where many members of the board and management team personally made confessions and faced accusations related to long-standing business practices, certainly awakened leaders at both companies to the rigors of party oversight and the danger of any kind of evasion and manipulation of state policy. The campaign made manifest the coercive potential of the state's legal apparatus and party-led mass movements, underlining the imperative for cooperation by corporate directors and managers if their companies were going to continue operating in the PRC. Thus, although both companies made it through the Five Antis Campaign intact, the process laid the groundwork for intensified state-private partnership in the move to public-private joint management, which was initiated the following year.

Public-Private Joint Management

The first national publishing conference and the Five Antis Campaign created a framework for Commercial Press and Zhonghua Book Company to operate as privately managed companies within the PRC, even as the state assumed increasingly direct control over the urban industrial economy. As discussed, both publishers tailored their publishing plans to state initiatives. They also participated in a collectively owned and managed distribution company under state oversight. Had such a system persisted, it would have allowed significant autonomy for private corporations within an overall framework of state planning and supervision. However, between the fall of 1953 and the spring of 1954, Commercial Press and Zhonghua Book Company, in parallel, negotiated new relationships with the PRC government, reorganizing as public-private joint-management companies. Both publishers had, in fact, previously petitioned to start public-private joint management in 1950, following the model of Kaiming Bookstore, but the government at the time had declined because it thought that "objective conditions were not mature and the subjective capability [of the companies was] insufficient."[44] Now, three years later after experimenting with a continued pattern of private ownership under state oversight, both the publishers and the government's cultural management apparatus moved to establish a closer partnership.

Part of the motivation for both the state and the private companies stemmed from a need to define more clearly the publishing mandates of each publisher. This imperative was clearest with Zhonghua Book Company. As of 1952, Zhonghua had been asked to focus on publishing books on agriculture, Russian language, and introducing the Soviet Union.[45] But by early 1953, this field of publishing specialization was significantly eroded as the Soviet Union transferred full control over Epoch Publishing Company (Shidai chubanshe) to the PRC government.[46] Beginning in 1954 Epoch focused on publishing Russian translations and books about the Soviet Union, which left Zhonghua with only an exclusive mandate for publishing agricultural and Russian-language books. In a context of coordinated specialization among publishers, area of specialization determined each press's effective market share, and Zhonghua's was shrinking.

At the same time, the PRC government was having trouble publishing varieties of books that it prioritized. Specifically, the GPA's Huang Luofeng 黄洛峰 reported to Xi Zhongxun 習仲勳 and Hu Qiaomu 胡喬木 in April 1953 that the Finance Committee's Compilation and Translation Office was failing to provide a stable foundation for establishing a Finance and Economics Publishing Company (Caijing chubanshe) because of a lack of appropriate leading cadres.[47] Huang's initial proposed solution was to make that committee into an office in the People's Publishing Company. But by November when representatives of eleven different ministries, offices, commissions, and state-owned enterprises met to discuss forming a Finance and Economics Publishing Company for their publishing needs, Zhonghua Book Company emerged as the consensus partner.[48] The group envisioned the Central Propaganda Department and Organizational Department appointing the main management staff (editor in chief, assistant editor in chief, manager, and director), with each interested government unit staffing each department. The initiative offered the prospect of significantly increased government involvement. It also granted Zhonghua a more substantial sector of the publishing market, which promised greater opportunities for institutional continuity and development.

In general, increased cooperation offered potential benefits for both the government and corporate sides, which came through clearly in the GPA party group's proposal for both companies' conversion to public-private joint-management enterprises in November 1953. The group perceived that "the two companies [Zhonghua and Commercial Press] have many editing and publishing cadres, skilled workers, and large-scale printing facilities that are very useful to the state. If they are reformed well, it could strengthen the state's publishing power."[49] Rather than setting up new publishing companies to specialize in higher-education materials and finance and economics publications, the government could build on the foundations of the existing companies.[50] In addition, the government already held significant portions of each company's shares, estimated at about 20 percent each, from confiscated "bureaucratic capital" and unclaimed shares, but it did not have a direct managerial presence in the existing corporate governance structures. Formalized joint management would allow state representatives to participate directly in planning and administration.

On the companies' side, the GPA party group surmised that each company had benefited economically by filling orders from the state and publishing manuscripts derived from government units.[51] Partnership with the state was increasingly the source of business opportunity. The GPA's judgment is confirmed by a letter Commercial Press chairman of the board Zhang Yuanji wrote to the company's Beijing office manager, Shi Jiuyun, in October 1953. Zhang saw Commercial Press's economic health to be improving under government guidance, and he viewed the new direction of publishing specialization of higher-education materials as promising to provide still further opportunities through state orders. Moreover, he believed distribution of the company's publications through the China Book Distribution Company and New China Bookstore to be a form of state capitalism in the form of collaboration with state-managed enterprises.[52] From Zhang's perspective, partnership with the state was the best mechanism to sustain Commercial Press's institutional health.

Reorganizing the two publishers as public-private joint-management companies was a two-way process that unfolded between October 1953 and May 1954. In October 1953 Commercial Press's Beijing office manager, Shi Jiuyun, held informal talks with the GPA's Publishing Management Bureau (Chuban guanli ju).[53] In a meeting on October 7, Shi expressed enthusiasm about the prospect of Commercial Press's taking responsibility for publishing higher-education textbooks. On October 22 Shi received a letter from Zhang Yuanji via Chen Shutong encouraging him to open discussions about the possibility of public-private joint management. In talks that day between bureau director Huang Luofeng and the publisher's representatives, Shi, Yuan Hanqing, and Dai Xiaohou, Huang outlined some of the parameters that would structure the agreement: Commercial Press would concentrate on higher-education publishing, its overseas operations would continue as before, and some publications would continue to carry the Commercial Press imprint. After hearing Shi's report on the discussions during a meeting on October 27 in Shanghai, board members offered feedback on proposals the company might offer.[54] In the board meeting of November 1, the directors "unanimously expressed [that they] enthusiastically welcome" public-private joint management.

Shi Jiuyun immediately returned to Beijing. On November 6, 9, 14, 18, and 26, he, Dai Xiaohou, and Yuan Hanqing met with GPA personnel and representatives of the Ministry of Higher Education to resolve a number of key points, such as maintaining the two trademarks and the company's overseas distribution system.[55] They established a time frame of the second quarter of 1954 to make the transition. They decided that only necessary staff would be transferred to Beijing, and they differentiated between matters to be handled before reorganization and those that could wait until after.

As described at the beginning of this chapter, in January a negotiating team that included members of the board and company management again went to Beijing to meet with GPA representatives. They held large-scale meetings on January 16 and 28, and small-scale meetings on January 20 and 27.[56] A striking feature of the records of these meetings was the sense of collaboration and cooperation they relate. For instance, board member Xu Fengshi 徐鳳石 in his account of the January meetings to fellow board members noted, "The general situation was harmonious. The government's abundant concern for our company at all times showed clearly in their words and expressions [yi yu yan biao]. It especially made us feel enthusiastic."[57] This sense of comity no doubt stemmed in part from the familiarity discussed earlier. In addition, Commercial Press's editor in chief, Yuan Hanqing, had been appointed by GPA director Hu several years before. Rather than tense negotiations between anonymous, hard-nosed state agents and self-interested capitalists, these meetings involved intellectuals with long histories in Chinese publishing and great personal familiarity. The meetings also included forms of elite sociability that tightened interpersonal bonds and might have obscured distinctions of power and authority. At the same time, though, the recent experience of the Five Antis Campaign meant that the state's coercive potential always hung in the background, conditioning the choices of board members and corporate managers.

Out of these meetings came the framework for reorganizing Commercial Press on a joint-management footing. With a target date of April 1, 1954 (later changed to the politically significant May 1, 1954), representatives from the government and corporate sides set up a preparatory office, with work groups in Shanghai and Beijing to coordinate the preparation.[58] The work groups conducted financial assessments of company assets to determine the new company's capital resources, orchestrated shareholders' meetings to facilitate corporate reorganization, and mobilized existing staff and workers to support the transition.[59] The resulting corporate structure included both public and private representatives but formalized government involvement in the company. The new board of directors was composed of twelve representatives of private shareholders and five representatives of public, or government, shareholders.[60] Significantly, government officials did not dictate who the new board members would be. But in discussions with the GPA, Hu Yuzhi and Huang Luofeng had "instructed that among the directors [representing] private shareholders [Commercial Press board members] should pay attention to drawing a clear political line"—that is, selecting people who were politically reliable and willing to cooperate with the state.[61] By articulating this expectation about the cooperativeness of private-shareholder directors, the government indirectly asserted its authority in corporate governance.[62]

In terms of management, the organizational rules stated that "both the public and private sides consult over nominations for this company's director [*shezhang*], assistant director, editor in chief [*zong bianji*], assistant editors in chief, manager [*jingli*], assistant manager(s), and report on them to the government's responsible institution to request approval of the appointment."[63] Yet discussions between the company and government officials had allocated positions in such a way as to give the government key positions of authority. "The company director and editor in chief will be appointed by the government; the managers will be chosen by the private side; the assistant directors, assistant editors in chief, and assistant managers will be appointed and chosen by the public and private sides both. Other important staff will be appointed by the director."[64] These state-appointed positions enabled the government to direct both the business and editorial sides of the company.[65]

At the same time, the personnel of Commercial Press was carried over en masse to the new company, with the exception of some staff who were nearing retirement age.[66] In addition, the bulk of the capital for the publisher was to be provided by Commercial Press. The company would have an overall capitalization of 4.3 million yuan in new currency, of which 4 million yuan was constituted from former Commercial Press assets and

300,000 yuan derived from government investment.[67] As a result of this process, then, the government acquired increasingly direct control over the corporate assets and personnel—that is, the financial, productive, and human capital—of Commercial Press. But Commercial Press persisted as a discrete institution with exclusive access to a sector of the book market— higher-education teaching materials—that it had been angling for since Wang Yunwu had initiated the University Series in 1931. Moreover, carrying over significant numbers of board members and editorial staff ensured significant institutional continuity.

Zhonghua Book Company's process of reorganization as a public-private joint-management company closely paralleled that of Commercial Press. On November 16, 1953, Zhonghua's provisional Editing Department director, Lu Wendi, met with the GPA's Huang Luofeng, Jin Canran 金燦然, and Fu Binran 傳彬然 to explore the idea of the publisher's reorganization.[68] Huang, who twelve days earlier had participated in the meeting with representatives from a range of state and party units to discuss reorganizing Zhonghua to publish finance and economics books, raised the idea of Zhonghua and the Finance and Economics Publishing Company constituting two imprints or trademarks within the same public-private joint-management company. Lu provisionally accepted the proposal, and on December 21 Zhonghua's board sent a formal request to the GPA to initiate public-private joint management.[69] Representatives of Zhonghua's board met with the GPA contemporaneously with Commercial Press's meetings there in January 1954.[70] As with Commercial Press, a planning office was established with representation from both the company and the government, and work groups were set up in both Beijing and Shanghai to manage the details of the corporate transformation.

Like Commercial Press, Zhonghua would now be one enterprise with two imprints or trademarks, the Finance and Economics Publishing Company (Caizheng jingji chubanshe) and Zhonghua Book Company.[71] The board was to have representatives of both public and private shareholders, with the chairman representing the latter and the vice-chairman representing the former. The director and editor in chief were appointed by the government, while the assistant director and assistant heads of the Editing Department were selected by the public and private sides together.[72] The main office was set up in Beijing, and a management office was set up in Shanghai. Again, the staff would carry over to the new company, except for those nearing retirement.[73] As with Commercial Press, because of a significant ownership stake, board representation, and the placement of government appointees in key managerial positions, the PRC government gained significantly more direct control over the human and financial capital of a major private publishing company and reoriented it toward its own publishing priorities. In turn, Zhonghua Book Company remained intact as an institution, and its new publishing specialization granted it exclusive access to a significant part of the publishing market having to do with finance and economics.[74]

The process of corporate transformation of these two companies is instructive for China's modern business history. In a recent essay collection, historian Sherman Cochran poses two fundamental questions about China's structural economic transformation in the 1950s. How fast or slow was that transformation (to which I would add the corollary question of how planned or intentional it was)? Why did some capitalists cooperate (or refuse to cooperate) with the emergent state-socialist PRC regime?[75]

In terms of the first question, the experience of China's two biggest private publishing companies suggests a process of change that was slow and, in some ways, halting or not fully planned. Both Commercial Press and Zhonghua Book Company continued to operate as privately owned joint-stock companies from 1949 through 1953. Their capital bases were intact as were their personnel, and their boards of directors functioned as they always had, with some adjustments for members who had left China in 1949. Without question both publishers adapted to new conditions. Some key managerial staff were appointed by the GPA. The companies invested in state initiatives, such as the China Book Distribution Company, adjusted their publication lists in accord with state agendas, and altered their Editing Departments to fit with new publishing directions. But, as shown in chapters 2 and 3, they had done as much under the Nationalist government and when facing wartime conditions during the 1930s and 1940s.

When more significant structural change happened in 1953 and 1954 both state and corporate sides initiated it. Moreover, the state's primary motivation was to reorient these companies to particular publishing agendas, not to take them over simply to meet an abstract model of state-socialist management. Based on assessments of publishing output during the first years of the PRC, GPA leaders came to view greater state involvement as a more efficient way to coordinate divisions of labor across a single industrial sector as more specialized publishing companies partnered with relevant government institutions. In line with recent analyses by Eddy U,

James Gao, and Thomas Mullaney, evidence from the publishing sector suggests that the early PRC party-state adapted structures and launched initiatives to achieve specific goals rather than imposing a predetermined, rigid structure of state socialism in a systematic way.[76] CCP adaptability and "opportunism," in Gao's parlance, were fundamental to the construction of public-private joint management in the publishing industry.[77]

In terms of why managers and shareholders of these two companies were willing to collaborate with the PRC state, the most convincing answer closely parallels Parks Coble's thesis in his essay about Zhou Zuomin in *The Capitalist Dilemma in China's Communist Revolution*. Coble emphasizes Zhou's "dedication to his enterprise" and his commitment to Jincheng Bank's institutional continuity.[78] Much like Zhou, men like Zhang Yuanji, Chen Shutong, and Shu Xincheng had given their lives to developing Commercial Press and Zhonghua Book Company because they saw them contributing to the "cultural enterprise" (*wenhua shiye*) of transforming China. During the long years of the War of Resistance and Civil War, they had made many adjustments to help their companies survive. Collaboration with the state merely offered a new mechanism for realizing that goal. In fact, through strictly defined divisions of labor among publishing companies, state involvement promised to secure particular kinds of market access and economic stability that competitive capitalism had so clearly failed to do in China during the 1930s and 1940s.

The publishers' corporate forms and their personnel might also have facilitated abandoning private enterprise for public-private collaboration. By the 1950s neither publisher had a single dominant corporate figure who owned most of the company and was primarily identified with it in the manner that Liu Hongsheng or the Rong family were with their enterprises. Members of the boards of directors and long-term employees owned significant shares in the companies and undoubtedly benefited economically from them. But shares were widely distributed, and shareholders' stake in their respective publishing company was as much cultural as it was economic. Moreover, by 1954 trading the economic benefits of private ownership for the social and political benefits of a positive cooperative relationship with the PRC government most likely seemed like a worthwhile exchange, especially after the campaigns of the early 1950s made clear the costs of resistance to government authority. Significantly, the shareholders' meetings that approved the transition to public-private joint management were heavily attended, and shareholders voted unanimously in support of corporate reorganization, suggesting no one involved in either publisher was fully invested in and dependent on these corporations' continuing as privately held economic entities.[79]

Public-private joint management enabled the two publishers to continue to operate as distinctive cultural producers in modern China, despite radical changes in government organization and economic structure. Certainly, both companies experienced significant structural changes. The company manager and editor in chief positions were now appointed by the government. Further, government representatives had a significant presence on the board of directors, though not a majority. These changes gave the government a direct line of authority in the companies' operations. Yet both companies' editorial staffs continued at each publisher, and many existing board members maintained their positions. These continuities in personnel ensured ongoing institutional memory, patterns of practice, and corporate identity.

Specializing Again

Introduction of public-private joint management entailed major adjustments to the Editing Departments at both Commercial Press and Zhonghua Book Company to provide a basis for new forms of publishing specialization. The GPA party committee had outlined these reorganization plans in its initial proposal to the Central Propaganda Department in November 1953.[80] For Commercial Press it suggested that the Ministry of Higher Education appoint the director as well as staff to participate in each section of the Editing Department.[81] Zhonghua would address the chronic shortage of specialized editorial personnel that it experienced during the early 1950s by drawing editorial staff from a variety of the government's economic management organs. These included the Central Finance Committee's Compiling and Translating Office as well as the Ministry of Finance, the Ministry of Commerce, Ministry of Foreign Trade, Ministry of Agriculture, Forestry Ministry, Ministry of Grain, People's Bank, and the General Cooperative Agency. The new Editing Department would "form several editorial rooms and publish books for each of the foregoing organs."[82]

Reorganization in these ways followed in 1954, leading to a new pattern of organizing editing work at both publishers. Incorporation of staff from the Ministry of Higher Education and a range of economic management units created Editing Departments where many personnel were oriented to the agendas and priorities of outside organizations. The integration seemed to work most effectively at Commercial Press. Yu Zhuo 於卓, who was one of the staff members of the Ministry of Higher Education Teaching Materials Compilation and Review Office transferred to Commercial Press, emphasizes his colleagues' fast transition into the Editing Department.[83] Relatively few colleagues from the ministry accompanied Yu—he estimates about a dozen—and the work style of the more experienced Commercial Press editors seems to have set the tone in the combined Editing Department. In fact, Yu suggests that Commercial Press's veteran editors effectively trained his transferred colleagues in basic compilation and editorial work.

At Zhonghua and the Finance and Economics Publishing Company, the newly reorganized Editing Department seems to have been plagued by a host of problems. After reorganization, the Editing Department had expanded to eighty-eight people, approaching the size of Zhonghua's prewar Editing Department.[84] During the spring of 1954, the GPA mobilized thirty-three editorial cadres from six different central government units and was actively recruiting additional staff members from two more.[85] Not surprisingly, cadres in different editorial sections who came from distinct ministries and commissions continued to identify with their units of origin, failing to draw together and work cooperatively. In the words of the publisher's work report from 1954,

> Between each department, office, and section, and even between the groups within an office, there was insufficient mutual understanding, sympathy, and coordination in their work. They regarded organic divisions of labor [fengong] as division of families [fenjia], and they emphasized their own difficulties and disregarded other departments. There existed localist ideas of selfish departmentalism [benwei zhuyi] with a lack of thinking about the whole situation. These all influenced vertical and horizontal relations to be abnormal, and they could not effectively unite and cooperate.[86]

These internal divisions generated inefficiency within the department, with some overworked and others sitting idle. True reorganization and integration seem to have been limited and incomplete.

This situation of internal fragmentation seems to have persisted even two years later when the Ministry of Culture party group's Qian Junrui 錢俊瑞[87]

assessed the situations at Commercial Press and Zhonghua.[88] In a report to Vice-Premier Chen Yun, he noted that within the Higher Education Publishing Company Dai Xiaohou ran an office of four people in Beijing specializing in Commercial Press editorial work while Ding Yinggui 丁英桂 ran an office of four people in Shanghai that was lithographing ancient books. At the Finance and Economics Publishing Company, in Beijing a staff of five continued to compile books under the Zhonghua imprint, while six did so in Shanghai, supported by a library staff of five people, led by Yao Shaohua. Commercial Press publications centered on popular science and Chinese medicine books, while Zhonghua published literary and historical books. The leading figures of these groups, such as Yao Shaohua for Zhonghua and Dai Xiaohou at Commercial Press, had worked at their companies for years and seem to have been maintaining a distinct corporate identity, through both their personnel and publishing agendas, within the larger reorganized companies.

In reflecting on the situation at the two publishers, Qian Junrui sketched in a more formal report to Chen Yun a few weeks later a rationale for reconstituting Commercial Press and Zhonghua Book Company as independent units.[89] Qian emphasized that the two publishers' long backlists of publications were underutilized, and their presence in overseas markets in Hong Kong and Southeast Asia was languishing. As noted, Qian was aware that the two companies' editorial staffs preserved a certain degree of integrity and independent initiative. He saw the potential to "use even more the names of Commercial Press and Zhonghua to organize publication of academic-quality books and reference books to enable Commercial Press and Zhonghua to play an even greater role in publishing circles" and to publish for overseas markets. However, Qian saw two conditions as essential to reestablishing Commercial Press and Zhonghua as independent publishing units: strengthening their editorial resources and identifying yet again "a certain direction of specialization to serve as a focal point, and at the same time to guarantee considerable breadth in their publishing scope to enable them to exist and be active for the long term."[90] Shifts in the government's own publishing priorities during the late 1950s created the conditions for each company to be reconstituted independently with publishing agendas and personnel that corresponded closely to their historical roots.

The dynamics of this process are clearest with Zhonghua Book Company. Contemporaneous with Qian Junrui's observations about organizational systems and personnel at Commercial Press and Zhonghua in 1956, officials in the Ministry of Culture began advocating for increased republication of classical texts and ancient books. For instance, a report from the Ministry of Culture party group to the Central Propaganda Department in May 1956 noted that there had been some modest publishing of classical texts during the early PRC, but it was largely critical of the "bourgeois" and "decadent" approach of state-owned publishers, who selected rare editions of obscure titles without concern for their research or pedagogical value.[91] "There has not been planned and timely publication of important ancient books that have real value based on the situation of academic research work and the needs of a broad group of readers. Rather, they have published some inaccessible and uncommon volumes that have no value or are not essential."[92] Moreover, the group found lithographed editions to be prohibitively expensive, and they were critical of the selection of editions and sloppy or incomplete annotation work. In September that year a *People's Daily* editorial further emphasized the value of classical publishing and called for a greater state role in coordinating it.[93] As a regime whose ideology was based on historical materialism, management of the historical archive was essential. At the same time, we can see in these calls for state management an implicit concern with the new PRC state's acting as steward of China's cultural heritage.[94]

Party and government leaders were responding in part to growing market demand from academic and educational circles, a concern that comes through clearly in Qi Yanming's 齊燕銘[95] (Ministry of Culture) report to the Central Propaganda Department in January 1958.

In the most recent few years, because of the rapid development of research work and higher education, and because of the uninterrupted rise in the level of the people's cultural life, the demand for ancient books has increased day by day. Science workers, propaganda and education workers, culture and art workers, and even ordinary cadres all need generally relevant ancient books to serve as reference material. But the books on the market are already fewer and fewer, and some are simply rare items that are hoarded. The current situation of ancient book publishing is that supply does not meet demand, and they are not closely enough connected to readers' needs. Many urgently needed important works have not been published.[96]

Qi rationalized this initiative by reference to Mao's "On New Democracy," which called for critical organization and selection of elements from China's "brilliant ancient culture" as a "necessary condition for developing the nation's new culture and raising the nation's self-confidence."[97] However, Qi also critically assessed contemporary publishers' limited editorial resources for classical books, estimating that there were no more than fifty people nationwide currently participating in classical publishing work. Moreover, he viewed the work itself as unsystematic, lacking comprehensive long-term planning.[98]

In response, with approval from the State Council's Scientific Planning Commission, Qi established a Planning Small Group for Organizing and Publishing Ancient Books (Guji zhengli chuban guihua xiaozu) that was subordinate to it.[99] The goals for the group were to set policies for classical-text publishing work, determine annual and long-term plans for ancient-book publishing, and make plans for cultivating talent to engage in classical publishing work. By mid-February the plan to establish the group had been approved by the Central Secretariat.[100] The group's roster included government officials and party cadres with backgrounds in publishing or cultural work (Ye Shengtao, Jin Canran, Wu Han 吳晗, Fan Wenlan 範文瀾, and Qi himself), leading scholars (e.g., Chen Yinke 陳寅恪 and Feng Youlan 馮友蘭), as well as intellectuals with decades of publishing experience, including in reprinting classical texts (Jin Zhaozi, Zheng Zhenduo, and Zhang Yuanji). So, figures from the private publishing industry were incorporated into the state's own process for planning the direction of publishing work. At the same time, Qi advocated for Zhonghua Book Company to be reestablished as a separate publishing entity and to be merged with the Ancient-Book Publishing Company (Guji chubanshe) to carry out the publishing initiatives of the small group.[101] This plan was endorsed by the Central Propaganda Department later in February.[102] Zhonghua's Shanghai office incorporated that city's Classical Literature Press (Gudian wenxue chubanshe) to form Zhonghua Book Company's Shanghai Editing Department.[103]

Commercial Press also reorganized as a separate publishing entity parallel to the change at Zhonghua. In February 1958 the Central Propaganda Department endorsed a plan for Commercial Press to focus independently on publishing international scholarly works in translation.[104] The Central Propaganda Department's Bao Zhijing and Zhou Yang tapped Chen Hanbo 陳翰伯, editor of that department's journal *Study* (*Xuexi*), to serve as the new editor in chief.[105] Commercial Press was also supposed to be guided and supported by a central-government-organized Planning Small Group for the Translation and Publication of World Scholarly Works.[106] But Chen himself was responsible for organizing the group, which failed to come together, suggesting Commercial Press had less institutional support than Zhonghua, perhaps because of the foreign focus of the publisher's list at a time of rapidly cooling relations with the Soviet Union.[107] On the board of directors, the private side representatives, many of whom had been involved since the late 1940s, remained in place, while representatives of the Ministry of Higher Education were removed, replaced by Chen, the new general manager, Guo Jing 郭敬, and the Propaganda Department's Wang Yi 王益.[108]

Zhonghua's former board of directors and Compilation and Review Committee were to provide the organizational foundation for the reconstituted Zhonghua Book Company. The board of directors was to correspond closely to the group that had orchestrated the transition to public-private joint management.[109] The Compilation and Review Committee, which was a consultative body, was to draw on the following original members: Director Shu Xincheng, with Fu Binran (formerly of the Ancient-Book Publishing Company) and Jin Zhaozi as assistant directors, with Lu Wendi, Xu Diaofu 徐調孚, Yao Shaohua, Zeng Ciliang 曾次亮 (also from Ancient-Book Publishing), Zhang Jinglu 張靜廬, Zhang Xichen 章錫琛, and Chen Naiqian 陳乃乾 as committee members. To this group the Ministry of Culture planned to introduce only Zhang Beichen 張北辰 and Jin Canran[110] to the committee, with Jin also serving as assistant director, as well as general manager and concurrent editor in chief. This approach effectively placed Jin Canran, as representative of the Ministry of Culture, over an editorial committee made up mostly of longtime Zhonghua staff editors and other old publishing hands.

However, as Qi Yanming's original proposal suggested, Zhonghua's editorial resources needed to be strengthened to fulfill its mandate.[111] This view was echoed by longtime Zhonghua compiler and Shanghai Editing Department director Jin Zhaozi, who assessed the Shanghai office's personnel needs in a July 1958 letter to Jin Canran in the following terms.

After Zhonghua and Classical Literature [publishing companies] merged, the work increased, but the editorial strength was insufficient by a wide margin. Classical Literature's original editorial staff [*bianji renyuan*] tended toward classical literature, and their capability from the start was not strong. Because of a lack of editorial staff, up to the present we have not had a way to establish history and philosophy groups. At the same time, we suspect that the proofreading strength is not enough. Currently, we depend on outside forces to proofread two-thirds of manuscripts. (At the same time, there is also some connection to the period of the rectification, when there were many meetings.) Now we urgently need to increase editorial cadres [*bianjiao ganbu*] who are strong in both politics and professional work. If we do not resolve this problem, in terms of work it will be difficult to develop.[112]

According to Zhonghua director Jin Canran's secretary at the time, Yu Xiaoyao 俞篠堯, Zhonghua's leadership initially relied in part for its personnel on "old publishing hands [*chubanjia*] and old editors, as well as a limited number of specialized scholars within the country in the fields of editions and bibliography, ancient philology, and ancient astronomy, calendrical calculations, and so forth."[113] Figures like Yao Shaohua, Zhang Xichen, and Lu Wendi corresponded to the petty intellectuals (i.e., Yu's "old publishing hands and editors") who had been core members of the major publishers' editing departments in the 1920s and 1930s. Chen Naiqian, whom Zhonghua had recruited in 1958, was an archetypal late Qing literatus. A classically trained scholar of editions who qualified as one of Yu's "few specialized scholars," from the late Qing through the Republican period Chen had collected and republished ancient books on his own.[114] At Zhonghua Chen oversaw the photolithographic reprinting of classical texts.[115] Jin also arranged for some younger scholars to be transferred to Zhonghua from nearby universities.

In recruiting publishing stalwarts and literati classical scholars, Zhonghua's leaders tapped social groups that could be suspect in the new political and social hierarchies of the socialist state as petty bourgeois intellectuals.[116] In fact, staff editors and managers from the former commercial publishing companies sometimes found themselves to be targets during the many political campaigns of the 1950s. For example, Commercial Press's Dai Xiaohou, who had reluctantly assumed the role of assistant manager (*xieli*) after Xie Renbing's untimely death, became a target of criticism during the Campaign to Suppress Hidden Counterrevolutionaries (Sufan yundong) in 1955.[117] At Zhonghua Book Company, longtime editor Lu Wendi, who had been assistant editor in chief of the Finance and Economics Publishing Company, had taken the lead in "airing views" during the Hundred Flowers Campaign and consequently lost his position and was demoted to be an ordinary editor of the fifth rank during the Anti-Rightist Campaign.[118]

Yet intellectuals in the publishing industry's leadership positions like Jin Canran and Qi Yanming still utilized these groups because their expertise was necessary for particular state-initiated projects, such as the republication of classical texts. Dai and Lu, for instance, both continued to do editorial work, despite having been targets of political campaigns.[119] Yu Xiaoyao's remembrance of Jin Canran makes explicit the social politics of this way of mobilizing marginalized intellectuals.

> During those few years, not a few intellectuals were mistakenly labeled as "rightists" or were criticized for being "bourgeois reactionary academic authorities" [*zichan jieji fandong xueshu quanwei*]. Comrade Canran thought that among these intellectuals some possessed special skills for organizing ancient books, that using this portion of strength to organize ancient books should be emphasized, and that it was necessary to do this from weighing the overall benefits to socialism. As a result, he raised with relevant leaders the suggestion of "picking up what others discard," transferring those then mistakenly labeled as "rightists" who really had a special proficiency as well as those experts with real talent and learning who had been criticized as "reactionary academic authorities" to come to Zhonghua Book Company to work.[120]

Cadre Wang Chun 王春 estimates that as many as twenty members of Zhonghua's editorial staff were those labeled "rightist" or politically "unreliable."[121] As in academic and technical fields in the early Soviet Union,[122] a dearth of expertise in the area of publishing and academic scholarship compelled the early PRC state to "recycle" groups that were politically suspect or socially problematic, in view of the new social order the state sought to institute, in order to realize some of its goals of cultural production.

Relying primarily on older scholars and experienced editorial staff, however, created real concerns, some practical and others political. In a document prepared for a forum on ancient-book publishing in the spring of 1957, Zhonghua leaders expressed concern that, because of the age of the veteran staff they had recruited, within five or ten years they would lack qualified personnel for collation and translation of classical texts.[123] From the government's side, Qi Yanming noted that "currently, those who are competent to do the work of organizing ancient books are commonly those more than forty or fifty years old who received relatively deeply feudal and capitalist educations."[124] To address the dearth of personnel capable of compiling classical texts for republication, Qi was reconciled to drawing on that pool, as Jin Canran was doing, but he viewed ongoing thought reform as necessary.[125] In fact, political study meetings were a routine aspect of office work in publishing companies during the late 1950s and early 1960s.[126]

At the same time, Qi also called for reaching out to universities to recruit experts there and to have them train students prepared to do compiling work, creating "revolutionary successors" in the cultural realm. "We have consulted with [Minister of Higher Education] Comrade Yang Xiufeng [楊秀峰] and gotten his initial agreement, and we plan to open a special course of study [xueke] at Beijing University and each year recruit thirty or so students."[127] The following year Jin Canran, Qi Yanming, and Wu Han worked with Yang Xiufeng to create a new Classical Documents Program (Gudian wenxian zhuanye) in Beijing University's Chinese Department that would train students in collating ancient books, the study of editions and bibliography, and interpretation of the classics. The program effectively prepared a cohort of young people with the specific skills needed for Zhonghua Book Company's new mandate of organizing and republishing classical texts.[128] It recruited students starting in the fall of 1959. When they began graduating in 1964 and 1965, a number of them immediately became editors and compilers at Zhonghua Book Company. Through coordination with the state, publishers like Zhonghua no longer had to depend on competitive labor markets to recruit staff, as they had before 1949. Instead, higher-education programs could be tailored specifically to publishing objectives.

The final arm of Zhonghua to be reorganized was the *Cihai* Editing Department based in Shanghai. The origin of this initiative was a discussion between Shu Xincheng and Chairman Mao when he was visiting Shanghai in September 1957. Shu convinced his Hunanese *tongxiang* of the value of revising *Cihai* to capture the substantial linguistic, intellectual, and political changes since its publication in 1936–1937.[129] The following spring the Shanghai Municipal Party Committee, responding to a directive from Mao himself, began organizing a *Cihai* Editing Department in Shanghai under supervision of the committee's Propaganda Department, with Shu Xincheng taking the lead.[130] The party committee proposed assigning staff for the project from local government and party organs as well as from area universities, while Shu Xincheng advocated drawing on the former Zhonghua staff editors who had been involved in compiling *Cihai* in the first place. The initial editorial staff came from the former Zhonghua Book Company, New China Bookstore's Shanghai office, and the Dictionary Compiling Office of New Knowledge Publishing Company (Xin zhishi chubanshe).[131] In the spring of 1959 the Shanghai Municipal Party Committee separated the *Cihai* Editing Department from the Zhonghua Book Company Shanghai Editing Department. It set up an editorial committee with Shu Xincheng as chair and with director of the Shanghai Municipal Publishing Department Luo Zhufeng 羅竹風\and secretary of the Municipal Social Science Association (Shelian) Cao Manzhi 曹漫之as assistant chairs.[132] In 1959 and 1960 *Cihai* adopted a mass-based approach that shifted the focus of editorial work away from the Editing Department to a variety of academic and professional organizations. When a full, reorganized editorial committee stabilized as of the summer of 1961, it included local government and party representatives and experts from local academic and cultural units of various kinds. But some of the core staff members were editors who had been at Zhonghua or other Shanghai publishers since the 1920s or 1930s, several of whom had worked on the original *Cihai*.[133] That group included Zhou Songdi, Liu Fanyou, Yang Yinshen, Fu Donghua 傅東華, and Jin Zhaozi. As with the reconstituted Commercial Press and Zhonghua Book Company, the early PRC's publishing infrastructure in these key areas of reference books, classical publishing, and translated foreign scholarship was built on the foundations of the pre-1949 private corporations, drawing heavily on their editorial resources.

Commercial Press's and Zhonghua Book Company's leaders successfully navigated the companies' transition to socialism during the 1950s. The publishers emerged from the process as distinct institutions in the PRC state's cultural apparatus, responsible for publishing foreign academic resources, classical texts and scholarship, and reference books. State agents now had central positions in the companies as directors, editors in chief, and members of the board, giving them direct lines of authority over the companies' operations. Moreover, publishing initiatives had to be vetted with the party's and state's cultural organs and were sometimes passed down from them. Yet each company maintained a corporate identity that was continuous with that developed under the competitive capitalism of the Republican period. Zhonghua was still a producer of reference books and classical texts for a wide audience, and Commercial Press was still a conduit for foreign learning. There were also striking continuities in the organization, leadership, and staff. Many members of the publishers' reconstituted boards of directors had been involved in the companies since before 1949, and numerous old publishing hands worked in their Editing Departments through the 1950s and into the 1960s, especially at Zhonghua.

These continuities did not result from inertia. As shown, during the initial period of public-private joint management from 1954 to 1958, the state experimented with tightly integrating the publishers with state entities, such as the Ministry of Higher Education and a range of economic ministries and commissions. But this new structure failed to generate increased production in the intended areas and largely stifled the publishing initiatives of the staff editors at Commercial Press and Zhonghua that state agents had wanted to tap into in the first place. The reconstitution of each publisher after 1958 marked an acknowledgment that both enterprises were more valuable to the government operating with their own personnel according to long-standing dynamics as they had during the early 1950s, but with greater state supervision and integration into a coordinated publishing plan. Whether the ownership structure was capitalist and private or socialist and public, these companies were valued because they produced books efficiently for mass readerships. Maintaining these enterprises' basic corporate organization and personnel after the transition to socialism marked a tacit recognition of the effectiveness of the mode of industrial publishing developed in late Qing and Republican China.

The new corporate forms that emerged in the 1950s grew out of dynamic engagement between publishing company leaders and state and party agents. The system of "division of labor and cooperation" (*fengong hezuo*), which served as a fundamental operating principle of state-led publishing during the early PRC, had clear precedents in the Nationalist Party's system of distributed market share for textbook publishing during the War of Resistance. These dynamics reflected to some extent Morris Bian's hypothesis about the war crisis shaping the modern Chinese state enterprise system.[134] But the system of public-private joint management that developed in the publishers differed substantially from the system of bureaucratic governance Bian describes. Moreover, the precise form of state-socialist coordination of enterprises had by no means been determined before the 1950s; rather, it was worked out in stages through the immediate post-1949 period, the Five Antis Campaign, development of joint management, and then reorganization in 1958.

Neither did the PRC state immediately impose a uniform system of direct and comprehensive state control of the media on a Soviet model.[135] The divergent fates of World Book Company, Kaiming Bookstore, Commercial Press, and Zhonghua Book Company, not to mention the state-owned publishing entities developed in the 1940s and 1950s, make this clear. Instead, fluid interactions between state agents and publishing-company leaders generated experimentation with several different approaches to state supervision and corporate management during the first seventeen years of the PRC. In the end, Commercial Press and Zhonghua came to operate under state management according to a centrally coordinated division of labor alongside other state publishers. However, tighter integration of these publishing companies with state institutions between 1954 and 1958 was abandoned to allow them to operate according to long-established internal institutional patterns. The continued salience of prewar approaches to publishing emerges even more clearly in the explorations in chapter 7 of the compilation and editing practices at Commercial Press and Zhonghua Book Company during the 1950s and early 1960s.

CHAPTER VII

Negotiated Cultural Production in the Pedagogical State

Throughout the economic crisis and corporate restructuring that marked the publishing sector's transition into the early PRC period, the compilation and publication of books continued unabated. During the Civil War, for example, Commercial Press staff editors were organized into teams to work on particular sections of a revised, abridged version of *Ciyuan*, with Zhang Yuanji overseeing the process.[1] When Commercial Press was finally ready to publish it at the end of June 1949, Shanghai was already under CCP control, so the company took an additional year to supplement it with terminology associated with the new state, with experienced staff editor Wu Zeyan 吳澤炎 doing most of that work.

Directly following the *Ciyuan* revision in the fall of 1949, Commercial Press's Editing Department sought to fashion a usable, general dictionary, the *Four-Corner New Dictionary* (*Sijiao haoma xin cidian*), which did not include specialized or rare characters and terms, targeting an audience of upper-primary and lower-middle-level students and those with a comparable level of education.[2] With Commercial Press's corporate administration in disarray, editors took the lead with this project and revived the mode of collaborative book production that had characterized the Commercial Press Editing Department during the late Qing and early Republic. They formed a small editorial group of eight members, which included longtime staff members Yang Yinshen and Jin Yunfeng. The group together worked out the scope of the dictionary, its search methods, and way of writing entries. To develop a common approach to writing definitions, they each individually wrote up entries for ten sample characters, then they shared them with one another and discussed their different strategies. Subsequently, each editor was responsible for the entries in one section of the dictionary, but they were reviewed by the whole group and decided upon collectively, following closely the textbook and reference book compilation process used by Commercial Press editors nearly five decades earlier. In the absence of an authoritative executive editor and a hierarchal work structure, staff editors managed this project collectively, on the study-society model. The resulting dictionary, which was first published in August 1950, was immensely successful, going through twenty printings by August 1952, suggesting the scale of the latent demand for up-to-date dictionaries. It incorporated new terms associated with Marxism-Leninism and revolutionary socialism, while also redefining older terms "based on new standpoints and points of view" (*genju xin de lichang he guandian*).[3]

As these examples from Commercial Press reveal, modes of book production developed during the first half of the twentieth century extended into the early PRC period, with the participation of longtime editors. Open to question was whether commercial publishers' personnel and production methods would continue to meet the needs of the new state, which approaches to book production would best fit the Mao era's shifting cultural politics, and how editorial practices might be transformed in the context of greater government involvement in the publishing industry. Throughout the 1950s and early 1960s, amid calls generally to expand the kinds and scope of publications for the common people, the PRC government encouraged publishers to "emphasize relatively popular books and periodicals in order to meet the need of cultivating large numbers of talented people for basic construction . . . [and] also publish relatively specialized works in order to meet the need for cultivating talent for high-level construction."[4] How publishing plans to meet these goals were set and implemented and how the content of particular publications was determined involved complex negotiations between government agency and party bureau cultural cadres, on the one hand, and publishing house administrators and editors on the other.

The expertise organized in Commercial Press's and Zhonghua Book Company's Editing Departments and their long histories as distinct organizations helped to constitute them as what Stephen Kotkin, writing about

Stalin's Soviet Union, has called fields of action.[5] The publishers' institutional integrity provided a basis for development of a negotiated form of cultural production in which state and party agencies claimed increasing amounts of cultural authority. But because of their knowledge and skills, elite and petty intellectuals working with or in publishing companies continued to play a vital role in state projects, pursue their own cultural agendas, and claim certain kinds of privilege. This chapter tracks the development of these dynamics by analyzing the compilation of three genres of text that had been vital to Commercial Press and Zhonghua Book Company during the Republican period and remained central to their portfolios during the early PRC: series publications; reprinted classical texts; and reference books, especially dictionaries.[6]

New Knowledge for New China: Series Publications

Formation of the new socialist state and drives for economic, social, and cultural construction created demand for publications that introduced corresponding areas of knowledge. Perception of these nascent markets stimulated production of series publications throughout the 1950s and early 1960s. Approaches to series production generally followed those pioneered during the 1920s and 1930s. Publishers organized editing departments of staff editors and experts in particular subject areas to produce manuscripts in-house, or they tapped networks of academic and professional experts outside the company to produce titles for thematic series. But the socialist state's formation of "organs of cultural management" (wenhua guanli bumen) also allowed coordination of multiple publishers for particular series publishing initiatives, as in the case of the Knowledge Series (Zhishi congshu) under Hu Yuzhi's tutelage. Yet even cooperative ventures like these drew on Republican precedents.

Establishment of the PRC created immediate demand for books about the Soviet Union, Marxism-Leninism, and science and technology, which provided opportunities for publishers.[7] At Zhonghua Book Company, under Shu Xincheng's direction, there was a rapid reorientation in publishing direction during this initial period, but the publisher still produced books in familiar ways. As noted in chapter 6, in 1948–1949 Zhonghua actively recruited five editorial staff members with Russian-language skills and set up classes for editors to study Marxism-Leninism.[8] These measures created the expertise within the company's Editing Department to produce translations from Russian and books on Marxist themes. As a result, in its initial post-1949 publication list distributed in the summer of 1950, Zhonghua offered two robust series of titles on Marxism-Leninism and the Soviet Union that were translated from Russian, the New Era Small Series (Xin shidai xiao congshu) and the Soviet Knowledge Small Series (Sulian zhishi xiao congshu).[9]

Commercial Press similarly responded to new areas of demand, but it took longer to reorganize and reorient its Editing Department. Immediately after the founding of the PRC, the company drew on its existing editorial resources and backlist in an effort to meet new publishing expectations, such as for children's reading materials.[10] During the next few years, Commercial Press built up its Editing Department to be able to offer topical series more directly relevant to the new era of socialist construction. After Yuan Hanqing was commissioned by GPA director Hu Yuzhi to direct the Editing Department at Commercial Press in 1951, he incorporated several of his former colleagues from the Bureau to Popularize Science (Kexue puji ju) and staff from Wang Tianyi's mass science periodicals.[11] The new personnel allowed Commercial Press to produce numerous new series on the themes of science and technology. These included the Small Series of China's Resources (Zhongguo fuyuan xiao congshu), the Translated Series of Scientific Monographs from the Soviet Union (Sulian kexue zhuanzhu yicong), Practical Electrical Engineering Series (Shiyong diangong congshu), Science Small Library (Kexue xiao wenku), the Soviet Mass Science Series (Sulian dazhong kexue congshu), and the Youth Science Series (Shaonian kexue congshu).[12] Mobilization of editors with expertise in scientific publishing allowed Commercial Press to dramatically expand its list in these areas. The company also continued to publish science and technology books for the University Series, extending Wang Yunwu's initiative that had persisted through the war years.[13] For these publications, the publisher still solicited manuscripts from scholars outside the company.[14]

As publishers' areas of specialization stabilized during the latter part of the 1950s, they developed more thematically specific series, sometimes with the initiative coming from state or party leaders working through government offices or party departments for cultural management. Zhonghua Book Company's Chinese History Small Series (Lishi xiao congshu) offers a prime example.[15] Beijing deputy mayor Wu Han initiated this series in 1958 with the goal of producing accessible historical works that teachers could use as reference materials.[16] To build up the series Wu established an editorial committee of scholars from outside the publisher that would solicit manuscripts and review submissions. Wu himself remained actively involved in the series, despite his official mayoral duties. He called regular editorial committee meetings, solicited manuscripts, and reviewed manuscripts quickly and rigorously.[17] The practical editing work, however, was done by staff editors organized as a Historical Series Group (Lishi congshu zu) in Zhonghua Book Company's Editing Department. The compilers and editors in the group had a demanding job, taking manuscripts written by specialized scholars and reshaping them into readable manuscripts of ten thousand to twenty thousand characters. The compilers sometimes also built on their own experience to write volumes for the series. These work processes directly paralleled those of earlier series compilation projects, such as the Complete Library, where publishers both solicited manuscripts from experts outside the company and tapped the resources of their own editing departments.

The compilers were drawn primarily from among the kinds of staff editors with a basic education described in chapter 2. Zhu Yanfu 朱彥頫 had previously been a middle school teacher and had compiled textbooks for Zhonghua Book Company for decades.[18] Li Gengxu 李賡序 and Gong Shaoying 鞏紹英 had both previously been editors under Jin Canran at People's Education Press, whom he recruited to work on this series.[19] Li represents a particularly interesting example of how the publishers "recycled" scholars with problematic class or political backgrounds for the sake of particular cultural projects. Li had been branded a rightist (youpai) in the Anti-Rightist Campaign of 1957, but Jin Canran was able to have him transferred from the rural area in Shanxi to which he had been sent for labor reform to Zhonghua Book Company so that his skills could be used for this series.

Zhu and Li each wrote titles for the Chinese History Small Series that were noteworthy for their clear organization and vivid writing. They also contributed extensive editorial work to transforming dry scholarly works into accessible popular readers, as the following statement by their colleague Wang Daiwen suggests.

For some manuscripts, the choice of topic and the materials were good, but they were poorly written, and even if the author revised the text repeatedly, he would have difficulty continuing to improve it. When it reached his [Zhu Yanfu's] hands, he would make some adjustments to the sections, polish the writing, and patch things up, then he could greatly improve the quality to reach the level of sending the manuscript to be published. Comrade Jin Canran greatly appreciated his ability to handle difficult manuscripts and "bring the dead back to life."[20]

As had been true during the first half of the twentieth century, publishers like Zhonghua used staff editors with generalist educations, sound writing skills, and editorial experience to reshape scholarly knowledge into books that were popularly accessible. Though the ownership structure had changed, the core objectives of industrial publishing—making a diverse array of modern and classical knowledge available to a mass public—remained the same. Staff editors, with their basic educations and life experiences that resonated with those of general readers, were essential to that process.

A somewhat different approach to organizing series publications characterized the Knowledge Series. In 1961 Hu Yuzhi, former director of the GPA who at that time was assistant director at the Ministry of Culture in charge of publishing, initiated the series. In May that year Hu hosted a meal at the Sichuan Restaurant in Beijing with the director of the Propaganda Department's Publishing Office, Bao Zhijing 包之靜, the director of the Publishing Office of the Ministry of Culture, Wang Yi 王益, along with the People's Publishing Company's Wang Ziye 王子野, Commercial Press's Chen Hanbo, and Zhonghua Book Company's Jin Canran.[21] At the meal Hu Yuzhi floated the idea of publishing a series to raise the cultural level of China's cadres, with each volume introducing them to intermediate-level knowledge on a cultural, scientific, or practical topic. Hu asserted that the basic level of knowledge presented in the series meant that the authors need not be elite experts; rather, staff editors at the publishers could write most of the manuscripts, as they had at Commercial Press, Zhonghua Book Company, and Kaiming Bookstore before the war. As models Hu's protégé Chen Yuan 陳原 cited Commercial Press's Complete Library but also the international examples of Everyman's Library and the Little Blue Book series. Hu's colleagues immediately supported the initiative and voiced suggestions for identifying series authors among "compilers, teachers, and engineers and technicians [gongcheng jishu renyuan]."

Hu further raised specific ideas about the content of the series, suggesting a focus on reading materials on science and technology and on "problems that were currently of the greatest concern to the masses [*qun-zhong zui guanxin de wenti*]."[22] In the aftermath of the Great Leap Forward, when cadres' mismanagement played a role in creating an economic disaster, the need for raising cadres' technical knowledge was quickly acknowledged by Hu's colleagues. In contrast, they balked at the idea of publishing volumes on questions like, "Why is the market in short supply?" or, "Why is there a lack of nonstaple foods?" These issues related to the state's economic policies, which could change quickly. In the wake of the Lushan Plenum and Peng Dehuai's purge, they were viewed as too politically sensitive.[23] Similarly, several people raised the possibility of texts that introduced basic elements of Marxist-Leninist theory, but the Central Propaganda Department's Bao Zhijing warned that publishing volumes on what were essentially contested concepts in Marxist theory could also be politically sensitive. He suggested leaving this work to a group in the Central Propaganda Department that was writing books explaining the basic principles of Marxism. In these discussions, we see government and party leaders responsible for managing the publishing industry and representatives of several leading publishers negotiating how to address a clear market demand while limiting risk, in a context in which culture was increasingly politicized.

Based on these discussions, on May 15, 1961, the Ministry of Culture's party group submitted a preliminary proposal to the Central Propaganda Department.[24] The party group planned for a consortium of six publishers to produce some two thousand volumes between 1961 and 1965, with each averaging fifty thousand characters, or about a hundred pages. It proposed organizing an editorial committee composed of "leading comrades of cultural and academic circles, figures in academic circles, and relevant publishing companies' editors in chief" to oversee and support the project. The thematic areas covered would include theoretical knowledge (but not Marxism-Leninism), historical knowledge, world knowledge, knowledge about production skills and daily life, and knowledge about literature and the arts. Given the division of labor among China's publishing companies after the industry's reorganization during the 1950s, the six publishers would each focus on a specific subject area. People's Publishing Company would concentrate on philosophy and social science; People's Literature Publishing Company would cover literature and the arts; Zhonghua would take up Chinese history and cultural heritage; Commercial Press would engage foreign history and cultural heritage; the Science Publishing Company would specialize in science, technology, and productive life; while the

World Knowledge Publishing Company would address international knowledge. Each company was then to formulate a list of titles for its subject area and solicit manuscripts to serve as models for its part of the list. The models were to be published in the fourth quarter of 1961. Significantly, the division of labor instituted in the publishing industry during the 1950s now posed a barrier to the kind of comprehensive publishing project that party and government cultural managers and publishing company leaders perceived to be a pressing need.

On May 18 the Central Propaganda Department held a meeting to discuss the initial proposal. The Ministry of Culture's Qi Yanming, Hu Yuzhi, and Chen Yuan attended, along with the Propaganda Department's director, Lu Dingyi 陸定一, and assistant directors Zhou Yang 周揚, Zhang Ziyi 張子意, Lin Mohan 林默涵, and Yao Qin 姚溱, as well as Bao Zhijing and Xu Liyi 許力以 from the Publishing Office, and Lin Jianqing 林澗清 from the Science Office.[25] On May 23, the Ministry of Culture submitted a slightly revised plan that was approved by the Central Propaganda Department on June 8.[26] The most significant change was moderation of the scale, with a goal of publishing three hundred to four hundred books in two to three years. Further, based on a comment by Zhou Yang about emphasizing richness of content over political viewpoint, the final plan still allowed publishers like Commercial Press and Zhonghua with large backlists to select appropriate books for republication. In this approval process, Ministry of Culture officials collaborated with publishing company directors to formulate a plan that was acceptable to cadres in the CCP's Propaganda Department.

Work on the series began in August 1961 with a meeting of the expanded editorial committee. But Hu Yuzhi quickly realized that the editorial committee, composed as it was of leading cultural and political figures who were widely dispersed, could not serve as an immediate managing body for the series.[27] Instead, he organized a standing editorial committee (changwu bianwei) composed of representatives of each of the participating publishers, who could meet once or twice a month to manage the series.[28] To brainstorm titles for each component subject area of the series, Hu initiated a string of forums between outside experts and representatives of the publishers to discuss possible topics of focus. Forums were held that year on economics, international issues, and philosophy.[29] Drawing on the forums, the Ministry of Culture's Chen Yuan, Wang Cheng 王城, and Han Zhongmin 韩仲民 formulated a list of about a thousand topics, on the model of an encyclopedia, echoing 1920s projects like the Universal Library and ABC Series. The standing editorial committee then worked with the publishers to identify volumes that fit the series. For instance, at Zhonghua Jin Canran engaged the linguist Wang Li 王力 to write a volume of fifty thousand to sixty thousand characters about poetic meter. Written in an accessible language, it was eagerly adopted by the committee as a model; the committee also felt that its focus on Chinese cultural heritage was relatively safe politically.

Overall, this pattern of series production closely paralleled that of the 1920s and 1930s. Publishers' executive editors engaged outside experts or organized staff editors in their own editing departments to produce specific titles for a thematically organized list. An editorial board provided a resource for choosing topics and soliciting manuscripts, but the direct management of the publication series remained in the hands of publishing companies' editors in chief, here organized as a standing editorial committee. The series, in turn, provided a venue for leading intellectuals like Wang Li to write more accessible books to reach a broader audience, much as they had before 1949.[30]

Where the publication process of the Knowledge Series differed from the processes of the pre-1949 period was in its coordination of multiple publishing companies in a common publishing venture. This coordination was necessitated by the strict imposition of thematic divisions of labor in the publishing industry during the 1950s. But the coordination was also facilitated by the development of the Ministry of Culture and the Central Propaganda Department as cultural management organs of the state and party, respectively. The networks of interaction that developed during the 1950s as publishers were reorganized and negotiated their publishing plans with these cultural management organs provided a basis for cooperation on a project like the Knowledge Series. Yet there were also notable precedents of cooperation among publishers, such as the coordinated printing and distribution of national standard textbooks during the 1940s, which also underpinned the collective publishing work of a new era.

Old Books for Current Use

During the first years of the PRC, classical publishing was a secondary concern compared with the importance placed on publications directly related to socialist construction, and it was not a primary mandate of either Commercial Press or Zhonghua Book Company. Zhonghua, for instance, when it listed its areas of publishing specialization in 1950 and then again in 1952, focused on the areas of agriculture, medicine, Russian-language texts, and publications introducing the Soviet Union, without mention of classical publishing.[31] A global assessment of ancient-book publishing during the early 1950s noted, "Since the start of the War of Resistance until two or three years into liberation, classical publishing work stopped for many years."[32]

By the mid-1950s, both Commercial Press and Zhonghua were again engaging in some forms of classical publishing, in part tapping into personnel and resources that were legacies of the Republican period. Longtime editor Zhao Shouyan 趙守儼, for example, describes in his memoir how classical texts were one of the main publishing areas for the remnant Commercial Press Editing Department housed in the Reference Book Group (Gongjushu zu) of the reorganized Higher-Education Publishing Company.[33] Initially, the group had only four people carried over from the previous Commercial Press, including Wu Zeyan 吳翠炎 and Zhou Yunqing 周雲青, who had worked in the Editing Department for some time. Between 1954 and 1958, it published several different categories of books, including technical classical books, the *Reduced-Size Most Reliable Editions of the Twenty-Four Dynastic Histories* (*Suoyin bainaben ershisi shi*), classical bibliographies and language books, notes on textual research, as well as collections of historical materials and notes on classical histories. Significantly, with a number of these collections Zhao and his colleagues drew on Commercial Press's previous legacy of classical publishing, such as Zhang Yuanji's set of dynastic histories from the 1920s and 1930s. Similarly, Commercial Press's Shanghai Editing Department commented in 1957 that its classical publishing was secondary to its primary focus on university and technical textbooks, encompassing just eighty titles that were based mostly on the company's old printing plates, with some additional editorial work.[34]

In the same period, Zhonghua Book Company assessed its own classical-book publishing as being fairly limited in scope.

Since joint management in 1954, according to directives from the leadership, we also published some ancient books, but because of limited manpower and because our comrades' levels [of classical education] were not good, our contributions to this aspect were very few.

There was also insufficient review in terms of the selection of ancient books. In recent years our company has generally published seventy-some titles of ancient books. The varieties can generally be divided into language, grammar, history, classical studies, ancient philosophers' works, agricultural books, texts of addresses [*jiangci*], and miscellaneous works.[35]

For both Commercial Press and Zhonghua during the mid-1950s, publication of classical texts was secondary to their main areas of concentration, demanding relatively little editorial energy.

Starting in 1956 and 1957, however, as the PRC began to separate itself from the Soviet Union and national distinctiveness became a greater concern, voices inside and outside the government began calling for a renewed emphasis on publication of classical texts.[36] In May 1956 the Ministry of Culture's party group reported to the CCP's Central Propaganda Department on the current state of classical-book publishing.[37] The report acknowledged some contributions in classical publishing during the early PRC period, but overall it criticized the lack of comprehensive planning among the many publishing companies that were each publishing different kinds of classical texts on their own initiative. Further, the party group criticized the publishers' "lack of a mass viewpoint" (*qunzhong guandian*), asserting that companies were issuing texts without regard to "the situation of academic research work and the needs of a broad group of readers." The publishers, the party group asserted, had an elitist, "bourgeois and decadent ideology" that emphasized rare, early editions without regard to their usefulness to the reader. The report was followed later that year by newspaper editorials extolling the value of ancient books and the need to preserve and develop ancient-book publishing.[38]

The following spring the Central Propaganda Department solicited feedback on ancient-book publishing from experienced figures in the publishing industry in Beijing and Shanghai, who wrote statements and held forums in response. These discussions developed in step with the Hundred Flowers Campaign in the publishing industry, which extended from late April into early June of 1957.[39] In his diary entry on the meeting in Shanghai on April 12, Shu Xincheng reported that the group included representatives from Zhonghua, Commercial Press, and the Classical Literature Publishing Company, along with two professors from Fudan and a member of the Literature Association (Wenyihui)—fourteen people in all.[40]

A summary report of these discussions in Shanghai, which also synthesized written statements by a range of publishing figures involved in ancient-book publishing, asserted that political stability after 1949 had led to a revival of cultural life, the Hundred Flowers Campaign had stimulated academic research, and development of high-school education had led to growing interest in classical literature.[41] All these factors created a positive demand for ancient books in two dimensions: "One aspect pertains to improvement, which is to supply academic research reference materials; one aspect pertains to popularization, which is to supply classical reading materials to students and teachers of the lower-middle-school level and above."[42] For improvement, Shanghai's classical-publishing hands suggested publishing in photolithograph form unpublished, very early, or rare editions gathered from the nation's libraries. They called for publishing the books in unadulterated form, without making alterations, as Ming scholar-publishers had done, or adding a "note on alterations" (*yougai bizhu*), when changes had been made.[43] In terms of popularization, they suggested meeting with high school teachers and university faculty members to get their views on the most valuable books to publish. Books to be published for this market could be composed of selections or translated to make them more accessible.

The Shanghai classical-publishing hands also highlighted several important issues related to the publishing process of ancient books. At the level of planning and coordination, they suggested establishing a comprehensive planning organization that included participants from production units and experts in classical learning. They also called for division of labor and coordination across publishing units. Further, they expressed real concern over mobilizing experienced personnel for this kind of publishing work. "The work of reprinting ancient books requires specialized talent. For instance, in the past with Commercial Press's *Sibu congkan*, without the venerable Zhang Jusheng, it could not have done its work well."[44] Zhonghua Book Company's accompanying report noted a dearth of personnel for the kinds of selection, collation, annotation, proofreading, and translation work required for classical publishing, emphasizing that the absence of capable classical-text editors would worsen in coming years as those now doing the work aged.[45] In response, the Shanghai publishers advocated recruiting new talent. Similarly, Zhonghua's Wu Tiesheng, in his written comments, observed that "currently, there are many publishers and talent is dispersed and not concentrated. Editorial staff are few, managers are many." He then asserted that "concentrating strength, making overall arrangements, correctly dividing labor, and avoiding redundancy and waste are all issues worth study by the leading organs."[46]

The leading organs apparently did study the issues and suggestions raised in these forums and written statements, for when the Ministry of Culture's Qi Yanming wrote to the Central Propaganda Department early in 1958 calling for renewed efforts to publish ancient books, he echoed many of their points.[47] Qi emphasized that study of ancient books should not be neglected, nor should it be a narrow, pedantic exercise. "The objective of organizing and publishing ancient books is to prepare relatively perfect conditions for critically putting in order our country's ancient culture."[48] Following the logic of the discussions in Shanghai, Qi asserted that "the target readers of ancient books by and large can be divided into two parts: one part is research workers and cultural and educational workers who have relatively high cultural levels; one part is ordinary readers, including cadres and students who have a secondary school cultural level or higher."[49] Experts, Qi reasoned, needed research and reference material, which required selection of editions and collation. Given the specialized and narrowly defined readership of these works, Qi suggested that some publications could be for internal circulation only (*neibu faxing*). Educators and culture workers with relatively high cultural levels, Qi observed, needed "our country's ancient representative academic and literary works." These required more organizational work in terms of punctuation and annotation, with the possibility of using old notes if appropriate resources were available, echoing comments by Shanghai's Hu Daojing 胡道靜 and Wu Tiesheng. For common readers, who needed selections of famous ancient works, the additional work would be even greater in terms of punctuation, annotation, publishing explanations, and even translation into the vernacular.

On the organizational side, Qi's proposal effectively took up each of the main concerns raised by the Shanghai publishers. Establishment of the Planning Small Group addressed the issue of long-term planning and coordination under state leadership. Designating Zhonghua Book Company as the main publisher of classical texts effected the concentration of publishing resources Wu Tiesheng had advocated. And initiation of the Classical Documents Program at Beida (see chapter 6) aimed to address the long-term concern about specialized staff for this kind of publishing. Significantly, Qi also placed great emphasis on the immediate dearth of expertise for compiling ancient books. "According to investigation, the editorial staff throughout the country currently engaged in ancient-book publishing overall is just fifty-some people. But during the Ming more than twenty-one hundred people participated in compiling the *Yongle Compendium*, and during compilation of *Siku quanshu* in the Qing dynasty there were more than three hundred people who directly participated in the work and can be identified by name. By comparison, we appear to be too few."[50]

Qi's observation carved out a place for classically trained scholars in Zhonghua's Editing Department during the late 1950s and early 1960s. In general, Qi's initiative to reinvigorate classical publishing echoed the recommendations of publishing hands with experience in classical publishing, suggesting give-and-take between intellectuals in publishing companies and cadres in positions of authority in the party and state.

During the period of the Great Leap Forward, however, classical publishing was difficult to justify in an atmosphere that was increasingly utopian and future oriented. In particular, during the spring of 1958, Chen Boda 陳伯達 formulated the slogan "Emphasize the present over the past" (*hou jin bo gu* 厚今薄古) in the Science Planning Commission, which was widely perceived as an attack on classical publishing.[51] In a series of talks that summer, Qi Yanming responded and argued strongly for the current value of engagement with the past: "Chairman Mao instructed us not to separate out part of history [*geduan lishi*]. The roots of today's problems reside in history; we must have a concrete understanding of those roots to be able to understand the present. If we do not study feudal society, we cannot understand the village. . . . Historical heritage is also the basis of new culture; new culture must assimilate historical things, and only in that way can we better cultivate new culture."[52]

In good historical-materialist form, Qi rationalized renewed commitment to classical scholarship as a way to historically situate and respond to current social and political problems. For him, the essential issue was studying the past in order to illuminate and improve the present, rather than just studying and exploring it for its own sake.[53] Despite criticism from leftists like Chen Boda, Qi made a compelling case for classical publishing as part of the revolutionary project.

As discussed in chapter 6, to implement the Ministry of Culture's initiative for classical publishing, Zhonghua Book Company reorganized in 1958 with an editorial committee composed of many old publishing hands and classically trained scholars, like Jin Zhaozi, Yao Shaohua, Lu Wendi, and Chen Naiqian. In addition, scholars with experience with classical texts were transferred in from other units, and recent college graduates were recruited, creating an Editing Department whose composition closely paralleled that of the major publishing companies during the 1920s and 1930s.[54] During this same period, the staff at Zhonghua formulated publishing plans in conjunction with members of the Planning Small Group for Organizing and Publishing Ancient Books, outside scholars, and other members of the Ministry of Culture and Central Propaganda Department. Tracking this process illuminates how publishing projects were initiated, organized, and executed during this period.

In June 1958 the Planning Small Group drafted an initial plan for organization and publication of ancient books, organized according to the three areas of literature, philosophy, and history. This plan was circulated among academic institutions and cultural organs, which offered feedback during the second half of 1958.[55] At the same time, intellectuals and government officials could initiate proposals for particular classical-publishing projects. For example, in October 1958 Wu Han and Fan Wenlan, both members of the Planning Small Group, acting in response to a directive from Mao Zedong, proposed preparing punctuated versions of the first four dynastic histories.[56] They met with Zhonghua general manager and executive editor Jin Canran and discussed the allocation of work on the four initial manuscripts, two of which were assigned, respectively, to Gu Jiegang and the Chinese Academy of Science History Institute and the other two of which were to be handled by Zhonghua Book Company directly.[57] They agreed on a common method of punctuation, and they decided that Zhonghua Book Company would formulate a further plan to punctuate the remaining twenty dynastic histories and the Qing draft history.

Drawing on feedback, Zhonghua Book Company's staff formulated a preliminary publishing plan for 1959–1962. The plan was framed in terms of the need to satisfy demand from a "broad group of cadres" (*guangda ganbu*) and "specialized research workers" (*zhuanmen yanjiu gongzuozhe*), echoing Qi Yanming's talks and communications during the previous year.[58] The company would publish different kinds of materials to address these two constituencies. For cadres of middle and upper cultural levels, it proposed reading materials that "carefully select from our country's ancient books some representative important works, organize them, and separately publish several sets of series." To make them suitable for the cultural level of the readers, depending on the text, they would require varying forms of punctuation, annotation, introductory explanation, or translation into modern Chinese. For the needs of academic researchers and experts, they proposed,

From one aspect organize and publish several sets of basic series classified by category, such as a classical literature basic series, an ancient philosophy basic series, basic historical books from successive dynasties, and so forth. From another aspect, we also must organize and publish some books of materials compiled by category and some that are overview collections and books with relatively important reference value and reference books that do not circulate much and are not convenient to acquire.[59]

The draft plan then offered specific lists of titles for each category of philosophy, literature, and history.

Focusing on the history section, the plan made a basic distinction between ancient history on the one hand and Qing and modern history on the other.[60] The former was divided into fourteen categories: dynastic histories, comprehensive histories, chronicles, specialized histories, systems of decrees and regulations, memorials and edicts, geography, crafts materials, astronomy and calendars, historical materials on Sino-foreign communication, examination of historical materials, category books and comprehensive reference books, collections of materials, and literary collections. The latter was divided into seven categories: comprehensive historical materials, archival historical materials, historical materials on specialized topics, literary collections and memorials, letters and diaries, collections of notes on Qing-dynasty historical materials, and collections of notes on modern historical materials. For each category, the publisher had to make a careful selection and prioritize. For instance, the company planned a selection of Song and Yuan gazetteers and looked ahead to needing to consult further with experts to determine which of the many Ming and Qing gazetteers to selectively republish. In general, Jin Canran consulted heavily with members of the Planning Small Group and other relevant scholars. With the section on historical publishing, for example, Jin wrote to Wu Han asking for specific feedback: "With the History Section's catalog, especially the Ming dynasty portion . . . we ask you to make a special effort to consider whether there is anything we should add or take out, or in terms of editions, what places do we need to be attentive to? Optimally, we ask that you first make revisions to the plan's initial draft."[61] In the fall of 1960, the Planning Small Group sent a revised plan covering the years 1960 to 1967 to universities and research institutes through the Ministry of Education and the Academy of Science to solicit suggestions about specific titles and volunteers to participate in the organization and compilation work on specific ancient books. Zhonghua Book Company was responsible for receiving and processing the responses.[62] During the period of the plan the company anticipated publishing some fourteen hundred fifty titles, including both materials and reference books for research and instruction and selected and annotated works for cadres and students.[63]

The republication of punctuated dynastic histories initiated by Mao and proposed by Fan Wenlan and Wu Han became Zhonghua's signature large-scale classical-publishing project during this period. When the project was launched, the company initially experimented with a new dynamic of collating and editing the *Twenty-Four Dynastic Histories* that augured a more "collective" or "socialist" mode of cultural production. Many segments of the dynastic histories were initially sent to academic institutions throughout the country, where teams of scholars and graduate students were to carry out collation and punctuation work.[64] Specifically, Gu Jiegang (then at the Chinese Academy of Science) worked on the *Records of the Grand Historian (Shiji)*; Northwestern University's History Department was responsible for the *Hanshu*; Shandong University's History Department was responsible for the histories of the Southern Dynasties; Wuhan University's History Department took on the histories of the Northern Dynasties; Sun Yat-sen University's History Department was to handle the *Tangshu*; the Liao, Jin, Yuan, and other non-Han dynasties of the middle period would be compiled by the Nationalities Institute; and the Ming-Qing History Research Lab of Nankai University collated and punctuated the *Mingshi*.[65] Other histories were punctuated and collated by individual editors. For instance, Chen Naiqian compiled the *Annals of the Three Kingdoms (Sanguozhi)*. Coordinating the efforts of teams of expert scholars from across the country who worked independently, this editorial strategy seemed to point toward a completely new dynamic of socialist cultural work.

But this collective and "socialist" mode of compiling simply did not function effectively. According to Zhao Shouyan, "Each history being punctuated and collated separately in the institutes and schools of outside areas was often interrupted by duties of teaching and research, carried out in fits and starts. In this way, not only did the timing not have any guarantee, influencing the rate of progress, but along with that problems also occurred with the quality."[66] For scholars and students not directly affiliated with the publisher, the collating and punctuation work associated with the *Twenty-Four Dynastic Histories* was simply not a high priority, leading to work that was delayed and of poor quality. In response, in 1963 Jin Can-ran consulted with Qi Yanming, then vice-minister of culture, and Zhou Yang, deputy director of the Central Propaganda Department, to concentrate work on the histories at the publisher's office in Beijing. This entailed either transferring scholars to Zhonghua to work on particular volumes or asking compilers and editors at the publisher to review and revise the work that had been shared out to university history departments.[67] We see writer and longtime staff editor Fu Donghua, for instance, taking up compilation of the *Hanshu*.[68] The resulting compilation process closely resembled that of the large-scale projects undertaken by the commercial publishers during the Republican period. Dedicated teams composed of staff editors and hired experts were organized under executive editors who delegated discrete tasks to each of the team's members. Centralized coordination proved essential to producing quality work. What changed was the organizational capacity of the socialist state, which was now able to transfer scholars from far-flung academic institutions to Zhonghua's offices in Beijing for work on a specific project.

In general, classical publishing during the first seventeen years of the Maoist period developed through multiple cycles of exchange between intellectuals working in the publishing companies, cadres working in state institutions and party organizations, and scholars in universities and research institutes. For the signature punctuated version of the *Twenty-Four Dynastic Histories* project, Zhonghua initially experimented with distributing the work to academic units throughout the country, but the results were disappointing. In response, Zhonghua gathered intellectuals in its Editing Department for centralized coordination of the work in ways similar to Commercial Press's encyclopedia and series publications of the 1920s. But unlike Wang Yunwu, who depended on competitive labor markets to recruit staff, Zhonghua in the 1960s benefited from the state's ability to allocate (*fenpei*) intellectual labor in unprecedented ways. A mode of coordinated production developed during a period of competitive capitalism was facilitated by the labor-allocation mechanisms of state socialism.

Reference Books for the People

The 1950s witnessed a dramatic transformation of the Chinese vocabulary with increased use of politicized rhetoric, universal adoption of

Marxism-Leninism as a conceptual framework for the New Society, and exposure to new forms of global knowledge derived from new alignments with state-socialist countries. Much as linguistic and conceptual shifts in the late Qing and May Fourth periods provided motivations for compiling, respectively, *Ciyuan* and *Cihai*, the transition to socialism created a pressing demand for new dictionaries and other reference books to provide authoritative definitions of new terms and concepts. But initial efforts at dictionary compilation in the 1950s, such as Commercial Press's initiatives described at the beginning of the chapter, were ad hoc, taken up by individual publishing companies, and borrowed heavily from prior dictionary projects. As the Shanghai Municipal Party Committee put it in a communication to the Central Committee regarding the beginning of the *Cihai* revision process, "These years there is not even one decent dictionary to use to investigate, which really is a great shortcoming of publishing work."[69] Only after 1957 did publishing companies and state and party cultural management organs cooperate to launch a comprehensive revision of *Cihai* to stabilize the vocabulary of Chinese socialism.[70] Yet many of the approaches to reference-book production ultimately used in the *Cihai* revision had started in the 1920s and 1930s, and the kinds of personnel used for dictionary compilation paralleled the kinds of earlier periods.

The initiative to revise *Cihai* apparently grew out of discussions between Shu Xincheng and Mao Zedong, the two Hunan natives, when Mao was visiting Shanghai in the fall of 1957. According to writer Li Chunping's account, Shu reported meeting with Mao on September 17, 1957, during which Mao expressed enthusiastic support for Shu to lead revision of *Cihai* and then continue on to publish an encyclopedia.[71]

On May 19, 1958, the Central Propaganda Department approved a plan for the Shanghai Municipal Party Committee to oversee revision of *Cihai* within the organizational structure of Zhonghua Book Company.[72] In the parlance of the Shanghai Municipal Committee, "In Shanghai set up the *Cihai* Editing Department. In name it will still belong to Zhonghua Book Company's organizational system. Administratively it will be concretely led by the locality [i.e., the Shanghai Municipal Government]."[73] The project was justified on the basis of the linguistic and cultural changes generated by the Chinese revolution and global developments: "*Cihai* has already been published for twenty years. In the past twenty years, the world has gone through great changes, and China has already gone through great changes. New terms are everywhere, and they are numerous. When revising *Cihai*, these new terms must be gathered together, organized, and incorporated in a timely way."[74] The Shanghai Municipal Committee estimated an overall cost of 1.5 million yuan over five years, designated Shu Xincheng to take primary responsibility for the project, and allocated level-one cadres from two departments and more than twenty common staff to carry out the project. It also called for further support from the State Council's Science Planning Commission, the Chinese Academy of Science, the Central Ministry of Culture, and the Central Ministry of Education. Moreover, the Shanghai Municipal Committee asked that "the [Party] Center take editorial staff that are scattered in various areas but which *Cihai* urgently needs and transfer them as soon as possible in order to benefit the work."[75]

However, when work on the *Cihai* revision process began in earnest in the spring of 1959, the Shanghai Municipal Committee spearheaded another approach, which drew more widely on academic units for their expertise. The *Cihai* Editorial Committee designated "universities and colleges, research institutions, and units with relevant business" to take responsibility for drafting entries in the subject areas in which they specialized. *Cihai* assistant director Hang Wei 杭葦[76] enumerated the participating units in a report to the Shanghai Publishing Bureau party committee in February 1960:

> Up to the present, the groups from which we have commissioned manuscript sections include 28 universities and colleges (of which 20 are in this city), 21 research institutions (of which 13 are in this city), and 41 business units (all of which are in this city). From the foregoing 90 units (if we take university departments as units, then there are 142), we estimate the number of people compiling [entries] to be more than 2,600 (of which upper-level students are about 700).[77]

Following Great Leap Forward patterns of mass mobilization of labor across units, the scale of coordination was huge, and large amounts of material were to be processed and compiled very quickly. For example, Li Chunping describes the Geography Department at East China Normal University mobilizing fifteen faculty and graduate students along with forty third-year students to compile one thousand entries in the course of one week in November 1959.[78]

After gathering the compiled entries from research and academic units in the spring of 1960, the Editing Department coordinated a mass review of the entries. Mass line tactics—mobilizing ordinary people for collective work on a party-led project—continued with a large-scale review of the manuscript during schools' summer vacation in 1960. As described again by Hang Wei in a report to the Shanghai Publishing Bureau's party group, the company would "during summer vacation this year [1960] widely mobilize teachers and students in the relevant departments in each of this city's universities and colleges, along with a portion of middle school teachers and business-department cadres to participate in checking."[79] Altogether they expected that 174 units and 1,299 people would participate, with the units ranging from research institutions, university and college departments, to factories and enterprises, party committees, and secondary schools.[80]

As with the Zhonghua Editing Department's coordinated approach to compiling the *Twenty-Four Dynastic Histories*, though, the *Cihai* Editing Department's mass line compiling strategy encountered numerous practical problems. Academic departments often provided uneven and grudging support for a project foisted on them by an outside unit. The quality of the dictionary's entries suffered accordingly. Hang Wei identified this issue early on in his February 1960 report to the Shanghai Publishing Bureau: "There are also some units that take this to be an extra burden, their attitude is not serious enough, the manuscript they write is of poor quality, or their work progress is very slow. For example, Fudan University's Chinese Department, its Foreign Literature Department, Normal University's Education Department, its Biology Department, and so forth."[81] According to Hang, some units refused to cooperate at all, like the Beijing Military Science Academy (Junshi kexue yuan), whose insight into military terms was viewed as essential. In other instances the units had a biased approach to the terminology, as did several units involved in drafting religious terminology. This decentralized process allowed for little quality control, since cooperating units were not necessarily as committed to this project as was the publisher, and entries grudgingly produced could be poorly researched and written. Li Chunping also indicates that in the summer of 1960 *Cihai*'s editorial leaders were increasingly aware of the limitations of crowd sourcing the manuscript's revision and review.[82]

An expanded Editorial Board Conference on February 6, 1961, repudiated the mass line approach of dictionary revision and review used during the Great Leap period. Instead, it initiated a process of concentrated revision undertaken by experts in each discipline who would be gathered at Shanghai's Pujiang Hotel during the spring and summer of 1961.[83] As with the Great Leap more generally, mass-mobilization-based industrial produc-tion was replaced by more established and effective approaches to indus-trial labor. Soon thereafter, 114 experts from academic units in Shanghai, Hangzhou, Nanjing, Hefei, and Beijing settled into the Pujiang Hotel for collective review and revision of the manuscript.[84]

Work dynamics on the *Cihai* revision greatly resembled group compil-ing projects from earlier periods, with elite scholars working collaboratively. Participants who lived nearby walked daily to the Pujiang Hotel for work, those living further away in Shanghai were driven to the hotel each day, while those from outside Shanghai stayed at the hotel. Compilers were organized according to discipline. Each disciplinary group shared a room in the hotel that was used as a makeshift office, with multiple desks or tables arranged in it. Compilers worked in close proximity through the hot Shanghai summer, unwilling even to open windows in fear of papers from drafts and notes being blown around.[85] Meals were shared, and often work discussions continued during and after meals and into the night. Gathering so many scholars in close proximity fostered an academic atmosphere that resembled the Commercial Press Editing Department of the first decade of the twentieth century, when late Qing literati had predominated, and the 1920s, when Wang Yunwu had amassed a brain trust of scholars returned from overseas study. As during those periods, compilation work gave rise to and was enriched by academic-style debates over competing theories, interpretations, and practical choices in compilation.[86] But all this work was now coordinated by the representatives of the Shanghai Municipal Pub-lishing Bureau, Luo Zhufeng and Hang Wei, who directed the project in ways similar to the executive editors of the pre-1949 period at Zhonghua and Commercial Press.

Coordinating experts to formulate entries for particular sections of the dictionary's encyclopedic terms also generated its own problems, as revealed in an October 1962 report from the *Cihai* Editing Department to the Shang-hai Publishing Bureau party group on the workings of the editorial com-mittee.[87] Scholars complained about those chosen as executive editors' (*zhu bianji*) not being up to the task and about effective, hardworking colleagues' work not being recognized and rewarded. Scholars sometimes held differ-ing opinions about whether revisions were necessary, and some angrily resisted colleagues' revising the entries they had written. Tensions arose between scholars from different universities, with an especially sharp rivalry developing between Fudan University and East China Normal.

Zhonghua's *Cihai* Editing Department reported, "Based on what is reflected in the car from Normal University to Pujiang, there is often, '*Cihai* emphasizes Fudan and looks down on Normal,' and 'the important staff members who are committee chairmen and executive editors have many from Fudan and few from Normal.'"[88] Disciplinary working groups varied considerably in the frequency of attendance and the rigor of their work. Some scholars spoke frankly about the tensions between work at their home institutions and work at *Cihai*. Shen Zhibai 沈知白 (a department chair at the Shanghai Conservatory and assistant executive editor for the music section) asked to return to his school because people there laughed at him for being diverted by the work on *Cihai* and complained about covering his classes.[89] Overall, scholars' continued affiliations with their home institutions and personal academic agendas limited their commitment to *Cihai* in a variety of ways.

Because of the technical and political nature of the encyclopedic entries of the revised dictionary, the *Cihai* Editing Department launched a process of broad consultation about the finished entries that was to take place in the fall and winter of 1961–1962.[90] In September 1961 the *Cihai* Editing Department prepared a "trial edition" (*shixingben*) in fifteen sample volumes divided by disciplinary area to send out to party, government, academic, and professional units throughout the country.[91] In addition, in December 1961 and January 1962, three work groups were sent to more than twenty cities to directly solicit commentary on the trial edition.[92]

The Northern Route Work Group in Beijing, for instance, got help from the Ministry of Culture to set up seventeen large and small forums to solicit feedback on specific disciplinary sections of the trial edition, and the team also met with some scholars individually.[93] The forums' overall evaluation of *Cihai* was quite positive, but specialists offered criticisms of specific disciplinary areas. For example, in regard to natural science, the summary of the criticism was, "In the mathematics category, there are relatively many problems with the explanatory text for the abacus and many errors with the data. Generally speaking, the explanatory text tends to be somewhat specialized and too abstract. For the physics and chemistry explanatory text, the material is out of date, and it does not reflect stable new achievements."[94] Further, political issues came up in regard to entries on theoretical problems in relation to current party approaches. But they could also be more specific: "Terms related to Asia, Africa, and Latin America were commonly felt to be few. But the terms related to the Soviet Union, in comparison, are relatively many."[95] At the same time, scholars expressed a hope that *Cihai* could contribute to the process of standardizing (*guifanhua*) foreign terms and academic terminology more generally, which had been a goal of Chinese intellectuals since the end of the Qing.[96]

The work groups also met independently with leading figures in the party to solicit their views. The Southern Route Working Group, led by Ding Jingtang 丁景唐, for example, met in Guangzhou with Zhou Yang on December 30, 1961, and with both Zhou and Kang Sheng 康生 on January 9, 1962. The discussions were wide ranging. In his individual meeting with the work group, Zhou Yang raised the issue of listing the names of all the compilers to ensure they take responsibility for their entries, asked for a list of all the terms they had cut and suggested consultation about those decisions, and recommended looking at how Diderot's *Encyclopédie* and the *Encyclopedia Britannica* handled evaluation of historical figures.[97] Kang Sheng, for his part, noted that with many entries there were open debates in academic circles and that party plans and policies were fluid, so *Cihai* could not hope to be definitive and absolute. He also pointed out the difficulty of crafting definitive entries for contested terms like "nationality" (*minzu*), where Stalin's orthodox definition did not accord with the realities of liberation movements in the developing world. Further, he raised the complex issue of how different historical figures should be evaluated, and whether or not there should be an entry for Chairman Mao, a question he suggested that they refer to the Central Secretariat.[98] Zhou Yang summarized their perspective by saying, "Toward *Cihai* there are two overall requirements: one is that it reflect the level of all academic circles, which is to reach a definite level; the second is to avoid errors in politics and general knowledge."[99]

In response to this extensive commentary from both academic experts and party leaders, the *Cihai* Editing Department began revising internally in the spring of 1962 and planned another period of concentrated revision with about a hundred compilers that summer.[100] As before, the Shanghai Municipal Committee proposed to bring in experts from outside when the academic resources in Shanghai were not sufficient. It also planned to have the *Cihai* Editing Department formulate an initial strategy for standardizing translated names and to coordinate with the State Science and Technology Committee and the Chinese Academy of Science on refining that strategy. But on the thorny issue of finalizing entries that were politically sensitive, the Shanghai Municipal Committee asked the Central

Propaganda Department to review and revise the entries. In May 1962 the *Cihai* Editing Department formulated a list of some three hundred terms that had the potential to create political problems.[101] By July 1963, after the *Cihai* Editorial Committee had carried out yet another round of revision, it had winnowed down the politically sensitive entries to 126 for the Party Center's review.[102] The Shanghai Municipal Committee planned in the summer of 1963 for the *Cihai* Editorial Committee to do a final concentrated revision to finalize the manuscript (*dinggao*), and it asked for approval to start typesetting and printing it in September of that year.

In December 1963 the Central Propaganda Department sent the Central Secretariat and Chairman Mao a recommendation that the dictionary be published without entries on politically sensitive terms like "Mao Zedong thought," "the Great Leap Forward," "people's communes," "politics in command," and Mao himself.[103] Apparently, after five months of mulling over the 126 entries Shanghai had sent the Party Center, the party leadership decided the judicious thing to do was to remove many of them altogether. The Propaganda Department also raised the question of whether *Cihai* should initially be published openly or in limited numbers for internal circulation only. On January 7, 1964, the Central General Office directed the Shanghai Municipal Committee to follow the Central Propaganda Department's recommendations and first publish several tens of thousands of copies to be circulated internally on a trial basis.[104] After five years of revision work, the fraught process of settling definitive explanations of key figures, events, and policies in Chinese Communist history confounded efforts to finalize a reliable comprehensive dictionary for a broad reading public.[105]

Cihai's extensive revision and review process between 1960 and 1964 encapsulates the form of negotiated cultural production that emerged during the first two decades of the PRC. This process was coordinated by the Shanghai Municipal Committee and the *Cihai* Editing Department, which included local government cultural managers, like Hang Wei and Luo Zhufeng, and old publishing hands, like Jin Zhaozi, Zhou Songdi, Yang Yinshen, and Qian Zihui. The department reached out to academic and professional specialists to ensure that entries reflected China's highest level of academic achievement. The Editing Department incorporated experts at key junctures, carried out revisions itself, and solicited reviews from academic and professional experts working outside the press for evaluation of specific kinds of entries. All three dynamics paralleled major commercial publishers' approaches to in-house book production and collaboration with academics during the 1920s and 1930s. In addition, *Cihai*'s editors vetted the selection of entries and specific text of definitions with party and government leaders to protect against political errors, adding a more comprehensive and rigorous level of political oversight than had ever existed before 1949. Organs and individual leaders of the CCP, in other words, had a direct hand in efforts to consolidate a new lexicon and conceptual universe during the 1950s and 1960s. And the supervision of editors' and experts' compilation work involved not only company directors but also several layers of political institutions.

Livelihood and Lifestyle in Culture Work

Persistent demand for books during the 1950s and early 1960s created opportunities for old publishing hands, elite scholars, and the newly educated to participate in cultural production. Although the CCP and PRC government set publishing agendas for publishers and intervened in the publishing process in unprecedented ways, authors, compilers, and editors fashioned niches to pursue personally meaningful work within the "fields of activity" constituted by early PRC editing departments. They also lived a relatively privileged existence, despite the new economic and sociopolitical realities of Maoist state socialism. State investment in publishing provided comfortable wage levels and sometimes additional perquisites for authors and editors working on prioritized projects. As before 1949, demand for diversified mass production imposed constraints on authors and editors but also created opportunities for them.

As had been true during the first half of the twentieth century, work at or with publishing companies had real material benefits for authors and editors. Editorial staff in the major publishing companies had relatively high wage levels for the early PRC, with remarkable continuity with salaries during the pre-1949 period. We get a sense of publishing staffs' levels of compensation from a 1956 directive from the Ministry of Culture setting wage levels for workers in cultural enterprises. The ministry determined to "further improve the wage system and carry out the principle of pay according to work to encourage cultural workers to improve their work skills and labor efficiency and to promote the development of cultural undertakings."[106] That is, relatively high wages were to provide incentives to encourage more efficient and higher-quality production from writers and editors.

In practice, for editorial staff and administrators at top-tier, central publishing companies, this meant wages that ranged from a high of 377 yuan per month for editors in chief (*zong bianji*) and reviewing editors (*bianshen*) to a low of 54 yuan per month for assistant editors (*zhuli bianji*).[107] There was little differentiation between editorial-room directors (*bianjishi zhuren*) and editors (*bianji*), whose wages for the most part ranged between 90 and 247 yuan per month, depending on grade. The close correspondence of these pay rates to those of the 1930s is quite remarkable. Although, given the lower cost of living after the transition to socialism, it is likely the real value of the wages during the 1950s was considerably higher. In comparative terms, editorial staff wages ranged somewhat higher than administrative staff in top-tier, central cultural enterprises.[108] Authors and editors also benefited from continuation of the manuscript fee and royalty system, which also offered extra income at rates comparable to if somewhat higher than those of the Republican period.[109] Although subject to persistent debates about whether they were necessary to stimulate cultural production or represented an unfair privilege that separated intellectuals from the masses, manuscript fees and royalties continued through the first decade and a half of the Mao era.[110] Older editors who had received company shares as a form of compensation or bonus before 1949 could also continue to draw dividends to enhance their earnings well into the Mao era.[111]

Beyond relatively high wages, cultural experts and editorial staff working in the publishing industry also experienced certain forms of comfort and privilege that marked their status. In particular, they had access to certain forms of consumption and special treatment that were not available to many others. For example, at Zhonghua older editors with scholarly or editorial experience, like Chen Naiqian and Zhang Xichen, sometimes got approval to work from home or had assistants to help them with copying, which could generate resentment among other staff members.[112] In other cases, spouses could be transferred to work at the company so they could live together instead of being posted to distant units.

When we assess the compiling teams for the *Cihai* revision in 1960 and 1961, we see clear signs of the forms of privilege editors and intellectuals could sometimes experience during the early Mao era. The Shanghai Municipal Party Committee intentionally set up favorable work conditions for the scholars and editors mobilized to work on the project in order to motivate them. In the party committee's words, "In the revision process, because we have strengthened intellectuals' political ideology education, respect their knowledge, promote free discussion academically, and at the same time give them convenient material conditions, so everyone's mood is happy, enthusiasm has been high, and the work attitude is conscientious."[113] In terms of housing, transportation, food, and leisure, they enjoyed a quality of life accessible to only a small minority at the time. Shanghai-based participants who lived some distance from the Pujiang Hotel had dedicated vehicles to transport them from Fudan, East China Normal, or the Shanghai Academy of Social Sciences to the hotel; experts from outside Shanghai lived at the hotel.[114] More striking yet, even during the Great Leap Famine, the scholars ate extremely well.

> In order that the experts' lives would not be [adversely] influenced, Shi Ximin [the Shanghai Municipal Party Committee's Culture and Education secretary] together with the relevant departments implemented a special, biased policy, doing their utmost to arrange good food. At that time pork had already become a luxury item in people's lives, and most residents depended on ration coupons for extremely small amounts of pork of one *jin* per person per month. At the Pujiang not only was there unlimited meat to eat, there were also large amounts of chicken, duck, and fish. Many staples were specially allocated here from outside areas to serve as a special supply. At every table of eight to ten people, there were four dishes and a soup, all of which were large plates so that they could eat their fill. At first, for these learned and refined scholars who lacked any fat on their stomachs, when they saw these fine meals, as soon as they swept aside their usual refinement, they ate voraciously. Cao Ying [草嬰] joked with several colleagues, saying, "Chairman Mao said let one hundred schools contend; we here have one hundred schools competing to eat!"[115]

Project leaders also secured access to plentiful supplies of cigarettes and liquor and arranged regular screenings of films for the editorial teams. In a society marked by rationing of even staple goods, such forms of privileged consumption marked these intellectual experts' elite status. Despite these special conditions, some compilers complained about the food or compared the treatment compiling *Cihai* unfavorably with treatment during an earlier project compiling textbooks at the International Hotel, indicating that such treatment was relatively common among culture workers in Shanghai and Beijing at this time.[116]

Just as important as material benefits, work for or at publishing companies during the early Mao period continued to provide opportunities for scholars and editors to pursue their own intellectual agendas and present their work. Series publications, because of the wide range of titles they gathered, offered particularly good outlets for scholarship. Commercial Press's continued publication of the University Series into the early 1950s, for example, provided an avenue of publication for manuscripts on science and technology subjects that in many cases had initially been drafted during the war years and in some cases had sat gathering dust throughout long years of conflict.[117] To be sure, after 1949 authors had to adapt to new ideological and academic frameworks. Thus, when Wu Xiang revised his *Outline of Physiology* for publication with Commercial Press in 1952, he reframed it in terms of Pavlov's theories, which better fit a Marxist-Leninist outlook.[118] Commercial Press nonetheless served as a vehicle for academic publishing, as it had since the 1910s. A decade later, the Knowledge Series provided leading scholars like Wang Li and Zhu Kezhen with a venue to publish books on topics that interested them. Although they had to accommodate the length requirements and adapt their style to meet the populist goals of the series, this was no more than they had done when publishing in Wang Yunwu's series during the 1920s and 1930s.[119] Zhonghua's Shanghai Editing Department, for its part, published several collective projects of literary criticism by young faculty and students from the Chinese Departments at Fudan University and Nanjing University, providing another conduit for scholarly publishing.[120]

Even work on a basic reference book, like *Cihai*, became a context for scholars to express their academic views and enshrine them in print. The high stakes for inclusion or exclusion of one's academic perspective underpinned heated debates among the dictionary's editorial committee members. For example, Li Chunping recounts how evolutionary biologists, supporting the competing perspectives of the American Morgan and the Russian Michurin, debated definitions during a concentrated revision session.[121] Similarly, Nanjing University professor Hong Cheng 洪誠 raged at Miao Yizhi 繆一之 and Bao Yuke 包玉珂 over revision of entries he had written that were based on many years of research on the *Songs of Chu*.[122] Work on the dictionary's revision became a powerful medium for publicizing one's scholarly views to a broader reading public and establishing them as definitive. During the Mao era, publishing, in short, remained a resource for knowledge production and for building or maintaining academic reputations, generating symbolic capital for intellectuals.[123]

When editors had a chance to voice their frustrations in the forums on publishing during the Hundred Flowers Campaign, they expressed some concerns about outlets for intellectual development and scholarly activity. As captured in a report summarizing forums for editors in the spring of 1957, "Editors raised many opinions regarding the eight-hour workday, not having opportunities to participate in academic activities, not hearing reports, wages being less than high-ranking intellectuals' outside the press, the issue of editors' advanced studies [jinxiu], the vacation system, and so forth."[124] Comments like these make clear that expectations about editorial work and opportunities for intellectual development and participation in academic life persisted during the 1950s and 1960s, even if the conditions at some publishers made these hopes harder to realize. After Zhonghua's reorganization in 1958, Jin Canran sought to create an environment that fostered editors' and cadres' intellectual lives by offering classes on classical Chinese, organizing specialized lectures, and encouraging editors to keep familiar with the scholarship on their areas of work.[125]

In many cases, outlets for editors to pursue their own scholarly interests persisted into the 1960s. For example, Zhonghua Book Company's agenda of classical publishing enabled Chen Naiqian to continue under state socialism his vocation of classical scholarship and discovery and republication of classical texts. As part of the *Twenty-Four Dynastic Histories* project, Chen was responsible for punctuation and collation of the *Annals of the Three Kingdoms*.[126] Apart from his contribution to this large-scale project, though, at Zhonghua Chen's group also published volumes of Ming-era statecraft writings and military records from the Ming Wanli period (1573–1620) and planned a series of Tang-era handwritten books recovered from Dunhuang. Chen himself compiled a collection of book notes on the collation, annotation, revision, and supplementing of the *Twenty-Four Dynastic Histories*. He also hoped to organize a group of younger scholars to work with him to gather and systematize the scholarly notes of Qing-era scholars, presumably on philology and other forms of evidential textual research.[127] On the one hand, Chen's ability to determine and prioritize projects was undoubtedly conditioned in new ways by party and government oversight. Contribution to state-driven projects like the *Twenty-Four Dynastic Histories* was a fundamental condition of his ongoing employment in Zhonghua's

Photostatic Printing Group. On the other hand, government investment and management overall provided more consistent and considerable support—financial and scholarly—for the kinds of projects to which Chen had dedicated his life than he had been able to tap when he worked as an independent scholar.

Similarly, as before 1949, series publications afforded opportunities for editors to write manuscripts to fill out the list. In fact, the growing emphasis during the early PRC period on books' accessibility to the common reader opened the door further to generalist editors' drafting manuscripts rather than specialized scholars. As with the Chinese History Small Series at Zhonghua, staff editor Li Gengxu wrote a volume for the series, *The War of Yiling* (*Yiling zhi zhan*), which the editorial committee received positively.[128] Similarly, Hu Yuzhi emphasized the value of mobilizing staff editors to compile manuscripts when introducing the Knowledge Series.[129] At the same time, the young editors cultivated in the Zhonghua Book Company Editing Department carried out their own research on topics as diverse as Zhu Xi and historical dramas and wrote related scholarly articles.[130] Overall, the emphasis on accessible texts for ordinary readers in the early PRC made it possible for staff editors to write manuscripts that helped their companies while also giving them chances to pursue their research interests.

The early PRC was without question a "propaganda state," in Peter Kenez's formulation.[131] As Chang-tai Hung and others have shown, it readily used the media, arts, public ritual, exhibitions, and a range of social organizations to spread explicitly political doctrines and mobilize different sectors of the population for mass political action.[132] Yet this chapter demonstrates that it was also a pedagogical state. That is, it actively supported and facilitated the production and dissemination of knowledge for the purposes of promoting economic development, preserving national culture, and cultivating its citizenry. At least two forces drove the pedagogical orientation of the early PRC government. As heir to the legacy of the late imperial Chinese model of the state, the PRC leadership inherited fundamental assumptions about governments being responsible for "transforming the people through education" (*jiaohua*) in both moral and intellectual terms.[133] In addition, undeniable economic backwardness led party and government leaders to prioritize economic development, for which the spread of technical knowledge, especially, was seen to be essential. The pedagogical goals of the state, which required targeting particular social groups with distinct forms of knowledge in published form, underpinned the perceived demand for different genres of publication seen throughout this chapter.

In fact, during the first seventeen years of the PRC, party and state cultural administrators persistently conceptualized the publishing process in terms of satisfying popular consumer demand. Whether they were discussing accessible punctuated versions of classical texts for students, general knowledge readers for cadres, or translations of Soviet scientific and technical writings for universities and technical schools, party and government leaders like Qi Yanming, Zhou Yang, and Hu Yuzhi sought to diversify the range of publications to satisfy the educational and intellectual needs of different sectors of the population. Although the fundamental motivating factor after 1949 was cultural construction rather than profit, the effort to meet demand drove the publishing process under state socialism as it had during the competitive capitalism of the late Qing and Republican periods. Insofar as Mao-era cultural construction preserved some of the agendas of intellectuals' cultural enterprise during the first half of the twentieth century—dissemination of Western learning, promulgation of science and technology for national development, preservation of the nation's cultural heritage—the continuities in publishing goals must have appeared even greater to old publishing hands like Shu Xincheng, Zhang Yuanji, or Jin Zhaozi.

The aim of diversifying production to meet various forms of social demand in publishing work fostered an emphasis on productive efficiency over the cultural politics of production. Persistent resource constraints also made optimizing efficiency paramount. We have seen this prioritization play out in several dimensions. For one, when celebrated models of mass line cultural production introduced during the Great Leap period proved to be ineffective, publishing company leaders and culture work administrators in the party and state reorganized compilation and editing processes according to familiar models developed under the conditions of competitive capitalism before 1949. But the new powers of the state to allocate personnel allowed publishers to align the staffing of editing departments to meet the needs of specific projects in ways that had been difficult, if not impossible, to sustain long term in the competitive labor markets of the 1920s and 1930s. The socialist labor-allocation process was not always smooth, as the tensions between faculty members at East China Normal and Fudan University during the *Cihai* revision process remind us. Yet the publishing sector's ability to mobilize talent—a goal stretching back to Zhang Yuanji's earliest days at Commercial Press—within the state socialist economy was most impressive. During the early PRC, as before 1949, editors and authors were subject to the demands of a production process that emphasized efficiency over all else. What changed was that productive efficiency after 1949 served socialist construction rather than corporate profit, with parameters set by party and state cultural administrators rather than company managers and boards of directors.

The need for specific kinds of talent to carry out projects to meet forms of knowledge production that the party prioritized also created opportunities for experienced editorial staff workers and various kinds of intellectuals to continue to play central roles in the publishing sector into the early 1960s. We see this most clearly with classical publishing, which depended on the efforts of literati editors like Chen Naiqian, their protégés like Hu Daojing, and old publishing hands like Jin Zhaozi and Zhang Xichen. But it was equally salient with other projects, like the production of series and reference books, where both specialized content knowledge and experience with book production were essential. The clearest indication of how productive efficiency trumped cultural politics during this period is the way verdicts in the Anti-Rightist Campaign were ignored, and punishments of exile reversed, to create editing departments suitable for specific publishing projects.

Because of their ongoing importance to cultural production, publishing hands, specialized intellectuals, and a new generation of college-educated staff editors enjoyed decent wages, certain perquisites of consumption, and opportunities to pursue their own intellectual agendas. These modes of distinction and cultural activity served to mark them as intellectuals. They also had some say in how the party and state defined and executed publishing initiatives. Throughout the first seventeen years of the PRC, we see a negotiated form of cultural production, where there was real interplay between the agendas of party and state cultural administrators, on the one hand, and, on the other, the expertise and experience of publishing-company managers, staff editors, and intellectuals. Reconstructing this interplay contributes to the ongoing effort to understand the complex relationship the CCP had with intellectuals and cultural producers during the second half of the twentieth century.[134]

The emphasis on publishing as a way to produce and disseminate transformative knowledge allowed specialists in particular subject areas and editorial staff in publishing companies themselves to assume meaningful roles in setting and realizing party and state agendas. Certainly, publishing managers and editors in the 1950s and early 1960s did not have as much latitude in setting publishing trends and shaping culture as they had during the Republican period or as did Paola Iovene's early Reform-era editors.[135] But neither were they simply drones working at the beck and call of party and government leaders. Patronage relationships between cultural administrators and intellectuals working in or with publishing companies created opportunities for the latter to advocate for or pursue certain projects, as was the case with Wu Han's and Hu Yuzhi's forays into series publishing.[136] Further, as noted with classical publishing, state-run forums like those associated with the Hundred Flowers Campaign, apart from their overtly political functions, generated fertile ideas for publishing initiatives from the level of staff editors in the publishers. Even with projects mandated by the highest leadership, such as revising *Cihai* and punctuating the *Twenty-Four Dynastic Histories*, editors and intellectuals affected the organization and content of the publications by drawing on their expertise in publishing and particular content areas. Through participation in the publishing process, Chinese intellectuals influenced the process of knowledge production in the early PRC, right until the eve of the Cultural Revolution.

Conclusion

"The unfairness for the editor is that year after year editors are always making wedding clothes for others' benefit, but they themselves can never sit in the 'bridal sedan chair.'"

—LUO MO [LUO ZHUFENG], "ECLECTICS"

I myself had also been an editor for several years and had tasted a little of the sweetness and bitterness of editors' work . . . but it had never produced the gloomy feeling of "making wedding clothes for others' benefit." . . . "Actually, in a socialist society, what worker's labor is not serving 'other people'?"

—YAO WENYUAN, "TWO EDITOR COMRADES' MIND-SETS"

In May 1962 Luo Zhufeng, acting director of the Shanghai Municipal Government's Publishing Bureau and assistant director of the *Cihai* revision project, wrote a brief essay (*zawen*) called "Eclectics" (Zajia) for the Shanghai newspaper *Wenhuibao*.[1] In the fall of 1961 the paper's editor in chief, Chen Yusun 陳虞孫, had convened a forum of people from news and publishing circles, which included both Luo and Yao Wenyuan 姚文元, to discuss regular publication of essays in the paper to create a livelier atmosphere. Chen's initiative came in a context of relative openness for intellectual discourse starting in the spring of 1961 that was perhaps best exemplified by the essay columns in Beijing newspapers, such as "The Long and Short" (Chang duan lu), "Evening Chats at Yan Mountain" (Yanshan yehua), and "Notes from Three-Family Village" (Sanjiacun zhaji), by Deng Tuo, Wu Han, Liao Mosha, and others.[2] Participants at the forum thought Luo Zhufeng was the perfect person to initiate the essay trend in Shanghai.

Luo Zhufeng's May essay was written under the pen name Luo Mo 駱漠 and framed as an encounter between the author and a nameless editor, who stops by to visit on a rainy night.[3] The course of the discussion turns to the nature of editorial work, which the narrator declares to be "eclectic" because the work is hard to characterize, echoing comments on the generalist nature of the editorial profession going back to Mao Dun's self-designation as a "handyman" (*daza*) in the 1910s. The editor in Luo's account then uses the discussion to complain about the treatment of editors, "being given the cold shoulder [*zuoleng bandeng*]," particularly focusing on their marginal or secondary status, as voiced in the epigraph about their never being the bride. The narrator in contrast emphasizes the joys of editing work, such as unearthing literary treasures that have social value, and maintains that the very eclecticism in editorial work was itself a kind of professionalism. Yet he also suggests that "responsible cadres" "have a sincere talk with them to understand a little better editors' work situation to help resolve some problems that can be resolved." Luo, here, spoke for the nameless editorial staff workers who served as the main agents of cultural production in the publishing industry from the 1930s into the early 1960s, with little recognition and limited reward. He voiced their desires for more recognition and perhaps the occasional opportunity to "sit in the bridal sedan chair" as authors. The persistence of these concerns reflects the stability in both the dynamics of book production and its reliance on petty intellectuals as cultural producers in China for the better part of four decades.

But Luo's piece immediately drew fire from the city's emergent cultural leftists. A week after the publication of "Eclectics," Yao Wenyuan wrote a sharp critical response in *Wenhuibao* that imitated the stylistic framing of Luo's essay (a discussion with an editor comrade), but it deployed a Maoist rhetoric and pointed comments aimed at discrediting the views of Luo's editor.[4] As the epigraph from Yao's article suggests, he used his own experience to question the legitimacy of the complaints voiced in Luo's essay. But more importantly, he articulated a view of social labor that envisioned everyone in all fields working selflessly for the greater good.

"But I always feel that authors and editors should be closely cooperating comrades in arms for the flourishing of the socialist literary enterprise and should not mutually complain. If there are contradictions, they can be discussed to reach a negotiated settlement. As for the leadership emphasizing the cultivation of artists, that is viewed from the overall situation of the whole socialist cultural undertaking and is not for a particular actor or author individually. We editors should give a fuller measure of effort."[5]

Yao, here, dismisses the individual concerns of editors voiced by Luo as a failure of socialist consciousness and commitment. Cultural workers, whether editors or authors, he suggests, should dedicate themselves to the collective project of state socialist cultural production.

Popular response to this clash of pens strongly favored Luo's perspective. In the weeks after Yao's article was published, *Wenhuibao* received more than sixty letters criticizing it, claiming that Yao was "sitting in the bridal sedan chair making sarcastic remarks."[6] But leftists in the Shanghai party apparatus, led by Zhang Chunqiao 張春橋, then managing cultural and education work in the Municipal Party Committee, used "Eclectics" as a pretext to attack intellectuals in Shanghai's cultural establishment. Zhang first suppressed a forum *Wenhuibao* planned on the subject of editorial work. Subsequently, in a thought work conference in 1963, Zhang spoke of the "Eclectics incident" as "a capitalist restoration on the ideological front." Then in a comment on a work summary, Zhang accused the essay's author of "assuming a capitalist standpoint and directly targeting [i.e., 'pointing the spearhead at'] the party." These accusations led to a large struggle meeting against Luo Zhufeng, who was forced to make a self-criticism and step down from his post as acting head of Shanghai's Publishing Bureau.[7] Luo subsequently immersed himself in editorial work on *Cihai.*[8]

The tempest around "Eclectics" served as a bellwether of the end of an era. It marked a shift from a concern with the efficiency of cultural production to meet social needs to an exclusive focus on the politics of cultural production. It also represented a turn away from a system in which cultural producers could reasonably express their goals for the content, direction, and conditions of their work to one in which unquestioning dedication to the collective was paramount. It is not surprising that the leading edge of this cultural criticism occurred in Shanghai and in relation to a cultural cadre like Luo, who was closely involved with *Cihai.* As discussed, in the *Cihai* revision project an old guard of publishing hands and specialized scholars continued to collaborate for book production in ways similar to the capitalist publishing circles of the pre-1949 period. It is also no coincidence that Luo Zhufeng's critics were Yao Wenyuan and Zhang Chunqiao, two eventual members of the Cultural Revolution's Gang of Four. In hindsight, the conflict around "Eclectics" can be seen as an opening attack on leaders in publishing circles and the intellectual establishment by cultural leftists, who sought to make the social and cultural politics of publishing a focus of criticism. It was soon followed by the 1964 rectification campaign in the Ministry of Culture, in which critics declared it to be the "ministry of emperors, kings, generals, and ministers" (*di wang jiang xiang bu*), "the ministry of gifted scholars and beautiful ladies" (*caizi jiaren bu*), and "the ministry of dead men and foreigners" (*siren yangren bu*). The ministry's party secretary and Zhonghua Book Company's great patron, Qi Yanming, became a focus of attack, made a self-criticism, and was transferred to a provincial post, casting a pall over Zhonghua's publishing work.[9]

When the Cultural Revolution broke out two years later, Commercial Press and Zhonghua Book Company were among the leading cultural institutions attacked because of their close associations with Wu Han, one of the main targets of the movement.[10] In July 1966 Commercial Press's director, Chen Hanbo, was labeled a "counterrevolutionary" because of the company's publication of Wu's Foreign History Small Series.[11] Zhonghua, because of its publishing of politically sensitive historical materials and connections not only with Wu Han but also with the Ministry of Culture's Qi Yanming, became an even bigger target of attack. Editor in Chief Jin Canran and Associate Editor Li Kan were immediately criticized along with Wu Han as "ox demons and snake spirits."[12] In addition, some of the practices that had fueled Zhonghua's resurgence after 1958, such as the rehabilitation and mobilization of "rightists" for editorial work, now served as fodder for indictments against Jin Canran and his colleagues.[13] Overall, Yu Xiaoyao estimates that more than one-third of Zhonghua Book Company's personnel were denounced and made the target of struggle.[14] Similarly, at the *Cihai* Editing Department in Shanghai, both elite intellectuals and staff editors became subject to criticism and attack, with Zhang Chunqiao declaring in 1967 that 96 percent of the *Cihai* Editorial Committee were "ox demons and snake spirits."[15] Starting in September 1969, most cadres from the Ministry of Culture and associated publishing companies in Beijing were sent to May 7 Cadre Schools in Xianning county, Hubei, while those associated with the *Cihai* revision went to Shanghai's Fengxian county.[16]

During the Cultural Revolution decade, almost all the cultural projects discussed in this book were interrupted. Between 1967 and 1972, work on *Cihai* was suspended.[17] The Knowledge Series ceased publication during the Cultural Revolution, after having published eighty-three titles by 1965.[18] Zhonghua Book Company's Chinese History Small Series became an immediate focus of criticism in meetings and big-character posters, and publication was suspended.[19] Work on the *Twenty-Four Dynastic Histories* project stopped because of political struggles in 1966, revived temporarily in 1967, and then ceased again from 1969 to 1971 as the majority of Zhonghua's editorial staff were sent down to the countryside.[20] Recruitment for the classical-documents program at Beida, which was one of Zhonghua's primary channels for cultivating new talent, was suspended for most of the Cultural Revolution decade (1966–1976).[21] In sum, the radical social criticism embodied in the Cultural Revolution completely disrupted the form of negotiated cultural production developed during the early PRC, which built on the institutions and depended on the personnel developed by Republican-period publishing companies. In fact, disrupting, uprooting, and replacing these institutions and personnel can be seen as one of the central motivations of the cultural side of the Cultural Revolution. During the Cultural Revolution decade, the restricted official cultural production of the propaganda state took center stage, even as interstitial informal and local and private cultures proliferated.[22] A new generation of cultural cadres sought to ensure their cultural authority by suspending the knowledge production for socialist construction pursued by the leading publishers.

This book has reconstructed the distinctive form of industrial book production that developed in China during the first two-thirds of the twentieth century. Commercial Press, Zhonghua Book Company, then World Book Company created new dynamics of cultural production in an effort both to make money and to transform Chinese culture, society, and politics through the production and dissemination of knowledge. During the late Qing and early Republic, mass production of textbooks and reference books held the most promise for accomplishing these dual goals, using the industrialized printing facilities described by Christopher Reed. The major publishers adapted to rapid changes to primary- and secondary-school curricula from the first decade of the twentieth century through the 1930s by developing large editing departments that could quickly generate new series of textbooks on demand. Once organized, these editing departments proved equally amenable to mobilization of mental labor for producing other kinds of publications. The development of academic disciplines and institutions starting in the 1910s, along with a powerful nationalism that demanded general education for all citizens, as well as preservation and circulation of the national heritage, created persistent demand for diverse genres of books, including reference books, series publications, and classical reprints. Chinese publishers' large editing departments of several dozen to several hundred editors and authors were globally distinctive, as Wang Yunwu and Shu Xincheng discovered when they surveyed publishers throughout Europe, North America, and Japan in the 1930s.

Large editing departments had historical precedents in late imperial literati compilation projects, which helped naturalize them in postimperial China. They persisted throughout the first half of the twentieth century because they allowed publishers to meet market demand and because they were relatively easy to staff. Social conditions that consistently generated surpluses of literate, knowledgeable people facilitated mobilization of talent into the early 1950s, though the available pool of educated people was constantly shifting with China's modern social changes. When Zhang Yuanji sought talent for Commercial Press's Editing Department to produce textbooks and reference books starting in the late Qing, he tapped into sprawling networks of classically trained literati from Jiangnan who had also acquired some degree of foreign learning, whether through formal schooling or self-study, and were seeking new career outlets after the end of the examination system in 1905. As Lufei Kui and Wang Yunwu launched series publications that included modern academic disciplines in the 1920s, they experimented with hiring foreign-educated or Chinese-trained experts to staff their editing departments. The disarray of Chinese higher education during the 1920s made publishing an attractive alternative, at least temporarily, for these elite scholars, but their expense and mobility limited their value for publishers over the long term. By the 1920s, moreover, China's educational system was generating a new surplus of high school and university graduates for whom editorial work promised stable wages, an academic atmosphere, and opportunities for advancement. This last group of petty intellectuals became the dominant force in the major publishers' editing departments by the end of the 1920s. Cheap and adaptable, they allowed Chinese publishers to maintain relatively large editing departments and produce a wide variety of publications into the early PRC period. Like the nameless code writers and content providers in the contemporary culture industry, petty intellectuals played a vital role in China's cultural production during the mid-twentieth century, a contribution that has often been overlooked.

Late imperial cultural patterns helped ensure these different groups of intellectuals' commitment to editorial work and underpin the operations of editing departments. A cultural preference for brushwork that distinguished intellectuals from nonliterate social groups consistently made editorial work attractive, even as editors' educational backgrounds shifted. The literati tendency to be an eclectic generalist made for editorial staffs that were flexible and adaptable. The persistence in editorial departments of literati leisure culture—banquets, drinking parties, poetry readings, book-buying excursions, opera (and later film) viewing, literary circles, mentoring relationships—meant that editors could live in a community of letters and share cultural practices that marked them as elite, even if they were not particularly wealthy. Those shared cultural practices also muted wealth and status distinctions among groups of intellectuals and obscured, to varying degrees, the commercial nature of the publishing enterprise. These dynamics all suggest that in China historically rooted cultural attitudes and practices helped sustain the labor mobilization and work culture that shaped the development of modern industrial publishing.

As personnel and the competitive environment shifted during the first decades of the century, so, too, did the dynamics of cultural production. Initially, literati editors developed a collaborative model of textbook and reference-book production that reflected modes of interaction in their study societies and political associations. By the 1920s, foreign-trained scholars and academics were bringing to the publishers new individualist models of monographic book production, where each editor or author covered a subject with a text. As Chinese-educated petty intellectuals came to dominate editing departments and competitive pressure to produce ever-greater varieties and numbers of print commodities increased, factory-based models of production became more common. Editing department directors like Wang Yunwu, Shu Xincheng, and Xu Weinan coordinated staff editors in generating and (re)packaging fungible text for textbooks, reference books, and series publications. Thus, we see a secular trend during the first half of the twentieth century from more horizontal and self-determined forms of cultural production to more vertical and hierarchical ones. That transformation depended on both the demand for efficiency in industrial capitalism and new social dynamics related to China's educational system.

The resulting proliferation of texts, especially during the 1920s and 1930s, earned significant profits for the three leading publishers, but it was also culturally and socially productive. In part 2 I reconstructed the production processes of several different kinds of publications and assessed their impact on Chinese thought and culture. Textbook and dictionary publishing helped stabilize a new lexicon, define new concepts, and popularize new writing styles. Reprinted ancient texts democratized access to rare books in unprecedented ways and reconfigured the source base for the modern project of "organizing the national heritage." Series publications introduced foreign academic disciplines and subjects to a broad readership while also reformulating them for the Chinese context through synthetic construction that drew on foreign scholarship. Based on these examples, I contend that the publishing sector in China operated for a time as an alternative to the university as the primary institution of modern knowledge production and to the state as both steward of national heritage and agent of cultural change.

As authors and editors produced texts, they also produced themselves and communities of readers. Authors of series monographs established themselves as leading experts in particular fields. Compilers of ancient-book reprints demonstrated their facility with classical scholarship and, in some cases, their status as book collectors and connoisseurs. Moreover, staff editors working on textbooks, dictionaries, and series publications distinguished themselves as scholars working with their pens rather than their hands. Industrialization of publishing created opportunities for late Qing literati, elite scholars, and those with basic modern educations to affect the development of modern Chinese culture and to constitute themselves as modern intellectuals in a variety of ways. As writing served to demonstrate cultural literacy and technical mastery, as well as to configure domains of knowledge, publishing became a central mechanism by which modern intellectuals defined themselves as a social group. Operating in conjunction with academic credentials and professional positions, publishing offered perhaps the most capacious and flexible field for literate people to represent themselves publicly and shape the category of intellectual.

By marketing monograph and classical-reprint series to libraries, secondary and higher schools, and government or commercial offices of various kinds, the publishers also constructed a "general reading public" (*yiban dushujie*). That reading community was minimally composed of secondary-level students and graduates, government officials, and urban professionals, as well as the remnants of the late Qing literati. Through exposure to the new forms of modern knowledge and reorganized classical culture encapsulated in these publications, this nascent reading public increasingly came to be associated with the image of the informed, modern citizenry. In proportion to China's overall population, this was a relatively narrow, culturally elite group. But in absolute terms it was a fairly large market that allowed companies like Commercial Press to earn a growing share of its profits from general interest books rather than textbooks alone.

Company managers and editing department directors increasingly configured publications to capture as much of this market of citizen readers as possible. They organized the fungible text produced by staff editors into newly packaged commodities. With monographic book production, company managers set word limits and defined the subject areas for series and titles. These became the parameters within which even elite academics had to operate in order to publish their work for a general audience. Consequently, during the Republican period increasing commodification of thought and scholarly production, to create and satisfy market niches as well as limit the cost and time of production, conditioned what could be published through the three leading publishers. Authors could always turn to smaller companies to publish their work with fewer constraints, but doing so limited the potential that their work would reach a wide readership and be able to shape culture and to make their reputations as they hoped. So, from the 1920s through the early 1950s, series publications presented the most recent Chinese scholarly work, despite the restrictions imposed by industrialized firms, because they provided authors access to readers.

Commodification of culture allowed publishing houses to persist as centers of cultural activity that offered intellectuals opportunities for self-expression and personal fulfillment. The editing department at a major company formed a community of scholars, where intellectuals could interact in a range of ways, forming dense social networks. These networks were actualized through forms of literati leisure culture, which persisted from the late Qing into the Mao era, even as they changed in some of their dynamics. In somewhat more formalized ways, library resources and supplemental classes that publishers provided to strengthen publications could also be used to enrich staff editors' intellectual lives. At the same time, constant demand for new publications enabled editors to pursue their own intellectual projects by writing articles and books that interested them. Even participation in large-scale collective publishing projects, like *Ciyuan* and *Cihai*, engendered pride among staff editors for their contributions to major cultural achievements. In sum, editing departments provided a context for editors to pursue their cultural agendas and live as intellectuals.

Many of the publishing dynamics developed under the competitive capitalism of China's Republican period continued during the first seventeen years of state socialism. The ongoing operation of Commercial Press and

Zhonghua Book Company in the PRC was not the result of an oversight by the CCP, nor was it merely a stopgap measure during the early years of post-1949 reconstruction. Rather, party and state cultural administrators valued and sought to exploit the productive capacity and techniques the two publishers had built up over several decades. In particular, the expertise and experience of their editorial staffs made them valuable for producing genres of text—especially reference books, classical reprints, and basic knowledge resources for a general readership—that had been vital to Republican publishing companies and remained a priority for the new PRC state. For Commercial Press and Zhonghua, collaboration with the socialist state held out much promise, despite the shift to state ownership. They each gained monopoly access to a valuable share of the book market while shedding the liabilities of their printing and distribution systems. Partnership with the state allowed publishing hands to continue the cultural enterprise of the first half of the twentieth century while being shielded from the most damaging features of competitive capitalism.

The complex dialogic relationship Commercial Press and Zhonghua Book Company established with the PRC government complicates a straightforward picture of Soviet-style publishing where central political authorities impose production imperatives on publishers.[23] The long history of Chinese commercial publishing during the first half of the twentieth century coupled with the limited organizational and economic resources of the new PRC encouraged development of a modus vivendi between the CCP and companies like Zhonghua and Commercial Press. Also key was the fact that the PRC government sought to be not only a propaganda state that imparted political messages and mobilized its citizenry but also a pedagogical state that instilled in its people knowledge fundamental to national construction and economic development. Commercial Press and Zhonghua Book Company publications—especially in the form of series publications and classical reprints—aimed at both specialized cultural workers and a broader community of general readers allowed the PRC to realize to some extent its pedagogical goals during the first seventeen years after 1949.

Because the early PRC state sought to reach large populations of readers with a wide array of publications to support the process of socialist construction, publishers still faced imperatives for diversifying products and maximizing productive efficiency. To meet these demands, Commercial Press and Zhonghua consistently turned to the personnel and techniques they had developed before 1949. Old publishing hands drawn from among the staff editors of the Republican period continued to play vital roles at both publishers into the 1950s and 1960s. Newly recruited editorial staff largely fit the petty intellectual profile of the old staff editors. To be sure, publishers and party and state cultural administrators experimented with more "socialist" approaches to compiling and editing during the late 1950s and early 1960s, with companies cooperating with academic units and leveraging mass mobilization in new ways. But the inefficiencies of these "revolutionary" approaches led to quick reversion to tried-and-true methods. Continuities in methods of production suggest that print industrialism's imperatives of efficiency for diversified mass production, rather than ownership structure (private versus public), were most decisive in shaping the dynamics of socialist cultural production during the early Maoist period.

During the early PRC, state and party agents intervened in the publishing process in unprecedented ways. They configured divisions of labor among publishing companies that set parameters on publishers' field of operations. They also held veto power over publishing plans and vetted final publications. Yet publishers, because of their expertise in particular content areas and in the publishing process itself, had significant input into the state's publishing agendas and were able to propose specific publishing initiatives within the state's parameters. The result was a negotiated form of cultural production in which cultural administrators and publishing hands both had a say. Moreover, publishers benefited greatly from the socialist state's new capacity to allocate labor, which allowed them to mobilize talent for particular publishing projects in ways unimaginable with the competitive labor markets of the first half of the twentieth century. As before 1949, Mao-era editing departments provided contexts for intellectuals to pursue their own scholarly agendas and live relatively privileged lives marked through various forms of intellectual exchange and cultural consumption.

The complexity of the negotiations in the publishing field, and intellectuals' ability to pursue their own agendas, suggests that the relationship between intellectuals and the PRC state before 1966 cannot be reduced to a one-way dynamic of state domination. Certainly, editors and groups of intellectuals experienced periods of state repression during rectification campaigns and the Anti-Rightist Campaign, and publishers needed to adapt their production processes to meet political imperatives during the Great Leap Forward. But the government remained dependent on these groups to realize its pedagogical goals, a fact brought home by the striking rehabilitation of so-called rightist intellectuals and editors in the reestablishment of Zhonghua Book Company in 1958. That very dependence, I maintain, threatened existentially the cultural authority and power of political cadres who did not share the cultural capital and publishing experiences of old publishing hands. That insecurity animated the attacks of the Cultural Revolution. It was no accident that Commercial Press and Zhonghua Book Company were among the first targets of that movement, for these cultural enterprises sustained and realized to a very high degree the intellectual autonomy and cultural authority of China's intellectuals during the Mao era. Criticism of the minor privileges, work culture, and publications of the intellectuals and editors associated with the two companies were not framed as "crimes" only to justify attacks against political rivals, although they were most certainly that. They were also a strategic assault on the forms of productive cultural power and authority that Chinese intellectuals had successfully cultivated in the publishing field since the start of the twentieth century.

Histories of twentieth-century China have largely been dominated by the narrative of revolutionary politics, which undoubtedly has profoundly impacted intellectual and cultural life. But this study also argues that the emergence of industrial capitalism played a huge role in shaping scholarship and culture. Industrial publishing provided intellectuals with a powerful resource to transform Chinese culture. Moreover, for the first half of the twentieth century, commercial publishing companies provided intellectuals with bases for activity that were relatively insulated from incursions by political forces. As centers of cultural prestige and productive expertise, they even offered intellectuals some leverage in negotiating with PRC state agents after the transition to socialism during the 1950s. At the same time, as demonstrated, industrial dynamics of cultural production shaped how Chinese intellectuals made books, and thus knowledge, over the course of the twentieth century. Forms of collective production developed in response to competitive commercial print markets during the first half of the twentieth century continued to affect the publishing sector under state socialism. And intellectuals' self-definition and public roles were in many ways mediated through their writing for commercial and then socialist book markets. Overall, we cannot fully understand the development of cultural and intellectual life in the twentieth century without exploring the nexus between culture and the industrial economy with the same rigor and intensity that we have dedicated to the intersection between culture and politics.

In the initial years of the Reform and Opening period (1978–present), publishing-industry figures who had been attacked during the Cultural Revolution were rehabilitated, companies and editing departments were reconstructed along familiar lines, and work on many projects under way in the early 1960s resumed. Former Commercial Press director Chen Hanbo became temporary party secretary of the State Publishing Bureau (Chubanju) starting in 1978.[24] Qi Yanming was rehabilitated in 1978 and took a leading role in the People's Political Consultative Conference, among other positions.[25] In March 1978 Commercial Press and Zhonghua Book Company were reestablished, initially with a joint-management office and then independently in August 1979.[26] In January 1978 the *Cihai* Editing Department was reconstituted as the Lexicographical Publishing Company (Cishu chubanshe) and later that year started once again revising *Cihai*. Xia Zhengnong 夏征農, Fudan University's party secretary, directed the reestablished *Cihai* Editorial Committee, but the practical manager of daily work on the project was none other than Luo Zhufeng, the target of criticism for the "Eclectics" incident who suffered numerous attacks during the Cultural Revolution. Significantly, the *Cihai* editors revived the concentrated revision process, drawing on a mix of company-based editors and academic experts, as they had in the 1960s, and using the pre–Cultural Revolution unfinished manuscript as their base text. This group pushed through the revision process in a matter of months to ensure the revised *Cihai* could be published as a gift to honor the thirtieth anniversary of the founding of the PRC in October 1979.[27] As these examples indicate, people and processes from the early Mao era played an important role in the revival of publishing during the reform era.

Recent studies of Reform-era literary publishing by Paola Iovene and Shuyu Kong suggest that metropolitan editors of journals and book series have revived the entrepreneurial and independent publishing initiatives characteristic of early Mao-era negotiated cultural production and even Republican-period commercial publishing.[28] But much about how cultural production has developed since the early 1980s remains opaque. Who are the current staff in publishers' editing departments, and how are they recruited? Have the collective-production dynamics developed in China during the early twentieth century and continued during the Maoist period persisted under conditions of market reform? How has market competition affected relations among publishers and between publishers and the state's cultural-management organs? Has the advent of digital publishing and the internet impacted industrial cultural production at major publishing companies? What opportunities and constraints do authors and editors face in the current publishing climate? These questions point in new directions for understanding the publishing industry and cultural production more broadly in present-day China.

Notes

Introduction

1. Each of these figures is discussed extensively in the chapters that follow.
2. Robert Culp, *Articulating Citizenship: Civic Education and Student Politics in Southeastern China, 1912–1940* (Cambridge, Mass.: Harvard University Asia Center, 2007), 44–47; Wang Jianjun 王建军, *Zhongguo jindai jiaokeshu fazhan yanjiu* 中国近代教科书发展研究 (Study of the development of China's modern textbooks) (Guangzhou: Guangdong jiaoyu chubanshe, 1996), 105–13; Ji Shaofu 吉少甫, *Zhongguo chuban jianshi* 中国出版简史 (An elementary history of Chinese publishing) (Shanghai: Xuelin chubanshe, 1991), 299–300, 330–32.
3. Li Jiaju 李家驹, *Shangwu yinshuguan yu jindai zhishi wenhua de chuanbo* 商務印書館與近代知識文化的传播 (Commercial Press and the transmission of modern knowledge and culture) (Beijing: Shangwu yinshuguan, 2005), chap. 4; Zhou Qihou 周其厚, *Zhonghua shuju yu jindai wenhua* 中華書局與近代文化 (Zhonghua Book Company and modern culture) (Beijing: Zhonghua shuju, 2007).
4. For the multiple causes and wide-ranging impacts of the end of the imperial civil service examination, see Benjamin A. Elman, *A Cultural History of Civil Examinations in Late Imperial China* (Berkeley: University of California Press, 2000), chap. 11.
5. Hao Chang, *Chinese Intellectuals in Crisis: The Search for Order and Meaning* (Berkeley: University of California Press, 1987); Joseph R. Levenson, *Confucian China and Its Modern Fate*, 3 vols. (Berkeley: University of California Press, 1958–1964).
6. Xiaoping Cong, *Teachers' Schools and the Making of the Modern Chinese Nation-State, 1897–1937* (Vancouver: University of British Columbia Press, 2007); Timothy B. Weston, *The Power of Position: Beijing University, Intellectuals, and Chinese Political Culture, 1898–1929* (Berkeley: University of California Press, 2004); Wen-hsin Yeh, *The Alienated Academy: Culture and Politics in Republican China, 1919–1937* (Cambridge, Mass.: Harvard University Asia Center, 1990).

7. Robert Culp, Eddy U, and Wen-hsin Yeh, *Knowledge Acts in Modern China: Ideas, Institutions, and Identities* (Berkeley: Institute of East Asian Studies, University of California, 2016); Xiaoqun Xu, *Chinese Professionals and the Republican State: The Rise of Professional Associations in Shanghai, 1912–1937* (Cambridge: Cambridge University Press, 2001).

8. Wen-hsin Yeh, *Provincial Passages: Culture, Space, and the Origins of Chinese Communism* (Berkeley: University of California Press, 1996); Jonathan D. Spence, *Mao Zedong* (New York: Viking, 1999).

9. In focusing on quotidian daily practices, this book follows other recent books that have concentrated on material life and "everyday modernity" in modern China. See, for example, Frank Dikötter, *Things Modern: Material Culture and Everyday Life in China* (London: Hurst, 2007); Madeleine Yue Dong and Joshua Goldstein, eds., *Everyday Modernity in China* (Seattle: University of Washington Press, 2006). But I also seek to connect new forms of daily social practice to the emergence of larger cultural and intellectual trends, as I did with Yeh, U, and our collaborators in *Knowledge Acts*.

10. Cynthia J. Brokaw and Kai-wing Chow, eds., *Printing and Book Culture in Late Imperial China* (Berkeley: University of California Press, 2005); Cynthia J. Brokaw, *Commerce in Culture: The Sibao Book Trade in the Qing and Republican Periods* (Cambridge, Mass.: Harvard University Asia Center, 2007); Joseph P. McDermott, *A Social History of the Chinese Book: Books and Literati Culture in Late Imperial China* (Hong Kong: Hong Kong University Press, 2006).

11. Kai-wing Chow, *Publishing, Culture, and Power in Early Modern China* (Stanford, Calif.: Stanford University Press, 2004).

12. Benedict Anderson, *Imagined Communities: Reflections on the Origin and Spread of Nationalism* (London: Verso, 1983). See also Michael Warner, *The Letters of the Republic: Publication and the Public Sphere in Eighteenth-Century America* (Cambridge, Mass.: Harvard University Press, 1990).

13. Kai-wing Chow, *Publishing*, 71–73.

14. Christopher A. Reed, *Gutenberg in Shanghai: Chinese Print Capitalism, 1876–1937* (Vancouver: University of British Columbia Press, 2004), 8–10.

15. Reed, *Gutenberg in Shanghai*, chap. 4.

16. Giles Richter, "Marketing the World: Publishing Entrepreneurs in Meiji Japan, 1870–1912" (PhD diss., Columbia University, 1999), 187, 198–99.

17. Richard Venezky with Carl F. Kaestle, "From McGuffey to Dick and Jane: Reading Textbooks," in *A History of the Book in America, Volume 4: Print in Motion; The Expansion of Publishing and Reading in the United States, 1880–1940*, ed. Carl F. Kaestle and Janice A. Radway (Chapel Hill: University of North Carolina Press, 2009), 425.

18. Richard Ohmann, "Diverging Paths: Books and Magazines in the Transition to Corporate Capitalism," in Kaestle and Radway, *History of the Book*, 108–9.

19. James L. West III, *American Authors and the Literary Marketplace since 1900* (Philadelphia: University of Pennsylvania Press, 1990). West observes that most publishers in Great Britain were even smaller and less internally diversified than their American counterparts.

20. Yue Meng, *Shanghai and the Edges of Empires* (Minneapolis: University of Minnesota Press, 2006), 33–42.

21. Benjamin A. Elman, *From Philosophy to Philology: Intellectual and Social Aspects of Change in Late Imperial China* (Cambridge, Mass.: Council on East Asian Studies, Harvard University, 1984), 104–5, 109.

22. Nancy Armstrong and Leonard Tennenhouse, *The Imaginary Puritan: Literature, Intellectual Labor, and the Origins of Personal Life* (Berkeley: University of California Press,

1992), 121–26; André Gorz, "The Tyranny of the Factory: Today and Tomorrow," in *The Division of Labour: The Labour Process and Class-Struggle in Modern Capitalism*, ed. André Gorz (Atlantic Highlands, N.J.: Humanities Press, 1976), 55–58; Alfred Sohn-Rethel, *Intellectual and Manual Labour: A Critique of Epistemology* (London: Macmillan, 1978), 145–63. The very concentration of organizational control by managers can seem to legitimize status differences between management and workers. Further, part of the intellectual work of the managerial stratum can take the form of ideological justification of a qualitative distinction between management and other kinds of labor.

23. Richard Florida, *The Rise of the Creative Class: And How It's Transforming Work, Leisure, Community, and Everyday Life* (New York: Basic Books, 2002), 8. See also Michael Hill's thoughtful definition of "mental labor" in *Lin Shu, Inc.: Translation and the Making of Modern Chinese Culture* (Oxford: Oxford University Press, 2013), 8.

24. William Whyte, for example, demonstrated that research and development work in postwar American industrial corporations became increasingly collective, discrete, technical, and routinized (*Organization Man* [Philadelphia: University of Pennsylvania Press, 2013]). Ohmann and Radway, similarly, describe the commodification of text, which publishers packaged and repackaged in various ways to engage diverse print markets. But Ohmann further notes that American publishers did not adopt new corporate forms to rationalize industrial production in the ways contemporaneous Chinese publishers did (Ohmann, "Diverging Paths," 109–13).

25. Michel Foucault, "What Is an Author?," in *Language, Counter-Memory, Practice: Selected Essays and Interviews*, ed. Donald F. Bouchard, trans. Donald F. Bouchard and Sherry Simon, 113–38 (Ithaca, N.Y.: Cornell University Press, 1977).

26. Lucien Febvre and Henri-Jean Martin, *The Coming of the Book: The Impact of Printing, 1450–1800*, trans. David Gerard (London: Verso, 1997 [1958]), 109.

27. Only a few business-history studies have considered the question of how technical personnel were recruited, trained, and managed, and they have focused largely on the managerial, service, or marketing dimensions. See, for instance, Sherman G. Cochran, *Big Business in China: Sino-Foreign Rivalry in the Cigarette Industry, 1890–1930* (Cambridge, Mass.: Harvard University Press, 1980); Elisabeth Köll, "The Making of the Civil Engineer in China: Knowledge Transfer, Institution Building, and the Rise of a Profession," in Culp, U, and Yeh, *Knowledge Acts*, 148–73; and Wen-hsin Yeh, *Shanghai Splendor: Economic Sentiments in the Making of Modern China, 1843–1949* (Berkeley: University of California Press, 2007), especially chaps. 4–5.

28. On different models for the formation of professions in Europe and America, see Andrew Abbott, *The System of Professions: An Essay on the Division of Expert Labor* (Chicago: University of Chicago Press, 1988); Magali Sarfatti Larson, *The Rise of Professionalism: A Sociological Analysis* (Berkeley: University of California Press, 1979).

29. For professionalization of those fields, see Xu, *Chinese Professionals*, and Culp, U, and Yeh, *Knowledge Acts*, part 2.

30. See, for example, Wen-hsin Yeh, *Shanghai Splendor*.

31. Culp, *Articulating Citizenship*; Peter Zarrow, *Educating China: Knowledge, Society, and Textbooks in a Modernizing World, 1902–1937* (Cambridge: Cambridge University Press, 2015).

32. Note, for instance, Eugenia Lean's innovative argument about how industrialist Chen Diexian ordered and authenticated scientific and industrial knowledge through compilation, editing, and publication of collectanea ("Proofreading Science: Editing and Experimentation in Manuals by a 1930s Industrialist," in *Science and Technology in Modern China, 1880s–1940s*, ed. Jing Tsu and Benjamin A. Elman, 185–208 [Leiden: Brill, 2014]).

33. Bruno Latour, *Pandora's Hope: Essays on the Reality of Science Studies* (Cambridge, Mass.: Harvard University Press, 1999), 67–79.

34. Michel Foucault, *The Archaeology of Knowledge*, trans. A. M. Sheridan Smith (New York: Pantheon Books, 1972), 27.

35. Literature was certainly a significant portion of these companies' publications. At Commercial Press, for instance, between 1897 and 1949 at least 11 percent of its overall publications were in the categories of Chinese or foreign literature; Li Jiaju, *Shangwu yinshuguan*, 168–69. Literary publishing in Shanghai's publishing circles has already been the focus of a series of outstanding recent books by Lee, Link, Hill, Des Forges, Hockx, and others. This book seeks to complement their contributions by focusing on nonliterary publications that contributed to knowledge production in classical scholarship and a variety of modern academic disciplines; Alexander Des Forges, *Mediasphere Shanghai: The Aesthetics of Cultural Production* (Honolulu: University of Hawai`i Press, 2007); Hill, *Lin Shu, Inc.*; Michel Hockx, *Questions of Style: Literary Societies and Literary Journals in Modern China, 1911–1937* (Leiden: Brill, 2011); Leo Ou-fan Lee, *Shanghai Modern: The Flowering of a New Urban Culture in China, 1930–1945* (Cambridge, Mass.: Harvard University Press, 1999); E. Perry Link Jr., *Mandarin Ducks and Butterflies: Popular Fiction in Early Twentieth-Century Chinese Cities* (Berkeley: University of California Press, 1981).

36. Studies of the development of academic fields are attentive to the content of scholarly publications but pay scant attention to the dynamics of the publishing process through which scholarship took material form and circulated; Brian Moloughney and Peter Zarrow, eds., *Transforming History: The Making of a Modern Academic Discipline in Twentieth-Century China* (Hong Kong: Chinese University Press, 2011); Arif Dirlik with Guannan Li and Hsiao-pei Yen, *Sociology and Anthropology in Twentieth-Century China: Between Universalism and Indigenism* (Hong Kong: Chinese University Press, 2012).

37. For that bifurcation of elite and popular audiences in the United States at this time, see Janice A. Radway, "Learned and Literary Print Cultures in an Age of Professionalization and Diversification," in Kaestle and Radway, *History of the Book*, 197–233; Joan Shelley Rubin, *The Making of Middlebrow Culture* (Chapel Hill: University of North Carolina Press, 1992).

38. Febvre and Martin, *Coming of the Book*, 249–59.

39. For Jiangnan's regional dominance of evidential studies scholarship and the collections of rare books necessary to pursue it, see Benjamin A. Elman, *Classicism, Politics, and Kinship: The Ch'ang-chou School of New Text Confucianism in Late Imperial China* (Berkeley: University of California Press, 1990).

40. Tse-tsung Chow, *The May 4th Movement: Intellectual Revolution in Modern China* (Cambridge, Mass.: Harvard University Press, 1960), 317–20; Tze-ki Hon, *Visions of Modernity: The Cultural and Historical Debates in Late Qing and Republican China* (Leiden: Brill, 2015); Laurence A. Schneider, "National Essence and the New Intelligentsia," in *The Limits of Change: Essays on Conservative Alternatives in Republican China*, ed. Charlotte Furth, 57–89 (Cambridge, Mass.: Harvard University Press, 1976).

41. Robert Darnton, *The Business of Enlightenment: A Publishing History of the "Encyclopédie," 1775–1800* (Cambridge, Mass.: Harvard University Press, 1979), 196–201, 467, 474–76.

42. Darnton, *The Business of Enlightenment*, 522.

43. Pierre Bourdieu, *The Field of Cultural Production: Essays on Art and Literature*, ed. Randal Johnson (New York: Columbia University Press, 1993), 29–144.

44. Bourdieu, *Field of Cultural Production*, 75.

45. Pierre Bourdieu, *Homo Academicus*, trans. Peter Collier (Stanford, Calif.: Stanford University Press, 1988).

46. Pierre Bourdieu, *Distinction: A Social Critique of the Judgement of Taste*, trans. Richard Nice (Cambridge, Mass.: Harvard University Press, 1984).

47. Roger Chartier, "Communities of Readers," in *The Order of Books: Readers, Authors, and Libraries in Europe between the Fourteenth and Eighteenth Centuries*, trans. Lydia G. Cochrane, 1–23 (Stanford, Calif.: Stanford University Press, 1994); Anindita Ghosh, *Power in Print: Popular Publishing and the Politics of Language and Culture in a Colonial Society, 1778–1905* (Oxford: Oxford University Press, 2006).

48. David Johnson, "Communication, Class, and Consciousness in Late Imperial China," in *Popular Culture in Late Imperial China*, ed. David Johnson, Andrew J. Nathan, and Evelyn S. Rawski (Berkeley: University of California Press, 1985), 59.

49. Zhonghua jiaoyu gaijin she 中華教育改進社, *Zhongguo jiaoyu tongji gailan* 中國教育統計概覽 (A survey of China's educational statistics) (Shanghai: Shangwu yinshuguan, 1923), 1–2.

50. Zhongguo di'er lishi dang'anguan 中國第二歷史檔案館, comp., *Zhonghua minguoshi dang'an ziliao huibian, Diwuji, Di'yibian, Jiaoyu* 中華民國史檔案資料彙編第五輯第一編 教育 (Collection of archival materials on the history of the Chinese Republic, Collection 5, Set 1, Education), 2 vols. (Nanjing: Jiangsu guji chubanshe), 1:579, 588–89; Culp, *Articulating Citizenship*, 304. Between 1930 and 1937, 1.5 to 2.5 million primary students were graduating annually, joining the ranks of fully literate active readers.

51. Brokaw suggests that a wide range of social groups in the Qing period possessed functional, specialized, or fragmented literacy (*Commerce in Culture*, 559–68).

52. Although, economic concerns related to market share, salaries, and royalties continued to be an issue into the 1960s.

53. Christopher A. Reed and Nicolai Volland, "Epilogue: Beyond the Age of Cultural Entrepreneurship, 1949–Present," in *The Business of Culture: Cultural Entrepreneurs in China and Southeast Asia, 1900–1965*, ed. Christopher Rea and Nicolai Volland, 259–82 (Vancouver: University of British Columbia Press, 2015), 261–69.

54. Mao famously established this revolutionary basis for evaluating literary and cultural work during the Yan'an Forum on Literature and Art in 1942; see Bonnie S. McDougall, *Mao Zedong's "Talks at the Yan'an Conference on Literature and Art": A Translation of the 1943 Text with Commentary*, Michigan Papers in Chinese Studies, no. 39 (Ann Arbor: Center for Chinese Studies, University of Michigan, 1980).

55. For the etymology and definition of these terms in left-wing discourse during the Republican period, see Eddy U, "Reification of the Chinese Intellectual: On the Origins of the CCP Concept of '*Zhishifenzi*,'" *Modern China* 35, no. 6 (November 2009): 604–31.

56. Armstrong and Tennenhouse, in their study of early modern English literature, likewise identify writing as the key activity defining the modern intellectual. They further see writing as socially productive in constituting modern, rational subjectivity and the "imagined community" of the nation (*The Imaginary Puritan*, 114–216).

57. Tani Barlow, "*Zhishifenzi* [Chinese Intellectuals] and Power," *Dialectical Anthropology* 16 (1991): 209–32; Arif Dirlik, *The Origins of the Chinese Communist Party* (New York: Oxford University Press, 1989); Jerome B. Grieder, *Intellectuals and the State in Modern China: A Narrative History* (New York: Free Press, 1983); Tse-tsung Chow, *The May 4th Movement*; Vera Schwarcz, *The Chinese Enlightenment: Intellectuals and the Legacy of the May Fourth Movement of 1919* (Berkeley: University of California Press,

1986). In his new comprehensive history *The Intellectual in Modern Chinese History* (Cambridge: Cambridge University Press, 2015), Timothy Cheek suggests that print capitalism provided the "hardware" for the circulation of intellectuals' ideas (35–39). Yet he focuses primarily on newspapers, and he sees the three processes of reform, revolution, and rejuvenation as the main dynamics conditioning intellectuals' definition and development.

58. Rea and Volland, *The Business of Culture*. See also Michael Hill's innovative study of the translator Lin Shu and Michel Hockx's brilliant analysis of Republican-period writers' stylistic positioning in the literary field: Hill, *Lin Shu, Inc.*; Hockx, *Questions of Style*.

59. Michel Foucault, *The History of Sexuality, Volume 1: An Introduction*, trans. Robert Hurley (New York: Vintage, 1980), 92.

60. Y. C. Wang, *Chinese Intellectuals and the West, 1872–1900* (Chapel Hill: University of North Carolina Press, 1966); Weili Ye, *Seeking Modernity in China's Name: Chinese Students in the United States, 1900–1927* (Stanford, Calif.: Stanford University Press, 2001).

61. Weston, *The Power of Position*, 216–28.

62. Robert Culp and Eddy U, "Introduction: Knowledge Systems, Knowledge Producers, and China's Distinctive Modernity," in Culp, U, and Yeh, *Knowledge Acts*, 1–3.

63. In the early 1920s there were only 141,662 secondary students in China. By 1935 the number had increased significantly to 522,625, but it was still proportionally quite small given an overall population of more than 400 million; Culp, *Articulating Citizenship*, 304. The number of university students and graduates was even smaller, reaching only 27,755 in 1934; Wen-hsin Yeh, *The Alienated Academy*, 282–83.

64. Cong, *Teachers' Schools*; Wen-hsin Yeh, *Shanghai Splendor*, chaps. 5–6.

65. Florida, *Rise of the Creative Class*, 8.

66. For one characterization of that tension, see Florida, *Rise of the Creative Class*, 37–43.

67. James Gao, *The Communist Takeover of Hangzhou: The Transformation of City and Cadre, 1949–1954* (Honolulu: University of Hawai`i Press, 2004); Thomas S. Mullaney, *Coming to Terms with the Nation: Ethnic Classification in Modern China* (Berkeley: University of California Press, 2011); Eddy U, *Disorganizing China: Counter-Bureaucracy and the Decline of Socialism* (Stanford, Calif.: Stanford University Press, 2007).

68. These questions are raised and engaged most directly in Sherman G. Cochran, ed., *The Capitalist Dilemma in China's Communist Revolution* (Ithaca, N.Y.: East Asia Program, Cornell University, 2014); and Morris Bian, *The Making of the State Enterprise System in Modern China: The Dynamics of Institutional Change* (Cambridge, Mass.: Harvard University Press, 2005).

69. For the model of the propaganda state, see Peter Kenez, *The Birth of the Propaganda State: Soviet Methods of Mass Mobilization, 1917–1929* (Cambridge: Cambridge University Press, 1985). For application of this model to the early PRC, see Chang-tai Hung, *Mao's New World: Political Culture in the early People's Republic* (Ithaca, N.Y.: Cornell University Press, 2010); Cheek, *The Intellectual*, 125–32.

70. For the genealogy of the pedagogical bent in the PRC state, see Donald Munro, *The Concept of Man in Contemporary China* (Ann Arbor: University of Michigan Press, 1977).

71. My understanding of this distinction between ideology (*yishi xingtai*) or propaganda (*xuanchuan*) and knowledge (*zhishi*) as it was expressed in the early PRC context is informed by discussion at the conference "Organized Knowledge and State Socialism in Mao's China" held at the Center for Chinese Studies, University of California, Berkeley, December 5–6, 2014. I thank the participants for their insights on this and many other issues.

1. Becoming Editors

1. The following account is drawn from Liu Hecheng 柳和城, *Sun Yuxiu pingzhuan* 孙毓修评传 (A critical biography of Sun Yuxiu) (Shanghai: Shanghai renmin chubanshe, 2011), 1–28.

2. Christopher A. Reed, *Gutenberg in Shanghai: Chinese Print Capitalism, 1876–1937* (Vancouver: University of British Columbia Press, 2004), 188–99; Yue Meng, *Shanghai and the Edges of Empires* (Minneapolis: University of Minnesota Press, 2006), 33–40.

3. Song Yuanfang 宋原放, ed., *Zhongguo chuban shiliao: Jindai bufen* 中國出版史料：近代部份 (Historical materials of Chinese publishing: Modern portion), vol. 3 (Wuhan: Hubei jiaoyu chubanshe, 2004), 6.

4. Reed, *Gutenberg in Shanghai*, 197–98; Manying Ip, *The Life and Times of Zhang Yuanji, 1867–1959: From Qing Reformer to Twentieth-Century Publisher* (Beijing: Commercial Press, 1985), 119–28; Meng, *Shanghai*, 37; Fei-hsien Wang, "Creating New Order in the Knowledge Economy: The Curious Journey of Copyright in China, 1868–1937" (PhD diss., University of Chicago, 2012), 105.

5. Robert Culp, "Building a National Print Market: A Preliminary Analysis of Book Distribution in Late Qing and Republican China," in *Chengshi chuanbo: Jiyu Zhongguo chengshi de lishi yu xianshi* 城市传播：基于中国城市的历史与现实 (Urban dissemination: Based on the history and reality of China's cities), ed. Huang Dan, 194–222 (Shanghai: Jiaotong University Press, 2016).

6. Li Jiaju 李家驹, *Shangwu yinshuguan yu jindai zhishi wenhua de chuanbo* 商務印書館與近代知識文化的传播 (Commercial Press and the transmission of modern knowledge and culture) (Beijing: Shangwu yinshuguan, 2005), 44–46; Wang Jiarong 汪家熔, *Shangwu yinshuguan shi ji qita—Wang Jiarong chubanshi yanjiu wenji* 商務印書館史及其他—汪家熔出版史研究文集 (The history of Commercial Press and other things: Wang Jiarong's collected writings on his research on the history of publishing). Beijing: Zhongguo shuji chubanshe chuban, 1998), 89–90.

7. See, for instance, Philip A. Kuhn and Susan Mann Jones, "Dynastic Decline and the Roots of Rebellion," in *The Cambridge History of China, Volume 10: Late Ch'ing, 1800–1911, Part 1*, ed. John K. Fairbank (New York: Cambridge University Press, 1986), 111–16; Shen Fu, *Six Records of a Floating Life* (Harmondsworth, Middlesex, UK: Penguin, 1983).

8. Zhang Yuanji 張元濟, *Zhang Yuanji riji* 张元济日记 (Zhang Yuanji's diary), 2 vols., organized by Zhang Renfeng 张人凤 (Shijiazhuang: Hebei jiaoyu chubanshe, 2000), 1:4–5, 7, 12–15, 23, 29–30.

9. Zhang Yuanji, *Zhang Yuanji riji*, 1:4–5.

10. Zhang Yuanji, *Zhang Yuanji riji*, 1:7.

11. Zhang Yuanji, *Zhang Yuanji riji*, 1:15.

12. Zhang Yuanji, *Zhang Yuanji riji*, 1:2, 5, 7, 11–3, 15, 23, 37, 40.

13. Jiang Weiqiao 蒋维乔, "Jiang Weiqiao riji zhailu (xu'er)" 蒋维乔日记摘录（续二）(Excerpts from Jiang Weiqiao's diary [continuation two]), *Shangwu yinshuguan guanshi ziliao* 商務印書館館史資料 (Commercial Press company history materials), no. 47 (June 10, 1991): 16–20, 22–24; Jiang Weiqiao, "Jiang Weiqiao riji (xuzhong)" 蒋维乔日记（续中）(Jiang Weiqiao's diary [middle continuation]), *Shangwu yinshuguan guanshi ziliao*, no. 48 (April 10, 1992): 13–16, 18, 20; Jiang Weiqiao, "Jiang Weiqiao riji (xuwan)" 蒋维乔日记（续完）(Jiang Weiqiao's diary [final continuation]), *Shangwu yinshuguan guanshi ziliao*, no. 50 (October 5, 1993): 16, 20.

14. Zhang Yuanji, *Zhang Yuanji riji*, 1:5, 11, 17–18, 57.

15. Zhang Yuanji, *Zhang Yuanji riji*, 1:23, 27.

16. Zhang Yuanji, *Zhang Yuanji riji*, 1:11, 15–16.

17. Fei-hsien Wang, "Creating New Order," chap. 5.

18. Zhang Yuanji, *Zhang Yuanji riji*, 1:3.

19. Zhang Yuanji, *Zhang Yuanji riji*, 1:12, 14.

20. On the importance of literati networks to late Qing and early Republican publishing ventures, see Lin Pan 林盼, "Wanqing xinshi meiti yu guanxi wang: *Zhongwai ribao* (1898–1908) yanjiu" 晚清新式媒體與關係網：《中外日報》(1898–1908)研究 (The late Qing new media and relational networks: A study of the *Sino-Foreign Daily* [1898–1908]) (PhD diss., Fudan University, 2013).

21. Zhang Yuanji, *Zhang Yuanji riji*, 1:4

22. Zhang Yuanji, *Zhang Yuanji riji*, 1:2; see also 1:12.

23. Zhang Yuanji, *Zhang Yuanji riji*, 1:6.

24. Zhang Yuanji, *Zhang Yuanji riji*, 1:11.

25. Zhang Yuanji, *Zhang Yuanji riji*, 1:17.

26. *SYJ*2, 87. Although, this did not keep him from requesting special treatment or getting a somewhat higher rate for manuscript fees; see Zhang Yuanji, *Zhang Yuanji riji*, 1:5.

27. Hu Shi 胡適, *Hu Shi de riji* 胡適的日記 (Hu Shi's diary), ed. Zhongguo shehui kexue yuan jindaishi yanjiusuo 中國社會科學院近代史研究所 and Zhonghua minguoshi yanjiushi 中華民國史研究室 (Hong Kong: Zhonghua shuju Xianggang fenju, 1985). 152.

28. Kaiming Bookstore's Editing Department, for instance, had large numbers of former Commercial Press editors, several of whom moved after Wang Yunwu dramatically cut that company's editorial staff after the Japanese bombing of its office and factory complex in January 1932; Wang Zhiyi 王知伊, comp., *Kaiming shudian jishi* 开明书店纪事 (A record of Kaiming Bookstore) (Taiyuan: Shanxi renmin chubanshe, 1991), 90–91.

29. *Zhonghua shuju wunian gaikuang* 中華書局五年概況 (The general situation at Zhonghua Book Company in 1916) ([Shanghai]: Zhonghua shuju, 1916), 1, 9.

30. By the early 1930s the comparative distinctiveness of Chinese publishers' editing departments became clear to keen observers like Shu Xincheng and Wang Yunwu as they studied developments in publishing industries in Europe, America, and Japan; see Shu Xincheng 舒新城, "Zhonghua shuju bianjisuo" 中華書局編輯所 (Zhonghua Book Company's Editing Department), in *Kuanggulu* 狂顧錄 (Record of wild reflections) (Shanghai: Zhonghua shuju, 1936); Wang Shounan 王壽南, comp., *Wang Yunwu xiansheng nianpu chugao* 王雲五先生年譜初稿 (Initial draft of the chronological biography of Mr. Wang Yunwu), 4 vols. (Taipei: Taiwan Shangwu yinshuguan, 1987), 1:234–35.

31. *Shangwu yinshuguan zhilüe* 商務印書館志略 (A general outline of Commercial Press) ([Shanghai]: Shangwu yinshuguan, 1926), 10–11.

32. Qian Binghuan 钱炳寰, *Zhonghua shuju dashi jiyao* 中华书局大事纪要 (Summary of major events at Zhonghua Book Company) (Beijing: Zhonghua shuju 2002), 15, 22–23; *Zhonghua shuju wunian gaikuang*, 2, 11.

33. For an account of curricular shifts during the late Qing and Republican periods, see Robert Culp, *Articulating Citizenship: Civic Education and Student Politics in Southeastern China, 1912–1940* (Cambridge, Mass.: Harvard University Asia Center, 2007), chap. 1; Li Huaxing 李华兴 et al., *Minguo jiaoyushi* 民国教育史 (Republican education history) (Shanghai: Shanghai jiaoyu chubanshe, 1997). Textbooks changed accordingly. Zhuang Yu, for instance, describes new textbook production for most years between 1902 and 1931. *SYJ*, 62–72.

34. *SYJ*, 66.

35. For a survey of Commercial Press and Zhonghua Book Company publications from the late Qing into the Republican period, see *Minguo sannian chun Zhonghua shuju gaikuang* 民國三年春中華書局概況 (Zhonghua Book Company's general situation in spring 1914) ([Shanghai: Zhonghua shuju, 1914]), 11–15; *Shangwu yinshuguan zhilüe*, 10–14; *Zhonghua shuju shisan nian gaikuang* 中華書局十三年概況 (The general situation at Zhonghua Book Company in 1924) ([Shanghai]: Zhonghua shuju, 1924), 8–10.

36. *SYJ*, 112, 151–52, 206. For other examples of prominent degree holders, see *SYJ*, 207–8.

37. Reed, *Gutenberg in Shanghai*, 168–70; *SYJ*, 73–75, 205; Ip, *Life and Times*, chaps. 2–4; Wang Jianjun 王建军, *Zhongguo jindai jiaokeshu fazhan yanjiu* 中国近代教科书发展研究 (Study of the development of China's modern textbooks) (Guangzhou: Guangdong jiaoyu chubanshe, 1996), 116–19; Xu Youchun 徐友春 et al., eds., *Minguo renwu da cidian* 民國人物大辭典 (Biographical dictionary of Republican China) (Shijiazhuang: Hebei renmin chubanshe, 1991), 746. Meng Yue makes a similar point about the broad cultural literacy of the "philologist editors" who led the Commercial Press Editing Department during the first two decades of the twentieth century (*Shanghai*, 34–42).

38. For a partial list of the editors at Zhonghua during the 1910s, see *Zhonghua shuju wunian gaikuang*, 11.

39. *HZS*, 1:234–35.

40. *HZS*, 1:27–28.

41. *HZS*, 1:235.

42. Xu Youchun et al., *Minguo renwu da cidian*, 704, 1574.

43. Jiang Weiqiao 蒋维乔, "Jiang Weiqiao riji zhailu" 蒋维乔日记摘录 (Excerpts from Jiang Weiqiao's diary), *Shangwu yinshuguan guanshi ziliao* 商務印書館館史資料 (Commercial Press company history materials), no. 45 (April 20, 1990): 2–16.

44. Jiang Weiqiao 蒋维乔, "Jiang Weiqiao riji zhailu (xuyi)" 蒋维乔日记摘录（续一） (Excerpts from Jiang Weiqiao's diary [continuation one]), *Shangwu yinshuguan guanshi ziliao* 商務印書館館史資料 (Commercial Press company history materials), no. 46 (September 20, 1990): 22; Jiang Weiqiao, "Jiang Weiqiao riji zhailu (xu'er)," 16–17, 21, 25.

45. Jiang Weiqiao, "Jiang Weiqiao riji zhailu," 11.

46. Jiang Weiqiao, "Jiang Weiqiao riji zhailu (xu'er)," 15–16, 19; Jiang Weiqiao, "Jiang Weiqiao riji (xuzhong)," 18.

47. Jiang Weiqiao, "Jiang Weiqiao riji (xuwan)," 17.

48. Jiang Weiqiao, "Jiang Weiqiao riji (xuwan)," 23.

49. Jiang Weiqiao, "Jiang Weiqiao riji zhailu (xuyi)," 14.

50. Jiang Weiqiao, "Jiang Weiqiao riji zhailu (xuyi)," 15, 20.

51. Jiang Weiqiao, "Jiang Weiqiao riji zhailu (xuyi)," 22.

52. Jiang Weiqiao, "Jiang Weiqiao riji zhailu (xu'er)," 17.

53. Jiang Weiqiao, "Jiang Weiqiao riji zhailu (xu'er)," 21, 25.

54. Jiang Weiqiao, "Jiang Weiqiao riji (xuzhong)," 13.

55. Jiang Weiqiao, "Jiang Weiqiao riji (xuzhong)," 21–22.

56. Jiang Weiqiao, "Jiang Weiqiao riji (xuzhong)," 11, 21–22; Jiang Weiqiao, "Jiang Weiqiao riji zhailu (xuyi)," 15.

57. By "habitus," Bourdieu means the structural patterns created by past social and cultural practices that condition the horizon of possibility and patterns of action in the present (*Outline of a Theory of Practice*, trans. Richard Nice [Cambridge: Cambridge University Press, 1977]; *The Logic of Practice*, trans. Richard Nice [Stanford, Calif.: Stanford University Press, 1990]). Bourdieu's formulation of habitus has been criticized by some for portraying social action and cultural expression as overly static and

unselfconscious. I find it helpful for analyzing how past cultural patterns can continue to inform perceptions, choices, and actions even in periods of rapid change. Moreover, I emphasize here how late Qing literati took an active role in reproducing their group habitus in the midst of a modern, industrial capitalist enterprise.

58. For further examples of recruitment through recommendations, see Li Jiaju, *Shangwu yinshuguan*, 98–100; *SYJ*, 57, 73–74, 107–8, 140–43; *HZS*, 1:18–24.
59. *SYJ*, 146, 151–52.
60. *Zhonghua shuju wunian gaikuang*, 2–3.
61. *SYJ*, 144.
62. For discussion of the teahouse in intermediate market towns as a site for local elite leisure and social and political activity, see G. William Skinner, "Marketing and Social Structure in Rural China, Part I," *Journal of Asian Studies* 24, no. 1 (1964): 27, 41–42; see also Qin Shao, "Tempest over Teapots: The Vilification of Teahouse Culture in Early Republican China," *Journal of Asian Studies* 57, no. 4 (November 1998): 1014–15.
63. *SYJ*, 143–44, 146.
64. Jiang Weiqiao, "Jiang Weiqiao riji zhailu," 12; Jiang Weiqiao, "Jiang Weiqiao riji zhailu (xuyi)," 21; Jiang Weiqiao, "Jiang Weiqiao riji zhailu (xu'er)," 21. See also *SYJ2*, 89–90.
65. *SYJ*, 205–8.
66. *Zhonghua shuju wunian gaikuang*, 10–12.
67. *SYJ*, 143–45.
68. G. William Skinner, "Mobility Strategies in Late Imperial China: A Regional Systems Analysis," in *Regional Analysis, Volume I: Economic Systems*, ed. Carol A. Smith (New York: Academic Press, 1976), 336–50; Kuhn and Jones, "Dynastic Decline," 111–28.
69. *SYJ*, 144–83.
70. *SYJ*, 178.
71. Chen Jiang 陈江, "Guji zhenglijia yu Zhongguo tonghua de chuangshiren—Sun Yuxiu" 古籍整理家与中国童话的创始人—孙毓修 (Organizer of ancient books and originator of Chinese children's stories: Sun Yuxiu), in *Zhongguo chuban shiliao: Jindai bufen* 中国出版史料：近代部分, vol. 3, ed. Wang Jiarong 汪家熔 (Wuhan: Hubei jiaoyu chubanshe, 2004), 468–70; Liu Hecheng, *Sun Yuxiu pingzhuan*; *SYJ*, 149–50, 154–55.
72. *SYJ*, 112–13.
73. *SYJ*, 152, 207.
74. E.g., Jiang Weiqiao, "Jiang Weiqiao riji zhailu (xuyi)," 12–14; Jiang Weiqiao, "Jiang Weiqiao riji zhailu (xu'er)," 16–24; Jiang Weiqiao, "Jiang Weiqiao riji (xuzhong)," 12–19; Jiang Weiqiao, "Jiang Weiqiao riji (xuwan)," 15–24.
75. *SYJ*, 150–52.
76. Stephen C. Averill, "The Cultural Politics of Local Education in Early Twentieth-Century China," *Twentieth-Century China* 32, no. 2 (April 2007): 12–14; Marianne Bastid, *Educational Reform in Early Twentieth-Century China*, trans. Paul Bailey (Ann Arbor: Center for Chinese Studies, University of Michigan, 1988); R. Keith Schoppa, *Chinese Elites and Political Change: Zhejiang Province in the Early Twentieth Century* (Cambridge, Mass.: Harvard University Press, 1982); Joan Judge, *Print and Politics: 'Shibao' and the Culture of Reform in Late Qing China* (Stanford, Calif.: Stanford University Press, 1996).
77. For instance, Commercial Press and Zhonghua Book Company staff members were heavily involved in the late Qing and early Republican Jiangsu Education Association and National Federation of Education Associations; see Paul J. Bailey, *Reform the People: Changing Attitudes Towards Popular Education in Early Twentieth Century China* (Vancouver: University of British Columbia Press, 1990), 66–67, 136–38, 208.
78. Jiang Weiqiao, "Jiang Weiqiao riji zhailu," 16.

79. Jiang Weiqiao, "Jiang Weiqiao riji zhailu (xuyi)," 12.

80. Jiang Weiqiao, "Jiang Weiqiao riji zhailu (xuyi)," 12–14.

81. *SYJ*, 60–61; see also *SYJ*, 74.

82. Bao Tianxiao also describes a highly collaborative process for revising the higher-primary Chinese textbook in 1912. With every three or four chapters he wrote, he could consult with Zhuang Yu and Yan Lianru, and he would also get advice from Jiang Weiqiao and Gao Mengdan; *SYJ2*, 90.

83. Lu Erkui 陸爾逵, "*Ciyuan* shuolüe" 辭源說略 (A summary of *Ciyuan*), in *Ciyuan* 辭源, ed. Lu Erkui, 2 vols. (Shanghai: Shangwu yinshuguan, 1915), 4; Wang Jiarong 汪家熔, "*Ciyuan, Cihai* de kaichuangxing" 辭源辭海的开创性 (The innovativeness of *Ciyuan* and *Cihai*), *Cishu yanjiu* 辞书研究, no. 4 (2001): 132–33.

84. Lu Erkui, "*Ciyuan* shuolüe," 4–5; Wang Jiarong, "*Ciyuan, Cihai*," 133; Jiang Weiqiao, "Jiang Weiqiao riji (xuwan)," 21–23.

85. Qian Binghuan, *Zhonghua shuju dashi jiyao*, 2–3; Reed, *Gutenberg in Shanghai*, 225–26, 229–30; *HZS*, 1:71.

86. Jiang Weiqiao, "Jiang Weiqiao riji (xuwan)," 19–20; Zhang Yuanji, *Zhang Yuanji riji*, 1:37, 49–50, 52. See also Hu Shi, *Hu Shi de riji*, 149–50.

87. Jiang Weiqiao, "Jiang Weiqiao riji (xuwan)," 22.

88. Zhang Yuanji, *Zhang Yuanji riji*, 1:60–62.

89. Similar dynamics marked discussions with Hu Shi about how to reorganize the Commercial Press Editing Department in 1921; Hu Shi, *Hu Shi de riji*, 144–243.

90. Habits of the scholar-official's lifestyle also persisted at institutions of higher learning, such as Beijing University; Timothy B. Weston, *The Power of Position: Beijing University, Intellectuals, and Chinese Political Culture, 1898–1929* (Berkeley: University of California Press, 2004), 103.

91. *SYJ*, 146, 157–58.

92. Skinner, "Mobility Strategies," 353–54. Henrietta Harrison's valuable biography of Liu Dapeng captures how study in an academy and pursuit of academic degrees inserted young men into "a community of elite men whose lives were focused round the structures of the state" (*The Man Awakened from Dreams: One Man's Life in a North China Village, 1857–1942* [Stanford, Calif.: Stanford University Press, 2005], 32–33). Catherine Yeh demonstrates that brothels and courtesan culture also continued to be a haven for literati working in publishing and academic circles in late Qing and Republican Shanghai, in part because many elite men continued to live and work in all-male environments and be away from home for long periods ("The Life-Style of Four *Wenren* in Late Qing Shanghai," *Harvard Journal of Asiatic Studies* 57, no. 2 [December 1997]: 419–70).

93. E.g., Jiang Weiqiao 蔣維喬, "Yinshizhai riji bufenjuan" 因是齋日記不分卷 (The diary of Yinshizhai [Jiang Weiqiao]), October–December, 1913 (manuscript, Shanghai Municipal Library [digital file]).

94. Jiang Weiqiao, "Jiang Weiqiao riji zhailu (xu'er)," 17–20.

95. Jiang Weiqiao, "Jiang Weiqiao riji zhailu (xu'er)," 20.

96. *SYJ*, 158–59.

97. Jiang Weiqiao, "Jiang Weiqiao riji zhailu (xu'er)," 15, 20.

98. Jiang Weiqiao, "Jiang Weiqiao riji (xuwan)," 13.

99. *SYJ*, 152–54.

100. *SYJ*, 149–57.

101. Jiang Weiqiao, "Jiang Weiqiao riji zhailu," 12.

102. For accounts of Jiangnan literati leisure culture in the late imperial period, see, for example, Shen Fu, *Six Records*; Timothy Brook, "Family Continuity and Cultural

Hegemony: The Gentry of Ningbo, 1368–1911," in *Chinese Local Elites and Patterns of Dominance*, ed. Joseph W. Esherick and Mary B. Rankin, 27–50 (Berkeley: University of California Press, 1976); and Catherine Yeh, "Life-Style of Four *Wenren*."

103. Jiang Weiqiao, "Jiang Weiqiao riji zhailu (xu'er)," 21. For other examples of dinner parties, see Jiang Weiqiao, "Jiang Weiqiao riji zhailu (xuyi)," 21; Jiang Weiqiao, "Jiang Weiqiao riji zhailu (xu'er)," 18; Jiang Weiqiao, "Jiang Weiqiao riji (xuwan)," 13, 19–20.

104. Jiang Weiqiao, "Jiang Weiqiao riji zhailu (xu'er)," 22; see also Jiang Weiqiao, "Jiang Weiqiao riji (xuwan)," 14.

105. Hu Shi's visit to the Commercial Press Editing Department during the summer of 1921 was also marked by numerous banquets, dinner parties, bookstore excursions, and business lunches; see Hu Shi, *Hu Shi de riji*, 141–243.

106. Jiang Weiqiao, "Jiang Weiqiao riji zhailu (xuyi)," 19.

107. Jiang Weiqiao, "Jiang Weiqiao riji (xuzhong)," 10.

108. Jiang Weiqiao, "Jiang Weiqiao riji (xuwan)," 17. Farewell banquets were also common; see Jiang Weiqiao, "Jiang Weiqiao riji zhailu (xu'er)," 23.

109. Zhang Yuanji, *Zhang Yuanji riji*, 1:33–34, 40, 43, 70.

110. Zhang Yuanji, *Zhang Yuanji riji*, 1:59.

111. Jiang Weiqiao, "Jiang Weiqiao riji zhailu (xu'er)," 19, 22; Jiang Weiqiao, "Jiang Weiqiao riji (xuwan)," 14.

112. Reed, *Gutenberg in Shanghai*.

113. Michel Foucault, *Discipline and Punish: The Birth of the Prison*, trans. Alan Sheridan (New York: Vintage, 1979); Timothy Mitchell, *Colonising Egypt* (Berkeley: University of California Press, 1991); E. P. Thompson, "Time, Work-Discipline, and Industrial Capitalism," *Past and Present*, no. 38 (December 1967): 56–97.

2. Universities or Factories?

1. Hu Shi 胡適, *Hu Shi de riji* 胡適的日記 (Hu Shi's diary), ed. Zhongguo shehui kexue yuan jindaishi yanjiusuo 中國社會科學院近代史研究所 and Zhonghua minguoshi yanjiushi 中華民國史研究室 (Hong Kong: Zhonghua shuju Xianggang fenju, 1985), 162.

2. Wang Shounan 王壽南, comp., *Wang Yunwu xiansheng nianpu chugao* 王雲五先生年譜初稿 (Initial draft of the chronological biography of Mr. Wang Yunwu), 4 vols. (Taipei: Taiwan Shangwu yinshuguan, 1987), 1:110–11.

3. Wang Shounan, *Wang Yunwu*, 1;111.

4. Wang Shounan, *Wang Yunwu*, 1:111–12.

5. *Zhonghua shuju dongshihui yijue'an* 中華書局董事會議決案 (Resolutions of the Zhonghua Book Company board of directors), January 21, 1920, ZSA511.9.942(1948).

6. Zuo Shunsheng 左舜聖, *Jin sanshi nian jianwen zaji* 近三十年見聞雜記 (Random notes on my experiences of the past thirty years) (Jiulong: Ziyou chubanshe, 1952), 21–22.

7. For background on the Young China Association, see Tse-tsung Chow, *The May 4th Movement: Intellectual Revolution in Modern China* (Cambridge, Mass.: Harvard University Press, 1960), 251–53.

8. Zou Zhenhuan 邹振环, "Xin wenhua congshu: Xinzhi chuanshu yu xinxue yinling" 新文化丛书：新知传输与新学引领 (The New Culture Series: The transmission of new knowledge and eager anticipation of new learning), in *Zhonghua shuju yu Zhongguo jin xiandai wenhua* 中华书局与中国近现代文化 (Zhonghua Book Company and China's modern culture), ed. Fudan daxue lishixi, Chuban bowuguan, Zhonghua shuju,

Shanghai cishu chubanshi (Shanghai: Shanghai renmin chubanshe, 2013), 169–70.

9. Li Da and Tian Han had studied in Japan, and Yu Jiaju had studied in England; Xu Youchun 徐友春 et al., eds., *Minguo renwu da cidian* 民國人物大辭典 (Biographical dictionary of Republican China) (Shijiazhuang: Hebei renmin chubanshe, 1991), 154–55, 246–47, 402. Zou Zhenhuan surmises that Zhang Wentian worked at Zhonghua after stints studying first in Japan and then in the United States; Zou, "Xin wenhua congshu," 170–71; see also Xu Youchun et al., *Minguo renwu da cidian*, 967.

10. *Zhonghua shuju wunian gaikuang* 中華書局五年概況 (The general situation at Zhonghua Book Company in 1916) ([Shanghai]: Zhonghua shuju, 1916), 2–3.

11. *Zhonghua shuju shisan nian gaikuang* 中華書局十三年概況 (The general situation at Zhonghua Book Company in 1924) ([Shanghai]: Zhonghua shuju, 1924), 2–3.

12. *Zhonghua shuju gaikuang* 中華書局概況 (Zhonghua Book Company's general situation) ([Shanghai: Zhonghua shuju], 1936), 8–23.

13. Zou, "Xin wenhua congshu," 169–84; Zuo, *Jin sanshi nian*, 20–23.

14. Hu Shi, *Hu Shi de riji*, 143–44; *SYJ*, 51; Zhang Renfeng 张人凤 and Liu Hecheng 柳和城, comps., *Zhang Yuanji nianpu changbian* 张元济年谱长编 (Chronological chronicle of Zhang Yuanji's life), 2 vols. (Shanghai: Jiaotong daxue chubanshe, 2011), 1:621.

15. Hu Shi, *Hu Shi de riji*, 145, 150, 151.

16. Hu Shi, *Hu Shi de riji*, 144, 150, 152, 178–79.

17. Hu Shi, *Hu Shi de riji*, 151, 156.

18. Hu Shi, *Hu Shi de riji*, 162.

19. Hu Shi, *Hu Shi de riji*, 185.

20. Hu Shi, *Hu Shi de riji*, 157, 158, 191.

21. Hu Shi, *Hu Shi de riji*, 191, 194, 204, 208, 251–53. Wang Shounan, *Wang Yunwu*, 1:108–9.

22. "Shangwu yinshuguan dongshi huiyi lu" 商務印書館董事會議錄 (Record of the Commercial Press board of directors meetings), unpublished manuscript of excerpted notes, 1922–1954, meeting no. 268, January 19, 1922.

23. *SYJ*, 253–55; Wang Jianhui 王建輝, *Wenhua de Shangwu—Wang Yunwu zhuanti yanjiu* 文化的商務—王雲五專題研究 (Cultural Commercial Press: Specialized research on Wang Yunwu) (Beijing: Shangwu yinshuguan, 2000), 31–39; Wang Shounan, *Wang Yunwu*, 1:108.

24. Hu Shi, *Hu Shi de riji*, 157; *SYJ*, 254.

25. Rea and Volland define the cultural entrepreneur as someone who takes risks and invests cultural and economic capital in cultural ventures for profit or accumulation of symbolic capital (Christopher Rea and Nicolai Volland, eds., *The Business of Culture: Cultural Entrepreneurs in China and Southeast Asia, 1900–1965* [Vancouver: University of British Columbia Press, 2015]).

26. Wang Shounan, *Wang Yunwu*, 1:114.

27. Wang Yunwu 王雲五, *Shangwu yinshuguan yu xin jiaoyu nianpu* 商務印書館與新教育年譜 (Yearly record of Commercial Press and the new education) (Taipei: Taiwan Shangwu yinshuguan, 1973), 119. See also "Bianyisuo zhiyuanlu" 編譯所職員錄 (Record of the staff in the Editing Department), mimeographed record, Shangwu yinshuguan [1926]; *SYJ*, 118–20, 303–5.

28. Xu Youchun et al., *Minguo renwu da cidian*, 539.

29. Xu Youchun et al., *Minguo renwu da cidian*, 1081–82.

30. Wang Yunwu, *Shangwu yinshuguan*, 119.

31. *Shangwu yinshuguan zhilüe* 商務印書館志略 (A general outline of Commercial Press) ([Shanghai]: Shangwu yinshuguan, 1926), 3–4; see also *SYJ*, 118–20.

32. *Shangwu yinshuguan zhilüe*, 4; *SYJ*, 118–20.

33. Tao Menghe 陶孟和, [*Xin xuezhi gaozhong jiaokeshu*] *shehui wenti* 新學制高中教科書社會問題 ([New School System high school textbook] social issues) (Shanghai: Shangwu yinshuguan, 1924); Zhang Qiyun 張其昀, [*Xin xuezhi gaoji zhongxue jiaokeshu*] *benguo dili* 新學制高級中學教科書本國地理 ([New School System upper-middle-school textbook] Chinese geography), 2 vols. (Shanghai: Shangwu yinshuguan, 1928 [1926–1928]).

34. Contracts for royalty payments for jointly held copyright and manuscript fees for purchased copyrights were both standard at Zhonghua Book Company; "[Zhonghua shuju] zong bianjibu banshi chengxu" 中華書局總編輯部辦事程序 (Management procedures for the General Editing Department [Zhonghua Book Company]), unpublished manuscript, 1935, category 2: contracts.

35. Bao Tianxiao 包天笑, *Chuanyinglou riji* 釧影樓日記 (Diary from Chuanying Hall), manuscript, Shanghai Municipal Library, September 30, 1925 (*yichou* 己丑), March 24–26, 31, 1926 (*bingyin* 丙寅), January 7, 1927 (*dingmao* 丁卯), January 22, 1929 (*jisi* 己巳).

36. [Shen] Zhifang [沈]知方, "Cong jihua dao chushu" 從計劃到出書 (From planning to publication), *Shijie* 世界 1, no. 1 (1928): 15; "Touxian" 頭銜 (Official title), *Shijie* 世界 1, no. 1 (1928): 35–36; "ABC congshu zhuzuozhe xiaoxi" ABC叢書著作者消息 (News about the ABC Series' authors), *Shijie* 世界 1, no. 1 (1928): 37.

37. For examples of scholars and authors arranging to publish translations, monographs, and literary works with Commercial Press, see *SYJ*, 306–7, 308–10, 314–15, 358–61.

38. Deng Yongqiu 鄧詠秋, "Minguo shiqi bianji he chuban ren de shengcun zhuangkuang" 民國時期編輯和出版人的生存狀況 (The living situation of editors and publishing people during the Republican period), *Chuban shiliao* 出版史料, no. 2 (2007): 116.

39. For in-depth treatment of the economic crisis at Beijing's universities during the early 1920s, see Timothy B. Weston, *The Power of Position: Beijing University, Intellectuals, and Chinese Political Culture, 1898–1929* (Berkeley: University of California Press, 2004), 216–28. For its impact on the career choices of one Commercial Press editor, see Wang Shihua 王湜華, *Wang Boxiang zhuan* 王伯祥傳 (Biography of Wang Boxiang) (Beijing: Zhonghua shuju, 2008), 25–27.

40. *SYJ*, 329; "Zhu Kezhen shengping yu gongxian" 竺可楨生平與貢獻 (Zhu Kezhen's life and contributions), in *Zhu Kezhen wenji* 竺可楨文集 (Zhu Kezhen's collected works) (Beijing: Kexue chubanshe, 1979), v–vi.

41. *SYJ*, 304.

42. Xu Youchun et al., *Minguo renwu da cidian*, 1081–82.

43. Xu Youchun et al., *Minguo renwu da cidian*, 220.

44. Shu Xincheng 舒新城, "Zhonghua shuju bianjisuo" 中華書局編輯所 (Zhonghua Book Company's Editing Department), in *Kuanggulu* 狂顧錄 (Record of wild reflections) (Shanghai: Zhonghua shuju, 1936), 151.

45. In the early 1920s there were only 141,662 secondary students nationwide. By 1935 the number had increased significantly to 522,625. In 1934 there were 27,755 university students; Robert Culp, *Articulating Citizenship: Civic Education and Student Politics in Southeastern China, 1912–1940* (Cambridge, Mass.: Harvard University Asia Center, 2007), 304; Wen-hsin Yeh, *The Alienated Academy: Culture and Politics in Republican China, 1919–1937* (Cambridge, Mass.: Harvard University Asia Center, 1990), 282–83.

46. Wang Shounan, *Wang Yunwu*, 1:114.

47. Christopher A. Reed, *Gutenberg in Shanghai: Chinese Print Capitalism, 1876–1937* (Vancouver: University of British Columbia Press, 2004), 241–49.

48. Zhu Lianbao 朱聯保, "Guanyu Shijie shuju de huiyi" 關於世界書局的回憶 (My recollections of World Book Company), *Chuban shiliao* 出版史料 1987, no. 2 (overall no. 8): 57.

49. "Xiaoxue bu zengtian bianjiyuan" 小學部增添編輯員 (The Primary School Division added editorial staff members), *Shijie yuekan* 世界月刊, no. 1 (1924), "Zalu" 雜錄 (Miscellaneous records): 1.

50. "Xiaoxue bu you tian bianjiyuan liangren" 小學部又添編輯員兩人 (The Primary School Division further added two editorial staff members), *Shijie yuekan* 世界月刊, no. 2 (1924), "Zalu" 雜錄 (Miscellaneous records): 1.

51. Note the parallel examples of Jin Zhaozi (金兆梓, 1889–1975) and Wang Boxiang; see *HZS*, 1:18–22, 227–28; *SYJ*, 272; Wang Shihua, *Wang Boxiang zhuan*, 27–28.

52. *HZS*, 1:150, 155, 158.

53. "Kaoxuan xiaoxi" 考選消息 (News of selection by examination), *Shangwu yinshuguan tongxinlu* 商務印書館通信錄, no. 400 (August 10, 1934): 18. The original pool of nominees included fifty-eight graduates from thirteen schools, of which thirty-two were invited to take the recruiting test; see "Kaoxuan xiaoxi," *Shangwu yinshuguan tongxinlu*, no. 398 (June 10, 1934): 19.

54. "Zhaokao bianyisheng" 招考編譯生 (Recruitment examination for compilation and translation students), *Shangwu yinshuguan tongxinlu* 商務印書館通信錄, no. 417 (January 20, 1936): 10.

55. For the limited work outlets for educated men during the Republican period, see Wen-hsin Yeh, *The Alienated Academy*, 186–93.

56. Source: "Lianxiyuan jinguan kaishi lianxi" 練習員進館開始練習 (Trainees enter the company and begin training), *Shangwu yinshuguan tongxinlu* 商務印書館通信錄, no. 401 (September 10, 1934): 10–11.

57. Source: "Zhaokao bianyisheng," 10.

58. For other examples of recruitment by examination, see Qian Binghuan 钱炳寰, *Zhonghua shuju dashi jiyao* 中华书局大事纪要 (Summary of major events at Zhonghua Book Company) (Beijing: Zhonghua shuju, 2002), 144–45; Shu, "Zhonghua shuju bianjisuo," 151; Zhu Lianbao, "Guanyu Shijie shuju," 53; *HZS*, 1:155.

59. Jin Yunfeng 金雲峰, "Wo he Shangwu yinshuguan" 我和商務印書館 (Me and Commercial Press), *Shangwu yinshuguan guanshi ziliao* 商務印書館館史資料 (Commercial Press company history materials), no. 4 (December 20, 1980): 8–9.

60. "Zhonghua shuju zhaokao lianxisheng zhangwuyuan chushi timu (minguo ershiliu nian chunji diyici zhaokao)" 中華書局招考練習生帳務員初試題目（民國二十六年春季第一次招考）(Preliminary topics for Zhonghua Book Company's recruitment exam for trainees and accounting staff [first recruitment exam of spring 1937]), *Chuban yuekan* 出版月刊, no. 2 (May 5, 1937): 16–19; "Zhaokao bianyisheng," 10.

61. "Lianxiyuan fuwu ji daiyu guize" 練習員服務及待遇規則 (Rules for trainee service and compensation), *Shangwu yinshuguan tongxinlu* 商務印書館通信錄, no. 397 (May 10, 1934): 13.

62. "Lianxiyuan bayuefen shixi chengxu yilanbiao" 練習員八月份實習程序一覽表 (Overview table of the August practice procedures for the trainees), *Shangwu yinshuguan tongxinlu* 商務印書館通信錄, no. 401 (September 10, 1934): 11.

63. "Lianxiyuan jinguan kaishi lianxi," 9–10.

64. *HZS*, 1:150–52; Jin Yunfeng, "Wo he Shangwu yinshuguan," 12; *SYJ*, 390–94.

65. *SYJ*, 118–20; "Bianyisuo zhiyuanlu."

66. Zhang Xichen asserts that 196 of these 240 editors had joined Commercial Press after 1921 and that there had been systematic elimination of many of those with the greatest seniority; *SYJ*, 120. Li Jiaju and Wang Jiarong also see significant turnover during this period; Li Jiaju 李家驹, *Shangwu yinshuguan yu jindai zhishi wenhua de chuanbo* 商務印書館與近代知識文化的传播 (Commercial Press and the transmission of modern knowledge and culture) (Beijing: Shangwu yinshuguan, 2005), 69; Wang Jiarong

汪家熔, *Shangwu yinshuguan shi ji qita—Wang Jiarong chubanshi yanjiu wenji* 商務印書館史及其他—汪家熔出版史研究文集 (The history of Commercial Press and other things: Wang Jiarong's collected writings on his research on the history of publishing) (Beijing: Zhongguo shuji chubanshe chuban, 1998), 96.

67. Qian Binghuan, *Zhonghua shuju dashi jiyao*, 177.

68. Hu Shi, *Hu Shi de riji*, 152; see also Deng, "Minguo shiqi bianji," 116. The table is reproduced in chapter 1.

69. Wang Shounan, *Wang Yunwu*, 1:241.

70. "Shangwu yinshuguan dongshi huiyi lu," special meeting, April 1, 1921; special meeting, April 15, 1922; meeting no. 281, April 19, 1923; meeting no. 292, March 25, 1924; meeting no. 303, March 10, 1925; *Shangwu yinshuguan gufen youxian gongsi jiesuan baogao* 商務印書館股份有限公司結算報告 (Final budget report for the Commercial Press joint stock company limited) ([Shanghai: Shangwu yinshuguan], 1925, 1929, 1930). The exception was 1927, when the company showed a profit of 326,088 yuan. *Shangwu yinshuguan gufen youxian gongsi jiesuan baogao*, 1927.

71. Qian Binghuan, *Zhonghua shuju dashi jiyao*, 177.

72. Qian Binghuan, *Zhonghua shuju dashi jiyao*, 103, 111, 121, 129, 134, 150.

73. Wang Shounan, *Wang Yunwu*, 1:234–35.

74. Shangwu yinshuguan 商務印書館, comp., *Shangwu yinshuguan fuye hou gaikuang* 商務印書館復業後概況 (Commercial Press's general situation after its revival of operations) ([Shanghai]: [Shangwu yinshuguan], [1934]), 2.

75. "Dongshihui tebie weiyuanhui tonggao, diyihao" 董事會特別委員會通告，第一號 (Notice number one of the special committee of the board of directors), *Shangwu yinshuguan tongxinlu* 商務印書館通信錄, no. 376 (July 10, 1932): 14; "Shanhou banshichu fenzi tonggao (zhaideng), fenzi di'er hao" 善後辦事處分字通告 (摘登)，分字第二號 (Rehabilitation office separate announcements [selected records], announcement number two)," *Shangwu yinshuguan tongxinlu* 商務印書館通信錄, no. 376 (July 10, 1932): 19.

76. "Shangwu yinshuguan dongshi huiyi lu," meeting no. 399, August 3, 1932.

77. "Zong guanlichu zuzhi xitong biao" 總管理處組織系統表 (Organizational chart for the General Management Office), *Shangwu yinshuguan tongxinlu* 商務印書館通信錄, no. 377 (September 15, 1932): 63, and "Zong guanlichu zhiyuan lu" 總管理處職員錄 (Roster of the staff in the General Management Office), *Shangwu yinshuguan tongxinlu* 商務印書館通信錄, no. 377 (September 15, 1932): 64.

78. For Wang Yunwu's justification of the policy of "one new title each day" (*meiri chu xinshu yizhong*) initiated during the press's revival in 1932, see "Shangwu yinshuguan dongshi huiyi lu, meeting no. 404, November 16, 1932.

79. "Bianshen weiyuanhui zhanxing banshi guize" 編審委員會暫行辦事規則" (Provisional work rules for the Compilation and Review Committee) (August 27, 1932), *Shangwu yinshuguan tongxin lu* 商務印書館通信錄, no. 377 (September 15, 1932): 20–21. In terms of magazine staff, in the fall of 1933 *Eastern Miscellany* had five staff members who did not overlap with other members of the Compilation and Review Committee; "Zong guanlichu tongren lu" 總管理處同人錄 (Roster of the colleagues in the General Management Office), *Shangwu yinshuguan tongxinlu*, no. 388 (August 10, 1933): 39.

80. *SYJ*, 261–62, 390–94; Jin Yunfeng, "Wo he Shangwu yinshuguan," 8–11; "Zhaokao jiaoduiyuan" 招考校對員 (Recruitment exam for proofreaders), *Shangwu yinshuguan tongxinlu* 商務印書館通信錄, no. 387 (July 10, 1933): 15.

81. Wen-hsin Yeh, "Progressive Journalism and Shanghai's Petty Urbanites: Zou Taofen and the *Shenghuo* Enterprise, 1926–1945," in *Shanghai Sojourners*, ed. Frederic Wakeman Jr. and Wen-hsin Yeh (Berkeley: Institute of East Asian Studies, University of

California, 1992), 191–205; Wen-hsin Yeh, *Shanghai Splendor: Economic Sentiments in the Making of Modern China, 1843–1949* (Berkeley: University of California Press, 2007), chaps. 5–6. For editorial staff's pay range, see Hu Shi, *Hu Shi de riji*, 152.

82. Wang Min 王敏, *Shanghai baoren shehui shenghuo* 上海报人社会生活 (Shanghai journalists' social lives [1872–1949]) (Shanghai: Shanghai cishu chubanshe, 2008), 210–11. Managers and a small group of gifted writers and correspondents earned considerably more.

83. Jiang Wenjun 江文君, *Jindai Shanghai zhiyuan shenghuoshi* 近代上海职员生活史 (History of the social lives of modern Shanghai's office workers) (Shanghai: Cishu chubanshe, 2011), 228–31, 248, 255–57. For teachers' salaries, see Cong, *Teachers' Schools and the Making of the Modern Chinese Nation-State, 1897–1937* (Vancouver: University of British Columbia Press, 2007), 101–2.

84. Fu Lan 富蘭, "Lun Shanghai shenghuofei jizeng zhi kejing" 論上海生活費激增之可驚 (On the surprising sudden increase in Shanghai's cost of living), *Qianye yuebao* 钱业月报 10, no. 3 (1930), "Lunzhu" 論著 (Treatises): 9–14.

85. For the editorial staff's role in organizing and promoting the Association to Advance Virtue, see Qian Binghuan, *Zhonghua shuju dashi jiyao*, 54.

86. Sheng Z W 生 Z W, "Shanghai zhongdeng shehui de shengji" 上海中等社會的生計 (The livelihood of Shanghai's midlevel society), *Jinde jikan* 進德季刊 [1], no. 1 (1922), "Yanlun" 言論 (Open discussion): 10–12. For an editor's statement linking increased cost of living and labor unrest in 1925, see "Zhonghua shuju zuori yibufen fuye" 中華書局昨日一部分復業 (Yesterday a group resumed work at Zhonghua Book Company), *Shenbao*, August 30, 1925.

87. Sheng, "Shanghai zhongdeng," "Yanlun," 12.

88. Jiang Bozhen 蔣伯震, "Xianzai zhongliu jieji de tongku he youlu" 現在中流階級的痛苦和憂慮 (The difficulties and concerns of the current middling class), *Jinde jikan* 進德季刊 582, no. 1 (1923), "Yanlun" 言論 (Open discussion): 11–14.

89. Jiang Bozhen, "Xianzai," "Yanlun," 13.

90. Zhu Lianbao, "Guanyu Shijie shuju," 61.

91. Shu Xincheng 舒新城, *Wo he jiaoyu* 我和教育 (Me and education) (Taipei: Longwen chubanshe, 1990), 321–22; *HZS*, 1:149–51; Qian Binghuan, *Zhonghua shuju dashi jiyao*, 92, 97.

92. Drawn from a letter from Shu Xincheng to Lufei Kui on October 17, 1939, as quoted in Qian Binghuan, *Zhonghua shuju dashi jiyao*, 97, 173–74.

93. For Wang's initial encyclopedia proposal, see Wang Shounan, *Wang Yunwu*, 1:113.

94. *SYJ*, 118–20, 255–56.

95. *SYJ*, 260; see also Wang Shounan, *Wang Yunwu*, 1:123.

96. Wang Shounan, *Wang Yunwu*, 1:240.

97. Wang Shaozeng 王紹曾, "Shangwu yinshuguan Jiaoshichu de huiyi" 商務印書館校史處的回憶 (Reminiscences of Commercial Press's Office for Historical Collation), in *Mulu banben jiaokan xue lunji* 目錄版本校勘學論集 (Collected writings on cataloging, editions, and collation), ed. Gu Meihua 顧美華 (Shanghai: Guji chubanshe, 2005), 734–37; *SYJ*, 261–62.

98. Robert Culp, "Mass Production of Knowledge and the Industrialization of Mental Labor: The Rise of the Petty Intellectual," in *Knowledge Acts in Modern China: Ideas, Institutions, and Identities*, ed. Robert Culp, Eddy U, Wen-hsin Yeh (Berkeley: Institute of East Asian Studies, University of California, 2016), 223–24. See also *HZS*, 1:149–53, 157, 163–64; Lufei Kui 陸費達, "Bianyin yuanqi" 編印緣起 (An account of the impetus for compilation and publication), in *Cihai* 辭海, vol. 1, ed. Shu Xincheng 舒新城, Shen Yi 沈頤, Xu Yuangao 徐元誥, and Zhang Xiang 張相 et al. (Shanghai: Zhonghua shuju, 1936).

99. "[Zhonghua shuju] zong bianjibu banshi chengxu."

100. *SYJ*, 390–94.

101. We see similar opportunities for upward mobility in Mao Dun's case, where he went from correcting English assignments for a correspondence course to editing *Fiction Monthly* (*Xiaoshuo yuebao*) in the course of a few years; *SYJ*, 141–94.

102. "Bianshen weiyuanhui zhanxing banshi guize," 20–21; "Bianshenbu zhanxing banshi guize" 編審部暫行辦事規則 (Provisional work rules for the Compilation and Review Department), *Shangwu yinshuguan tongxin lu* 商務印書館通信錄, no. 403 (November 10, 1934): 5–7.

103. "[Zhonghua shuju] zong bianjibu banshi chengxu."

104. Publishing company leaders at the time were starting to conceptualize mental labor in terms of the managerial or planning function. In a lecture in 1924, Lufei Kui asserted that "invention, craftsmanship/design [*yijin*], planning, direction [*zhihui*] all are a step further in mental labor" Lufei Bohong 陸費伯鴻, "Jingji zhi yuansu" 經濟之元素 (The economy's elements), *Jinde jikan* 進德季刊 3, no. 2 (1924), "Yanjiang" 演講 (Lectures): 2.

105. Benjamin A. Elman, *From Philosophy to Philology: Intellectual and Social Aspects of Change in Late Imperial China* Cambridge, Mass.: Council on East Asian Studies, Harvard University, 1984), 104–5, 109. Moreover, in other industries there were long histories of refined divisions of labor and mass production; see Lothar Ledderose, *Ten Thousand Things: Module and Mass Production in Chinese Art* (Princeton, N.J.: Princeton University Press, 2000), especially chap. 4.

106. Shu, "Zhonghua shuju bianjisuo," 150.

107. The extent of this control was likely no greater than that of, say, Ruan Yuan's control over his project compilers. But the patronage relations governing late-imperial projects entailed a high degree of personal interaction and reciprocity, which was quite different from the dynamics of wage labor.

108. *HZS*, 1:19–20, 227–29.

109. Fu Weiping offers a parallel example from Commercial Press. After working as a textbook compiler during the 1910s and 1920s, he became director of one of the encyclopedia divisions in the 1920s and a reviewing editor (*bianshenyuan*) with the formation of the Compilation and Review Committee in 1932; *SYJ*, 255; "Zong guanli chu zhiyuanlu," *Shangwu yinshuguan tongxinlu*, no. 377 (September 15, 1932): 64.

110. Wang Runhua 王潤華, "Qianyan" 前言 (Foreword), in *Wang Boxiang riji* 王伯祥日記 (Wang Boxiang's diary), by Wang Boxiang 王伯祥, 44 vols. (Beijing: Guojia tushuguan chubanshe, 2011), 1:1.

111. Wang Shihua, *Wang Boxiang zhuan*, 29, 39.

112. Wang Boxiang, *Wang Boxiang riji*, 4:208–348.

113. Wang Boxiang, *Wang Boxiang riji*, 4:347.

114. Wang Boxiang, *Wang Boxiang riji*, 4:347.

115. Wang Boxiang, *Wang Boxiang riji*, 4:348.

116. Note the parallel example of Yang Yinshen writing a literary history during the 1930s; *SYJ*, 392–93.

117. The following account is drawn primarily from "Gongchao zhiyao" 工潮誌要 (Brief account of the labor protest), *Lizhi zazhi* 勵志雜誌, no. 3 (1925): 59–73; "Shangwu yinshuguan dongshi huiyi lu," special meeting, August 23, 1925; meeting no. 308, September 22, 1925; Wang Boxiang, *Wang Boxiang riji*, 2:246–53. For day-to-day coverage of the strike, see *Shenbao*, August 23–29, 1925.

118. "Tongren Wusa shijian houyuanhui weiyuanhui zuzhi ji jingguo" 同人五卅事件後援會委員會組織及經過 (Organization and process of our colleagues' May Thirtieth

Incident Support Association Committee), *Lizhi zazhi* 勵志雜誌, no. 3 (1925): 56–59; "Shangwu yinshuguan dongshi huiyi lu," meeting no. 306, June 23, 1925.

119. Wang Shihua, *Wang Boxiang zhuan*, 36–37; Wang Boxiang, *Wang Boxiang riji*, 2:165–66.

120. "Gongchao zhiyao," 61–72.

121. "Gongchao zhiyao," 61–72; "Shangwu yinshuguan dongshi huiyi lu," meeting no. 308, September 22, 1925.

122. Qian Binghuan, *Zhonghua shuju dashi jiyao*, 72–74; *Shenbao*, August 29–31, 1925; September 3, 1925.

123. Qian Binghuan, *Zhonghua shuju dashi jiyao*, 84–89; *Shenbao*, July 3–7, 11–13, 25–28, 30–31, 1927; August 2, 19, 1927.

124. On the organization of the CCP at Commercial Press, see Reed, *Gutenberg*, 220–23.

125. Culp, "Mass Production of Knowledge," 227–30.

126. For the durability of this status distinction from late imperial society, see Jiang Wenjun, *Jindai Shanghai zhiyuan*, 206–7, which draws on Fei Xiaotong 費孝通, "Lun zhishi jieji" 論知識階級 (On intellectuals), *Guancha* 觀察 3, no. 8 (October 18, 1947): 11–15.

127. Mao Tun, *Spring Silkworms and Other Stories*, trans. Sidney Shapiro (Beijing: Foreign Languages Press, 1956), 164–88. I thank Chris Reed for pointing out this story's relevance to this discussion and recommend his thoughtful interpretation of it in *Gutenberg*, 275.

128. Mao, *Spring Silkworms*, 167.

129. [Zuo] Shunsheng [左]舜聖, "Ji benju tongren zuijin de yuxue yanjiu re" 記本局同人最近的語學研究熱 (Recording the recent craze of language study among this company's colleagues), *Jinde jikan* 進德季刊 [1], no. 3 (1922), "Yanlun" 言論 (Open discussion): 17–18.

130. [Zuo] Shunsheng, "Ji benju tongren," "Yanlun," 18.

131. [Zuo] Shunsheng, "Ji benju tongren," "Yanlun," 18.

132. *SYJ*, 206–7.

133. Hu Shi, *Hu Shi de riji*, 145, 150, 151, 162.

134. "Dongfang tushuguan" 東方圖書館 (Eastern Library), *Lizhi zazhi* 勵志雜誌, no. 1 (1925): 87; "Kaimu shengkuang" 開幕盛況 (The flourishing situation of the opening ceremony), *Lizhi zazhi* 勵志雜誌, no. 2 (1926): 126–28.

135. *HZS*, 1:172–75. See also Wang Youpeng, "Research Note: Shanghai's Lexicographical Publishing House Library as a Resource for Research on Republican Period Popular Culture and Education," trans. Robert Culp, *Republican China* 22, no. 2 (April 1997): 103–9.

136. *SYJ*, 146, 152, 155, 158.

137. *SYJ*, 154.

138. Lu Tianbai 盧天白, "Wo zai Shangwu yinshuguan sinian jianwen" 我在商務印書館四年見聞 (What I saw and heard in four years at Commercial Press), in *Zhonghua wenshi ziliao wenku* 中華文史資料文庫 (Chinese cultural and historical materials treasury), vol. 16, *Wenhua jiaoyu bian* 文化教育編 (Culture and education volume), comp. Quanguo zhengxie wenshi ziliao weiyuanhui 全國政協文史資料委員會 (Beijing: Zhongguo wenshi chubanshe, 1996), 523–24.

139. "Ma Runqing xiansheng fu Mei liuxue" 馬潤卿先生赴美留學 (Mr. Ma Runqing will go to America to study), *Jinde jikan* 進德季刊 3, no. 1 (1924), "Huiwu baogao" 會務報告 (Association affairs reports): 7.

140. *HZS*, 1:68–69.

141. [Li] Jinhui [黎]錦暉, "Zhe shi ying zhuyi de yidian" 這是應注意的一點 (This is a point that should be paid attention to), *Jinde jikan* 進德季刊 2, no. 1 (1923), "Tiyi" 提議 (Proposals): 3.

142. [Li] Jinhui, "Zhe shi ying zhuyi," "Tiyi," 4.

143. *SYJ*, 347; *SYJ*, 304.

144. *SYJ*, 349–50.

145. *SYJ*, 348.

146. As with Gao, Wang's memoir from the 1950s vividly recalled the atmosphere of intellectual community at Commercial Press during the 1920s and early 1930s; see *SYJ*, 276–77.

147. Wang Shihua, *Wang Boxiang zhuan*, 34–35; Wang Boxiang, *Wang Boxiang riji*, 2:142–45.

148. For examples of Wang's involvement, see Wang Boxiang, *Wang Boxiang riji*, 1:14, 16–17, 23.

149. For examples of these kinds of social activities, see Wang Boxiang, *Wang Boxiang riji*, 1:13, 16–19; 2:248, 365, 369; 4:222, 230, 240.

150. Moishe Postone, *Time, Labor, and Social Domination: A Reinterpretation of Marx's Critical Theory* (Cambridge: Cambridge University Press, 1996).

151. Alfred Sohn-Rethel, *Intellectual and Manual Labour: A Critique of Epistemology* (London: Macmillan, 1978), 145–63; André Gorz, "The Tyranny of the Factory: Today and Tomorrow," in *The Division of Labour: The Labour Process and Class-Struggle in Modern Capitalism*, ed. André Gorz (Atlantic Highlands, N.J.: Humanities Press, 1976), 55–58.

152. Michel de Certeau, *The Practice of Everyday Life*, trans. Steven Rendall (Berkeley: University of California Press, 1984), 24–30.

Part I Epilogue

1. Zhu Lianbao 朱聯保, "Guanyu Shijie shuju de huiyi" 關於世界書局的回憶 (My recollections of World Book Company), *Chuban shiliao* 出版史料, no. 2 (1987): 59.

2. Zhonghua shuju gufen youxian gongsi dongshihui 中華書局股份有限公司董事會, *Shinianlai zhi baogao (Minguo ershiliu nian zhi sanshiwu nian)* 十年來之報告 (民國二十六年至三十五年) (Ten-year report [1937–1946]) ([Shanghai: Zhonghua shuju,] 1948), 1–4.

3. Wang Yuguang 王余光 and Wu Yonggui 吴永贵, *Zhongguo chuban tongshi: Minguo juan* 中国出版通史：民国卷 (Comprehensive history of Chinese publishing: Volume on the Republic) (Beijing: Zhongguo shuji chubanshe, 2008), 131–32; Zhonghua shuju gufen youxian gongsi dongshihui, *Shinianlai zhi baogao*, 11; Qian Binghuan 钱炳寰, *Zhonghua shuju dashi jiyao* 中华书局大事纪要 (Summary of major events at Zhonghua Book Company) (Beijing: Zhonghua shuju 2002), 159; Wang Jiarong 汪家熔, *Shangwu yinshuguan shi ji qita—Wang Jiarong chubanshi yanjiu wenji* 商務印書館史及其他—汪家熔出版史研究文集 (The history of Commercial Press and other things: Wang Jiarong's collected writings on his research on the history of publishing) (Beijing: Zhongguo shuji chubanshe chuban, 1998), 133–37.

4. Wang Yunwu coincidentally was in Chongqing attending the Citizens' Consultative Conference (Guomin canzhenghui) when the invasion of Hong Kong happened, so he was not cut off from the interior in Hong Kong; Wang Jiarong, *Shangwu yinshuguan*, 164; Chongqing chubanzhi bianzuan weiyuanhui 重庆出版志編纂委员会, comp., *Chongqing chuban jishi, diyiji* 重庆出版纪实，第一辑 (A true record of publishing in Chongqing, first collection) (Chongqing: Chongqing chubanshe, 1988), 3. For exposition of the Zhonghua General Management Office's relocation to Chongqing after Pearl Harbor, see "Li Zongjingli baogao shixiang" 李總經理報告事項 (General

[282]   2. UNIVERSITIES OR FACTORIES?

Manager Li's report on various matters), in *Zhonghua shuju gufen youxian gongsi zai Yu dongshi diyici tanhuahui* 中華書局股份有限公司在渝董事第一次談話會 (First discussion meeting of the directors in Chongqing of the Zhonghua Book Company Ltd.), manuscript, July 3, 1943, 2–6, ZSA511.9.952; Zhonghua shuju gufen youxian gongsi dongshihui, *Shinianlai zhi baogao*, 5, 13–14. See also Qian Binghuan, *Zhonghua shuju dashi jiyao*, 187.

5. Qian Binghuan, *Zhonghua shuju dashi jiyao*, 161; Wang and Wu, *Zhongguo chuban tongshi: Minguo juan*, 129.

6. Qian, *Zhonghua shuju dashi jiyao*, 177.

7. Qian, *Zhonghua shuju dashi jiyao*, 195–96.

8. Wang Jiarong, *Shangwu yinshuguan*, 138–39.

9. Chongqing chubanzhi bianzuan weiyuanhui, *Chongqing chuban jishi*, 3–6, 16–17, 33–34.

10. "Shangwu yinshuguan dongshi huiyi lu" 商務印書館董事會議錄 (Record of the Commercial Press board of directors meetings), unpublished manuscript of excerpted notes, 1922–1954 meeting no. 434, April 8, 1939; see also Wang Jiarong, *Shangwu yinshuguan*, 144.

11. Zhongguo di'er lishi dang'anguan 中國第二歷史檔案館, comp., *Zhonghua minguoshi dang'an ziliao huibian, Diwuji, Di'erbian, Jiaoyu* 中華民國史檔案資料彙編第五輯第二編教育 (Collection of archival materials on the history of the Chinese Republic, Collection 5, Set 2, Education), 2 vols. (Nanjing: Jiangsu guji chubanshe, 1997), 1:495–96.

12. Ch'en Li-fu, *The Storm Clouds Clear over China: The Memoir of Ch'en Li-fu*, ed. Sidney H. Chang and Ramon Myers (Stanford, Calif.: Hoover Press, 1994), 101.

13. Zhongguo di'er lishi dang'anguan, *Zhonghua minguoshi*, 1:496.

14. Wang Yunwu 王雲五, *Shangwu yinshuguan yu xin jiaoyu nianpu* 商務印書館與新教育年譜 (Yearly record of Commercial Press and the new education) (Taipei: Taiwan Shangwu yinshuguan, 1973), 784; Zhu Lianbao, "Guanyu Shijie shuju," 58–59; "Li Zongjingli baogao shixiang," 2–6.

15. Prior to the war, Commercial Press, Zhonghua, World, and Kaiming Bookstore had dominated the textbook market, producing, for instance, more than 80 percent of the secondary textbooks approved by the government for use during the 1930s; see Robert Culp, *Articulating Citizenship: Civic Education and Student Politics in Southeastern China, 1912–1940* (Cambridge, Mass.: Harvard University Asia Center, 2007), 45–46; Wang Jianjun 王建军, *Zhongguo jindai jiaokeshu fazhan yanjiu* 中国近代教科书发展研究 (Study of the development of China's modern textbooks) (Guangzhou: Guangdong jiaoyu chubanshe, 1996).

16. "Li Zongjingli baogao shixiang," 5–6; Wang and Wu *Zhongguo chuban tongshi: Minguo juan*, 139; Wang Jiarong, *Shangwu yinshuguan*, 170.

17. *Zhonghua shuju gufen youxian gongsi zai Yu dongshi di'erci tanhuahui* 中華書局股份有限公司在渝董事第二次談話會 (Second discussion meeting of the directors in Chongqing of the Zhonghua Book Company Ltd.), manuscript, May 27, 1946, 11–12, 20, ZSA511.9.952; Zhu Lianbao, "Guanyu Shijie shuju," 59.

18. "Li Zongjingli baogao shixiang," 5.

19. Zhonghua shuju gufen youxian gongsi dongshihui, *Shinianlai zhi baogao*, 13–14.

20. Wang Yunwu, *Shangwu yinshuguan*, 784–86.

21. Chongqing chubanzhi bianzuan weiyuanhui, *Chongqing chuban jishi*, 3–6.

22. Zhou Wu 周武, "Cong quanguoxing dao difanghua: 1945 zhi 1956 nian Shanghai chubanye de bianqian" 从全国性到地方化：1945至1956年上海出版业的变迁 (From national to localized: The change in Shanghai's publishing industry, 1945–1956), *Shilin* 史林, no. 6 (2006): 72–80; Nicolai Volland, "Cultural Entrepreneurship in the

Twilight: The Shanghai Book Trade Association, 1945–1957," in *The Business of Culture: Cultural Entrepreneurs in China and Southeast Asia, 1900–1965*, ed. Christopher Rea and Nicolai Volland (Vancouver: University of British Columbia Press, 2015), 238–44.

23. "Benju jianshi" 本局簡史 (A simple history of this company), unpublished manuscript, 1950, ZSA511.9.957, 11; "Zhonghua shuju quanti zhigong tongji biao" 中華書局全體職工統計表 (Statistical table of the overall staff and workers of Zhonghua Book Company) (August 1950), ZSA511.9.957.

24. *SYJ2*, 394.

3. Transforming Word and Concept Through Textbooks and Dictionaries

1. "Minguo ershisan nian yiyue qiri guoyu tongyi choubei weiyuanhui di ershijiu ci changwu weiyuanhui de yijue'an" 民國二十三年一月七日國語統一籌備委員會第二十九次常務委員會的議決案 (January 7, 1934 National Language Unification Preparatory Committee Twenty-Ninth Standing Committee meeting resolutions), *Guoyu zhoukan* 國語週刊, no. 123 (February 5, 1934): 1.

2. The work of Reinhart Koselleck and his colleagues in the *Geschichtliche Grundbegriffe* project has shaped my understanding of the genealogical development of terms and concepts, along with their changing social meanings and roles. Concepts are associated with particular words but are not subsumed by them. Rather, concepts have ambiguous and contested meanings and operate at a higher level of generality than most common words. "Social and political concepts possess a substantial claim to generality and always have many meanings . . . a word becomes a concept when the plenitude of a politicosocial context of meaning and experience in and for which a word is used can be condensed into one word" (Reinhart Koselleck, "*Begriffgeschichte* and Social History," in *Futures Past: On the Semantics of Historical Time*, trans. Keith Tribe [Cambridge, Mass.: MIT Press, 1985], 83–84). For an overview of the history of concepts approach, see Tribe's "Translator's Introduction" (x–xv) in the same volume.

3. Sang Bing, "The Convergence and Divergence of China's Written and Spoken Languages: Reassessing the Vernacular Language During the May Fourth Period," *Twentieth-Century China* 38, no. 1 (January 2013): 71–93.

4. Lynda Mugglestone, for instance, demonstrates how the *Oxford English Dictionary* came to be an authoritative text, even though it was intended to describe past and current language use (*Lost for Words: The Hidden History of the Oxford English Dictionary* [New Haven, Conn.: Yale University Press, 2005], esp. chap. 5).

5. Michael W. Apple and Linda K. Christian-Smith, "The Politics of the Textbook," in *The Politics of the Textbook*, ed. Michael W. Apple and Linda K. Christian-Smith (New York: Routledge, 1991), 4.

6. For these educational reforms and the introduction of textbooks, see Robert Culp, *Articulating Citizenship: Civic Education and Student Politics in Southeastern China, 1912–1940* (Cambridge, Mass.: Harvard University Asia Center, 2007), chap. 1; Peter Zarrow, *Educating China: Knowledge, Society, and Textbooks in a Modernizing World, 1902–1937* (Cambridge: Cambridge University Press, 2015), chap. 1.

7. For a thorough assessment of the importance of this set of textbooks, see Wang Jianjun 王建軍, *Zhongguo jindai jiaokeshu fazhan yanjiu* 中国近代教科书发展研究 (Study of

the development of China's modern textbooks) (Guangzhou: Guangdong jiaoyu chu-banshe, 1996), 105–13.

8. Wang Youpeng 王有朋, *Zhongguo jindai zhong xiao xue jiaokeshu zongmu* 中國近代中小學教科書總目 (Comprehensive catalog of China's modern secondary and primary text-books) (Shanghai: Cishu chubanshe, 2010), 98, 120–21; Ji Shaofu 吉少甫, *Zhongguo chuban jianshi* 中国出版简史 (An elementary history of Chinese publishing) (Shanghai: Xuelin chubanshe, 1991), 299–300, 330; Wang Jianjun, *Zhongguo jindai jiaokeshu*, 113. For one educator's account of choosing Commercial Press publications, see Quan Hua 權驊, "Jiaoyu shiyan xinde" 教育實驗心得 (The results of education research), *Jiaoyu zazhi* 教育雜誌 3, no. 2 (February 10, 1911), "Zhengwen" 徵文 (Solicited writings): 18.

9. Wang Yunwu 王雲五, *Shangwu yinshuguan yu xin jiaoyu nianpu* 商務印書館與新教育年譜 (Yearly record of Commercial Press and the new education) (Taipei: Taiwan Shangwu yinshuguan, 1973), 323.

10. *Wenyan* style was, of course, complex, highly nuanced, and changing quickly during the late nineteenth and early twentieth centuries. For a thorough analysis of the new and old prose forms appearing in late Qing and early Republican newspapers, see Bar-bara Mittler, *A Newspaper for China? Power, Identity, and Change in Shanghai's News Media, 1872–1912* (Cambridge, Mass.: Harvard University Asia Center, 2004). For a more wide-ranging discussion of early twentieth-century prose style, see Edward Gunn, *Rewriting Chinese: Style and Innovation in Twentieth-Century Chinese Prose* (Stan-ford, Calif.: Stanford University Press, 1991), 32–37. This set of Commercial Press textbooks, and others of the late Qing and early Republic, incorporated various sty-listic elements.

11. For accounts of this longer process of lexical change, see Michael Lackner, Iwo Ame-lung, and Joachim Kurtz, eds., *New Terms for New Ideas: Western Knowledge and Lexical Change in Late Imperial China* (Leiden: Brill, 2001); Lydia H. Liu, *Translingual Practice: Literature, National Culture, and Translated Modernity—China, 1900–1937* (Stanford, Calif.: Stanford University Press, 1995); and Federico Masini, *The Formation of the Mod-ern Chinese Lexicon and Its Evolution Toward a National Language: The Period from 1840 to 1898* (Berkeley: Project on Linguistic Analysis, 1993).

12. Gao Fengqian 高鳳謙, Zhang Yuanji 張元濟, and Jiang Weiqiao 蔣維喬, *[Zuixin] gaodeng xiaoxue guowen jiaokeshu* 最新高等小學國文教科書 (Newest higher-primary Chinese textbook), 8 vols. (Shanghai: Shangwu yinshuguan, 1907).

13. Liu defines "return graphic loans" as terms whose combination of Chinese charac-ters had existed in China during earlier periods but whose meaning changed signifi-cantly in modern Japan. These terms were then reimported into China from Japan beginning in the 1890s, with their new meanings intact (*Translingual Practice*, 32–34).

14. Gao, Zhang, and Jiang, *[Zuixin] gaodeng xiaoxue guowen*, 1:2–5.

15. Jiang Weiqiao 蔣維喬 and Zhuang Yu 莊俞 (with Yang Yutong 楊瑜統), *[Zuixin] guowen jiaokeshu* 最新國文教科書 ([Newest] Chinese textbook), 10 vols. (Shanghai: Shangwu yinshuguan, 1906–1907 [1905–1906]), 10:60. The chapter was titled "Without Lack-ing Confidence" (Wu zinei).

16. Jiang and Zhuang, *[Zuixin] guowen jiaokeshu*, 7:4–5; 10:39–40; Gao, Zhang, and Jiang, *[Zuixin] gaodeng xiaoxue guowen*, 1:51–2; 4:7–8.

17. Prasenjit Duara, *Rescuing History from the Nation: Questioning Narratives of Modern China* (Chicago: University of Chicago Press, 1995), 17–23; Qin Shao, *Culturing Modernity: The Nantong Model, 1890–1930* (Stanford, Calif.: Stanford University Press, 2004), 30–33, 176–88.

18. Rowe has drawn parallels between Qing-era *li* and European conceptions and practices of civility (William T. Rowe, *Saving the World: Chen Hongmou and Elite*

Consciousness in Eighteenth-Century China [Stanford, Calif.: Stanford University Press, 2001], 442–45). Although these comparisons are suggestive, "civilization" as expressed through the modern loanword *wenming* differed significantly in its emphasis on technological competence as a mode of measuring difference as well as its concern for modes of behavior adapted to open public contexts like parks, factories, and schools.

19. Christopher A. Reed, *Gutenberg in Shanghai: Chinese Print Capitalism, 1876–1937* (Vancouver: University of British Columbia Press, 2004), 230–31.

20. I explore early Republican language textbooks in some depth in "Teaching *baihua*: Textbook Publishing and the Production of Vernacular Language and a New Literary Canon in Early Twentieth-Century China," *Twentieth-Century China* 34, no. 1 (November 2008): 14–17.

21. Wang Jianjun 王建军, "Lun jindai baihuawen jiaokeshu de shengchan 论近代白话文教科书的生产 (The production of modern vernacular-language textbooks), *Huadong shifan daxue xuebao* 华东师范大学学报, no. 2 (1996): 64. Elisabeth Kaske links growing conservatism in education-oriented language policies to the turn toward Confucianism under Yuan Shikai's regime (*The Politics of Language in Chinese Education, 1895–1919* [Leiden: Brill, 2008], 416–20).

22. Wang Jiarong 汪家熔, "*Ciyuan, Cihai* de kaichuangxing" 辞源辞海的开创性 (The innovativeness of *Ciyuan* and *Cihai*), *Cishu yanjiu* 辞书研究, no. 4 (2001): 132; Zhang Renfeng 张人凤 and Liu Hecheng 柳和城, comps., *Zhang Yuanji nianpu changbian* 张元济年谱长编 (Chronological chronicle of Zhang Yuanji's life), 2 vols. (Shanghai: Jiaotong daxue chubanshe, 2011), 1:263.

23. Qiao Yong 乔永, "*Ciyuan* bianzuan xiuding bainian jishi" 辞源编纂修订百年记事 (Account of one hundred years of compiling and revising *Ciyuan*), *Chuban shiliao* 出版史料, no. 1 (2009): 121.

24. Lu Erkui 陸爾逵, "*Ciyuan* shuolüe" 辭源說略 (A summary of *Ciyuan*), in *Ciyuan* 辭源, ed. Lu Erkui et al., 2 vols. (Shanghai: Shangwu yinshuguan, 1915), 1:4.

25. Lu Erkui, "*Ciyuan* shuolüe," 1:4; Wang Jiarong, "*Ciyuan, Cihai*," 132–33.

26. Lu Erkui, "*Ciyuan* shuolüe," 1:5.

27. For those reviews, see Shi Jianqiao 史建桥, Qiao Yong 乔永, and Xu Congquan 徐从权, eds., *Ciyuan yanjiu lunwen ji* 辞源研究论文集 (Collection of writings on *Ciyuan*) (Beijing: Shangwu yinshuguan, 2009), 302–14.

28. Wang Yunwu, *Shangwu yinshuguan yu xin jiaoyu nianpu*, 331.

29. Lu Erkui 陸爾逵 et al., *Ciyuan* 辭源, 2 vols. (Shanghai: Shangwu yinshuguan, 1915), "Zi" 子, 83. According to Liu, this term had "round-trip diffusion," returning to China with a new meaning via Japan. Liu, *Translingual Practice*, 281.

30. Lu Erkui et al., *Ciyuan*, "Zi," 279. Similarly, the entry on the "Republican polity" (*gonghe guoti* 共和國體) stressed popular sovereignty: "The state's sovereignty resides in the whole body of the people and does not establish a sovereign" ("Zi," 294).

31. Lu Erkui et al., *Ciyuan*, "Zi," 282.

32. Lu Erkui et al., *Ciyuan*, "Zi," 149. See also the entry for *rendao* 人道 (humanity, humanitarianism), "Zi," 149.

33. Stephen C. Angle, *Human Rights and Chinese Thought: A Cross-Cultural Inquiry* (Cambridge: Cambridge University Press, 2002), chap. 6. By contrast, Jin and Liu see a more liberal formulation of rights developing during the late Qing and early Republic; Jin Guantao 金觀濤 and Liu Qingfeng 劉青峰, *Guannianshi yanjiu: Zhongguo xiandai zhongyao zhengzhi shuyu de xingcheng* 觀念史研究：中國現代重要政治術語的形成 (Studies in the history of ideas: The formation of important modern Chinese political terms) (Hong Kong: Research Center for Contemporary Chinese Culture, Chinese University of Hong Kong, 2008), 9–10.

34. Lu Erkui et al., *Ciyuan*, "Zi," 149.

35. Culp, *Articulating Citizenship*, chap. 2; Frank Dikötter, *The Discourse of Race in Modern China* (Stanford, Calif.: Stanford University Press, 1992), chaps. 3–4; Duara, *Rescuing History*, chap. 2.

36. Lu Erkui et al., *Ciyuan*, "Zi," 150.

37. Lu Erkui et al., *Ciyuan*, "Zi," 149–50, 279–81.

38. Lu Erkui et al., *Ciyuan*, "Zi," 202, 279.

39. Lu Erkui et al., *Ciyuan*, "Zi," 168–71.

40. The terms, though, had different provenance. *Zhuti* was a return graphic loan that had originated in classical Chinese and accreted new meanings in Meiji Japan; Liu, *Translingual Practice*, 339. *Zhuguan* was what Liu calls a Sino-Japanese-European loanword, meaning a term newly coined in Japan using Chinese characters to express a foreign meaning (297).

41. Lu Erkui et al., *Ciyuan*, "Zi," 83.

42. Lu Erkui et al., *Ciyuan*, "Zi," 83.

43. Lu Erkui et al., *Ciyuan*, "Zi," 148.

44. Zheng Wang, *Women in the Chinese Enlightenment: Oral and Textual Histories* (Berkeley: University of California Press, 1999), 50, 53–54.

45. As Koselleck observes, the introduction of new terms can provide a basis for articulating new concepts, which in turn allows for the consolidation of new social identities and relations: "Increasingly, concepts of the future were created; positions that were to be captured had first to be formulated linguistically before it was possible to even enter or permanently occupy them" ("*Begriffgeschichte* and Social History," 78).

46. Li Huaxing 李华兴 et al., *Minguo jiaoyushi* 民国教育史 (Republican education history) (Shanghai: Shanghai jiaoyu chubanshe, 1997), 111–18.

47. Wang Jianjun, "Lun jindai baihuawen," 64–66.

48. Zheng Guomin 郑国民, *Cong wenyanwen jiaoxue dao baihuawen jiaoxue—woguo jin xiandai yuwen jiaoyu de biange licheng* 从文言文教学到白话文教学——我国近现代语文教育的变革历程 (From literary-language instruction to vernacular-language instruction: The process of reform for our country's modern-language education) (Beijing: Beijing shifan daxue chubanshe, 2000), chap. 1.

49. Vera Schwarcz, *The Chinese Enlightenment: Intellectuals and the Legacy of the May Fourth Movement of 1919* (Berkeley: University of California Press, 1986), 76–82.

50. Kaske, *Politics of Language*, 442–43; Li Jinxi 黎錦熙, *Guoyu yundong shigang* 國語運動史綱 (A historical outline of the national language movement) (Shanghai: Shanghai shudian, 1990), 108–12; Wang Jianjun, "Lun jindai baihua," 66.

51. Li Jinxi, *Guoyu yundong shigang*, 109.

52. For a theorization of the struggle in modern societies to establish and maintain an "official" language and the role of education in that process, see Pierre Bourdieu, *Language and Symbolic Power*, trans. Gino Raymond and Matthew Adamson (Cambridge, Mass.: Harvard University Press, 1991), chap. 1.

53. For instances of resistance within government circles to changing textbook language during the 1910s, see Li Jinxi, *Guoyu yundong shigang*, 107–8.

54. Li Jinxi, *Guoyu yundong shigang*, 117; Zhang Yuanji 張元濟, *Zhang Yuanji riji* 張元济日记 (Zhang Yuanji's diary), 2 vols., organized by Zhang Renfeng 张人凤 (Shijiazhuang: Hebei jiaoyu chubanshe, 2000), 2:893–94.

55. Wang Jianjun, "Lun jindai baihua," 66.

56. Qian Binghuan, *Zhonghua shuju dashi jiyao*, 53; Zhou Qihou 周其厚, *Zhonghua shuju yu jindai wenhua* 中華書局與近代文化 (Zhonghua Book Company and modern culture) (Beijing: Zhonghua shuju, 2007), 92–93.

57. *SYJ*, 65, 70–72. The New School System was instituted in 1922 at the urging of the National Federation of Educational Associations, which issued new curriculum standards in 1923 in draft form. The school system shifted to an American-style 6-3-3-4 system, reflecting the ascendancy of American-trained educators and educational methods during the late 1910s and early 1920s. For more in-depth discussion of the New School System and curricular changes as they pertained to secondary schools, see Culp, *Articulating Citizenship*, chap. 1; Barry Keenan, *The Dewey Experiment in China: Educational Reform and Political Power in the Early Republic* (Cambridge, Mass.: Harvard University Press, 1977).

58. Xiaoxue bu tongren 小學部同人, "Benju bianjisuo xin xuezhi xiaoxue jiaokeshu xuan-yan" 本局編輯新學制小學教科書宣言 (Declaration regarding the New School System primary-school textbooks compiled by this company), *Shijie yuekan* 世界月刊, no. 1 (1924), "Lunzhu" 論著 (Treatises): 6–7.

59. Xiaoxue bu tongren, "Benju bianjisuo," "Lunzhu," 7.

60. "Zhengqiu xiaoxue jiaocai jiang jiexiao" 徵求小學教材將揭曉 (Going to announce the solicitation of primary teaching materials), *Shijie yuekan* 世界月刊, no. 1 (1924), "Zalu" 雜錄 (Miscellaneous records): 1; "Zhengqiu xiaoxue jiaokeshu bianji fangfa yi jieshu" 徵求小學教科書編輯方法已結束 (Solicitation for methods of compiling primary-school textbooks has already concluded), *Shijie yuekan* 世界月刊, no. 1 (1924), "Zalu" 雜錄 (Miscellaneous records): 1.

61. Li Jinxi, *Guoyu yundong shigang*, 108–20; Quanguo jiaoyuhui lianhehui xin xuezhi kecheng biaozhun qicao weiyuanhui 全國教育會聯合會新學制課程標準起草委員會, ed., *Xin xuezhi kecheng biaozhun gangyao* 新學制課程標準綱要 (Outline of the curriculum standards for the New School System) (N.p.: n.p., 1924 [1923]), "Xiaoxue guoyu kecheng gangyao" (Curriculum outline for primary-school national language), 1–5; "Chuji zhongxue guoyu kecheng gangyao" (Curriculum outline for lower-middle-school national language), 12–21; Zheng Guomin, *Cong wenyanwen jiaoxue*, 51–62. Note that Commercial Press's Wu Yanyin wrote the curriculum standards for the New School System primary-school national-language curriculum.

62. Hu Shi 胡適, "Guoyu biaozhun yu guoyu" 國語標準與國語 (National language standards and national language) (Preface to *Fellow Student Directory of the National Language Short-Term Training School* [*Guoyu jiangxisuo tongxuelu xu* 國語講習所同學錄序]), *Xin jiaoyu* 新教育 3, no. 1 (February 1920): 1–4.

63. Zhou Qihou, *Zhonghua shuju*, 92–94.

64. Sei Jeong Chin, "Print Capitalism, War, and the Remaking of Mass Media in 1930s China," *Modern China* 40, no. 4 (2014): 403–6.

65. Zhuang was a native of Wujin, Jiangsu. After studying at Waseda University in Japan, he taught at Changzhou's Guanying Primary School before joining Commercial Press; Wu Yanyin 吳研因, Zhuang Shi 莊適, and Shen Qi 沈圻, *Xin xuezhi guoyu jiaokeshu* 新學制國語教科書 (New School System national-language textbook) (Shanghai: Shangwu yinshuguan, 1923; repr., Tianjin: Tianjin guji chubanshe, 2013), "Zuozhe jianjie" 作者簡介 (Brief introduction of the authors).

66. Wu (1886–1975) was a native of Jiangyin, Jiangsu. In 1903 he attended Shanghai Banjingyuan Normal Lecture Course, and in 1906 he graduated from the Longmen Academy in Shanghai. Returning to Jiangyin, he taught at Guanyin Temple Municipal Number Nine Primary School. He subsequently became an expert on one-room education and became director of the one-room division of the Jiangyin Municipal Number Nine Primary School; Wu, Zhuang, and Shen, *Xin xuezhi guoyu jiaokeshu* (2013), "Zuozhe jianjie."

67. This was one of Commercial Press's most successful textbooks, going through hundreds of printings stretching into the early 1930s; Wang Youpeng, *Zhongguo jindai*, 109.

68. Hu Shunhua 胡舜華 et al., [*Xin jiaoyu jiaokeshu*] *guoyu duben* 新教育教科書國語讀本 ([New-education textbook] national-language reader), 8 vols. (Shanghai: Zhonghua shuju, 1920–1921); Zhuang Shi 莊適, Wu Yanyin 吳研因, and Shen Qi 沈圻, *Xin xuezhi guoyu jiaokeshu* 新學制國語教科書 (New School System national-language textbook), 8 vols. (Shanghai: Shangwu yinshuguan, 1923–1924 [1923]); Wei Bingxin 魏冰心 et al., eds., [*Xiaoxue chuji xuesheng yong*] *guoyu duben* 小學初級學生用國語讀本 ([For use by lower-primary students] national-language reader) (Shanghai: Shijie shuju, [1932]; repr., Shanghai: Shanghai kexue jishu wenxian chubanshe, 2005).

69. Ye Shaojun 葉紹鈞, [*Xiaoxue chuji xuesheng yong*] *Kaiming guoyu keben* 小學初級學生用開明國語課本 (Kaiming's national-language textbook for lower-primary students), 8 vols. (Shanghai: Kaiming shudian, 1932).

70. Wu, Zhuang, and Shen, *Xin xuezhi guoyu jiaokeshu* (2013), 391–92.

71. The fable and fairy-tale motifs were particularly common in the Commercial Press and World Book Company publications; see Zhuang, Wu, and Shen, *Xin xuezhi guoyu jiaokeshu*; Wei et al., [*Xiaoxue chuji xuesheng yong*] *guoyu duben*. For extensive dialogue, see also see Ye, [*Xiaoxue chuji xuesheng yong*] *Kaiming guoyu duben*.

72. Hu Shunhua et al., [*Xin jiaoyu jiaokeshu*] *guoyu duben*, 6:21–23; see also 7:24–26, which recounts a trip around the world.

73. Wei et al., [*Xiaoxue chuji xuesheng yong*] *guoyu duben*, 2:154; see also 2:56–57, 65–67.

74. Hu Shunhua et al., [*Xin jiaoyu jiaokeshu*] *guoyu duben*, 6:1–6; Wu, Zhuang, and Shen, *Xin xuezhi guoyu jiaokeshu* (2013), 360–62, 436–39.

75. Shu Xincheng 舒新城, [*Xin zhongxue jiaokeshu*] *chuji gongmin keben* 新中學教科書初級公民課本 ([New middle-school textbook] lower-level civics textbook), 3 vols. (Shanghai: Zhonghua shuju, 1923–1924).

76. Wei et al., [*Xiaoxue chuji xuesheng yong*] *guoyu duben*, 2:51–54. The typeface for this lesson approximated brush-written calligraphy, which likely enhanced its power for being perceived as a potential model by students.

77. Hu Shunhua et al., [*Xin jiaoyu jiaokeshu*] *guoyu duben*, 6:17–18.

78. For other examples, see Wu, Zhuang, and Shen, *Xin xuezhi guoyu jiaokeshu* (2013), 294–95; Hu Shunhua et al., [*Xin jiaoyu jiaokeshu*] *guoyu duben*, 6:20–21; 7:3–4; Ye, [*Xiaoxue chuji xuesheng yong*] *Kaiming guoyu duben*, 2:51; 7:74–78.

79. Wei et al., [*Xiaoxue chuji xuesheng yong*] *guoyu duben*, 2:43–44. See also Hu Shunhua et al., [*Xin jiaoyu jiaokeshu*] *guoyu duben*, 4:2–3; 7:1.

80. Hu Shunhua et al., [*Xin jiaoyu jiaokeshu*] *guoyu duben*, 7:6–9. Kaiming reprinted actual news reports; Ye, [*Xiaoxue chuji xuesheng yong*] *Kaiming guoyu duben*, 7:14–15.

81. Hu Shunhua et al., [*Xin jiaoyu jiaokeshu*] *guoyu duben*, 7:8.

82. For instance, Wei Bingxin's textbook embedded lectures within letters two student friends exchanged with each other; Wei et al., [*Xiaoxue chuji xuesheng yong*] *guoyu duben*, 2:51–54. Hu Shunhua's presented notes about a lecture in a lesson with a student diary; Hu Shunhua et al., [*Xin jiaoyu jiaokeshu*] *guoyu duben*, 7:1. Wu Yanyin and Zhuang Shi's textbook also offered a number of legal cases, in which an official's voice was presented in a colloquial form of more analytic writing; Wu, Zhuang, and Shen, *Xin xuezhi guoyu jiaokeshu* (2013), 395–97, 398–404, 429–30. Ye Shengtao's Kaiming textbook provided vernacular sentence patterns for students to practice writing; Ye, [*Xiaoxue chuji xuesheng yong*] *Kaiming guoyu duben*.

83. Tao Menghe 陶孟和, [*Xin xuezhi gaozhong jiaokeshu*] *shehui wenti* 新學制高中教科書社會問題 ([New School System high school textbook] social issues) (Shanghai: Shangwu yinshuguan, 1924), 11–12. See also Gu Shusen 顧樹森 and Pan Wen'an 潘文安, [*Xinzhu*] *gongmin xuzhi* 新著公民須知 ([The newly written] essential knowledge for citizens), 3 vols. (Shanghai: Shangwu yinshuguan, 1924 [1923]).

84. Gunn, *Rewriting Chinese*, 225–67.

85. For a parallel example from a civics textbook, see Zhou Gengsheng 周鯁生, [*Xin xuezhi*] *Gongmin jiaokeshu* 新學制公民教科書 ([New School System] civics textbook) (Shanghai: Shanwu yinshuguan, 1923–1926), 1 (1923): 64. Zhou had studied politics, economics, and law in Edinburgh and Paris. He taught at Beida during the mid-1920s. For a full biography, see Xu Youchun 徐友春 et al., eds., *Minguo renwu da cidian* 民國人物大辭典 (Biographical dictionary of Republican China) (Shijiazhuang: Hebei renmin chubanshe, 1991), 539.

86. Merle Goldman, "Left-Wing Criticism of the *Pai-hua* Movement," in *Reflections on the May Fourth Movement: A Symposium*, ed. Benjamin I. Schwartz (Cambridge, Mass.: Harvard University Press, 1972), 85–88; E. Perry Link Jr., *Mandarin Ducks and Butterflies: Popular Fiction in Early Twentieth-Century Chinese Cities* (Berkeley: University of California Press, 1981), 19.

87. "Shubao jieshao" 書報介紹 (Book and journal introductions), *Chudeng jiaoyu* 初等教育 1, no. 2 (1923): 295.

88. "Jiaoyubu shending Shijie shuju jiaokeshu" 教育部審定世界書局教科書 (Ministry of Education authorizes World Book Company textbooks), *Xuedeng* 學燈 1, no. 15 (January 15, 1925): 4.

89. Li Jinxi, *Guoyu yundong shigang*, 121.

90. Dong Renjian 董任堅, "Jieshao yibu ertong guoyu jiaokeshu" 介紹一部兒童國語教科書 (Introducing a children's national language textbook), *Tushu pinglun* 圖書評論 1, no. 2 (1932): 69.

91. Shen Shoumei 沈瘦梅, "Ping Shijie shuju chuban de guoyu wen duben" 評世界書局初版的國語文讀本 (Critiquing the national-language reader published by World Book Company), *Minguo ribao: Juewu* 民國日報：覺悟 1, no. 23 (January 23, 1926): 2–3.

92. "Minguo ershisan nian."

93. "Xunling di yierjiu hao (jiunian eryue shisanri)" 訓令第一二九號（九年二月十三日） (Order number 129 [February 13, 1920]), *Jiangxi jiaoyu xingzheng yuebao* 江西教育行政月報 3, no. 2 (1920): 38; "Xunling di ererba hao (Shisi nian siyue sanri)" 訓令第二二八號（十四年四月三日） (Order number 228 [April 3, 1925]), *Fujian jiaoyu yuekan* 福建教育月刊 2, no. 8 (1925): 27–28; "Guoyu tongyi choubeihui gonghan" 國語統一籌備會公函 (Public letter of the National Language Unification Preparation Committee), *Zhuji jiaoyu yuekan* 諸暨教育月刊, no. 23 (1925): 1–2.

94. Huang Fengling 黃鳳嶺, "Chongming Youzhu xiang di'er chuji xiaoxuexiao shishi gaikuang" 崇明友助鄉第二初級小學校實施概況 (The situation of implementation at Chongming Youzhu Township's Number Two Lower-Primary School), *Xiaoxue jiaoyu yuekan* 小學教育月刊 1, no. 1 (June 1925): 1–2; Da Bingshan 笪炳善, "Jurong disi xuequ diwu chuji xiaoxuexiao shishi gaikuang" 句容第四學區第五初級小學實施概況 (The situation of implementation at the Number Five Lower-Primary School of Jurong's Fourth Academic District), *Xiaoxue jiaoyu yuekan* 小學教育月刊 1, no. 5 (November 1925): 1–2; Wu Moyi 吳默宜, "Qingpu xianli diyi xiaoxuexiao guoyu jiaoxue guocheng" 青浦縣立第一小學校國語教學過程 (The process of national-language instruction at Qingpu County Number One Primary School), *Jiangsu di'er shifan qu xiaoxue jiaoshi yanjiuhui niankan* 江蘇第二師範區小學教師研究會年刊 (May 1924): 239; "Qingpu xian Guyan Xiangjiahui xiang gongli diyi xiaoxuexiao guoyu ke jiaoxue shili" 青浦縣固堰香鄉匯鄉公立第一小學校國語科教學實例 (A real example of national-language instruction for the Public First Primary School of Guyan Xiangjiahui Township in Qingpu County), *Jiangsu di'er shifan qu xiaoxue jiaoshi yanjiuhui niankan* 江蘇第二師範區小學教師研究會年刊 (May 1924): 198; "Jiading Qiyun xuexiao guoyuke jiaoxue shili," 嘉定企雲學校國語科教學實例 (Real examples of

national-language instruction at Jiading's Qiyun school), *Jiangsu di'er shifan qu xiaoxue jiaoshi yanjiuhui niankan* 江蘇第二師範區小學教師研究會年刊 (May 1924): 153.

95. Qin Shuqiu 秦書秋, "Qingpu xianli di'er xiaoxuexiao guoyuke jiaoxue guocheng juli" 青浦縣立第二小學校國語科教學過程舉例 (An example of the process of national-language instruction at Qingpu County Second Primary School), *Jiangsu di'er shifan qu xiaoxue jiaoshi yanjiuhui niankan* 江蘇第二師範區小學教師研究會年刊 (May 1924): 194.

96. Guoli bianyiguan 國立編譯館, *Chuji xiaoxue guoyu changshi keben* 初級小學國語常識課本 (Lower-primary national language and common knowledge textbook), 8 vols. (N.p.: Guoding zhongxiao xue jiaokeshu qijia lianhe gongyingchu, 1947). As stated in the "Key Points of Compilation," "This book compiles in coordination common knowledge and national language, using common-knowledge teaching materials as the warp [*jing*], and using national-language teaching materials to connect with it."

97. Guoli bianyiguan, *Chuji xiaoxue*, 2:31.

98. Guoli bianyiguan, *Chuji xiaoxue*, 5:13.

99. Guoli bianyiguan, *Chuji xiaoxue*, 5:41. As with the previous generation of textbooks, more expository writing was presented in later volumes of the introductory textbooks.

100. Guoli bianyiguan, *Chuji xiaoxue*, 3:3.

101. Guoli bianyiguan, *Chuji xiaoxue*, 3:14.

102. Guoli bianyiguan, *Chuji xiaoxue*, 5:7.

103. Guoli bianyiguan, *Chuji xiaoxue*, 5:9. See also the rules for a commemorative meeting for Sun Yat-sen, 5:3.

104. "Qita shiji wenti" 其他實際問題 (Other practical questions), *Jinxiu banyuekan* 進修半月刊 6, no. 19 (1937): 839.

105. Lufei Kui 陸費逵, "Bianyin yuanqi" 編印緣起 (An account of the impetus for compilation and publication), in *Cihai* 辭海, vol. 1, ed. Shu Xincheng 舒新城, Shen Yi 沈頤, Xu Yuangao 徐元誥, and Zhang Xiang 張相 et al. (Shanghai: Zhonghua shuju, 1936), 1; Qian Binghuan, *Zhonghua shuju dashi jiyao*, 21.

106. *Cihai digao* 辭海底稿 (*Cihai* initial draft), 8 vols., manuscript (N.p.: Cishu chubanshe tushuguan, 192?).

107. Lufei Kui's preface to *Cihai* suggests that Shu Xincheng took over editing the project in 1927; Lufei Kui, "Bianyin yuanqi," 1. Zhou Songdi, one of the core staff members of the project, states that Shu Xincheng became executive editor of the project in April 1928; *HZS*, 1:150. Shu Xincheng confirms the later date in his diary; see Qian Binghuan, *Zhonghua shuju dashi jiyao*, 143; Shu Xincheng 舒新城, *Shu xincheng riji* 舒新城日記 (Shu Xincheng's diary [1929–1960]), 34 vols. (Shanghai: Shanghai cishu chubanshe, 2013), 7:282–84 (April 10, 1936).

108. Lufei Kui, "Bianyin yuanqi," 1.

109. Lufei Kui, "Bianyin yuanqi," 1; *HZS*, 1:163–64.

110. *HZS*, 1:153.

111. *HZS*, 1:151, 155–56, 162–65.

112. Robert Culp, "Mass Production of Knowledge and the Industrialization of Mental Labor: The Rise of the Petty Intellectual," in *Knowledge Acts in Modern China: Ideas, Institutions, and Identities*, ed. Robert Culp, Eddy U, Wen-hsin Yeh (Berkeley: Institute of East Asian Studies, University of California, 2016), 223–24. See also *HZS*, 1:149–53, 157, 163–64; Lufei Kui, "Bianyin yuanqi," 1.

113. "Bianji dagang" 編輯大綱 (Editorial outline), *Cihai* 辭海, 5 *zhong*, 7th ed., ed. Shu Xincheng 舒新城 et al. (N.p.: Zhonghua shuju, 1941), 2; *HZS*, 1:151–52.

114. Li Jinxi, "Xu" (Preface), *Cihai* 辭海, 5 *zhong*. 7th ed., ed. Shu Xincheng 舒新城 et al. (N.p.: Zhonghua shuju, 1941), 6.

115. "Bianji dagang," 1.

116. Shu et al., *Cihai*, "Chen" 辰, 68–69; "Si" 巳, 204; "You" 酉, 100.

117. Shu et al., *Cihai*, "You," 100; "Xu" 戌, 152.

118. Shu et al., *Cihai*, "Zi," 137.

119. Shu et al., *Cihai*, "Zi," 334.

120. Shu et al., *Cihai*, "Zi," 45.

121. Shu et al., *Cihai*, "Chen," 270.

122. Shu et al., *Cihai*, "Chen," 270.

123. Shu et al., *Cihai*, "Zi," 90–93.

124. Shu et al., *Cihai*, "Zi," 328.

125. Qian Binghuan, *Zhonghua shuju dashi jiyao*, 142–43.

126. *HZS*, 1:165.

127. Zhou Shushan 周曙山, "*Cihai* 'dangshi' bufen zhengmiu" 辭海黨史部份正謬 (Correcting errors in *Cihai*'s party-history portion), *Shengli zazhi* 勝利雜誌, new no. 3 (1943): 22.

128. Zhou Shushan, "*Cihai* 'dangshi' bufen zhengmiu," 22.

129. For an overview of these developments, see Robert Culp and Eddy U, "Introduction: Knowledge Systems, Knowledge Producers, and China's Distinctive Modernity," in *Knowledge Acts in Modern China: Ideas, Institutions, and Identities*, ed. Robert Culp, Eddy U, and Wen-hsin Yeh, 1–26 (Berkeley: Institute of East Asian Studies, University of California, 2016).

130. Shu et al., *Cihai*, "Zi," 328–32.

131. Shu et al., *Cihai*, "Zi," 348; Lu Erkui et al., *Ciyuan*, "Zi," 294–95. See also entries for "differentiation" (*fenhua* 分化) and "law of distribution" (*fenbulu* 分佈率) in Shu et al., *Cihai*, "Zi," 377, 380.

132. Lu Erkui et al., *Ciyuan*, "Zi," 228.

133. Shu et al., *Cihai*, "Zi," 266.

134. Shu et al., *Cihai*, "Chen," 270. For the most comprehensive account of the folklore studies movement, see Laurence A. Schneider, *Ku Chieh-kang and China's New History: Nationalism and the Quest for Alternative Traditions* (Berkeley: University of California Press, 1971).

135. Shu et al., *Cihai*, "Zi," 99–100.

136. Shu et al., *Cihai*, "Zi," 174.

137. For Nationalist Party efforts to control academic knowledge, see John Israel, *Lianda: A Chinese University in War and Revolution* (Stanford, Calif.: Stanford University Press, 1998); J. Megan Greene, "Looking Toward the Future: State Standardization and Professionalization of Science in Wartime China," in *Knowledge Acts in Modern China: Ideas, Institutions, Identities*, ed. Robert Culp, Eddy U, and Wen-hsin Yeh, 275–303 (Berkeley: Institute of East Asian Studies, University of California, 2016).

138. Linguist Li Jinxi was a consultant for the New School System national-language reader compiled by Li Jinhui (Li Jinxi's brother) and Lufei Kui, but such direct involvement by experts was the exception, not the rule; Qian Binghuan, *Zhonghua shuju dashi jiyao*, 63.

4. Repackaging the Past

1. Jiangnan, which literally means "south of the [Yangzi] river," connotes the cultural and economic core areas of southern Jiangsu and northern Zhejiang.

2. Given the length and clumsiness of the English translations of the titles of this collection and the others discussed in this chapter, for the sake of concision I refer to them throughout primarily by their Chinese titles.

3. Sun Yuxiu 孫毓修, "Jiangnan yueshu ji" 江南閱書記 (Record of reviewing books in Jiangnan), manuscript, Shanghai Municipal Library (digital file), 1919, 6–29; Liu Hecheng 柳和城, *Sun Yuxiu pingzhuan* 孫毓修评传 (A critical biography of Sun Yuxiu) (Shanghai: Shanghai renmin chubanshe, 2011), 236–37; *SYJ*, 180–83. Mao Dun conflates several trips and mistakenly places them all in the summer of 1919.

4. Peter K. Bol, *"This Culture of Ours": Intellectual Transitions in T'ang and Sung China* (Stanford, Calif.: Stanford University Press, 1992); R. Kent Guy, *The Emperor's Four Treasuries: Scholars and the State in the Late Ch'ien-lung Era* (Cambridge, Mass.: Council on East Asian Studies, Harvard University, 1987); Angela Zito, *Of Body and Brush: Grand Sacrifice as Text/Performance in Eighteenth-Century China* (Chicago: University of Chicago Press, 1997); Benjamin A. Elman, *From Philosophy to Philology: Intellectual and Social Aspects of Change in Late Imperial China* (Cambridge, Mass.: Council on East Asian Studies, Harvard University, 1984).

5. Joseph R. Levenson, *Confucian China and Its Modern Fate*, 3 vols. (Berkeley: University of California Press, 1958–1964).

6. Lydia Liu identifies "national essence" as a Sino-Japanese-European loanword and "national learning" as a return graphic loan from classical Chinese whose meaning changed when reintroduced from Japan (*Translingual Practice: Literature, National Culture, and Translated Modernity—China, 1900–1937* [Stanford, Calif.: Stanford University Press, 1995], 293, 326).

7. "Fujian sheng zhengfu jiaoyuting, xunling tongzi di liushi hao" 福建省政府教育廳訓令通字第六十號 (Fujian provincial government Department of Education order no. 60), *Fujian jiaoyu zhoukan* 福建教育週刊, no. 188 (1934): 20–21.

8. Yue Meng, *Shanghai and the Edges of Empires* (Minneapolis: University of Minnesota Press, 2006), 47–51.

9. Bourdieu distinguishes between different forms of capital, which is ultimately a consequence of the accumulation of labor. Social capital takes the form of resources related to social networks. Cultural capital derives from various forms of cultural mastery, which can be embodied in skills, techniques, and practices, materialized in objects, or institutionalized through systematic recognition, such as with academic degrees (Pierre Bourdieu, "The Forms of Capital," in *Handbook of Theory and Research for the Sociology of Education*, ed. John G. Richardson, 241–58 [Westport, Conn.: Greenwood Press, 1986]).

10. Christopher A. Reed, *Gutenberg in Shanghai: Chinese Print Capitalism, 1876–1937* (Vancouver: University of British Columbia Press, 2004), 168–70; Manying Ip, *The Life and Times of Zhang Yuanji, 1867–1959: From Qing Reformer to Twentieth-Century Publisher* (Beijing: Commercial Press, 1985), chaps. 2–4.

11. Chen Jiang 陈江, "Guji zhenglijia yu Zhongguo tonghua de chuangshiren—Sun Yuxiu" 古籍整理家与中国童话的创始人—孙毓修 (Organizer of ancient books and originator of Chinese children's stories: Sun Yuxiu), in *Zhongguo chuban shiliao: Jindai bufen* 中国出版史料：近代部分, vol. 3, ed. Wang Jiarong 汪家熔 (Wuhan: Hubei jiaoyu chubanshe, 2004), 466–67; Liu Hecheng, *Sun Yuxiu pingzhuan*, 2–14.

12. *SYJ*, 149–54.

13. Hu Shi 胡適, *Hu Shi de riji* 胡適的日記 (Hu Shi's diary), ed. Zhongguo shehui kexue yuan jindaishi yanjiusuo 中國社會科學院近代史研究所 and Zhonghua minguoshi yanjiushi 中華民國史研究室 (Hong Kong: Zhonghua shuju Xianggang fenju, 1985), 181.

14. Liu Hecheng, *Sun Yuxiu pingzhuan*, 195–96.

15. Liu Hecheng, *Sun Yuxiu pingzhuan*, 196.

16. Liu Hecheng, *Sun Yuxiu pingzhuan*, 209–28.

17. Liu Hecheng, *Sun Yuxiu pingzhuan*, 230–31. Sun Yuxiu, "Sibu juyao shuolüe" 四部舉要說略 (Summary of *Sibu juyao*), manuscript, Shanghai Municipal Library (digital file),

n.d. This manuscript was subsequently published with only minor editorial changes as the introductory essay for the *Sibu congkan* project, which by then had been renamed; see "Yinxing *Sibu congkan* qi" 印行四部叢刊啟 (Explaining the publication of *Sibu congkan*), in *Sibu congkan shulu* 四部叢刊書錄 (Reading notes for *Sibu congkan*), ed. Hanfenlou 涵芬樓 ([Shanghai: Shangwu yinshuguan], n.d.).

18. Fu Zengxiang (1872–1950) was a native of Jiang'an, Sichuan, who won the *jinshi* degree in 1898. He served as a compiler in the Hanlin Academy and in a number of educational positions, including a stint in Japan. After 1911 he served in several government positions, including minister of education from 1917 to 1919. He was also a scholar of editions; Xu Youchun 徐友春 et al., *Minguo renwu dacidian* 民國人物大辭典 (Biographical dictionary of Republican China) (Shijiazhuang: Hebei renmin chubanshe, 1991), 1163.

19. Zhang Renfeng 张人凤 and Liu Hecheng 柳和城, comps., *Zhang Yuanji nianpu changbian* 张元济年谱长编 (Chronological chronicle of Zhang Yuanji's life), 2 vols. (Shanghai: Jiaotong daxue chubanshe, 2011), 1:411.

20. They also consulted with Shen Zipei 沈子培 about the catalog; Zhang Yuanji 張元濟, *Zhang Yuanji riji* 张元济日记 (Zhang Yuanji's diary), 2 vols., organized by Zhang Renfeng 张人凤 (Shijiazhuang: Hebei jiaoyu chubanshe, 2000), 1:36.

21. Zhang Yuanji 張元濟, *Zhang Yuanji quanji* 張元濟全集 (Zhang Yuanji's complete works), 10 vols. (Beijing: Shangwu yinshuguan, 2007), 1:544–45; Liu Hecheng, *Sun Yuxiu pingzhuan*, 231–33.

22. For a synopsis of the debate on photomechanical reproduction versus typesetting, see *SYJ*, 180.

23. Zhang and Liu, *Zhang Yuanji nianpu changbian*, 1:545.

24. Liu Hecheng, *Sun Yuxiu pingzhuan*, 233.

25. Zhang Yuanji, *Zhang Yuanji quanji*, 1:547–49.

26. Zhang Yuanji, *Zhang Yuanji quanji*, 1:546–48; Liu Hecheng, *Sun Yuxiu pingzhuan*, 242–43.

27. Liu Hecheng, *Sun Yuxiu pingzhuan*, 243–46. Although, Liu Hecheng notes that Qu's editions were often significantly rarer.

28. Zhang and Liu, *Zhang Yuanji nianpu changbian*, 1:542.

29. Pierre Bourdieu, *Distinction: A Social Critique of the Judgement of Taste*, trans. Richard Nice (Cambridge, Mass.: Harvard University Press, 1984).

30. Zhang Yuanji, *Zhang Yuanji riji*, 2:881–82; *SYJ*, 325.

31. Zhang Yuanji, *Zhang Yuanji riji*, 2:987; Zhang and Liu, *Zhang Yuanji nianpu changbian*, 1:683, 713–14, 2:792–93.

32. Liu Hecheng, *Sun Yuxiu pingzhuan*, 241–42; Zhang Yuanji, *Zhang Yuanji riji*, 2:980.

33. *Sibu congkan shulu*.

34. Sun Yuxiu, "Jiangnan yueshu ji," 26; *SYJ*, 181.

35. Liu Hecheng, *Sun Yuxiu pingzhuan*, 234–35.

36. Zhang Yuanji, *Zhang Yuanji riji*, 2:678.

37. Sun Yuxiu, "Jiangnan yueshu ji," 30.

38. Liu Hecheng, *Sun Yuxiu pingzhuan*, 236; "Yinxing *Sibu congkan* qi."

39. Sun Yuxiu, "Jiangnan yueshu ji," 12.

40. Sun Yuxiu, "Jiangnan yueshu ji," 17.

41. Sun Yuxiu, "Jiangnan yueshu ji," 16.

42. Sun Yuxiu, "Jiangnan yueshu ji," 22.

43. Sun Yuxiu, "Jiangnan yueshu ji," 41.

44. Liu Hecheng, *Sun Yuxiu pingzhuan*, 238.

45. Sun Yuxiu, "Jiangnan yueshu ji," 48–54.

46. Liu Hecheng, *Sun Yuxiu pingzhuan*, 240; *SYJ*, 182–83.

47. Liu Hecheng, *Sun Yuxiu pingzhuan*, 240–41; *Sibu congkan shulu*.

48. *SYJ*, 181.

49. Zhang Yuanji, *Zhang Yuanji riji*, 2:820.

50. Liu Hecheng, *Sun Yuxiu pingzhuan*, 246–52.

51. Liu Hecheng, *Sun Yuxiu pingzhuan*, 254.

52. Liu Hecheng, *Sun Yuxiu pingzhuan*, 254–55; Lizhou 蠹舟, "Lun Shangwu yinshuguan chuban zhi *Sibu congkan*" 論商務印書館出版之四部叢刊 (On the *Sibu congkan* published by Commercial Press), *Tushuguanxue jikan* 圖書館學季刊 3, nos. 1–2 (1929): 289–92.

53. Lizhou, "Lun Shangwu yinshuguan," 291.

54. Zhou Qihou 周其厚, *Zhonghua shuju yu jindai wenhua* 中華書局與近代文化 (Zhonghua Book Company and modern culture) (Beijing: Zhonghua shuju, 2007), 213.

55. For the comprehensive English-language account of the compilation of the *Four Treasuries*, see Guy, *The Emperor's Four Treasuries*.

56. Zheng Hesheng 鄭鶴聲, "Yingyin *Siku quanshu* zhi jingguo" 影印四庫全書之經過 (The process of the photographic reprinting of the *Complete Book of Four Treasuries*), *Tushu pinglun* 圖書評論 2, no. 2 (1933): 67–69.

57. "Shangwu yinshuguan jieyin *Siku quanshu* jihuashu" 商務印書館借印四庫全書計劃書 (Commercial Press's plan to borrow and publish the *Complete Book of Four Treasuries*) (n.d.), in *Shangwu yinshuguan ni yin Siku quanshu shimo* 商務印書館擬印四庫全書始末 (The whole story of Commercial Press's planning to reprint the *Complete Book of Four Treasuries*), manuscript documents, Shanghai Municipal Library, 1924–19??.

58. "Shangwu yinshuguan jieyin *Siku quanshu* yuanqi" 商務印書館借印四庫全書緣起 (An account of the impetus for Commercial Press's borrowing and publishing the *Complete Book of Four Treasuries*), in *Shangwu yinshuguan ni yin Siku quanshu shimo*.

59. "Shangwu yinshuguan jieyin *Siku quanshu* jiliie" 商務印書館借印四庫全書紀略 (A general record of Commercial Press's borrowing and publishing the *Complete Book of Four Treasuries*) (n.d.), in *Shangwu yinshuguan ni yin Siku quanshu shimo*.

60. Petitions to the Ministry of Communication on March 22 and April 3, 1924; response from the ministry on April 1, 1924; *Shangwu yinshuguan ni yin Siku quanshu shimo*.

61. Letter from the Hu-Ning Railroad Management Bureau on April 10, 1924; *Shangwu yinshuguan ni yin Siku quanshu shimo*.

62. "Shangwu yinshuguan jieyin *Siku quanshu* jiliie." The statement was issued on April 8, but according to its record of events, Commercial Press apparently became aware of it through a public notice on April 10.

63. "Da zongtongfu mishuting zhi guowuyuan gonghan" 大總統府秘書廳致國務院公函 (Public correspondence of the secretariat of the President's Office to the cabinet) (April 8, 1924), in *Shangwu yinshuguan ni yin Siku quanshu shimo*.

64. "Zhang jun Yuanji zhi guowuyuan Sun zongli han" 張君元濟致國務院孫總理函 (Mr. Zhang Yuanji's letter to the cabinet's Premier Sun) (April 15, 1924), in *Shangwu yinshuguan ni yin Siku quanshu shimo*.

65. "Guowuyuan Sun zongli fu Zhang jun han" 國務院孫總理覆張君函 (Cabinet Premier Sun replying to Mr. Zhang's letter) (May 3, 1924), in *Shangwu yinshuguan ni yin Siku quanshu shimo*.

66. Zheng Hesheng, "Yingyin *Siku quanshu*," 72, 79.

67. Zheng Hesheng, "Yingyin *Siku quanshu*," 72–79. See also "Linshi zhizhengling" 臨時執政令 (Provisional executive order), *Anhui jiaoyu gongbao* 安徽教育公報, no. 59 (1925), "Mingling" 命令 (Directives): 1.

68. Zheng Hesheng, "Yingyin *Siku quanshu*," 77–79; "*Siku quanshu* yingyin zhi zhong-chuo" 四庫全書影印之中輟 (Suspension in midcourse for reprinting of the *Complete Book of Four Treasuries*), *Tushuguanxue jikan* 圖書館學季刊 1, no. 3 (1926): 540.

69. "*Siku quanshu* de jinxi" 四庫全書的今昔 (The past and present of the *Complete Book of Four Treasuries*), *Xinghua zhoukan* 興華週刊29, no. 48 (1932): 4; Wang Yunwu 王雲五, *Shangwu yinshuguan yu xin jiaoyu nianpu* 商務印書館與新教育年譜 (Yearly record of Commercial Press and the new education) (Taipei: Taiwan Shangwu yinshuguan, 1973), 433.

70. Wang Yunwu, *Shangwu yinshuguan*, 432–34.

71. "*Siku quanshu* chuban wenti" 四庫全書出版問題 (Publishing issues for the *Complete Book of Four Treasuries*), *Hubei jiaoyu yuekan* 湖北教育月刊 1, no. 1 (September 1933): 192–95; Zhang and Liu, *Zhang Yuanji nianpu changbian*, 2:923–32.

72. Zhang and Liu, *Zhang Yuanji nianpu changbian*, 2:934; "*Siku quanshu* zhenben chuji" 四庫全書珍本初集 (First collection of the rare books in the *Complete Book of Four Trea-suries*), in *Sibu congkan sanbian mulu* 四部叢刊三編目錄 (Catalog for the third compila-tion of *Sibu congkan*) ([Shanghai]: Shangwu yinshuguan, 1935).

73. Yu Xiaoyao 俞筱堯 and Liu Yanjie 劉彥捷, eds., *Lufei Kui yu Zhonghua shuju* 陸費逵 與中華書局 (Lufei Kui and Zhonghua Book Company) (Beijing: Zhonghua shuju, 2002), 453.

74. Yu and Liu, *Lufei Kui yu Zhonghua shuju*, 447.

75. Yu and Liu, *Lufei Kui yu Zhonghua shuju*, 447–49. For Lufei Chi's biography, see Arthur H. Hummel, *Eminent Chinese of the Ch'ing Period (1644–1912)*, vol. 1. (Wash-ington, D.C.: U.S. Government Printing Office, 1943), 1:542–43.

76. Yu and Liu, *Lufei Kui yu Zhonghua shuju*, 452.

77. Yu and Liu, *Lufei Kui yu Zhonghua shuju*, 447.

78. *Sibu beiyao shumu tiyao* 四部備要書目提要 (Catalog and abstracts of *Sibu beiyao*) (Shang-hai: Zhonghua shuju, n.d.), vol. 1.

79. Yu and Liu, *Lufei Kui yu Zhonghua shuju*, 448.

80. Yu and Liu, *Lufei Kui yu Zhonghua shuju*, 449.

81. Yu and Liu, *Lufei Kui yu Zhonghua shuju*, 449.

82. *Sibu beiyao shumu tiyao*, vol. 1; Yu and Liu, *Lufei Kui yu Zhonghua shuju*, 453.

83. Chen Gaoyong 陳高傭, "Zhongguo wenhua yu Zhongguo guji: *Sibu beiyao* chongyin ganyan" 中國文化與中國古籍：四部備要重印感言 (Chinese culture and Chinese ancient books: Reflections on the reprinting of *Sibu beiyao*), *Xin Zhonghua* 新中華 2, no. 5 (1934): 29.

84. "Hubei cungu xuetang ge xueke fennian jiaofa" 湖北存古學堂各學科分年教法 (Teach-ing methods for each course by year at Hubei's School for Preserving the Heritage), in *Zhongguo jindai xuezhi shiliao* 中國近代學制史料 (Historical materials on China's modern school system), part 2, vol. 2, ed. Zhu Youhuan 朱有瓛 et al. (Shanghai: Hua-dong shifan daxue chubanshe, 1987), 507–8.

85. Liang Qichao 梁啓超, "Guoxue rumen shu yaomu ji qi dufa" 國學入門書要目及其讀法 (An essential syllabus of introductory books for national studies and their reading method), *Dongfang zazhi* 東方雜誌 20, no. 8 (1923): 135–53.

86. Lufei Kui 陸費逵, "Zuidi xiandu dang du zhi guoxue shu" 最低限度當讀之國學書 (The minimal level of national-learning books one should read), *Jinde jikan* 進德季刊 3, no. 2 (1924), "Yanlun" 言論 (Open discussion): 8–12.

87. *Sibu congkan shulu*.

88. Zhou Qihou, *Zhonghua shuju*, 210; Yu and Liu, *Lufei Kui yu Zhonghua shuju*, 447–48; *HZS*, 1:82. Gao Shixian was a native of Hangzhou and a *juren* of the late Qing period. He joined Zhonghua in 1913 and served on the board of directors and its standing

committee at various points. He directed the Arts Division of the Editing Department as well as the Ancient Books Division. He had a noteworthy collection of calligraphy and paintings. Ding Fuzhi was a native of Hangzhou who was an expert in inscriptions and seal carving, an artist, and a collector; see *HZS*, 1:33–35.

89. Yu and Liu, *Lufei Kui yu Zhonghua shuju*, 447, 452.

90. *HZS*, 1:83.

91. Zhou Qihou, *Zhonghua shuju*, 216–17; Liang Yan 梁彥, ed., *Zhonghua shuju shoucang xiandai mingren shuxin shouji* 中华书局收藏现代名人书信手迹 (Handwritten letters by famous modern people held by Zhonghua Book Company) (Beijing: Zhonghua shuju, 2012), 120–21.

92. Yu and Liu, *Lufei Kui yu Zhonghua shuju*, 453–55.

93. Zhou Qihou, *Zhonghua shuju*, 217.

94. Yu and Liu, *Lufei Kui yu Zhonghua shuju*, 456–57.

95. Yu and Liu, *Lufei Kui yu Zhonghua shuju*, 456.

96. Yu and Liu, *Lufei Kui yu Zhonghua shuju*, 456–57.

97. For an account of the production process, see Lothar Ledderose, *Ten Thousand Things: Module and Mass Production in Chinese Art* (Princeton, N.J.: Princeton University Press, 2000), 140–42.

98. *HZS*, 1:168.

99. Yu and Liu, *Lufei Kui yu Zhonghua shuju*, 457. Sun Luoren suggests other libraries were contacted as well; *HZS*, 1:169.

100. *HZS*, 1:168; Yu and Liu, *Lufei Kui yu Zhonghua shuju*, 458.

101. *HZS*, 1:169.

102. *HZS*, 1:170.

103. "*Siku quanshu* zhenben chuji."

104. *Sibu congkan mulu, fu qi fanli yuyue zhangcheng yangben* 四部叢刊目錄附啟例預約章程樣本 (*Sibu congkan* catalog with appendixes of announcement, introduction, advance-order rules, and sample) (N.p.: n.p., [1920?]). Note that payment in full by October 1920 garnered steep discounts, leading to a final price of 500 yuan for the Lianshi paper edition and 400 yuan for the Maobian paper edition. A pocket-size edition published in 1936 sold for somewhat less, 250 yuan for 110 hardbound volumes or 200 yuan for 440 paperback volumes; see *Suoben Sibu congkan chubian shulu* 縮本四部叢刊初編書錄 (Reading notes for the first series of the pocket-size *Sibu congkan*) ([Shanghai]: Shangwu yinshuguan, 1936).

105. "*Sibu beiyao* yuyue zhangcheng" 四部備要預約章程 (Advance-order regulations for *Sibu beiyao*), in *Sibu beiyao yangben* 四部備要樣本 (Sample book of *Sibu beiyao*) ([Shanghai]: Zhonghua shuju, n.d.).

106. *HZS*, 1:82–83. Promotional materials sent to the Fujian government in 1934 quoted an advance-order price for the larger five-*kai* version of 600 yuan; "Fujian sheng zhengfu," 20–21.

107. "*Siku quanshu* zhenben chuji."

108. Yu and Liu, *Lufei Kui yu Zhonghua shuju*, 457; *HZS*, 1:168. Although, full advance payment garnered a discount of 50 percent; *Gujin tushu jicheng yangben* 古今圖書集成樣本 (Sample book for *Complete Collection of Past and Present Books and Illustrations*) ([Shanghai]: Zhonghua shuju, n.d.).

109. Yu and Liu, *Lufei Kui yu Zhonghua shuju*, 448.

110. Liu Hecheng, *Sun Yuxiu pingzhuan*, 231.

111. Chen Gaoyong, "Zhongguo wenhua yu Zhongguo guji," 29.

112. "Jiangsu jiaoyuting xunling di erqian liubai qishiqi hao" 江蘇教育廳訓令第二千六百七十七號 (Jiangsu Department of Education order no. 2677), *Jiangsu sheng gongbao*

江蘇省公報, no. 2881 (1922), "Xunling" 訓令 (Orders): 4–5. See also "Fujian sheng zhengfu," 20–21.

113. "Xunling quanxuesuo zhuanzhi benyi xuejie zhuoliang daigou *Sibu congkan*" 訓令勸 學所轉知本邑學界酌量採購四部叢刊 (Order to the Education Promotion Office to in turn notify this city's academic circles to consider buying *Sibu congkan*), *Jiangshan gong-bao* 江山公報, no. 3 (1920): 13–15.

114. As Cynthia J. Brokaw and Kai-wing Chow have shown, standard editions of classical texts and commentaries had circulated widely in woodblock form during the late imperial period (*Printing and Book Culture in Late Imperial China* [Berkeley: University of California Press, 2005]; Cynthia J. Brokaw, *Commerce in Culture: The Sibao Book Trade in the Qing and Republican Periods* [Cambridge, Mass.: Harvard University Asia Center, 2007]).

115. For Jiangnan's local dominance of evidential studies scholarship and the collections of rare books necessary to pursue it, see Benjamin A. Elman, *Classicism, Politics, and Kinship: The Ch'ang-chou School of New Text Confucianism in Late Imperial China* (Berkeley: University of California Press, 1990). But Steve Miles has also demonstrated how the Pearl River Delta emerged as a competing center for scholarship and cultural production during the nineteenth century; see Steven B. Miles, *The Sea of Learning: Mobility and Identity in Nineteenth-Century Guangzhou* (Cambridge, Mass.: Harvard University Asia Center, 2006).

116. Lizhou, "Lun Shangwu yinshuguan," 292.

117. Lucien Febvre and Henri-Jean Martin, *The Coming of the Book: The Impact of Printing, 1450–1800*, trans. David Gerard (London: Verso, 1997 [1958]).

118. Laurence A. Schneider, "National Essence and the New Intelligentsia," in *The Limits of Change: Essays on Conservative Alternatives in Republican China*, ed. Charlotte Furth, 57–89 (Cambridge, Mass.: Harvard University Press, 1976); Tse-tsung Chow, *The May 4th Movement: Intellectual Revolution in Modern China* (Cambridge, Mass.: Harvard University Press, 1960), 317–20; Tze-ki Hon, *Visions of Modernity: The Cultural and Historical Debates in Late Qing and Republican China* (Leiden: Brill, 2015); Zhou Qihou, *Zhonghua shuju*, 203–8; Chen Gaoyong, "Zhongguo wenhua yu Zhongguo guji," 28.

119. Note, for instance, how textual exegesis became a prominent scholarly approach at Beijing University during the 1920s, an approach that required a rich, varied source base; see Xiaoqing Diana Lin, *Peking University: Chinese Scholarship and Intellectuals, 1898–1937* (Albany: State University of New York Press, 2005), 99–108.

5. Introducing New Worlds of Knowledge

1. "Pinqing Daxue congshu weiyuanhui weiyuan han" 聘請大學叢書委員會委員函 (Letter of invitation for members of the University Series Committee), *Shangwu yinshuguan tongxinlu* 商務印書館通信錄, no. 379 (November 15, 1932): 12–13.

2. "Yinxing Daxue congshu tiaoli" 印行大學叢書條例 (Regulations for publication of the University Series [October 1932]), *Shangwu yinshuguan tongxinlu* 商務印書館通信 錄, no. 379 (November 15, 1932): 3–4.

3. "Bianyin Daxue congshu xuxun" 編印大學叢書續訊 (Further news about the publishing of the University Series), *Shangwu yinshuguan tongxinlu* 商務印書館通信錄, no. 388 (August 10, 1933): 19–22.

4. Kenneth C. Davis, *Two-Bit Culture: The Paperbacking of America* (Boston: Houghton Mifflin, 1984), 1–82; Janice A. Radway, "Learned and Literary Print Cultures in an

Age of Professionalization and Diversification," in *A History of the Book in America, Volume 4: Print in Motion; The Expansion of Publishing and Reading in the United States, 1880–1940*, ed. Carl F. Kaestle and Janice A. Radway, 197–233 (Chapel Hill: University of North Carolina Press, 2009); Joan Shelley Rubin, *The Making of Middlebrow Culture* (Chapel Hill: University of North Carolina Press, 1992).

5. Gérard Genette, *Paratexts: Thresholds of Interpretation*, trans. Jane E. Lewin (Cambridge: Cambridge University Press, 1997 [1987]).

6. Kai-wing Chow, *Publishing, Culture, and Power in Early Modern China* (Stanford, Calif.: Stanford University Press, 2004), 111–18; Joachim Kurtz, "Framing European Technology in Seventeenth-Century China: Rhetorical Strategies in Jesuit Paratexts," in *Cultures of Knowledge: Technology in Chinese History*, ed. Dagmar Schäfer, 209–32 (Leiden: Brill, 2011).

7. Lydia H. Liu, *Translingual Practice: Literature, National Culture, and Translated Modernity—China, 1900–1937* (Stanford, Calif.: Stanford University Press, 1995); Michael Gibbs Hill, *Lin Shu, Inc.: Translation and the Making of Modern Chinese Culture* (Oxford: Oxford University Press, 2013), 20.

8. Benjamin A. Elman, *On Their Own Terms: Science in China, 1550–1900* (Cambridge, Mass.: Harvard University Press, 2005), 321–32, 359–68, 413.

9. For examples of the institutionalization of modern academic disciplines in Europe and the United States, see Peter Novick, *That Noble Dream: The "Objectivity Question" and the American Historical Profession* (Cambridge: Cambridge University Press, 1999); George Stocking, *Victorian Anthropology* (New York: Free Press, 1987). For the development of particular academic disciplines in late nineteenth- and early twentieth-century Japan, see Stefan Tanaka, *Japan's Orient: Rendering Pasts into History* (Berkeley: University of California Press, 1993); J. Victor Koschmann, ed., *International Perspectives on Yanagita Kunio and Japanese Folklore Studies* (Ithaca, N.Y.: China-Japan Program, Cornell University, 1985); Kenneth B. Pyle, *The New Generation in Meiji Japan: Problems of Cultural Identity, 1885–1895* (Stanford, Calif.: Stanford University Press, 1987); Andrew Barshay, *The Social Sciences in Modern Japan: The Marxian and Modernist Traditions* (Berkeley: University of California Press, 2004).

10. Y. C. Wang, *Chinese Intellectuals and the West, 1872–1900* (Chapel Hill: University of North Carolina Press, 1966); Weili Ye, *Seeking Modernity in China's Name: Chinese Students in the United States, 1900–1927* (Stanford, Calif.: Stanford University Press, 2001).

11. Zhou Qihou 周其厚, *Zhonghua shuju yu jindai wenhua* 中華書局與近代文化 (Zhonghua Book Company and modern culture) (Beijing: Zhonghua shuju, 2007), 170–73; Zou Zhenhuan 邹振环, "Xin wenhua congshu: Xinzhi chuanshu yu xinxue yinling" 新文化丛书：新知传输与新学引领 (The New Culture Series: The transmission of new knowledge and eager anticipation of new learning), in *Zhonghua shuju yu Zhongguo jin xiandai wenhua* 中华书局与中国近现代文化 (Zhonghua Book Company and China's modern culture), ed. Fudan daxue lishixi, Chuban bowuguan, Zhonghua shuju, Shanghai cishu chubanshi (Shanghai: Shanghai renmin chubanshe, 2013), 168–70.

12. Zuo was a native of Changsha who studied in a series of schools there before transferring to the Zhendan Academy in Shanghai in 1914, where he studied for three years. In 1917 he went to Nanjing, where he worked as a private tutor. He joined the Young China Association in 1919 and became a member of the advisory council. In the spring of 1920 he went to work for Zhonghua Book Company; Xu Youchun 徐友春 et al., eds., *Minguo renwu da cidian* 民國人物大辭典 (Biographical dictionary of Republican China) (Shijiazhuang: Hebei renmin chubanshe, 1991), 152–53.

13. Zuo Shunsheng 左舜聖, *Jin sanshi nian jianwen zaji* 近三十年見聞雜記 (Random notes on my experiences of the past thirty years) (Jiulong: Ziyou chubanshe, 1952), 22.

14. Zou, "Xin wenhua congshu," 174–76. The group publishing multiple volumes included Ma Junwu 马君武 (7 titles), Liu Boming 刘佰明 (3 titles), Chang Naizhi 常乃悳 (3 titles), Li Da 李达 (2 titles), Liu Bingli 刘炳藜 (2 titles), and Sun Lianggong 孙良工 (2 titles).

15. Zuo, *Jin sanshi*, 22; see also Ma Junwu, *Da'erwen wuzhong yuanshi Da'erwen wuzhong yuanshi* 達爾文物種原始 (Darwin's *Origin of Species*) (Shanghai: Zhonghua shuju, 1926 [1920]), "Xuci" 序詞 (Preface).

16. Zou, "Xin wenhua congshu," 174.

17. William P. Alford, *To Steal a Book Is an Elegant Offense: Intellectual Property Law in Chinese Civilization* (Stanford, Calif.: Stanford University Press, 1995), 41–43, 50–51. After the Nationalist government promulgated its copyright law in 1928, translations themselves could be registered for copyright, but no provision was made for compensation for the copyright holder of the original work. "The Copyright Law," trans. N. F. Allman, *China Law Review* 4, no. 2 (November 1929): 2. Fei-hsien Wang has established that, apart from legal provisions, the Shanghai publishing guild itself was the main enforcer of copyright in Republican China, and commercial publishers had no incentive to enforce international copyright laws; Fei-hsien Wang, "Creating New Order in the Knowledge Economy: The Curious Journey of Copyright in China, 1868–1937" (PhD diss., University of Chicago, 2012).

18. Liu Boming, lecturer, *Jindai xiyang zhexue shi dagang* 近代西洋哲學史大綱 (An outline of the history of modern Western philosophy), comp. Miao Fenglin 繆鳳林 (Shanghai: Zhonghua shuju, 1922 [1921]), "Fanli" 凡例 (Reading instructions); Liu Bingli, *Shehui wenti gangyao* 社會問題綱要 (An outline of social problems) (Shanghai: Zhonghua shuju, 1930), "Xu" 序 (Preface).

19. Rudolf Eucken, *Rensheng zhi yiyi yu jiazhi* 人生之意義與價值 (The significance and value of human life), trans. Yu Jiaju 余家菊 (Shanghai: Zhonghua shuju, 1920), "Yizhe de duanyu" 譯者的短語 (Phrases from the translator).

20. Guotai 郭泰, Li Da 李達, trans., *Weiwu shiguan jieshuo* 唯物史觀解說 (Explanation of historical materialism) (Shanghai: Zhonghua shuju, 1921), "Yizhe fuyan" 譯者附言 (Appended words from the translator).

21. J. Smith, *Su'e de funü* 蘇俄的婦女 (The Soviet Union's women), trans. Cai Yongchang 蔡詠裳 and Dong Shaoming 懂紹明 (Shanghai: Zhonghua shuju, 1930), "Tiji" 題記 (Introductory notes).

22. [Eugen] Philippovich, *Jiaotong zhengce* 交通政策 (Transportation policies), trans. Ma Junwu 馬君武 (Shanghai: Zhonghua shuju, 1924), "Xuwen" 序文 (Preface).

23. Jin Guobao 金國寶, *Tongji xinlun* 統計新論 (New discourse on statistics) (Shanghai: Zhonghua shuju, 1925); Liu Bingli 劉炳藜, *Shehui kexuejia yu shehui yundongjia* 社會科學家與社會運動家 (Social scientists and leaders of social movements) (Shanghai: Zhonghua shuju, 1931), "Kanci" 刊辭 (Words upon publication); Xu Sitong 徐嗣同, *Shehui kexue mingzhu tijie* 社會科學名著題解 (Explanatory notes on famous works of social science) (Shanghai: Zhonghua shuju, 1932), "Xuyan" 序言 (Preface); Liu Bingli, *Shehui wenti gangyao*, "Xu."

24. Xu Sitong, *Shehui kexue mingzhu tijie*, "Xuyan."

25. Wenzhou 文宙, "Suigan: Shijie congshu, Xinwenhua congshu" 隨感：《世界叢書》《新文化叢書》 (Informal essay: World Series and New Culture Series), *Shaonian shehui banyuekan* 少年社會半月刊 2, no. 6 (1920): [27].

26. Wang Yunwu 王雲五, *Shangwu yinshuguan yu xin jiaoyu nianpu* 商務印書館與新教育年譜 (Yearly record of Commercial Press and the new education) (Taipei: Taiwan Shangwu yinshuguan, 1973), 119.

27. Wang Shounan 王壽南, comp., *Wang Yunwu xiansheng nianpu chugao* 王雲五先生年譜初稿 (Initial draft of the chronological biography of Mr. Wang Yunwu), 4 vols. (Taipei: Taiwan Shangwu yinshuguan, 1987), 1:112–13.

28. Wang, *Shangwu yinshuguan*, 119–20.

29. These were all subjects covered in the most comprehensive of the early series, the Universal Library (Baike xiao congshu).

30. Pamela O. Long, *Openness, Secrecy, Authorship: Technical Arts and the Culture of Knowledge from Antiquity to the Renaissance* (Baltimore: Johns Hopkins University Press, 2003), 1; Magaret Somers, "The Privatization of Citizenship: How to Unthink a Knowledge Culture," in *Beyond the Cultural Turn: New Directions in the Study of Society and Culture*, ed. Victoria E. Bonnell and Lynn Hunt, 121–61 (Berkeley: University of California Press, 1999), 124–35.

31. It is now clear that throughout the late imperial period Confucian theoretical and moral knowledge coexisted with emergent forms of technical knowledge, although the latter were often evaluated through the lens of a Confucian value system. See Dagmar Schäfer, ed., *Cultures of Knowledge: Technology in Chinese History* (Leiden: Brill, 2011). And certainly Daoism and Buddhism always offered alternative frameworks for evaluating knowledge.

32. "Wanyou wenku bianyi fanli" 萬有文庫編譯凡例 (Introduction to the compiling of the Complete Library), in *Wanyou wenku diyiji yiqianzhong mulu* 萬有文庫第一集一千種目錄 (Catalog of one thousand titles of the first collection of the Complete Library), ed. Wang Yunwu 王雲五 et al. ([Shanghai]: Shangwu yinshuguan, [1929]), 2.

33. For a synthetic analysis of the civic republican approach to national citizenship in twentieth-century China, see Robert Culp, "Synthesizing Citizenship in Modern China," *History Compass* 5/6 (2007): 1833–61.

34. Prior studies of the series have not closely analyzed the intellectual labor needed to produce it. See, for instance, Leo Ou-fan Lee, *Shanghai Modern: The Flowering of a New Urban Culture in China, 1930–1945* (Cambridge, Mass.: Harvard University Press, 1999), 55–63; Li Jiaju 李家駒, *Shangwu yinshuguan yu jindai zhishi wenhua de chuanbo* 商務印書館與近代知識文化的传播 (Commercial Press and the transmission of modern knowledge and culture) (Beijing: Shangwu yinshuguan, 2005), 239–54; Wang Jianhui 王建輝, *Wenhua de Shangwu—Wang Yunwu zhuanti yanjiu* 文化的商務—王雲五專題研究 (Cultural Commercial Press: Specialized research on Wang Yunwu) (Beijing: Shangwu yinshuguan, 2000), 105–12.

35. *SYJ*, 309, 359–61, 372.

36. Other examples of leading scholars working in the Editing Department who authored, translated, compiled, and reviewed multiple volumes for these series include He Bingsong, Fu Donghua, Tao Menghe, Zhang Qiyun, Ren Hongjun, Lü Simian, Bing Zhi, and Gao Juefu. As noted, textbook compilers like Wang Boxiang might also contribute multiple titles; see Wang Yunwu et al., *Wanyou wenku diyiji yiqianzhong mulu*.

37. For an account of Zhu's education and the relationship between his academic work and publishing work, see *SYJ*, 328–29.

38. I use here Commercial Press's own translation of Wanyou wenku 萬有文庫, Complete Library, rather than Leo Lee's more direct and accurate translation of *All-Comprehensive Repository*; see Lee, *Shanghai Modern*, 55. I do so, in part, because Wang Yunwu conceived of this set of books as a self-contained library that covered all bases of modern learning.

39. Wang Yunwu 王雲五, "Yinxing Wanyou wenku yuanqi" 印行萬有文庫緣起 (Genesis of the publication of the Complete Library), in Wang Yunwu et al., *Wanyou wenku*

diyiji yiqianzhong mulu. For the number of titles associated with each series included in the Complete Library, see "Wanyou wenku bianyi fanli."

40. Wang Yunwu 王雲五, "Yinxing Wanyou wenku di'er ji yuanqi" 印行萬有文庫第二集緣起 (Genesis of the publication of the second collection of the Complete Library), in *Wanyou wenku di'er ji mulu* 萬有文庫第二集目錄 (Catalog for the second collection of the Complete Library), ed. Wang Yunwu 王雲五 et al. (Shanghai: Shangwu yinshuguan, [1934]).

41. "Wanyou wenku diyiji yuyue jianzhang" 萬有文庫第一集預約簡章 (Advance-order procedures for the Complete Library, first collection), in Wang Yunwu et al., *Wanyou wenku diyiji yiqianzhong mulu.* The price for the second series was comparable.

42. Wang Yunwu, "Yinxing Wanyou wenku di'er ji yuanqi"; Wang Yunwu 王雲五, "Yinxing Wanyou wenku di yi er ji jianbian yuanqi" 印行萬有文庫第一二集簡編緣起 (Genesis of the abridged first and second collections of the Complete Library), in *Wanyou wenku diyi er ji jianbian mulu* 萬有文庫第一二集簡編目錄 (Catalog of the first and second abridged collections of the Complete Library), ed. Wang Yunwu 王雲五 et al. ([Shanghai]: Shangwu yinshuguan, [1939]), 1–2.

43. For overviews of the content of the Complete Library, see Lee, *Shanghai Modern,* 56–63; Li Jiaju, *Shangwu yinshuguan,* 345–51. Material for the following paragraph is drawn from these synthetic sources and Wang Yunwu et al., *Wanyou wenku diyiji yiqianzhong mulu*; Wang Yunwu et al., *Wanyou wenku di'er ji mulu.*

44. Li Jiaju, *Shangwu yinshuguan,* 246–48. Liu surveys 1,043 titles, which incorporates titles from the first and second collections.

45. Tong Lam, *A Passion for Facts: Social Surveys and the Construction of the Chinese Nation-State, 1900–1949* (Berkeley: University of California Press, 2011); Janet Y. Chen, *Guilty of Indigence: The Urban Poor in China, 1900–1953* (Princeton, N.J.: Princeton University Press, 2012), chap. 2.

46. Wang Yunwu et al., *Wanyou wenku diyiji yiqianzhong mulu.*

47. Wang Shounan, *Wang Yunwu xiansheng,* 110–11. For discussion of the contemporaneous shift from viewing books as discrete objects to viewing text as fungible content in American publishing, see Carl F. Kaestle and Janice A. Radway, "Introduction: Section II. The Publishing Trades," in *A History of the Book in America, Volume 4: Print in Motion; The Expansion of Publishing and Reading in the United States, 1880–1940* (Chapel Hill: University of North Carolina Press, 2009), 49, 55. Note, too, Rubin's account of the way Simon and Schuster generated publication ideas and then solicited texts, which were marketed heavily (Joan Shelley Rubin, *The Making of Middlebrow Culture* [Chapel Hill: University of North Carolina Press, 1992], 245–46).

48. For reference, Gamble, in his survey of the living standards of families in Beijing during the early 1930s, found that only 13 percent had incomes of more than 100 yuan per month. In addition, only the group of families earning more than 125 yuan per month spent more than 100 yuan annually on education and might have been able to afford the installment payments for the Complete Library; see Sidney D. Gamble, *How Chinese Families Live in Peiping: A Study of the Income and Expenditure of 283 Chinese Families Receiving from $8 to $550 Silver per Month* (New York: Funk and Wagnalls, 1933), 3–4, 165–69, 335.

49. Wang Yunwu, " Yinxing Wanyou wenku yuanqi."

50. Wang Yunwu, *Shangwu yinshuguan,* 250.

51. Wang Yunwu, *Shangwu yinshuguan,* 250.

52. "Wanyou wenku changxiao" 萬有文庫暢銷 (The Complete Library sells briskly), *Dushu yuekan* 讀書月刊 1, no. 2 (1930): 209–10.

53. Gao Zheyi (Robert Culp), "Wei putong duzhe qunti chuangzao 'zhishi shijie': Shangwu yinshuguan yu Zhongguo xueshu jingying de hezuo" 为普通读者群体创造 '知识世界'——商务印书馆与中国学术精英的合作 (A world of knowledge for the circle of common readers: Commercial Press's partnership with China's academic elite), *Shilin* 史林, no. 3 (2014): 103.

54. Wang Yunwu, "Yinxing Wanyou wenku di'er ji yuanqi," 2.

55. "Tushuguan jinxun size" 圖書館近訊四則 (Four items of recent news about the library), *Jiaoda sanrikan* 交大三日刊, no. 12 (1929): 2; "Di'erqi Wanyou wenku dao xiao" 第二期 萬有文庫到校 (The second installment of the Complete Library arrived at the school), *Jimei zhoukan* 集美週刊, no. 258 (1930): 8–9; "Wanyou wenku di yi er qi yi jidao" 萬有 文庫第一二期已寄到 (The first and second installments of the Complete Library have already been mailed to the school), *Wuzhong zhoukan* 五中週刊, no. 90 (May 18, 1931): 1. See also Lu Danlin 陸丹林, "Daolu xiehui gouji Wanyou wenku bianyan" 道路協會 購庋萬有文庫弁言 (Introductory remark on the Road Association purchasing the Complete Library), *Daolu yuekan* 道路月刊 28, no. 2 (1929): 3.

56. *Zhonghua shuju gaikuang* 中華書局概況 (Zhonghua Book Company's general situation) ([Shanghai: Zhonghua shuju], 1936), 13–22.

57. The New Culture Series, for example, peaked at forty titles in all.

58. Xu Weinan 徐慰南, "ABC congshu fakan zhiqu" ABC 叢書發刊旨趣 (The purpose of launching the ABC Series), in *Baoxianxue ABC* 保險學 ABC (The ABCs of insurance), ed. Zhang Bozhen 張伯箴 (Shanghai: Shijie shuju, 1929).

59. Xu Weinan, "ABC congshu fakan zhiqu."

60. Charles Hayford, *To the People: James Yen and Village China* (New York: Columbia University Press, 1990); Emily Honig, *Sisters and Strangers: Women in the Shanghai Cotton Mills, 1919–1949* (Stanford, Calif.: Stanford University Press, 1987), 202–43.

61. [Shen] Zhifang [沈]知方, "Cong jihua dao chushu" 從計劃到出書 (From planning to publication), *Shijie* 世界 1, no. 1 (1928): 14.

62. [Shen] Zhifang, "Cong jihua dao chushu," 14.

63. Elman, *On Their Own Terms*, 28–29, 44–46, 51–53.

64. [Shen] Zhifang, "Cong jihua dao chushu," 15.

65. "Touxian" 頭銜 (Official title), *Shijie* 世界 1, no. 1 (1928): 35.

66. "ABC congshu mulu" (Catalog for the ABC Series), in *Baoxianxue ABC* 保險學ABC (The ABCs of insurance), ed. Zhang Bozhen 張伯箴 (Shanghai: Shijie shuju, 1929).

67. Eugenia Lean, "Proofreading Science: Editing and Experimentation in Manuals by a 1930s Industrialist," in *Science and Technology in Modern China, 1880s–1940s*, ed. Jing Tsu and Benjamin A. Elman, 185–208 (Leiden: Brill, 2014).

68. William T. Rowe, "Political, Social, and Economic Factors Affecting the Transmission of Technical Knowledge in Early Modern China," in *Cultures of Knowledge: Technology in Chinese History*, ed. Dagmar Schäfer (Leiden: Brill, 2011), 43.

69. Yin Shouguang 殷壽光, *Fenpei lun ABC* 分配論 ABC (The ABCs of theories of distribution) (Shanghai: Shijie shuju, 1928), "Liyan" 例言 (Introduction); Tang Binhua 湯彬華, *Funu yundong ABC* 婦女運動 ABC (The ABCs of the women's movement) (Shanghai: Shijie shuju, 1929 [1928]), "Xu."

70. After graduating from Beida in 1918, Sun won government funding to study in the United States, studying at the University of Illinois and Columbia University before getting his PhD at New York University in 1925; Xu Youchun, *Minguo renwu*, 779; Sun Benwen 孫本文, *Shehuixue ABC* 社會學 ABC (The ABCs of Sociology) (Shanghai: Shijie shuju, 1929); Sun Benwen, *Renkou lun ABC* 人口論 ABC (The ABCs of population theories) (Shanghai: Shijie shuju, 1928).

71. Yang Zheming 楊哲明, *Shizheng zuzhi ABC* 市政組織 ABC (The ABCs of municipal government organization) (Shanghai: Shijie shuju, 1930); Yang Zheming, *Shizheng jihua ABC* 市政計畫 ABC (The ABCs of urban planning) (Shanghai: Shijie shuju, 1929); Yang Zheming, *Shizheng guanli ABC* 市政管理 ABC (The ABCs of municipal management) (Shanghai: Shijie shuju, 1928); Yang Zheming, *Shizheng gongcheng ABC* 市政工程 ABC (The ABCs of municipal government engineering) (Shanghai: Shijie shuju, 1929).

72. Gao Xisheng 高希聖, *Chan'er xianzhi ABC* 產兒限制 ABC (The ABCs of birth control) (Shanghai: Shijie shuju, 1929), "Liyan"; Huang Menglou 黃夢樓, *Gongsifa ABC* 公司法 ABC (The ABCs of company law) (Shanghai: Shijie shuju, 1931), "Liyan"; Zhang Jiatai 張家泰, *Gongshang guanli ABC* 工商管理 ABC (The ABCs of industrial and commercial management) (Shanghai: Shijie shuju, 1929), "Xu"; Wang Danru 王瀣如, *Guoji maoyi ABC* 國際貿易 ABC (The ABCs of international trade) (Shanghai: Shijie shuju, 1928), "Liyan"; Wang Yiyai 王益厓, *Haiyang xue ABC* 海洋學 ABC (The ABCs of oceanography) (Shanghai: Shijie shuju, 1929), "Xu"; Li Quanshi 李權時, *Caizheng xue ABC* 財政學 ABC (The ABCs of finance) (Shanghai: Shijie shuju, 1928), "Liyan"; Feng Zikai 豐子愷, *Goutu fa ABC* 構圖法 ABC (The ABCs of composition) (Shanghai: Shijie shuju, 1928), "Liyan"; Sun Benwen, *Renkou lun ABC*, "Liyan"; Sun Benwen, *Shehuixue ABC*, "Liyan"; Wu Jingshan 吳靜山, *Sheying xue ABC* 攝影學 ABC (The ABCs of photography) (Shanghai: Shijie shuju, 1928), "Liyan"; Jiang Xiangqing 蔣湘青, *Tianjing sai ABC* 田徑賽 ABC (The ABCs of track-and-field competitions) (Shanghai: Shijie shuju, 1928), "Xu"; Li Zongwu 李宗武, *Renwen dili ABC* 人文地理 ABC (The ABCs of human geography) (Shanghai: Shijie shuju, 1929), "Xu."

73. Wang Yunwu, *Shangwu yinshuguan*, 120.

74. "Wanyou wenku bianyi fanli," 2.

75. Lou Tongsun 樓桐孫, *Zujie wenti* 租界問題 (The problem of the concessions) (Shanghai: Shangwu yinshuguan, 1932), "Xu"; Xiang Da 向達, *Zhongwai jiaotong xiaoshi* 中外交通小史 (Communications between China and Foreign Lands with Respect to Cultural Diffusion) (Shanghai: Shangwu yinshuguan, 1930), "Zuozhe zhuiyan" 作者贅言 (The author's repetitious statement); Gao Jiansi 高踐四, *Minzhong jiaoyu* 民眾教育 (Popular education) (Shanghai: Shangwu yinshuguan, 1933), "Fanli"; Qian Mu 錢穆, *Mozi* 墨子 (Shanghai: Shangwu yinshuguan, 1930), "Xu."

76. Shen Qianyi 沈乾一, *Zhongyi qianshuo* 中醫淺說 (Chinese medicine) (Shanghai: Shangwu yinshuguan, 1931), "Fanli," 2.

77. Wang Yunwu et al., *Wanyou wenku diyiji yiqianzhong mulu*.

78. "Daxue congshu weiyuanhui tiaoli" 大學叢書委員會條例 (Regulations for the University Series Committee) (October 24, 1932), *Shangwu yinshuguan tongxinlu* 商務印書館通信錄, no. 379 (November 15, 1932): 3.

79. "Pinqing Daxue congshu," 12–13.

80. "Pinqing Daxue congshu," 13.

81. "Daxue congshu bianyin jinkuang" 大學叢書編印近況 (The recent situation of the publishing of the University Series), *Shangwu yinshuguan tongxinlu* 商務印書館通信錄, no. 385 (May 10, 1933): 19–20; *Daxue congshu mulu* 大學叢書目錄 (The catalog for the University Series) ([Shanghai]: Shangwu yinshuguan, 1935), 159.

82. "Daxue congshu weiyuanhui tiaoli," 3.

83. "Daxue congshu bianyin jinkuang," 19–20.

84. "Bianyin Daxue congshu xuxun," 19.

85. For the final catalog, see *Daxue congshu mulu*.

86. Megan Greene documents how the Nationalist government moved to centralize university curricula starting in 1938 ("Looking Toward the Future: State Standardization

and Professionalization of Science in Wartime China," in *Knowledge Acts in Modern China: Ideas, Institutions, Identities*, ed. Robert Culp, Eddy U, and Wen-hsin Yeh [Berkeley: Institute of East Asian Studies, University of California, 2016], 283–84).

87. Wen-hsin Yeh, *The Alienated Academy: Culture and Politics in Republican China, 1919–1937* (Cambridge, Mass.: Harvard University Asia Center, 1990), chap. 5.

88. "Daxue congshu kemu yu benguan yiyou shugao shumu bijiao biao" 大學叢書科目與本館已有書稿數目比較表 (A comparative statistical table of University Series subjects and manuscripts that this company already has), in *Daxue congshu mulu*.

89. "Bianyin Daxue congshu xuxun," 20–21.

90. Liang Junli 梁鋆立, "Duiyu Shangwu yinshuguan Daxue congshu mulu zhong falu ji zhengzhi bufen zhi shangque" 對於商務印書館大學叢書目錄中法律及政治部份之商榷 (A discussion of the law and politics sections of Commercial Press's University Series catalog), *Tushuguan pinglun* 圖書館評論 2, no. 2 (1933): 9.

91. "Daxue congshu kemu yu benguan."

92. "Bianyin Daxue congshu xuxun," 22.

93. "Daxue congshu weiyuanhui tiaoli," 3.

94. "Yinxing Daxue congshu tiaoli," 4.

95. "Yinxing Daxue congshu tiaoli," 4.

96. "Daxue congshu kemu yu benguan." Fifty-one titles were being written for science subjects, and twenty-eight for engineering.

97. "Shangwu yinshuguan dongshi huiyi lu" 商務印書館董事會議錄 (Record of the Commercial Press board of directors meetings), unpublished manuscript of excerpted notes, 1922–1954, meeting no. 434, April 8, 1939.

98. "Ershiwu niandu gudong changhui huiyi jilu" 二十五年度股東常會會議紀錄 (Record of the 1936 annual shareholders' meeting), *Shangwu yinshuguan tongxinlu* 商務印書館通信錄, no. 420 (April 20, 1936): 12–15.

99. "Ershiliu niandu gudong changhui huiyi jilu" 二十六年度股東常會會議紀錄 (Record of the 1937 annual shareholders' meeting), *Shangwu yinshuguan tongxinlu* 商務印書館通信錄, no. 434 (June 20, 1937): 20–24.

100. Li Chaoying 李超英, *Bijiao caizheng zhidu* 比較財政制度 (Comparative finance systems) ([Chongqing]: Shangwu yinshuguan, 1944 [1943]), "Zixu" and "Fuzhi" 附誌 (Appended note). See also Zhang Jiangshu 張江樹, *Lilun huaxue shiyan* 理論化學實驗 (Experiments in theoretical chemistry) (Shanghai: Shangwu yinshuguan, 1949 [1945]), "Xuyan," which was completed in 1943 but printed for the first time only after the war at the end of 1945. See also C. H. Richardson, *Tongji fenxi daolun* 統計分析導論 (An introduction to statistical analysis), trans. Luo Dafan 羅大凡 and Liang Hong 梁宏 (Shanghai: Shangwu yinshuguan, 1948), "Yizhe xu" 譯者序 (Translators' preface).

101. Chongqing chubanzhi bianzuan weiyuanhui 重庆出版志编纂委员会, comp., *Chongqing chuban jishi, diyiji* 重庆出版纪实, 第一辑 (A true record of publishing in Chongqing, first collection) (Chongqing: Chongqing chubanshe, 1988), 5–6; Wang Yunwu, *Shangwu yinshuguan*, 785.

102. Tang Xifen 唐惜分 Chen Lijiang 陳禮江, Cui Daiyang 崔戴陽, Xu Xiling 徐錫齡, Zhuang Zexuan 莊澤宣, Chen Ziming 陳子明, and Hu Yi 胡毅, *Geguo jiaoyu de zhexue beijing* 各國教育的哲學背境 (The philosophical background of each country's education) (Shanghai: Shangwu yinshuguan, 1934), "Yixu" 譯序 (Translators' preface). See also Chang Daozhi 常導之, *De Fa Ying Mei siguo jiaoyu gaiguan* 德法英美四國教育概觀 (Overview of education in the four countries of Germany, France, England, and America) (Shanghai: Shangwu yinshuguan, 1932 [1930]), "Bianyan" 弁言 (Foreword); Zhuang Zexuan 莊澤宣, *Geguo jiaoyu bijiao lun* 各國教育比較論 (Comparative education) (Shanghai: Shangwu yinshuguan, 1929), "Zixu."

103. Wu Junsheng 吳俊升, *Jiaoyu zhexue dagang* 教育哲學大綱 (Outline of educational philosophy) (Shanghai: Shangwu yinshuguan, 1935), "Zixu," 1. See also Shu Xincheng 舒新城, *Xiandai jiaoyufa* 現代教育法 (Modern educational methods) (Shanghai: Shangwu yinshuguan, 1930), "Xu."

104. See, for example, Wang Junsheng 王駿聲, *Youzhiyuan jiaoyu* 幼稚園教育 (Kindergarten education) (Shanghai: Shangwu yinshuguan, [1926]), "Zixu"; Cheng Xiangfan 程湘帆, *Zhongguo jiaoyu xingzheng* 中國教育行政 (Educational administration in China) (Shanghai: Shangwu yinshuguan, 1930), "Zhongguo jiaoyu xingzheng xu" 中國教育行政序 (Preface to *Educational Administration in China*), 2; Liao Shicheng 廖世承, *Zhongxue jiaoyu*, 中學教育 (Middle-school education) (Shanghai: Shangwu yinshuguan, 1947 [1924]), "Zixu."

105. See, for example, Zhong Luzhai 鍾魯齋, *Bijiao jiaoyu* 比較教育 (Comparative education) (Shanghai: Shangwu yinshuguan, 1935), "Xuyan"; Wu Shirui 吳世瑞, *Jingjixue yuanli* 經濟學原理 (Principles of economics) (Shanghai: Shangwu yinshuguan, 1935), "Zixu"; Sun Benwen 孫本文, *Shehuixue yuanli* 社會學原理 (Principles of sociology) (Shanghai: Shangwu yinshuguan, 1935), "Liyan"; Zheng Lanhua 鄭蘭華, *Shiyan putong huaxue* 實驗普通化學 (Experimental regular chemistry) (Shanghai: Shangwu yinshuguan, 1935 [1934]), "Bianyan."

106. Yang Zheming, *Shizheng guanli ABC*, "Liyan"; Yang Zheming, *Shizheng jihua ABC*, "Liyan"; Jiang Xiangqing, *Tianjing sai ABC*, "Xu"; Zhang Jiatai, *Gongshang guanli ABC*, "Xu"; Xie Liuyi 謝六逸, *Shenhua xue ABC* 神話學 ABC (The ABCs of mythology) (Shanghai: Shijie shuju, 1928), "Xu." Similar comments were found in the prefaces of books from the New Culture Series. See, for instance, Xu Sitong, *Shehui kexue mingzhu tijie*, "Xuyan"; Liu Bingli, *Shehui wenti gangyao*, "Xu"; Zengdiyongzhilang 增地庸治朗, *Jingying jingji xue* 經營經濟學 (The study of operational economics), trans. Pan Nianzhi 潘念之 (Shanghai: Zhonghua shuju, 1931), "Yixu" 譯序 (Translator's preface).

107. Wang Yunwu et al., *Wanyou wenku diyiji yiqianzhong mulu*, 21; Liu Binglin, *Lishite* 劉秉麟 (Friedrich List) (Shanghai: Shangwu yinshuguan, 1930), "Zixu"; Liu Binglin, *Lijiatu* 理嘉圖 (David Ricardo) (Shanghai: Shangwu yinshuguan, 1926), "Ziba" 自跋 (Author's postscript).

108. See the references in note 71.

109. Sun Benwen, *Shehuixue ABC*; Sun Benwen, *Renkou lun ABC*; Sun Benwen, *Shehuixue yuanli*; Sun Benwen 孫本文, *Shehui xinlixue* 社會心理學 (Social psychology) (Shanghai: Shangwu yinshuguan, 1946); Sun Benwen 孫本文, *Xiandai Zhongguo shehui wenti* 現代中國社會問題 (Modern Chinese social problems), 4 vols. (Chongqing: Shangwu yinshuguan, 1942–1946).

110. For examples from several series, see Hao Liyu 郝立輿, *Lingshi caipanquan wenti* 領事裁判權問題 (A study on consular jurisdiction) (Shanghai: Shangwu yinshuguan, 1926 [1925]), "Luo Junren xiansheng xu" 羅鈞任先生序 (Preface of Mr. Luo Junren); Jin Guobao, *Tongji xinlun*, "Tongji xinlun xuyi" 統計新論序一 (First preface of *New Discourse on Statistics*), "Xu'er" 序二 (Second preface), "Xusan" 序三 (Third preface); Li Zongwu 李宗武 and Mao Yongtang 毛泳棠, trans., *Ren de shenghuo* 人的生活 (People's lives) (Shanghai: Zhonghua shuju, 1922), "Xu"; Dong Wenqiao 董問樵, *Guofang jingji lun* 國防經濟論 (Discussion of national defense economics) (Chongqing: Shangwu yinshuguan, 1943 [1940]), "Ma xu" 馬序 (Preface by Ma [Yinchu]).

111. Lin Kui 林骙, *Maersasi renkou lun* 馬爾薩斯人口論 (Malthus on population) (Shanghai: Shangwu yinshuguan, 1926), "Xu."

112. Dong Wenqiao, *Guofang jingji lun*, "Zixu."

113. Dong Wenqiao, *Guofang jingji lun*, "Zixu," 3.

114. The examples are too numerous to cite. Beginning with the Beijing University Series and the New Culture Series, authors described themselves as compiling university lectures from disparate sources and using them as the foundation for a book; Liu Boming, *Jindai xiyang zhexue shi dagang*, "Fanli"; Liu Bingli, *Shehui wenti gangyao*, "Xu"; Zhang Weici 張慰慈, *Zhengzhixue dagang* 政治學大綱 (Outline of political science) (Shanghai: Shangwu yinshuguan, 1927 [1923]), "Xu," 1; Tao Menghe 陶孟和, *Shehui yu jiaoyu* 社會與教育 (Society and education) (Shanghai: Shangwu yinshuguan, 1922), "Xuyan," 1.

115. Wu Shirui, *Jingjixue yuanli*, "Zixu."

116. Yue Meng, *Shanghai and the Edges of Empires* (Minneapolis: University of Minnesota Press, 2006), 38. For her definition of "transcompilation," see p. 37. My emphasis on the constructive agency of Chinese authors who drew from Western scholarly literature and reconstituted it for the Chinese context also parallels the approaches of Lydia Liu and Michael Hill, although Hill focuses more strictly on literary translation; Liu, *Translingual Practice*; Hill, *Lin Shu, Inc.*).

117. For a thoughtful analysis of Sun Benwen's academic influences and his role in establishing the discipline of sociology in China, see Guannan Li, "The Synthesis School and the Founding of 'Orthodox' and 'Authentic' Sociology in Nationalist China: Sun Benwen's Sociological Thinking and Practice," in *Sociology and Anthropology in Twentieth-Century China: Between Universalism and Indigenism*, ed. Arif Dirlik, with Guannan Li and Hsiao-pei Yan, 63–87 (Hong Kong: Chinese University Press, 2012).

118. Sun Benwen, *Shehuixue ABC*, "Liyan."

119. Sun Benwen, *Shehuixue yuanli*, "Liyan."

120. Sun Benwen, *Shehuixue yuanli*, "Xu" and "Liyan."

121. Sun Benwen, *Shehuixue yuanli*, "Xu," 2.

122. Zhong Luzhai, *Bijiao jiaoyu*, "Xuyan."

123. Zhong Luzhai, *Bijiao jiaoyu*, "Xuyan."

124. Wu Junsheng, *Jiaoyu zhexue dagang*, "Zixu," 4. For other examples in the same series, see Huang Juemin 黃覺民, *Jiaoyu xinli xue* 教育心理學 (Educational psychology) (Shanghai: Shangwu yinshuguan, 1935), "Zixu"; Shu, *Xiandai jiaoyufa*, "Xu," 4; J. K. Stableton, *Zhong xiao xue xundao shishifa* 中小學訓導實施法 (Your problems and mine in the guidance of youth), trans. Zhang Shengzu 張繩祖 (Shanghai: Shangwu yinshuguan, 1933), "Yizhe fuji" 譯者附記 (Translator's appended remarks) and "Yizhe yan" 譯者言 (Words from the translator).

125. Zhong Luzhai, *Bijiao jiaoyu*, "Xuyan," 3; Li Chaoying, *Bijiao caizheng zhidu*, "Zixu"; Zhang Jiangshu, *Lilun huaxue shiyan*, "Xuyan"; Richardson, *Tongji fenxi daolun*, "Yizhe xu"; Jin Guobao 金國寶, *Tongji xue dagang* 統計學大綱 (Outline of statistics) (Shanghai: Shangwu yinshuguan, 1935), "Yinyan" 引言 (Foreword).

126. Sun Benwen, *Shehuixue yuanli*, "Liyan," 3.

127. Li Chaoying, *Bijiao caizheng zhidu*, "Zixu"; Chen Xuanshan 陳選善, *Jiaoyu ceyan* 教育測驗 (Educational tests) (Shanghai: Shangwu yinshuguan, 1935 [1933]), "Zixu"; Wang Shulin 王書林, *Jiaoyu tongji xue* 教育統計學 (Educational statistics) (Shanghai: Shangwu yinshuguan, 1937), "Zixu"; Wang Shijie 王世杰, *Bijiao xianfa* 比較憲法 (Comparative constitutions) (Shanghai: Shangwu yinshuguan, 1933 [1927]), "Chuban xu" 初版序 (Preface to the first edition), 3.

128. Zhang Yinian 章頤年, *Xinli weisheng gailun* 心理衛生概論 (A general discussion of mental hygiene) (Shanghai: Shangwu yinshuguan, 1936), "Xu," 2.

129. Susan L. Glosser, "The Truths I have Learned," in *Chinese Femininities / Chinese Masculinities: A Reader*, ed. Susan Brownell and Jeffrey N. Wasserstrom, 120–44 (Berkeley: University of California Press, 2004); Zheng Wang, *Women in the Chinese*

Enlightenment: Oral and Textual Histories (Berkeley: University of California Press, 1999).

130. Wang Shijie, *Bijiao xianfa*, "Chuban xu," 2–3; Zhang Yinian, *Xinli weisheng gailun*, "Xu."

131. William T. Rowe, *Saving the World: Chen Hongmou and Elite Consciousness in Eighteenth-Century China* (Stanford, Calif.: Stanford University Press, 2001); Donald Munro, *The Concept of Man in Contemporary China* (Ann Arbor: University of Michigan Press, 1977).

132. Note historian Zhang Kaiyuan's revealing account of using the Complete Library for supplemental reading while a secondary student in Sichuan during the War of Resistance; Wang Jianhui, *Wenhua de Shangwu*, "Xu," 1–2.

133. Pierre Bourdieu, *The Field of Cultural Production: Essays on Art and Literature*, ed. Randal Johnson (New York: Columbia University Press, 1993); Pierre Bourdieu, *Homo Academicus*, trans. Peter Collier (Stanford, Calif.: Stanford University Press, 1988).

6. Print Industrialism and State Socialism

1. For accounts of the January meetings, see "Shangwu yinshuguan dongshi huiyi lu" 商務印書館董事會議錄 (Record of the Commercial Press board of directors meetings), unpublished manuscript of excerpted notes, 1922–1954, meeting no. 524, February 10, 1954; *SYJ*, 434–35; and PRCCS1954, 38–44, 61–63. A full account of the transition to public-private joint management follows in the chapter.

2. Zhou Wu 周武, "Cong quanguoxing dao difanghua: 1945 zhi 1956 nian Shanghai chubanye de bianqian" 从全国性到地方化：1945至1956年上海出版业的变迁 (From national to localized: The change in Shanghai's publishing industry, 1945–1956), *Shilin* 史林, no. 6 (2006): 73–74.

3. Wang Zhiyi 王知伊, *Kaiming shudian jishi* 开明书店纪事 (Historical record of Kaiming Bookstore) (Taiyuan: Shanxi renmin chubanshe, 1991), 178–80.

4. PRCCS1949, 539–40.

5. Zhou Wu, "Cong quanguoxing dao difanghua," 77–78.

6. "Benju jianshi" 本局簡史 (A simple history of this company), unpublished manuscript, 1950, 6, ZSA511.9.957.

7. *SYJ*2, 387–88.

8. "Benju jianshi," 7.

9. Nicolai Volland, "The Control of the Media in the People's Republic of China" (PhD diss., University of Heidelberg, 2003), chaps. 4–5.

10. Volland, "Control of the Media," 283–86. See also Zhou Wu, "Cong quanguoxing dao difanghua," 80–81; Fang Houshu 方厚枢 and Wei Yushan 魏玉山, *Zhongguo chuban tongshi: Zhonghua renmin gongheguo juan* 中国出版通史：中华人民共和国卷 (Comprehensive history of Chinese publishing: Volume on the People's Republic of China) (Beijing: Zhongguo shuji chubanshe, 2008), chap. 2.

11. PRCCS1949, 188–89, 535–36, 539–40.

12. PRCCS1950, 18–19, 28–29.

13. PRCCS1950, 95.

14. PRCCS1950, 647; PRCCS1950, 642–44.

15. Qian Binghuan 钱炳寰, *Zhonghua shuju dashi jiyao* 中华书局大事纪要 (Summary of major events at Zhonghua Book Company) (Beijing: Zhonghua shuju 2002), 239–40.

16. *SYJ*2, 378–79.

17. PRCCS1950, 669–78.

18. Qian Binghuan, *Zhonghua shuju dashi jiyao*, 243; "Shangwu yinshuguan dongshi huiyi," meeting no. 503 (December 24, 1950); Fang and Wei, *Zhongguo chuban tongshi*, 54; *SYJ2*, 390. Initial capitalization was 3 billion yuan, which was increased several times in 1951. Each company paid a proportional share. The new company had a combined management committee drawn from representatives of each publisher.

19. PRCCS1950, 642–43.

20. *SYJ2*, 377.

21. "Benju jianshi," 11.

22. "Benju jianshi," 14–15.

23. Qian Binghuan, *Zhonghua shuju dashi jiyao*, 247.

24. Qian Binghuan, *Zhonghua shuju dashi jiyao*, 250.

25. Qian Binghuan, *Zhonghua shuju dashi jiyao*, 252; *Zhonghua shuju dongshihui huiyi jilu, 1952 nian yiyue zhi 1953 nian sanyue* 中華書局董事會會議紀錄,1952年一月至1953年三月 (Minutes of the Zhonghua Book Company board of directors meetings, January 1952–March 1953), January 14, 1952, ZSA 511.9.820 (1).

26. *Zhonghua shuju dongshihui huiyi jilu*, August 8, 1952; October 26, 1952, ZSA 511.9.820 (1).

27. *SYJ2*, 377.

28. *SYJ*, 432–34.

29. *SYJ*, 441–43.

30. "Shangwu yinshuguan dongshi huiyi lu," meeting no. 514 (July 26, 1952). The company aimed at an overall proportion that year of 71.6 percent for technical books and periodicals versus 28.4 percent for other kinds of books.

31. Zhou Wu, "Cong quanguoxing dao difanghua," 81.

32. Song Yuanfang 宋原放, ed., *Zhongguo chuban shiliao: Xiandai bufen* 中国出版史料：现代部分 (Historical materials for Chinese publishing: Contemporary portion), vol. 3.1 (Jinan: Shandong jiaoyu chubanshe, 2000), 131.

33. For a detailed account of the Five Antis campaign in nearby Hangzhou, see James Gao, *The Communist Takeover of Hangzhou: The Transformation of City and Cadre, 1949–1954* (Honolulu: University of Hawai`i Press, 2004), 164–79. For its impact on the business community throughout China, see Sherman G. Cochran, ed., *The Capitalist Dilemma in China's Communist Revolution* (Ithaca, N.Y.: East Asia Program, Cornell University, 2014).

34. *Zhonghua shuju dongshihui huiyi jilu*, February 13, 1952, ZSA 511.9.820 (1).

35. *Zhonghua shuju dongshihui huiyi jilu*, June 1, 1952, ZSA 511.9.820 (1).

36. *Zhonghua shuju dongshihui huiyi jilu*, June 1, 1952, ZSA 511.9.820 (1).

37. *Zhonghua shuju dongshihui huiyi jilu*, August 8, 1952, ZSA 511.9.820 (1). That figure did not include fines for local branches; *Zhonghua shuju dongshihui huiyi jilu*, December 11, 1952, ZSA 511.9.820 (1). See also Qian Binghuan, *Zhonghua shuju dashi jiyao*, 254.

38. PRCCS1951, 488.

39. "Shangwu yinshuguan dongshi huiyi lu," meeting no. 511 (February 9, 1952).

40. SMA S313-4-93, 30–39.

41. "Shangwu yinshuguan dongshi huiyi lu," meeting no. 512 (March 22, 1952).

42. "Shangwu yinshuguan dongshi huiyi lu," meeting no. 513 (May 29, 1952).

43. "Shangwu yinshuguan dongshi huiyi lu," meeting no. 514 (July 26, 1952). The overall illegal income of the main office was calculated to be 332,230,000 yuan, not including branch offices.

44. PRCCS1953, 591; see also *SYJ2*, 379. Kaiming started the process of becoming a public-private joint-management company in 1950; "Kaiming shudian qingqiu yu

guojia heying chengwen" 开明书店请求与国家合营呈文 (Kaiming Bookstore's petition for joint state management), in *Kaiming shudian jishi* 开明书店记事 (A record of Kaiming Bookstore), comp. Wang Zhiyi 王知伊 (Taiyuan: Shanxi renmin chubanshe, 1991), 177–82. Kaiming later merged with the Youth Publishing Company (Qingnian chubanshe) to become the China Youth Publishing Company (Zhongguo qingnian chubanshe) in April 1953; Fang and Wei, *Zhongguo chuban tongshi*, 53–54.

45. *Zhonghua shuju dongshihui huiyi jilu*, February 20, 1953, ZSA 511.9.820(1), 41–42.

46. Nicolai Volland, *Socialist Cosmopolitanism: The Chinese Literary Universe, 1945–1965* (New York: Columbia University Press, 2017), 36–37.

47. PRCCS1953, 287.

48. PRCCS1953, 587–88.

49. PRCCS1953, 593–95; the quotation is on p. 594.

50. This perception of private publishers' value as resources the state could tap was echoed in other contexts as well; see Song, *Zhongguo chuban shiliao: Xiandai bufen*, 3.1, 131–32; Fang and Wei, *Zhongguo chuban tongshi*, 50.

51. PRCCS1953, 593–94.

52. PRCCS1953, 602–3.

53. "Shangwu yinshuguan dongshi huiyi lu," meeting no. 522, November 1, 1953.

54. In October, the board also solicited statements of support from the company's unions in Beijing and Shanghai.

55. "Shangwu yinshuguan dongshi huiyi lu," meeting no. 523, December 2, 1953; PRCCS1953, 604–6.

56. "Shangwu yinshuguan dongshi huiyi lu," meeting no. 524, February 10, 1954.

57. "Shangwu yinshuguan dongshi huiyi lu," meeting no. 524, February 10, 1954.

58. See "Guanyu Shangwu yinshuguan shixing quanmian gong si heying gaizu wei Gaodeng jiaoyu chubanshe de huitan jiyao" 關於商務印書館實行全面公私合營改組為高等教育出版社的會談紀要 (Summary of the talks regarding Commercial Press's implementation of comprehensive public-private joint management and reorganization into the Higher Education Publishing Company) and "Gaodeng jiaoyu chubanshe choubeichu jianze" 高等教育出版社籌備處簡則 (Simplified regulations of the Higher Education Publishing Company Preparatory Office), in "Shangwu yinshuguan dongshi huiyi lu," meeting no. 524, February 10, 1954.

59. PRCCS1954, 99–108, 109–15.

60. "Gongsi heying Gaodeng jiaoyu chubanshe zhangcheng" 公私合营高等教育出版社章程 (Regulations for the public-private joint management Higher Education Press) (September 26, 1954), in SMA B167-1-47, 4–5.

61. "Shangwu yinshuguan dongshi huiyi lu," meeting no. 524, February 10, 1954. The GPA also cautioned the government in Shanghai to have the companies dislodge "known counterrevolutionaries and traitorous elements" from the new boards of directors; PRCCS1954, 95.

62. In practice, the existing board representing private shareholders largely remained intact; PRCCS1954, 174.

63. "Gongsi heying Gaodeng jiaoyu chubanshe zhangcheng," 4–5.

64. "Guanyu Shangwu yinshuguan shixing quanmian gong si heying gaizu wei Gaodeng jiaoyu chubanshe de huitan jiyao," in "Shangwu yinshuguan dongshi huiyi lu," meeting no. 524, February 10, 1954.

65. PRCCS1954, 72–73.

66. "Guanyu Shangwu yinshuguan shixing quanmian gong si heying gaizu wei Gaodeng jiaoyu chubanshe de huitan jiyao" in "Shangwu yinshuguan dongshi huiyi lu," meeting no. 524, February 10, 1954.

67. "Gongsi heying Gaodeng jiaoyu chubanshe dongshihui di'erci huiyi jilu" 公私合營高等教育出版社董事會第二次會議記錄 (Minutes of the second meeting of the board of directors of the public-private jointly managed Higher Education Press), August 5, 1955, in SMA B167-1-47, 2–3.

68. PRCCS1953, 607–8.

69. Qian Binghuan, *Zhonghua shuju dashi jiyao*, 264–65.

70. PRCCS1954, 38–44; *HZS*, 1:221–23.

71. PRCCS1954, 38–44; Qian Binghuan, *Zhonghua shuju dashi jiyao*, 267–68.

72. PRCCS1954, 72–73.

73. PRCCS1954, 111.

74. For that market allocation, see PRCCS1954, 120–22.

75. Cochran, *Capitalist Dilemma*, 1–17.

76. Gao, *Communist Takeover*; Thomas S. Mullaney, *Coming to Terms with the Nation: Ethnic Classification in Modern China* (Berkeley: University of California Press, 2011); Eddy U, *Disorganizing China: Counter-Bureaucracy and the Decline of Socialism* (Stanford, Calif.: Stanford University Press, 2007).

77. Gao, *Communist Takeover*, 247–51.

78. Parks Coble, "Zhou Zuomin and the Jincheng Bank," in *The Capitalist Dilemma in China's Communist Revolution*, ed. Sherman Cochran (Ithaca, N.Y.: East Asia Program, Cornell University, 2014), 168–74.

79. PRCCS1954, 112.

80. PRCCS1953, 594–95.

81. This approach was echoed in Commercial Press's own proposals for the reorganization; see PRCCS1953, 598.

82. PRCCS1953, 595. See also ZSA 511.9.748, 44–45.

83. *SYJ*, 453–55.

84. "Caizheng jingji chubanshe chengli yilai gongzuo baogao (yijiuwusi nian jiuyue)" 財政經濟出版社成立以來工作報告 (一九五四年九月) (Work report of the Finance and Economics Publishing Company since its founding [September 1954]), manuscript, 3. The Zhonghua office in Shanghai also had a combined Editing and Proofreading Section of twenty people, pushing the combined editorial personnel to more than a hundred for the first time since before the war; "Caizheng jingji chubanshe Shanghai banshichu 1956 nian gongzuo zongjie" 財政經濟出版社上海辦事處1956年工作總結 (Work summary for the Shanghai office of the Finance and Economics Publishing Company in 1956), manuscript, March 29, 1957, in SMA B167.1.138, 116.

85. PRCCS1954, 118.

86. "Caizheng jingji chubanshe chengli yilai gongzuo baogao," 5.

87. Qian (1908–1985) was a native of Wuxi and a 1926 graduate of Jiangsu Provincial Third Normal School. He participated in the National Revolution as a member of the Nationalist Party and was expelled in the 1927 purge. In 1933 he worked for TASS's Shanghai office and joined the League of Left-Wing Writers. His association with Hu Yuzhi began in 1934, when they founded the journal *World Knowledge* (*Shijie zhishi*). He joined the CCP in September 1935 and served in a variety of cultural and educational positions during the War of Resistance and Civil War periods. In 1954 he became assistant director of the Ministry of Culture and secretary of its party group; Xu Youchun 徐友春 et al., eds., *Minguo renwu da cidian* 民國人物大辭典 (Biographical dictionary of Republican China) (Shijiazhuang: Hebei renmin chubanshe, 1991), 1529.

88. PRCCS1956, 129–30.

89. PRCCS1956, 147–49.

90. PRCCS1956, 148–49.

91. PRCCS1956, 94–95.

92. PRCCS1956, 95.

93. PRCCS1956, 234–35.

94. For analysis of the late imperial state as a cultural patron, see R. Kent Guy, *The Emperor's Four Treasuries: Scholars and the State in the Late Ch'ien-lung Era* (Cambridge, Mass.: Council on East Asian Studies, Harvard University, 1987).

95. Qi (1907–1978) was ethnically Mongol and a native of Beijing. In his youth he studied engraving and calligraphy, and in 1930 he graduated from the National Learning Department (Guoxuexi) of Beiping's China University (Zhongguo daxue). He subsequently taught in various schools in northern China and started several journals. At the start of the War of Resistance, he joined military units in western Shandong, working in a cultural capacity, and joined the CCP in 1938. He served in a variety of educational and cultural posts during the War of Resistance and Civil War periods. At the time of this report, he was director of the Bureau of Experts (Zhuanjiaju) in the State Council. Starting in February 1960 he was a vice-minister of culture and secretary of the ministry's party group; Xu Youchun et al., *Minguo renwu da cidian*, 1337.

96. PRCCS1957–1958, 337.

97. PRCCS1957–1958, 339.

98. PRCCS1957–1958, 338.

99. PRCCS1957–1958, 337–38.

100. PRCCS1957–1958, 347.

101. PRCCS1957–1958, 340–41.

102. PRCCS1957–1958, 360–61; see also *HZS*, 2:24–25.

103. *HZS*, 2:25–26.

104. PRCCS1957–1958, 362–63.

105. *SYJ*, 459–61.

106. PRCCS1957–1958, 361.

107. *SYJ*, 460.

108. PRCCS1957–1958, 363. The private-share board members included Chairman of the Board Zhang Yuanji and Directors Xu Fengshi 徐鳳石, Yu Mingshi 俞明時, Wei Fuqing 韋傅卿, Chen Suzhi 陳夙之, Yu Houpei 郁厚培, Yu Huancheng 俞寰澄, Jiang Huanqing 江寰清, and Tao Gongze 陶公擇.

109. PRCCS1957–1958, 362–64.

110. Jin (1913–1972), a Shandong native, had attended Beida and went to Yan'an in 1938, joining the CCP at that time. Later he served as a researcher in the History Research Office of the Marxism Leninism Institute. After 1949 he served as office director of the Compilation and Review Bureau of the GPA, director of the Ministry of Culture's Publishing Department, and member of the Small Group for Planning the Organization and Publication of Ancient Books; Liao Gailong 廖盖龙, Luo Zhufeng 罗竹风, and Fan Yuan 范源, eds., *Zhongguo renming da cidian: Dangdai renwu juan* 中国人名大辞典：当代人物卷 (China's biographical dictionary: Volume on contemporary figures) (Shanghai: Cishu chubanshe, 1992), 1350. In the capacity of his roles in the GPA and Ministry of Culture, Jin had played a central role in the reorganization of both Commercial Press and Zhonghua as joint-management companies in 1953–1954.

111. PRCCS1957–1958, 341.

112. Jin Zhaozi to Jin Canran, July 4, 1958, in SMA B167.1.275, 54–55; copy to Shanghai Municipal Publishing Bureau. (Underlining included in the copy on file in the Publishing Bureau [Chubanju] archive.).

113. *HZS*, 2:26.

114. *HZS*, 1:131–36.

115. *HZS*, 2:103–4.
116. For one account of the construction of these social and political categories in Shanghai, see Lynn T. White, *Policies of Chaos: The Organizational Causes of Violence in China's Cultural Revolution* (Princeton, N.J.: Princeton University Press, 1989).
117. *SYJ2*, 391–93.
118. *HZS*, 2:246–47.
119. *HZS*, 2:71; *SYJ2*, 392.
120. *HZS*, 2:30; see also *HZS*, 2:69–71. Note that Qi Yanming had also been reconciled to such mobilization of politically suspect rightists because of the need for staff with compiling skills when he launched the proposal for Zhonghua's reorganization; PRCCS1957–1958, 341.
121. *HZS*, 2:71.
122. Sheila Fitzpatrick, *The Cultural Front: Power and Culture in Revolutionary Russia* (Ithaca, N.Y.: Cornell University Press, 1992), 38–64.
123. "Chuxi guji zuotanhui yijian" 出席古籍座谈会意见 (Suggestions for the forum on ancient books), unpublished manuscript, [1957], ZSA 10.01.1.
124. PRCCS1957–1958, 341.
125. PRCCS1957–1958, 341, 451–52, 456–57.
126. *HZS*, 2:246–47; "Yijiuliuwu nian Shanghai chuban gongzuo zongjie baogao" 一九六五年上海出版工作总结报告 (1965 final report on Shanghai's publishing work), in SMA B167.1.762, 15–18.
127. PRCCS1957–1958, 341.
128. *HZS*, 2:30–31, 106–10.
129. Li Chunping 李春平, *Cihai jishi* 辞海纪事 (An account of *Cihai*) (Shanghai: Cishu chubanshe, 2000), 68–70.
130. PRCCS1957–1958, 419–21.
131. Li Chunping, *Cihai jishi*, 70–71; Shu Xincheng 舒新城, *Shu Xincheng riji* 舒新城日記 (Shu Xincheng's diary [1929–1960]), 34 vols. (Shanghai: Shanghai cishu chubanshe, 2013), 31:387, 393–95, 401–2, 405–6, 438–40 (March 18, 21, 25, 27, 1958; April 14, 1958).
132. Li Chunping, *Cihai jishi*, 72–73.
133. "*Cihai* bianji weiyuanhui mingdan (cao'an)" 辭海編輯委員會名單（草案） (Draft of the *Cihai* Editorial Committee name list) (August 28, 1961), in SMA B167-1-476, 12–16.
134. Morris Bian, *The Making of the State Enterprise System in Modern China: The Dynamics of Institutional Change* (Cambridge, Mass.: Harvard University Press, 2005). Significantly, there was little prewar state coordination of the publishing industry of the kind that William Kirby observed in his analysis of state planning institutions during the Nanjing decade ("Engineering in China: Birth of the Developmental State, 1928–1937," in *Becoming Chinese: Passages to Modernity and Beyond*, ed. Wen-hsin Yeh, 137–60 [Berkeley: University of California Press, 2000]).
135. For the Soviet approach to book publishing, see Jeffrey Brooks, *Thank you, Comrade Stalin! Soviet Public Culture from Revolution to Cold War* (Princeton, N.J.: Princeton University Press, 2000), 239–45; Gregory Walker, "Soviet Publishing Since the October Revolution," in *Books in Russia and the Soviet Union: Past and Present*, ed. Miranda Beaven Remnek (Wiesbaden: Harrassowitz, 1991), 64–70. By the mid-1920s private publishing in the USSR was reduced to almost nothing. Large state publishers, coordinated by subject area, dominated much book production along with specialized publishers associated with specific organizations and institutions in the state and academia. Comprehensive censorship expanded dramatically under Glavlit during the Stalinist period.

7. Negotiated Cultural Production in the Pedagogical State

1. *SYJ*, 405–8.

2. *SYJ*2, 414–18; Zhao Tingwei 趙廷為, Yang Yinshen 楊蔭深, Huang Weirong 黃維榮, Hu Wenkai 胡文楷, Jin Yunfeng 金雲峯, Li Jikai 李季開, Mu Shaoliang 沐紹良, and Zhu Gongchui 朱公垂, *Sijiao haoma xin cidian* 四角號碼新詞典 (Four-corner new dictionary) (Shanghai: Shangwu yinshuguan, 1951), "Bianji dayi" 編輯大意 (Main points of compilation).

3. *SYJ*2, 418; Zhao et al., *Sijiao haoma xin cidian*, "Bianji dayi." For examples of new Marxist-Leninist terms and redefined older terms, see pp. 156, 165–66, 169, 175–77.

4. PRCCS1950, 647–48.

5. Stephen Kotkin, *Magnetic Mountain: Stalinism as a Civilization* (Berkeley: University of California Press, 1997), 21–23.

6. This chapter does not include discussion of textbooks, whose publication came to be monopolized by the state-owned People's Education Press (Renmin jiaoyu chubanshe) after 1953. Continued publication and distribution of primary and secondary textbooks by Commercial Press and Zhonghua Book Company in the early PRC was a stopgap measure and never considered a key component of their divisions of labor; see Fang Houshu 方厚枢 and Wei Yushan 魏玉山, *Zhongguo chuban tongshi: Zhonghua renmin gongheguo juan* 中国出版通史：中华人民共和国卷 (Comprehensive history of Chinese publishing: Volume on the People's Republic of China) (Beijing: Zhongguo shuji chubanshe, 2008), 23–25.

7. Nicolai Volland argues persuasively that the Soviet Union became the primary zone of a realigned cosmopolitan world order in China during the 1950s (*Socialist Cosmopolitanism: The Chinese Literary Universe, 1945–1965* (New York: Columbia University Press, 2017), 170–72.

8. "Benju jianshi" 本局簡史 (A simple history of this company), unpublished manuscript, 1950, 11, ZSA 511.9.957.

9. *Zhonghua shuju jiefanghou chuban xinshu mulu* 中华书局解放后出版新书目录 (Catalog of new books published by Zhonghua Book Company after Liberation) (N.p.: Zhonghua shuju, 1950), 4–12.

10. *SYJ*, 407–8. In 1949–1950 Commercial Press drew heavily from its backlist, especially series publications from the Republican period; see *Shangwu yinshuguan chuban xinshu* 商務印書館初版新書 (Commercial Press's first-edition new books), January–March 1950 (N.p.: Shangwu yinshuguan, 1950), 8–11.

11. *SYJ*, 432–33, 441–43.

12. *SYJ*, 443.

13. For examples of early PRC-period publication of science and technology books in the University Series, see Gu Yisun 顧宜孫 and Yang Yaoqian 楊耀乾, *Mucai jiegou xue* 木材結構學 (Study of the structure of wooden materials) (Shanghai: Shangwu yinshuguan, 1954 [1952]); Wang Zhen 王箴, *Putong huaxue* 普通化學 (General chemistry) (Shanghai: Shangwu yinshuguan, 1954 [1952]); Wu Xiang 吳襄, *Shenglixue dagang* 生理學大綱 (Outline of physiology) (Shanghai: Shangwu yinshuguan, 1952); Chen Shanlin 陳善林, *Tongji liebiao yu zhitu* 統計列表與製圖 (Statistical tables and charts) (Shanghai: Shangwu yinshuguan, 1954 [1952]); Zhou Shaolian 周紹濂, *Weifen jihe* 微分幾何 (Differential geometry) (Shanghai: Shangwu yinshuguan, 1951 [1950]).

14. Yuan Hanqing 袁翰青, "Yuan xu" 袁序 (Yuan's preface), in Wang Zhen, *Putong huaxue*.

15. Wu Han also initiated a Foreign History Small Series (Waiguo lishi xiao congshu) that was published at Commercial Press; *SYJ2*, 460–61.

16. *HZS*, 2:16, 124–27.

17. *HZS*, 2:16–17.

18. *HZS*, 2:104–5.

19. *HZS*, 2:125–26.

20. *HZS*, 2:125–26

21. Song Yuanfang 宋原放, ed., *Zhongguo chuban shiliao: Xiandai bufen* 中国出版史料：现代部分 (Historical materials for Chinese publishing: Contemporary portion), vol. 3.1 (Jinan: Shandong jiaoyu chubanshe, 2000), 187–89.

22. Song, *Zhongguo chuban shiliao: Xiandai bufen*, 189–91.

23. On the political implications of the Lushan Plenum, see Kenneth Lieberthal, "The Great Leap Forward and the Split in the Yenan Leadership," in *The Cambridge History of China, Volume 14: The People's Republic, Part 1; The Emergence of Revolutionary China, 1949–1965*, ed. Roderick MacFarquhar and John K. Fairbank, 291–359 (Cambridge: Cambridge University Press, 1987).

24. PRCCS1961, 152–55.

25. Song, *Zhongguo chuban shiliao: Xiandai bufen*, 192–94.

26. PRCCS1961, 156–58.

27. Song, *Zhongguo chuban shiliao: Xiandai bufen*, 194–98.

28. The committee was composed of Fan Yong 範用 (representing People's Press), Chen Hanbo (representing Commercial Press), Ding Shuqi 丁樹奇 (representing Zhonghua Book Company), Meng Chao 孟超 (representing People's Literature Press), Feng Binfu 馮賓符 (representing World Knowledge Press), and Huang Shuntong 黃順桐 (representing the Science and Technology Association and Popular Science Press). The Central Propaganda Bureau's Xu Liyi 許力以 also frequently participated; Song, *Zhongguo chuban shiliao: Xiandai bufen*, 195.

29. Song, *Zhongguo chuban shiliao: Xiandai bufen*, 196–97.

30. Wang Li had written multiple volumes on request for Commercial Press during the 1930s; see *SYJ*, 359–61.

31. "Ben ju jianshi," 14; Qian Binghuan, *Zhonghua shuju dashi jiyao*, 252; *Zhonghua shuju dongshihui huiyi jilu,1952 nian yiyue zhi 1953 nian sanyue* 中華書局董事會會議紀錄,1952年一月至1953年三月 (Minutes of the Zhonghua Book Company board of directors meetings, January 1952–March 1953), February 20, 1953, ZSA 511.9.820(1), 41–42.

32. "Shanghai guji chuban gongzuo qingkuang, wenti, he jianyi" 上海古籍出版工作情況，問題和建议 (Shanghai's ancient-book-publishing work situation, problems, and suggestions) [April 1957], ZSA 10.01.1.

33. *SYJ2*, 396–400.

34. "Shangwu yinshuguan heying hou guji chuban qingkuang" 商務印書館合營後古籍出版情况 (Commercial Press's ancient-book-publishing situation after joint management) (April 22, 1957), ZSA 10.01.1.

35. "Chuxi guji zuotanhui yijian" 出席古籍座谈会意见 (Ideas for attending the ancient-book forum) [April 1957], ZSA 10.01.1.

36. Julia Andrews describes a parallel resurgence of interest in Chinese-style ink-and-brush painting (*guohua*) during this period (*Painters and Politics in the People's Republic of China, 1949–1979* [Berkeley: University of California Press, 1994], 169–202).

37. PRCCS1956, 94–95.

38. PRCCS1956, 233–34.

39. For an overview of the Hundred Flowers Campaign in the publishing industry in Beijing and Shanghai, see Fang and Wei, *Zhongguo chuban tongshi*, 97–100.

40. Shu Xincheng 舒新城, *Shu Xincheng riji* 舒新城日記 (Shu Xincheng's diary [1929–1960]), 34 vols. (Shanghai: Shanghai cishu chubanshe, 2013), 31:11–12 (April 12, 1957).

41. "Shanghai guji chuban gongzuo qingkuang," ZSA 10.01.1.

42. "Shanghai guji chuban gongzuo qingkuang," ZSA 10.01.1

43. Hu Daojing 胡道靜, "Cong duzhe jiaodu kan dui chongyin keji guji de yixie yaoqiu" 從讀者角度看對重印科技古籍的一些要求 (From the reader's perspective viewing some demands for reprinting ancient books on technology), 2–3, ZSA 10.01.1.

44. "Shanghai guji chuban gongzuo qingkuang," ZSA 10.01.1.

45. "Chuxi guji zuotanhui yijian," 2, ZSA 10.01.1.

46. Wu Tiesheng, 吳铁声, "Duiyu jinhou guji chuban guihua de yijian" 对于今后古籍出版规划的意见 (Opinions regarding future plans for publishing ancient books), 3, ZSA 10.01.1.

47. PRCCS1957–1958, 336–41. Similar points were echoed in later talks by Qi and Zhou Yang; see PRCCS1957–1958, 348–52; PRCCS1959–1960, 62–63.

48. PRCCS1957–1958, 339.

49. PRCCS1957–1958, 339.

50. PRCCS1957–1958, 338. Qi voiced similar concerns more than a year later at an expanded meeting of the Small Group; PRCCS1959–1960, 69.

51. *HZS*, 2:4–5.

52. PRCCS1957–1958, 450.

53. PRCCS1957–1958, 449–57.

54. *HZS*, 2:26–27, 79–81.

55. "Guji zhengli chuban guihua, 1959–1962 nian zhengli he chuban guji jihua (cao'an)" 古籍整理出版規劃，1959–1962年整理和出版古籍計畫（草案）(Ancient-book organizing and publishing plan, 1959–1962 [draft]), in ZSA, Zhonghua shuju, *juanhao* 4 中華書局，卷號4 (Zhonghua Book Company, file no. 4).

56. PRCCS1957–1958, 529.

57. PRCCS1957–1958, 530.

58. "Guji zhengli chuban guihua, 1959–1962," "Shuoming" 說明 (Explanation).

59. "Guji zhengli chuban guihua, 1959–1962," "Shuoming" 說明 (Explanation).

60. "Guji zhengli chuban guihua, 1959–1962," "Lishi bufen" 歷史部分 (Historical section).

61. Jin Canran to Wu Han, May 9, 1959, in ZSA, Zhonghua shuju, *juanhao* 4.

62. "Zhonghua renmin gongheguo Jiaoyubu guanyu qing youguan gaodeng xuexiao xiezhu zhengli guji de tongzhi" 中华人民共和国教育部关于请有关高等学校协助整理古籍的通知 (The PRC Ministry of Education notice regarding the request that relevant higher-level schools assist in the organization of ancient books), October 18, 1960; Guji zhengli chuban guihua xiaozu 古籍整理出版規劃小組, "Cuixun guji zhengli guihua de anpai luoshi qingkuang" 催询古籍整理规划的安排落实情况 (Urgent query about the situation of arranging to carry out the plan for organizing ancient books), December 2, 1960, in ZSA, Zhonghua shuju, *juanhao* 8.

63. Guji zhengli chuban guihua xiaozu 古籍整理出版規劃小組 (Planning Small Group for organizing and publishing ancient books), "San zhi ba nian zhengli chuban guji de zhongdian guihua (cao'an)"《三至八年整理出版古籍的重點規劃（草案）》(Plan of the important points of organizing and publishing ancient books for years three to eight [draft]), October 1960, in ZSA, Zhonghua shuju, *juanhao* 8.

64. *HZS*, 2:113–14.

65. *HZS*, 2:113–14; "Guji zhengli chuban guihua, 1959–1962," "Jia: Gudaishi bufen, 1; Ershisishi, jia: Biaodianben" 甲。古代史部分1，二十四史，甲。標點本 (A: Ancient history section, 1; Twenty-four dynastic histories, [a] Punctuated volumes).

66. *HZS*, 2:116.

67. *HZS*, 2:116.

68. *HZS*, 2:115.

69. PRCCS1957–1958, 420. For thoughtful analysis of earlier efforts to categorize and define new terms in dictionaries during the Mao era, see Jennifer E. Altehenger, "On Difficult New Terms: The Business of Lexicography in Mao Era China," *Modern Asian Studies* 51, no. 3 (2017): 622–61.

70. An effort to revise *Ciyuan* was initiated at the same time, but it was to focus on ancient Chinese terms and etymology to complement *Cihai*'s modern focus. Undertaken by Commercial Press, the *Ciyuan* revision, which was overseen largely by Wu Zeyan, also closely followed pre-1949 approaches to reference-book compilation; see Shi Jianqiao 史建桥, Qiao Yong 乔永, and Xu Congquan 徐从权, eds., *Ciyuan yanjiu lunwen ji* 辞源研究论文集 (Collection of writings on *Ciyuan*) (Beijing: Shangwu yinshuguan, 2009), 29–34, 75–78.

71. Li Chunping 李春平, *Cihai jishi* 辞海纪事 (An account of *Cihai*) (Shanghai: Cishu chubanshe, 2000), 68–70.

72. PRCCS1957–1958, 419–20.

73. PRCCS1957–1958, 420.

74. PRCCS1957–1958, 421.

75. PRCCS1957–1958, 420–21. Zhou Yang was charged by Lu Dingyi with overseeing the transfer of staff.

76. Hang was a Wuxi native who joined the Communist Youth League in 1929, graduated from the Shanghai Art Academy in 1931, and joined the CCP in 1941. Before 1949 he served in a number of administrative and educational positions. After 1949 he served in several positions in the Shanghai Municipal Education Bureau before becoming assistant director of the *Cihai* Editing Committee; Liao Gailong 廖盖龙, Luo Zhufeng 罗竹风, and Fan Yuan 范源, eds., *Zhongguo renming da cidian: Dangdai renwu juan* 中国人名大辞典：当代人物卷 (China's biographical dictionary: Volume on contemporary figures) (Shanghai: Cishu chubanshe, 1992), 1281.

77. Hang Wei to Municipal Publishing Bureau Party Committee (February 4, 1960), in SMA B167-1-396, 53.

78. Li Chunping, *Cihai jishi*, 74–76.

79. Hang Wei to Municipal Publishing Bureau Party Committee (February 22, 1960), in SMA B167-1-396, 59.

80. "*Cihai* chugao shuqi shencha ge danwei canjia renshu zongji (cao'an)" 《辞海》初稿暑期审查各单位参加人数总计（草案） (Overall calculation of the numbers of people participating from each unit in the *Cihai* preliminary draft summer review [draft]) (June 30, 1960); "*Cihai* chugao shuqi shencha dazhuan yuanxiao canjia renshu tongji biao (cao'an)" 《辞海》初稿暑期审查大专院校参加人数统计表（草案） (Statistical table for the number of people participating in the *Cihai* preliminary draft summer review from colleges and universities [draft]), in SMA B167-1-396, 62–63.

81. Hang Wei to Municipal Publishing Bureau Party Committee (February 4, 1960), in SMA B167-1-396, 54–55.

82. Li Chunping, *Cihai jishi*, 80–83.

83. Li Chunping, *Cihai jishi*, 83–84.

84. Li Chunping, *Cihai jishi*, 84–85.

85. Li Chunping, *Cihai jishi*, 90, 93, 98.

86. Li Chunping, *Cihai jishi*, 92–94.

87. "*Cihai* dinggao gongzuo zhong de yixie qingkuang" 《辞海》定稿工作中的一些情况 (Some situations with work on the *Cihai* finalized manuscript) (October 15, 1962), in SMA B167.1.550, 48–53.

88. "*Cihai* dinggao gongzuo," 49.

89. "*Cihai* dinggao gongzuo," 52–53.

90. *Cihai* Editing Department (Hang Wei) to [Shanghai Municipal] Publishing Bureau and also report to the Municipal Committee Propaganda Department, the Education and Hygiene Work Department, and Comrade Shi Ximin (July 21, 1961), in SMA B167.1.476, 39–40.

91. Zhonghua Book Company to Shanghai Municipal Publishing Bureau's party group, with "Fenfa fanwei ji banfa (cao'an)" 分发范围及办法（草案）(Scope and methods of distribution [draft]) appended, in SMA B167.1.476, 18–20.

92. PRCCS1962–1963, 35–36.

93. Beilu *Cihai* shixingben zhengqiu yijian gongzuozu 北路辞海试行本征求意见工作组, "Zai Beijing de huodong" 在北京的活动 (Activities in Beijing), in SMA B167.1.476, 53.

94. Beilu *Cihai* shixingben, "Zai Beijing de huodong," 54.

95. Beilu *Cihai* shixingben, "Zai Beijing de huodong," 54.

96. Beilu *Cihai* shixingben, "Zai Beijing de huodong," 53–54.

97. "Zhou Yang tongzhi tanhua jiyao (mijian)" 周扬同志谈话纪要 （密件）(Summary of discussion with Comrade Zhou Yang [classified document]) (January 6, 1962), in SMA B167.1.550, 74–75.

98. "Kang Sheng, Zhou Yang tongzhi jiejian *Cihai* zhengqiu yijian gongzuo zu de tanhua jilu" 康生，周扬同志接见《辞海》征求意见工作组的谈话记录 (Record of the discussion of Comrades Kang Sheng, Zhou Yang with the working group soliciting opinions on *Cihai*) (January 9, 1962), in SMA B167.1.550, 75–83.

99. "Kang Sheng, Zhou Yang tongzhi jiejian *Cihai*," 82.

100. PRCCS1962–1963, 37–38.

101. Hang Wei to the [Shanghai Municipal] Publishing Bureau party group and reporting to the Municipal Committee Propaganda Department (May 16, 1962), in SMA B167.1.550, 33–34.

102. PRCCS1962–1963, 254–55.

103. PRCCS1964–1966, 14–15.

104. PRCCS1964–1966, 13. In response, the *Cihai* Editing Department scrambled in the spring of 1964 to erase politically sensitive entries and to purge discredited figures from the entries that were included; see Li Chunping, *Cihai jishi*, 109–10.

105. Fifteen thousand copies of the "unfinished manuscript" (*weidinggao*) were published in April 1965; Li Chunping, *Cihai jishi*, 110.

106. PRCCS1956, 169.

107. PRCCS1956, 176–77. Shanghai's large publishers were to calculate wages according to the standard for top-tier, central enterprises.

108. PRCCS1956, 178–79.

109. Timothy Cheek, *Propaganda and Culture in Mao's China: Deng Tuo and the Intelligentsia* (Oxford: Clarendon Press, 1997), 247.

110. For government directives on and debates regarding manuscript fees and royalties, see PRCCS1957–1958, 469–75, 535–39, 543–45; PRCCS1959–1960, 45–46, 153–55, 181–85, 357–61; PRCCS1961, 235–36; PRCCS1962–1963, 9–11, 56–58; PRCCS1964–1966, 223–25, 365–68.

111. *HZS*, 2:250–51.

112. *HZS*, 2:75.

113. PRCCS1962–1963, 36.

114. Li Chunping, *Cihai jishi*, 88–91.

115. Li Chunping, *Cihai jishi*, 89.

116. "*Cihai* dinggao gongzuo," 53.

117. Wang Zhen, *Putong huaxue*, "Zixu" 自序 (Author's preface); Gu and Yang, *Mucai jiegou xue*, "Xuyan" 序言 (Preface).

118. Wu Xiang, *Shenglixue dagang*, "Xu" 序 (Preface).

119. Song, *Zhongguo chuban shiliao: Xiandai bufen*, 3.1:197–99.

120. "Zhonghua shuju Shanghai bianjisuo 1960 nian chushu qingkuang zongjie" 中華書局上海編輯所1960 年出書情況總結" (Summary of the Zhonghua Book Company Shanghai Editing Department situation of putting out books in 1960) (February 1961), in SMA B167.1.387, 116.

121. Li Chunping, *Cihai jishi*, 92.

122. "*Cihai* dinggao gongzuo," 50. For other examples of similar debates, see pp. 49–50.

123. Christopher A. Reed and Nicolai Volland, "Epilogue: Beyond the Age of Cultural Entrepreneurship, 1949–Present," in *The Business of Culture: Cultural Entrepreneurs in China and Southeast Asia, 1900–1965*, ed. Christopher Rea and Nicolai Volland (Vancouver: University of British Columbia Press, 2015), 261–69.

124. PRCCS1957–1958, 178.

125. *HZS*, 2:28–29.

126. *HZS*, 2:114.

127. *HZS*, 2:103–4.

128. *HZS*, 2:126.

129. Song, *Zhongguo chuban shiliao*, 187–88.

130. *HZS*, 2:105.

131. Peter Kenez, *The Birth of the Propaganda State: Soviet Methods of Mass Mobilization, 1917–1929* (Cambridge: Cambridge University Press, 1985).

132. Chang-tai Hung, *Mao's New World: Political Culture in the early People's Republic* (Ithaca, N.Y.: Cornell University Press, 2010); Timothy Cheek, *The Intellectual in Modern Chinese History* (Cambridge: Cambridge University Press, 2015), 125–32; Hung Wu, *Remaking Beijing: Tiananmen Square and the Creation of a Political Space* (Chicago: University of Chicago Press, 2005); Andrews, *Painters and Politics*; Denise Y. Ho, *Curating Revolution: Politics on Display in Mao's China* (Cambridge: Cambridge University Press, 2018). But Matthew Johnson also captures the limitations, unevenness, and pluralism in the institutions of the propaganda state ("Beneath the Propaganda State: Official and Unofficial Cultural Landscapes in Shanghai, 1949–1965," in *Maoism at the Grassroots: Everyday Life in China's Era of High Socialism*, ed. Jeremy Brown and Matthew D. Johnson, 199–229 [Cambridge, Mass.: Harvard University Press, 2015]).

133. Donald Munro, *The Concept of Man in Contemporary China* (Ann Arbor: University of Michigan Press, 1977).

134. Andrews, *Painters and Politics*; Cheek, *Propaganda and Culture*; Brian James DeMare, *Mao's Cultural Army: Drama Troupes in China's Rural Revolution* (Cambridge: Cambridge University Press, 2015); Merle Goldman, *Literary Dissent in Communist China* (New York: Atheneum, 1971); Yang Kuisong 杨奎松, *Renbuzhu de "guanhuai": 1949 nian qianhou de shusheng yu zhengzhi* 忍不住的"关怀"：1949年前后的书生与政治 (Unbearable "care": Scholars and politics before and after 1949) (Guilin: Guangxi shifan daxue chubanshe, 2013).

135. Paola Iovene, *Tales of Futures Past: Anticipation and the Ends of Literature in Contemporary China* (Stanford, Calif.: Stanford University Press, 2014), chap. 3.

136. For an analysis of the dynamics of cultural patronage during the early PRC, see Elizabeth J. Perry, *Anyuan: Mining China's Revolutionary Tradition* (Berkeley: University of California Press, 2012).

Conclusion

1. My account of the "Eclectics" incident is based on Shanghai chubanzhi bianzuan weiyuanhui 上海出版志编纂委员会, *Shanghai chubanzhi* 上海出版志 (Shanghai publishing gazetteer) (Shanghai: Shanghai shehui kexue yuan chubanshe, 2000), 1185–86; Li Chunping 李春平, *Cihai jishi* 辞海纪事 (An account of *Cihai*) (Shanghai: Cishu chubanshe, 2000), 106–7; Fang Houshu 方厚枢 and Wei Yushan 魏玉山, *Zhongguo chuban tongshi: Zhonghua renmin gongheguo juan* 中国出版通史：中华人民共和国卷 (Comprehensive history of Chinese publishing: Volume on the People's Republic of China) (Beijing: Zhongguo shuji chubanshe, 2008), 114–15.

2. For a detailed assessment of these developments, see Timothy Cheek, *Propaganda and Culture in Mao's China: Deng Tuo and the Intelligentsia* (Oxford: Clarendon Press, 1997), 235–55.

3. Luomo 骆漠 [Luo Zhufeng 罗竹风], "Zajia—yige bianji tongzhi de xiangfa" 杂家——一个编辑同志的想法 (Eclectics—an editor comrade's way of thinking), *Wenhuibao* 文汇报, May 6, 1962.

4. Yao Wenyuan 姚文元, "Liangge bianji tongzhi de xiangfa 两个编辑同志的想法 (Two editor comrades' mind-sets), *Wenhuibao* 文汇报, May 13, 1962.

5. Yao, "Liangge bianji tongzhi."

6. Shanghai chubanzhi bianzuan weiyuanhui, *Shanghai chubanzhi*, 1185.

7. The editors at *Wenhuibao* who had solicited Luo's essay were also subjected to struggle meetings and had to make self-criticisms.

8. Li Chunping, *Cihai jishi*, 107.

9. *HZS*, 2:11–12.

10. For the initial attacks on Wu Han, see Yan Jiaqi and Gao Gao, *Turbulent Decade: A History of the Cultural Revolution*, trans. and ed. D. W. Y. Kwok (Honolulu: University of Hawai`i Press, 1990), 23–37; Roderick MacFarquhar and Michael Schoenhals, *Mao's Last Revolution* (Cambridge, Mass.: Harvard University Press, 2006), 15–19, 27–31.

11. Fang and Wei, *Zhongguo chuban tongshi*, 124.

12. *HZS*, 2:16.

13. *HZS*, 2:76, 250.

14. *HZS*, 2:38.

15. Li Chunping, *Cihai jishi*, 115–29.

16. Fang and Wei, *Zhongguo chuban tongshi*, 125; *HZS*, 2:38, 76–77, 251; Li Chunping, *Cihai jishi*, 126–29.

17. Li Chunping, *Cihai jishi*, 116–29.

18. Song Yuanfang 宋原放, ed., *Zhongguo chuban shiliao: Xiandai bufen* 中国出版史料：现代部分 (Historical materials for Chinese publishing: Contemporary portion), vol. 3.1 (Jinan: Shandong jiaoyu chubanshe, 2000), 200.

19. *HZS*, 2:129–30.

20. *HZS*, 2:81–82, 116–18.

21. *HZS*, 2:110.

22. Barbara Mittler, *A Continuous Revolution: Making Sense of Cultural Revolution Culture* (Cambridge, Mass.: Harvard University Asia Center, 2012), 19–20.

23. As Gregory Walker characterizes the system, "the high degree to which Party and state authorities determine the development and operation of Soviet publishing leaves to the individual publishing-house a severely limited number of directions in which it, as an enterprise, can make important decisions between different options" (*Soviet Book Publishing Policy* [Cambridge: Cambridge University Press, 1978], 41–44, 48–67;

the quotation is from p. 48). Walker describes formal structural relationships. Lived practice in the USSR, as per Kotkin, was likely more complex.

24. Fang and Wei, *Zhongguo chuban tongshi*, 198.
25. *HZS*, 2:14.
26. Fang and Wei, *Zhongguo chuban tongshi*, 214.
27. Li Chunping, *Cihai jishi*, 148–55; Luo Zhufeng 罗竹风 and Wang Yue 王岳, "*Cihai liushi nian*" 辞海》六十年 (Sixty years of *Cihai*), *Cishu yanjiu* 辞书研究 5 (1996): 51–53; Fang and Wei, *Zhongguo chuban tongshi*, 220–21.
28. Paola Iovene, *Tales of Futures Past: Anticipation and the Ends of Literature in Contemporary China* (Stanford, Calif.: Stanford University Press, 2014), chap. 3; Shuyu Kong, *Consuming Literature: Best Sellers and the Commercialization of Literary Production in Contemporary China* (Stanford, Calif.: Stanford University Press, 2005), chap. 2.

Bibliography

Abbott, Andrew. *The System of Professions: An Essay on the Division of Expert Labor.* Chicago: University of Chicago Press, 1988.

"ABC congshu mulu" (Catalog for the ABC Series). In *Baoxianxue ABC* 保險學 ABC (The ABCs of insurance), ed. Zhang Bozhen 張伯箴. Shanghai: Shijie shuju, 1929.

"ABC congshu zhuzuozhe xiaoxi" ABC叢書著作者消息 (News about the ABC Series' authors). *Shijie* 世界 1, no. 1 (1928): 37.

Alford, William P. *To Steal a Book Is an Elegant Offense: Intellectual Property Law in Chinese Civilization.* Stanford, Calif.: Stanford University Press, 1995.

Allen, Oliver E. "This Great Mental Revolution." *Audacity* (Summer 1996): 52–61.

Altehenger, Jennifer E. "On Difficult New Terms: The Business of Lexicography in Mao Era China." *Modern Asian Studies* 51, no. 3 (2017): 622–61.

Anderson, Benedict. *Imagined Communities: Reflections on the Origin and Spread of Nationalism.* London: Verso, 1983.

Andrews, Julia F. *Painters and Politics in the People's Republic of China, 1949–1979.* Berkeley: University of California Press, 1994.

Angle, Stephen C. *Human Rights and Chinese Thought: A Cross-Cultural Inquiry.* Cambridge: Cambridge University Press, 2002.

Apple, Michael W., and Linda K. Christian-Smith. "The Politics of the Textbook." In *The Politics of the Textbook,* ed. Michael W. Apple and Linda K. Christian-Smith, 1–23. New York: Routledge, 1991.

Armstrong, Nancy, and Leonard Tennenhouse. *The Imaginary Puritan: Literature, Intellectual Labor, and the Origins of Personal Life.* Berkeley: University of California Press, 1992.

Averill, Stephen C. "The Cultural Politics of Local Education in Early Twentieth-Century China." *Twentieth-Century China* 32, no. 2 (April 2007): 4–32.

Ayers, William. *Chang Chih-tung and Educational Reform in China.* Cambridge, Mass.: Harvard University Press, 1971.

Bailey, Paul J. *Reform the People: Changing Attitudes Towards Popular Education in Early Twentieth Century China.* Vancouver: University of British Columbia Press, 1990.

Bao Tianxiao 包天笑. *Chuanyinglou riji* 釧影樓日記 (Diary from Chuanying Hall). Manuscript, Shanghai Municipal Library, 1925–1935.

Barlow, Tani. "*Zhishifenzi* [Chinese Intellectuals] and Power." *Dialectical Anthropology* 16 (1991): 209–32.

Barshay, Andrew. *The Social Sciences in Modern Japan: The Marxian and Modernist Traditions.* Berkeley: University of California Press, 2004.

Bastid, Marianne. *Educational Reform in Early Twentieth-Century China.* Trans. Paul Bailey. Ann Arbor: Center for Chinese Studies, University of Michigan, 1988.

"Benju jianshi" 本局簡史 (A simple history of this company). Unpublished manuscript, 1950. ZSA511.9.957.

Bian, Morris. *The Making of the State Enterprise System in Modern China: The Dynamics of Institutional Change.* Cambridge, Mass.: Harvard University Press, 2005.

"Bianji dagang" 編輯大綱 (Editorial outline). *Cihai* 辭海, 5 *zhong*. 7th ed. Ed. Shu Xincheng 舒新城 et al. N.p.: Zhonghua shuju, 1941.

"Bianshenbu zhanxing banshi guize" 編審部暫行辦事規則 (Provisional work rules for the Compilation and Review Department). *Shangwu yinshuguan tongxin lu* 商務印書館通信錄, no. 403 (November 10, 1934): 5–7.

"Bianshen weiyuanhui zhanxing banshi guize" 編審委員會暫行辦事規則" (Provisional work rules for the Compilation and Review Committee) (August 27, 1932). *Shangwu yinshuguan tongxin lu* 商務印書館通信錄, no. 377 (September 15, 1932): 20–21.

"Bianyin Daxue congshu xuxun" 編印大學叢書續訊 (Further news about the publishing of the University Series). *Shangwu yinshuguan tongxinlu* 商務印書館通信錄, no. 388 (August 10, 1933): 19–24.

"Bianyisuo zhiyuanlu" 編譯所職員錄 (Record of the staff in the Editing Department). Mimeographed record, Shangwu yinshuguan [1926].

Bol, Peter K. *"This Culture of Ours": Intellectual Transitions in T'ang and Sung China.* Stanford, Calif.: Stanford University Press, 1992.

Bourdieu, Pierre. *Distinction: A Social Critique of the Judgement of Taste.* Trans. Richard Nice. Cambridge, Mass.: Harvard University Press, 1984.

——. *The Field of Cultural Production: Essays on Art and Literature.* Ed. Randal Johnson. New York: Columbia University Press, 1993.

——. "The Forms of Capital." In *Handbook of Theory and Research for the Sociology of Education*, ed. John G. Richardson, 241–58. Westport, Conn.: Greenwood Press, 1986.

——. *Homo Academicus.* Trans. Peter Collier. Stanford, Calif.: Stanford University Press, 1988.

——. *Language and Symbolic Power.* Trans. Gino Raymond and Matthew Adamson. Cambridge, Mass.: Harvard University Press, 1991.

——. *The Logic of Practice.* Trans. Richard Nice. Stanford, Calif.: Stanford University Press, 1990.

——. *Outline of a Theory of Practice.* Trans. Richard Nice. Cambridge: Cambridge University Press, 1977.

Brokaw, Cynthia J. *Commerce in Culture: The Sibao Book Trade in the Qing and Republican Periods.* Cambridge, Mass.: Harvard University Asia Center, 2007.

Brokaw, Cynthia J., and Kai-wing Chow, eds. *Printing and Book Culture in Late Imperial China.* Berkeley: University of California Press, 2005.

Brook, Timothy. "Family Continuity and Cultural Hegemony: The Gentry of Ningbo, 1368–1911." In *Chinese Local Elites and Patterns of Dominance*, ed. Joseph W. Esherick and Mary B. Rankin, 27–50. Berkeley: University of California Press, 1976.

Brooks, Jeffrey. *Thank You, Comrade Stalin! Soviet Public Culture from Revolution to Cold War.* Princeton, N.J.: Princeton University Press, 2000.

Brown, Shana J. "Archives at the Margins: Luo Zhenyu's Qing Documents and Nationalism in Republican China." In *The Politics of Historical Production in Late Qing and Republican China*, ed. Tze-ki Hon and Robert Culp, 249–70. Leiden: Brill, 2007.

——. *Pastimes: From Art and Antiquarianism to Modern Chinese Historiography*. Honolulu: University of Hawai`i Press, 2011.

"Caizheng jingji chubanshe chengli yilai gongzuo baogao (yijiuwusi nian jiuyue)" 財政經濟出版社成立以來工作報告（一九五四年九月）(Work report of the Finance and Economics Publishing Company since its founding [September 1954]). Manuscript, ZSA.

Certeau, Michel de. *The Practice of Everyday Life*. Trans. Steven Rendall. Berkeley: University of California Press, 1984.

Chang, Hao. *Chinese Intellectuals in Crisis: The Search for Order and Meaning*. Berkeley: University of California Press, 1987.

Chang Daozhi 常導之. *De Fa Ying Mei siguo jiaoyu gaiguan* 德法英美四國教育概觀 (Overview of education in the four countries of Germany, France, England, and America). Shanghai: Shangwu yinshuguan, 1932 [1930].

Chartier, Roger. "Communities of Readers." In *The Order of Books: Readers, Authors, and Libraries in Europe between the Fourteenth and Eighteenth Centuries*, trans. Lydia G. Cochrane, 1–23. Stanford, Calif.: Stanford University Press, 1994.

Cheek, Timothy. *The Intellectual in Modern Chinese History*. Cambridge: Cambridge University Press, 2015.

——. *Propaganda and Culture in Mao's China: Deng Tuo and the Intelligentsia*. Oxford: Clarendon Press, 1997.

Chen, Janet Y. *Guilty of Indigence: The Urban Poor in China, 1900–1953*. Princeton, N.J.: Princeton University Press, 2012.

Ch'en, Li-fu. *The Storm Clouds Clear over China: The Memoir of Ch'en Li-fu*. Ed. Sidney H. Chang and Ramon Myers. Stanford, Calif.: Hoover Press, 1994.

Chen Gaoyong 陳高傭. "Zhongguo wenhua yu Zhongguo guji: *Sibu beiyao* chongyin ganyan" 中國文化與中國古籍：四部備要重印感言 (Chinese culture and Chinese ancient books: Reflections on the reprinting of *Sibu beiyao*). *Xin Zhonghua* 新中華 2, no. 5 (1934): 27–29.

Cheng Xiangfan 程湘帆. *Zhongguo jiaoyu xingzheng* 中國教育行政 (Educational administration in China). Shanghai: Shangwu yinshuguan, 1930.

Chen Jiang 陳江. "Guji zhenglijia yu Zhongguo tonghua de chuangshiren—Sun Yuxiu" 古籍整理家与中国童话的创始人—孙毓修 (Organizer of ancient books and originator of Chinese children's stories: Sun Yuxiu). In *Zhongguo chuban shiliao: Jindai bufen* 中國出版史料：近代部分, vol. 3, ed. Wang Jiarong 汪家熔, 465–71. Wuhan: Hubei jiaoyu chubanshe, 2004.

Chen Shanlin 陳善林. *Tongji liebiao yu zhitu* 統計列表與製圖 (Statistical tables and charts). Shanghai: Shangwu yinshuguan, 1954 [1952].

Chen Xuanshan 陳選善. *Jiaoyu ceyan* 教育測驗 (Educational tests). Shanghai: Shangwu yinshuguan, 1935 [1933].

Chin, Sei Jeong. "Print Capitalism, War, and the Remaking of Mass Media in 1930s China." *Modern China* 40, no. 4 (2014): 393–425.

Chongqing chubanzhi bianzuan weiyuanhui 重庆出版志编纂委员会, comp. *Chongqing chuban jishi, diyiji* 重庆出版纪实，第一辑 (A true record of publishing in Chongqing, first collection). Chongqing: Chongqing chubanshe, 1988.

Chow, Kai-wing. *Publishing, Culture, and Power in Early Modern China*. Stanford, Calif.: Stanford University Press, 2004.

——. *The Rise of Confucian Ritualism in Late Imperial China: Ethics, Classics, and Lineage Discourse*. Stanford, Calif.: Stanford University Press, 1994.

Chow, Tse-tsung. *The May 4th Movement: Intellectual Revolution in Modern China*. Cambridge, Mass.: Harvard University Press, 1960.

Cihai digao 辭海底稿 (*Cihai* initial draft). 8 vols. Manuscript. N.p.: Cishu chubanshe tushuguan, 192?.

Coble, Parks. "Zhou Zuomin and Jincheng Bank." In *The Capitalist Dilemma in China's Communist Revolution*, ed. Sherman Cochran, 151–74. Ithaca, N.Y.: East Asia Program, Cornell University, 2014.

Cochran, Sherman G. *Big Business in China: Sino-Foreign Rivalry in the Cigarette Industry, 1890–1930*. Cambridge, Mass.: Harvard University Press, 1980.

——, ed. *The Capitalist Dilemma in China's Communist Revolution*. Ithaca, N.Y.: East Asia Program, Cornell University, 2014.

Cong, Xiaoping. *Teachers' Schools and the Making of the Modern Chinese Nation-State, 1897–1937*. Vancouver: University of British Columbia Press, 2007.

"The Copyright Law." Trans. N. F. Allman. *China Law Review* 4, no. 2 (November 1929): 1–5.

"Cuishe juan gou Wanyou wenku" 萃社捐購萬有文庫 (The Gathering Society contributes funds to buy the Complete Library). *Sili lingnan daxue xiaobao* 私立嶺南大學校報 2, no. 2 (1930): 11.

Culp, Robert. *Articulating Citizenship: Civic Education and Student Politics in Southeastern China, 1912–1940*. Cambridge, Mass.: Harvard University Asia Center, 2007.

——. "Building a National Print Market: A Preliminary Analysis of Book Distribution in Late Qing and Republican China." In *Chengshi chuanbo: Jiyu Zhongguo chengshi de lishi yu xianshi* 城市传播：基于中国城市的历史与现实 (Urban dissemination: Based on the history and reality of China's cities), ed. Huang Dan, 194–222. Shanghai: Jiaotong University Press, 2016.

——. "Mass Production of Knowledge and the Industrialization of Mental Labor: The Rise of the Petty Intellectual." In *Knowledge Acts in Modern China: Ideas, Institutions, and Identities*, ed. Robert Culp, Eddy U, Wen-hsin Yeh, 207–41. Berkeley: Institute of East Asian Studies, University of California, 2016.

——. "Synthesizing Citizenship in Modern China." *History Compass* 5/6 (2007): 1833–61.

——. "Teaching *baihua*: Textbook Publishing and the Production of Vernacular Language and a New Literary Canon in Early Twentieth-Century China." *Twentieth-Century China* 34, no. 1 (November 2008): 4–41.

Culp, Robert, and Eddy U. "Introduction: Knowledge Systems, Knowledge Producers, and China's Distinctive Modernity." In *Knowledge Acts in Modern China: Ideas, Institutions, and Identities*, ed. Robert Culp, Eddy U, and Wen-hsin Yeh, 1–26. Berkeley: Institute of East Asian Studies, University of California, 2016.

Culp, Robert, Eddy U, and Wen-hsin Yeh, eds. *Knowledge Acts in Modern China: Ideas, Institutions, and Identities*. Berkeley: Institute of East Asian Studies, University of California, 2016.

Da Bingshan 笪炳善. "Jurong disi xuequ diwu chuji xiaoxuexiao shishi gaikuang" 句容第四學區第五初級小學校實施概況 (The situation of implementation at the Number Five Lower-Primary School of Jurong's Fourth Academic District). *Xiaoxue jiaoyu yuekan* 小學教育月刊 1, no. 5 (November 1925): 1–12.

Darnton, Robert. *The Business of Enlightenment: A Publishing History of the "Encyclopédie," 1775–1800*. Cambridge, Mass.: Harvard University Press, 1979.

Davis, Kenneth C. *Two-Bit Culture: The Paperbacking of America*. Boston: Houghton Mifflin, 1984.

"Daxue congshu bianyin jinkuang" 大學叢書編印近況 (The recent situation of the publishing of the University Series). *Shangwu yinshuguan tongxinlu* 商務印書館通信錄, no. 385 (May 10, 1933): 19–21.

"Daxue congshu kemu yu benguan yiyou shugao shumu bijiao biao" 大學叢書科目與本館已有書稿數目比較表 (A comparative statistical table of University Series subjects and manuscripts that this company already has). In *Daxue congshu mulu* 大學叢書目錄 (The catalog for the University Series). [Shanghai]: Shangwu yinshuguan, 1935.

Daxue congshu mulu 大學叢書目錄 (The catalog for the University Series). [Shanghai]: Shangwu yinshuguan, 1935.

"Daxue congshu weiyuanhui tiaoli" 大學叢書委員會條例 (Regulations for the University Series Committee) (October 24, 1932). *Shangwu yinshuguan tongxinlu* 商務印書館通信錄, no. 379 (November 15, 1932): 3.

"Daxue congshu weiyuanhui weiyuan mingdan" 大學叢書委員會委員名單 (Name list of the University Series Editorial Committee's members). In *Daxue congshu mulu* 大學叢書目錄 (The catalog for the University Series). [Shanghai]: Shangwu yinshuguan, 1935.

DeFrancis, John. *Nationalism and Language Reform in China*. Princeton, N.J.: Princeton University Press, 1950.

DeMare, Brian James. *Mao's Cultural Army: Drama Troupes in China's Rural Revolution*. Cambridge: Cambridge University Press, 2015.

Deng Yongqiu 鄧詠秋. "Minguo shiqi bianji he chuban ren de shengcun zhuangkuang" 民國時期編輯和出版人的生存狀況 (The living situation of editors and publishing people during the Republican period). *Chuban shiliao* 出版史料, no. 2 (2007): 115–17.

Des Forges, Alexander. *Mediasphere Shanghai: The Aesthetics of Cultural Production*. Honolulu: University of Hawai`i Press, 2007.

"Di'erqi Wanyou wenku dao xiao" 第二期萬有文庫到校 (The second installment of the Complete Library arrived at the school). *Jimei zhoukan* 集美週刊, no. 258 (1930): 8–9.

Dikötter, Frank. *The Discourse of Race in Modern China*. Stanford, Calif.: Stanford University Press, 1992.

——. *Things Modern: Material Culture and Everyday Life in China*. London: Hurst, 2007.

"Dinggou Wanyou wenku" 訂購萬有文庫 (Ordering the Complete Library). *Wuzhong zhoukan* 五中週刊, no. 85 (March 16, 1931): 1.

Dirlik, Arif. *The Origins of the Chinese Communist Party*. New York: Oxford University Press, 1989.

Dirlik, Arif, with Guannan Li and Hsiao-pei Yen, eds. *Sociology and Anthropology in Twentieth-Century China: Between Universalism and Indigenism*. Hong Kong: Chinese University Press, 2012.

Dong, Madeleine Yue, and Joshua Goldstein, eds. *Everyday Modernity in China*. Seattle: University of Washington Press, 2006.

"Dongfang tushuguan" 東方圖書館 (Eastern Library). *Lizhi zazhi* 勵志雜誌, no. 1 (1925): 87.

"Dongfang tushuguan" 東方圖書館 (Eastern Library). *Lizhi zazhi* 勵志雜誌, no. 2 (1926): 126–28.

Dong Renjian 董任堅. "Jieshao yibu ertong guoyu jiaokeshu" 介紹一部兒童國語教科書 (Introducing a children's national language textbook). *Tushu pinglun* 圖書評論 1, no. 2 (1932): 69–76.

"Dongshihui tebie weiyuanhui tonggao, diyihao" 董事會特別委員會通告，第一號 (Notice number one of the special committee of the board of directors). *Shangwu yinshuguan tongxinlu* 商務印書館通信錄, no. 376 (July 10, 1932): 14.

Dong Wenqiao 董問樵. *Guofang jingji lun* 國防經濟論 (Discussion of national defense economics). Chongqing: Shangwu yinshuguan, 1943 [1940].

Duara, Prasenjit. *Rescuing History from the Nation: Questioning Narratives of Modern China*. Chicago: University of Chicago Press, 1995.

Elman, Benjamin A. *Classicism, Politics, and Kinship: The Ch'ang-chou School of New Text Confucianism in Late Imperial China*. Berkeley: University of California Press, 1990.

——. *A Cultural History of Civil Examinations in Late Imperial China.* Berkeley: University of California Press, 2000.

——. *From Philosophy to Philology: Intellectual and Social Aspects of Change in Late Imperial China.* Cambridge, Mass.: Council on East Asian Studies, Harvard University, 1984.

——. *On Their Own Terms: Science in China, 1550–1900.* Cambridge, Mass.: Harvard University Press, 2005.

"Ershiliu niandu gudong changhui huiyi jilu" 二十六年度股東常會會議紀錄 (Record of the 1937 annual shareholders' meeting). *Shangwu yinshuguan tongxinlu* 商務印書館通信錄, no. 434 (June 20, 1937): 18–27.

"Ershiwu niandu gudong changhui huiyi jilu" 二十五年度股東常會會議紀錄 (Record of the 1936 annual shareholders' meeting). *Shangwu yinshuguan tongxinlu* 商務印書館通信錄, no. 420 (April 20, 1936): 11–17.

Eucken, Rudolf. *Rensheng zhi yiyi yu jiazhi* 人生之意義與價值 (The significance and value of human life). Trans. Yu Jiaju 余家菊. Shanghai: Zhonghua shuju, 1920.

Fang Houshu 方厚樞 and Wei Yushan 魏玉山. *Zhongguo chuban tongshi: Zhonghua renmin gongheguo juan* 中国出版通史:中华人民共和国卷 (Comprehensive history of Chinese publishing: Volume on the People's Republic of China). Beijing: Zhongguo shuji chubanshe, 2008.

Febvre, Lucien, and Henri-Jean Martin. *The Coming of the Book: The Impact of Printing, 1450–1800.* Trans. David Gerard. London: Verso, 1997 [1958].

Fei Xiaotong 費孝通. "Lun zhishi jieji" 論知識階級 (On intellectuals). *Guancha* 觀察 3, no. 8 (October 18, 1947): 11–15.

"Fengtian chaobu *Siku quanshu*" 奉天抄補四庫全書 (Fengtian copies to supplement the *Complete Book of Four Treasuries*). *Xinghua* 興華 23, no. 3 (1926): 44.

Feng Zikai 豐子愷. *Goutu fa ABC* 構圖法 ABC (The ABCs of composition). Shanghai: Shijie shuju, 1928.

Fitzpatrick, Sheila. *The Cultural Front: Power and Culture in Revolutionary Russia.* Ithaca, N.Y.: Cornell University Press, 1992.

Florida, Richard. *The Rise of the Creative Class: And How It's Transforming Work, Leisure, Community, and Everyday Life.* New York: Basic Books, 2002.

Foucault, Michel. *The Archaeology of Knowledge.* Trans. A. M. Sheridan Smith. New York: Pantheon Books, 1972.

——. *Discipline and Punish: The Birth of the Prison.* Trans. Alan Sheridan. New York: Vintage, 1979.

——. *The History of Sexuality, Volume 1: An Introduction.* Trans. Robert Hurley. New York: Vintage, 1980.

——. "What Is an Author?" In *Language, Counter-Memory, Practice: Selected Essays and Interviews,* ed. Donald F. Bouchard, trans. Donald F. Bouchard and Sherry Simon, 113–38. Ithaca, N.Y.: Cornell University Press, 1977.

"Fujian sheng zhengfu jiaoyuting, xunling tongzi di liushi hao" 福建省政府教育廳訓令通字第六十號 (Fujian provincial government Department of Education order no. 60). *Fujian jiaoyu zhoukan* 福建教育週刊, no. 188 (1934): 20–21.

Fu Lan 富蘭. "Lun Shanghai shenghuofei jizeng zhi ke jing" 論上海生活費激增之可驚 (On the surprising sudden increase in Shanghai's cost of living). *Qianye yuebao* 錢業月報 10, no. 3 (1930), "Lunzhu" 論著 (Treatises): 9–14.

Gamble, Sidney D. *How Chinese Families Live in Peiping: A Study of the Income and Expenditure of 283 Chinese Families Receiving from $8 to $550 Silver per Month.* New York: Funk and Wagnalls, 1933.

Gao, James. *The Communist Takeover of Hangzhou: The Transformation of City and Cadre, 1949–1954.* Honolulu: University of Hawai`i Press, 2004.

Gao Fengqian 高鳳謙, Zhang Yuanji 張元濟, and Jiang Weiqiao 蔣維喬. [*Zuixin*] *gaodeng xiao-xue guowen jiaokeshu* 最新高等小學國文教科書 (Newest higher-primary Chinese text-book). 8 vols. Shanghai: Shangwu yinshuguan, 1907.

Gao Jiansi 高踐四. *Minzhong jiaoyu* 民眾教育 (Popular education). Shanghai: Shangwu yin-shuguan, 1933.

Gao Xisheng 高希聖. *Chan'er xianzhi ABC* 產兒限制 ABC (The ABCs of birth control). Shanghai: Shijie shuju, 1929.

Gao Zheyi 高哲一 (Robert Culp). "Wei putong duzhe qunti chuangzao 'zhishi shijie': Shangwu yinshuguan yu Zhongguo xueshu jingying de hezuo" 为普通读者群体创造'知识世界'——商务印书馆与中国学术精英的合作 (A world of knowledge for the circle of common readers: Commercial Press's partnership with China's academic elite). *Shilin* 史林, no. 3 (2014): 92–108.

Genette, Gérard. *Paratexts: Thresholds of Interpretation.* Trans. Jane E. Lewin. Cambridge: Cambridge University Press, 1997 [1987].

Ghosh, Anindita. *Power in Print: Popular Publishing and the Politics of Language and Culture in a Colonial Society, 1778–1905.* Oxford: Oxford University Press, 2006.

Glosser, Susan L. "The Truths I Have Learned." In *Chinese Femininities / Chinese Masculini-ties: A Reader*, ed. Susan Brownell and Jeffrey N. Wasserstrom, 120–44. Berkeley: University of California Press, 2004.

Goldman, Merle. "Left-Wing Criticism of the *Pai-hua* Movement." In *Reflections on the May Fourth Movement: A Symposium*, ed. Benjamin I. Schwartz, 85–94. Cambridge, Mass.: Harvard University Press, 1972.

——. *Literary Dissent in Communist China.* New York: Atheneum, 1971.

"Gongchao zhiyao" 工潮誌要 (Brief account of the labor protest). *Lizhi zazhi* 勵志雜誌, no. 3 (1925): 59–73.

Gorz, André. "The Tyranny of the Factory: Today and Tomorrow." In *The Division of Labour: The Labour Process and Class-Struggle in Modern Capitalism*, ed. André Gorz, 55–61. Atlantic Highlands, N.J.: Humanities Press, 1976.

"Gou zhi Wanyou wenku" 購製萬有文庫 (Purchasing the Complete Library). *Chengdu shi shi zhengfu gongbao* 成都市市政府公報, no. 11 (1929), "Zhengwu jiyao" 政務紀要 (Summary of government affairs): 1–2.

Greene, J. Megan. "Looking Toward the Future: State Standardization and Professional-ization of Science in Wartime China." In *Knowledge Acts in Modern China: Ideas, Institu-tions, Identities*, ed. Robert Culp, Eddy U, and Wen-hsin Yeh, 275–303. Berkeley: Institute of East Asian Studies, University of California, 2016.

Grieder, Jerome B. *Intellectuals and the State in Modern China: A Narrative History.* New York: Free Press, 1983.

Gujin tushu jicheng yangben 古今圖書集成樣本 (Sample book for *Complete Collection of Past and Present Books and Illustrations*). [Shanghai]: Zhonghua shuju, n.d.

Gunn, Edward. *Rewriting Chinese: Style and Innovation in Twentieth-Century Chinese Prose.* Stanford, Calif.: Stanford University Press, 1991.

Guoli bianyiguan 國立編譯館. *Chuji xiaoxue guoyu changshi keben* 初級小學國語常識課本 (Lower-primary national language and common knowledge textbook). 8 vols. N.p.: Guoding zhongxiao xue jiaokeshu qijia lianhe gongyingchu, 1947.

Guotai 郭泰, Li Da 李達, trans. *Weiwu shiguan jieshuo* 唯物史觀解說 (Explanation of histori-cal materialism). Shanghai: Zhonghua shuju, 1921.

"Guoyu tongyi choubeihui gonghan" 國語統一籌備會公函 (Public letter of the National Language Unification Preparation Committee). *Zhuji jiaoyu yuekan* 諸暨教育月刊, no. 23 (1925): 1–2.

Gu Shusen 顧樹森 and Pan Wen'an 潘文安. [*Xinzhu*] *gongmin xuzhi* 新著公民須知 ([The newly written] essential knowledge for citizens). 3 vols. Shanghai: Shangwu yinshuguan, 1924 [1923].

Guy, R. Kent. *The Emperor's Four Treasuries: Scholars and the State in the Late Ch'ien-lung Era.* Cambridge, Mass.: Council on East Asian Studies, Harvard University, 1987.

Gu Yisun 顧宜孫 and Yang Yaoqian 楊耀乾. *Mucai jiegou xue* 木材結構學 (Study of the structure of wooden materials). Shanghai: Shangwu yinshuguan, 1954 [1952].

Han Wei 漢�. "*Siku quanshu di beijing*" 四庫全書底背景 (The background of the *Complete Book of Four Treasuries*). *Minguo ribao: Juewu* 民國日報: 覺悟 2, no. 18 (February 18, 1924): 6–7.

Hao Liyu 郝立輿. *Lingshi caipanquan wenti* 領事裁判權問題 (A study on consular jurisdiction). Shanghai: Shangwu yinshuguan, 1926 [1925].

Harrison, Henrietta. *The Man Awakened from Dreams: One Man's Life in a North China Village, 1857–1942.* Stanford, Calif.: Stanford University Press, 2005.

Hayford, Charles. *To the People: James Yen and Village China.* New York: Columbia University Press, 1990.

He Bingsong 何炳松. *Lishi yanjiufa* 歷史研究法 (History research methods). Shanghai: Shangwu yinshuguan, 1927.

Hill, Michael Gibbs. *Lin Shu, Inc.: Translation and the Making of Modern Chinese Culture.* Oxford: Oxford University Press, 2013.

Ho, Denise Y. *Curating Revolution: Politics on Display in Mao's China.* Cambridge: Cambridge University Press, 2018.

Hockx, Michel. *Questions of Style: Literary Societies and Literary Journals in Modern China, 1911–1937.* Leiden: Brill, 2011.

Hon, Tze-ki. *Visions of Modernity: The Cultural and Historical Debates in Late Qing and Republican China.* Leiden: Brill, 2015.

Honig, Emily. *Sisters and Strangers: Women in the Shanghai Cotton Mills, 1919–1949.* Stanford, Calif.: Stanford University Press, 1987.

Huang Fengling 黃鳳嶺. "Chongming Youzhu xiang di'er chuji xiaoxuexiao shishi gaikuang" 崇明友助鄉第二初級小學校實施概況 (The situation of implementation at Chongming Youzhu Township's Number Two Lower-Primary School). *Xiaoxue jiaoyu yuekan* 小學教育月刊 1, no. 1 (June 1925): 1–6.

Huang Juemin 黃覺民. *Jiaoyu xinli xue* 教育心理學 (Educational psychology). Shanghai: Shangwu yinshuguan, 1935.

Huang Menglou 黃夢樓. *Gongsifa ABC* 公司法 ABC (The ABCs of company law). Shanghai: Shijie shuju, 1931.

"Hubei cungu xuetang ge xueke fennian jiaofa" 湖北存古學堂各學科分年教法 (Teaching methods for each course by year at Hubei's School for Preserving the Heritage). In *Zhongguo jindai xuezhi shiliao* 中國近代學制史料 (Historical materials on China's modern school system), part 2, vol. 2, ed. Zhu Youhuan 朱有瓛 et al., 507–12. Shanghai: Huadong shifan daxue chubanshe, 1987.

Hummel, Arthur H. *Eminent Chinese of the Ch'ing Period (1644–1912).* Vol. 1. Washington, D.C.: U.S. Government Printing Office, 1943.

Hung, Chang-tai. *Mao's New World: Political Culture in the early People's Republic.* Ithaca, N.Y.: Cornell University Press, 2010.

——. *War and Popular Culture: Resistance in Modern China, 1937–1945.* Berkeley: University of California Press, 1994.

Hu Shi 胡適. "Guoyu biaozhun yu guoyu" 國語標準與國語 (National language standards and national language) (Preface to *Fellow Student Directory of the National Language*

Short-Term Training School [*Guoyu jiangxisuo tongxuelu xu* 國語講習所同學錄序]). *Xin jiaoyu* 新教育 3, no. 1 (February 1920): 1–4.

——. *Hu Shi de riji* 胡適的日記 (Hu Shi's diary). Ed. Zhongguo shehui kexue yuan jindaishi yanjiusuo 中國社會科學院近代史研究所 and Zhonghua minguoshi yanjiushi 中華民國史研究室. Hong Kong: Zhonghua shuju Xianggang fenju, 1985.

Hu Shunhua 胡舜華 et al. [*Xin jiaoyu jiaokeshu*] *guoyu duben* 新教育教科書國語讀本 ([New education textbook] national-language reader). 8 vols. Shanghai: Zhonghua shuju, 1920–1921.

Iovene, Paola. *Tales of Futures Past: Anticipation and the Ends of Literature in Contemporary China*. Stanford, Calif.: Stanford University Press, 2014.

Ip, Manying. *The Life and Times of Zhang Yuanji, 1867–1959: From Qing Reformer to Twentieth-Century Publisher*. Beijing: Commercial Press, 1985.

Israel, John. *Lianda: A Chinese University in War and Revolution*. Stanford, Calif.: Stanford University Press, 1998.

"Jiading Qiyun xuexiao guoyuke jiaoxue shili" 嘉定企雲學校國語科教學實例 (Real examples of national-language instruction at Jiading's Qiyun school). *Jiangsu di'er shifan qu xiaoxue jiaoshi yanjiuhui niankan* 江蘇第二師範區小學教師研究會年刊 (May 1924): 153–56.

Jia Fengzhen 賈豐臻. "Jinhou xiaoxue jiaoke zhi shangque" 今後小學教科之商榷 (A discussion of primary instruction from now on). In *Zhongguo jindai xuezhi shiliao* 中國近代學制史料, part 3, vol. 1, ed. Zhu Youhuan 朱有瓛 et al., 163–68. Shanghai: Huadong shifan daxue chubanshe, 1990.

Jiang Bozhen 蔣伯震. "Xianzai zhongliu jieji de tongku he youlu" 現在中流階級的痛苦和憂慮 (The difficulties and concerns of the current middling class). *Jinde jikan* 進德季刊 2, no. 1 (1923), "Yanlun" 言論 (Open discussion): 11–14.

"Jiangsu jiaoyuting xunling di erqian liubai qishiqi hao" 江蘇教育廳訓令第二千六百七十七號 (Jiangsu Department of Education order no. 2677). *Jiangsu sheng gongbao* 江蘇省公報, no. 2881 (1922), "Xunling" 訓令 (Orders): 4–5.

Jiang Weiqiao 蔣维乔. "Jiang Weiqiao riji zhailu" 蔣维乔日记摘录 (Excerpts from Jiang Weiqiao's diary). *Shangwu yinshuguan guanshi ziliao* 商務印書館館史資料 (Commercial Press company history materials), no. 45 (April 20, 1990): 2–16.

——. "Jiang Weiqiao riji zhailu (xu'er)" 蔣维乔日记摘录 (续二) (Excerpts from Jiang Weiqiao's diary [continuation two]). *Shangwu yinshuguan guanshi ziliao* 商務印書館館史資料 (Commercial Press company history materials), no. 47 (June 10, 1991): 15–28.

——. "Jiang Weiqiao riji (xuwan)" 蔣维乔日记 (续完) (Jiang Weiqiao's diary [final continuation]). *Shangwu yinshuguan guanshi ziliao* 商務印書館館史資料 (Commercial Press company history materials), no. 50 (October 5, 1993): 13–24.

——. "Jiang Weiqiao riji zhailu (xuyi)" 蔣维乔日记摘录 (续一) (Excerpts from Jiang Weiqiao's diary [continuation one]). *Shangwu yinshuguan guanshi ziliao* 商務印書館館史資料 (Commercial Press company history materials), no. 46 (September 20, 1990): 12–22.

——. "Jiang Weiqiao riji (xuzhong)" 蔣维乔日记 (续中) (Jiang Weiqiao's diary [middle continuation]). *Shangwu yinshuguan guanshi ziliao* 商務印書館館史資料 (Commercial Press company history materials), no. 48 (April 10, 1992): 11–25.

——. "Yinshizhai riji bufenjuan" 因是齋日記不分卷 (The diary of Yinshizhai [Jiang Weiqiao]). Manuscript, Shanghai Municipal Library (digital file), 1912–1922.

Jiang Weiqiao 蔣维喬 and Zhuang Yu 莊俞 (with Yang Yutong 楊瑜統). [*Zuixin*] *guowen jiaokeshu* 最新國文教科書 ([Newest] Chinese textbook). 10 vols. Shanghai: Shangwu yinshuguan, 1906–1907 [1905–1906].

Jiang Wenjun 江文君. *Jindai Shanghai zhiyuan shenghuoshi* 近代上海职员生活史 (History of the social lives of modern Shanghai's office workers). Shanghai: Cishu chubanshe, 2011.

Jiang Xiangqing 蔣湘青. *Tianjing sai ABC* 田徑賽 ABC (The ABCs of track-and-field competitions). Shanghai: Shijie shuju, 1928.

"Jiaoyubu shending Shijie shuju jiaokeshu" 教育部審定世界書局教科書 (Ministry of Education authorizes World Book Company textbooks). *Xuedeng* 學燈 1, no. 15 (January 15, 1925): 4.

"Jiaoyu jianxun" 教育簡訊 (Brief news about education). *Shandong jiaoyu xingzheng zhoubao* 山東教育行政週報, no. 61 (1929): 24.

Jin Guantao 金觀濤 and Liu Qingfeng 劉青峰. *Guannianshi yanjiu: Zhongguo xiandai zhongyao zhengzhi shuyu de xingcheng* 觀念史研究：中國現代重要政治術語的形成 (Studies in the history of ideas: The formation of important modern Chinese political terms). Hong Kong: Research Center for Contemporary Chinese Culture, Chinese University of Hong Kong, 2008.

Jin Guobao 金國寶. *Tongji xinlun* 統計新論 (New discourse on statistics). Shanghai: Zhonghua shuju, 1925.

——. *Tongji xue dagang* 統計學大綱 (Outline of statistics). Shanghai: Shangwu yinshuguan, 1935 [1934].

Jingyin Siku quanshu hanchuanben ni mu 景印四庫全書罕傳本擬目 (Planned catalog for photolithographic printing of rarely circulating books in the *Complete Book of Four Treasuries*). N.p.: n.p., 1933.

Jin Yunfeng 金雲峰. "Wo he Shangwu yinshuguan" 我和商務印書館 (Me and Commercial Press). *Shangwu yinshuguan guanshi ziliao* 商務印書館館史資料 (Commercial Press company history materials), no. 4 (December 20, 1980): 8–18.

Ji Shaofu 吉少甫. *Zhongguo chuban jianshi* 中国出版简史 (An elementary history of Chinese publishing). Shanghai: Xuelin chubanshe, 1991.

Johnson, David. "Communication, Class, and Consciousness in Late Imperial China." In *Popular Culture in Late Imperial China*, ed. David Johnson, Andrew J. Nathan, and Evelyn S. Rawski, 34–72. Berkeley: University of California Press, 1985.

Johnson, Matthew D. "Beneath the Propaganda State: Official and Unofficial Cultural Landscapes in Shanghai, 1949–1965." In *Maoism at the Grassroots: Everyday Life in China's Era of High Socialism*, ed. Jeremy Brown and Matthew D. Johnson, 199–229. Cambridge, Mass.: Harvard University Press, 2015.

Judge, Joan. *Print and Politics: 'Shibao' and the Culture of Reform in Late Qing China*. Stanford, Calif.: Stanford University Press, 1996.

Kaestle, Carl F., and Janice A. Radway. "Introduction, Section II, The Publishing Trades." In *A History of the Book in America, Volume 4: Print in Motion; The Expansion of Publishing and Reading in the United States, 1880–1940*, ed. Carl F. Kaestle and Janice A. Radway, 49–55. Chapel Hill: University of North Carolina Press, 2009.

"Kaiming shudian qingqiu yu guojia heying chengwen" 开明书店请求与国家合营呈文 (Kaiming Bookstore's petition for joint state management). In *Kaiming shudian jishi* 开明书店记事 (A record of Kaiming Bookstore), comp. Wang Zhiyi 王知伊, 177–83. Taiyuan: Shanxi renmin chubanshe, 1991.

"Kaoxuan xiaoxi" 考選消息 (News of selection by examination). *Shangwu yinshuguan tongxinlu* 商務印書館通信錄, no. 398 (June 10, 1934): 19.

"Kaoxuan xiaoxi" 考選消息 (News of selection by examination). *Shangwu yinshuguan tongxinlu* 商務印書館通信錄, no. 400 (August 10, 1934): 18.

Kaske, Elisabeth. *The Politics of Language in Chinese Education, 1895–1919*. Leiden: Brill, 2008.

Keenan, Barry. *The Dewey Experiment in China: Educational Reform and Political Power in the Early Republic*. Cambridge, Mass.: Harvard University Press, 1977.

——. *Imperial China's Last Classical Academies: Social Change in the Lower Yangzi, 1864–1911*. Berkeley: University of California Press, 1994.

Kenez, Peter. *The Birth of the Propaganda State: Soviet Methods of Mass Mobilization, 1917–1929.* Cambridge: Cambridge University Press, 1985.

Kirby, William. "Engineering in China: Birth of the Developmental State, 1928–1937." In *Becoming Chinese: Passages to Modernity and Beyond*, ed. Wen-hsin Yeh, 137–60. Berkeley: University of California Press, 2000.

Köll, Elisabeth. "The Making of the Civil Engineer in China: Knowledge Transfer, Institution Building, and the Rise of a Profession." In *Knowledge Acts in Modern China: Ideas, Institutions, and Identities*, ed. Robert Culp, Eddy U, and Wen-hsin Yeh, 148–73. Berkeley: Institute of East Asian Studies, University of California, 2016.

Kong, Shuyu. *Consuming Literature: Best Sellers and the Commercialization of Literary Production in Contemporary China.* Stanford, Calif.: Stanford University Press, 2005.

Koschmann, J. Victor, ed. *International Perspectives on Yanagita Kunio and Japanese Folklore Studies.* Ithaca, N.Y.: China-Japan Program, Cornell University, 1985.

Koselleck, Reinhart. "*Begriffgeschichte* and Social History." In *Futures Past: On the Semantics of Historical Time*, trans. Keith Tribe, 73–91. Cambridge, Mass.: MIT Press, 1985.

Kotkin, Stephen. *Magnetic Mountain: Stalinism as a Civilization.* Berkeley: University of California Press, 1997.

Kuhn, Philip A., and Susan Mann Jones. "Dynastic Decline and the Roots of Rebellion." In *The Cambridge History of China, Volume 10: Late Ch'ing, 1800–1911, Part 1*, ed. John K. Fairbank, 107–62. New York: Cambridge University Press, 1986.

Kurtz, Joachim. "Framing European Technology in Seventeenth-Century China: Rhetorical Strategies in Jesuit Paratexts." In *Cultures of Knowledge: Technology in Chinese History*, ed. Dagmar Schäfer, 209–32. Leiden: Brill, 2011.

Lackner, Michael, Iwo Amelung, and Joachim Kurtz, eds. *New Terms for New Ideas: Western Knowledge and Lexical Change in Late Imperial China.* Leiden: Brill, 2001.

Lam, Tong. *A Passion for Facts: Social Surveys and the Construction of the Chinese Nation-State, 1900–1949.* Berkeley: University of California Press, 2011.

Larson, Magali Sarfatti. *The Rise of Professionalism: A Sociological Analysis.* Berkeley: University of California Press, 1979.

Latour, Bruno. *Pandora's Hope: Essays on the Reality of Science Studies.* Cambridge, Mass.: Harvard University Press, 1999.

Lean, Eugenia. "Proofreading Science: Editing and Experimentation in Manuals by a 1930s Industrialist." In *Science and Technology in Modern China, 1880s–1940s*, ed. Jing Tsu and Benjamin A. Elman, 185–208. Leiden: Brill, 2014.

Ledderose, Lothar. *Ten Thousand Things: Module and Mass Production in Chinese Art.* Princeton, N.J.: Princeton University Press, 2000.

Lee, Leo Ou-fan. *Shanghai Modern: The Flowering of a New Urban Culture in China, 1930–1945.* Cambridge, Mass.: Harvard University Press, 1999.

Levenson, Joseph R. *Confucian China and Its Modern Fate.* 3 vols. Berkeley: University of California Press, 1958–1964.

Li, Guannan. "The Synthesis School and the Founding of 'Orthodox' and 'Authentic' Sociology in Nationalist China: Sun Benwen's Sociological Thinking and Practice." In *Sociology and Anthropology in Twentieth-Century China: Between Universalism and Indigenism*, ed. Arif Dirlik, with Guannan Li and Hsiao-pei Yan, 63–87. Hong Kong: Chinese University Press, 2012.

Liang Junli 梁鋆立. "Duiyu Shangwu yinshuguan Daxue congshu mulu zhong falu ji zhengzhi bufen zhi shangque" 對於商務印書館大學叢書目錄中法律及政治部份之商榷 (A discussion of the law and politics sections of Commercial Press's University Series catalog). *Tushuguan pinglun* 圖書館評論 2, no. 2 (1933): 3–9.

Liang Qichao 梁啓超. "Guoxue rumen shu yaomu ji qi dufa" 國學入門書要目及其讀法 (An essential syllabus of introductory books for national studies and their reading method). *Dongfang zazhi* 東方雜誌 20, no. 8 (1923): 135–53.

Liang Yan 梁彦, ed. *Zhonghua shuju shoucang xiandai mingren shuxin shouji* 中华书局收藏现代名人书信手迹 (Handwritten letters by famous modern people held by Zhonghua Book Company). Beijing: Zhonghua shuju, 2012.

"Lianxiyuan bayuefen shixi chengxu yilanbiao" 練習員八月份實習程序一覽表 (Overview table of the August practice procedures for the trainees). *Shangwu yinshuguan tongxinlu* 商務印書館通信錄, no. 401 (September 10, 1934): 11.

"Lianxiyuan fuwu ji daiyu guize" 練習員服務及待遇規則 (Rules for trainee service and compensation). *Shangwu yinshuguan tongxinlu* 商務印書館通信錄, no. 397 (May 10, 1934): 13–14.

"Lianxiyuan jinguan kaishi lianxi" 練習員進館開始練習 (Trainees enter the company and begin training). *Shangwu yinshuguan tongxinlu* 商務印書館通信錄, no. 401 (September 10, 1934): 9–11.

Liao Gailong 廖盖龙, Luo Zhufeng 罗竹风, and Fan Yuan 范源, eds. *Zhongguo renming da cidian: Dangdai renwu juan* 中国人名大辞典：当代人物卷 (China's biographical dictionary: Volume on contemporary figures). Shanghai: Cishu chubanshe, 1992.

"Liaoning Jiaoyuting cheng, di 316 hao" 遼寧教育廳呈第三一六號 (Submitted by the Liaoning Department of Education, no. 316). *Liaoning jiaoyu yuekan* 遼寧教育月刊 1, no. 9 (1929): 121–22.

Liao Shicheng 廖世承. *Zhongxue jiaoyu* 中學教育 (Middle-school education). Shanghai: Shangwu yinshuguan, 1947 [1924].

Li Chaoying 李超英. *Bijiao caizheng zhidu* 比較財政制度 (Comparative finance systems). [Chongqing]: Shangwu yinshuguan, 1944 [1943].

Li Chunping 李春平. *Cihai jishi* 辞海纪事 (An account of *Cihai*). Shanghai: Cishu chubanshe, 2000.

Lieberthal, Kenneth. "The Great Leap Forward and the Split in the Yenan Leadership." In *The Cambridge History of China, Volume 14: The People's Republic, Part 1; The Emergence of Revolutionary China, 1949–1965*, ed. Roderick MacFarquhar and John K. Fairbank, 291–359. Cambridge: Cambridge University Press, 1987.

Li Huaxing 李华兴 et al. *Minguo jiaoyushi* 民國教育史 (Republican education history). Shanghai: Shanghai jiaoyu chubanshe, 1997.

Li Jiaju 李家驹. *Shangwu yinshuguan yu jindai zhishi wenhua de chuanbo* 商務印書館與近代知識文化的传播 (Commercial Press and the transmission of modern knowledge and culture). Beijing: Shangwu yinshuguan, 2005.

[Li] Jinhui [黎]錦暉. "Zhe shi ying zhuyi de yidian" 這是應注意的一點 (This is a point that should be paid attention to). *Jinde jikan* 進德季刊 2, no. 1 (1923), "Tiyi" 提議 (Proposals): 3–5.

Li Jinxi 黎錦熙. *Guoyu yundong shigang* 國語運動史綱 (A historical outline of the national-language movement). Shanghai: Shanghai shudian, 1990.

——. "Xu" 序 (Preface). *Cihai* 辭海. 5 zhong. 7th ed. Ed. Shu Xincheng 舒新城 et al. N.p.: Zhonghua shuju, 1941.

Lin, Xiaoqing Diana. *Peking University: Chinese Scholarship and Intellectuals, 1898–1937*. Albany: State University of New York Press, 2005.

"Ling gexian jiaoyuju, shengli tushuguan, sheng sili ge da zhong xiao xuexiao xiaozhang cuicu ding gou Wanyou wenku you" 令各縣教育局，省立圖書館，省私立各大，中，小學校校長催促定購萬有文庫由 (Order to the provincial library, each county's bureau of education, and each of the province's private universities, secondary and primary schools urging them to buy the Complete Library). *Fujian jiaoyuting zhoukan* 福建教育廳週刊, no. 50 (1929): 53.

Link, E. Perry, Jr. *Mandarin Ducks and Butterflies: Popular Fiction in Early Twentieth-Century Chinese Cities*. Berkeley: University of California Press, 1981.

Lin Kui 林骙. *Maersasi renkou lun* 馬爾薩斯人口論 (Malthus on population). Shanghai: Shangwu yinshuguan, 1926.

Lin Pan 林盼. "Wanqing xinshi meiti yu guanxi wang: *Zhongwai ribao* (1898–1908) yanjiu" 晚清新式媒體與關係網:《中外日報》(1898–1908)研究 (The late Qing new media and relational networks: A study of the *Sino-Foreign Daily* [1898–1908]). PhD diss., Fudan University, 2013.

"Linshi zhizhengling" 臨時執政令 (Provisional executive order). *Anhui jiaoyu gongbao* 安徽教育公報, no. 59 (1925), "Mingling" 命令 (Directives): 1.

Li Quanshi 李權時. *Caizheng xue ABC* 財政學ABC (The ABCs of finance). Shanghai: Shijie shuju, 1928.

Liu, Lydia H. *Translingual Practice: Literature, National Culture, and Translated Modernity—China, 1900–1937*. Stanford, Calif.: Stanford University Press, 1995.

Liu Bingli 劉炳藜. *Shehui kexue jia yu shehui yundong jia* 社會科學家與社會運動家 (Social scientists and leaders of social movements). Shanghai: Zhonghua shuju, 1931.

——. *Shehui wenti gangyao* 社會問題綱要 (An outline of social problems). Shanghai: Zhonghua shuju, 1930.

Liu Binglin 劉秉麟. *Lijiatu* 理嘉圖 (David Ricardo). Shanghai: Shangwu yinshuguan, 1926.

——. *Lishite* 李士特 (Friedrich List). Shanghai: Shangwu yinshuguan, 1930.

Liu Boming 劉伯明, lecturer. *Jindai xiyang zhexue shi dagang* 近代西洋哲學史大綱 (An outline of the history of modern Western philosophy). Comp. Miao Fenglin 繆鳳林. Shanghai: Zhonghua shuju, 1922 [1921].

Liu Hecheng 柳和城. *Sun Yuxiu pingzhuan* 孫毓修評传 (A critical biography of Sun Yuxiu). Shanghai: Shanghai renmin chubanshe, 2011.

Lizhou 蠡舟. "Lun Shangwu yinshuguan chuban zhi *Sibu congkan*" 論商務印書館出版之四部叢刊 (On the *Sibu congkan* published by Commercial Press). *Tushuguanxue jikan* 圖書館學季刊 3, nos. 1–2 (1929): 289–92.

Li Zongwu 李宗武. *Renwen dili ABC* 人文地理ABC (The ABCs of human geography). Shanghai: Shijie shuju, 1929.

Li Zongwu 李宗武 and Mao Yongtang 毛泳棠, trans. *Ren de shenghuo* 人的生活 (People's lives). Shanghai: Zhonghua shuju, 1922.

Long, Pamela O. *Openness, Secrecy, Authorship: Technical Arts and the Culture of Knowledge from Antiquity to the Renaissance*. Baltimore: Johns Hopkins University Press, 2003.

Lou Tongsun 樓桐孫. *Zujie wenti* 租界問題 (The problem of the concessions). Shanghai: Shangwu yinshuguan, 1932.

Lu Danlin 陸丹林. "Daolu xiehui gouji Wanyou wenku bianyan" 道路協會購庋萬有文庫弁言 (Introductory remark on the Road Association purchasing the Complete Library). *Daolu yuekan* 道路月刊 28, no. 2 (1929): 3.

Lu Erkui 陸爾逵. "*Ciyuan* shuolüe" 辭源說略 (A summary of *Ciyuan*). In *Ciyuan* 辭源, ed. Lu Erkui et al. 2 vols. Shanghai: Shangwu yinshuguan, 1915.

Lu Erkui 陸爾逵 et al. *Ciyuan* 辭源. 2 vols. Shanghai: Shangwu yinshuguan, 1915.

Lufei Bohong 陸費伯鴻. "Jingji zhi yuansu" 經濟之元素 (The economy's elements). *Jinde jikan* 進德季刊 3, no. 2 (1924), "Yanjiang" 演講 (Lectures): 1–4.

Lufei Kui 陸費逵. "Bianyin yuanqi" 編印緣起 (An account of the impetus for compilation and publication). In *Cihai* 辭海, vol. 1, ed. Shu Xincheng 舒新城, Shen Yi 沈頤, Xu Yuangao 徐元誥, and Zhang Xiang 張相 et al. Shanghai: Zhonghua shuju, 1936.

———. "Zuidi xiandu dang du zhi guoxue shu" 最低限度當讀之國學書 (The minimal level of national-learning books one should read). *Jinde jikan* 進德季刊 3, no. 2 (1924), "Yanlun" 言論 (Open discussion): 8–12.

Luomo 駱漠 [Luo Zhufeng 罗竹风]. "Zajia—yige bianji tongzhi de xiangfa" 杂家———一个编辑同志的想法 (Eclectics—an editor comrade's way of thinking). *Wenhuibao* 文汇报, May 6, 1962.

Luo Zhufeng 罗竹风 and Wang Yue 王岳. "*Cihai* liushi nian" 《辞海》六十年 (Sixty years of *Cihai*). *Cishu yanjiu* 辞书研究, 5 (1996): 49–54.

Lu Tianbai 盧天白. "Wo zai Shangwu yinshuguan sinian jianwen" 我在商務印書館四年見聞 (What I saw and heard in four years at Commercial Press). In *Zhonghua wenshi ziliao wenku* 中華文史資料文庫 (Chinese cultural and historical materials treasury), vol. 16, *Wenhua jiaoyu bian* 文化教育編 (Culture and education volume), comp. Quanguo zhengxie wenshi ziliao weiyuanhui 全國政協文史資料委員會, 518–25. Beijing: Zhongguo wenshi chubanshe, 1996.

MacFarquhar, Roderick, and Michael Schoenhals. *Mao's Last Revolution*. Cambridge, Mass.: Harvard University Press, 2006.

Ma Junwu 馬君武. *Da'erwen wuzhong yuanshi* 達爾文物種原始 (Darwin's *Origin of Species*). Shanghai: Zhonghua shuju, 1926 [1920].

Mao Tun. *Spring Silkworms and Other Stories*. Trans. Sidney Shapiro. Beijing: Foreign Languages Press, 1956.

"Ma Runqing xiansheng fu Mei liuxue" 馬潤卿先生赴美留學 (Mr. Ma Runqing will go to America to study). *Jinde jikan* 進德季刊 3, no. 1 (1924), "Huiwu baogao" 會務報告 (Association affairs reports): 7.

Masini, Federico. *The Formation of the Modern Chinese Lexicon and Its Evolution Toward a National Language: The Period from 1840 to 1898*. Berkeley: Project on Linguistic Analysis, 1993.

McDermott, Joseph P. *A Social History of the Chinese Book: Books and Literati Culture in Late Imperial China*. Hong Kong: Hong Kong University Press, 2006.

McDougall, Bonnie S. *Mao Zedong's "Talks at the Yan'an Conference on Literature and Art": A Translation of the 1943 Text with Commentary*. Michigan Papers in Chinese Studies, no. 39. Ann Arbor: Center for Chinese Studies, University of Michigan, 1980.

Meng, Yue. *Shanghai and the Edges of Empires*. Minneapolis: University of Minnesota Press, 2006.

Miles, Steven B. *The Sea of Learning: Mobility and Identity in Nineteenth-Century Guangzhou*. Cambridge, Mass.: Harvard University Asia Center, 2006.

"Minguo ershisan nian yiyue qiri guoyu tongyi choubei weiyuanhui di ershijiu ci changwu weiyuanhui de yijue'an" 民國二十三年一月七日國語統一籌備委員會第二十九次常務委員會的議決案 (January 7, 1934 National Language Unification Preparatory Committee Twenty-Ninth Standing Committee meeting resolutions). *Guoyu zhoukan* 國語週刊, no. 123 (February 5, 1934): 1–2.

Minguo sannian chun Zhonghua shuju gaikuang 民國三年春中華書局概況 (Zhonghua Book Company's general situation in spring 1914). [Shanghai: Zhonghua shuju, 1914].

Mitchell, Timothy. *Colonising Egypt*. Berkeley: University of California Press, 1991.

Mittler, Barbara. *A Continuous Revolution: Making Sense of Cultural Revolution Culture*. Cambridge, Mass.: Harvard University Asia Center, 2012.

———. *A Newspaper for China? Power, Identity, and Change in Shanghai's News Media, 1872–1912*. Cambridge, Mass.: Harvard University Asia Center, 2004.

Moloughney, Brian, and Peter Zarrow, eds. *Transforming History: The Making of a Modern Academic Discipline in Twentieth-Century China*. Hong Kong: Chinese University Press, 2011.

Mugglestone, Lynda. *Lost for Words: The Hidden History of the Oxford English Dictionary*. New Haven, Conn.: Yale University Press, 2005.

Mullaney, Thomas S. *Coming to Terms with the Nation: Ethnic Classification in Modern China*. Berkeley: University of California Press, 2011.

Munro, Donald. *The Concept of Man in Contemporary China*. Ann Arbor: University of Michigan Press, 1977.

Novick, Peter. *That Noble Dream: The "Objectivity Question" and the American Historical Profession*. Cambridge: Cambridge University Press, 1999.

Ohmann, Richard. "Diverging Paths: Books and Magazines in the Transition to Corporate Capitalism." In *A History of the Book in America, Volume 4: Print in Motion; The Expansion of Publishing and Reading in the United States, 1880–1940*, ed. Carl F. Kaestle and Janice A. Radway, 102–15. Chapel Hill: University of North Carolina Press, 2009.

Perry, Elizabeth J. *Anyuan: Mining China's Revolutionary Tradition*. Berkeley: University of California Press, 2012.

Philippovich, [Eugen]. *Jiaotong zhengce* 交通政策 (Transportation policies). Trans. Ma Junwu 馬君武. Shanghai: Zhonghua shuju, 1924.

"Pinqing Daxue congshu weiyuanhui weiyuan han" 聘請大學叢書委員會委員函 (Letter of invitation for members of the University Series Committee). *Shangwu yinshuguan tongxinlu* 商務印書館通信錄, no. 379 (November 15, 1932): 12–13.

Postone, Moishe. *Time, Labor, and Social Domination: A Reinterpretation of Marx's Critical Theory*. Cambridge: Cambridge University Press, 1996.

Pyle, Kenneth B. *The New Generation in Meiji Japan: Problems of Cultural Identity, 1885–1895*. Stanford, Calif.: Stanford University Press, 1987.

Qian Binghuan 钱炳寰. *Zhonghua shuju dashi jiyao* 中华书局大事纪要 (Summary of major events at Zhonghua Book Company). Beijing: Zhonghua shuju 2002.

Qian Mu 錢穆. *Mozi* 墨子. Shanghai: Shangwu yinshuguan, 1930.

Qiao Yong 乔永. "*Ciyuan* bianzuan xiuding bainian jishi" 辞源编纂修订百年记事 (Account of one hundred years of compiling and revising *Ciyuan*). *Chuban shiliao* 出版史料, no. 1 (2009): 121–24.

"Qingdao tebie shi zhengfu xunling, di 288 hao" 青島特別市政府訓令第二八八號 (Order number 288 of the Qingdao Special Municipality government). *Jilin sheng jiaoyuhui yuebao* 吉林省教育會月報, no. 11 (1929): 75–76.

"Qingpu xian Guyan Xiangjiahui xiang gongli diyi xiaoxuexiao guoyu ke jiaoxue shili" 青浦縣固堰香郊匯鄉公立第一小學校國語科教學實例 (A real example of national-language instruction for the Public First Primary School of Guyan Xiangjiahui Township in Qingpu County). *Jiangsu di'er shifan qu xiaoxue jiaoshi yanjiuhui niankan* 江蘇第二師範區小學教師研究會年刊 (May 1924): 198–202.

Qin Shuqiu 秦書秋. "Qingpu xianli di'er xiaoxuexiao guoyuke jiaoxue guocheng juli" 青浦縣立第二小學校國語科教學過程舉例 (An example of the process of national-language instruction at Qingpu County Second Primary School). *Jiangsu di'er shifan qu xiaoxue jiaoshi yanjiuhui niankan* 江蘇第二師範區小學教師研究會年刊 (May 1924): 194–98.

"Qita shiji wenti" 其他實際問題 (Other practical questions). *Jinxiu banyuekan* 進修半月刊 6, no. 19 (1937): 839.

Quanguo jiaoyuhui lianhehui xin xuezhi kecheng biaozhun qicao weiyuanhui 全國教育會聯合會新學制課程標準起草委員會, ed. *Xin xuezhi kecheng biaozhun gangyao* 新學制課程標準綱要 (Outline of the curriculum standards for the New School System). N.p.: n.p., 1924 [1923].

Quan Hua 權驊. "Jiaoyu shiyan xinde" 教育實驗心得 (The results of education research). *Jiaoyu zazhi* 教育雜誌 3, no. 2 (February 10, 1911), "Zhengwen" 徵文 (Solicited writings): 17–23.

Radway, Janice A. "Learned and Literary Print Cultures in an Age of Professionalization and Diversification." In *A History of the Book in America, Volume 4: Print in Motion; The Expansion of Publishing and Reading in the United States, 1880–1940*, ed. Carl F. Kaestle and Janice A. Radway, 197–233. Chapel Hill: University of North Carolina Press, 2009.

Rea, Christopher, and Nicolai Volland, eds. *The Business of Culture: Cultural Entrepreneurs in China and Southeast Asia, 1900–1965*. Vancouver: University of British Columbia Press, 2015.

Reed, Christopher A. *Gutenberg in Shanghai: Chinese Print Capitalism, 1876–1937*. Vancouver: University of British Columbia Press, 2004.

Reed, Christopher A., and Nicolai Volland. "Epilogue: Beyond the Age of Cultural Entrepreneurship, 1949–Present." In *The Business of Culture: Cultural Entrepreneurs in China and Southeast Asia, 1900–1965*, ed. Christopher Rea and Nicolai Volland, 259–82. Vancouver: University of British Columbia Press, 2015.

"Renji biye tongxue mujuan goumai Wanyou wenku" 仁級畢業同學募捐購買萬有文庫 (The Renji graduating class raises funds to purchase the Complete Library). *Jimei zhoukan* 集美週刊, no. 264 (1931): 11.

Richardson, C. H. *Tongji fenxi daolun* 統計分析導論 (An introduction to statistical analysis). Trans. Luo Dafan 羅大凡 and Liang Hong 梁宏. Shanghai: Shangwu yinshuguan, 1948.

Richter, Giles. "Marketing the World: Publishing Entrepreneurs in Meiji Japan, 1870–1912." PhD diss., Columbia University, 1999.

Rogaski, Ruth. *Hygienic Modernity: Meanings of Health and Disease in Treaty-Port China*. Berkeley: University of California Press, 2004.

Rowe, William T. "Political, Social, and Economic Factors Affecting the Transmission of Technical Knowledge in Early Modern China." In *Cultures of Knowledge: Technology in Chinese History*, ed. Dagmar Schäfer, 25–44. Leiden: Brill, 2011.

——. *Saving the World: Chen Hongmou and Elite Consciousness in Eighteenth-Century China*. Stanford, Calif.: Stanford University Press, 2001.

Rubin, Joan Shelley. *The Making of Middlebrow Culture*. Chapel Hill: University of North Carolina Press, 1992.

Sang Bing. "The Convergence and Divergence of China's Written and Spoken Languages: Reassessing the Vernacular Language During the May Fourth Period." *Twentieth-Century China* 38, no. 1 (January 2013): 71–93.

Schäfer, Dagmar, ed. *Cultures of Knowledge: Technology in Chinese History*. Leiden: Brill, 2011.

Schneider, Laurence A. *Ku Chieh-kang and China's New History: Nationalism and the Quest for Alternative Traditions*. Berkeley: University of California Press, 1971.

——. "National Essence and the New Intelligentsia." In *The Limits of Change: Essays on Conservative Alternatives in Republican China*, ed. Charlotte Furth, 57–89. Cambridge, Mass.: Harvard University Press, 1976.

Schoppa, R. Keith. *Chinese Elites and Political Change: Zhejiang Province in the Early Twentieth Century*. Cambridge, Mass.: Harvard University Press, 1982.

Schwarcz, Vera. *The Chinese Enlightenment: Intellectuals and the Legacy of the May Fourth Movement of 1919*. Berkeley: University of California Press, 1986.

"Shandong sheng zhengfu jiaoyuting bei'an wenshu yilan biao" 山東省政府教育廳備案文書一覽表 (Overview table of the correspondence on file from the Shandong Provincial Government Department of Education). *Shandong jiaoyu xingzheng zhoubao* 山東教育行政週報, no. 109 (1930), "Biaoge" 表格 (Tables): 14–15.

Shanghai chubanzhi bianzuan weiyuanhui 上海出版志編纂委员会. *Shanghai chubanzhi* 上海出版志 (Shanghai publishing gazetteer). Shanghai: Shanghai shehui kexue yuan chubanshe, 2000.

Shangwu yinshuguan 商務印書館, comp. *Shangwu yinshuguan fuye hou gaikuang* 商務印書館
復業後概況 (Commercial Press's general situation after its revival of operations). [Shang-
hai]: [Shangwu yinshuguan], [1934].

——, comp. *Shangwu yinshuguan jiushinian, 1897–1987—Wo he Shangwu yinshuguan* 商务印书
馆九十年 1897–1987—我和商务印书馆 (Ninety years of Commercial Press, 1897–1987:
Me and Commercial Press). Beijing: Shangwu yinshuguan, 1987.

——, comp. *Shangwu yinshuguan jiushiwu nian, 1897–1992—Wo he Shangwu yinshuguan* 商务
印书馆九十五年 1897–1992—我和商务印书馆 (Ninety-five years of Commercial Press,
1897–1992: Me and Commercial Press). Beijing: Shangwu yinshuguan, 1992.

Shangwu yinshuguan chuban xinshu 商務印書館初版新書 (Commercial Press's first-edition new
books). January–March 1950. N.p.: Shangwu yinshuguan, 1950.

"Shangwu yinshuguan dongshi huiyi lu" 商務印書館董事會議錄 (Record of the Commercial Press board of directors meetings). Unpublished manuscript of excerpted notes,
1922–1954.

"Shangwu yinshuguan fanyin *Siku quanshu*" 商務印書館翻印四庫全書 (Commercial Press's
republication of the *Complete Book of Four Treasuries*). *Aiguobao* 愛國報, no. 22 (1924):
28–29.

Shangwu yinshuguan gufen youxian gongsi jiesuan baogao 商務印書館股份有限公司結算報告 (Final
budget report for the Commercial Press joint stock company limited). [Shanghai:
Shangwu yinshuguan], 1925, 1927, 1929, 1930.

Shangwu yinshuguan ni yin Siku quanshu shimo 商務印書館擬印四庫全書始末 (The whole story
of Commercial Press's planning to reprint the *Complete Book of Four Treasuries*). Manuscript documents, Shanghai Municipal Library, 1924–19??.

"Shangwu yinshuguan shixing bianyi gongzuo baochou biaozhun banfa jiufen ji" 商務印
書館試行編譯工作報酬標準辦法糾紛記 (Record of the controversy over Commercial
Press's trial methods for pay standards for compiling and translating work). In *Zhongguo
xiandai chuban shiliao* 中國現代出版史料 (Historical materials for modern Chinese publishing), Ding bian 丁編 (Fourth series), ed. Zhang Jinglu 張靜盧, 2:414–22. Beijing:
Zhonghua shuju, 1959.

Shangwu yinshuguan zhilüe 商務印書館志略 (A general outline of Commercial Press). [Shang-
hai]: Shangwu yinshuguan, 1926.

"Shanhou banshichu fenzi tonggao (zhaideng), fenzi di'er hao" 善後辦事處分字通告 (摘登)，分字
第二號 (Rehabilitation office separate announcements [selected records], announcement number two)." *Shangwu yinshuguan tongxinlu* 商務印書館通信錄, no. 376 (July 10,
1932): 19.

Shao, Qin. *Culturing Modernity: The Nantong Model, 1890–1930*. Stanford, Calif.: Stanford
University Press, 2004.

——. "Tempest over Teapots: The Vilification of Teahouse Culture in Early Republican
China." *Journal of Asian Studies* 57, no. 4 (November 1998): 1009–41.

Shen Fu. *Six Records of a Floating Life*. Harmondsworth, Middlesex, UK: Penguin, 1983.

Shen Qianyi 沈乾一. *Zhongyi qianshuo* 中醫淺說 (Chinese medicine). Shanghai: Shangwu
yinshuguan, 1931.

Shen Shoumei 沈瘦梅. "Ping Shijie shuju chuban de guoyu wen duben" 評世界書局初版的
國語文讀本 (Critiquing the national-language reader published by World Book Company). *Minguo ribao: Juewu* 民國日報：覺悟 1, no. 23 (January 23, 1926): 2–3.

Shen Yi 沈頤 et al. [*Xinbian chunji shiye*] *Zhonghua guowen jiaokeshu* 新編春季始業中華國文教
科書 ([New edition] spring-start Zhonghua Chinese textbook). 6 vols. Shanghai: Zhonghua shuju, 1915 [1914].

[Shen] Zhifang [沈]知方. "Cong jihua dao chushu" 從計劃到出書 (From planning to publication). *Shijie* 世界 1, no. 1 (1928): 13–16.

Sheng Z W 生 Z W. "Shanghai zhongdeng shehui de shengji" 上海中等社會的生計 (The livelihood of Shanghai's midlevel society). *Jinde jikan* 進德季刊 [I], no. I (1922), "Yan-lun" 言論 (Open discussion): 10–12.

Shi Jianqiao 史建桥, Qiao Yong 乔永, and Xu Congquan 徐从权, eds. *Ciyuan yanjiu lunwen ji* 辞源研究论文集 (Collection of writings on *Ciyuan*). Beijing: Shangwu yinshuguan, 2009.

"Shubao jieshao" 書報介紹 (Book and journal introductions). *Chudeng jiaoyu* 初等教育 I, no. 2 (1923): 295–96.

Shu Xincheng 舒新城. *Shu xincheng riji* 舒新城日記 (Shu Xincheng's diary [1929–1960]). 34 vols. Shanghai: Shanghai cishu chubanshe, 2013.

——. *Wo he jiaoyu* 我和教育 (Me and education). Taipei: Longwen chubanshe, 1990.

——. *Xiandai jiaoyufa* 現代教育法 (Modern educational methods). Shanghai: Shangwu yin-shuguan, 1930.

——. [*Xin zhongxue jiaokeshu*] *chuji gongmin keben* 新中學教科書初級公民課本 ([New middle-school textbook] lower-level civics textbook). 3 vols. Shanghai: Zhonghua shuju, 1923–1924.

——. "Zhonghua shuju bianjisuo" 中華書局編輯所 (Zhonghua Book Company's Editing Department). In *Kuanggulu* 狂顧錄 (Record of wild reflections). Shanghai: Zhonghua shuju, 1936.

Shu Xincheng 舒新城, Shen Yi 沈頤, Xu Yuangao 徐元誥, and Zhang Xiang 張相 et al., eds. *Cihai* 辭海. 2 vols. Shanghai: Zhonghua shuju, 1936–1937.

Sibu beiyao shumu tiyao 四部備要書目提要 (Catalog and abstracts of *Sibu beiyao*). Shanghai: Zhonghua shuju, n.d.

Sibu beiyao yangben 四部備要樣本 (Sample book of *Sibu beiyao*). [Shanghai]: Zhonghua shuju, n.d.

Sibu congkan mulu, fu qi fanli yuyue zhangcheng yangben 四部叢刊目錄附啟凡例預約章程樣本 (*Sibu congkan* catalog with appendixes of announcement, introduction, advance-order rules, and sample). N.p.: n.p., [1920?].

Sibu congkan shulu 四部叢刊書錄 (Reading notes for *Sibu congkan*). [Shanghai: Shangwu yin-shuguan], n.d.

"*Siku quanshu* chuban wenti" 四庫全書出版問題 (Publishing issues for the *Complete Book of Four Treasuries*). *Hubei jiaoyu yuekan* 湖北教育月刊 I, no. I (September 1933): 192–95.

"*Siku quanshu* de jinxi" 四庫全書的今昔 (The past and present of the *Complete Book of Four Treasuries*). *Xinghua zhoukan* 興華週刊29, no. 48 (1932): 4.

"*Siku quanshu* yingyin zhi zhongchuo" 四庫全書影印之中輟 (Suspension in midcourse for reprinting of the *Complete Book of Four Treasuries*). *Tushuguanxue jikan* 圖書館學季刊 I, no. 3 (1926): 540.

"*Siku quanshu* zhenben chuji" 四庫全書珍本初集 (First collection of the rare books in the *Complete Book of Four Treasuries*). In *Sibu congkan sanbian mulu* 四部叢刊三編目錄 (Catalog for the third compilation of *Sibu congkan*). [Shanghai]: Shangwu yinshuguan, 1935.

Skinner, G. William. "Marketing and Social Structure in Rural China, Part I." *Journal of Asian Studies* 24, no. I (1964): 3–43.

——. "Mobility Strategies in Late Imperial China: A Regional Systems Analysis." In *Regional Analysis, Volume I: Economic Systems*, ed. Carol A. Smith, 327–64. New York: Academic Press, 1976.

Smith, J. *Su'e de funü* 蘇俄的婦女 (The Soviet Union's women). Trans. Cai Yongchang 蔡詠裳 and Dong Shaoming 懂紹明. Shanghai: Zhonghua shuju, 1930.

Sohn-Rethel, Alfred. *Intellectual and Manual Labour: A Critique of Epistemology*. London: Mac-millan, 1978.

Somers, Magaret. "The Privatization of Citizenship: How to Unthink a Knowledge Culture." In *Beyond the Cultural Turn: New Directions in the Study of Society and Culture*, ed. Victoria E. Bonnell and Lynn Hunt, 121–61. Berkeley: University of California Press, 1999.

Song Yuanfang 宋原放, ed. *Zhongguo chuban shiliao: Jindai bufen* 中國出版史料：近代部份 (Historical materials of Chinese publishing: Modern portion). Vol. 3. Wuhan: Hubei jiaoyu chubanshe, 2004.

——, ed. *Zhongguo chuban shiliao: Xiandai bufen* 中国出版史料：现代部分 (Historical materials for Chinese publishing: Contemporary portion). Vol. 3.1. Jinan: Shandong jiaoyu chubanshe, 2000.

Spence, Jonathan D. *Mao Zedong*. New York: Viking, 1999.

Stableton, J. K. *Zhong xiao xue xundao shishifa* 中小學訓導實施法 (Your problems and mine in the guidance of youth). Trans. Zhang Shengzu 張繩祖. Shanghai: Shangwu yinshuguan, 1933.

Stocking, George. *Victorian Anthropology*. New York: Free Press, 1987.

Sun Benwen 孫本文. *Renkou lun ABC* 人口論 ABC (The ABCs of population theories). Shanghai: Shijie shuju, 1928.

——. *Shehui xinlixue* 社會心理學 (Social psychology). Shanghai: Shangwu yinshuguan, 1946.

——. *Shehuixue ABC* 社會學 ABC (The ABCs of Sociology). Shanghai: Shijie shuju, 1929.

——. *Shehuixue yuanli* 社會學原理 (Principles of sociology). Shanghai: Shangwu yinshuguan, 1935.

——. *Xiandai Zhongguo shehui wenti* 現代中國社會問題 (Modern Chinese social problems). 4 vols. Chongqing: Shangwu yinshuguan, 1942–1946.

Sun Yuxiu 孫毓修. "Jiangnan yueshu ji" 江南閱書記 (Record of reviewing books in Jiangnan). Manuscript, Shanghai Municipal Library (digital file), 1919.

——. "*Sibu juyao* shuolüe" 四部舉要說略 (Summary of *Sibu juyao*). Manuscript, Shanghai Municipal Library (digital file), n.d.

Suoben Sibu congkan chubian shulu 縮本四部叢刊初編書錄 (Reading notes for the first series of the pocket-size *Sibu congkan*). [Shanghai]: Shangwu yinshuguan, 1936.

Tanaka, Stefan. *Japan's Orient: Rendering Pasts into History*. Berkeley: University of California Press, 1993.

Tang, Xiaobing. *Global Space and the Nationalist Discourse of Modernity: The Historical Thinking of Liang Qichao*. Stanford, Calif.: Stanford University Press, 1996.

Tang Binhua 湯彬華. *Funü yundong ABC* 婦女運動 ABC (The ABCs of the women's movement). Shanghai: Shijie shuju, 1929 [1928].

Tang Xifen 唐惜分, Chen Lijiang 陳禮江, Cui Daiyang 崔戴陽, Xu Xiling 徐錫齡, Zhuang Zexuan 莊澤宣, Chen Ziming 陳子明, and Hu Yi 胡毅. *Geguo jiaoyu de zhexue beijing* 各國教育的哲學背境 (The philosophical background of each country's education). Shanghai: Shangwu yinshuguan, 1934.

Tao Menghe 陶孟和. *Shehui yu jiaoyu* 社會與教育 (Society and education). Shanghai: Shangwu yinshuguan, 1922.

——. [*Xin xuezhi gaozhong jiaokeshu*] *shehui wenti* 新學制高中教科書社會問題 ([New School System high school textbook] social issues). Shanghai: Shangwu yinshuguan, 1924.

Thompson, E. P. "Time, Work-Discipline, and Industrial Capitalism." *Past and Present*, no. 38 (December 1967): 56–97.

Thompson, Roger. *China's Local Councils in the Age of Constitutional Reform, 1898–1911*. Cambridge, Mass.: Harvard University Press, 1995.

"Ting ling ge jiaoju beikuan dinggou Wanyou wenku" 廳令各教局備款定購萬有文庫 (The department orders each bureau of education to prepare funds to order the Complete Library). *Fujian jiaoyuting zhoukan* 福建教育廳週刊, no. 137 (1932): 17.

"Tongren Wusa shijian houyuanhui weiyuanhui zuzhi ji jingguo" 同人五卅事件後援會委員會組織及經過 (Organization and process of our colleagues' May Thirtieth Incident Support Association Committee). *Lizhi zazhi* 勵志雜誌, no. 3 (1925): 56–59.

"Touxian" 頭銜 (Official title). *Shijie* 世界 1, no. 1 (1928): 35–36.

Trouillot, Michel-Rolph. *Silencing the Past: Power and the Production of History.* Boston: Beacon Press, 1995.

"Tushuguan jinkuang" 圖書館近況 (The recent situation at the library). *Guangdong Guomin daxue zhoubao* 廣東國民大學週報 2, no. 4 (1929): 15.

"Tushuguan jinxun size" 圖書館近訊四則 (Four items of recent news about the library). *Jiaoda sanrikan* 交大三日刊, no. 12 (1929): 2.

U, Eddy. *Disorganizing China: Counter-Bureaucracy and the Decline of Socialism.* Stanford, Calif.: Stanford University Press, 2007.

——. "Reification of the Chinese Intellectual: On the Origins of the CCP Concept of 'Zhishifenzi.'" *Modern China* 35, no. 6 (November 2009): 604–31.

Venezky, Richard, with Carl F. Kaestle. "From McGuffey to Dick and Jane: Reading Textbooks." In *A History of the Book in America, Volume 4: Print in Motion; The Expansion of Publishing and Reading in the United States, 1880–1940*, ed. Carl F. Kaestle and Janice A. Radway, 415–30. Chapel Hill: University of North Carolina Press, 2009.

Volland, Nicolai. "The Control of the Media in the People's Republic of China." PhD diss., University of Heidelberg, 2003.

——. "Cultural Entrepreneurship in the Twilight: The Shanghai Book Trade Association, 1945–1957." In *The Business of Culture: Cultural Entrepreneurs in China and Southeast Asia, 1900–1965*, ed. Christopher Rea and Nicolai Volland, 234–58. Vancouver: University of British Columbia Press, 2015.

——. *Socialist Cosmopolitanism: The Chinese Literary Universe, 1945–1965.* New York: Columbia University Press, 2017.

Wagner, Rudolf G. "The Canonization of May Fourth." In *The Appropriation of Cultural Capital: China's May Fourth Project*, ed. Milena Doleželová-Velingerová and Oldřich Král, with Graham Sanders, 66–120. Cambridge, Mass.: Harvard University Asia Center, 2001.

Walker, Gregory. *Soviet Book Publishing Policy.* Cambridge: Cambridge University Press, 1978.

——. "Soviet Publishing Since the October Revolution." In *Books in Russia and the Soviet Union: Past and Present*, ed. Miranda Beaven Remnek, 59–91. Wiesbaden: Harrassowitz, 1991.

Wang, Fei-hsien. "Creating New Order in the Knowledge Economy: The Curious Journey of Copyright in China, 1868–1937." PhD diss., University of Chicago, 2012.

Wang, Q. Edward. *Inventing China through History: The May Fourth Approach to Historiography.* Albany: State University of New York Press, 2001.

Wang, Y. C. *Chinese Intellectuals and the West, 1872–1900.* Chapel Hill: University of North Carolina Press, 1966.

Wang, Youpeng. "Research Note: Shanghai's Lexicographical Publishing House Library as a Resource for Research on Republican Period Popular Culture and Education." Trans. Robert Culp. *Republican China* 22, no. 2 (April 1997): 103–9.

Wang, Zheng. *Women in the Chinese Enlightenment: Oral and Textual Histories.* Berkeley: University of California Press, 1999.

Wang Boxiang 王伯祥. *Wang Boxiang riji* 王伯祥日記 (Wang Boxiang's diary). 44 vols. Beijing: Guojia tushuguan chubanshe, 2011.

Wang Danru 王澹如. *Guoji maoyi ABC* 國際貿易 ABC (The ABCs of international trade). Shanghai: Shijie shuju, 1928.

Wang Jianhui 王建輝. *Wenhua de Shangwu—Wang Yunwu zhuanti yanjiu* 文化的商務—王雲五專題研究 (Cultural Commercial Press: Specialized research on Wang Yunwu). Beijing: Shangwu yinshuguan, 2000.

Wang Jianjun 王建军. "Lun jindai baihuawen jiaokeshu de shengchan" 论近代白话文教科书的生产 (The production of modern vernacular-language textbooks). *Huadong shifan daxue xuebao* 华东师范大学学报, no. 2 (1996): 63–72.

——. *Zhongguo jindai jiaokeshu fazhan yanjiu* 中国近代教科书发展研究 (Study of the development of China's modern textbooks). Guangzhou: Guangdong jiaoyu chubanshe, 1996.

Wang Jiarong 汪家熔. "Ciyuan, Cihai de kaichuangxing" 辞源辞海的开创性 (The innovativeness of *Ciyuan* and *Cihai*). *Cishu yanjiu* 辞书研究, no. 4 (2001): 130–45.

——. *Shangwu yinshuguan shi ji qita—Wang Jiarong chubanshi yanjiu wenji* 商務印書館史及其他—汪家熔出版史研究文集 (The history of Commercial Press and other things: Wang Jiarong's collected writings on his research on the history of publishing). Beijing: Zhongguo shuji chubanshe chuban, 1998.

Wang Junsheng 王駿聲. *Youzhiyuan jiaoyu* 幼稚園教育 (Kindergarten education). Shanghai: Shangwu yinshuguan, [1926].

Wang Min 王敏. *Shanghai baoren shehui shenghuo 1872–1949* 上海报人社会生活 (1872–1949) (Shanghai journalists' social lives [1872–1949]). Shanghai: Shanghai cishu chubanshe, 2008.

Wang Runhua 王潤華. "Qianyan" 前言 (Foreword). In *Wang Boxiang riji* 王伯祥日記 (Wang Boxiang's diary), by Wang Boxiang 王伯祥, vol. 1. Beijing: Guojia tushuguan chubanshe, 2011.

Wang Shaozeng 王紹曾. "Shangwu yinshuguan Jiaoshichu de huiyi" 商務印書館校史處的回憶 (Reminiscences of Commercial Press's Office for Historical Collation). In *Mulu banben jiaokan xue lunji* 目錄版本校勘學論集 (Collected writings on cataloging, editions, and collation), ed. Gu Meihua 顧美華. Shanghai: Guji chubanshe, 2005.

Wang Shihua 王湜華. *Wang Boxiang zhuan* 王伯祥傳 (Biography of Wang Boxiang). Beijing: Zhonghua shuju, 2008.

Wang Shijie 王世杰. *Bijiao xianfa* 比較憲法 (Comparative constitutions). Shanghai: Shangwu yinshuguan, 1933 [1927].

Wang Shounan 王壽南, comp. *Wang Yunwu xiansheng nianpu chugao* 王雲五先生年譜初稿 (Initial draft of the chronological biography of Mr. Wang Yunwu). 4 vols. Taipei: Taiwan Shangwu yinshuguan, 1987.

Wang Shulin 王書林. *Jiaoyu tongji xue* 教育統計學 (Educational statistics). Shanghai: Shangwu yinshuguan, 1937.

Wang Yiyai 王益厓. *Haiyang xue ABC* 海洋學 ABC (The ABCs of oceanography). Shanghai: Shijie shuju, 1929.

Wang Youpeng 王有朋. *Zhongguo jindai zhong xiao xue jiaokeshu zongmu* 中國近代中小學教科書總目 (Comprehensive catalog of China's modern secondary and primary textbooks). Shanghai: Cishu chubanshe, 2010.

Wang Yuguang 王余光 and Wu Yonggui 吳永贵. *Zhongguo chuban tongshi: Minguo juan* 中國出版通史:民国卷 (Comprehensive history of Chinese publishing: Volume on the Republic). Beijing: Zhongguo shuji chubanshe, 2008.

Wang Yunwu 王雲五. *Shangwu yinshuguan yu xin jiaoyu nianpu* 商務印書館與新教育年譜 (Yearly record of Commercial Press and the new education). Taipei: Taiwan Shangwu yinshuguan, 1973.

——. "Yinxing Wanyou wenku di'er ji yuanqi" 印行萬有文庫第二集緣起 (Genesis of the publication of the second collection of the Complete Library). In *Wanyou wenku di'er ji mulu* 萬有文庫第二集目錄 (Catalog for the second collection of the Complete Library), ed. Wang Yunwu 王雲五 et al. Shanghai: Shangwu yinshuguan, [1934].

——. "Yinxing Wanyou wenku di yi er ji jianbian yuanqi" 印行萬有文庫第一二集簡編緣起 (Genesis of the abridged first and second collections of the Complete Library). In *Wanyou wenku diyi er ji jianbian mulu* 萬有文庫第一二集簡編目錄 (Catalog of the first and second abridged collections of the Complete Library), ed. Wang Yunwu 王雲五 et al. [Shanghai]: Shangwu yinshuguan, [1939].

——. "Yinxing Wanyou wenku yuanqi" 印行萬有文庫緣起 (Genesis of the publication of the Complete Library). In *Wanyou wenku diyiji yiqianzhong mulu* 萬有文庫第一集一千種目錄 (Catalog of one thousand titles of the first collection of the Complete Library), ed. Wang Yunwu 王雲五 et al. [Shanghai]: Shangwu yinshuguan, [1929].

Wang Yunwu 王雲五 et al., eds. *Wanyou wenku di'er ji mulu* 萬有文庫第二集目錄 (Catalog for the second collection of the Complete Library). Shanghai: Shangwu yinshuguan, [1934].

——, eds. *Wanyou wenku diyi er ji jianbian mulu* 萬有文庫第一二集簡編目錄 (Catalog of the first and second abridged collections of the Complete Library). Shanghai: Shangwu yinshuguan, [1939].

——, eds. *Wanyou wenku diyiji yiqianzhong mulu* 萬有文庫第一集一千種目錄 (Catalog of one thousand titles of the first collection of the Complete Library). [Shanghai]: Shangwu yinshuguan, [1929].

Wang Zhen 王箴. *Putong huaxue* 普通化學 (General chemistry). Shanghai: Shangwu yinshuguan, 1954 [1952].

Wang Zhiyi 王知伊. *Kaiming shudian jishi* 开明书店纪事 (Historical record of Kaiming Bookstore). Taiyuan: Shanxi renmin chubanshe, 1991.

"Wanyou wenku bianyi fanli" 萬有文庫編譯凡例 (Introduction to the compiling of the Complete Library). In *Wanyou wenku diyiji yiqianzhong mulu* 萬有文庫第一集一千種目錄 (Catalog of one thousand titles of the first collection of the Complete Library), ed. Wang Yunwu 王雲五 et al. [Shanghai]: Shangwu yinshuguan, [1929].

"Wanyou wenku changxiao" 萬有文庫暢銷 (The Complete Library sells briskly). *Dushu yuekan* 讀書月刊 1, no. 2 (1930): 209–10.

"Wanyou wenku di yi er qi yi jidao" 萬有文庫第一二期已寄到 (The first and second installments of the Complete Library have already been mailed to the school). *Wuzhong zhoukan* 五中週刊, no. 90 (May 18, 1931): 1.

"Wanyou wenku diyiji yuyue jianzhang" 萬有文庫第一集預約簡章 (Advance-order procedures for the Complete Library, first collection). In *Wanyou wenku diyiji yiqianzhong mulu* 萬有文庫第一集一千種目錄 (Catalog of one thousand titles of the first collection of the Complete Library), ed. Wang Yunwu 王雲五 et al. [Shanghai]: Shangwu yinshuguan, [1929].

Warner, Michael. *The Letters of the Republic: Publication and the Public Sphere in Eighteenth-Century America*. Cambridge, Mass.: Harvard University Press, 1990.

Watson, James L. "Rites or Beliefs? The Construction of a Unified Culture in Late Imperial China." In *China's Quest for National Identity*, ed. Lowell Dittmer and Samuel S. Kim, 80–103. Ithaca, N.Y.: Cornell University Press, 1993.

Wei Bingxin 魏冰心 et al., eds. [*Xiaoxue chuji xuesheng yong*] *guoyu duben* 小學初級學生用國語讀本 ([For use by lower-primary students] national-language reader). Shanghai: Shijie shuju, [1932]. Reprint, Shanghai: Shanghai kexue jishu wenxian chubanshe, 2005.

Wenzhou 文宙. "Suigan: Shijie congshu, Xinwenhua congshu" 隨感：《世界叢書》《新文化叢書》" (Informal essay: World Series and New Culture Series). *Shaonian shehui banyuekan* 少年社會半月刊 2, no. 6 (1920): [27].

West, James L., III. *American Authors and the Literary Marketplace since 1900*. Philadelphia: University of Pennsylvania Press, 1990.

Weston, Timothy B. *The Power of Position: Beijing University, Intellectuals, and Chinese Political Culture, 1898–1929*. Berkeley: University of California Press, 2004.

White, Lynn T. *Policies of Chaos: The Organizational Causes of Violence in China's Cultural Revolution*. Princeton, N.J.: Princeton University Press, 1989.

Whyte, William H. *Organization Man*. Philadelphia: University of Pennsylvania Press, 2013.

Wu, Hung. *Remaking Beijing: Tiananmen Square and the Creation of a Political Space*. Chicago: University of Chicago Press, 2005.

Wu Jingshan 吳靜山. *Sheying xue ABC* 攝影學 ABC (The ABCs of photography). Shanghai: Shijie shuju, 1928.

Wu Junsheng 吳俊升. *Jiaoyu zhexue dagang* 教育哲學大綱 (Outline of educational philosophy). Shanghai: Shangwu yinshuguan, 1935.

Wu Moyi 吳默宜. "Qingpu xianli diyi xiaoxuexiao guoyu jiaoxue guocheng" 青浦縣立第一小學校國語教學過程 (The process of national-language instruction at Qingpu County Number One Primary School). *Jiangsu di'er shifan qu xiaoxue jiaoshi yanjiuhui niankan* 江蘇第二師範區小學教師研究會年刊 (May 1924): 239–43.

Wu Shirui 吳世瑞. *Jingjixue yuanli* 經濟學原理 (Principles of economics). Shanghai: Shangwu yinshuguan, 1935.

Wu Xiang 吳襄. *Shenglixue dagang* 生理學大綱 (Outline of physiology). Shanghai: Shangwu yinshuguan, 1952.

Wu Yanyin 吳研因, Zhuang Shi 莊適, and Shen Qi 沈圻. *Xin xuezhi guoyu jiaokeshu* 新學制國語教科書 (New School System national-language textbook). Shanghai: Shangwu yinshuguan, 1923. Reprint, Tianjin: Tianjin guji chubanshe, 2013.

Xiang Da 向達. *Zhongwai jiaotong xiaoshi* 中外交通小史 (Communications between China and Foreign Lands with Respect to Cultural Diffusion). Shanghai: Shangwu yinshuguan, 1930.

Xiaoxue bu tongren 小學部同人. "Benju bianjisuo xin xuezhi xiaoxue jiaokeshu xuanyan" 本局編輯新學制小學教科書宣言 (Declaration regarding the New School System primary-school textbooks compiled by this company). *Shijie yuekan* 世界月刊, no. 1 (1924), "Lunzhu" 論著 (Treatises): 6–7.

"Xiaoxue bu you tian bianjiyuan liangren" 小學部又添編輯員兩人 (The Primary School Division further added two editorial staff members). *Shijie yuekan* 世界月刊, no. 2 (1924), "Zalu" 雜錄 (Miscellaneous records): 1.

"Xiaoxue bu zengtian bianjiyuan" 小學部增添編輯員 (The Primary School Division added editorial staff members). *Shijie yuekan* 世界月刊, no. 1 (1924), "Zalu" 雜錄 (Miscellaneous records): 1.

Xie Liuyi 謝六逸. *Shenhua xue ABC* 神話學 ABC (The ABCs of mythology). Shanghai: Shijie shuju, 1928.

Xu, Xiaoqun. *Chinese Professionals and the Republican State: The Rise of Professional Associations in Shanghai, 1912–1937*. Cambridge: Cambridge University Press, 2001.

"Xunling di ererba hao (shisi nian siyue sanri)" 訓令第二二八號（十四年四月三日）(Order number 228 [April 3, 1925]). *Fujian jiaoyu yuekan* 福建教育月刊 2, no. 8 (1925): 27–28.

"Xunling di yierjiu hao (jiunian eryue shisanri)" 訓令第一二九號（九年二月十三日）(Order number 129 [February 13, 1920]). *Jiangxi jiaoyu xingzheng yuebao* 江西教育行政月報 3, no. 2 (1920): 38.

"Xunling ge xian jiaoyuju zhongdeng yishang xuexiao shengli tushuguan ling zhuoliang qingxing caigou Shangwu yinshuguan Wanyou wenku you" 訓令各教育局中等以上學校省立圖書館令酌量情形採購商務印書館萬有文庫由 (Order to each county bureau of education, middle school and higher, and the provincial library to consider the circumstances and purchase Commercial Press's Complete Library). *Jiangxi jiaoyu gongbao* 江西教育公報 3, no. 12 (1929): 28–29.

"Xunling quanxuesuo zhuanzhi benyi xuejie zhuoliang daigou *Sibu congkan*" 訓令勸學所轉知本邑學界酌量採購四部叢刊 (Order to the Education Promotion Office to in turn notify this city's academic circles to consider buying *Sibu congkan*). *Jiangshan gongbao* 江山公報, no. 3 (1920): 13–15.

Xu Sitong 徐嗣同. *Shehui kexue mingzhu tijie* 社會科學名著題解 (Explanatory notes on famous works of social science). Shanghai: Zhonghua shuju, 1932.

Xu Weinan 徐慰南. "ABC congshu fakan zhiqu" ABC 叢書發刊旨趣 (The purpose of launching the ABC Series). In *Baoxianxue ABC* 保險學 ABC (The ABCs of insurance), ed. Zhang Bozhen 張伯箴. Shanghai: Shijie shuju, 1929.

Xu Youchun 徐友春 et al., eds. *Minguo renwu da cidian* 民國人物大辭典 (Biographical dictionary of Republican China). Shijiazhuang: Hebei renmin chubanshe, 1991.

Yang, Chia-ling, and Roderick Whitfield, eds. *Lost Generation: Luo Zhenyu, Qing Loyalists and the Formation of Modern Chinese Culture*. London: Saffron, 2013.

Yang Kuisong 杨奎松. *Renbuzhu de "guanhuai": 1949 nian qianhou de shusheng yu zhengzhi* 忍不住的"关怀"：1949年前后的书生与政治 (Unbearable "care": Scholars and politics before and after 1949). Guilin: Guangxi shifan daxue chubanshe, 2013.

Yang Zheming 楊哲明. *Shizheng gongcheng ABC* 市政工程 ABC (The ABCs of municipal government engineering). Shanghai: Shijie shuju, 1929.

——. *Shizheng guanli ABC* 市政管理 ABC (The ABCs of municipal management). Shanghai: Shijie shuju, 1928.

——. *Shizheng jihua ABC* 市政計畫 ABC (The ABCs of urban planning). Shanghai: Shijie shuju, 1929.

——. *Shizheng zuzhi ABC* 市政組織 ABC (The ABCs of municipal government organization). Shanghai: Shijie shuju, 1930.

Yan Jiaqi and Gao Gao. *Turbulent Decade: A History of the Cultural Revolution*. Trans. and ed. D. W. Y. Kwok. Honolulu: University of Hawai`i Press, 1990.

Yao Wenyuan 姚文元. "Liangge bianji tongzhi de xiangfa" 两个编辑同志的想法 (Two editor comrades' mind-sets). *Wenhuibao* 文汇报, May 13, 1962.

Ye, Weili. *Seeking Modernity in China's Name: Chinese Students in the United States, 1900–1927*. Stanford, Calif.: Stanford University Press, 2001.

Yeh, Catherine Vance. "The Life-Style of Four *Wenren* in Late Qing Shanghai." *Harvard Journal of Asiatic Studies* 57, no. 2 (December 1997): 419–70.

Yeh, Wen-hsin. *The Alienated Academy: Culture and Politics in Republican China, 1919–1937*. Cambridge, Mass.: Harvard University Asia Center, 1990.

——. "Progressive Journalism and Shanghai's Petty Urbanites: Zou Taofen and the *Shenghuo* Enterprise, 1926–1945." In *Shanghai Sojourners*, ed. Frederic Wakeman Jr. and Wen-hsin Yeh, 186–238. Berkeley: Institute of East Asian Studies, University of California, 1992.

——. *Provincial Passages: Culture, Space, and the Origins of Chinese Communism*. Berkeley: University of California Press, 1996.

——. *Shanghai Splendor: Economic Sentiments in the Making of Modern China, 1843–1949*. Berkeley: University of California Press, 2007.

Ye Shaojun 葉紹鈞. [*Xiaoxue chuji xuesheng yong*] *Kaiming guoyu keben* 小學初級學生用開明國語課本 (Kaiming's national-language textbook for lower-primary students). 8 vols. Shanghai: Kaiming shudian, 1932.

"Yingyin *Siku quanshu* heyi puji wenhua" 影印四庫全書何以普及文化 (How will reprinting the *Complete Book of Four Treasuries* spread culture?). *Xinghua* 興華 22, no. 39 (1925): 3.

Yin Shouguang 殷壽光. *Fenpei lun ABC* 分配論 ABC (The ABCs of theories of distribution). Shanghai: Shijie shuju, 1928.

"Yinxing Daxue congshu tiaoli" 印行大學叢書條例 (Regulations for publication of the University Series [October 1932]). *Shangwu yinshuguan tongxinlu* 商務印書館通信錄, no. 379 (November 15, 1932): 3–4.

"Yinxing *Sibu congkan* qi" 印行四部叢刊啟 (Explaining the publication of *Sibu congkan*). In *Sibu congkan shulu* 四部叢刊書錄 (Reading notes for *Sibu congkan*), ed. Hanfenlou 涵芬樓. [Shanghai: Shangwu yinshuguan], n.d.

Yu Xiaoyao 俞筱堯 and Liu Yanjie 劉彥捷, eds. *Lufei Kui yu Zhonghua shuju* 陸費逵與中華書局 (Lufei Kui and Zhonghua Book Company). Beijing: Zhonghua shuju, 2002.

Zarrow, Peter. *Educating China: Knowledge, Society, and Textbooks in a Modernizing World, 1902–1937*. Cambridge: Cambridge University Press, 2015.

Zengdiyongzhilang 增地庸治朗. *Jingying jingji xue* 經營經濟學 (The study of operational economics). Trans. Pan Nianzhi 潘念之. Shanghai: Zhonghua shuju, 1931.

Zhang Jiangshu 張江樹. *Lilun huaxue shiyan* 理論化學實驗 (Experiments in theoretical chemistry). Shanghai: Shangwu yinshuguan, 1949 [1945].

Zhang Jiatai 張家泰. *Gongshang guanli ABC* 工商管理 ABC (The ABCs of industrial and commercial management). Shanghai: Shijie shuju, 1929.

Zhang Qiyun 張其昀. [*Xin xuezhi gaoji zhongxue jiaokeshu*] *benguo dili* 新學制高級中學教科書本國地理 ([New School System upper-middle-school textbook] Chinese geography). 2 vols. Shanghai: Shangwu yinshuguan, 1928 [1926–1928].

Zhang Renfeng 张人凤 and Liu Hecheng 柳和城, comps. *Zhang Yuanji nianpu changbian* 张元济年谱长编 (Chronological chronicle of Zhang Yuanji's life). 2 vols. Shanghai: Jiaotong daxue chubanshe, 2011.

Zhang Weici 張慰慈. *Zhengzhixue dagang* 政治學大綱 (Outline of political science). Shanghai: Shangwu yinshuguan, 1927 [1923].

Zhang Xichen 章錫琛. "Mantan Shangwu yinshuguan" 漫談商務印書館 (Casual discussion of Commercial Press). In *Zhonghua wenshi ziliao wenku* 中華文史資料文庫 (Chinese cultural and historical materials treasury), vol. 16, *Wenhua jiaoyu bian* 文化教育編 (Culture and education volume), ed. Quanguo zhengxie wenshi ziliao weiyuanhui 全國政協文史資料委員會, 488–508. Beijing: Zhongguo wenshi chubanshe, 1996.

Zhang Yinian 章頤年. *Xinli weisheng gailun* 心理衛生概論 (A general discussion of mental hygiene). Shanghai: Shangwu yinshuguan, 1936.

Zhang Yuanji 張元濟. *Zhang Yuanji quanji* 張元濟全集 (Zhang Yuanji's complete works). 10 vols. Beijing: Shangwu yinshuguan, 2007.

——. *Zhang Yuanji riji* 张元济日记 (Zhang Yuanji's diary). 2 vols. Organized by Zhang Renfeng 张人凤. Shijiazhuang: Hebei jiaoyu chubanshe, 2000.

"Zhaokao bianyisheng" 招考編譯生 (Recruitment examination for compilation and translation students). *Shangwu yinshuguan tongxinlu* 商務印書館通信錄, no. 417 (January 20, 1936): 10.

"Zhaokao jiaoduiyuan" 招考校對員 (Recruitment exam for proofreaders). *Shangwu yinshuguan tongxinlu* 商務印書館通信錄, no. 387 (July 10, 1933): 15.

"Zhaoqu diyi jie lianxiyuan jianzhang" 招取第一屆練習員簡章 (Concise regulations for recruiting and selecting the first group of trainees). *Shangwu yinshuguan tongxinlu* 商務印書館通信錄, no. 397 (May 10, 1934): 12–13.

Zhao Tingwei 趙廷為, Yang Yinshen 楊蔭深, Huang Weirong 黃維榮, Hu Wenkai 胡文楷, Jin Yunfeng 金雲峯, Li Jikai 李季開, Mu Shaoliang 沐紹良, and Zhu Gongchui 朱公垂. *Sijiao haoma xin cidian* 四角號碼新詞典 (Four-corner new dictionary). Shanghai: Shangwu yinshuguan, 1951.

Zheng Guomin 郑国民. *Cong wenyanwen jiaoxue dao baihuawen jiaoxue—woguo jin xiandai yuwen jiaoyu de biange licheng* 从文言文教学到白话文教学———我国近现代语文教育的变革历程 (From literary-language instruction to vernacular-language instruction: The process of reform for our country's modern-language education). Beijing: Beijing shifan daxue chubanshe, 2000.

Zheng Hesheng 鄭鶴聲. "Yingyin *Siku quanshu* zhi jingguo" 影印四庫全書之經過 (The process of the photographic reprinting of the *Complete Book of Four Treasuries*). *Tushu pinglun* 圖書評論 2, no. 2 (1933): 67–105.

Zheng Lanhua 鄭蘭華. *Shiyan putong huaxue* 實驗普通化學 (Experimental regular chemistry). Shanghai: Shangwu yinshuguan, 1935 [1934].

"Zhengqiu xiaoxue jiaocai jiang jiexiao" 徵求小學教材將揭曉 (Going to announce the solicitation of primary teaching materials). *Shijie yuekan* 世界月刊, no. 1 (1924), "Zalu" 雜錄 (Miscellaneous records): 1.

"Zhengqiu xiaoxue jiaokeshu bianji fangfa yi jieshu" 徵求小學教科書編輯方法已結束 (Solicitation for methods of compiling primary-school textbooks has already concluded). *Shijie yuekan* 世界月刊, no. 1 (1924), "Zalu" 雜錄 (Miscellaneous records): 1.

Zhongguo chuban kexue yanjiusuo 中国出版科学研究所 and Zhongyang dang'anguan 中央档案馆, comps. *Zhonghua renmin gongheguo chuban shiliao (yijiusijiu nian)* 中华人民共和国出版史料 （一九四九年） (Historical materials for publishing in the People's Republic of China [1949]). Beijing: Zhongguo shuji chubanshe, 1995.

Zhongguo chuban kexue yanjiusuo 中国出版科学研究所 and Zhongyang dang'anguan 中央档案馆, comps. *Zhonghua renmin gongheguo chuban shiliao (yijiuwuling nian)* 中华人民共和国出版史料第二卷 （一九五零 年） (Historical materials for publishing in the People's Republic of China [1950]). Beijing: Zhongguo shuji chubanshe, 1996.

Zhongguo chuban kexue yanjiusuo 中国出版科学研究所 and Zhongyang dang'anguan 中央档案馆, comps. *Zhonghua renmin gongheguo chuban shiliao (yijiuwusan nian)* 中华人民共和国出版史料 （一九五三年） (Historical materials for publishing in the People's Republic of China [1953]). Beijing: Zhongguo shuji chubanshe, 1999.

Zhongguo chuban kexue yanjiusuo 中国出版科学研究所 and Zhongyang dang'anguan 中央档案馆, comps. *Zhonghua renmin gongheguo chuban shiliao (yijiuwusi nian)* 中华人民共和国出版史料 （一九五四年） (Historical materials for publishing in the People's Republic of China [1954]). Beijing: Zhongguo shuji chubanshe, 1999.

Zhongguo chuban kexue yanjiusuo 中国出版科学研究所 and Zhongyang dang'anguan 中央档案馆, comps. *Zhonghua renmin gongheguo chuban shiliao (yijiuwuliu nian)* 中华人民共和国出版史料 （一九五六年） (Historical materials for publishing in the People's Republic of China [1956]). Beijing: Zhongguo shuji chubanshe, 2001.

Zhongguo chuban kexue yanjiusuo 中国出版科学研究所 and Zhongyang dang'anguan 中央档案馆, comps. *Zhonghua renmin gongheguo chuban shiliao (yijiuwuqi, yijiuwuba nian)* 中华人民共和国出版史料 （一九五七·一九五八年） (Historical materials for publishing in the People's Republic of China [1957–1958]). Beijing: Zhongguo shuji chubanshe, 2004.

Zhongguo chuban kexue yanjiusuo 中国出版科学研究所 and Zhongyang dang'anguan 中央档案馆, comps. *Zhonghua renmin gongheguo chuban shiliao (yijiuwujiu, yijiuliuling nian)* 中华人民共和国出版史料 （一九五九·一九六零年） (Historical materials for publishing in the People's Republic of China [1959–1960]). Beijing: Zhongguo shuji chubanshe, 2005.

Zhongguo chuban kexue yanjiusuo 中国出版科学研究所 and Zhongyang dang'anguan 中央档案馆, comps. *Zhonghua renmin gongheguo chuban shiliao (yijiuliuyi nian)* 中华人民共和国出版史料 （一九六一年） (Historical materials for publishing in the People's Republic of China [1961]). Beijing: Zhongguo shuji chubanshe, 2007.

Zhongguo chuban kexue yanjiusuo 中国出版科学研究所 and Zhongyang dang'anguan 中央档案馆, comps. *Zhonghua renmin gongheguo chuban shiliao (yijiuliuer, yijiuliusan nian)* 中华人民共和国出版史料 （一九六二·一九六三年） (Historical materials for publishing in the People's Republic of China [1962–1963]). Beijing: Zhongguo shuji chubanshe, 2009.

Zhongguo chuban kexue yanjiusuo 中国出版科学研究所 and Zhongyang dang'anguan 中央档案馆, comps. *Zhonghua renmin gongheguo chuban shiliao (yijiuliusi nian zhi yijiuliuliu nian)* 中华人民共和国出版史料（一九六四年至一九六六年）(Historical materials for publishing in the People's Republic of China [1964–1966]). Beijing: Zhongguo shuji chubanshe, 2009.

Zhongguo di'er lishi dang'anguan 中國第二歷史檔案館, comp. *Zhonghua minguoshi dang'an ziliao huibian, Diwuji, Di'erbian, Jiaoyu* 中華民國史檔案資料彙編第五輯第二編教育 (Collection of archival materials on the history of the Chinese Republic, Collection 5, Set 2, Education). 2 vols. Nanjing: Jiangsu guji chubanshe, 1997.

——, comp. *Zhonghua minguoshi dang'an ziliao huibian, Diwuji, Di'yibian, Jiaoyu* 中華民國史檔案資料彙編第五輯第一編教育 (Collection of archival materials on the history of the Chinese Republic, Collection 5, Set 1, Education). 2 vols. Nanjing: Jiangsu guji chubanshe, 1994.

Zhonghua jiaoyu gaijin she 中華教育改進社. *Zhongguo jiaoyu tongji gailan* 中國教育統計概覽 (A survey of China's educational statistics). Shanghai: Shangwu yinshuguan, 1923.

Zhonghua shuju bianjibu 中华书局编辑部, comp. *Huiyi Zhonghua shuju* 回忆中华书局 (Remembering Zhonghua Book Company). 2 books in 1 vol. Beijing: Zhonghua shuju, 2001 [1987].

Zhonghua shuju dongshihui huiyi jilu, 1952 nian yiyue zhi 1953 nian sanyue 中華書局董事會會議紀錄, 1952年一月至1953年三月 (Minutes of the Zhonghua Book Company board of directors meetings, January 1952–March 1953). ZSA 511.9.820 (1).

Zhonghua shuju dongshihui yijue'an 中華書局董事會議決案 (Resolutions of the Zhonghua Book Company board of directors). 1917–1925. ZSA511.9.942(1948).

Zhonghua shuju gaikuang 中華書局概況 (Zhonghua Book Company's general situation). [Shanghai: Zhonghua shuju], 1936.

Zhonghua shuju gufen youxian gongsi dongshihui 中華書局股份有限公司董事會. *Shinianlai zhi baogao (Minguo ershiliu nian zhi sanshiwu nian)* 十年來之報告（民國二十六年至三十五年）(Ten-year report [1937–1946]). [Shanghai: Zhonghua shuju,] 1948.

Zhonghua shuju gufen youxian gongsi fuyuan hou dishici dongshi jiancha lianxi huiyi 中華書局股份有限公司復員後第十次董事監察聯席會議 (Tenth joint meeting of the directors and auditors of the Zhonghua Book Company Ltd. after demobilization). Manuscript, December 15, 1947. ZSA511.9.943(1).

Zhonghua shuju gufen youxian gongsi zai Yu dongshi di'erci tanhuahui 中華書局股份有限公司在渝董事第二次談話會 (Second discussion meeting of the directors in Chongqing board members of the Zhonghua Book Company Ltd.). Manuscript, May 27, 1946. ZSA511.9.952.

Zhonghua shuju gufen youxian gongsi zai Yu dongshi diyici tanhuahui 中華書局股份有限公司在渝董事第一次談話會 (First discussion meeting of the directors in Chongqing of the Zhonghua Book Company Ltd.). Manuscript, July 3, 1943. ZSA511.9.952.

Zhonghua shuju jiefanghou chuban xinshu mulu 中华书局解放后出版新书目录 (Catalog of new books published by Zhonghua Book Company after Liberation). N.p.: Zhonghua shuju, 1950.

Zhonghua shuju shisan nian gaikuang 中華書局十三年概況 (Zhonghua Book Company's situation in 1924). [Shanghai]: Zhonghua shuju, 1924.

Zhonghua shuju wunian gaikuang 中華書局五年概況 (The general situation at Zhonghua Book Company in 1916). [Shanghai]: Zhonghua shuju, 1916.

"Zhonghua shuju zhaokao lianxisheng zhangwuyuan chushi timu (minguo ershiliu nian chunji diyici zhaokao)" 中華書局招考練習生帳務員初試題目（民國二十六年春季第一次招考）(Preliminary topics for Zhonghua Book Company's recruitment exam for trainees and accounting staff [first recruitment exam of spring 1937]). *Chuban yuekan* 出版月刊, no. 2 (May 5, 1937): 16–19.

"[Zhonghua shuju] zong bianjibu banshi chengxu" 中華書局總編輯部辦事程序 (Management procedures for the General Editing Department [Zhonghua Book Company]). Unpublished manuscript, 1935. ZSA.

"Zhonghua shuju zuori yibufen fuye" 中華書局昨日一部分復業 (Yesterday Zhonghua Book Company partially resumed work). *Shenbao*, August 30, 1925.

Zhong Luzhai 鍾魯齋. *Bijiao jiaoyu* 比較教育 (Comparative education). Shanghai: Shangwu yinshuguan, 1935.

Zhou Gengsheng 周鯁生. *[Xin xuezhi] gongmin jiaokeshu* 新學制公民教科書 ([New School System] civics textbook). Shanghai: Shanwu yinshuguan, 1923–1926 [1923].

Zhou Qihou 周其厚. *Zhonghua shuju yu jindai wenhua* 中華書局與近代文化 (Zhonghua Book Company and modern culture). Beijing: Zhonghua shuju, 2007.

Zhou Shaolian 周紹濂. *Weifen jihe* 微分幾何 (Differential geometry). Shanghai: Shangwu yinshuguan, 1951 [1950].

Zhou Shushan 周曙山. "Cihai 'dangshi' bufen zhengmiu" 辭海黨史部份正謬 (Correcting errors in *Cihai*'s party-history portion). *Shengli zazhi* 勝利雜誌, new no. 3 (1943): 22.

Zhou Wu 周武. "Cong quanguoxing dao difanghua: 1945 zhi 1956 nian Shanghai chubanye de bianqian" 从全国性到地方化：1945至1956年上海出版业的变迁 (From national to localized: The change in Shanghai's publishing industry, 1945–1956). *Shilin* 史林, no. 6 (2006): 72–95.

Zhuang Shi 莊適, Wu Yanyin 吳研因, and Shen Qi 沈圻. *Xin xuezhi guoyu jiaokeshu* 新學制國語教科書 (New School System national-language textbook). 8 vols. Shanghai: Shangwu yinshuguan, 1923–1924 [1923].

Zhuang Zexuan 莊澤宣. *Geguo jiaoyu bijiao lun* 各國教育比較論 (Comparative education). Shanghai: Shangwu yinshuguan, 1929.

"Zhu Kezhen shengping yu gongxian" 竺可楨生平與貢獻 (Zhu Kezhen's life and contributions). In *Zhu Kezhen wenji* 竺可楨文集 (Zhu Kezhen's collected works). Beijing: Kexue chubanshe, 1979.

Zhu Lianbao 朱聯保. "Guanyu Shijie shuju de huiyi" 關於世界書局的回憶 (My recollections of World Book Company). *Chuban shiliao* 出版史料 1987, no. 2 (overall no. 8): 52–68.

Zhu Weibo 朱蔚伯. "Wang Yunwu yu Shangwu yinshuguan" 王雲五與商務印書館 (Wang Yunwu and Commercial Press). In *Zhonghua wenshi ziliao wenku* 中華文史資料文庫 (Chinese cultural and historical materials treasury), vol. 16, *Wenhua jiaoyu bian* 文化教育編 (Culture and education volume), comp. Quanguo zhengxie wenshi ziliao weiyuanhui 全國政協文史資料委員會, 509–17. Beijing: Zhongguo wenshi chubanshe, 1996.

Zito, Angela. *Of Body and Brush: Grand Sacrifice as Text/Performance in Eighteenth-Century China*. Chicago: University of Chicago Press, 1997.

"Zong guanlichu tongren lu" 總管理處同人錄 (Roster of the colleagues in the General Management Office). *Shangwu yinshuguan tongxinlu* 商務印書館通信錄, no. 388 (August 10, 1933): 39–40.

"Zong guanlichu zhiyuan lu" 總管理處職員錄 (Roster of the staff in the General Management Office). *Shangwu yinshuguan tongxinlu* 商務印書館通信錄, no. 377 (September 15, 1932): 64–65.

"Zong guanlichu zuzhi xitong biao" 總管理處組織系統表 (Organizational chart for the General Management Office). *Shangwu yinshuguan tongxinlu* 商務印書館通信錄, no. 377 (September 15, 1932): 63.

Zou Zhenhuan 邹振环. "Xin wenhua congshu: Xinzhi chuanshu yu xinxue yinling" 新文化丛书：新知传输与新学引领 (The New Culture Series: The transmission of new knowledge and eager anticipation of new learning). In *Zhonghua shuju yu Zhongguo jin xiandai wenhua* 中华书局与中国近现代文化 (Zhonghua Book Company and China's modern culture), ed. Fudan daxue lishixi, Chuban bowuguan, Zhonghua shuju, Shanghai cishu chubanshi, 167–87. Shanghai: Shanghai renmin chubanshe, 2013.

[Zuo] Shunsheng [左]舜聖. "Ji benju tongren zuijin de yuxue yanjiu re" 記本局同人最近的語學研究熱 (Recording the recent craze of language study among this company's colleagues). *Jinde jikan* 進德季刊 [I], no. 3 (1922), "Yanlun" 言論 (Open discussion): 17–18.

Zuo Shunsheng 左舜聖. *Jin sanshi nian jianwen zaji* 近三十年見聞雜記 (Random notes on my experiences of the past thirty years). Jiulong: Ziyou chubanshe, 1952.

"Zuo Shunsheng xiansheng jiang fu Fa" 左舜生先生將赴法 (Mr. Zuo Shunsheng will go to France). *Jinde jikan* 進德季刊 3, no. I (1924), "Huiwu baogao" 會務報告 (Association affairs reports): 7.

Index

ABC Series (ABC congshu; World Book Company), 23, 60, 69, 156, 167–70, 174–76, 222; synthetic construction of, 176, 178; and University Series, 172, 174

academic disciplines, 266n36, 298n119; and *Cihai*, 118, 121–22, 123; and new terms and concepts, 102, 117, 125; professionalization of, 158; in series publications, 156, 157, 163, 167–68, 170, 172–80, 182, 252, 253; Western, 15, 157–58, 163, 170, 255

academic institutions: cultural production in, 12–17; employment in, 3, 60–61; lifestyle of, 78–79, 81–83, 235, 252–54, 256, 273n90, 282n146; professionalization of, 179; recruitment from, 1, 59, 68, 175–80, 176, 182, 210, 216, 234–35, 243; and revised *Cihai*, 233, 242; and series publications, 23, 155, 180; and the state, 273n92, 304n86; terms and concepts in, 22, 96, 237; training in, 210, 226, 252; writing style of, 111–12

Advancing Virtue Quarterly, 74, 78, 81

Alford, William, 158

Ancient-Book Publishing Company (Guji chubanshe), 206

Anderson, Benedict, 4

Angle, Stephen, 102

Annals of the Three Kingdoms (Sanguozhi), 230, 243

Anti-Rightist Campaign (1957), 209, 218, 246, 258

Apple, Michael, 96

Archaeology of Knowledge (Foucault), 11

Assembled Essentials of the Complete Book of Four Treasuries (Siku quanshu huiyao), 141

authors: in editing departments, 5–6, 14, 19–20, 85, 96, 219, 239, 253; vs. editors, 248–50; editors as, 48–49, 73–74, 85; female, 180; intellectuals as, 18, 19–20; lifestyle of, 67, 239–44; outside, 30–31, 60; payments to, 18, 29, 30, 32, 60, 67, 73, 156, 173, 180, 240; in Reform period, 261; restrictions on, 19, 182, 246, 256, 261; of series publications, 23, 59, 157, 168–70, 175–80, 254, 255, 256; status of, 9, 13–14, 15, 16, 18, 176, 255; in U.S. publishing, 6. *See also* compilers; editors

Bao Tianxiao, 32, 60, 273n82

Bao Xianchang, 28, 47

Bao Xian'en, 28

Bao Yuke, 242

Bao Zhijing, 206, 219, 220, 221

Beijing: *Four Treasuries* in, 136–37, 138, 139, 140; publishing in, 60, 87; transfer of personnel to, 91, 191, 197, 199, 204

Bian, Morris, 212–13

bindings, book, 144, 145, 146, 148

Bing Zhi, 69, 171, 301n36

Blumenbach, Johann Friedrich, 123

Book of Changes (*Zhou yi*), 135

book production: collaborative, 7, 8, 22, 44–47, 56, 100–101, 179, 214–15, 238–39, 254, 273n82; continuities in, 195, 201–2, 212–16, 245, 246, 258; efficiency in, 250, 254, 257, 258; and fungibility of text, 70–71, 85, 173, 254, 256, 302n47; industrialization of, 5–6, 8, 9, 17, 22, 31, 51, 53–86, 153, 172, 180, 212, 219, 254, 255, 259; mass mobilization for, 233–35, 245, 258; negotiated, 21, 24, 214–47, 252, 257, 258, 260; in PRC, 7–9, 18, 20–21, 24, 185–247; systematization of, 19–20, 22

Bourdieu, Pierre, 13–16, 131, 182, 271n57, 293n9

Buddhism, 37–38, 301n31

Cai Qimin, 62, 64

Cai Yongchang, 159

Cai Yuanpei, 28, 47, 61, 119, 171

Campaign to Suppress Hidden Counterrevolutionaries (Sufan yundong; 1955), 208

Cao Chensi, 64

Cao Chu, 55

Cao Kun, 139

Cao Manzhi, 211

Cao Ying, 241

capital: cultural, 131–32, 140, 153, 259, 293n9; financial, 200; human, 29, 128, 198–99, 200; social, 84, 85–86, 130, 133–34, 140, 153, 293n9; symbolic, 13, 17, 243, 275n25

Capital Normal Library (Jingshi tushuguan; Beijing), 136, 139

capitalism: and elites, 3, 17, 50–52; industrial, 3, 17, 21, 24, 47–48, 50–52, 201, 212, 245, 254, 259; methods of, 24, 250, 256–57; print, 4–5, 38–39, 268n57; state, 196; vs. state socialism, 16, 21, 201, 212, 245, 256–57

Capitalist Dilemma in China's Communist Revolution, The (Coble), 201

censorship, 140–41, 154, 187, 313n135

Central Propaganda Department (PRC), 20, 192, 195, 202, 205, 206; and negotiated production, 220–22, 224, 226, 228; and revised *Cihai*, 232, 237–38

Central Weekly (*Zhongyang zhoukan*), 121

Certeau, Michel de, 85

Chartier, Roger, 15

Chen Boda, 227

Chen Chengze, 35, 42, 43

Chen Diexian, 169, 265n32

Chen Gaoyong, 151

Chen Hanbo, 206, 207, 219, 251, 260, 315n28

Chen Li, 142

Chen Lifu, 119

Chen Menglei, 147

Chen Naiqian, 207, 208, 227, 230, 240, 243–44, 246

Chen Qitian, 55

Chen Shutong, 186, 188, 196, 201

Chen Suzhi, 312n108

Chen Yin, 46

Chen Yinke, 206

Chen Yuan, 219, 221

Chen Yun, 204

Chen Yusun, 248

Chen Zhonghe, 150

Cheng Yingzhang, 69

Chiang Kai-shek, 89

China, People's Republic of (PRC): book production in, 3, 7–9, 18, 20–21, 24, 185–247; economy of, 220, 244–45, 257; intellectuals in, 21, 239–44, 258–59; investment by, 243–44; as pedogogical state, 244–45, 257, 258; as propaganda state, 244, 252, 257, 319n134; state-publisher negotiations in, 214–47; and USSR, 20, 188, 207, 213, 224, 314n7

China Book Distribution Company (Zhongguo tushu faxing gongsi), 190, 196, 200

China Youth Publishing Company (Zhongguo qingnian chubanshe), 310n44

Chinese Communist Party (CCP): and Five Antis Campaign, 192, 193, 194; and negotiated knowledge, 245–47; and negotiated production, 215, 216, 220, 227, 231, 243–44; in Republican period, 75, 76, 120; and revised *Cihai*, 236–39; and series publications, 159, 217; and state socialism, 200–201; and wartime publishers, 187, 188

Chinese History Small Series (Lishi xiao congshu; Zhonghua), 217–18, 244, 251

Chinese language: academic writing in, 111–12, 237; classical (*wenyan*), 3, 96, 97, 100, 107–8, 112, 116, 124, 285n10; and dictionaries, 95–125; and editing departments, 78, 125; and language reform, 105–6, 107, 108, 112, 113, 125; loanwords in, 287n40, 293n6; models for, 105, 107–12, 116, 124; new genres in, 96, 109–10, 115–16, 124; new terms and concepts in, 96–105, 117, 124–25, 231–39, 284n2, 287n45; parallel style (*piantiwen*) in, 129; professionalized, 111–12; pronunciation of, 95; in recruitment examinations, 64; return graphic loans in, 285n13, 287n40, 293n6; spoken, 108–9, 111, 114–15, 116; in textbooks, 95–125; transliterated terms in, 103; vernacular (*baihua*), 3, 13, 22, 95–97, 107–16, 124, 139; Westernized, 100; written, 96, 109–10, 111, 114–15, 116

Chinese Socialist Party, 37

Chinese Translations of World-Famous Works (series; Commercial Press), 162, 164

Chongqing, 87, 88, 174, 282n4

Chow, Kai-wing, 4, 5

Christianity, 158

Christian-Smith, Linda, 96

Cihai dictionary (Zhonghua), 62, 69, 70, 190, 256; new terms and concepts in, 22, 96, 116–24, 125; revision of, 1, 210–11, 232–42, 245, 247, 250, 251, 260, 318n105

circulation (*liutong*), 127, 130, 147, 150, 154, 252

circulation, internal (*neibu faxing*), 226, 238

citizens (*gongmin*), 101, 120; reading public as, 15, 21, 124, 161–62, 181–82, 252, 255–56, 257

citizenship (*guomin*), 98, 124

civil service examinations, 4, 16, 150; end of, 1, 2, 28, 33, 253; and literati, 18, 27–28, 35, 36, 128, 131

Civil War, Chinese, 90, 150, 187–88, 201, 214–15

civilization (*wenming*), 98–99, 286n18

Ciyuan dictionary (Commercial Press), 43, 116, 190, 232, 256; vs. *Cihai*, 120–24, 125; collaborative compilation of, 46, 100–101; new terms and concepts in, 22, 96, 101–5; revised edition of, 214, 317n70

class struggle (*jieji douzheng*), 118

classical learning, 15, 225; democratization of, 23, 150–53; of editors, 34–38, 42, 44, 51, 52, 128, 131, 133, 150; language of, 3, 37, 96

Classical Literature Press (Gudian wenxue chubanshe), 206, 207–8, 224

classical texts: accessibility of, 128, 129–30, 136, 141, 147, 150–53; in Cultural Revolution, 252; expertise in, 225–27; on history, 228, 230; rare editions of, 16, 127, 128, 152, 154, 205, 224, 225; readers of, 4, 16, 37, 38; woodblock editions of, 4, 5, 298n114

classical texts, republication of, 2, 11, 126–54, 164; commentaries in, 142, 143, 152, 154; by Commercial Press, 23, 126–41, 150–53, 191, 223, 224; and Confucianism, 127, 153; democratized access to, 12, 23, 150–53, 255; in early PRC, 186, 210–11, 247; editors for, 6, 14, 17, 23, 44, 66, 127, 210, 225; experts for, 225–27, 234–35, 237, 238, 246–47; and intellectuals, 18, 153, 179, 206, 209, 225, 228, 231; and libraries, 151–52; literati role in, 14, 28, 125, 127, 128–36, 140, 148, 150, 153, 154, 246; negotiated production in, 216, 222–31, 257; and popularization, 141–46, 150, 225; prices of, 130, 137, 139, 148, 151; punctuation in, 230, 245; and rare editions, 127, 128, 152, 154, 205; readers for, 15–16, 18, 151–52, 252, 255; reconfiguration of, 153–54; reorganization for, 70, 205, 230–31; state involvement in, 136–41, 191, 216, 222–31, 257; thematic organization in, 147–50; by Zhonghua, 23, 24, 127, 128, 141–53, 186, 206, 210,

classical texts (*continued*)
212, 223–28, 230, 231, 234. *See also
particular texts*

Coble, Parks, 201

Cochran, Sherman, 200

Colleagues' Association to Advance Virtue
(Jindehui), 67

Collected Glosses on the Classics
(*Jingji zuangu*; compilation), 6

*Collection of Chinese Classical,
Historical, Philosophical, and Literary
Works* (*Sibu congkan*), 28, 43, 128–36,
225; and accessibility, 23, 151, 152,
154; criticism of, 135–36; vs. *Four
Treasuries*, 138, 140; goals for,
129–30; vs. *Gujin tushu jicheng*, 148;
prices of, 130, 297n104; research
for, 126–27; vs. *Sibu beiyao*, 141,
143, 144

Collection of Household Knowledge
(Jiating changshi huibian; Chen
Diexian), 169

*Collection of Obscure Books from the
Hanfenlou* (*Hanfenlou miji*; Commercial
Press), 129

Coming of the Book, The (Febvre and
Martin), 9

Commercial Press (Shangwu yinshuguan):
academic atmosphere at, 53, 78–84,
235, 242, 282n146; bombing of, 66, 71,
77, 79–81, 163, 270n28; and Chinese
language, 96–100, 106–8, 114, 116, 125;
in Civil War, 214–15; and classical
reprints, 23, 126–41, 150–53, 154, 191,
223, 224; collaborative production at, 8,
44–45, 46, 47, 56; compensation at,
31–33; Compilation and Review
Committee of, 71, 171, 172, 173;
continuities at, 198, 201–2, 212–16,
246, 260; dictionaries of, 31, 59, 66,
100–105, 116–25, 214–15, 232, 317n70;
in early PRC, 8, 20–21, 23, 90, 91, 186;
editing departments of, 5–7, 8, 21–22,
34, 39, 40, 41, 42, 51, 65, 277n66;
founding of, 1, 28; and Hu Shi, 32, 53,
57, 58, 65, 78, 79, 273n89, 274n105;
industrialization in, 69–74; and labor
activism, 74, 75, 76–77; leisure culture
of, 49–50, 52, 84; libraries of, 48, 57,
79–81, 129–31, 133, 164; literati at, 1,

27–52; and Mao Dun, 35, 39, 40,
42–43, 47, 48, 81, 133–34; and
negotiated production, 214–25, 231,
257; New Books Division of, 55; and
new terms and concepts, 97–100;
overseas operations of, 196–97, 204;
political attacks on, 192, 193, 251, 252,
259; profits of, 65–66, 174, 256;
public-private joint management of,
194–99, 200, 312n110; recruitment by,
22, 27, 28–30, 55–56, 57, 61, 62, 253;
reorganizations of, 20, 23, 57–60,
66–67, 68, 202–3, 204, 205, 206–7, 212;
series publications of, 23, 155, 160–66,
217, 219, 220; specialization at, 24, 59,
66, 191; staff of, 21–22, 31, 54, 62–63,
64, 68–69, 84, 271n37, 272n77; state
control of, 23–24, 185–86, 188, 189,
211–13, 256–57; textbooks of, 34, 89,
96, 97–100, 106, 107, 113, 114, 116,
283n15, 314n6; training at, 62–65; in
wartime, 87–88, 187; vs. World, 167,
168. *See also particular titles*

compensation: for authors, 18, 30, 60, 67,
240; in bonuses, 48, 65, 75, 77; and
copyrights, 300n17; for editors, 60–61,
65–68, 78, 85, 239–40, 243, 246; for
expertise, 150, 172; and labor activism,
75–76; for manuscripts, 29, 30, 32, 60,
73, 156, 173, 180, 240, 276n34; in PRC,
239–40, 243, 246, 253, 318n109; in
Republican period, 19, 29, 31–33, 48,
52, 78, 88, 240; in royalties, 29, 30,
34, 60, 156, 173, 180, 240, 267n52,
276n34; in shares, 189, 201, 240

compilation, 6–7, 10, 23, 28, 72;
collaborative, 44–46, 97, 100–101,
215, 254. *See also* series publications;
particular titles

compilers, 1, 14, 18, 62–64, 66, 100–101,
177; in early PRC, 218, 232, 235,
237, 239–44, 241; and industrialization
of production, 71, 86. *See also*
editors

Complete Book of Four Treasuries (*Siku
quanshu*), 23, 136–41, 154, 227; *Siku
quanshu zhenben*, 150, 151, 172

*Complete Collection of Past and Present Books
and Illustrations* (*Gujin tushu jicheng*), 23,
127, 147–50, 151

Complete Library (Wanyou wenkou; Commercial Press), 155, 161–66, 167, 218, 219, 301n38; vs. ABC Series, 170; cataloging of, 164–65; marketing of, 70, 164–66; price of, 163, 164–65, 182; readers of, 23, 308n132; vs. University Series, 90, 174, 175

Confucianism, 21, 96, 103, 286n21, 301n31; and classical reprints, 127, 153; and elites, 2, 18, 176; and knowledge, 12, 161, 181

constitutional monarchy (*junzhu lixian*), 98, 99

copyrights, 30, 159, 162, 276n34, 300n17

correspondence courses, 34, 42, 43, 46

cultural entrepreneurs, 17, 275n25

cultural production, 8–21, 153, 186, 254; industrialization of, 85, 86; negotiated, 21, 24, 214–47, 252, 257, 258, 260; in Reform period, 260, 261; socialist, 249–50, 258

Cultural Revolution (1966–1976), 24, 186, 247, 251–52, 259

culture: commodification of, 256; and economy, 17, 259; imperial, 253–54; knowledge, 122, 161–62, 182; literati leisure, 10, 14, 22, 38–39, 49–51, 52, 57, 83–84, 186, 235, 254, 256; literati workplace, 39–42; material, 103; national, 127–28, 129; new Chinese, 3–4, 178; and new terms and concepts, 100, 103, 104–5, 118

Dagongbao (*L'Impartial*; newspaper), 187

Dai Daxi, 63

Dai Kedun, 33, 36, 42, 46, 49

Dai Kegong, 42

Dai Keshao, 42

Dai Xiaohou, 186, 188, 196, 197, 204, 208, 209

Daoism, 301n31

Darwin, Charles, 37, 158

Deng Tuo, 248

dictionaries, 1, 22–23, 142; authority of, 96–97, 101, 102, 105, 119, 124, 125, 284n4; and Chinese language, 95–125; and classical reprints, 142, 153; collaborative compilation of, 45–46, 100–101; of Commercial Press, 31, 59,

66, 100–105, 116–25, 214–15, 232, 317n70; industrialized production of, 70, 255; negotiated production of, 214–16; new terms and concepts in, 22, 96, 100, 101–5, 116–24, 125, 215, 232, 254; of Zhonghua Book Company, 117. *See also particular titles*

Diderot, Denis, 12, 237

Ding Fuzhi, 143, 144, 153, 297n88

Ding Jingtang, 237

Ding Juntao, 187

Ding Shuqi, 315n28

Ding Xiaoxian, 75

Ding Yinggui, 204

distribution, 5, 15, 153; in early PRC, 188, 194, 257; joint companies for, 89, 189–90, 196, 200; overseas, 46, 197; of textbooks, 89, 114, 222

Dong Maotang, 30

Dong Shaoming, 159

Dong Wenqiao, 176

Du Yaquan, 29, 31–32, 40, 43, 44, 100

Duan Fuqun, 58

Duan Qirui, 139

Duan Yucai, 142

Eastern Library (Dongfang tushuguan; Commercial Press), 79, 80, 81, 164

Eastern Miscellany (*Dongfang zazhi*; journal), 43, 88, 278n79

"Eclectics" (Zajia; Luo Mo), 248–50, 260

economy, 8–10, 11, 13; and culture, 17, 259; and middle class, 67–68; of PRC, 220, 244–45, 257; and series publications, 159

editing departments, 1–10; academic atmosphere in, 22, 78–79, 82–83, 235, 253, 256; authors in, 5–6, 14, 19–20, 85, 96, 219, 239, 253; careers in, 27–52, 70–71; and Chinese language, 78, 125; in Civil War, 214–15; and classical reprints, 150, 227–28; collaboration in, 7, 8, 22, 44–47, 56, 97, 100–101, 179, 214–15, 238–39, 254, 273n82; of Commercial Press, 5–7, 8, 21–22, 34, 39, 40, 41, 42, 51, 65, 277n66; as communities, 19, 28; continuity of, 212–16; and cultural production, 9–10,

editing departments (*continued*)
14, 17; and dictionaries, 211, 233–34, 238; division of labor in, 72, 84, 85, 117; downsizing of, 88, 90–91; in early PRC, 8, 239–44, 257–58; factionalism in, 40, 42; flow production in, 84; generalist work style in, 42–44, 51, 52; horizontal vs. vertical relations in, 44, 47, 71–74; independent contractors to, 30, 31, 34; industrialization of, 69–74; kinship in, 40, 42; large size of, 33–34, 51, 65, 66, 252–53; literati leisure culture in, 10, 14, 22, 38–39, 49–51, 52, 57, 83–84, 186, 235, 254, 256; mobility in, 72–73, 85; native place affiliations, 40–41, 42; and negotiated production, 216, 217, 218, 222, 227–28; new school graduates in, 19, 22, 61, 62, 63, 65, 67, 68, 71, 84, 210, 227–28, 253; organization of, 39–42; and outside organizations, 202–3; and political issues, 246; in Reform period, 260; reorganizations of, 55–60, 162, 202–11, 273n89; in Sino-Japanese War (War of Resistance) period, 88; and social networks, 38–39, 50, 82, 84, 85–86, 253, 256; social status in, 22, 74, 254, 264n22; specialization in, 58–59, 66, 190–91, 195, 196, 200, 204–11, 209, 215, 217, 223; training in, 62–65; types of intellectuals in, 68–69, 84, 253, 256, 258, 301n36; of Western publishers, 66, 77, 270n30; work schedules in, 48–49, 51; of Zhonghua, 21–22, 34, 39, 40, 41, 42, 51, 65, 311n84. *See also* recruitment
editions, study of (*banbenxue*), 129, 131, 133, 135, 153, 208, 210, 294n18
editors, 1–10; as authors, 20, 48–49, 73–74, 85; and Chinese language, 96–97, 125; classical learning of, 34–38, 42, 44, 51, 52, 128, 131, 133, 150; of classical reprints, 6, 14, 17, 23, 44, 66, 127, 210, 225, 226; compensation of, 29, 31–33, 60–61, 65–68, 78, 85, 239–40, 243, 246; in early PRC, 21, 239–44, 257–58; foreign learning of, 22, 51, 52, 60–61, 84, 254; as generalists, 43–44, 51, 52; hybrid learning of, 34–38, 51; incentives for, 69–70, 77, 85, 246; and industrialization of production, 71, 86;

influence of, 12–13, 19–20, 24, 247; and labor activism, 74–76; with modern educations, 36, 61–62, 71, 84, 254; and negotiated production, 210, 218–19, 226, 231, 232, 233; political criticism of, 248–52; politically suspect, 218, 251, 258, 260; PRC allocation of, 245–46; and reform movements, 35–38, 51, 97–98, 102; in Reform period, 261; and social production, 13, 14, 16; social status of, 67–68, 77, 78, 85, 255; training of, 62–65, 210, 226, 252; vs. workers, 84–85, 86. *See also* intellectuals; literati, Qing-Republican
education: as career, 2, 10, 14, 18, 19, 27; and Confucianism, 2, 12, 18, 161, 176, 181, 286n21; of editors, 14, 22, 30, 36, 60–63, 65, 68, 71, 81, 84, 254; foreign, 1, 2, 13, 18–19, 22, 30, 57, 58, 60–61, 75, 81, 84, 111, 128, 150, 158, 176, 235, 253, 254, 275n9; higher, 59–60, 155, 172, 180, 196, 199, 253; hybrid, 34–38; and language reform, 105–7; mass, 167, 168; modern, 2, 27, 28, 34, 36, 61–63, 65, 68, 70, 71, 84, 153, 160, 181, 252, 254, 255; numbers of students receiving, 267n50, 268n63, 276n45; opportunities for, 78–79, 81; primary, 98, 113–14; vs. propaganda, 20–21; reforms of, 11, 97, 106, 108, 111, 113, 272n77, 288n57, 292n138; and series publications, 155, 160, 167, 168, 172, 175, 176, 178–79, 181, 253. *See also* classical learning; textbooks
Education Monthly (*Jiaoyu zazhi*), 43, 46, 101
Education Press (Jiaoyu chubanshe), 188
elites, educated. *See* intellectuals; literati, Qing-Republican
Elman, Benjamin, 157, 168
encyclopedias, 54, 59, 69–70, 105, 231, 232
Encyclopédie (Diderot), 12, 237
England, 111, 176, 264n19, 275n9
English language, 30, 58, 64
English-Chinese New Dictionary (*Ying Hua xin zidian*; Commercial Press), 31
Epoch Publishing Company (Shidai chubanshe), 195
Essential Writings from the Four Categories of Learning (*Sibu beiyao*), 23, 127, 141–46;

and access to classical texts, 151, 152;
commentaries in, 142, 143, 152, 154;
goals of, 141–43; imitation-Song fonts
of, 143–45, 147; prices of, 297n106; vs.
Sibu congkan, 141, 143, 144
Eucken, Rudolf, 159
Europe, 4–5, 11–12, 77, 99, 157,
253, 270n30. *See also* Western
learning
Everyman's Library, 219
evidential learning, 143

fairy tales, 108, 289n71
Fan Wenlan, 206, 228, 230
Fan Yong, 315n28
Fan Yuanlian, 35–36, 117
Fan Yunliu, 168
Febvre, Lucien, 9
Feng Binfu, 315n28
Feng Youlan, 206
Fiction Monthly (*Xiaoshuo yuebao*), 129,
280n101
Finance and Economics Publishing
Company (Caizheng jingji chubanshe,
Caijing chubanshe; Zhonghua), 185,
195, 199, 203, 204, 209
Five Antis Campaign (1952), 192–94, 197,
213
Foreign History Small Series (Waiguo
lishi xiao congshu; Commercial Press),
251, 315n15
Foucault, Michel, 11
Four Books, 142
Four Treasuries. See *Complete Book of
Four Treasuries*
Four-Corner New Dictionary (*Sijiao haoma
xin cidian*; Commercial Press), 214–15
Franklin, Benjamin, 108, 109
Free Marriage (*Ziyou jiehun*; journal), 37
Fu Binran, 199, 207
Fu Donghua, 211, 231, 301n36
Fu Sinian, 153, 171
Fu Weiping, 69, 70, 171
Fu Zengxiang, 130, 294n18

Gang of Four, 250
Gao, James, 201
Gao Fengchi, 28, 47, 50
Gao Fengqian. *See* Gao Mengdan
Gao Juefu, 82, 301n36

Gao Mengdan (Fengqian), 29, 35,
40, 49, 50, 99, 100; and classical
reprints, 138; and collaborative
production, 44–48; and pay rates, 32,
33; and reorganization, 53, 57; and
series publications, 160; and textbooks,
97, 273n82
Gao Shixian (Yehou), 143, 147, 153,
296n88
Ge Suicheng, 88
General Publishing Administration
(Chuban zongshu; GPA), 185–86; and
Five Antis Campaign, 193; and
public-private joint management,
195, 196, 197, 198, 199, 200; and
reorganization of publishers, 202, 203;
and traitorous elements, 310n61; and
transition to state control, 188, 190,
191, 192; and World Book Company,
189
genres, new, 22, 96, 109–10, 115–16, 124,
216
Ghosh, Anindita, 15
Golden Harbor Press (Kinkōdō; Japan),
5–6, 29, 44
Gong Shaoying, 218
Great China Book Company (Da
Zhongguo tushuju), 187
Great East Book Company (Dadong
shuju), 89
Great Leap Forward, 220, 227, 241; mass
mobilization in, 233, 234, 235, 245, 258
Gu Jiegang, 59, 153, 171, 228, 230
Guan Huaicong, 62, 64
Guangxu, Emperor, 35
Gujin tushu jicheng. See *Complete Collection
of Past and Present Books and Illustrations*
Gunn, Edward, 112
Guo Bingwen, 101
Guo Jing, 207
Guo Renyuan, 171–72

Haeckel, Ernst, 158
Han Zhongmin, 221
Hanfeizi, 37
Hanfenlou Library (Commercial Press),
48, 57, 79, 81, 129–31, 133
Hang Wei, 233, 234, 235, 238, 317n76
Hanshu, 230, 231
Harrison, Henrietta, 273n92

He Bingsong, 59, 68, 69, 83, 85, 171, 301n36

High School National Language Textbook, 70

High School Series (Zhongxue congshu; Commercial Press), 90

Higher Education Publishing Company (Gaodeng jiaoyu chubanshe; Commercial Press), 185, 204, 223

Hill, Michael, 157, 307n116

History of Chinese Philosophy (*Zhongguo zhexue shi dagang*; Hu Shi), 173

History of the Taiping Heavenly Kingdom Revolution (*Taiping tianguo geming shi*; Wang Boxiang), 73–74

Homo Academicus (Bourdieu), 13, 14

Hong Cheng, 242

Hong Kong, 174, 193, 204, 282n4

Hong Liangji, 142

Hu Daojing, 226, 246

Hu Peihui, 142

Hu Qiaomu, 195

Hu Shi, 105, 107, 143, 153, 171, 173; and Commercial Press, 32, 53, 57, 58, 65, 78, 79, 273n89, 274n105

Hu Shunhua, 109, 110, 114, 289n82

Hu Yuzhi, 83, 185, 191, 192, 198, 311n87; and negotiated production, 216, 217, 219, 220, 221, 244, 245, 247

Huainanzi, 37

Huang Luofeng, 195, 196, 198, 199

Huang Shaoxu, 70

Huang Shuntong, 315n28

Hundred Days Reform (1898), 3, 35, 128

Hundred Flowers Campaign, 209, 224, 225, 243, 247

Hung, Chang-tai, 244

industrialism, print, 5–6, 8, 9, 17, 84, 252, 258; and classical reprints, 153; and literati culture, 31, 51; state control of, 185–213

intellectuals (*zhishifenzi*), 268n57; and *Cihai*, 121–22, 234–35, 237, 238, 250; and classical reprints, 153, 206, 225, 246; communities of, 82–83, 239–44, 282n146; and continuities in publishing, 245–46; and Cultural Revolution, 24; diverse types of, 18–21, 100, 104; in early PRC, 21, 239–44; in editing departments, 18, 22, 60–69, 253, 256,

258; elite, 68, 167, 216, 221–22, 239–44, 253–55, 256, 301n36; as experts, 175–77, 216, 225, 234–38, 240, 246–47, 253, 260, 292n138; fields of activity of, 216, 239; foreign-educated, 58–59, 162, 168–69, 177; influence of, 21, 246–47; leisure culture of, 83–84, 239–44; modern, 17, 20, 175–77, 267n56; and negotiated production, 21, 216, 221–22, 225, 228, 231, 259; and new academic disciplines, 121–22, 125; and new terms and concepts, 96–97, 101–2, 106, 112, 123, 124; political attacks on, 249, 259; politically suspect, 209–10, 258; privileges of, 240–42, 246, 258; in Reform period, 260; reputations of, 175–80, 182, 243; research opportunities for, 242–43, 246; and series publications, 155–56, 158, 168–69, 171–72, 175–81, 253; social status of, 2, 14, 17, 18, 78, 255; specialized, 61, 250; and state socialism, 21, 197, 201; and textbooks, 105, 106, 292n138; and unpaid labor, 179–80. *See also* labor, intellectual; literati, Qing-Republican

intellectuals, petty (*xiao zhishifenzi*), 17, 19–23, 150; and *Cihai*, 117; in early PRC, 208, 216, 249, 258; in editing departments, 60–69, 85, 86, 253, 254; independent projects of, 19–20, 73–74; and negotiated book production, 216; and new terms and concepts, 96–97, 125; political attacks on, 249; social status of, 73, 77

International Concession (Shanghai), 77, 87

introductions (*liyan*), 156, 176

Iovene, Paola, 247, 260

January 28 Incident (1932), 66, 71, 77, 79–81, 163, 270n28

Japan: attacks on China by, 66, 71, 73, 77, 79–81, 87, 114, 140, 163, 174, 270n28; influence of, 35, 99, 157; publishing in, 5–6, 44, 253; study in, 35, 57, 275n9; study tour of, 66, 77, 270n30

Japanese language, 64, 98–99, 103, 112, 285n13, 287n40

Jiang Baili, 176

Jiang Boxun, 42

Jiang Bozhen, 68, 74, 78
Jiang Fucong, 140
Jiang Huanqing, 312n108
Jiang Kanghu, 37
Jiang Menglin, 171, 179
Jiang Weiqiao, 43, 49, 99; and *Ciyuan*, 100,
102; and collaborative production,
44–45, 46, 52, 97; hybrid learning
of, 36–37; and staffing of editorial
departments, 29, 30, 33, 40; and
textbooks, 44, 97, 273n82; work
schedule of, 47, 48
Jiang Zuoyu, 126, 133, 134
Jiangnan Arsenal publications, 36, 161
Jiangnan Library (Nanjing), 126; and *Sibu
congkan*, 132, 133–34, 140
Jiangnan region, 21, 29, 38, 154, 253;
scholarly dominance of, 152, 266n39,
298n115
Jiao Xun, 142
Jin Canran, 199, 206–10, 243, 312n110; and
negotiated production, 218, 219, 222,
228, 229, 231; political attacks on, 251
Jin Haiguan, 55
Jin Yunfeng, 214
Jin Yuxiu, 62
Jin Zhaoyan, 42
Jin Zhaozi, 1, 42, 72–73, 85, 88, 206,
207; and *Cihai*, 120, 211, 238; and
continuities in publishing, 211,
245; and negotiated production, 227,
246
Johnson, David, 16
journalism, 2, 18, 19, 107–8, 117, 268n57
journals, 2, 51, 59, 71, 85, 90; in-house
production of, 6, 34, 67
Justice Daily (Gongli ribao), 75

Kaiming Bookstore (Kaiming shudian),
33, 187, 189, 213, 219, 270n28; and
public-private joint management, 194,
309n44; and textbooks, 89, 108, 283n15,
289n82
Kang Sheng, 237
Kang Youwei, 35
Kinkōdō (Golden Harbor Press), 5–6, 29,
44
knowledge (*zhishi*), 168, 265n32, 268n71;
commodification of, 7, 8–9, 11, 256;
and Confucianism, 301n31; culture of,

122, 161–62, 182; democratization of,
128, 136, 153; global, 15, 23, 84, 101,
103, 232
knowledge, production of, 11–13, 153,
255; and intellectuals, 246, 247;
and pedogogical state, 244–45; and
reference books, 11, 242–43, 252;
and series publications, 23, 181;
for socialist construction,
21, 252
Knowledge Series (Zhishi congshu), 216,
219–22, 242, 244, 251
Kong, Shuyu, 260
Koselleck, Reinhart, 118, 284n2,
287n45
Kotkin, Stephen, 215–16
Kropotkin, Peter, 119

labor: costs of, 32, 63; industrial,
148, 152, 235; markets for, 32, 42,
210, 231, 245–46, 254, 258; mass
mobilization of, 233–35, 245; state
allocation of, 231, 245–46, 258; wage,
72, 280n107
labor, division of, 148, 258, 280n105;
among publishers, 219–20; and
cooperation (*fengong hezuo*), 212; in
early PRC, 186, 190–91; and negotiated
production, 220, 225, 226; and
public-private joint management,
200; in Qing-Republican period,
53–54, 72, 84; thematic, 222
labor, intellectual: on classical reprints,
132, 143, 148; collaborative, 7, 8, 22,
44–47, 56, 97, 100–101, 179, 214–15,
238–39, 254, 273n82; on content, 7–8,
19–20, 52; on content vs. management,
69, 71, 72–73, 85; division of, 53–54;
and economic production, 9–10; and
flow production, 72; industrialization
of, 53–86, 69–74, 265n24; and literati
culture, 38–39; male vs. female, 180; on
management, 7–8, 19, 52–54, 69,
280n104; mechanization of, 74, 84–86;
mobility of, 72–73, 85; and status, 14,
17, 18, 77–78, 241, 255, 264n22
labor activism, 74–76
Latour, Bruno, 11
Lean, Eugenia, 169, 265n32
Lenin, V.I., 118

Leninisn, 120

Lexicographical Publishing Company (Cishu chubanshe), 260

Li Chunping, 232, 233, 234, 242

Li Da, 55, 159, 275n9

Li Gengxu, 218, 244

Li Jiaju, 163

Li Jinhui, 82, 83, 106, 292n138

Li Jinxi, 118, 292n138

Li Kan, 251

Li Kenong, 64

Li Shicen, 83

Li Shizeng, 189

Li Shuming, 90

Li Yongchun, 142

Li Yuanhong, 121

Liang Qichao, 35, 143

Liang Sicheng, 173

Lianying Bookstore, 189

Liao Mosha, 248

libraries, 85, 256; marketing to, 151–52, 164, 166; at publishing companies, 14, 28, 48, 53, 57, 66, 78, 79–81

Lin Jianqing, 221

Lin Kui, 176

Lin Mohan, 221

Lin Shu, 164

List, Friedrich, 161, 176

literacy, 16, 267n50, 267n51, 271n37; cultural (*wen*), 99, 255

literary publishing, 4, 6, 30, 61, 266n35

Literary Research Association (Wenxue yanjiuhui), 83

literati, Qing-Republican: and accessiblity of texts, 154, 167; careers for, 1–4, 18–19, 27–52, 253; and civil service examinations, 18, 27–28, 35, 36, 128, 131; and classical reprints, 14, 28, 125, 127, 128–36, 140, 148, 150, 153, 154, 246; and collaborative production, 7, 8, 22, 44–47, 56, 97, 100–101, 179, 214–15, 238–39, 254, 273n82; cultural literacy of, 99; as editors, 98, 100–105, 253–54; and foreign learning, 27–28, 34–38, 51, 52; vs. foreign-educated intellectuals, 177; habitus of, 272n57; hybrid learning of, 34–38; leisure culture of, 10, 14, 22, 38–39, 49–51, 52, 57, 83–84, 186, 235,

254, 256, 273n92; low-ranking, 12, 128, 133; and market demands, 54, 62–63; vs. new school graduates, 19, 22, 61–63, 65, 67, 68, 71, 84, 85; and new terms and concepts, 100–105; political suspicion of, 208; and print industrialism, 5, 31, 51; recruitment of, 28–34, 39, 47, 50; and reform movements, 28, 35–38, 51; social networks of, 29–30, 31, 38–39, 50, 51, 52; social status of, 2, 13–14, 255; workplace culture of, 39–42, 235

Literature Weekly (*Wenxue zhoubao*), 83

Little Friend Library (Xiao pengyou wenku; Zhonghua), 55

Liu, Lydia, 157, 293n6, 307n116

Liu Baonan, 142

Liu Bingli, 159

Liu Binglin, 175–76

Liu Boming, 159

Liu Dapeng, 273n92

Liu Fanyou, 117, 211

Liu Hongsheng, 201

"Livelihood of Shanghai's Middle-Class Society" (in *Advancing Virtue Quarterly; Jinde jikan*), 67

Lu Dingyi, 221, 317n75

Lu Dongping, 168

Lu Erkui, 100

Lu Jialiang, 81

Lu Qiuxin, 32

Lü Simian, 173, 301n36

Lu Tianbai, 81

Lu Weishi, 49

Lu Wendi, 186, 199, 207, 208–9, 227

Lu Yunbiao, 62

Lufei Chi, 141

Lufei Kui (Bohong), 44, 117, 280n104; and classical reprints, 141–45, 151, 153; and organization of production, 7, 55, 85; and series publications, 180, 253; and textbooks, 46, 292n138; and Zhonghua, 33, 36, 46, 48

Lufei Shuchen, 150

Luo Jialun, 171

Luo Zhufeng (Luo Mo), 211, 235, 238, 248–50, 260

Lushan Plenum, 220

Ma Junwu, 158, 159, 171
Ma Runqing, 81
Malthus, 176
management: vs. content production, 69, 71, 72–73, 85; and cooperation, 24; of intellectual labor, 7–8, 19, 52–54, 69, 280n104; and literati leisure culture, 50, 52; organs of cultural (*wenhua guanli bumen*), 216; scientific, 8, 72, 77, 78; and status, 264n22
management, public-private joint (*gong si heying*), 20, 23–24, 90, 194–202, 213; benefits of, 195–96, 202; of Commercial Press, 194–99, 200, 312n110; as experiment, 212; and reorganizations, 202–3, 207; requests for, 187; shares in, 189, 196; transition to, 185–86; and World Book Company, 189; of Zhonghua, 194, 195, 199–200, 223, 312n110
Manchurian Incident (1931), 140
manuscripts: acquisition of, 34, 60, 69; compensation for, 29, 30, 32, 60, 73, 156, 173, 180, 240, 276n34; independent production of, 19–20, 48, 73–74, 90; in-house production of, 5–6, 14, 19–20, 85, 96, 219, 239, 253; and literati culture, 39, 50, 51, 52; rights to, 30–31; for series publications, 155, 158, 162, 169; solicitation of, 71, 88, 90, 162, 169, 191, 217, 218, 221, 222
Mao Dun (Shen Yanbing), 41, 75, 76, 83, 112, 188, 280n101; and classical reprints, 126–27; at Commercial Press, 35, 39, 40, 42–43, 47, 48, 81, 133–34; as handyman (*daza*), 43, 248; and *Sibu congkan*, 132, 133, 134; on social status, 77–78
Mao Jin, 4–5
Mao Zedong, 206, 227, 230, 267n54; and *Cihai*, 210, 232, 237, 238
marketing: to communities of readers, 14, 15; to government offices, 152, 166; to libraries, 151–52, 164, 166; to new school graduates, 160, 255, 267n50; of series publications, 70, 152, 164–66
markets, book: of citizen readers, 256; for classical texts, 129, 148, 205–6, 225, 228; decline of, 88, 90; in early PRC, 245; and editors, 43–44, 52, 252; and

intellectuals, 239, 256; and labor organization, 52, 54–55, 84, 85; and literati, 39, 51, 54, 62–63; and negotiated production, 216–17, 220, 225, 228, 257; in Reform period, 260; for Russian language, 216, 217; for series publications, 156, 160–61, 163–64, 181–82; for textbooks, 89, 97, 100, 106, 114, 125, 283n15
Martin, Henri-Jean, 9
Marx, Karl, 176
Marxism-Leninism, 118, 215, 232, 242; series publications on, 216, 217, 220
May Fourth Movement, 3, 55, 82, 118, 124, 126; and language reform, 112, 117, 125, 232
May Thirtieth Movement, 74–75
Meng Chao, 315n28
Meng Haoran Collection, 132–33
Meng Sen, 101
Meng Xiancheng, 179
Meng, Yue, 6, 127–28, 177, 271n37
Miao Fenglin, 159
Miao Quansun, 129
Miao Yizhi, 242
middle class, 67–68
Mingshi, 230
Ministry of Culture (PRC), 236, 311n87; and negotiated production, 219–22, 224, 226, 227, 228; rectification campaign in, 250–51; and reorganizations of publishers, 203–4, 205, 207
Ministry of Education (Nationalist), 139, 140, 172; and language reform, 95, 105, 106, 107; and textbooks, 89, 113
Ministry of Education (PRC), 188, 197, 233
Ministry of Higher Education (PRC), 202, 207, 212
Monistic Philosophy (Haeckel), 158
monographs, 23, 122, 124, 127, 171–74; lecture notes as, 159, 175, 177, 178. *See also* series publications
Mu Jixiang, 64
Mullaney, Thomas, 201

National Federation of Education Associations (Quanguo jiaoyuhui lianhehui), 106

national heritage, reorganizing (*zhengli guogu*), 12, 18, 23, 153, 255
National Language Unification Preparatory Committee (Guoyu tongyi choubeihui), 95, 97, 105, 113
national learning (*guoxue*), 142, 144, 163, 293n6
National Learning Basic Series (Commercial Press), 164
National Learning Small Series (Commercial Press), 162
National Literature Monthly (*Guowen yuekan*), 187
National Office of Compilation and Translation (Guoli bianyiguan; Nationalist), 90, 114–16
National Publishing Conference, 189, 190, 191, 194
nationalism, 4, 12, 75, 76, 161–62, 252
Nationalist government, 76, 188, 189, 200, 304n86; and *Cihai*, 120, 121, 124; and classical reprints, 136–41, 147, 153; and copyrights, 300n17; and education, 11, 89, 95, 105–7, 113, 139, 140, 172; and series publications, 171, 172, 181; and textbooks, 88–89, 113, 114–16
Nationalist Party, 87, 121, 124, 171, 172, 187, 212
New Character Dictionary (*Xin zidian*; Commercial Press), 100
New China Bookstore (Xinhua shudian), 188, 190, 196, 211
New China Semi-monthly (*Xin Zhonghua banyuekan*), 187
New Culture Movement, 54, 118, 126; and *Ciyuan*, 101, 103–4, 105; and series publications, 157–60, 169
New Culture series (Xin wenhua congshu; Zhonghua), 55, 155, 158, 160, 161, 169, 307n114
New Education series (Zhonghua), 110
New Era Small Series (Xin shidai xiao congshu; Commercial Press), 217
New Fiction (*Xin xiaoshuo*), 37
New Form (Xinti) textbooks (Commercial Press), 106
New Knowledge Publishing Company (Xin zhishi chubanshe), 211
New People's Journal (*Xinminbao*), 37

New School System (Xin xuezhi), 106, 111, 288n57; textbooks for, 108, 113, 292n138
New World, The (Bowman), 162
New Zhonghua magazine, 90
New-Era History and Geography Series (Commercial Press), 162
Newest Textbook series (Zuixin jiaokeshu; Commercial Press), 97, 99
newspapers, 107–8, 117, 268n57
Northern Expedition (1927), 76
Notes and Commentaries of the Thirteen Classics, 142

Ogburn, William, 178
Ohmann, Richard, 265n24
"On New Democracy" (Mao Zedong), 206
On Population (Malthus), 176
Origin of Species (Darwin), 37, 158
Outline of History (*Shijie shi gang*; Wells), 173
Ouyang Hancun, 42
Ouyang Pucun, 42

Pan Daren, 192
Pan Gongzhan, 76
paratext, 132, 156
Paris Commune, 120
patronage, 50, 72, 132, 133, 173, 247, 280n107
Pavlov, Ivan, 242
Pedagogical Series (Shifan congshu; Commercial Press), 175
Pedagogical Small Series, 179
Peng Dehuai, 220
People's Base Publishing Company (Minben chubanshe), 191, 195
People's Daily, 205
People's Education Press (Renmin jiaoyu chubanshe), 218, 314n6
People's Literature Publishing Company, 220
People's Publishing Company (Renmin chubanshe), 219, 220
People's Publishing Houses (Renmin chubanshe), 188

Philippovich, Eugen, 159
photolithography, 16, 147; of *Four Treasuries*, 138, 140, 141; of *Sibu beiyao*, 143, 145; of *Sibu congkan*, 127, 130–33, 136, 138, 144
Planning Small Group for Organizing and Publishing Ancient Books (Guji zhengli chuban guihua xiaozu), 206, 226, 228, 229
political campaigns, 192–94, 197, 201, 208–10, 213, 250–51, 258
political issues, 37–38, 194, 246; and *Cihai*, 118, 120–21; and *Ciyuan*, 101, 105; and new terms and concepts, 22, 96, 98, 100, 117; and revised *Cihai*, 236–39, 250, 251, 259, 318n105
popularization: and classical reprints, 141–46, 150, 225; of new styles, 254–55; and series publications, 156, 166–70, 181; vs. specialization, 177, 181
postscripts (*bawen*), 156
Practical Electrical Engineering Series (Shiyong diangong congshu; Commercial Press), 217
prefaces (*xu, xuyan*), 4, 176, 179; in series publications, 156–57, 159, 174
preservation (*baocun*), 127, 137, 138, 147, 252
Primary Education (Chudeng jiaoyu; journal), 113
Principles of Sociology (Sun Benwen), 178
proofreading, 62, 64–67, 70, 71, 77; of classical reprints, 43, 128, 129, 135, 142–46, 148
propaganda (*xuanchuan*): vs. knowledge (*zhishi*), 268n71; in PRC, 20–21; and the state, 244, 252, 257, 319n134. *See also* Central Propaganda Department
publishing circles (*chubanjie*), 10
Publishing Weekly (Chuban zhoukan; Commercial Press), 70
Pujiang Hotel (Shanghai), 234, 235, 236, 241

Qi Yanming, 260, 313n120; and classical reprints, 209, 210, 221, 226–28, 231, 245, 312n95; political attacks on, 251; and reorganization of publishing, 205–7
Qi Yaolin, 132

Qian Junrui, 203–4, 311n87
Qian Xuantong, 105
Qian Zihui, 238
Qing New Policies, 3
Qu Liangshi, book collection of, 131–32, 136
Qu Qiubai, 112

race (*renzhong*), 102, 123, 124
rare books (*shanbenshu*), 127–32, 136, 142, 143, 152, 154
Rare Editions of the Twenty-Four Dynastic Histories (Bainaben ershisi shi), 70
Rea, Christopher, 17
readers, 12, 14; as citizens, 15, 21, 124, 161–62, 181–82, 252, 255–56, 257; of classical reprints, 15–16, 18, 151–52, 226, 252, 255; of classical texts, 4, 16, 37, 38; communities of, 9, 11, 15, 16, 18, 255; in "general reading public" (*yiban dushu jie*), 15, 156, 162, 255; of series publications, 156, 182, 255
reading instructions (*fanli*), 156
Reading Monthly (Dushu yuekan), 165
Records of the Grand Historian (Shiji), 230
recruitment: from academic institutions, 1, 59, 68, 175–80, 182, 210, 216, 234–35, 243; by Commercial Press, 22, 27, 28–30, 55–56, 57, 61, 62, 253; examinations for, 62, 64; of literati, 28–34, 39, 47, 50; and modern education, 61–62, 65; in PRC, 210, 252; in Reform period, 260; and social networks, 29–30, 31, 51, 52, 253, 256; by World Book Company, 22, 33, 61–62, 68–69; of young staff, 55–56, 57; by Zhonghua, 22, 29, 33, 61, 62, 68–69, 84
Reduced-Size Most Reliable Editions of the Twenty-Four Dynastic Histories (Suoyin bainaben ershisi shi; Commercial Press), 223
Reed, Christopher, 5, 252, 281n127
reference books, 2, 6, 12, 14–18; *Ciyuan* as, 103, 105; collaborative compilation of, 215, 254; and Commercial Press, 90, 191; in early PRC, 186, 191, 211; education for producing, 51, 61; flow production of, 84; industrial production of, 19, 22, 53–54, 71, 85;

reference books (*continued*)
in-house production of, 6, 34, 67; and knowledge production, 11, 242–43, 252; and literati culture, 39, 125; negotiated production of, 216, 231–39, 257; readers of, 15, 16; repackaging text for, 53, 164, 173, 254, 256, 265n24; series publications as, 181; and specialization, 59, 246; standardization of, 19, 74; in wartime, 88; Western, 117; and Zhonghua, 24, 186, 212. *See also* dictionaries

Reform and Opening period (1978–present), 260

reform movements: and classical reprints, 153; and dictionaries, 101, 104, 105, 120; and editors, 35–38, 51, 52, 97–98, 102; and language, 3, 22, 105–6, 107, 108, 112, 113, 125; and literati, 28, 35–38, 44, 51, 128; and textbooks, 52, 97–98; women's, 104, 169

Ren Hongjun, 58, 61, 68, 171, 301n36

Republican Chinese Language Textbook (Gonghe guowen jiaokeshu), 34

Revolution of 1911, 3, 43, 46

Ricardo, David, 176

rights (*quan*), 98, 101–2, 103, 104, 124

Rong family, 201

Rousseau, Jean Jacques, 12

Ruan Yuan, 6, 142, 280n107

Russian language, 188, 195, 216, 217, 223

Sanlian Bookstore, 188, 189

science, 24, 161, 191, 242; in *Cihai*, 118, 122; new terminology for, 117; in series publications, 157, 163, 169, 172, 216, 219

Science Publishing Company, 220

Science Small Library (Kexue xiao wenku; Commercial Press), 217

series publications (*congshu*), 2, 11–19, 155–82; academic disciplines in, 156, 157, 163, 167–68, 170, 172–80, 182, 252, 253; accessibility of, 15, 166, 181, 182, 219, 244; authors of, 23, 59, 157, 168–70, 175–80, 254, 255, 256; and copyright issues, 159; in early PRC, 90, 257; in-house production of, 6, 12, 13, 22; and intellectuals, 155–56, 158,

168–69, 171–72, 175–81; lecture notes in, 159, 175, 177, 178, 307n114; markets for, 156, 160–61, 163–64, 181–82; and national development, 159, 161, 172, 175, 181–82; negotiated production of, 216–22, 231, 246, 247; political topics in, 220, 222; readers of, 15, 16, 156, 182, 255, 256; repackaging of text for, 164, 173, 254; and research opportunities, 242, 244; restrictions on, 19, 182, 256; and social status, 13–14, 255. *See also particular titles*

Seven-Company Associated Supply Office (Qijia lianhe gongying chu), 89

Shanggong Primary School (Commercial Press), 82

Shanghai, 12, 19, 29, 37, 266n35; beginnings of Cultural Revolution in, 248–50; booksellers' associations in, 30–31, 193; and *Cihai*, 210–11, 232, 233; classical reprints in, 138–39, 153; in early PRC, 90, 91, 192, 198, 199, 204, 225; Japanese attacks on, 66, 71, 77, 79–81, 163, 270n28; liberation of, 187; publishing guild of, 300n17; wartime, 87, 88, 163, 186–87, 214; Westernized language in, 100

Shanghai Municipal Library, 174

Shanghai Municipal Party Committee, 237, 238, 240–41, 250, 310n61; and revised *Cihai*, 210, 211, 232, 233

Shanghai Publishing Bureau, 234, 235

Shen Duoshan, 49, 71, 117, 118, 120–21, 125

Shen Qi, 108

Shen Qianyi, 170

Shen Shoumei, 113

Shen Yanbing. *See* Mao Dun

Shen Yi, 46, 49

Shen Zhibai, 236

Shen Zhifang, 7, 33, 46, 69, 71, 85; and series publications, 167, 168, 170, 180, 182

Shen Zipei, 294n20

Shenbao, 129

Shi Jiuyun, 186, 196–97

Shi Ximin, 241

Shu Xincheng, 147, 186, 270n30; and *Cihai*, 69, 117, 118, 120–21, 125, 210–11, 232, 233, 291n107; and industrialized production, 7, 61, 69, 71, 72, 79, 85, 254; and institutional continuity, 201, 207; and negotiated production, 216, 224, 245

Sibu beiyao. See *Essential Writings from the Four Categories of Learning*

Sibu congkan. See *Collection of Chinese Classical, Historical, Philosophical, and Literary Works*

Siku quanshu. See *Complete Book of Four Treasuries*

Sima Guang, 115

Sino-Japanese War (1937), 73, 87, 114, 174

Small Series of China's Resources (Zhongguo fuyuan xiao congshu; Commercial Press), 217

Smith, Adam, 176

social Darwinism, 99, 118

Social Issues (Shehui wenti) textbook, 111–12

social networks, 173, 179, 197, 293n9; and classical reprints, 128, 131–32, 140, 148, 153; in editing departments, 38–39, 50, 82, 84, 85–86; and recruitment, 29–30, 31, 51, 52, 253, 256

social production, 9, 13–18, 22

social sciences, 24, 112, 122–23, 157, 159, 163, 169

social status: of authors, 9, 13–14, 15, 16, 18, 176, 255; in editing departments, 22, 74, 254, 264n22; of editors, 67–68, 77, 78, 85, 86, 240, 255; of mental labor, 2, 14, 17, 18, 77–78, 241, 255, 264n22; middle-class, 67–68; production of, 13–18

socialism, state, 23–24; and allocation of labor, 231, 245–46, 258; vs. capitalism, 16, 21, 201, 212, 245, 256–57; and CCP, 200–201; and cultural production, 10, 16; and intellectuals, 21, 197, 201, 239; and negotiated book production, 214–47; new vocabulary of, 215, 232; transition to, 20, 211–13

socialist construction, 9, 15, 246, 257; and classical reprints, 223; cultural production for, 17, 24; knowledge production for, 21, 252

Song Jiaxiu, 63

Songs of Chu, 242

Soviet Knowledge Small Series (Sulian zhishi xiao congshu), 217

Soviet Mass Science Series (Sulian dazhong kexue congshu; Commercial Press), 217

Soviet Union (USSR), 245; and PRC, 20, 188, 207, 213, 224, 314n7; publishing in, 209, 257, 313n135, 321n23; and revised *Cihai*, 236–37; series publications on, 159, 216, 217, 223; and Zhonghua Book Company, 191, 195. *See also* Russian language

Stalin, Joseph, 237

State Publishing Bureau, 260

Student Magazine (Xuesheng zazhi), 43

Student National Learning Series (Commercial Press), 164

Study (Xuexi; journal), 206

study societies (*xuehui*), 7, 22, 39, 50, 52, 85; and collaborative production, 44, 45, 47, 56, 215, 254

Su Jiqing, 88

Subao (newspaper), 36

Sun Baoqi, 139

Sun Benwen, 1, 170, 176, 178, 179, 303n70

Sun Kanghou (Jun), 126, 132, 133

Sun Lianggong, 70

Sun Luoren, 148, 150

Sun Xingyan, 142

Sun Yat-sen, 121

Sun Yirang, 142

Sun Yuxiu (Xingru), 1, 23, 27–29, 35, 49, 52, 81; and *Ciyuan*, 100; and classical reprints, 126–36, 140, 141, 143, 144, 151, 153; and rare editions, 43, 48, 79, 154

Sun Zhuang, 138

synthetic construction, 23, 157, 177–79, 181, 255, 307n116

Taiping Rebellion, 137

Taiwan, 193

Tan Jun, 63

Tan Lianxun, 30

Tang Cheng, 58, 61, 68, 69, 82, 83, 171

Tang Yongtong, 179

Tangshu, 230

Tao Gongze, 312n108

Tao Menghe, 58–61, 68, 69, 111–12, 171, 301n36

Taylorism (scientific management; *kexue guanli*), 8, 72, 77, 78

technology: in *Cihai*, 118; and civilization, 99; and Confucianism, 301n31; new terms for, 98, 100; and pedogogical state, 244–45; print, 5, 29, 152; in series publications, 163, 169, 172, 174, 216, 219–20; specialization in, 191, 217, 220

textbooks, 2, 12–18; Chinese language in, 13, 22–23, 95, 97–100, 104, 105–15, 171–72; collaborative production of, 39, 44–45, 46, 215, 222, 254, 273n82; of Commercial Press, 34, 89, 96, 97–100, 106, 107, 113, 114, 116, 283n15, 314n6; competition in, 125, 283n15; consortium for publication of, 89–90; dialogue in, 108–9, 110, 114–15, 289n82; division of labor for, 53–54; editors for, 12, 17, 28–29, 61–62; flow production of, 84; industrialized production of, 19, 22, 70, 71, 85, 255; in-house production of, 5–6, 12, 33–34, 51, 67; and knowledge production, 11–12, 252; markets for, 15–16, 70, 89, 97, 100, 106, 114, 125, 283n15; for modern education, 34, 61, 105–12, 113, 292n138; and Nationalist government, 88–89, 113, 114–16; new terms and concepts in, 17–18, 96, 97–100, 103, 153, 254; and political campaigns, 193; and reform movements, 52, 97–98; and series publications, 155, 171–72, 174, 181; and specialization, 58, 59, 60; standardization of, 19, 74, 114–16; state control of, 188, 192, 196, 314n6; of World Book Company, 109, 110, 113, 114, 116, 283n15; of Zhonghua, 90, 109, 110, 114, 116, 283n15, 314n6. *See also particular titles*

Thomas, William I., 178

Three Kingdoms, 73–74

Three Principles of the People (*sanmin zhuyi*), 120

Tian Han, 55, 275n9

Tongwen Book Company, 148

Translated Series of Scientific Monographs from the Soviet Union (Sulian kexue zhuanzhu yicong; Commercial Press), 217

translations: for Commercial Press, 24, 62–63, 64; copyrights for, 300n17; of foreign scholarship, 157, 186, 206; by literati, 6, 28, 48; rates for, 30; Russian, 195, 217; in series publications, 157, 158–59, 162, 163, 164, 173, 177, 181; and synthetic construction, 177, 178

transmission (*liuchuan*), 127, 147, 150

Travels in the New World (Xindalu youji), 37

Tushu jicheng, 190

Twenty-Four Dynastic Histories (Ershisi shi), 70, 223, 230–31, 234, 243, 247, 251

typefaces, 289n76; imitation-Song, 143–45, 147

U, Eddy, 200

United Front, 76

United States (U.S.), 157, 179, 181, 275n9, 288n57; popularized knowledge in, 156; print capitalism in, 4–5; publishing in, 6, 165, 253, 264n19, 265n24, 270n30, 302n47; study tour of, 66, 77, 270n30

Universal Library (Baike xiao congshu; Commercial Press), 162, 163, 167, 170, 176, 222, 301n29

University Series (Daxue congshu; Commercial Press), 88, 90, 155, 171–81, 217, 242, 307n114; catalog for, 172–73; readers of, 23, 171, 181, 199; subjects in, 173, 175; unpaid labor on, 180

Veritable Records (compilation), 6

Vernacular Chinese History (Baihua benguoshi; Lü Simian), 173

Victory Magazine (Shengli zazhi), 121

Volland, Nicolai, 17, 90, 188, 314n7

Wang, Fei-hsien, 31, 300n17

Wang Boxiang, 73–74, 75, 83, 85, 301n36

Wang Cheng, 221

Wang Chun, 209

Wang Daiwen, 218

Wang Li, 222, 242, 315n30

Wang Qixi, 63

Wang Shijie, 171

Wang Shiyuan, 133

Wang Tianyi, 191, 217
Wang Yanfan, 63
Wang Yi, 207, 219
Wang Yinzhi, 142
Wang Yunwu: flight to Taiwan of, 193; and industrialized production, 7, 57–60, 65, 68, 69, 70, 71, 85, 254; and Japanese attacks, 270n28, 282n4; managerial plan of, 53–54; vs. PRC publishing, 231, 242; production policies of, 84, 155, 278n78; and recruitment, 61, 111, 169, 235; and series publications, 155, 160–68, 170–73, 180, 182, 199, 217, 253; study tour of, 66, 77, 270n30; and Taylorism, 8, 77, 78
Wang, Zheng, 104
Wang Zhenzhi, 126, 134
Wang Zhonggu, 32
Wang Ziye, 219
War of Resistance, 174, 187, 201, 212–13
"Wartime" (You di er zhang; Mao Dun), 77
Wei Bingxin, 108, 109, 114, 168, 289n82
Wei Fuqing, 312n108
Wei Tao, 133
Wei's Suzhou Collection, 133
Wells, H. G., 173
Weng Wenhao, 171
Wenhuibao (newspaper), 248–50, 320n7
Wenjinge (at Summer Palace, Rehe), 136, 139, 140
Wenlan Pavilion, 148
Wentong Book Company (Wentong shuju), 89
Wenyuange (at the Palace Museum, Beijing), 136
Western influence: and *Cihai*, 121–22, 123, 124, 237; and *Ciyuan*, 101, 105; in editing departments, 42, 253; on literati, 27–28, 34–38, 44, 51, 52; and new terms and concepts, 96, 102
Western learning: of literati, 22, 28, 35, 44, 52, 253; vs. national learning, 144; and readers, 15, 43; in series publications, 157–60, 161, 162, 175–76; syntheses of, 11–12, 159, 176, 177–78; translations of, 157, 186, 206, 211
Whyte, William, 265n24

women, 104, 159, 169, 180, 273n92
woodblock (xylographic) printing, 4, 5, 142, 144, 152, 298n114
World (*Shijie*; World Book Company journal), 168
World Agency (Shijie she), 189
World Book Company (Shijie shuju), 5, 60, 76; founding of, 2, 61; industrialized production at, 8, 72, 252; and new terms and concepts, 96, 106–7, 108; in PRC, 189, 213; recruitment by, 22, 33, 61–62, 68–69; series publications of, 23, 155–56, 160, 162, 164, 167–70, 176; textbooks of, 89, 109, 110, 113, 114, 116, 283n15; in wartime, 87. *See also* ABC Series
World Knowledge Publishing Company, 221
World Series, 160
Writer's Study (Zuojia shuwu), 187
Wu Han, 206, 210, 247, 248; and classical texts, 228, 229, 230; political attacks on, 251; and series publications, 217–18, 315n15
Wu Jingheng (Zhihui), 119
Wu Junsheng, 175, 179
Wu Pengfei, 63
Wu Shengzu, 63
Wu Shirui, 177
Wu Tiesheng, 225, 226
Wu Xiang, 242
Wu Yanyin, 108, 114, 288n66, 289n82
Wu Zengqi (Yiting), 35, 42, 79
Wu Zeyan, 63, 214, 223, 317n70
Wu Zhihui, 189
Wuchang Uprising, 46, 121

Xi Zhongxun, 195
Xia Jingguan, 131
Xia Ruifeng, 28
Xiaolutian collection, 131
Xie Liuyi, 83
Xie Meng, 36
Xie Renbing, 188, 189, 190, 208
Xu Diaofu, 187, 207
Xu Fengshi, 197, 312n108
Xu Furu, 49
Xu Ke (Zhongke), 35
Xu Liyi, 221, 315n28
Xu Sitong, 159

Xu Weinan, 7, 69, 71, 85, 167,
    168, 169, 254
Xu Yuangao, 36, 117

Yan Fu, 37, 102, 164
Yan Lianru, 49, 273n82
Yan'an Forum on Literature and Art
    (1942), 267n54
Yang Chiyu, 44, 49
Yang Gengguang, 176
Yang Xianjiang, 83
Yang Xiufeng, 210
Yang Yinshen, 70, 85, 211, 214, 238,
    280n116
Yang Yutong, 97
Yang Zheming, 170, 176
Yao Pengzi, 187
Yao Qin, 221
Yao Shaohua, 88, 204, 207, 208, 227
Yao Wenyuan, 248–50
Ye Dehui, 131
Ye Shengtao, 75, 83, 108, 146, 185, 206,
    289n82
Yeh, Catherine, 273n92
Yeh, Wen-hsin, 67
Yongle Compendium, 137, 138, 227
Young China Association (Shaonian
    Zhongguo xuehui), 55, 158, 160,
    299n12
Young China Association Series
    (Zhonghua), 55
Youth Publishing Company (Qingnian
    chubanshe), 310n44
Youth Science Series (Shaonian kexue
    congshu; Commercial Press), 217
Youth Society Semi-monthly (Shaonian shehui
    banyuekan), 160
Yu Fu, 152
Yu Houpei, 312n108
Yu Huancheng, 312n108
Yu Jiaju, 55, 159, 275n9
Yu Mingshi, 312n108
Yu Shaohua, 31
Yu Xiaoyao, 208, 209, 251
Yu Zhuo, 203
Yuan Hanqing, 191, 196, 197, 217
Yuan Shikai, 286n21

Zeng Ciliang, 207
Zeng Xinshan, 62, 64

Zhang Beichen, 207
Zhang Boling, 171
Zhang Chunqiao, 250
Zhang Jingjiang, 189
Zhang Jinglu, 207
Zhang Jusheng. See Zhang Yuanji
Zhang Qiyun, 59, 60, 162, 301n36
Zhang Shizhao, 139, 140
Zhang Wentian, 55, 81, 275n9
Zhang Xiang, 36
Zhang Xianzhi, 120–21
Zhang Xichen, 207, 208, 240, 246, 277n66
Zhang Yinian, 180
Zhang Yuanji (Jusheng), 35, 48, 57, 99,
    187, 225; and classical reprints, 23, 70,
    126, 138–39, 141, 150, 153, 206, 223; and
    collaborative production, 44, 46, 97;
    and institutional continuity, 201, 245,
    246; and literati leisure culture, 49, 50;
    and new terms and concepts, 97, 100;
    and pay rates, 31–32, 33; in PRC, 188,
    196, 214, 312n108; and rare editions,
    79, 154; recruitment by, 21, 27–28, 29,
    30, 31, 253; and series publications, 160;
    and Sibu congkan, 128–32, 134, 136, 140
Zhang Yuli, 63
Zhang Zhidong, 143
Zhang Ziyi, 221
Zhao Jing, 64
Zhao Shouyan, 223, 230
Zheng Guomin, 105
Zheng Taipu, 188
Zheng Zhenduo, 75, 83, 171, 206
Zheng Zhenwen, 40, 42, 57, 83, 171
Zhengzhong Book Company
    (Zhengzhong shuju), 89
Zhong Jizhou, 192
Zhong Luzhai, 178–79
Zhong Wenzheng, 142
Zhonghua Book Company (Zhonghua
    shuju), 1–2, 272n77; academic
    atmosphere at, 78–79, 81, 82, 235, 242,
    243–44; and Cihai, 211, 232; classical
    reprints of, 23, 24, 127, 128, 141–53,
    186, 206, 210, 212, 223–28, 230, 231,
    234; collaborative production at, 5, 8,
    46, 47; vs. Commercial Press, 100; in
    Cultural Revolution, 252; in early
    PRC, 7, 8, 20–21, 90–91, 213, 240,
    311n84; editing department of, 21–22,

34, 36, 39, 40, 41, 42, 51, 65; educational opportunities at, 78–79, 81; and Five Antis Campaign, 192–93; founding of, 2, 33, 46, 48; industrialized production at, 49, 70, 71, 72–73; institutional continuity of, 7, 201–2, 212–13, 215–16; and labor activism, 74, 76; literati at, 28, 34–35, 44, 52, 84; and negotiated production, 216–20, 223–24, 226–28, 230, 231, 257; New Books Division (Xinshubu) of, 55, 158; and new terms and concepts, 96, 106, 107, 108, 109, 110, 114, 116, 125; political attacks on, 250, 251, 259, 318n105; politically suspect staff at, 209, 251, 258–59, 313n120; public-private joint management of, 194, 195, 199–200, 223, 312n110; recruitment for, 22, 29, 33, 61, 62, 68–69, 84; in Reform period, 260; reorganizations of, 55–57, 56, 60, 202, 203, 204, 205, 207–8, 212; research opportunities at, 79, 242, 243–44; series publications of, 155, 158, 216–18, 219, 220; specialization of, 24, 61, 190–91; state control of, 23–24, 185–86, 188, 189, 257; textbooks of, 89, 109, 110, 114, 116, 283n15, 314n6; transition to socialism of, 211–13; wages at, 66, 67; in wartime, 87–88, 187; vs. World, 167, 168

Zhonghua Education Circles (journal), 187

Zhonghua's Great Dictionary (Zhonghua da zidian), 117

Zhongshan Dictionary, 70

Zhou Changshou, 83

Zhou Gengsheng, 58, 68, 290n85

Zhou Jianren, 185

Zhou Jimei, 30

Zhou Shushan, 121

Zhou Songdi, 211, 238, 291n107

Zhou Wu, 90, 187, 191–92

Zhou Yang, 206, 221, 237, 245, 317n75

Zhou Youqin, 42

Zhou Yueran, 42

Zhou Yunqing, 223

Zhou Yutong, 83, 187

Zhou Zuomin, 201

Zhou Zuoren, 105

Zhu Bin, 142

Zhu Jiahua, 171

Zhu Jingnong, 58, 83, 171

Zhu Kezhen, 1, 58, 61, 83, 162, 171, 242

Zhu Xi, 142, 145, 244

Zhu Yanfu, 218, 219

Zhu Yixin, 168

Zhuang Boyu, 49

Zhuang Shi, 108, 114, 289n82

Zhuang Yu, 29, 35, 40, 49, 52, 100; and textbooks, 34, 97, 273n82

Zou Zhenhuan, 158, 275n9

Zuo Shunsheng, 55, 56, 78–79, 81, 158, 299n12

STUDIES OF THE WEATHERHEAD EAST ASIAN INSTITUTE
Columbia University
Selected Titles
(Complete list at http://weai.columbia.edu/publications/studies-weai/)

The Power of Print in Modern China: Intellectuals and Industrial Publishing from the End of Empire to Maoist State Socialism, by Robert Culp. Columbia University Press, 2019.

Residual Futures: The Urban Ecologies of Literary and Visual Media of 1960s and 1970s Japan, by Franz Prichard. Columbia University Press, 2019.

Thought Crime: Ideology and State Power in Interwar Japan, by Max Ward. Duke University Press, 2019.

Statebuilding by Imposition: Resistance and Control in Colonial Taiwan and the Philippines, by Reo Matsuzaki. Cornell University Press, 2019.

Nation-Empire: Ideology and Rural Youth Mobilization in Japan and Its Colonies, by Sayaka Chatani. Cornell University Press, 2019.

The Invention of Madness: State, Society, and the Insane in Modern China, by Emily Baum. University of Chicago Press, 2018.

Fixing Landscape: A Techno-Poetic History of China's Three Gorges, by Corey Byrnes. Columbia University Press, 2018.

Japan's Imperial Underworlds: Intimate Encounters at the Borders of Empire, by David Ambaras. Cambridge University Press, 2018.

Heroes and Toilers: Work as Life in Postwar North Korea, 1953–1961, by Cheehyung Harrison Kim. Columbia University Press, 2018.

Electrified Voices: How the Telephone, Phonograph, and Radio Shaped Modern Japan, 1868–1945, by Kerim Yasar. Columbia University Press, 2018.

Making Two Vietnams: War and Youth Identities, 1965–1975, by Olga Dror. Cambridge University Press, 2018.

A Misunderstood Friendship: Mao Zedong, Kim Il-sung, and Sino–North Korean Relations, 1949–1976, by Zhihua Shen and Yafeng Xia. Columbia University Press, 2018.

Raising China's Revolutionaries: Modernizing Childhood for Cosmopolitan Nationalists and Liberated Comrades, by Margaret Mih Tillman. Columbia University Press, 2018.

Buddhas and Ancestors: Religion and Wealth in Fourteenth-Century Korea, by Juhn Y. Ahn. University of Washington Press, 2018.

Idly Scribbling Rhymers: Poetry, Print, and Community in Nineteenth-Century Japan, by Robert Tuck. Columbia University Press, 2018.

China's War on Smuggling: Law, Economic Life, and the Making of the Modern State, 1842–1965, by Philip Thai. Columbia University Press, 2018.

Forging the Golden Urn: The Qing Empire and the Politics of Reincarnation in Tibet, by Max Oidtmann. Columbia University Press, 2018.

The Battle for Fortune: State-Led Development, Personhood, and Power among Tibetans in China, by Charlene Makley. Cornell University Press, 2018.

Aesthetic Life: Beauty and Art in Modern Japan, by Miya Elise Mizuta Lippit. Harvard University Asia Center, 2018.

Where the Party Rules: The Rank and File of China's Communist State, by Daniel Koss. Cambridge University Press, 2018.

Resurrecting Nagasaki: Reconstruction and the Formation of Atomic Narratives, by Chad R. Diehl. Cornell University Press, 2018.

China's Philological Turn: Scholars, Textualism, and the Dao in the Eighteenth Century, by Ori Sela. Columbia University Press, 2018.

Making Time: Astronomical Time Measurement in Tokugawa Japan, by Yulia Frumer. University of Chicago Press, 2018.

Mobilizing Without the Masses: Control and Contention in China, by Diana Fu. Cambridge University Press, 2018.

Post-Fascist Japan: Political Culture in Kamakura after the Second World War, by Laura Hein. Bloomsbury, 2018.

China's Conservative Revolution: The Quest for a New Order, 1927–1949, by Brian Tsui. Cambridge University Press, 2018.

Promiscuous Media: Film and Visual Culture in Imperial Japan, 1926–1945, by Hikari Hori. Cornell University Press, 2018.

The End of Japanese Cinema: Industrial Genres, National Times, and Media Ecologies, by Alexander Zahlten. Duke University Press, 2017.

The Chinese Typewriter: A History, by Thomas S. Mullaney. The MIT Press, 2017.

Forgotten Disease: Illnesses Transformed in Chinese Medicine, by Hilary A. Smith. Stanford University Press, 2017.

Borrowing Together: Microfinance and Cultivating Social Ties, by Becky Yang Hsu. Cambridge University Press, 2017.

Food of Sinful Demons: Meat, Vegetarianism, and the Limits of Buddhism in Tibet, by Geoffrey Barstow. Columbia University Press, 2017.

Youth for Nation: Culture and Protest in Cold War South Korea, by Charles R. Kim. University of Hawai`i Press, 2017.

Socialist Cosmopolitanism: The Chinese Literary Universe, 1945–1965, by Nicolai Volland. Columbia University Press, 2017.

The Social Life of Inkstones: Artisans and Scholars in Early Qing China, by Dorothy Ko. University of Washington Press, 2017.

Darwin, Dharma, and the Divine: Evolutionary Theory and Religion in Modern Japan, by G. Clinton Godart. University of Hawai`i Press, 2017.

Dictators and Their Secret Police: Coercive Institutions and State Violence, by Sheena Chestnut Greitens. Cambridge University Press, 2016.

The Cultural Revolution on Trial: Mao and the Gang of Four, by Alexander C. Cook. Cambridge University Press, 2016.

Inheritance of Loss: China, Japan, and the Political Economy of Redemption after Empire, by Yukiko Koga. University of Chicago Press, 2016.

Homecomings: The Belated Return of Japan's Lost Soldiers, by Yoshikuni Igarashi. Columbia University Press, 2016.

Samurai to Soldier: Remaking Military Service in Nineteenth-Century Japan, by D. Colin Jaundrill. Cornell University Press, 2016.

The Red Guard Generation and Political Activism in China, by Guobin Yang. Columbia University Press, 2016.

Accidental Activists: Victim Movements and Government Accountability in Japan and South Korea, by Celeste L. Arrington. Cornell University Press, 2016.

Ming China and Vietnam: Negotiating Borders in Early Modern Asia, by Kathlene Baldanza. Cambridge University Press, 2016.